The History of Selkirkshire; or, Chronicles of Ettrick Forest.

Thomas Craig Brown

The History of Selkirkshire; or, Chronicles of Ettrick Forest.

Brown, Thomas Craig

British Library, Historical Print Editions

British Library

1886 ～ 54 years after Walter Scott's death

2 vol. ; 4°.

10370.i.17.

— 136 years before I bought it (in 2022)

The BiblioLife Network

This project was made possible in part by the BiblioLife Network (BLN), a project aimed at addressing some of the huge challenges facing book preservationists around the world. The BLN includes libraries, library networks, archives, subject matter experts, online communities and library service providers. We believe every book ever published should be available as a high-quality print reproduction; printed on- demand anywhere in the world. This insures the ongoing accessibility of the content and helps generate sustainable revenue for the libraries and organizations that work to preserve these important materials.

The following book is in the "public domain" and represents an authentic reproduction of the text as printed by the original publisher. While we have attempted to accurately maintain the integrity of the original work, there are sometimes problems with the original book or micro-film from which the books were digitized. This can result in minor errors in reproduction. Possible imperfections include missing and blurred pages, poor pictures, markings and other reproduction issues beyond our control. Because this work is culturally important, we have made it available as part of our commitment to protecting, preserving, and promoting the world's literature.

GUIDE TO FOLD-OUTS, MAPS and OVERSIZED IMAGES

In an online database, page images do not need to conform to the size restrictions found in a printed book. When converting these images back into a printed bound book, the page sizes are standardized in ways that maintain the detail of the original. For large images, such as fold-out maps, the original page image is split into two or more pages.

Guidelines used to determine the split of oversize pages:

• Some images are split vertically; large images require vertical and horizontal splits.
• For horizontal splits, the content is split left to right.
• For vertical splits, the content is split from top to bottom.
• For both vertical and horizontal splits, the image is processed from top left to bottom right.

2022
18 86
―――――――
136

SELKIRKSHIRE

OR

CHRONICLES OF ETTRICK FOREST

ANDREW PRINGLE, LORD ALEMOOR

THE HISTORY OF

SELKIRKSHIRE

OR

CHRONICLES OF ETTRICK FORES

BY

T. CRAIG-BROWN

VOL. II.

THE BURGH AND PARISH OF SELKIRK

APPENDIX

EDINBURGH: DAVID DOUGLAS

MDCCCLXXXVI

Prince. IS IT UPON RECORD ? OR ELSE REPORTED
     SUCCESSIVELY FROM AGE TO AGE ?
Buckingham. UPON RECORD, MY GRACIOUS LORD.
Prince. BUT SAY, MY LORD, IT WERE NOT REGISTER'D—
     METHINKS THE TRUTH SHOULD LIVE FROM AGE TO AGE.
               Richard III., ACT III. SC. 1.

CONTENTS.

ETYMOLOGY OF "SELKIRK," xi

CHAPTER I.

TO 1126 A.D.

Foundation of Selkirk Abbey—Selkirk then an old town—Ancient castle—Endowments of Abbey—Monks removed to Kelso—Virgin and Child in Burgh Seal, . . 1-8

CHAPTER II.

1126 TO 1512.

Castle frequent residence of Scottish kings—Early Parliaments at Selkirk—"Sorrowless-field:" tradition *versus* fact—Selkirk as a surname—Annexation to England—Recovered by the Douglases—Selkirk burned by Umfraville—Burgh Accounts in Exchequer Rolls—Quaint old names of Burgh lands—James IV. at Selkirk—Slaughter in the town—Again burned by Musgrave—Earliest Burgh Records—Instructions to Night-watch—Sumptuary edicts by Town Council—Philiphaugh's duties as Sheriff, ... 9-19

CHAPTER III.

1513 TO 1526.

Burgess-roll before Flodden—Summons from the king to assemble for war—Bailie's directions—Ramparts and ditches put in order—Ker of Greenhead, "weill-wisher" of Burgh—Two months' gap in Burgh Records—Accepted traditions erroneous—Sir William Brydone a "Pope's Knight"—"The Flodden Flag"—Ladywood-edge incident—Frequent service of heirs after Flodden—Inventories of household and personal effects—Quaint laws by Town Council—Frequent strengthening of Night-watch—Penalties for not rising to the fray, ... 20-32

CHAPTER IV.

1527 TO 1542.

Strange contract with Roland Hamilton about a maiden—Priests of chapels connected with church—Fear of pestilence—Town isolated—Approach of English : fortifica-

PAGE

tions strengthened—Gift by burgess to church for requiems for his soul—Jewels,
weapons, and rich dresses of deceased burgess—Grants of land and privileges by
James V.—Burgh Minstrel—Ale-brewing—Provost Muthag and Bailie Kein slain
in defence of town's lands—Scott of Buccleuch, Provost of Selkirk,   .   . 33-43

CHAPTER V.

1543 TO 1599.

Town frequently burned and plundered—Lukewarm support of Reformation—Treatment of a madman—The community against Murray of Philiphaugh—First M.P.
for the Burgh, and list of successors, ... 44-51

CHAPTER VI.

1600 TO 1660.

Shoemakers' Statutes—Scott of Haining's friends rescued from Bailies—Church offences
—Schoolmaster and precentor—Archery practice in kirkyard—Scourged and
banished for theft—Various lands transferred—Tolbooth broken by Sir Robert
Scott of Thirlestane—Old Scots couplets—Buccleuch and lairds of his clan enrolled
burgesses—Forty Selkirk men march against king's party in England—First in
breach at Newcastle—Exactions by Cromwell's troopers—Selkirk in possession of
English under Lord Howard—Ancient silver arrow—Visits of Royal Bodyguard—
Winners' names, ... 52-66

CHAPTER VII.

1661 TO 1699.

Persecuted Covenanters—Division of Selkirk Common—Boundaries of land awarded to
Burgh—Satchells on a Selkirk bailie—Extreme poverty of inhabitants—Riot by
Kers and dragoons, ... 67-74

CHAPTER VIII.

1700 TO 1715.

Church tyranny and intolerance—Funeral customs—Woman excommunicated—Town's
debt—Water supply—Burgh M.P. to vote against Union with England—Shirking
"the plate" on Sunday—Duel, and death of Laird of Raeburn—Coal prospecting at
Lindean—Lad and lass pilloried and banished—Craft precedence—Thief banished
—Sinfulness of curds and whey on Sunday—Drinking after ten prohibited—Pant
Well erected—Horse Races—First Jacobite Rebellion—Shoes supplied to Highland army—Torwoodlee to command Burgh troop,   .   .   . 75-92

CHAPTER IX.

1716 TO 1744.

PAGE

A domineering Council—Lawyer cursed in church—Duke of Douglas asserts his regality—King's birthday—Ceremony at Cross—Eminent services of Town-Clerk —Grammar-School pupils acting play—Horse-racing—Executioner appointed— Burgh "Champion"—Precautions against pestilence—Burning of Meg Lawson, a witch—Profanity of Harden—Excambions with Haining—Elders as privileged talebearers—Church patronage—Runaway marriage of schoolmaster and Miss Plummer—Earthquake in Selkirk—Hangman's ladle abolished—Ornaments for Cross and Pant Well—A souter sells his wife—New bridge—Extraordinary prayer for weather—Duke of Hamilton electioneering—Gift of £200—Indenture of Burgh hangman—Duke of Douglas again troubling—Laird of Haining expelled from Council—Great riot, ...   93-110

CHAPTER X.

1745 TO 1799.

Jacobites in Town Council—2000 pairs of shoes to rebel army—Highlanders and butcher—Bridge carried away—Prevalent wickedness—Church patronage disputed—Election bribes—Duke of Queensberry's interference—Drastic law against mad dogs—Lax treatment of prisoners—Demolition of ancient ports and Cross— Hangman borrowed from Jedburgh—Fatal storm—Invasion by brown rats—Fall of new bridge—Strange suicide—Present bridge built—Poverty and want—Sir John Moore made a burgess—Robert Burns in Selkirk—Town to furnish men for navy, ...   111-127

CHAPTER XI.

1800 TO 1834.

Sir Walter Scott appointed Sheriff—Petty local strife—Skeleton found in Bog—Old Tolbooth demolished—Professor Lawson's military ardour—False alarm—March of Volunteers—Southey's bad impression of Selkirk—Sir Walter Scott elected Burgh elder—Common-riding banquet at Three Brethren Cairn—French prisoners' balloon—Ridiculous duel at Linglee—Search for coal—Silver cup from Lord Dalkeith—Sir Walter on the bench—scenes in court—Emperor Nicholas in Selkirk—Mimic battle at Bowhill—Robert Owen's candidature discouraged— Prince Leopold made a burgess—Projected railway—Town's right in Haining Loch—Sir Walter Scott designs flag for Selkirk—Lingering superstitions—Scott's death—Touching incident at his monument—Reform Bill "rings out the old" in Selkirk, ...   128-160

CHAPTER XII.

PAGE

Old places: Trinity Hill, Peel Gait, Ring o' the Toun, Lady Well, St. Mungo's Well, Chicken Acre, Gallows Knowe and Moss-troopers' Graves, Tibby Tamson's—Old families and notables: the Andersons, Brydones, Clarksons; "Davie Gellatly;" Hendersons, Johnstons, Langs; Professor Lawson, Dr. Mercer; Mitchelhills, Rodgers; William Riddell, Sam Russell, Rev. William Sorley, John Thomson; Anguses, Ewarts, etc.—Old customs: cock-fighting on Fastern's E'en, King of the School—Old weapons, and other relics, ... 161-176

CHAPTER XIII.

Textile trade—Old Waulk-mills—Grants from Board of Manufactures—Linen trade—Incle-making—Customer-work—Tweed-trade—List of mills, . . 177-182

CHAPTER XIV.

Guildry Book—Merchant Company—Incorporations of Weavers, Shoemakers, Tailors, Fleshers and Hammermen—Extracts from minutes, and lists of deacons, . 183-217

CHAPTER XV.

Church and ministers of Selkirk—John Welsh, the Covenanter—Dr. Canaries, the Papist—The Old Church and its subsidiary chapels—Church burnt—Trades Aisles—Quaint paintings on "breast of loft"—Old tombstones—Ghost story, . 218-234

CHAPTER XVI.

Bowhill and the house of Buccleuch—Bridgelands—Broadmeadows—Carterhaugh, and the Handba' match—Fastheugh—Fauldshope and the Turnbulls—Foulshiels—Mungo Park—The Haining and its lairds: Scotts, Riddells, Pringles—Harehead—Hartwoodburn and the Currors—Heatherlie, Batts, etc.—Middlestead and the Plummers—Newark—Old Wark—Oakwood and the house of Harden (Polwarth)—Philiphaugh and its lairds: Turnbulls, Barbours, and Murrays—The Shaw—Sunderlandhall and its lairds: the Cockburns, Kers, and Scott-Plummers—Todrig, the home of a poet—Williamhope and the Stoddarts—The Yair—Greenhead—Whitmuir, ... 235-380

APPENDIX.

Charter of Selkirk Abbey—County items in Kelso Abbey rent-roll—Inventory of a laird of Gala (c. 1564)—Rent-roll of Gala estate, 1656—Report on Gala, 1797—County voters, 1790—Stock on Buccleuch farms, 1766—"Extent" of Ettrick Forest, 1628—Valuation Rolls, 1643, 1883, etc.—Growth of agriculture—Wool and sheep premiums, 1760 to 1830—Salmon-fishing and factory pollution—Population table, and Notes, ... 381-413

LIST OF ILLUSTRATIONS.

ON SEPARATE PAGES.

PORTRAIT OF LORD ALEMOOR, ...	*Frontispiece.*
SELKIRK CLAUSE IN KING MALCOLM'S CHARTER, 1159, . .	*facing page* 8
SELKIRK ACCOUNT IN EXCHEQUER ROLL, 1450, ...	14
MINUTE OF TOWN COUNCIL—LEVY FOR FLODDEN, ...	21
CHARTER BY JAMES V., 1535, ...	38
PLAN OF SELKIRK BURGH LANDS, ...	67
MAP OF HAINING (1757), SHOWING TOWN WALLS AND GATES, . .	105
PLAN OF OLD TOLBOOTH AND MARKET-PLACE, ...	130
SIR WALTER SCOTT SITTING AS SHERIFF, ...	140
PORTRAIT OF PROFESSOR LAWSON, ...	169
PLAN OF TOWN, 1823, ...	175
OAKWOOD TOWER, ...	235

IN THE TEXT.

	PAGE
ARMS AND MOTTO OF THE BURGH OF SELKIRK, ...	1
THE BRYDONE SWORD, ...	28
SELKIRK BURGH SEAL, ...	29
SELKIRK SILVER ARROW, ...	52
SELKIRK PRISON, ...	111
THE PANT WELL, ...	118
SELKIRK BURGESS CUP, ...	137
LETTER BY SIR WALTER SCOTT (FACSIMILE), . . .	151, 152
FLAG DESIGNED BY SIR WALTER SCOTT, ...	153
SCOTT'S COURT-HOUSE AND MONUMENT, ...	157
SELKIRK MARKET-PLACE, 1837, ...	183

		PAGE
THE SOUTERS' HALBERT,	.	200
SOUTERS' STONE AT ABBOTSFORD,	.	201
THE FLESHERS' HALBERT,	.	213
GATE OF OLD CHURCHYARD,	.	218
TOMBSTONES IN CHURCHYARD,	.	233
TAMLANE'S WELL,	.	283
PLAN OF NEWARK CASTLE,	.	326
STONE IN OAKWOOD TOWER,	.	330
THE YAIR,	.	375

ETYMOLOGY OF SELKIRK.

BURGH AND PARISH OF SELKIRK.

1119-24	Schelechyrch, . . .	Title of Earl David's Charter.—Dalrymple.
1159	Seleschirche, . . .	Charter of Malcolm IV.
1165-1214	Selekirche, ...	Charter of William the Lion.
1227	Celeschirch, ...	Great Seal, iii. 2308.
1232	Seleskirke, ...	Roll of Glasgow Diocese.
1265	Selekrik, ...	Exchequer Rolls, i. 30.
1292	Selechirche, ...	Rot. Scot., i. 7.
1306	Selkirk, ...	Eng. Charter to Aymer de Valence.
1309	Sellechirch, ...	Rot. Scot., i. 80.
1322	Selkyrc and Schelgrene,	Great Seal.
1402	Selkeryk, ...	Rot. Scot., ii. 163.
1429	Selkrik, ...	Rot. Scot., iv. 520.
	Selcraig, ...	
1560	Selcraig, ...	Acts of Parl., ii. 565.
1659	Salkraig, ...	Acts of Parl., vi. (2) 884.

Other Spellings.—Selchirche, Selekyrcke, Selekirke, Selkirke, Seleschyrche, Selechirc, Selekirc, Selechirk, Selkyrk, Selekirk, Selkirc, Selkyrck, Selkyrke.—Lib. de Kelso; Lib. de Melros; Chamb. Rolls, etc. etc.

Much ingenuity has been expended on the etymology of Selkirk. Sir James Dalrymple derived it from *Schelch* and *grech*, signifying the kirk in the wood; and this was accepted by C. C., the compilers of the Old and New Statistical Accounts. Mr. Chalmers advanced *Sel*, great ii. 963. or good, and *chyrc*, church, as the probable origin, offering the alternative of *Sele*, a hall or prince's court, for the first half of the name, which might thus mean the church of the prince's castle. Defensible guesses all three, though close study of the early spelling suggests another. Almost certainly, the first syllable of Selkirk is the same as the last in Galashiels, the earliest recorded spelling of the one being *Schel*chyrch, and of the other Galu*schel*. This being so, the proper interpretation would be—kirk of the shiels. *Schel* recurs as first syllable, and a significant fact is the occasional coupling of Selkirk with "Schelgrene" in early documents. All pasture lands and "forests" were dotted over with shielings; and near Peebles, which C. P., had much in common with Selkirk, there is a Shielgreen to this day. Peebles itself is from 56. the old British word for tents or movable habitations. A notable instance of the same use of the word "Sel" is Brus*sels*—originally Brocksele—shiel or hut on the marsh.

ARMS AND MOTTO OF THE BURGH OF SELKIRK.

CHAPTER I.

TO 1126 A.D.—SELKIRK ABBEY.

SELKIRK is singularly destitute of any outward sign of its great and undeniable antiquity. Of the castles, towers, gateways, tolbooths, and churches revealed by ancient record not one remains; and it is open to question if there be a building in the burgh which can claim an age of two centuries. But a visible and tangible milestone in the path backwards to the early days of Selkirk presents itself in the ruins of the ancient Abbey of Kelso. In one sense these are like a geological section—something of their history may be gathered from their architectural strata. High up, florid pinnacles and peaked arches reveal a period when Gothic architecture was supreme. Lower down are the round arches of the Norman style, while at the base sturdy Saxon piers tell of a taste earlier and more rude. Evidences of disfigurement recall the days, not now recent, when the fine old interior was rendered ugly enough to serve for the purposes of Presbyterian worship. Traces are still to be seen of the flames kindled when Hertford dealt the last blow to its stateliness. Imagination fills the spacious area with groups and processions of monks as they file from long stone passages towards the altar. Proud Border barons, with their followers, have knelt there in penitence, and there Scottish kings and English kings have acknowledged the King of kings. History spreads itself out like a map to the far-off day when David, newly crowned, moved in and out amongst the rising walls. After realising all this, one is in a position to comprehend the great age of Selkirk, for the monks who laid the first stone of Kelso Abbey came from the pre-existing monastery there.

To say this was in the year 1126, or 760 years ago, hardly enables one to grasp the period that has since gone by. Prince Charlie's passing is now nigh a century and a half back in history. But there was the battle of Philiphaugh 100 years before that, Flodden 130 years before Philiphaugh, Bannockburn 200 years before Flodden; and this removal of monks from Selkirk was 200 years before that again. There are flourishing Antiquarian Societies in New York and Boston devoted to the study and elucidation of the early history of the United States, or rather of the first British Colonies; but people were born, and lived and toiled in Selkirk, for 350 years before Columbus began to dream of a continent beyond the Western Sea which lashed its waves on Spain.

This is a degree of antiquity to satisfy the aspiration of any Scottish burgh, but Selkirk may claim still hoarier age. We have it on the authority of David I. himself, before he ascended the throne, that Selkirk was even then an "old town."

L. K., i. 3.

It is from the charter in which this statement is made, and from two others which followed it, that all information concerning old Selkirk is obtained. These are—Earl David's charter founding Selkirk Abbey (1119-24), his charter removing it to Kelso (c. 1126), and his grandson Malcolm's confirmation in 1159.

App.

While his three elder brothers followed each other on their father's throne, David, youngest son of Malcolm Canmore, spent much of his time in the Norman Courts of England and of France, acquiring a culture too rare in his native country. Having obtained a gift of Cumbria from the Scottish king, his brother, and Northumbria by marriage, David conceived the idea of settling in his own land some of those industrious monks whose beneficent works abroad he had often witnessed. He accordingly applied to Saint Bernard, founder of the Benedictine establishment at

Tiron, who spared him a draft of thirteen of his followers—men not only of Christian faith, but of skill in many branches of industry. They were masons, carpenters, smiths, painters, and husbandmen. To provide for this valuable band of colonisers, whom he located near his own strong castle of Selkirk, Earl David endowed them with wide possessions and valuable privileges—

"Like wealthy men who care not how they give."

First, he gave them "the land of Selkirk, from where a rivulet App. descending from the hills runs into Yarrow as far as that rivulet which, coming down from Crossinemere, flows into Tweed; and beyond the said rivulet which falls into Yarrow, a certain particle of land between the road which leads from the castle to the abbey and Yarrow—that is, towards the old town." Besides the towns of Midlem, Bowden, and Aldona (?), he gave them his whole lordship of Melrose, lands in Sprouston and Berwick, shares in fishing, parts of burgh dues, a tenth of the "kain" cheeses of Galloway, half the skins of his kitchen, a tenth of the hides of stags which his huntsmen killed, an equal share of his fishing water about Selkirk, and equal right to his woods and pastures. In England, land at Hardingstrop, besides the mill and fields near the bridge of Northampton. All this endowment David dedicated to the Abbey of Selkirk, "in honour of St. Mary and of St. John the Evangelist, for the weal of his own soul, of the souls of his father and mother, brothers and sisters, and all his ancestors," for ever inalienably, so that none of his successors should presume to exact anything from the monks but prayers only for the weal of their souls.

In this document, the important points are the boundaries of the land of Selkirk and the mention of "the *old* town." How old that old town was can only be conjectured, but, from its name, certainly not older than the Saxon occupation, which began about the sixth century. More B. S., 278, 390. than probably the *chirche* was planted beside the *scheles* on the revival of Christianity, in the time of Queen Margaret, after its eclipse in Scotland for nearly 500 years, which would make the name now about eight centuries old. The *scheles*, which must have been there before the church, were the nuts or clachans of shepherds in charge of flocks out at pasture. The word is Saxon, the Norse being *skalig*, from which is derived "scalengas" in monk-Latin—used to signify a right of pasture as distinct from a gift of land.

So that the probable evolution of Selkirk would be—(1) a collection of dwelling-places for herdsmen and hunters employed in the Royal Forest ; (2) the erection of a church, possibly by the Culdees of Old Melrose ; (3) the building of a castle ; (4) the settlement of a number of craftsmen under its protection, and the gradual gathering together of a community. This stage it had reached when the black-robed Tironensian monks came over from France to found the abbey.

Patro-
logiae,
v. 172,
p. 1426.
　　Gaufridus Grossus, a monk of Tiron, who wrote the life of St. Bernard, and who must have known the brethren who went to Selkirk, says :—

　　"About this time (1108) David, afterwards King of Scotland, came to hear by report of the signal merits of our most blessed father then still living. By dint of strenuous embassies he obtained no small number of disciples from the congregation ; and in Lothian he built them a house (*coenobium*) on a pleasant site near the river Tweed, which he sufficiently endowed with rents and wide possessions. After he had done this, desiring ardently to see the man of God, he set out from his northern home, and passing the bounds of many interjacent regions, braving the terrors of the British Sea, and crossing the provinces of Normandy, he arrived at Tiron. But he could not behold what he desired, for the holy father had already departed to heaven. Yet, lest he might appear ungrateful or careless of so great a man, he laid aside his royal dignity, and, on his bended knees, presented himself before the tomb with becoming reverence. The monastery, which he had already founded, he endowed with wider territory and revenues. And taking with him twelve monks with an Abbot of the Order, in addition to those he already had, at length reached his own kingdom."

App.
　　That the deed of foundation was important is evident from the number and rank of its witnesses—John, Bishop of Glasgow, the Countess Matilda (daughter of Henry I. of England, and David's niece), David's son Henry (a prince of promise, whose early death was a blow to Scotland), Robert Bruce (ancestor of the hero of Bannockburn), the Sheriff of Bamborough, and several knights of Norman lineage, whose names afterwards became famous in England.

Hist.
Coll.,
li. 237.
　　A striking commentary on the settlement at Selkirk is offered by Sir James Dalrymple, who endeavours to prove that the Abbacies founded by David were "calculat to propagat the Romish religion in this kingdom, upon the ruines and suppressions of the Culdean churches and monastries." He represents the popish Bishop of Glasgow as being greatly strengthened by the erection of Selkirk abbacy, and its annexation to his diocese. But popular clamour forced Bishop John to leave the country (making believe to go to Jerusalem), until ordered back by the Pope. Again driven from his diocese, he lived with the monks at Tours till, in the year 1138, King David commanded him to return, on pain of ecclesiastical censure. Dalrymple is of opinion that in 1125, when a papal legate came to hold the first Council

in Scotland, there was no popish abbacy but one at Selkirk. Be this as it may, it is not to be believed that Earl David was actuated solely, or even chiefly, by a desire to extend the sway of the Roman Pontiff. It is more credible that, being alive to the advantages conferred by learned and civilised monks on other countries, he wished his own to be brought under their humanising influence. The Culdees, worthy ministers of a simple faith though they were, seem to have been destitute of those arts which flourished amidst the brotherhoods acknowledging the Pope. They were too much akin to their rude flocks to initiate that controlling influence over them which the Church eventually developed. It may thus be maintained that David in founding Selkirk Abbey carried out a patriotic policy, and that the amelioration of life which followed the Benedictine settlement was cheaply purchased at the cost of Culdee independence. These stout old anti-innovators, however, did not surrender without a struggle. It has been already seen how they drove the Roman Bishop of Glasgow from his place; and the monkish strangers at Selkirk no doubt suffered their share of persecution. So near to the powerful Culdee monastery of Melrose, there must have been many partisans of the old faith ready to molest them, but for the protection afforded by the prince's castle of Selkirk, under the shadow of whose walls they commenced to rear their holy fane.

Much difficulty attends the identification of the "land of Selkirk," as App. defined in David's charter. In the first place, it is evident either that the river from the junction at Bowhill to Tweed must then have borne the name of Yarrow instead of Ettrick, or that the "land of Selkirk" must have lain between Yarrow and Tweed. The latter hypothesis is untenable, and the former, though it simplifies the difficulty, does not remove it. The first rivulet which falls into Tweed below the junction is that which divides Faldonside from Abbotsford; and if this be the *rivulus* of the charter, Faldonside lesser loch must be Crassansmer—*mer* or *mere* being the Saxon for lake, as in Grasmere, Windermere, etc. And if the Shaw Burn be that which "descends from the hills and runs into Yarrow," the "land of Selkirk" given to the monastery must have lain between it and Faldonside burn, while on the west side of Shaw Burn must have been the "certain particle of land between the river and the road leading from Castle to Abbey." Although, to understand the charter at all, it is necessary to look upon Yarrow as continuing its name till it reaches Tweed, it should not be over-looked that 100 years later, in 1232, the combined rivers were known as

Ettrick. Subsequent references to the lands might have cleared away the difficulty, but for confusion arising from two Selkirks being in the field— Abbot's Selkirk and King's Selkirk; in Latin, Selkirk-Abbatis and Selkirk-Regis respectively. Of the two the King's town would be the oldest, the Abbot's town consisting of certain cottages occupied by cultivators of the Abbey lands. For a century or two the distinction was kept up in ecclesiastical documents, but history does not record the date when Selkirk-Abbatis ceased to be a local habitation and a name. We are inclined to think that the property now and past memory known as The *Batts*, lying in the "land of Selkirk," as we interpret the charter, has something to do with the old designation.

L. K., var.

Lists of Glasgow diocesan charters from 1180 to 1232 mention the church of Selkirk and church of the other Selkirk. In a deed granted at

L. K., 300.

Seleschirche (1153-65), Malcolm IV. confirmed to Kelso "the church of Selkirk, with the half ploughgate of land which in the time of David my grandsire, lay dispersed about the fields (*per campum*); and as it is of little use so broken up, I give them an equal portion of land in one piece for the foresaid half ploughgate." A ploughgate was 104 Scots acres, equal to about 130 imperial acres. In a rent-roll of the time of Robert Bruce, the Abbey

L. K., 460.

property in Selkirk-Regis is said to consist of the land of Bridgelands, containing 16 acres, and of pasture in Minchmoor; but various gaps in the entry, and the words "Selkirk Abbatis" without remark of any kind, show the scribe to have been at sea—confused probably by the dual name. Further on we come upon the following entry :—

SELKIRK-ABBATIS.

"They have the said town of Abbots-Selkirk. One ploughgate and a half, which used to yield 10 merks yearly. Fifteen husbandlands, each containing an oxgang (13 acres) rented at 4 shillings. All the husbandmen have to give the Abbot ten days' work in autumn; two to furnish a cart for carrying peats from the moss to the Abbey, and two to provide a pack-horse for carrying goods from Berwick to the Abbey. They have to give the same service as Bowden husbandmen—to plough every year an acre and a half in the grange at Newtown; to harrow one day with a horse; to find a man to assist in washing, and another in shearing the sheep; to carry corn with a cart one day in autumn; to carry the Abbot's wool from the barony to the Abbey, and to find their own carriage beyond the muir towards Leshmahago (where the monks had a religious house, a sanctuary and great possessions). Besides the husbandlands there are 16 cottages in Selkirk-Abbatis with 10 acres of land between them; fifteen rented at 12 pence, and one at two shillings with nine days' harvest work, and assistance at sheep-shearing. Three breweries each pay 6s. 8d. per annum; and one corn-mill five merks. Beyond the lordships they have 30 acres yielding 5s., besides four acres, called 'Richard Cute's land,' yielding 6s. yearly."

A privilegium by Pope Innocent IV. (1243-54) is the last writ in L. K., which the distinction is mentioned, his Holiness confirming the Abbey in ^{350.} possession of Monks-Selkirk (Selechirche-Monachorum) and King's-Selkirk. The rectorial revenues of the churches of King's-Selkirk and Abbot's-Selkirk L. K., are given at £20 and 40s. respectively in the roll of 1300, and appear to ^{471.} correspond with entries in the roll of 1567 valuing the vicarage at £66, 13s. 4d., and the "Kirklands" at the old sum of 40s. The rectorial revenue of Abbot's-Selkirk had thus been changed to the rent of a field, known within memory as "Kirklands,"—the first on the left of the Bleachfield Road after leaving the old toll-house.

The disappearance of impalpable boundary lines is little to be wondered at, but it is marvellous how substantial walls which for thirteen years the monks of Selkirk were busy rearing should,

"like the baseless fabric of a vision,
Leave not a rack behind."

Not a tittle of direct evidence exists as to the site on which they stood, much less a sentence surviving from the olden time to convey an idea of their extent and plan. Neither in the archives of the diocese of Chartres, where Tiron is situated, nor in those of the ancient Benedictine Abbey of Solesmes (kindly searched by MM. L'Abbé Germond et L'Abbé Piotin at the writer's request), is there to be found a trace of the offshoot to Selkirk. Perhaps when the dark recesses of the Vatican come to be opened, some plodding antiquary will reveal the secret. Meantime, one has to be content with a dim tradition that the deserted walls stood scaffold-high for many years on what is now the south side of High Street, at the west corner of Tower Street.

No secret is made of the reason why the monks abandoned Selkirk and went to Kelso. It was "because the former was not suitable for a monastery;" and candour compels the admission that the monks made a good change in respect of climate. Probably, however, the strongest reason was David's growing preference for Roxburgh Castle—a preference which became more marked when he succeeded his brother on the throne in 1124. He then set about the translation of the monks, and in 1126 it was effected, the Bishop of Glasgow being a strong advocate of the change. All their Selkirk rights and lands (except the lordship of Melrose, conveyed to the new Abbey there) were confirmed to them at Kelso, others being added. And to these considerable additions had been made, when Malcolm in 1159 re-confirmed

Kelso Abbey in its extensive holdings. This document of confirmation, now
L. K., xliv., in the Roxburgh archives, is considered by Mr. Cosmo Innes "the most
remarkable of Scotch charters. It is carefully and even handsomely written;
but its chief interest is derived from an illuminated initial M, which
perpetuates a pair of the earliest Scotch portraits that have come down to
us"—King David I. and his grandson Malcolm IV., "whose youthful and
beardless face accounts for his *sobriquet* of *The Maiden* better than the
refuted tradition of his vow of chastity." A reduced facsimile is given of
that part which relates to Selkirk.

This transaction was the beginning of a close connection between the two
towns. David made it a condition of the change that the priests or abbots
of Selkirk should be court chaplains to himself and his successors—a privilege
R. S. recognised by Edward I. in 1296 when Adam de Selkirk was called "parson
of the chapel of the camp of Roxburgh," and so late as 1534 when Sir
B. R. William Bryden was styled "vicar of Selkirk and Auld Roxburgh."

Probably by way of compensating Selkirk for the loss of hides from the
King's kitchen and forest, its inhabitants were entitled to unusual privileges
in purchasing the same from Kelso, confirmed less than 200 years ago in a
Cor. mss. treaty of reciprocity, here slightly abridged :—

"At Kelso, 2 October 1697 : The which day George Pringle, bailie-depute of Kelso, sitting
in judgment in a lawful fenced court, having received a petition from the Magistrates, etc.,
of Selkirk, anent the privileges of their cordiners and burgesses in buying hides in the land-
market here, and having discoursed several neighbours anent the said privileges, found the
desire of their petition to be reasonable, and enacts that the free burgesses of Selkirk shall
have liberty to buy hides in the land-market of Kelso at any time of the day . . . likeas the
Magistrates of Selkirk declare that they will allow and defend any wonted privileges of the
merchants or tradesmen of Kelso ever had in their burgh of Selkirk."

Inheriting the fair-lined slippers of the abbot, the Duke of Roxburgh
procured and maintained the right of presentation to Selkirk parish church;
but the Patronage Abolition Act has snapped for ever the last cord of the
union formed between Selkirk and Kelso good seven hundred years ago.

Two things remained with Selkirk after the departure of the monks—the
name of the church, St. Mary's, and the seal, a representation of the Virgin
and Child. This, after being adopted as the town's coat-of-arms, has been
mixed up with an incident, real or fabled, of the return from Flodden, the
addition of a shield bearing the lion-rampant having been probably made in
the time of James V.

mam partem molendinorum. & terram dodni in eadem uilla. & terram Waltheui filii Ernebold. Et uillam de middelham & Bothueldene cum suis rectis diuisis. in terris & aquis. in boscho & plano. Et xxx acras terre de territoris Lillesclive. inter Alnam & riuulum qui diuidit t'ram de middelham et d'Lilles clive. & decimam molendini ipsius uille scilicet Lillesclive et Whitelawa. et Whitemere cum suis rectis diuisis. Et terram de Seleschirche cum suis diuisis in terris et aquis in boscho et plano. & aquas meas circa Seleschirche. communes ad piscandum suis p'p'is piscatoribus ut meis. & pasturas communes suis hominibus ut meis. & boschos meos domibus suis faciendis. et ad ardendum ut m'. Et ecclesiam de altera Seleschirche cum dimidia carrucata terrae. Et ecclesiam & terram d'Lesmagu cum suis rectis diuisis &c &c.

SELKIRK CLAUSE IN KING MALCOLM'S CHARTER. 1159.

CHAPTER II.

A.D. 1126 TO A.D. 1512.

THOUGH glory ecclesiastical had departed from Selkirk, its importance in other respects suffered no eclipse. In William the Lion's reign (1159-1214) it again became a favourite residence of royalty, many Acts of Government or Royal Decrees being issued by this monarch "before his full court assembled at Selkirk." In 1204, on the Sunday after Easter, the King decided at Selkirk a long-standing dispute between the monks of Kelso and Melrose concerning the boundaries of Bowden. On the 6th November four years later, his Majesty, having decided another question of boundary between Melrose Abbey and the Earl of Dunbar, took into consideration with his assembly of nobles a matter which displays in a very absurd light the musings of certain imaginative philologists.

"A very deep pit," says Sir T. D. Lauder, "was discovered recently in the old tower of Cowdenknowes, which was believed to have a communication with the house of Sorrowlessfield, on the opposite side of the water. This place belonged to an ancient family who, at one time, were all cut off in a battle, so that none remained to mourn for the rest, which circumstance gave rise to the strange name."

"The vivid freshness of Sir David Brewster's memory," says his biographer, "and his love of the legendary history of the Vale of Tweed, was displayed in every drive, and not only excited by an extra occasion. He used to tell with peculiar interest that 'Sorrowlessfield' was so named because in 1513 it was the only valley in Scotland where there was no sorrow —its every inhabitant, young and old, matron, maid, and infant, going forth to the death at Flodden."

Now this very piece of ground, fully 300 years before Flodden, was decided by William the Lion and his Court at Selkirk to belong to the monks of Melrose, as it was held by William Sorlees, from whom it derived the name of Sorleesfield! In all tradition there is nothing so doubtful as the story which accounts for a name.

From the number of peers and prelates who attended on these occasions and witnessed decrees, it is evident that the Castle of Selkirk must have been large and important. Where it stood is not so uncertain as the site of the monastery, probability pointing to the Peel Hill as its most likely stance. Not only do ancient documents favour the supposition, but the shape, size, and position of Peel Hill single it out as a most probable "coigne of vantage" for the king's stronghold. In those days of hand-to-hand fighting, and no missiles reaching further than arrows, it would be a good position to defend. To the north a steep slope stretched down without a break until it reached the brook now known as "the Clockie"—mayhap a survival from *cloaque*, Norman-French for drain or sewer. On the west and south its base was washed by the Haining Loch, much deeper then than now, with an arm stretching far round, past the Bog and the Foul Port, to Porches Pool— now a bowling-green near the new United Presbyterian Church. It was thus accessible only from the east, along the ridge now occupied by Castle Street (a modernised version of its old and finer name—the Peel Gait); but across the road stretched a deep ditch, visible to this day, spanned by a drawbridge for the passage of friends, but yawning like a grave before advancing enemies. On the height thus defended by nature and by art there was room enough for a castle of royal dimensions, able to shelter king and council with all their servants and retainers. That Selkirk once had such a castle has been abundantly proved in the course of these pages, and that it stood on the Peel Hill is almost certain. For many reasons. There is no other likely place. It corresponds with the notice of the castle in King David's charter. It is close to the Haining—"the hanite part" of a royal forest being near the castle. Moreover, Peel Hill and Haining went with the office of Constable of Selkirk, and afterwards with the Sheriffship of Selkirk, along with the burgh dues belonging directly to the King.

For.
Law.

Probably in the ruthless Border wars which followed Bruce's death Selkirk Castle was razed to the ground, and its site taken up by a small peel for the crown tacksman, which in its turn has wholly disappeared. Beneath the deep soil of decayed vegetation which now covers the hill, one comes upon stones which formed part of frowning battlements. Standing by the

"Old yew which graspeth at the stones"

on the apex of the mound, surrounded by a guard of lofty beeches, one must perforce moralise a little on departed greatness. Impressive it is to think that so many hundred years ago on this very spot kings summoned their nobles to peaceful council or to bloody war. Only one scene from that distant age would now be felt in keeping with the place—the scene when, accompanied by a retinue of nobles and huntsmen, David the Saint, or Malcolm the Maiden, or William the Lion issued from the castle gate to chase the stag by Ettrick braes or Yarrow.

> "O merry it was in the good green wood,
>   When the mavis and merle were singing,
> When the deer swept by, and the hounds were in cry,
>   And the hunter's horn was ringing."

In the scant records which survive of Alexander II.'s reign, Selkirk appears frequently as honoured by the royal presence. In 1223 he sat *in plena curia apud Seleschirk* upon a question between the monks of Newbattle and the canons of Holyrood. One charter signed by Alexander in 1227 is notable for the unique spelling of "Celeschirch;" but the most interesting of his Selkirk Acts is that dated 1234, in which he enjoined the monks of Kelso to devote certain lands on each side of the water to the perpetual maintenance of a bridge over Ettrick, whence the estate of Bridgelands derived its name. [L. M., 204, 216, 219, 250.] [A. P., i. 405.] [G. S., iii. 2308.] [L. K., 308, 309.]

During his prosperous and happy reign, Alexander III. does not appear to have been much at Selkirk, though there is mention of one visit. Probably in his time the castle was abandoned as a royal residence, and allowed to go to ruin; for it is not mentioned in the list of twenty-three surrendered by Edward to Baliol in 1292. In this reign, however, the word is first encountered as a personal surname. In 1273 Patricke de Selkirke became Abbot of Melrose, being most likely a monk connected with the place. As Abbot he is suspected to have been prime instigator of Baliol's ill-starred attempt to throw off the English yoke; but he was none the less fain to sign allegiance to Edward two years afterwards; and in 1305 he was one of ten Scotch commissioners who sat with twenty English at Westminster to draw out a plan of governing Scotland. First applied, no doubt, to people coming from Selkirk, the surname soon became common. Thomas of Selkirk and Peter of Selkirk were burgesses of Berwick, Hew of Selkirk being a burgess of Edinburgh. None of them, however, can be said to have shed so much lustre on their god-mother as their descendant in modern times, the prototype of Robinson Crusoe. [L. M., 274.] [R. S., i. 11.] [L. M., 336.] [R. C., 93.]

The town of Selkirk had its share in the ups and downs of the nation in the eight-and-twenty years between Alexander's death and Bannockburn.

The very year Edward I. awarded the crown to Baliol, he sent notice to the tenant of Selkirk Mills, one John le Tailleur, that the £28 of rent he was in arrear had been assigned to the executors of the will of Master Robert of Dumfries, lately Chancellor of OUR kingdom of Scotland! For a short while Wallace succeeded in holding Selkirk against the usurper, and is believed to have been made Guardian of the kingdom in its Church of St. Mary; but very soon afterwards the town fell again into southern possession. Edward I. was himself in Selkirk on his way back to England in 1304, and seems to have formed a high opinion of its importance. He immediately put the town and castle in the keeping of Aymer de Valence, Earl of Pembroke, a renowned English general, who at once set himself to strengthen the fortress. In 1309 de Valence received orders "to provision the castle of Selkirk with men and victuals with all expedition against the King's enemies and rebels," and next year Edward II. was there for nearly a week in September, directing operations against Robert the Bruce.

From the exactions of a hostile army Selkirk was freed by the victory of Bannockburn. In 1322, Robert I. appointed William Turnbull of Philiphaugh to the office of Constable of Selkirk, with all that belonged to that office in the time of Alexander III.; and the same year let the mill of Selkirk to Henry Gelchedall for two merks yearly, Thomas of Charteris (de Carnoto) accounting in 1329 for rent of mill, lately in the hands of Gelchedale, deceased. Horses and mares for the King's stud were brought from various places to Selkirk, and in 1330, 24s. was paid from the Royal Exchequer for salt for the King's venison at Selkirk. By the disastrous Scottish defeat at Halidon Hill in 1333, the town was again put under English domination, it and the castle being formally assigned in Baliol's shameful pact "to be held separately from the Crown of Scotland, and annexed to and incorporated with the Crown of England for ever." In virtue of this concession, the keeper of Selkirk Castle was notified that Antonio de Lucy had been appointed keeper of Berwick, and other Englishmen set over the annexed provinces in various administrative posts. Edward also confirmed a charter by William de Coucy in favour of his son William, of Selkirk and Traquair, with other property.

It does not appear, however, that Selkirk remained in English occupation for any considerable period, the Douglases being as determined to hold the forest granted to them by Bruce as the English king was to obtain it. The Knight of Liddesdale expelled the English in 1338; and when after

R. S.,
i. 13.

R. S.,
i. 54.

Dug.
Bar.,
i. 777.

R. S.,
i. 80.

R. S.,
i. 103.

G. S.,
i. 5.

R. C.,
31.
E. R.,
i. 149.

E. R., i.
71, 340,
313.

Rym.,
iv. 615,
616.

R. S.,
i. 352.

H. A., ii.
222, 243.

David II.'s defeat and capture at Neville's Cross in 1346 the southerners again became masters of the Border, William Douglas, first Earl of the name, once more drove them out. There could be no surer sign of its confirmed recovery to Scottish rule than payment of tribute to the Scottish king; and the "bailies of Selkirk" figure for 53s. 4d. in 1368. The jealousy with which the Kings reserved their personal interest in the town of Selkirk is illustrated in David II.'s charter to Robert de Dalyell, who got all the lands of Selkirk in 1365, "except our yearly returns from our burgh." Indeed, until its advancement to the dignity of a royal burgh in 1535, it was properly a burgh in the royal demesne. When Robert III. confirmed George, Earl of Angus, in his vast possessions, they comprised "the haill toun of Selkirk;" and the Douglas influence continued to preponderate until James II. himself took possession of their Selkirkshire estates in 1455. *[margin: E. R., ii. 302. — G. S., i. 45. — His. MSS., vii. 727.]*

While James I. was still a prisoner in the court of England, Douglas of Drumlanrig obtained confirmation of his hold on Selkirk. Six years later, in 1418, a raid across the Border led to a retaliatory invasion headed by Sir Robert Umfraville, Governor of Berwick, who burned the town of Selkirk—first recorded experience of a calamity afterwards almost familiar enough to breed contempt. *[margin: Bucc., ii. 22. — Harding, c. 218.]*

The return of James I. from captivity resulted in a stirring up of the towns throughout all Scotland—the King's object being the establishment of a power to support him against the overweening pretensions of his nobility. Following the inquiry he caused to be made respecting revenue from the customs, Selkirk reappears in the accounts of Exchequer. *[margin: E. R., iv. 419, 460, 495, 521, 551, 587, 663.]*

1424-6.—Memorandum that William Wood, bailie of the burgh of Selkirk, asserted that he had not yet received any burgh rents or petty customs; but the deputy chamberlain had measured the burgh-roods (*particatas burgales*), which extended to five times twenty and ten roods, of which each owed fivepence annually to the King, and for the rents of which he would account at next reckoning.

1426-8.—Account of John Spardur, bailie of Selkirk. He charges himself with £4, 9s. 8d. rents of the burgh for two years—namely, of five times twenty and ten burgess-roods. Also with 11s. 8d. petty customs for two years. With certain divisions of land, acknowledged to be in hands of the King, he does not charge himself, but will in next account. The account is balanced by two payments of £2, 10s. 10d. and £2, 12s. 6d. to Sir John Forrester and Master John Wyncestre respectively.

1428-9.—George Sparedur, one of the bailies of Selkirk. Year's rents, £2, 6s. 8d., petty customs, 6s. No yield from the lands of Gelchden, Crakewilly, le Pele, Sausarelande, Communwomanlande, Colvilslande, or Ewarslande, in the King's hands.

1429-30.—Bailie Geo. Spardur. Rents, £2, 6s. 8d., petty customs, 13s. 4d. Rent of lands of Gelchdene from Martinmas to Whitsunday, 2s. 6d.; of Crakwyly, 2d.; of Pell, 6d.;

of Saussarlande, 1d.; of Commonwommanlande, 1d. No rent for these lands from the term of Pentecost because they were waste, nor for the lands of Colvyllisande and Ewarislande, pledged by the Chamberlain.

1430-31.—Bailie John Sparder. Much as in last, but Gelchdene changed to Geldstaniscroft.

1433-34.—Bailie John "Spare-the-dur." Returns as in last.

E. R., v. 400, 440. 1434-1450.—Fifteen years. Accounts of the burgh of Selkirk rendered at Holyrood by Bailie John Sparedur. First, rents of burgess-roods, £35. Petty customs, £5. Gelchden, Crakwilly, le Pele, Sausareland, Comounwomanland, Colynlisland and Ewarisland, £5. Total £45. Discharge of the same—paid Cranstoun of Cranstoun for 11 years, as appears from the King's letters privately exhibited, £40, which sum the King's grace, by advice of his Council, gave to him for good service done to his King and country. And allowed to the inhabitants of the said burgh of Selkirk on account of their poverty and the devastation caused during the war with England, £5.

1450 to 1451.—Bailies Walter Turnbul and William Kene. Revenue as before.

Except le Pele, or Peelhill, these somewhat extraordinary names of King's lands other than burgess acres have long since disappeared, neither document nor tradition affording the slightest clue to their identity. Probably the land afterwards known as Kingcroft comprises them all.

A. P., ii. 63, 68. In 1449 and 1451 James II. executed identical charters confirming to William, Earl of Douglas, the forest lands of Ettrick on payment of a broad arrow at the hill of Selkirk; and in 1452, after his cowardly slaughter of the Earl, the King thought it necessary to march south with 30,000 men, Aslo. MSS., ii. 49. by way of overawing the murdered chief's retainers, Selkirk being one of the places visited. Little, however, was effected but the destruction of corn and orchards by the host, and the desolating of the lands of many who were the King's own friends.

For the year 1467-8 the total value of the King's dues from the burgh of Selkirk was £2, 6s. 8d., beside which a sum of £109 of arrears seems E. R., vii. 597, 671. stupendous. Next year it was cancelled, because Bailie Spardur, who was responsible, had left no distrainable heirs.

The accession of James IV. to the throne of his ill-used father, in 1488, was the signal for considerable changes in the ownership of land, those who had fought against the late King being rewarded at the expense of such as had defended him. Though the lordship of Selkirk was given to G. S., ii. 1827. George Douglas, son and heir of Angus, the town to all appearance remained Crown property; and was visited by its royal superior three T. A., 98, 104, 107, 185. months after he became King. Of date the 19th November 1488 there is entry of a payment "in Selkirk to the King, 20 half rose nobles, £18." This was while James was holding justiciary courts in various towns of

Selkyrk Compotu ...

Item compotus ...

S[umm]a ...

Expense eiusd[em] ...

S[umm]a ...

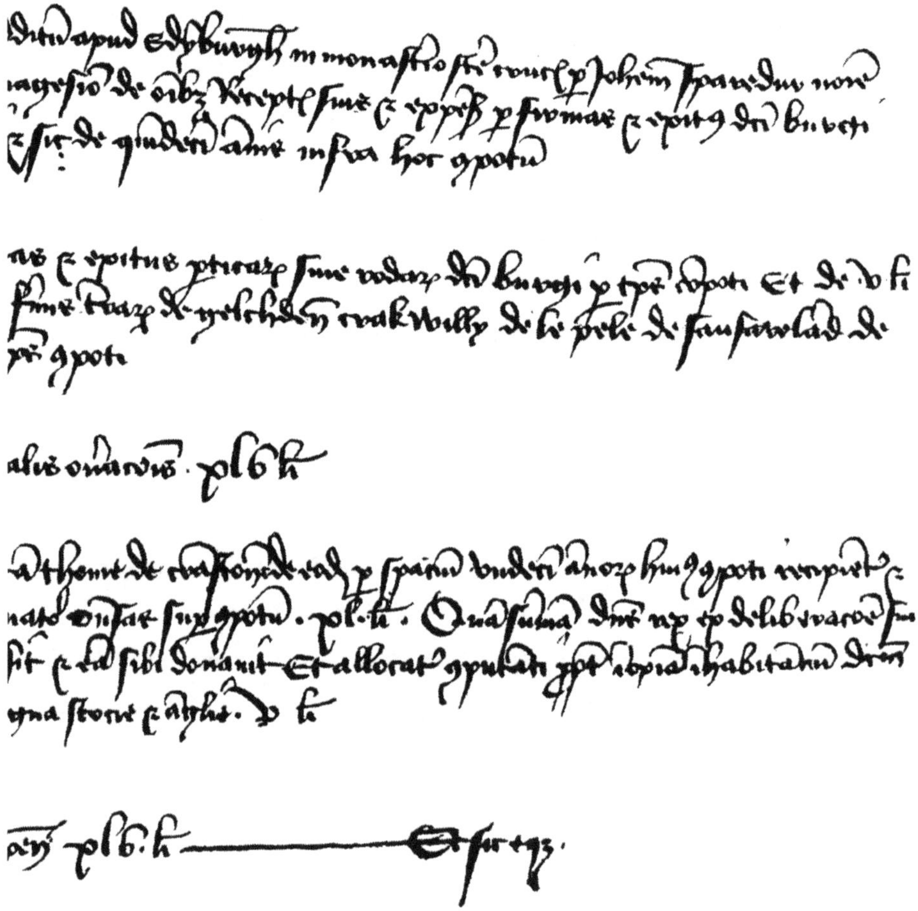

HEQUER ROLL, 1450.

the Border, the expenses for two days at Selkirk amounting to £12. In April 1489, 22s. was paid to Peter Ker, currour, for going with letters for the tax, to Selkirk, and other places; no less than £36, 16s. 8d. being allowed for the expenses of Lord Drummond's children, boys and horses, while on circuit. The King was passionately attached to Lord Drummond's daughter Margaret.

That there was abundant need for such courts is evident from the many cases of murder, theft, and outrage of every kind brought before them. At Jedburgh, Scot of Howpaslot and his accomplices had to answer for harrying Pit., i. 18. Harehead, in Yarrow, of 40 oxen and cows and 300 sheep. Hector Lauder, brother of the laird of Todrig (Parish of Selkirk), was accused of getting the Elliots to help him in stealing 5 score cows and oxen and the whole household goods from Whitmuir, and for bringing in the Forsters (great thieves) to the Pot-loch of Selkirk. From Fastheuch, ewes were stolen by men who were further accused of taking part in a horrible attack upon the secluded house of Ploro, slaying the goodwife and her two sons, and carrying away rich booty of live-stock and household plenishings. The proceedings at Selkirk, elsewhere recorded, throw a strong light on the fierce customs and unsettled life of Borderers at this time—evils against which residence in a town offered but indifferent protection. When in 1497 Surrey led an English army into Scotland, to counteract James iv.'s parade on behalf of Perkin Warbeck, and laid siege to Ayton Castle, the burgh of Selkirk sent its share of men to the Scottish army. In the Exchequer Rolls there is a note that a fine for E. R., 320. non-appearance will not be levied in the case of Bailie William Cranston of Selkirk, because at the time he was in the service of the King at Ayton, on the trial of Heron and certain Englishmen convicted there.

The sixteenth century brought no respite from the lawlessness which had pervaded the closing years of its predecessor. Murder followed murder, feud embittered feud, and robbery brought retaliation, in rapid and appalling succession. In 1500, Ninian Murray and George Vins slew John Porteous P. S., iii. 78, 76. in Selkirk; and shortly afterwards the crime was followed by the cruel slaughter of John Furde in the town of Selkirk by William Ker, Whitmuir, Pit., i. 32. and Alexander Gray in Greenhead, James Kein, Selkirk, and James Elwalde (Elliot), Whitmuir. A Justiciary Court was held in Selkirk, in 1502, by Lord Gray, but seems to have had little effect in reducing the turbulent inhabitants to order. Indeed, the times were not favourable for the prosecution of peaceful industries. Guided by Adam Turnbull, in Hornshole, Pit., i. 35.

Sir John Musgrave led a body of English suddenly to Selkirk, burning the town, and robbing the inhabitants of goods to the value of 1000 merks. In the light of such outrages it is not difficult to understand the eager readiness with which the men of Selkirk afterwards flocked to the King's banner when he promised to lead them against England.

About this time the ancient records of the Burgh become available for the purposes of history, and from them we learn in what manner its affairs were administered. It would appear as if the earliest manuscripts had perished in the flames lighted by Sir John Musgrave, for the first minute extant is dated 17th January 1503-4, the year after the burning. Unfortunately, the next leaves are lost as far as 1506. On the 19th May of that year, a letter from the King was read, authorising Ralph Ker of Primside to build a mill upon his lands of Bullsheugh ("Byllieshaugh" in record), and to extend them as far as may be found necessary on the common land of the burgh between Bullsheugh and Ettrick; to make a sufficient aqueduct from the south side through the said common ground, provided he obtain consent of the bailies, council, and community, build a sufficient bridge over the dam, and undertake to maintain it. As a matter of course, the King's letter was at once complied with by the "Inquest," as the Council of that time was termed. This "Inquest" was composed of the "best and worthiest of the burgh," presided over by an Alderman and Bailies, who were also the Magistrates of the town. Their names in 1506 were—

G. S.,
ii. 2966.

Adam Turnbull of Philiphaugh.	Ringan Brown.	Watt Hall.
George Scott.	Thomas Kene.	Thome Bryden.
Thomas Johnston.	James Minto.	David Bryden.
Woll Ker of Whitmuir.	Wolken Bryden.	David Henderson.
Woll Porteous.	John Smith.	Jas. Porteous.
Ringan Donaldson.	James Hall.	John Moys.

It is impossible to say what qualifications other than "goodness and worth" were necessary for members of the Inquest, but from the constant change of names in the sederunt, it would appear as if all were entitled to sit who had property—say, a burgess-acre. Of fifteen who met on 22d October 1509, only four were amongst the nineteen who ratified the King's letter about Bullsheugh Mill. The others are—

Woll Main.	Wolle Loremer.	James Scott.
John Johnston.	John Lauder.	John Loremer.
Andrew Sanderson.	Alex. Kein.	Robert Scott.
Jok Barker.	Wolzeame Ker.	

Among thirteen who were at a meeting a fortnight later, the new names are :—

David Brown.	John Chapman.	James Skirving.
Kentigern (Mungo) Brown.	Robert Porteous.	Arch^d Thomson.
	James Bryden.	

The following extracts from the minute-book reveal conditions of life offering a violent contrast to the calm and even tenor of Selkirk existence nowadays :—

1509, Oct. 22.—Decreed that aill should be sold from Sunday forth by all brewsters under pain of cheatery of the samen and 8 chalders to the Bailies. The baxters to have the bread of 20 ounces, and at ilk unce to have a pais. Nae unfreeman to bake nor brew, buy nor sell. . . . The meeting finds Robert Scott and Thomas Johnston convenient to the office of the Baillierie, and lays the samen on them.

1509, Dec. 5.—Ordains watches to be keepit by mens and not by laddies; and, as was ordanit befor, to walk on the back side within the boundis of their watchis. And nae watch maun gae to the potation and drink from time 9 hours forth under the pain of unlaw; and to wak quhyll cokraw (walk—perhaps keep awake—until cock-crow, or sunrise), and syne to warn Stewin of Lauder in the Wast Port, Thomas Johnson in the Under Port, and Wat Haw on the East Port.

1510, Oct. 7.—A watch of 18 men, neebors and housholders, nichtly to walk, weil abulzeit (armed) as they may best, to begin at 9 hours, and wak quhyll lawchful cokcraw, under pain at ilk failure of 12 pence, but favour. Two burgesses to be made at the Bailies, pleasure, the entry-money of one to be taen incontinent to beat the Towbooth (point it with lime), and one mark of the tother to be given to Robin Scott and Thomas Johnston (both bailies), for their costs when they rade to Edinburgh.

1511, Jany. 14.—Robert Chapman mentioned as having an annual rent from land on the south side of the Peel-gait (now Castle Street).

Feb. 23.—Watch of 9 men appointed, well-furnished, and instructed as to the time to leis (loose—cease watching). To inquire at Pat Kein, David Brown, and Thomas Brydone, gif it be time to leis—ilka watch to inquire for its own part of the town.

Mention of Hallwollhill on the West side of High Street.

Horse taken for debt and valued at 32s. Scots.

Sept. 30.—The haill community of the Burgh fand and made John of Murray of Fawlahill (and Philiphaugh), Sheriff of Selkirk, a Burgess of the same; and swore the aith.

Dec. 10.—Patrick Wilkieson prohibited from selling the mill-stane, for which he was pursued by John Scot. . . . Ordained ony nicht-walkers which are known should be punished in the stocks 24 hours, and sent out of the town for a year and a day.

1512, Feby. 17.—Nicol of Karncross, Baily-deput to my Lord of Melros, presented a commission under the common seal of the Abbey to borrow Matho Rannek from this present court, which the Bailies admitted. Resolution to proceed with edifice of church—"Our Lady work"—given elsewhere. Act against creelmen—men who went about selling goods from baskets. Any one selling bread to such to be fined 8s. for the Kirk-work.

July 27.—Schir William of Furde, chaplain, and David Brown relieve John Johnston, burgess of Selkirk of £15, 12s., for which he was surety to the Abbot of Jedburgh for certain bear and meal received by him and delivered to John Murray of Philiphaugh—under the pain of cursing.

Lands of Harisbuttis let by Bailie Scott to Mungo Brown.

The piece of land betwixt the old dam and the river under Maldisheugh declared to be common, as also the lands and haugh betwixt the dyke below Bullsheuch and the river.

In ordinary times nine men were enough to watch during night; but when an attack was apprehended the number was doubled or tripled, as the occasion warranted. It seems to have been arduous work to keep the watch efficient. A few months' peace lulled the guard into deputing their duties to boys; they became apt to linger about the middle of the town instead of walking "on the back side," that is, at the back of the walls, and to indulge in drinking. It must be kept in mind that the town was then enclosed in a triangle of earthwork fortification, with ports or gates at each corner. The gates were hung from large oaken beams lying across the streets, or on hinges built into strong walls on either side. An old Selkirk man who died about 1880, remembered hearing in his youth about the beam across the West Port from an old residenter who had seen it. Each gate was flanked by mason work for several yards before the earthen rampart commenced. When nine men were on the watch, three would have charge of each division of the town marked by a port. One being left at the gate, two might patrol from that point half-way to the two other gates, which would be a tolerably efficient cordon.

Nothing is more instructive than the glimpses of land customs revealed in these ancient manuscripts. Scrupulous regard was paid to the difference between land common to the whole community, and the burgess-acres, which, though held from the King, were the heritable property of individuals. In the beginning of the sixteenth century, letters were issued to the Sheriff of Selkirk to examine certain lands of Patrick Wallance, deceased, and to appraise their value, for relief of Richard Kene in the sum of £20. John Murray of Philiphaugh, Sheriff-depute (the same, by the way, who has been unanimously fixed upon as "The Outlaw!"), having found one husband-land called "Burgess Walleys" in the burgh belonging hereditarily to the said deceased Patrick, gave notice to all having an interest to appear before him on the soil of the said land, to hear it valued. None appearing, he, by thirteen trustworthy persons elected for the purpose, declared the land to be of the value of £20. And, because no person came forward to buy it at the price, the said Sheriff, by virtue of his office, assigned the land to Richard Kene, in satisfaction of his claim, according to Act of Parliament, subject to a right of

Kam.
Trac.
App.

redemption by the heirs of Patrick Wallance within seven years. In the same way, in 1507, Janet Forman having obtained a decree against Robert Scott G. s., ii. 3120. in Selkirk, for the balance of a debt, obtained from the King certain lands and the tower near the lake of Selkirk (the Haining loch), of the annual value of 20s., Harbutislands at 26s., Collanscroft at 20s., Pringle's croft and Crawfordscroft at 12s., and the lands of Langschot at 12s., with a mill upon the stream running past the said tower at 20s.; in all, £5 3s., within the burgh and liberty of Selkirk—reserving free possession of the mill to Janet Ker, mother of the said Robert Scott, and a right to Robert and his heir to redeem the property within seven years.

CHAPTER III.

1513 TO 1526.

ABOUT this date the term *curia burgalis capitalis,* or head burgh court, is used at intervals in place of *Inquisitio,* or inquest, to describe a meeting of Council. In the following return of the "Community of Burgesses of Selkirk," dated 25th May 1513, it is interesting to note many names which still linger among the old families of the place. Some, doubtless, were eliminated from the burgess-roll for ever, on the battlefield of Flodden four months later.

James Clerk, St.	Thomas Watson.	Nin. Donaldson.
James Hogg.	Matth. Sewright.	Nin. Minto.
Thos. Greenshel.	Nin. Donaldson.	John Sanderson.
John Burne.	Wm. Blake.	And. Swan.
John Wolson.	Dd. Minto.	Jas. Scott.
Cuthbert Turnbull.	John Hall.	Nichol Henderson.
John Hastie, St.	Andw. M'Dowell.	Wm. Chesame.
Geo. Scott.	John Hall.	John Curll.
John Boyle.	George Thompson.	John Forsyth.
Thos. Porteous.	Thos. Porteous.	Pat. Wilkieson.
Rob. Kerr.	Wm. Watson.	Thos. Legertwood.
Wm. Robertson.	John Kein.	Solomon Deephope.
Geo. Brown.	Walter Hall.	Geo. Kyll.
Ad. Wilkieson.	John Mows.	John Johnstone.
John Kowper.	Jas. Sanderson.	Wm. Main.
Thos. Kein.	Wm. Justice.	Hary Saloman.
And. Strang.	Wm. Robertson.	John Harper.
Rob. Porteous.	John Thomson.	Robert Brown.
John Loremer.	Antony Gibson.	Nicholas Wilkieson.
Peter Porteous.	John Dun.	Laird of Philiphaugh.
Egidius Porteous.	John Lumsden.	Allan Forsyth.
Wm. Turnbull.	James Mows.	Patrick Kene.
John Brydyne.	Wm. Freer.	Wm. Aitchison.
Thos. Talzeour.	John Freer.	Wm. Caidzow.
Dd. Brydyne.	James Brydyne.	Wm. Kene.
Matth. Dryster.	Matth. Couper.	John Kene.
Thos. Brydyne.	Andrew Laurie.	James Kene.

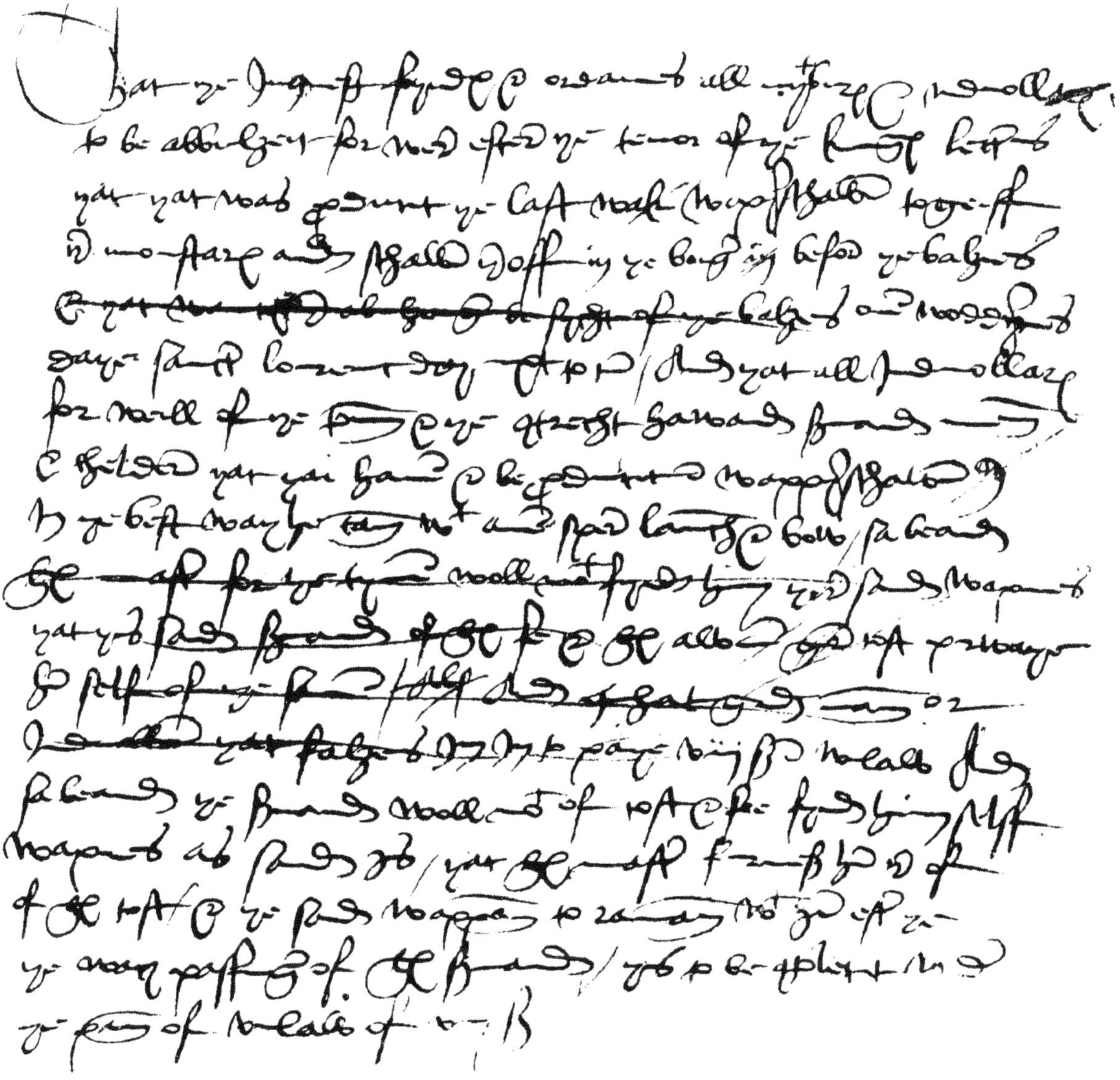

1513. AUGUST 2.—LEVY FOR FLODDEN—MINUTE OF TOWN COUNCIL.

Thomas Hall.
Thos. Mathoson.
Thos. Johnstone.
John Farle.
Wm. Persone.
John Wightman.
Simon Farle.
Allan Dawgless.
Geo. Stabill.
Jas. Inglisman.
Richard Young.
James Nithan.
John Learmont.
John Farle.
Robt. Todrik.
James Watson.
John Kune.
Pat. Moffat.
Jas. Porteous.
John Kaidzow.
Jas. Helme.
John Muthag.
Wm. Braidfoot.
John Scott.
Jas. Conchere.
Thos. Hall.
Jas. Brydyne.
John Cant.
John Lawson.
Jas. Harper.

John Kene.
John Mospatrick.
John Mulross.
Steph. Dalglees.
James Harper.
Richd. Chapman.
John Brydyn.
Wm. Couper.
John Cornwell.
Wm. Learmont.
Alex. Brown.
John Smith.
James Chisholm.
James Braidfoot.
Roger Murray.
John Cavers.
Andrew Maturk.
John Chapman.
James Robertson.
Mungo Brown.
David Brown.
Wm. Kerr.
John Freer.
Robert Gillies.
Ad. Thomson.
Thomas Crookshank.
Wm. Tait.
Robt. Chisholm.
John Barker.

John Lauder.
Geo. Chapman.
Wm. Loremer.
Thos. Minto.
Steph. Lawder.
Jas. Chapman.
John Porteous.
Thos. Tod.
Wm. Blake.
Robt. Brydyn.
John Thomson.
Robt. Benet.
Wm. Lidderdale.
Thomas Henderson.
Wm. Porteous.
And. Henderson.
John Robertson.
John Cowan.
Wm. Porteous.
James Skune.

THE ASSISTERS.
Robert Scott.
Stephen of Lauder.
Thomas Johnston.
George Scott.
David Brown.
Thos. Brydyn.
John Scott.

With reference to "the Assisters," it should be noted that all, except the first, are in the principal roll also. Probably they "assisted" the Bailie, Robert Scott, whose name heads the list, and who was either laird of Haining or related to him. Five pages on, the minutes bring us face to face with the King's mad expedition to England, the disastrous issue of which at Flodden has been so prominently identified with Selkirk history.

1513, August 2.—Finds and ordains all neighbours and indwellers to be abulzeit (furnished) for war, after the tenor of the King's letters produced at last wapinschawing, to give their monsteris (demonstration) and shewing thereof in the Bog before the Bailies on Wednesday, St. Laurence day (10th August). And that all indwellers, for the weal of the town and country, having servant men and children, that they be produced at wapingschawing in best way they can, with ane spear, lance, and bow. And sae bein he will nocht of coft (not buy) and free find himself weapons as said is, that his master furnish him thereof of his coft, the said weapons to remain with him after the waypassing of his servant. To be fulfilled under the unlaw of 8s. . . . . Also finds that neighbours about the hill lend their horse to bring 5 sledful of turf, and who has no horse, to come himself and give his pains for casting and laying of the turf; and that each indweller send one servant betwixt this and Sunday to the loch-end and places about the Bog where need is; and also all neighbours to cast their headrooms and fence-places, as required, betwixt this and the said day—to be completed under pain of 2s. to be poynded and paid on Saturday at even from the failers. And all places at the east and west end of the town, to be likewise ordered anent the stopping of headrooms, casting of stanches, and barrows making . . . The watch to stand as it is—no boys nor children, but the goodman of the house, or a sufficient man in the sight of the bailies. Also that all manner of men come to the kirkyaird when a fray happens to pass, with the bailies, under pain of 8s.

On the 22d of August James marched with his army from Edinburgh, the Border contingent probably joining him on the march. The same day Andrew Ker of Greenhead and Andrew Ker of Gateshaw having been made burgesses, the former was chosen to be "weill-wisher and supplear" to the town of Selkirk (it being found necessary to have one), as his father was before him, for one year. There is something almost touching in the town, fearful of coming danger, thus putting itself under protection of its powerful neighbour.

The battle of Flodden was fought on 9th September; but from 22d August till 25th October there is no entry in the Burgh Records, nor is the battle once alluded to, even indirectly, in the subsequent minutes. The clerk's handwriting remains the same, old names are repeated in the list of members, orders about the watch are given in much the same terms as formerly, but no mention of Flodden. It would seem as if a silent oath had been taken that the dreadful day should be blotted for ever out of record.

What authentic history refuses to divulge, unauthorised tradition has supplied with liberal hand. There is probably no incident in Scottish history so familiar as the part said to have been taken by Selkirk in the fatal fight, and it is regrettable to have to add that there are few stories so much indebted to imagination, and so little to facts. Of at least a score of different versions, the earliest is that which appears in Hodge's MSS., written about 1722, and preserved in the Advocates' Library :—

"King James IV., on the way to Flodden, where he engaged the English army, had from the burgh of Selkirk eighty well-armed men commanded by the town-clerk, who were all, except the clerk, cut in pieces. The clerk only returned, and brought with him one of the English banners and a halbert axe, which are yearly carried before the magistrates at the riding of their common and other public weaponschawings. James v. when he came to the Forest of Selkirk to expel the outlaw, and understanding the good services done by the burgh of Selkirk to King James iv. at Flodden, did make a grant to the burgh of Selkirk of 10,000 aikers of his forest to belong to them in property, for maintaining the royalty, with liberty to cut down as much of the forest as would rebuild the town. He appointed them sheriffs within themselves, with a power of repledging from any court, spiritual or temporal. He created the clerk and his successors knights, conform to a patent thereanent lying in the burgh's charter-chest—the onerous cause in the patent being for the good service done by Wm. Bryden, clerk of our burgh of Selkirk, to our predecessor at the field of Flodden : therefore we create him and his successors knights. He likeways granted to the burgh liberty to make incorporations, and particularly one of the sutors, and appointed the deacon to provide each newly admitted burgess with a maid, if the burgess require it. I am told several burgesses have some years ago pled their privilege, and were by the deacon provided to their satisfaction. At the time of the Field of Flodden, there was one of the burgess's wives with a child went out, thinking long for her husband, and was found dead at the root of a tree, and the child sucking her breast, on the edge of rising ground belonging to the town, which is called Ladywoodedge since that time to this day. The town's arms are a woman and child, mentioned in their charter as, 'a woman in a forest of wood lying dead at the root of a tree with a child sucking at her breast,' which bearing was appointed them by James v."

On this veracious narrative hang all the lies and stories clustered round the simple fact that Selkirk sent men to Flodden. To expose, in detail, the falsehoods of so obvious a fabrication may seem superfluous; but so much of it has been accepted by the credulous as to render it desirable to compare the incidents in various versions, often contradicted by ascertained facts. So far as known, the first published reference to the tradition is in an account of the parish, written by the minister in 1790. Instead of eighty, the contingent from Selkirk is put at the round number of one hundred; but of these "a few" returned besides the town-clerk,—the solitary survivor, according to Hodge. From the reverend pastor we learn for the first time that the standard was taken from the English by a member of the Corporation O. S. A., of Weavers; and that William Brydone (clerk at the time of James v.'s ii. 436. visit), was knighted for his valour. He also mentions what Hodge omitted to note—that the very sword worn by Brydone at the time was still in possession of his lineal descendants. Without analysing the innumerable minor accounts (for every historian, every note-making visitor, every ballad critic, every patriotic author, has repeated the story in some shape), it is

B. M.,
iii. 317.

desirable to examine the version given by Sir Walter Scott, not less on account of the eminence of the writer than of its world-wide circulation. Going a step further than the Rev. Mr. Robertson, Scott says the King knighted William Brydone on the field of battle; and repeats Hodge's explanation of the town's arms, displacing the tree-root, however, by a sarcophagus! "That William Brydone," continues Scott, "actually enjoyed the honour of knighthood, is ascertained by many of the deeds in which his name appears as a notary-public. John Brydone, lineal descendant of the gallant town-clerk, is still alive, and possessed of the relics mentioned. The old man, though in an inferior station of life, receives considerable attention from his fellow-citizens, and claims no small merit to himself on account of his brave ancestor." Recurring to Hodge's account, which may be correct enough in regard to the number eighty, it is necessary to accept with some reserve the statement that they were under command of the town-clerk. In those days that functionary was a clergyman of the Roman Catholic Church, and although lay abbots fought by the King at Flodden, there is no record of a priest unsheathing the sword. If the clerk was there at all, it was on a religious errand, to administer ghostly comfort to those in need of it—

A pious man whom duty brought
To dubious verge of battle fought,
To shrieve the dying, bless the dead.

The natural leader of the men of Selkirk was the laird of Haining, and the disappearance of the head of that family in 1513 makes it at least possible that he fell fighting near the King, who was also his immediate feudal superior. Next in Hodge's story to demand attention are the English banner and halbert axe. The latter may be dismissed with the remark that halberts, being the symbol of authority, were carried before burgh bailies long before Flodden; that two are still so carried; and that at one time each deacon of a craft was preceded by his own halberdier. It is odd that a substantial relic like a halbert should have totally disappeared; but that there ever really was an English weapon brought back from Flodden has never been asserted except by Hodge. It does not appear to have occurred to him that so heavy an addition to his impedimenta would have embarrassed the solitary clerk on his weary trudge from the battlefield. But what is to be said about the flag—the precious relic which for at least one hundred years has been to Selkirk what the statue of Minerva was to Troy? It has a romance to itself—

"From his order requiring all the male adults of each family to repair to his standard, the King excepted the eldest son, that he might be spared in order to maintain the females and junior members of the family in case the rest were cut off. There was one family of the name of Fletcher, consisting of five sons, the youngest of whom not relishing the King's order, fell a-crying, and expressed the utmost unwillingness to proceed upon so hazardous an enterprise. The eldest brother, enraged at such symptoms of cowardice, struck him upon the face, and said he would go himself. He did so, and in the event was the only person of his family that survived the conflict. He took from an English leader and brought home with him a pennon, which he presented to his own incorporation, the weavers. . . . It is (1829) of green silk, fringed round with pale silk twist, about four feet long, and tapering towards the extremity most remote from the staff. Some armorial bearings such as an eagle and a serpent were once visible upon it, but scarcely a lineament can be discerned amidst the tatters to which it is now reduced." _{Pict. Scot., i. 146.}

Unconscious of his pun, Mr. Chambers goes on to say that its *dilapidation* is to be ascribed to *stones* thrown at it by boys who used to call it the "weavers' dishclout." It is hardly necessary to balance the claims of Brydone and of Fletcher to the honour of bringing home the captured colour. If by either, it was by a Brydone, of which name there were many burgesses, while the roll of 1513 will be searched in vain for a Fletcher. Were further evidence needed to discredit the Fletcher episode, it is forthcoming in the fact that the Weavers' Corporation, of which this hero was a member, did not exist until nearly 100 years after the battle! Regarding the "armorial bearings like an eagle and a serpent," which Mr. Chambers is careful to say "were once visible," may not the device have been

> "Almost in shape of a camel?
> *Polonius.* By the mass, and 'tis like a camel, indeed.
> *Hamlet.* Methinks it is like a weasel.
> *Polonius.* It is backed like a weasel.
> *Hamlet.* Or, like a whale?
> *Polonius.* Very like a whale."

The only figures now discernible on the flag are two shuttles which stretch from side to side. These emblems of the craft of weaving, and the fact that the banner has always been in possession of the Weavers' Corporation, seem to indicate that the boys may have been near the truth, if somewhat inelegantly expressed, when they called it the "weavers' dishclout." Of course it is just possible that a band of English weavers under Surrey may have lost their standard in the battle, and that this may be it; but it is against such a supposition that while in the books both of the Town Council and the

Weavers' Corporation there is frequent mention of flags, there is not one allusion to an old flag brought from Flodden. It remains, however, to be said that not only have the people of Selkirk long believed in the flag as a genuine trophy from the famous fight, but that forty years ago the weavers were offered £10 for it by the Antiquarian Society; and undoubtedly whatever authority can be derived from tradition may properly be claimed for it.

Regarding a somewhat similar tradition at Hawick, the historian of that burgh says—

Wils.
Haw., 37,
49, 213.

"The inhabitants of Selkirk also display a flag at the riding of the Common, which is likewise reputed to have been taken from the English, while some affirm that both standards were won on the field of Flodden. Had these ensigns been trophies gained at Bannockburn, their origin would not have been so wonderful; but when the disasters of Flodden are recalled to mind, such a traditionary story becomes marked with absurdity."

Recognising the incredibility of the Flodden story, the Hawick people have altered the date of their legend from 1513 to 1514, when a band of English marauders were surprised by "the callants" and completely massacred. Moreover, the flag they now display is not asserted to be the identical colour then captured, but merely "the representative of the ancient relic."

Probably nothing that can be written will shake the belief cherished by every true "souter o' Selkirk" in the much-worshipped pennon. To this strong feeling forcible expression has been given in rhyme by a modern hero of Selkirk, whose deeds of rash bravery were the gossip of Crimean trenches, and who left an arm under the walls of the Redan :—

> Auld Flodden's flag! the bluid-stained rag!
>   We'll lo'e while we hae life.
> It thrills us still to hae the will
>   To join in ilka strife,
> Where "Scotland" is the watchword true,
>   And liberty the aim;
> For fause is he whae's feared to dee
>   For love o' his dear hame.

It is of course unnecessary to refute with evidence or argument Hodge's extraordinary account of James the Fifth's dealings with the ancient burgh. The marvellous stipulation by which the honourable craft of souters was converted into a sort of matrimonial agency for the supply of bachelor burgesses with wives is in one sense of service. It enables us to know for certain that Hodge was either imposed upon by a man who combined the faculty of lying with a keen sense of humour, or was such a man himself.

There is more of ignorance, however, than of anything else in his narrative of the knightly town-clerk. It is altogether beyond doubt that one William Brydone was town-clerk of Selkirk at or near the time of Flodden; and it is certain that in several documents he figures as Sir William. It seems as if some person, able to decipher ancient manuscripts, but unable to explain how a town-clerk should be Sir, had invented the whole story about Brydone's leading the Selkirk men to Flodden, and his bravery there, in order to account for the title. And its possession by other notaries about and after the time of James v.'s visit, has led him further to the palpable absurdity of making the knighthood applicable to all Brydone's successors,—a blunder excusable in Hodge or in Hodge's hoaxer, but to be wondered at in so erudite an antiquary as Sir Walter Scott. The proper explanation is simple. Sir William Brydone was of a class of priests known as Pope's knights for at least fifty years prior to the Reformation. They were invariably styled Sir, or Schir, and the only way to detect them from men of arms is by the omission of the word "knight" or *miles* after their names. Shakespeare was aware of the practice, and introduces it in the "Merry Wives of Windsor"—

Act iii.
Sc. 1.

"How now, master parson? Good-morrow, good Sir Hugh."

It is furthermore attested by Sir David Lindsay—

> The puir priest thinkis he gettis na richt,
> Be he noch stylit lyke ane knicht,
> And callit Schir afore his name,
> As Schir Thomas and Schir Williame.

Brydone's title of "Sir" is therefore no indication of knighthood; and the fact of "knight" being wanting to his name wherever it occurs, either before or after Flodden, is conclusive. Besides, the story bears one well-known mark of invention—it is hopelessly contradictory. Hodge says James v. conferred the honour in 1535 (22 years after Flodden); another authority says it was given by James iv. in token of the soldierlike appearance of the Selkirk company when they arrived in camp; while Sir Walter Scott asserts that the valiant monarch knighted Brydone for his courage on the field of battle. The fact of Sir William Brydone being a priest of course precludes the chance of his sword being in the possession of descendants, for the double reason that he probably never had a sword, and that he should have had no descendants. Some priests, however, "repudiated the doctrine of clerical celibacy; and for many of them who lived in concubinage there was doubtless the plea that morally they led a life of married domesticity. They lived with their wives in soberness and constancy, with consciences void of offence, doing what seemed to them right amid the difficulties by which they were surrounded." There were other Brydones in Selkirk, however, besides the priest, Sir William—men of substance and position. Almost certainly there were Brydones in the eighty who marched from Selkirk at their monarch's call, and what more likely than that stories of their prowess may have descended to the time of the first romancer? The sword bears every mark of age and of a trusty weapon; and though it never earned knighthood for a town-clerk of Selkirk, it may well have left its mark on many of the surging throng of Englishmen which pressed in upon the narrowing circle of James's bodyguard at Flodden.

The Brydone Sword.

Doubtless another instance of *post non propter* is the concluding fable about the dead woman and living child. The same ingenious individual who invented the heroism of the town-clerk to account for his title of "Sir," has improvised the incident of Ladywoodedge to account for the woman and child in the town's arms.

Any one who looks at the burgh arms as they appear in its ancient seal can have no difficulty in deciding what they represent. Beyond all cavil, it is the virgin and child. No halo would have surrounded the head of the warrior's widow, however sacred her memory; and equally out of place would be the ecclesiastical altar in the background. The seal is the seal of Kelso Abbey, plus the royal shield, with its "ruddy lion ramp'd in gold."

Selkirk Burgh Seal.

Stripped of the excrescences which "lawless and uncertain thoughts" have clustered round it, the story of Selkirk's share in Flodden may lose picturesqueness; but it now rests on a firm basis of fact. Actual written minutes of the time reveal to us the spirit with which the town answered its King's summons to the field, the eager promptitude with which its Bailies made arrangements for the muster, the impressment of every capable hand to the work of entrenching, and the prudent scheme by which protection was insured from the baron of Greenhead. It is no stretch of fancy to believe that the burgesses of Selkirk would quit them like men on that afternoon in autumn when,

> Linked in the serried phalanx tight
> Groom fought like noble, squire like knight,
>   As fearlessly and well.

Is there not something more expressive than any written word in the two months' utter blank in the town's records? Three weeks of feverish anxiety, while the fate of Scotland and the lives of their own strong men yet hung in the balance, a week of anguish and despair, a month of voiceless, effortless paralysis; power of deed and word recurring only when dread of the advancing foe called for keener watch and ward, and stronger earthworks. Quite as mournfully significant are the frequent services of heirs recorded after the battle, absence of the usual phrase, "while fighting under our Lord's banner," seeming to corroborate the existence of a resolute vow never even to mention the bloody day.

Relieved for a time from apprehension of an English foray, the people of Selkirk gradually settled down to their old ways, more alert in their nightly watch perhaps, and with more frequent eye towards the bale-fire peaks. Little of interest is to be gleaned from the Records at this time :—

1514, 30th Jany.—Conjunct infeftment of Robert Bryden, burgess, and his wife in part of the tenement under the cloister or enclosure, and all that house standing contiguous to the chamber of Sir Wm. Bryden.

1515, June 26.—Sasine of John Bryden, true and lawful heir of Thomas Bryden, burgess, his father, of a tenement lying in the Volgate (Gait or road of the Foul Port or South Port), and other properties, including Gargunnoch lands, 10 rigs in Eastfield, of which 4 lie on the west part of Dunsdale, which leads by the King's Way to the burgh and to Uplands.

Deprived of its most valiant and capable defenders, Selkirk became the prey of freebooters and Border thieves; while to add to its woes, a deadly plague which overspread the country wrought havoc in the widowed town. By command of the Lord-Governor, taxation to the extent of £16 was remitted to the Bailies of Selkirk, "becaus at thai war hereit be thevis and pestellence."

T. A., 1515-16.

1516, Feby. 9.—An interesting list of "heirship goods" belonging to William Porteous, heir of William Porteous his guidsir, and William Porteous his father, and held by James and Janet Brydon for his behoof :—A cauldron, muckle pot of 2 gallons, pewter charger or tray, pewter plate, pewter dish, saucer, tin pint, basin, laver, pair of wool combs, brazen chandler, crook, pair of "tayngis," "wondow claith," pair of plough-irons, spit, meat almry, vessel almry, crook, chest, a "nox-bed," with pertinents, masking-tub, wyrt-stand, a gilfalt, spear, axe, sword, chandler, a "quhythalc." He had likewise 2 rigs of Lady's Shaw, one in the Goslawdales and the other north of the Bawthorne.

1517, April 28.—The Council ordains a tron to be raised under the cross. All middens thereabout, and about the tolbooth, and upon the foregate about the cross, and along the Kirk Wynd, to be removed, forbidding any to lie in these places more than fifteen days at any time of year, under a penalty ! Also ordains the sir bailies to punish regrators (hucksters) of our common market, both anent flesh, fish, victual, butter, cheese, and salt. Also ordains our commons to be ridden next holiday.

Marriage-contract between Geo. Ormiston and Isbel, sister of "Master" Michael Scott—
"Master" being applied only to men of learning.

1518.—Mention of lands of Caldshields lying under the Peelhill. Adam Johnston, wabster, pursued by Thos. Johnston, burgess, acting for John Dalgliesh, for certain cloth arrested in his hands.

"Whaten man hes swine, to keep them out his neebor's skaith; and if any are apprehended, the apprehender nochte to slay them for their damages, but to follow the said swine to the owner of the same, and have for his skaith 2s. for ilk swine he has fund."

1519.—Ordained that the mill in future be put up to auction once a year from Lammas to Lammas. Followed by a tack to Janet, relict of George Scott, at 28 merks yearly. Ordained that all indwellers bring their girst to the common mill of Selkirk or to the mill of Mauldisheuch.

1520, Jany. 6.—John Melros deponed that the spouse of James Braidfoot granted to him that he should give ane pair of sheets, and ane cursch (kerchief) to his friend in marriage when David Cadzow should "marrow."

May 8.—The inquest advises you Sir Alderman and bailies to cause any parties at discussion to take four well-advised men and neighbours by consent of both parties, "that shall pass and mak ane mends where the fault beis;" and if these four cannot agree, the bailies to ordain them an overman, with consent of both parties, that all be agreed to within 15 days. "Gif ony gainstands that will not bide the decree as said is, to be inbrought to the next court, to lay the fault where it should be." And in time coming, whoever is known "tulzeour," doing wrong to his neighbour, drawing his blood wrongly, to be really punished in his goods, and to forswear the town, from his fault be known for a year and a day.

Oct. 22.—John Johnston, bailie of Selkirk, accounts for seven merks spent in the common profit of the town, except 3s. 10d., for which he gave pledges to Sir Wm. Brydin. Common good in the hands of Sir William Brydon and Robin Ker.

1521, August 9.—Ordains all men, indwellers in the burgh, with their servants, to come readily when any fray arises, well-armed, for the good of the town and of the country, and pass together at their power.

1522, April 29.—A weaponshow to be held on Sunday, at one afternoon, and all men to be furnished with jack (leathern coat), spear, lance, or fencible weapons, ilk man with his servants, under penalty.

1523, April 15.—Thirty men to be put on the watch.

This large increase—ten men to guard each ward, instead of three—was no doubt in consequence of non-renewal of the truce with England, and a threatened inroad from the opposite Border. Four or five months later, Lord Dacre led a force of ten thousand men from Yorkshire, and counties further north, against the town of Jedburgh, which they utterly destroyed by fire.

1524.—Mention of a deed written in 1512 by Schir John Mitchelbill, presbyter of Glasgow, and notary-public (another Pope's knight), in connection with the old croft commonly called Kilcroft.

Oct. 4.—"The backsters to bake their penny breid fairlie after the quantity, as they buy their wheat." No one to buy wheat until it has been shown in the market; "nae bagster to give nae mae breid bot ane to the dizzen, under pain of escheat;" and their stuff to be seen by the bailies before it is sold to creelmen.

1525, May 30.—The whole community, with the Alderman and bailies, to ride the Common in the north part, and cause thirteen "eldest and worthiest to pass afore the lave."

James Scoon to pay 2s. yearly for his forge which stands in the common street.

1526, Feby. 26.—Adam of Tweedy claimed a horse arrested in hands of John of Murray (in his capacity as sheriff), who asserted that Adam was at the King's horn when the horse was taken. Adam denied he ever was; offered to give Murray both the horse and £20 if he would produce the man's warrant that stole it; and deputed John Murray in Kirkhouse, his procurator, either to bring the horse again, or else his skin.

Oct. 16.—John Johnston and John Chisholm, bailies, compeared in the Hill of the Trinity at Selkirk, where Janet Scott owned to a debt in Stephen Lauder's books.

At this period the Scottish Border remained in a most unsettled state, and there is frequent mention in the records of penalties for not "rising to the fray."

CHAPTER IV.

1527 TO 1542.

MANNERS and customs betraying a characteristic union of simplicity and superstition are disclosed in a remarkable entry, of date 27th June 1527; according to which James Tait and his wife are ordained "to keep their maiden (madayne) surely to Martinmas, until this gentleman called Roland Hamilton bring a relic—failing thereof to lose (tyne) his claim to the sword, and if they keep not their maiden, to 'underlie the sowme of the said swerd.'" B. R.

An agreement, it seems, had been entered into between Tait and his wife on the one part, and Roland Hamilton on the other, that the pair would keep their maiden surely till Martinmas, when he would bring a bell "quhilk is callit St. Mahageo's bell." As a pledge he left his sword, which he was to forfeit if he failed; while if the Taits failed to keep the virgin, they were to forfeit a sum equal to its value.

The "inquest" then ordains Roland Hamilton to bring sufficient proof that he gave his sword to the maiden, failing which James and Christian Tait, as well as Thomas, are either to swear themselves free ("sakles airt and pairt red and consell") of the sword, or to make payment thereof.

From such slender material it is difficult to construct the story of this unusual transaction. Probably "this gentleman called Roland Hamilton" was a near relative of the first Earl of Arran, appointed Warden of the Marches a few years before. He may have been quartered in the town when smitten with the charms of James Tait's maiden, who, it may be observed, is nowhere called his daughter. Unable to take his sweetheart with him, Roland left his trusty blade, no doubt a valuable one, in token of his faithfulness. Under forfeiture of like value the honest burgess undertook to have the lassie waiting for him. St. Mahago's bell introduces rather a puzzling feature. It must have been a relic of that early Saint, preserved in his cell at Lesmahago; and as the Earl of Arran held great estates there, the bell adds to the probability of Roland being one of his family. Bells were sometimes given by way of atonement, and the bell of so ancient and reputable a

saint as Machutus would be looked upon as a priceless gift, bringing good
fortune to its possessor, and warding off evil. It may have been promised to
the Taits either by way of reparation for an outrage, or by way of exchange
for the girl. About the *dénouement* of this affair the records are disappoint-
ingly silent, but a hope may be expressed that the bravest of the brave proved
true to the fairest of the fair, and that its removal to Selkirk saved Saint
Mahago's bell from the destruction which overtook his bones and other relics
at the time of the Reformation.

1527, B. R.   The intimate relations between the civil power and the Church in Roman
Catholic times are illustrated in a list of Sunday offerings received by Sir
David Chapman, priest, in presence of Sir William Brydon, priest, Mungo
Brydon, and the two bailies, John Chapman and John Johnston. Sir Ninian
Brydon, priest, figures as a donor, the offerings being made on Saints' days.
Two years later "all Our Lady offerings" are ordered to be put daily in a box
with two keys—the vicar to keep the box, Symon the key, and Sir Ninian
the book of receivings and deliverings.

In 1527, mention is made of a house in Selkirk let by Robert Scott of Howpaslot to certain
of his servants; and of the Lairds of Glenrath as superiors of two houses in the burgh.

On the 18th February there was a special order to rise to the fray—probably in connection
with the struggle between Angus and other nobles for possession of the young King.

G. S., iii. 652.   One result of James's escape from Angus, and of the Earl's expulsion from
Scotland, was the acquisition by James Murray of Philiphaugh of twenty-one
forfeited husbandlands in the burgh of Selkirk. In 1534 seven husbandlands
and six shillings of a husbandland were assigned by Patrick, son of James
Murray, to Edmonston of that Ilk, in payment of a debt, but subject to
repurchase in seven years. Of these lands, one was held by John Bridin and
G. S., iii. 1419.   Isabella, widow of John Bridin, junior; two by the widow of George Scott and
the widow of Thomas Ker; one by Margaret, widow of George Haldane; one
by Robert Chepman and Symon Jameson; one by George and William
Chepman; one and the fragment by William Kene. By a letter from the
1533, P. S., ix. 191.   King, Robert Scott, burgess of Selkirk, obtained all the property of his brother
John, including a tenement and croft on the south side of the burgh between
the lands of William Ker of Shaw on the east, and the lands of William
Chepman on the west. That the Brydones were at this period people of
G. S., iii. 1513.   means and position is further evidenced by a charter, dated Greenhead, 12th
July 1534, in which Elizabeth Fallow, wife of John Bridin, burgess of Selkirk,
sells her half of the lands of Softlaw to Ker of Primside—the witnesses being

Sir William Bridin, vicar of Selkirk, Sir Ninian Bridin, Sir George Anderson, chaplain, James Bridin, M'Dowall of Makerston, and others. Connected with the same family a quaintly-worded deed is engrossed in the Council books :—

29th Aug. 1530.—It is compromettit and finally agreed betuix Janet Bryden, relek of umquh. Robt Bryden, and William Bryden, her son and appearand heir, that the said Janet should of her guid free will (nocht need by nae strength nor yet by nae claim nor richt by title of heirship) gif freelie William her son half ane daiker of barkit leather where it lies in the hole, after the vicar's distribution and discretion. *Item*, ane laid of bear for to be diligent to win the lave. *Item*, his dearest em (uncle) Sir William compromettis him als meikle bear as he will saw within Selkirk upon guid lands and competent, after guid use of maillers, and able thereto of his cost. *Also*, the said William Bryden grantis that his mother sold have the cauldron for her life-tyme, and the maskyn-falt (vat) ; and, when the said William needs them, to be between them thankfully as effeirs cost frie. *Also*, gif the saids Janet haldis the acre into her awin hands, the said vicar Schir William his cousin and dearest eme bindes him by faith and truth in his body to gif William his friend as mickle annual or lands as the acre is worth. *Item*, the said Janet obliges her faithfully that after she be married and clad with ane husband or other man, she shall gif over all claim and possession scho has to any lands, etc. Witnessed by Sir Wm Bryden, vicar in Selkirk, Sir David Scott, and Bailie Robert Chapman.

There is sometimes an element of fiction in conveyances of this period from ecclesiastics to cousins and nephews, the relationship of the beneficiary being often of a still closer description ; but there being no room for such a supposition in the present case, it becomes evident that even had Sir William belied his clerical profession and fought at Flodden, he did not leave descendants in possession of his Andrea Ferrara. Anc. Ch., p. 188.

1530, July 12.—Ordains the bailies and the community to go immediately after this court to those who have been at Edinburgh or any place infected with the pestilence, to command them to hold themselves in their houses by themselves until eight days be bypast ; and, "mair atour," we discharge (prohibit) all indwellers in the town, under pain of out putting from the town, that they pass without leave asked and given to any fairs either far or near, and specially into Lothian, where the sickness is openly known ; and at the least they shall be put out of the town 40 days. And for defence from the said sickness, we ordain four men at the east part, dwellers, to stand at the said end of the town and take each one sworn that he was (not) near any infected folk ; and these men "to stand every mercat day fra the sun rising while it pass to, that they check all men by their great aiths whether they were near infekkit pairts or nocht."

This was a wave of the pest known as "sweating sickness," which devastated Europe, especially its northern half, during 1528 and after. How

Heck.
Epi.,
p. 238.

many lives were lost in the outbreak is unknown; but by some historians it is distinguished from less terrible eruptions as "The Great Mortality."

1530-1, Feb. 14.—Ordains nae deaf men to walk in or stand as watches—specially auld Blair the cooper.

February 28.—The burgh having been called upon for £6 to sustain the King's wars against Donald of the Isles, there is a list of 89 contributing burgesses. From ten men 4s. each was levied, from thirty-two 2s., from twenty-seven 1s., and from twenty, 6d. each.

1531-2, February 26.—Walter Scott, tutor of Haining, freely confessed how his predecessors and righteous heritors of the Haining, his father and "gussar" (goodsir, grandfather), irrevocably and for ever mair ordained to be given 2s. Scots to the upholding the lights and service of the Holy Cross altar situate in the parish kirk of Selkirk, off two rigs lying within the freedom of Selkirk—one upon the knowe belonging to Sir Ninian Bryden, the other in Goslawdale; and ratifies the said gift to the said altar to be paid to Sir John Bryden, chaplain, of that Ilk.

In dread of an attack from the English, who under the leadership and instigation of the exiled Angus were making frequent inroads on the Scottish Border, the bailies ordered Selkirk to be put in posture of defence.

1532, October 30.—All the heidrowmes and stankis within or without the burgh, to be made and cast substantiously within 15 days; and each watch ordained to mend their own barrows honestly until they come to the yetts hanging, and then the yetts (gates) shall be hung at the common expense.

What could afford a more striking contrast to the energetic United Presbyterian evangelicalism of his descendants than the following gift by Thomas Johnson to insure requiems for his soul?

1534, May 20.—"In honour of the Fader, Sonne, and Haly Gaist and the Blessed Virgine Sanct Mary, and all the Sanctis in Hevin"—a worthy man, Thomas Johnson, burgess in Selkirk, has purely and simply resigned, by exhibition of a penny (as use is in the burgh), half a merk of rent, to be uptaken from a croft lying at the loch-end, within the burgh-roods (burgess-acres) of Selkirk, the land of John Curror being on the east, the Common called the Bog on the south, the King's street on the north, and the Haining loch on the west—service thereof being given to a venerable man Schir William Bryden, curate for the time, and to his successors curates of Selkirk, for ever, to cause solemnly and faithfully an *obit* to be done on Sunday after the day of the said Thomas's decease, devoutly in the parish kirk of Selkirk; the half-merk to be distributed in this wise—The vicar or curate 16d., every priest 12d., the clerk 4d. for the bell-ringing, and 4d. for the candle to burn on the grave—for the weal of my soul, Catherine Shiel my spouse, John Johnson, Mr. James Johnson, and Thomas Johnson's souls. And if Thos. Johnson and my heirs make not thankful payment, as God forbid they do, I ordain the curate of Selkirk to "exoner" the said Thomas and his heirs from the occupying of the said croft.

1534.—Jock Angus the swordslipper, Sandy Gledstanes, and Thomas Hendry, all put in the Bailies' will for troubling the good town in the night.

People of the present day, accustomed to lengthy and verbose proclamations by the Privy Council regarding cattle disease, must appreciate a short and pithy order by the Selkirk Town-Council three hundred and fifty years ago—"All infekkit nowt to be put at the Dry Loch, under a penalty." The following inventory of the personal effects of a well-to-do Selkirk man, a man of learning withal (the Mr. James Johnson whose soul was to be remembered in the vicar's prayers), is suggestive of considerable comfort and wealth :—

Ring with hoop of gold, silver spoon with knob on end, carved bed, carved press with lock and keys, Flanders counter with the forms, ten silver beads with a silver gaud, turned chair, four-foot stool, feather bed with pertinents, "haw-basin" of fine brass, goose-pan, best gown, inside hunting coat of worsted, a shot coat of velvet, hat, bonnet, best sark, best doublet, horse-shoes, pantons, boots, spurs, saddle, bridle, saddle-cloth, sword, buckler, furnished whinger, belt, purse, best piece of gold or other coins therein, tippet of silk or of camlet lined with "bugis" (fur), ten silver beads, a ring of thrown silver, a wheel and cards, a hackle, a "paysill," a pair of shears, pepper-quhern (mill), 12 silver spoons, etc. etc.

1534, Dec. 30.—Mention of "Sir William Bryden, vicar of Selkirk and Auld Roxburgh." Three months later, mention of "the lady of *Abbotside*," —a name we have failed to identify, but which may conceal a reference to Abbots-Selkirk, of the twelfth century.

A most important era in the history of Selkirk is now approached—its endowment by King James v. with various privileges and landed property.

During the four hundred years since its first mention by David i., Selkirk had remained a town or burgh in the King's demesne—the absolute property of the monarch, who often granted it to favourite partisans. One of these, a Douglas, appears to have created Selkirk a burgh of regality; but of this there is no evidence beyond a futile claim by the Duke of Douglas B. R. in 1717.

According to Mr. Hill Burton, the municipal corporations of Scotland are B. S., ii. relics of those planted by the Romans wherever they set foot. Being in their [84, *seq*.] essence little models of the great republic, their spirit was antagonistic to feudalism, and the conditions of their existence created an interest against the aristocracy which was apt to throw them into alliance with the King. It was especially so in Scotland, where the royal burgh was the direct creature of the Crown. There was this specialty in its constitution, that within the bounds of its privileges it could not sub-feu and create vassals subservient to it, as a great lord could on his domains. Every burgess was a direct vassal of the Crown. Besides royal burghs there were burghs of regality and burghs of barony, held in vassalage not of the Crown, but of some great lordship, the burgh of regality being of higher rank and swaying greater power than the barony. Both of these, however, required creation or confirmation by the King; so that in one way or other the Crown preserved its prerogative right of giving life to municipal corporations of all grades. The name by which they were called bears witness, says Mr. Hill Burton, to the purposes for which they were devised. Both in England and Lowland Scotland the word "broch" meant one who pledged himself for another; so in the Scots form of "burgh" it meant a community united together in a common lot and cause as pledges or securities for each other. "Their position could not be better expressed. Holding their own as they did against the powers of the feudal aristocracy, they found that in their hands the capacity of the numerous weak to stand up through the influence of combination against the individually strong, was sorely tested." It is, however, open to question whether the word be derived from *broch* or from the Saxon *byrig* or *burh*, signifying "strong man's fort." Development from a cluster of houses under protection of a castle is at least as natural as from a congregation of men pledged together for common defence. The former, at all events, we know to have been the history of the growth of Selkirk.

From the following charter by James v., which is the oldest in the town's possession, it would appear as if Selkirk had been constituted a free burgh by the King's ancestors. There is some difficulty in accepting this literally, certain facts being against it. Selkirk dues, instead of appearing with those of other burghs in Exchequer accounts, were commonly included in the revenue from Crown property. Nevertheless commissioners from Selkirk took their seats in Parliament in 1469 and 1478 along with those from other burghs.

A.P., ii.
93, 121.

At St. Andrews, 4 March 1535-6:

G. S.,
iii. 1555.
    Whereas the charters of the old foundation of the burgh of Selkirk and its liberties granted by the King's progenitors have for the most part been destroyed through assaults of war, pestilence, fire, and others, whereby the usages of trade have ceased among her burgesses, to the great hurt of them and of the commonweal, and to the prejudice and great damage of his Majesty in the matter of customs, the King has infeft of new to the burgesses and community the burgh of Selkirk, in free burgh, with the commons and possessions belonging to the same, with power of electing bailies, of holding a fair annually on St. Laurence day and during the octaves thereof, with court-house, prison, power of holding burgh courts, and with liberty to buy and sell wine, wax, ale, spices, broad and narrow woollen and linen, and other merchandise whatsoever, and of having bakers, brewers, vendors of fish and flesh, as freely and in the same manner as any other burgh within the kingdom: To hold of the Crown in fee and heritage

CHARTER BY JAMES V. TO BURGH OF SELKIRK. 1535.

and free burgage for ever, for the payment of the burgh fermes and other duties, use and wont as in times past.

So thoroughly alive were the burgesses to the value of this concession, B. R., 14 Mch. that ten days after its date they awarded William Chepman, their clerk, a fee of £57, 8s. 4d. for his labours in connection therewith. They further appointed John Chepman to keep the common seal; the charter-precept and all other evidence to be put in the common box, faithful copies being put in sure keeping, in three faithful men's hands. A month later all the South Common marches were ridden (except those of Whitmuir and Whitmuirhall) by cognition of certain well-belovit and ancient men, who found "nae wrang-dyking within their freedom." It may give some idea of the extent of Selkirk Common previous to its division, to mention the marches ridden at this time— Haining, Hartwoodburn, North Sinton, Wester Lilliesleaf, Friarshaw, Midlem, Prieston, Horserig, Whitlawhouse, Lindean, Kirkland, and Greenhead. Note is taken that Midlem claims loaning and pasturing of cattle in Mossmuir, girse and water from their townhead east through the Common of Selkirk to Cowblain burn and Preston dykes—"never stoppit by nae man, in nae man's days past memory of man, in simmer nor vinter." After perambulation of the North Common, Yair promised to put back a wrongous dyke.

Quickly following the charter came two letters, in which the King gave further marks of his favour to the ancient burgh :—

At Stirling, 20 June 1536 :

We, for the gude, treu, and thankfull service done and to be done to ws be oure lovittis, G. S., the ballies, burgessis, and communite of our burgh of Selkirk, and for certane otheris resonable iii. 1773. causis, grantis licence to thame and their successouris, to ryfe, outbreke, and teill yeirlie 1000 acris of thair commoun landis of oure said burgh in quhat part thairof thai pleise, for polecy, strenthing and bigging of the samyn for the wele of ws and of our liegis reparand thairto, and defence aganis our auld innemyis of Ingland, and uthir wayis; and will and grantis that thai sall nocht be callit, accusit, nor incur ony dangere or skaythe thairthrow in their personis, landis, nor gudis, notwithstanding ony our actis or statutis maid or to be maid in the contrar :— with power to thame to occupy the saidis landis with thair awin gudis, or to set thame to tennentis, as thai sall think maist expedient for the wele of our said burgh, with fre ische and entre, etc. Gevin under our signet, and subscrivit with our hand, etc.

At Kirkcaldy, 2 Sept. 1536 :

We, understanding that our burgh of Selkirk and inhabitantis thairof continualie sen the G. S., feild of Flodoun hes bene oppressit, heriit, and ourerun be thevez and tratouris, quhairthrow the iii. 1773. hant of merchandice hes cessit amangis thame of langtyme by gane, and thai heriit thairthrow, and we defraudit of oure custumes and dewiteis,—thairfor, and for divers utheris resonable causis moving ws, of oure kinglie power, fre motyve and autorite ryale, grantis to thame and their successouris, ane fair day, begynnand at the feist of the Conception of Oure Lady nixt to cum, and be the octavis of the samyn perpetualy in tyme cuming. Subscrivit, etc.

Taking occasion by the hand, the Council resolved their fair on St. Laurence Day should be proclaimed at all the mercat crosses, for which purpose criers with hand-bells were to pass through the great burgh towns, Hawick, Jedburgh, Kelso, Peebles, Melrose, Haddington, Lauder, Lanark, and Lythgo, in all goodly haste. Nine well-advised men of the Council assigned "every geir ane place," viz. :—Chapman merchants on the south side of the Cross; cordiners on the south side of the Tolbooth; wool, skin, cheese, and butter about the Tron; the meal-market where it was before; other victuals east to George Lidderdale's house; and all to be east of the Tolbooth. The market of horse, nolt, and sheep to be in the eastern part of the town, about the forges; the wood-market on Hallwell Hill. (Haly-well was another name for the Lady's well, still in use near the Volunteer Hall.)

1537, May 15.—George Roull appointed, as most able to make the town's service duly, and no other minstrel to be employed. The Council discharge all other minstrels except the said George, that none be received "to nae bridal nor feasts" but the said George, common minstrel, under pain of 8s., paid by those who receive any other. "Whether," says Sir Walter Scott, "the ballads were originally the composition of minstrels, professing the joint arts of poetry and music, or whether they were the occasional effusions of some self-taught bard, is a question into which I do not mean to inquire. But it is certain that till a very late period, the pipers, of whom there was one attached to each Border town of note, and whose office was often hereditary, were the great depositaries of oral and particularly of poetical traditions. About springtime and after harvest, it was the custom of these musicians to make a progress through a particular district of the country. The music and the tale repaid their lodging, and they were usually gratified with a donation of seed-corn. This order of minstrels is alluded to in the comic song of *Maggie Lauder*, who thus addresses a piper—

"'Live ye upo' the Border?'"

1536-7.—Mention of Thomas Murray of Bowhill as Sheriff-depute; also of David Dalgleish as "making oath upon the cross of a whinger."

Having obtained, in April 1538, another charter from the King, confirming the charter of 1535, and the two royal letters which followed it, the Council at once set about the perambulation of the common near Peelhill. An Inquest chosen by the Bailies passed and redd (cleared) the King's Street on the north part of Peelhill, and the common on the north and south sides

B. M., i. 224.

G. S., iii. 1773.

of the Peelhill. They began and sett at the north end of Lammascroft, toward the Castle; and made the King's Street 40 feet wide, as use is and was, evenly ascending the waterfall of the Peelseuch to other lands on the north side, to the King's Street called Caldshiels Gate and Peel-gate; with a vennel ascending up outside the "auld barros" cast in time of war, for ease of the town, and closing of that port, which is 14 feet in breadth; and the gavellar croft on the west side of the vennel; also a portion of common on the south side of the Peelhill and seuch, descending to the Haining Loch—the King's Street on the south side of the same. The which bounds were "stobbit and cairnit" with great stones and turf.

1538, May 14.—Order for weapon-shaw and common-riding by all between 60 and 70 years of age, under penalty of 8s. Bailies—James Braidfoot and James Kein.

November 22.—Mention of arrears owing to Sir Ninian Brydyn, common clerk, for a shrine in which to keep the common seal, charters, etc. John Muthag ordered to mend the said shrine and furnish it with locks and keys.

1539-40, January 27.—Finds that the bailies shall drink one gallon of ale of every man that brewed 16 penny ale at Yule, by tenor of the Act of Parliament; and in time coming all brewers that are free are remitted to brew worthy ale for common sale at Yule, Pasch, Whit-sunday, Our Lady day, and our fair-days, and to sell it after the discretion of two faithful "cunners" (experts) duly sworn, and a bailie with them, to "caulk" (chalk) every hosteler door a certain price according to the value of the ale, without fraud or guile. Who breaks their "cunnand" (covenant) to pay 8s. Ale now in the vessel to be sold for 12d., and after then (?) at 16d. per gallon; the cunners to pass with a bailie, and where it is not worth 16d. to caulk it for 12 pence.

1539, April 29.—Three men of each ward appointed to give in lists of the neighbours who can sustain the King's wars, horse, and gear, also footmen that can sustain themselves, and to consider how many will take the King's wages.

June 3.—Eight burgesses and five parishioners, being sworn upon the Holy Evangel, preferred Sir Adam Ker to Sir Thomas Scoon and Sir Stephen Wilkieson for the service of the rood altar—the qualifications being "the maist devote priest, lawliest, maist discreit to serve God and our altar."

June 12.—John Watson having built a house at the Yair burn-foot on the town's common, and said that he held it of the King's grace and the gentle-men of the Yair and Fairnalee, the whole community pulled it down!

October 15.—Town's bakers prohibited from selling 1½d. loaves to strangers in town and sheriffdom, under forfeit of the whole batch; and landward bakers prohibited from coming in.

1540, April 6.—The Green haugh on the north side of Mauldisheugh Mill and all the water-stones to the cauld back declared to have been common since the memory of man; and if James Wilkieson, our guild-brother and burgess, has taken the said Greenhaugh from Patrick Murray, our Sheriff, by word or writ, he is to be "annullit of his friedom and giltrie brether-hood, and never to be admittit amongst the burgesses, council, and community in time to come."

Still heaping favours upon "the glad aspiring little burgh," King James v. in a new charter added to its dignities and privileges :—

At St. Andrews, 2 Oct. 1540 :

The King—considering the burgh of Selkirk lies near to England, Liddesdale, and other pernicious and unpeaceful provinces, full of thieves, robbers, and traitors, by whom and other powerful men (for want of a noble and good man to defend it and its inhabitants) it has been often burnt, harried, destroyed, and oppressed—concedes to the bailies and community of Selkirk the power of annually electing a provost, which provost and bailies he creates sheriffs of Selkirk within the said burgh, holding office directly from the King. Moreover, the King exempts the said provost, bailies, inhabitants, and community from the jurisdiction of the sheriff of Selkirk, confirms the commutation of the burgh dues and petty customs for an annual payment of five pounds, and confers on the said provost, etc., the right to have walls, trenches, and water ditches around the said burgh.

This document cannot have been many days in Selkirk before the Council, at a meeting on 10th October, "found John Muthag able to be provost" for a year, and also Sheriff within the burgh; James Kein and James Scott being elected bailies. It is questionable if a tradesman such as Muthag, who in 1538 repaired the charter shrine, was quite a *nobilis et bonus vir* in the sense of the King's charter; but he set himself resolutely *defendere burgum et incolas ejus.* The task cost him his life—

1541, September 21.—Riding of the North Common by James Scot, bailie (John Muthag, provost, and James Kein, bailie, having been slain upon St. James' day, 25th July, in defence of our commons, by James Ker, Ralph Ker, and William Renton). The boundaries are described .as beginning from Heatherlie Loaning to Smith's Pool, up Billesheugh mill dam (with the north part of the mill) to Maldisheugh mill dam and syke, and old water-gait behind the mill, up the water stanes and middle of Ettrick, till opposite the meeting of that river and Yarrow, then a little west to Redheugh up the King's street that passes through the West-faulds to a path called the Vedy Path on the east part of Parlaw bank, up the water sands leaving by south of the same, "quhill ye come equivalently fornent" the west mains of the lordship of Selkirk; even (straight) up by Howden and a cairn of stones on the west part of the common beneath the Chamberlain ford of Ettrick, and then down by the old cairns of stones towards the bounds of Carterhaugh, lineally on the north side of Duckpool, even down by the cairn of stones to Yarrow Water, and through it even down the back of the mill dam of Philiphaugh, and then down about Philiphaugh dykes at the head of the Common haugh; even up till you come to path at Philiphaugh town-end and up the dykes to Harehead (occupied by them of Philiphaugh) and Flat woodshaws even at the head; then take north-west and follow by cairns of stones to the nether part of a meadow called Dynnesdale, and north-west by that over a sike up the great craigs and cairns of stones beside James Donaldson's bughts; and then northly descending to a green gate (path) lying under the hill called the Blacklaw and the stead of Fawside (Foulshiels), and follow out that gate over Blacklaw burn, straight up another green gate to cairns upon the watershed of the hill called Lamblaw. Straight up "swapand the 3 bridder" to the old cairn of stones on the height of the hill, and then even down northly the watershed of the hill as the cairns propones down to the dykes of the stead called the Yair, till ye come to the Friar croft dykes and Emmerlaw Burn, down till ye ride to the mid-stream of Tweed, till ye come to Howdenburnfoot, and then from it straight up Howdendikes, Sunderland dikes, Owen's Close (Ettrickbank) dykes till you come to Ettrick even down the mid-stream to the nether part of the town-haugh which James Ker of Brigheuch violently rave up and tilled in the year 1540, for which the community summoned him and his complices before the Lords and won it against him. For that plea and others our provost, John Muthag, and James Kein, were both slain when they were riding to lead the third production of proofs. Which end of the common haugh has a great old foundation of a dyke betwixt the Abbot of Kelso's lands called the Brigheuch, of which Jas. Ker "rave" out the mid part, which old dike lineally passes out to the house of the Brigheuch, and then under the brae up the "Edir," and back of James Kein's dike till it comes to the lands of Selkirk at Yperlaw Well.

In 1540, Patrick Murray of Philiphaugh had a renewal charter of Peelhill, with the dues G. S., and petty customs of the burgh, granted to his grandfather John Murray in 1509; and in iii. 2318, 1542 Lammasland, in the mains of Selkirk, formerly held by John Simson as vassal of Earl 2686. Angus, was confirmed in his possession by the King, to whom they had reverted after the Earl's forfeiture.

After the murder of their first provost, the burgesses seem to have thought the office too dangerous to be held by one of themselves like the ill-fated Muthag; and it became a bone of contention amongst the most powerful of the neighbouring barons.

In 1542 Gilbert Ker of Greenhead, afterwards Sir Gilbert, alleging that B. R. not only he, but his father Andrew and his grandfather Ralph, had been aldermen of the burgh of Selkirk, complains that now Walter Scott, alleging himself provost, is not worthy to bear the office of provostry because he is the King's rebel and at the horn for seven years bypast. Whereto Bailie John Bryden answers that the letters are old "cassen" letters of no effect, and that the said Walter Scott had been instantly released. Greenhead's appeal to the time when on the eve of Flodden his father was chosen "well-wisher and supplier" to the town was of no avail; for later on (in 1545) we find Thomas Scott acting for Sir Walter Scott of Branxholme, knight, provost of Selkirk, and letting the customs to Janet, widow of Provost Muthag.

CHAPTER V.

1543 TO 1599.

THE wretched inhabitants of Selkirk were now about to experience a renewal of the burnings, assaults, and devastations, their subjection to which since Flodden had excited the generous pity of King James v. From September 1543 to midsummer of the following year, the Scottish Border was exposed to a series of vindictive and destructive raids by Englishmen and by Scottish freebooters under English protection. Against the Clan Scott and its leader the Lord of Buccleuch, these attacks were especially directed; the recent efforts of "Wicked Wat" to break the power of Liddesdale thieves obtaining for the English hearty assistance from Armstrongs, Nicksons, and Batisons. After laying waste the entire valley of Ettrick, an English officer named Edward Story, by command of Sir Thomas Wharton, attacked the town of Selkirk on the last day of October, and burnt it, with eight great stacks of corn. It can hardly be doubted that next year when Buccleuch marched to the assistance of Angus against Sir Ralph Evers and Sir Brian Latoun, there would be burgesses of Selkirk in his company; and that the relentless cruelty of the English was in some measure avenged on the field of Ancrum. Exasperated by this defeat and by the loss of two such able generals, King Henry commissioned Hertford at once to head an avenging raid upon the Scottish Border. The unexampled barbarity of this expedition is dealt with in another page; and nothing could more clearly illustrate the ruin and poverty in which the raid of 1543-4 involved Selkirk, than that in 1545 Hertford, though within a few miles, did not consider it worth while to carry thither his flaming torch. In a third raid by Hertford (now Duke of Somerset) in 1547, Selkirk seems again to have escaped a visit from the destroyers; but in the disastrous battle of Pinkie there doubtless fell some of its "fencible men betwixt sixty and sixteen" who had answered the proclamation calling them to the fray. Short was the respite. To revenge the incarceration of their chiefs at Buccleuch's instigation, the Kerrs invited Lord Grey and the English to help them against their powerful enemy. These

Harl.
MSS.
B. M.,
1757,
293.

P. C.,
i. 74, *seq.*

unnatural allies wound up a series of bloody and destructive reprisals by burning and harrying the town of Selkirk, whereof Buccleuch was provost. So that the office which James v. had created for the purpose of giving Selkirk the protection of "a good and noble man," had up to this time only led it into grief and trouble, exposing it to additional danger.

Pinkie was the last field on which the Scots encountered their "auld enemies of England," the battles on Scottish ground after that date being fought not as between England and Scotland, but between one party and another. Yet although peace was proclaimed between the kingdoms it was not established on their borders; and an elaborate system of extradition had to be maintained to insure the punishment of broken men of the Marches. Letters were sent charging Selkirk to be in readiness to keep the days of [P. C., i. 138.] trew on the 1st and 4th March 1553 at Cocklaw and Eidam burn.

Of forty-two burghs of Scotland in 1556, Selkirk paid the same taxes as Peebles, Dunbar, Lauder, and other towns of similar insignificance; and although the lapse of a century and a half did not much change their relative position in respect of wealth and population, in 1695 the monthly assessment [Gib. Glas., 103, etc.] of Selkirk was £72, and of Peebles only £66.

By a most unfortunate and regrettable loss of the burgh archives from 1545 to 1635, we are left in ignorance of the attitude of the burgesses when John Knox brought about the Reformation; but circumstantial evidence is all in the direction of proving that the townspeople were not at first warm adherents of the new doctrine. Their hostility to John Welsh, the Covenanting minister, less than thirty years later, shows unmistakeably that the ancient Church had even then a strong hold upon their minds and hearts.

In 1564, the provost and bailies, along with the landholders of the Middle [P. C., i. 283.] March, were warned to give better service to the Warden, Sir Walter Ker of Cessford, who had complained of the slack manner in which he was supported. That the authorities were in no mind to be trifled with in matters of this sort, is evident from the sharp punishment dealt out to a Selkirk man for [P. S., xxxiv. 62.] "remaining and biding from our sovereign's host ordained to convene at Musselburgh, for passing forthward with their majesties to Edinburgh." Within three days of the muster, Andrew, *alias* Dand Elliot, otherwise called "Dande of the Kow," was put to the horn, and the escheat of his goods gifted to Walter Scott of Tushielaw. In the summer and autumn of 1566, proclamation was thrice made at the market-place for assembling under arms to pass [P. C., i. 476, 481.] with Queen Mary towards the Borders; and next year, after the Queen's abdication, Regent Murray charged the provost, bailies, and inhabitants of Selkirk and other towns to " prepair and have in reddines bakin breid, browin aill, hors meit, mannis meit, and uther neidfull ludgeing and provisioun agane the 8 day of November nixtocum," under pain of being held partakers with the thieves and traitors against whom he was about to march.

A. P.,
ii. 566.
To Archibald, Earl of Angus, Queen Mary ratified, in 1567, charters granted to his predecessors, of vast estates, including " the lands, lordship, and barony of Selkirk, with pendicles in free holding, and the fruits, mills, multures, woods, fisheries, belonging to the same, lying within the county of Selkirk."

About this time the representation of burghs in the Convention of Estates or Scottish Parliament was placed upon a new footing. It is generally supposed that after the Parliament of 1326 (which granted the tenth penny of all rents and profits of lands to King Robert Bruce, and obtained from him in return the important obligation that no tax should be levied by the Crown without consent of Parliament), the burgesses had representatives in every Convention; but as only a very few lists of burgh commissioners exist of earlier date than the beginning of the sixteenth century, there is no certainty upon the point. Commissioners for the burgh of Selkirk sat in 1469, in 1478, in 1560, and in 1567; but history does not record their names. In the latter year it was enacted that provosts of burghs, or commissioners for burghs, should be present in every Convention; and although the Act was for a while imperfectly observed, Selkirk appears to have taken full advantage of the privilege. In 1568 Thomas Scott took his seat in the Scottish Parliament for the burgh of Selkirk. In 1579 he was succeeded by John Mitchelhill, member of a substantial and prominent family of burgesses, which supplied representatives to Parliament during the next hundred years.

M.P.s FOR THE BURGH OF SELKIRK.

1469, 1478, 1560, 1567, not named.
1568. Thomas Scott.
1579. John Mitchelhill.
1583. Gavin Wilkie.
1585. George Halliwell.
1587. John Watson.
1593. James Scott.
1612. James Mitchelhill.

1617. James Mitchelhill and Mr. John Ker.
1621. William Elliot.
1630. Mr. John Ker.
1639. Bailie William Scott.
1640. William Mitchelhill.
1641. Bailie William Scott.
   „   Bailie Thomas Scott.

1644. William Elliot.
1645. Bailie Thomas Scott.
1648. William Elliot.
1649. Bailie Thomas Scott.
In 1654 Cromwell united Selkirk with Peebles, Haddington, Dunbar, Jedburgh, Lauder, and North Berwick, to return a representative to the Parliament at Westminster.
1654. William Thompson, burgess of Haddington.
1656. George Downing. Preferred to sit for Carlisle.
1656. John Vincent of Warnford, in Northumberland.
1658. Doctor Thomas Clarges. Knighted at Breda in 1660 for his efforts to restore Charles II. Afterwards M.P. for Oxford University.
In 1660, after the collapse of the Protectorate and restoration of the monarchy, Selkirk resumed sending its own representative to the Scottish Parliament.
1661. Bailie Robert Elliot.
1665. Bailie William Mitchelhill.
1667. Bailie William Mitchelhill.
1669. Patrick Murray.
1678. Bailie William Waugh.
1681. Andrew Angus, town-clerk.
1685. Bailie William Waugh.
1689. Mr. John Murray, Philiphaugh.
1702-6. Bailie Robert Scott.
On the union of the Parliaments Selkirk again lost its right of separate representation, and was joined with the burghs of Peebles, Lanark, and Linlithgow.
1707. Mungo Graham of Gorthie.
1708. Col. George Douglas, brother to the Earl of Morton.
1713. Sir Jas. Carmichael of Bonytown, Bart. (Petitioned against.)
1715. Col. George Douglas.
1722. Daniel Weir of Stonebyres, Lanarkshire. (Petition.)
1725. John Murray of Philiphaugh.

1734. Hon. Jas. Carmichael, son of Earl of Hyndford.
1741. John M'Kie of Palgowan, afterwards designed John Ross M'Kie of Hawkhead. Double return; the Hon. Jas. Carmichael waiving his claim.
1747. Hon. Jas. Carmichael. (Lawrence Dundas not duly elected.)
1754. John Murray of Philiphaugh.
1761. Admiral Sir John Ross of Balnagowan.
1768. James Dickson of Broughton and Kilbucho.
1772. Sir James Cockburn of Langton (on Mr. Dickson's death).
1784. Captain John Moore, afterwards Lieut.-Gen. Sir John Moore, who fell at Corunna.
1790. William Grieve, of London.
1796. Viscount Stopford.
1802. Lieut.-Col. Dickson of Kilbucho.
1806. Sir Charles Ross of Balnagowan. (Petition.)
1807. Wm. Maxwell of Carriden.
1812. Sir John Riddell of Riddell, Bart.
1818. John Pringle of Haining (on Sir John Riddell's death).
1820. Henry Monteith of Carstairs, thrice Lord Provost of Glasgow.
1826. Adam Hay, banker in Edinburgh, afterwards Sir Adam Hay, Bart., of Haystoune.
1830. Henry Monteith of Carstairs.
1831. Wm. D. Gillon of Wallhouse. Married (1820) a daughter of John Corse Scott of Sinton.
After the Reform Bill of 1832 and until that of 1868, the burgh of Selkirk was merged in the county. Mr. Disraeli united it with Hawick and Galashiels, the first member for the three towns being—
1868. George Otto Trevelyan: Junior Lord of Admiralty, 1869; Secretary to Admiralty, 1880; Chief Secretary for Ireland, and a Privy Councillor, 1882; Chancellor of Duchy of Lancaster, and member of Gladstone Cabinet, 1884.

One result of the re-invigorated Parliament appears to have been a determination to tolerate no longer the thieves who infested the Border, making the lives of peaceable folks not worth living. In April 1569, Bailie James Scott of Selkirk signed, along with Buccleuch and other of the Border barons, a bond to unite in suppressing these robbers with the utmost rigour. How much of the Bailie's heart was in such work may be guessed from the mention of his son's name along with those of his relations of Tushilaw as exactors of black mail from quiet crofters in Gattonside. In the same year (1578) an extraordinary case came before the Privy Council, on the complaint of Thomas Doby, burgess in Selkirk.

Robert Doby, burgess, and James Doby, indweller in Selkirk, are represented to have sent for Thomas to come and settle with them for certain sums and goods he had lent to them. He at last coming to them, "lippaning na ewill in thair handis," they being his own natural brothers, he behaving himself ever as a true and faithful brother to them, and disbursing his geir in great quantity at divers times for their relief, they most unnaturally, with John Dun in Brigheuch, tenant to Thomas Ker in Sunderlandhall, and Thomas Dun, indweller in Selkirk, after they had enticed him to Robert Doby his brother's house, and thence to his stable, unmercifully and inhumanly "dang him with mony bauch straikis, band him fute and hand, and spuilzeit him of his jak, plaitslevis, his pistolet, his belt and furneist quhinzear, his gartanis and his purse," with sundry pieces of money and writings therein, without any occasion or quarrel, as God knows.

The accused brothers alleged in defence that the said Thomas had been mad these divers years bygone—"lyke as he in his madnes hes sindrie tymes riddin day and nicht to and fra in the cuntrie, and specialie in the nicht, armit with jak, steilbonat, pistolet, sword, and lanse stalf, showtand and cryand maist feirfullie; as alsua hurt himself with his awin quhinzear, and put ane cord about his awin neck to have hangit himself"—which was why, being moved of brotherly love, they disarmed him.

Finding it impossible to decide their conflicting statements, the Council referred the whole case to the Provost and Bailies of Selkirk.

1584-5, March 3.—John Ker, son of Thomas Ker of Kippelaw, dwelling in Selkirk, accused of joining Scott of Halyden and others in going armed "in the gloming of the evening" to Haltree, where they stole "fyve oxin, foure ky, and ane broun naig."

1585-6.—Proclamations at the market cross for a muster at Stirling, a Justice-Court at Jedburgh, for relief of the Warden from vexatious applications, meeting of English and Scotch commissioners for the Border, forbidding of an intended combat between certain English

P. C., i. 651.

P. C., iii. 101.

P. C., iii. 107.

P. C., iii. 726.

P. C., iv. 28, 45, 46, 68, 81, 98.

and Scotch borderers, and for Scott of Buccleuch to find "sikker souirtie" for £10,000, that he will not attack Hay of Yester.

1586-7.—Proclamations at Selkirk market cross anent recent Justice-Court at Jedburgh, P. C., against riding in England in warlike manner, and urging the well-disposed to light bale-fires [147, 234] when alarmed.

1587-8.—Proclamations of meeting to preserve peace on Borders; of court for all persons P. C., harmed by the "reiffis, stowthis, heirschippis, and oppressionis of disordourit subjectis." [240, 259, 372, 395,]

1589.—Proclamation of muster "round his Majesty at Edinburgh," with spears and [791, 795.] hackbuts, to suppress certain enterprises against the true religion. Muster at Brechin, to be attended by the inhabitants of Selkirk and other burghs, for punishment of those engaged in late rebellion.

1590.—Proclamation of special committee of Privy Council for government of Border Marches; and for all fencibles between 60 and 16 to meet his Majesty at Peebles, in view of a raid to the Borders.

It requires little imagination to assist one in realising the constant unsettling and uneasy life of the indwellers of Selkirk while such proclamations were being issued. Reduced to poverty by English marauders, as well as by thieves on their own side of the Cheviots, striving hard to win sustenance from sterile and unkindly crofts, the burgesses had yet to provide their own share of the King's army and of the King's taxes. Life cannot have been so pleasant with them but that volunteers for the frequent levies would be plentiful. Their furnishing was probably a greater difficulty than their enrolment; and the town's burden would not be lightened by its share in the equipment of a ship for the convoying of his Majesty, "with the Queen, his dearest bedfellow," from Norway. Some of the inhabitants, however, were well off, there being frequent mention of the principal families as owners of land in other places. When James Douglas, Commendator of Melrose, in 1590, Wade. alienated lands to the feuars of Gattonside, he excepted two acres belonging Melr. [343.] to James Scott in Selkirk: no doubt the same who represented the burgh in Parliament in 1593. The same James Scott obtained a charter of tenements G. s., lying towards the sheep-market of Selkirk between the lands of Earl Angus [39-66.] on the east and west, the "Mid-stream of Acres" on the north, and the common road on the south. His name recurs in the following extract from the Records of the Privy Council :—

1590, May 15.—Bond of caution by James Hoppringle of Torsons (of that Ilk) and P. C., Williame Borthwick of Cruikstoun, for Robert Scott of Haining, in £1000, and for George [iv. 480.] Mitchelhill and Gawine Wilkie (Wilkene), bailies of Selkirk, James Scott, called Litle James, burgess there, John Sweit there, George Halywell there, Wm. Mitchelhill there, William Brydane, common clerk of Selkirk, John Brady, called Lang John, burgess there, William Scott, called Litle William, there, William Thomson, cordiner there, and Patrick Kene there, in £500 each,

VOL. II.   G that they will not harm Patrick Murray of Philiphaugh, or his dependants. Witnesses to the Selkirk signatures—John Melrose, burgess, Adam Murray, burgess, John Lidderdale, burgess, and Wm. Mairshaell; William Brydin, notary public, subscribing for Kene, Mairshaell, Litill Willie, Lang John, Thomson and Sweit, who cannot write.

May 20.—Caution by Patrick Murray of Philiphaugh, and by James Hoppringle of Wood-house and John Hoppringle of Buckholme, sureties for the said Patrick, for John Murray and Andrew Murray his brothers, James Murray, son natural to the late Patrick Murray of Philip-haugh, John Murray of Blackbarony, Mr Judeane (Gideon) and William Murray his brothers, Patrick Murray of Kirkhouse, Robert Murray of Orchard, George Turnbull in Philiphaugh, John his son, William Murray there, and Michael Watson, servant to the said Patrick, that they will not harm Robert Scott of Haining, James Scott, called "Mekle Jamie Eister," or any of the other 12 persons for whom caution had been found in the Act of May 15.

Evidence of a lingering attachment to the Romish Church—or at least of hostility to the Reformed preachers—is afforded by the attitude of members of prominent families in the town.

Vol. iv.
521.
1590, August 11.—It having been resolved to call before the Secret Council all Papists, Jesuits, priests, troublers of ministers, non-payers of stipend, etc., letters were sent to the following active pursuers and troublers of ministers in the execution of their function, and in the possessing of their manses and glebes—George Mitchelhill, George Haliwell, Wm. Mitchelhill, George Anisoun, John Turnbull, indwellers in Selkirk, and to James Scot, Wm. Mitchelhill and John Kene—to appear before the King and Council at Edinburgh on 25th September.

Notwithstanding the terms of the following complaint, it is hardly open to doubt that pride had less to do with the Selkirk folks' apparently defiant attitude than their chronic impecuniosity.

P. C.,
v. 450.
1598, March 17.—Complaint by Thomas Inglis, merchant burgess of Edinburgh. On 5th Nov. last, George Haliwell, John Lidderdale, and Walter Halliwell, burgesses of Selkirk, had been put to the horn for non-payment of £750 due to him. And because they remained (as they do yet) most proudly and contemptuously at the said process, Robert Scott of Haining, Provost-depute, James Scott and James Mitchelhill, bailies of Selkirk, had been charged to put them in "strait firmance and captivitie." The provost and bailies have, however, "maist proudlie" disobeyed the charge; and to the further contempt of his Majesty have resetted the said rebels within their burgh. Not appearing nor producing the said rebels, the provost and bailies were denounced rebels themselves.

1598, August 12.—Signature at Selkirk of band of peace between Gladstones and Maxwells.

Auth.
MSS.
In the last year of this century a deed was executed by which part of Selkirk glebe was sold by the minister, although it has been generally under-stood that prior to the Act of 1866 such a transaction could only be carried through by special Act of Parliament. It is dated Branxholm, 6th August 1599, the parties granting the feu being as follows :—

Mr. Patrick Shaw, minister at Selkirk.
    ,, John Knox,   ,,   Melrose.
    ,, John Smith,   ,,   Maxton.
    ,, Thos. Duncanson, ,,   Bowden.
    ,, Thos. Storrie,   ,,   (Westruther).
    ,, Geo. Byres,   ,,   (Legerwood).
    ,, Alex. Simpson,   ,,   Mertoun.
    ,, James Daes,   ,,   Arsiltoun.
    ,, Allan Lundie,   ,,   Lessudden.
    ,, Wm. Hogg,   ,,   Boldside.

brethren of the Presbytery of Melrose, with consent of—

Sir Walter Scott of Branxholm, Knight (Buccleuch).
Patrick Murray of Falahill (Philiphaugh).
Andrew Ker of Yair.
Robert Scott of Haining.
Robert Scott of Oakwood.
John Ker of Whitmuirhall.
Thomas Ker of Sunderlandhall.
James Scott, bailie.

John Melross, Wm. Synton, Patrick Kene, Robert Dobie, John Lidderdale, Geo. Turnbull, Mungo Johnston, James Turnbull, Wm. Nicol, and George Mitchelhill, bailiffs, burgesses of Selkirk, gentlemen, parishioners and inhabitants of Selkirk. The deed bears that for 100 merks Mr. Patrick Shaw conveys to George Anderson, burgess of Selkirk, "the onset back and fore with the yaird of the same and pertinents thereof pertaining to the said Mr. Patrick as part of his manse," to be held in free blench for payment of one penny at Whitsunday, " gif it is asked allenerlie." In the event of Anderson being molested in possession, Scott of Haining, Ker of Yair, and Scott of Hartwoodmyres, bind themselves to pay him 200 merks, of which the brethren of the Presbytery shall relieve them. Sir W. Scott signs "Bacleugh," the Bailie signs "James Scott at the Cross," and some of the town councillors with their hands at the pen of their common clerk (Henry Blaikie), because they cannot write.

Selkirk Silver Arrow.

CHAPTER VI.

1600 TO 1660.

Auth.
MSS.

FOUR leaves are all that survive of the Council Records from 1545 to 1635. Dated 1593, they contain minutes authorising the formation of trade guilds, and are signed by H. Blaikie, town-clerk. It does not appear that any of the crafts took immediate advantage of the Council's decree; but eight years afterwards twenty-seven master shoemakers drew up a code of acts and statutes for their "awin weills, commodity, and profit in their awin union and body." In this document deacons are unmentioned, transgressors being amenable to "the brethren," and the only officers are the four quarter-masters. Not until 1608 did the Council, in compliance with a petition from the wabster craft, issue a seal of cause granting the weavers power to elect a deacon, with other privileges of full and regular incorporation. Next year the cordiners (as the souters delighted to call themselves) obtained a charter, and were followed a year later by the tailors. For close on seventy years these three were the only incorporated crafts of Selkirk, the fleshers and hammermen not obtaining seals of cause until 1679 and 1681 respectively. Elsewhere the interesting history of these ancient guilds is detailed at length.

Birrel's
Diary.

In the year 1600 the Gowrie Conspiracy led to severe measures against those bearing the name of Ruthven. At first they were ordered to pass out of the country ; but a year later the edict was modified to the extent that they must change their names, and not come near the King by ten miles, on pain of treason. As a matter of fact, there are to this day Selkirk families who, though still spelling their name Ruthven, are addressed as " Ribbons," and so call themselves.

If we may believe a complaint by Bailies George Mitchelhill, Patrick P. C. Kene, and James Scott, the 1st of December 1608 must have been an exciting day in Selkirk. Armed with swords, gauntlets, plate-sleeves, and other weapons, John Scott, brother to Walter Scott of Woll, with John Turnbull his half-brother, under the special causing, hounding-out, and direction of Robert Scott of Haining, came that day about the sun-setting to the dwelling-house of John Jackson, "knok-keiper" (clock-keeper) and burgess of Selkirk, and therein entered violently with drawn swords in their hands. Fiercely setting upon the said John, they shamefully, cruelly, and unmercifully invaded and pursued him of his life, gave him many bloody wounds in divers parts of his body, and left him for dead. On information thereof the Bailies, for discharge of the duty of their office, repaired to the said persons and laid hold of them, in purpose to have them warded, "lippyning that nane durst have bene so insolent as to have taen them off thair handis." Yet William Scott, brother to Robert Scott of Haining, accompanied by Walter Gledstanes and John Gledstanes, servitors to the said goodman of Haining, Walter Scott of Huntly, William his brother, Walter Scott of Thirlstane, William Scott of Bowhill, James his brother, Walter Scott called auld Walter in Synton, John Turnbull, appearand of Hundalee, Robert and Andrew his brothers, and David Scott, brother of the deceased Scott of Synton, with divers others their accomplices, all furnished as if for war, likewise of the special causing of Haining, came in a tumultuous and unseemly manner to the said bailies upon the high causeway (hie calsay) of the said burgh, and there masterfully reft from them the prisoners, and carried them away, therethrough committing a most open riot and a high and proud contempt and indignity against his Majesty's highness and his authority. The rescued bravos failed to appear, were found guilty of wounding the clock-keeper as charged, and were directed to enter their persons within the Tolbooth of Edinburgh, and there abide at their own expense until the Lords should take further order anent their punishment.

1610, December 11.—Wattie Haliwell being charged with troubling the kirk of Selkirk, P. R. answered he made no trouble save that he sat down where he was accustomed. The minister said he had sat down there in great contempt, the men of Carterhaugh being appointed to sit there, as he well knew.   *Ordered to confess after sermon next Sabbath.*

P. R.   1613, July 13.—John Paterson, late schoolmaster of Selkirk, having complained of Mr. Patrick Shaw, the minister, taking the session-book out of his house and putting him unlawfully out of the school, Mr. Shaw answered (1) that the session-book was his own, and (2) that Paterson being insufficient both for reading and teaching, and the Council not liking him, he had given him warning at Candlemas and thereafter at the Pasche before Whitsunday.

1614, December 6.—Will Purves ordered to remove all his fuel (" eldin ") out of the kirkyard, and all other his material, with all diligence ; and that in time coming he " nather mell (meddle) with the kirk-zeard nor the dykis thereof, under all tynsole" (loss).

1616, July 2.—James Kein in Selkirk confessed to profaning the Sabbath of the Communion, taking it in the morning and riding away immediately with the goodman of Whitmuir to Muirton, where they drank all the day.

If the parishioners of Selkirk were not all that the presbytery could wish, it was not because of any shortcoming in their pastor.   At the presbyterial visitation Mr. Shaw was found to teach twice on the Sabbath ; to have prayers sometimes in the week-days, morning and evening, especially in winter ; to examine once a year ; to give Our Lord's Supper once a year, and to visit the sick when desired.   His reverend brethren nevertheless felt it their duty to admonish him to examine every Sabbath after the preaching, and to give communion twice a year at least.   Because he pled difficulty in obtaining P. R.   the elements, he was ordered to charge Mr. James Durham, parsoun, to furnish elements for four times a year.   The minister is also directed, with consent of the town, to seek for a good schoolmaster, to be tried by the presbytery before being appointed, " because he is to read in the Kirk, and take up the psalm singing."

Another instruction of the presbytery was that the butts should be put out of the churchyard, which was a place of burial and not of gaming.   Fully a century and a half before, an Act had been passed decreeing the disuse of football and golf, and ordaining the erection of bowmarks and a pair of butts A. P.,   at each parish church.   Every Sunday from Easter to Allhallowmass, all men ii. 48.   between fifty and twelve were to practise shooting, six arrows each at least, under pain of twopence, to be paid as drink-money to those present.

Dun.   1618.—One John Ker, town-clerk of Selkirk, writes a paper for Ker of Greenhead. MSS.

Pit.   There is record of what appears to be an inordinately severe sentence iii. 441.   for an almost trivial offence.   Gilbert Elliot, called " Gib the Galliard," was accused of stealing, " under silence and clud of nycht," a purse with forty pounds therein, " furth of Johnnie Airmestrang's breikis," with drinking ten merks of the money, and keeping the rest until he was challenged.   Elliot denied theft, " bot allanerlie that he being in Alexander Youngeis house in Selkirk, ryseing in the moirning, fand the purse upone the flure of the chalmer." The ten merks he drank he claimed as salvage-money, and the rest he had restored as soon as he understood whose it was. The jury having by the mouth of John Scott of Hundelishoip, foreman, pronounced Gilbert to be culpable of taking away the purse but cleansed him of stealing it, he was sentenced to be scourged through the burgh of Edinburgh, and to be banished from the realm for ever, under pain of death, without favour. This although the owner of the purse had declined to pursue Elliot for theft !

1620.—Transference of Selkirk property formerly belonging to John Scott, called of Selk. Bgh. Newark, from Andrew Scott, surgeon in Edinburgh, in favour of William Kemp, Musselburgh. Sas. It is minutely detailed as follows :—

Tenement of land between that of Gavin Murray on the east, Nittage's close or long close on the west, yard of James Waugh on south, and High Street on north.

Four " port "-lands lying near the West Port, between the High Street as it leads to the Mill-burn on the north and the Peelhill on the south, the lands of Wm. Mitchelhill on the west, and of —— on the east.

Hall's Croft near the east port, between the water of Ettrick on the north, James Mitchelhill's lands on the west, Bailie James Kene's lands on the east, and the King's highway on the south.

Tait's hill croft, between Simon Halliday's lands on the west, the lands of " Bawiethorne " on the east, lands occupied by John Fairgrieve on the south, and Simon Halliday's head-port on the north.

White's croft, between James Mitchelhill's lands on the north, the Portlands on the east, the Struthers meadow on the west, and the lands called Rattontails on the south.

Brother Croft (fraterna crofta), lying from the lower side of the lands of Reideilles, between the King's highway on the north, the Corslands on the east, Thomas Scott's lands on the south, and Thos. Halliwell's lands on the west.

About same date is a charter by George Halyday, maltman burgess of Selk. Bgh. Selkirk, to John his second son, of a tenement, with yard, etc., near the east Sas. port, between the land of Simon Halyday (granter's father) on the east and south, George Scot's house on the west, and the public street on the north. Also Gargunnock's croft north of the public street on the east side of the burgh, between the laird of Greenhead's lands on north, public street on south, the late James Wauch's lands on west, and the water of Ettrick on the north.

George Halyday also grants to Janet Brewis (Bruce) his wife, in liferent—

Dunsdale croft, containing six rigs of land between the laird of Greenhead's land on the east, John Fletcher's lands on south, Shawburn on the west, and Dunsdalehaugh on the north.

A rig on north side of Struther-meadow between Jas. Mitchelhill's lands on south, Mungo Burn's lands on north.

Two rigs on south side of Struther-meadow, between Wm. Mitchelhill's lands on south and said meadow on north.

Croft and piece of meadow called the Reidheild croft between John Dun's lands on east, Thomas Turnbull's on south, and public street on north.

Two rigs upon the Uplands between the lands of Robert Scott, called Wester, on the east and Bailie Wm. Elliot's lands on the west.

Two butts of land at the Stobstone gate, between Thomas Jackson's lands on south, Thomas Hardie's on north.

Also a butt of land above the Neppilands (?).

Anls. of Hawk., 195, *seq.*   1622-3.—Among the "persons of assize" or jurymen at Justiciary Courts held in Jedburgh and Dumfries were—

> James Keine, late bailie of Selkirk.
> Wm. Scott, called "of the Pillars," late bailie of Selkirk.
> John Turnbull of Howden.
> Wm. Ellott, bailie of Selkirk.
> James Murray, notar in Selkirk.
> Wm. Purves, Thesaurar of Selkirk.
> George Riddell in Selkirk.
> William Turnbull, portioner of Philiphaugh.

At Jedburgh, Pett Murray in Swineside was found guilty of stealing, from the Common of Selkirk, seven sheep belonging to Philiphaugh's tenants, three belonging to three other persons, five belonging to William Murray in Philiphaugh, and a wedder belonging to Sir John Murray of Philiphaugh (Sir John being one of the justices). He was hanged along with other eighteen Borderers convicted of like crimes.

For a vivid picture of the lawlessness and violence of Borderers—especially those of rank and influence—at this period, nothing surpasses the description of the Knight of Thirlestane's attempted escape from Selkirk prison.

P. C.   On the 5th day of January 1625, Bailies Andrew Ker and William Elliot were called to the middle wardhouse, wherein the following persons were warded for great sums of money—Sir Robert Scott of Thirlstane, Knight, Gawin Ellot of Burgh, George Davidson of Kames, Thomas Lytill of Mickledale, and John Skaillis, servitor to the said Sir Robert. The Bailies, having searched and viewed the wardhouse, found that the said persons had broken open a great part of the north side wall, and also had broken, digged, and wrought through the south wall close under the sole of the fore-window, "that they micht have sene the Hie Street tharthrow." Being asked "quhy they had brokin his Majesteis javell," to what intent, and which of them was plotter and mover of the rest, they confessed that they were all "upoun the counsall and knawledge of the breking," that it was plotted by Sir Robert Scott of Thirlstane, that they were all helpers except George Davidson, and that they all intended to escape the next night, except the said George, who was compelled by fear of his life to swear that he should conceal their flight. Thereafter the Bailies and Council searched the prisoners' beds, and found in the said Sir Robert's "ane coulter of ane pleuch brokin in thrie pairtis be workin at the wall, with ane uther new coulter, as also twa greit craw-irnes" (which Sir Robert confessed he had caused to be made for the better breaking of the ward), "with foure faddome towis or thereby, and spurris, and buitis and hors wandis, in everie ane of the six prisoners' beddis, and twa raper swordis within the said Sir Robert Scott his trunk." At the request of the Bailies, Robert Scott, notary, wrote an account of the affair, which was sent to the Privy Council. It was drawn up in presence of Mr. Patrick Shaw, minister of the parish, Mr. James Scott, minister of Yarrow, Mr. Alexander Kid, minister of Ashkirk, Mr. John Ker, sheriff-clerk, and James Sword, his servant.

Besides being Sheriff-Clerk, Mr. John Ker was twice representative of the burgh in A. P., Parliament, and in 1628, was commissioner in an agreement about teinds between the King ^{v. 195.} and his Scottish burghs.

1629.—Andrew Angus paid 40s. for "tuilzeing" (engaging in a broil) with Andrew Tait Cor. MSS. upon the market-day.

Although after the accession of James VI. to the throne of England, the language of educated Scotsmen became year by year more assimilated to English, the vernacular continued to be widely used. In legal proceedings, in Church Courts, in Town-Councils, the old Scots tongue prevailed, and even Hawk. in the schools, English had not yet displaced it. In a copy-book written at Soc. Selkirk in 1630, the set-lines are all in the native dialect, consisting of such 1869. couplets as—

> Quhen sair calamitie ouirsettis ane gentill hart,
> Quha bearis it pacientlie, he playis ane proudent pairt.

> Na plesoure is bot pane, as previs experiens,
> Thairfoir lat hoip remane, and tak in pacience.

> As efter snaw and sleet, sall cum the someris flowris,
> Thay ar nocht warth the sueit, that may nocht suffer souris.

> Ye sie the stormis blast garris cluddis fall out in rane,
> Bot quhan the schuar is past, the sky will cleare agane.

In common with a number of other burghs, Selkirk in 1633 obtained an Act of Parliament ratifying all the charters that had ever been granted in its A. P., favour, and confirming it in possession of all its lands and privileges, without prejudice to the rights of the Earl of Roxburgh, Riddell of Haining, Murray of Philiphaugh, and the Marquis of Douglas, in Selkirk Common. Evidently following this concession, the burgh mails and petty customs were sold to the town for 4000 merks by Sir John Murray. That these yielded considerable revenue appears from a payment of £4 by Mark Anderson for import-duty on a tun of wine, the same from Margaret Coutts for another tun, and £3 for three puncheons.

Slt. Clk.'s MSS.

B. R.

The proverbial want of harmony amongst musicians had its illustration in a riot by Adam Moffat, piper, against John Law, violer, in 1637, for which Adam had "to pay the piper" to the tune of £5, 8s. Scots.

With a view to confining the range of a pestilence which visited the Borders in the spring and early summer of 1637, various orders were issued to the county justices. Sir John Murray of Philiphaugh, as convener of Selkirkshire, preferred a complaint against the people of Selkirk for defying the regulations. Hearing that a burgess named James Murray was about to have a daughter married, and that great numbers were expected to gather for the occasion, he forbade the assemblage as dangerous, limiting the attendance to four or five witnesses. But the man was obstinate, and in reply to Sir John's remonstrances said, "If ye be feared, come not there." To a demand that they should put the man in prison the bailies gave no heed, and at the marriage next day 80 or 100 persons met "and drank together all that day till night."

P. C.

About this time William Nicol was complained against for the "bigging and re-edifying" of the west side of his house called "The Auld Forest's Peel," and thereby encroaching on the ground of William Smail.

B. R.

By a special Act of Parliament granted in 1641, the Bailies of Selkirk were empowered to hold a new fair on the 4th of July "callit St. Merteene of Bullion his day," and for eight days thereafter, in place of the old fair held on the 8th December. A graphic description of the difficulties attending the winter fair is given in the preamble, in which it is declared "altogether unprofitable, in respect of the shortness of the day, foulness of the weather, deepness of the soil, and greatness of the waters of Tweed, Ettrick, Yarrow, and others, which hinders both the bestial and goods to be transported and the lieges to come and go without great hazard of the loss of the goods and bestial, as well as the owners' and buyers' lives." It was further represented that Selkirk was the special and only royal burgh within his Majesty's lordship of

A. P., v. 545.

Ettrick Forest and sheriffdom of Selkirk, and that great quantities of nolt, sheep, wool, and other bestial and goods were sold in its markets and fairs.

Less success appears to have attended another supplication by Selkirk to Parliament, for moneys paid to Major-General Monro and his soldiers; but in 1644, the Estates authorised repayment of £800, with interest since August 1641. ^{A. P., v. 695.} ^{A. P., vi. (1) 173.}

1642, October.—In consequence of complaints concerning the slowness of burgesses in attending funerals outside the burgh, it is ordained that in all time coming 10 or 12 men appointed out of each watch, shall by turns accompany the bailies to any "outlandish burial" they go to. Those that have no horse of their own to fee one if they are able. ^{B. R.}

1643, January 6.—The said day Marion Hislop, spouse to William Cook, miller, convicted of stealing John Tait's barley out of his stack-yard, is sentenced to be taken to the Cross with the bear sheaves, and there openly proclaimed a thief; the officer to banish her the town, with her husband and whole family—never to return, under pain of scourging.

1643.—For half-year from April to October the total revenue of the common good of the burgh was 3061 merks—about £166 sterling.

When in the summer of 1643, the quarrel between King and Parliament, being at its height, the Estates of Scotland met in defiance of his Majesty's order, they resolved to send a large army to help the Roundheads in England. In the War Committee of Selkirkshire, Thomas Scott of Selkirk found a place, there being evidently the most perfect accord between the authorities of town and county. A signal proof of their co-operation was given on the 6th December, when nearly all the gentlemen of note within the Forest were created burgesses. It is recorded that the right noble and potent Earl, Francis, Earl of Buccleuch, was received a freeman, along with ^{A. P., vi. (1) 51.}

> David Scott, his Lordship's brother.
> Sir Wm. Scott, yr. of Harden (ancestor of Lord Polwarth).
> Patrick Scott of Thirlestane (ancestor of Lord Napier and Ettrick).
> Walter Scott of Goldielands.
> Thomas Scott of Todrig.
> Sir John Scott of Newburgh, Knight.
> John Scott, his son.
> Andrew Ker of Sunderlandhall (ancestor of Mr. Scott Plummer).
> John Ker, his brother.
> Wm. Scott of Tushielaw.
> Andrew Scott of Broadmeadows.
> William and Francis his sons.
> Robert Scott of Bowhill.
> Robert Scott, son to Sir Robert Scott of Haining.
> William Scott of Headshaw.
> William Scott of Hartwoodmyres.
> James Glover, servitor to Buccleuch.

George Scott, " callit of the Woll."
Thomas Porteous, servitor to David Scott (brother to Buccleuch).
John Scott of Gilmanscleuch.
John Scott, Provost of Creichton.
Walter Scott of Commonside.
William Scott, his brother.
Robert Scott of Glack.
Archibald Elliot of Philhope.
Archibald Elliot of Burnmouth.
John Murray of Sundhope.
Andrew Scott of Foulshiels.
Walter Scott of Chapel.
Wm. Thomson, servitor to Sir John Murray.
Adam Turnbull, servitor to Wm. Scott of Mangerton.
Walter Scott of Shielswood.
James   , portioner of Redpath.
William Scott of Sinton.

There can be little doubt that this imposing demonstration of friendship between landed men and burgesses was made in view of the impending campaign ; and it may well be that the lesser lairds were mindful of the privileges enjoyed by widows and orphans of freemen, should they fall in battle.   A month later, "considering the time for the expedition to England was near, and that it was very expedient their soldiers should have some competent sum to buy clothes and provisions for their voyage, and go out like themselves, to the credit of the burgh, being noways inferior to others, the Bailies ordained a stent to be cast among the burgh, extending to 1000 merks, so that to every soldier there might fall twenty merks, and to every sergeant £20 Scots."   On the 23d January 1644, the creditable number of forty-one "soldiers for the burgh," having been admitted burgesses gratis, marched out of the town to their rendezvous at Hawick, "for the expedition to England, for relief of the Protestants there, borne down through the tyranny and cruelty of the Papists," as it is put in the Council minute-book.   No excuse is offered for giving here the names of the Selkirk men who thus set out to take part in a campaign which may be said to have turned the current of British history.   What would we not give for the muster-roll of their ancestors, who a century and a half before were decimated around the king at Flodden ?

John Sword, elder.	Nicol Smith.	Andrew Dickson.
John Sword, yr.	Wm. Wilson.	Thomas Moffat.
Wm. Donaldson.	Jas. Fairbairn.	James Donaldson.
Wm. Cochrane. (?)	Andrew Emond.	Adam Jamieson.

John Darling.	John Jackson, mcht.	Ralph Cowan.
Thomas Mitchelhill. (?)	—— Glasgow.	John Young.
Andrew Angus.	Thomas Brydin.	Andrew Boston.
Rob. Blaikie.	James Bullerwell. (?)	Alex. Wallace.
Jas. Lennox.	John Fletcher, cordiner.	Adam Ballanden.
Walter Rae.	Adam Cowan.	Thomas Lambert.
Pat. Fletcher.	Jas. Thomson, serjeant.	Robert Renwick.
Wm. Donaldson, elder.	Jas. Caldwells, yr.	John Paterson.
Wm. Brown.	John Scoon.	Malcolm Kene.
Richard Brewhouse.	Gilbert Ballantyne.	

At the same time their officers, Colonel Home, Major Hadden, Captain William Wallace, and Captain George Campbell, received the freedom of the burgh, their regiment being that known as the Lord Chancellor's. After a fatiguing and trying march in wintry weather, the Scottish army "sat down" before Newcastle, which they besieged nine months without compelling the royalist garrison to surrender. At last, on the 19th October, eight storming parties attacked through breaches made by mines or artillery, the Selkirk company and Buccleuch's regiment entering together at Close Gate. Within the walls the victors found great penury, scarcity, and wretchedness, the miseries of a state of siege being aggravated by pestilence. Soon after the fall of Newcastle, the plague spread into Scotland, the Borders being once more ravaged by this resistless scourge. What with a deficient harvest, heavy taxation for war purposes, the drawing away of her ablest young men for the army, the devastation of many districts by hostile bands of soldiers, and the generally depressing effect of incessant preachings, prayings, fastings, and self-abasements, the Scotch were so reduced in vital power as to offer but too easy a prey to epidemic ; and Newcastle was bitterly avenged. *New. Repr. Lith- gow's Pphlet. Ch. Dom. Ann. ii. 156.*

During the absence of their own fencible men in England, the community of Selkirk had to complain of irregular and partial billeting of the officers of Lord Lothian's regiment, a stent of £360 Scots being raised from "the richer sort" to redress the inequality.

The dignity of the bailies seems to have risen with the importance of their emprises, two "souters" being fined 20s. each for "their rustic incivility in bringing and addressing themselves with their aprons about them, to convoy the bailies in ganging the fair." Ordained that in future no burgess attend any public meeting except he be honestly apparelled, under pain of £10.

It is a noteworthy fact that from 9th August to 22d October 1645, there is no entry in the public records of the burgh—its even tenor being evidently too much disturbed by the presence first of Montrose and his army, and then of the Covenanters and Leslie. Apparently with the view of writing in something when danger was over, a page and a half have been left blank, but so they remain to this day ; and thus we are without information concerning two months of supreme interest in the town's history. It was in Selkirk Tolbooth the Covenanters went through the hideous farce of trying Irish mercenaries taken prisoner at Philiphaugh before they hanged or shot them.

A. P., vi.
(1) 492.

Continued sacrifices were called for in order to maintain war against the King's party. In 1646, Selkirk had to furnish other ten men to recruit the army in England, and to raise 2000 merks for reducing the debt upon "the Commonwealth," as the State was already being called.

To meet "a want which had been suffered for ages," it was decided in 1647 to get a coble for the ferry across Ettrick ; and later on the boat was let to one William Brown for £3 per annum. It is evident from this entry that the bridge erected by Alexander III. at Bridgeheuch had long before disappeared.

Carlyle's
Crom-
well,
L. 77.

There is every reason to believe that in 1648, between the 9th and 14th October, no less a personage than Oliver Cromwell passed through Selkirk on his way from Dalkeith to Carlisle. As the "Lieutenant-General" took five days to the journey, it is not improbable he may have rested a night in the old burgh, and one may imagine the great soldier's interest in details of the battle which three years before had done such good service to "the cause."

A. P., vi.
(2) 458.

By a special Act of Parliament, Mr. Justice-depute Colville was directed to attend a Justiciary Court at Selkirk on the 10th of July 1649. Among the Justices nominated were Francis, Earl of Buccleuch, Sir William Scott of Harden, Sir Andrew Ker of Greenhead, Walter Scott of Whitslade, William Scott of Sinton, and Patrick Scott of Thirlestane. A tradition concerning the execution of ten men at a time in Selkirk is supposed to refer to a "vindica-tion of the law" after this court. An old woman who died in 1768, used to say her father was one of the guard during the night before their execution, one guard for each criminal being locked in by the provost, who slept all that night with the Tolbooth keys beneath his pillow. One of the condemned men asking for a knife to cut tobacco with, his comrade suspecting violence, cautioned the guard against giving it, saying, " there are enough to die already."

Nichol
Recol.

A. P., vi.
(2) 491,
535, 583.

1649.—Protest by Edinburgh against a revised taxt-roll for royal boroughs, in which Selkirk is entered at £120. Same year Parliament ordered the well-affected officers and soldiers who had fled from Ireland to be quartered in the shire and burgh of Selkirk and elsewhere, pending their incorporation in the Scottish army.

In June 1650, the committee for disposing of the forces ordered Colonel Scott and Lieutenant-Colonel Ker of Newton to draw their troops to Selkirk —no doubt in view of the threatened invasion by Cromwell, who crossed Tweed on the 16th July. After his victory at Dunbar, Cromwell spread part of his army over the south of Scotland, Major Robertson being in command Pgle. of a detachment in Selkirk, and a captain of the same regiment being Mem. quartered at Torwoodlee. By their unrelenting exactions, the people were reduced to great poverty, sometimes to absolute want. In 1653 the Laird of Haining raised an action against a great number of townspeople for appropriating wood and corn of his, left by the English, who had violently taken and brought in the wood and corn of the burgesses, for lack of firing in time of winter, when they had three regiments for eight days. The Council determined to defend the case.

An evidence of the dignified temper in which the authorities of Selkirk bore these trials, and their sacrifices for what they at least thought was their country's welfare, is afforded by their treatment of Michael Mitchelhill. This man, though a Councillor, cursed the stenters who were gathering contributions for the soldiers, upon which he was deprived of his councillorship, and his own contribution was returned to him.

In 1651, a committee of the Jedburgh Town-Council rode into Selkirk to declare to Lord Howard their town's innocence of certain outrages recently committed by mosstroopers; but a court-martial of the English J. R. officers held Jedburgh responsible, and fined the burgh £500. Hearing that ii. 195. the inhabitants had resolved not to pay, the English General despatched from Selkirk a body of troops, who took prisoner the Provost, Bailies, and several of the Councillors, and lodged them in jail. Whereupon Jedburgh, brought to its senses, agreed to pay the money, and ordained a stent for the purpose.

When in 1652, after having reduced the country by his iron hand to quietness, Cromwell put on a velvet glove and tried to woo Scotland to union with England, Mr. John Angus, commissioner for the burgh of A. P., vi. Selkirk, assented to the proposal in the preliminary convention held at (2) 792. Dalkeith, at all events; but he was absent from the next meeting in Edinburgh, for what reason was declared to be unknown. Probably Selkirk's admiration of the Articles of Union was like Master Slender's love for Mistress Anne Page: "There was little love for them at first sight, and it pleased God to decrease it on further acquaintance."

1654.—In consequence of complaints by townspeople of the corn-mills being taken by B. R.

bailies as partners, leading to slack service, and great loss to hostillers, bakers, and others, it is ordained that in future neither bailie, magistrate, dean of guild, treasurer, nor clerk should be tacksmen or partners of the mills, directly or indirectly.

1657.—To prevent confusion from Councillors speaking all at one time, rule passed that one of the Bailies be chosen preses, to whom in turn each man may address himself.

B. R.
1658.—No person indwelling within the burgh, man or woman, free or unfree, to go to harvest in Lothian or any other place abroad till such time as corn belonging to the burgh be shorn, under penalty of banishment and loss of freedom.

During Cromwell's protectorate, Selkirk seems to have enjoyed the blessedness of the people whose annals are dull, its burgh records being singularly prosaic and devoid of incident.

A. P., vi.
(2) 884.
In 1659, it had to submit, under the name of "Salkraig," to an assessment of £13, 6s. 4d. levied by the Parliament of the Commonwealth for the thwarting of false brethren, Papists and others, in their wicked and traitorous design of bringing in Charles Stuart—Bailies Gawain Murray and Francis Eliott being put on the Committee of War.

The effort was in vain, and next year, in the merry month of May, the arrival of King Charles II. sent a thrill of delight throughout the country, the reaction from long-faced austerity being nowhere more exuberant than in Scotland. The prospect of recovering comparative freedom of speech seems to have been too much for James Murray, brother to the Laird of Philiphaugh. According to the testimony of John Anderson and Hugh Black, that gentleman so far forgot himself as in the Tolbooth, and on the Sabbath Day, to swear

B. R.
by God's wounds that the people of the burgh of Selkirk were but all knaves and rascals!

Among many trophies treasured by Her Majesty's Scottish Bodyguard, the Royal Company of Archers, is the ancient silver arrow of Selkirk. It is at least doubtful whether this prize originally had any connection with a metropolitan or national society; for not only was it shot for some years before the Royal Company is known to have had a corporate existence, but its first nine winners were men of the Border—more than half of them sons of the Forest. Equally impossible is it to assign a definite age to the relic; for although the first winner's tablet is dated 1660, it may have been competed for long before that. It is possibly a survival from the time when burghs were ordered by Act of Parliament to encourage archery, and may have been the guerdon of many a proud young yeoman at forest wapinschaws. After Scott of Goldielands first tacked a medal to the arrow, it was won no fewer than nine times in the course of fourteen years; but after 1674, there occurs a gap of nearly a century and a half. Its history for that period would be like Voilet's—"a blank, my lord"—but for a brief entry in the Council minutes of 1728, recording that the clerk having delivered up the "town's silver arrow," with nine silver plates, it was put into the charter-chest. There it lay until unearthed by Sir Walter Scott.

On the 28th August 1818, by invitation from the Magistrates, a party of the Royal Archers came to Selkirk and competed once more for the arrow. Leaving Edinburgh at a quarter past six in the morning in two coaches-and-four, they breakfasted at Stow, and reached Selkirk at one. "The Magistrates and trades, with their respective colours displayed, accompanied the Royal Company to a field at the bridge over the Ettrick. The ground was very unfavourable, and at the first end there were nine arrows broken; it was also a very high wind. The shooting, notwithstanding, was very creditable to the Royal Company, and appeared highly gratifying to an immense concourse of people of all classes, assembled upon the occasion to witness this novel weaponshawing. The prize was carried by the town's officer before the victor to the hotel. It was borne upon a long staff decorated gaily with the finest flowers. . . . The Magistrates conferred the freedom of Selkirk upon all the members of the Royal Company who were present at dinner, observing all the ceremonies of the *birse*, and exhibiting the colours which were brought off by the Souters from the fatal field of Flodden, which were religiously touched by all of us." The party remained at Selkirk overnight and went to Peebles next day. The record of a visit to Selkirk in 1823 bears that "the road was lined by the people of the town and neighbouring country-side, all clean and neatly dressed," and that "the dinner was pretty good, and the wines very fair, particularly a riddle and a half of claret given by the town." Members not previously burgesses were admitted to that distinguished privilege upon going through all the forms of "licking the birse," etc.; and though "Mr. Paterson, the treasurer, left the chair at ten o'clock, some of the party kept up the festivity for a considerable time longer." An excursion in 1833 stimulated the poet of the Queen's Body Guard to rhyme—

(margin note: Hist. R. C. A., 184.)

> If a song must be sung, or a speech must be made,
> I'll recount the exploits of our archers' crusade,
> Of their doings at Selkirk, at Peebles their fun;
> Though, if all is recounted, I ne'er should be done
>   With Selkirk stories
>   Peebles glories—
> Sure such a Body-Guard never was seen.

After the convivialities of the evening mess at Selkirk, comes the avenging morn—

> Next morning the headaches, the small beer, the joke,
> The hot hand, the hot head, the pigs in the poke;
> The gay breakfast at Yair—and there's one that felt queer
> Till he got a good swig of Glenormiston beer—
> Where we had luncheon,
> And drank a puncheon
> In quenching the thirst of the King's Body-Guard.

The friendly feeling that had so far characterised the intercourse between archers and burgh was rudely broken in 1835. The Magistrates desired to throw open the competition to persons who were not members of the Royal Company, and demanded that the arrow should be returned to them. Although the council of the Royal Company considered they had an undoubted right to retain it until the next period of shooting for it, they gave it up to avoid unpleasant discussion, and ordered that the prize should be omitted in future from the annual roster. Mr. Pringle of Haining wrote expressing his regret that the Selkirk arrow was not to be shot for by the Royal Company, and intimated his desire to present to them on his own account an arrow to be competed for. To this the council replied thanking Mr. Pringle, but stating that they considered it impossible for the Royal Company to shoot at Selkirk for an arrow given by a private individual. In 1868 the Selkirk arrow was, at the request of the Magistrates, again restored to its place in the roster; and the historian of the Royal Company, after remarking that several competitions have followed the reconciliation, adds that "no warmer welcome is given to the Royal Company than by that ancient town on the occasion of their visits there."

Winners of the Arrow.

1660. Walter Scott of Goldielands.	1823. J. C. Wilson, W.S.
1661. John Scott of Woll.	1828. John Maxton.
1662. John Nicholl in Bellenten.	1830. Albert Cay.
1663. James Nicholl in Andleshope.	1833. W. S. Watson, Accountant.
1664. Do. do.	1868. P. Craig Maclagan, M.D.
1671. James Browne of Kelso.	1871. Charles Steuart, W.S.
1672. James Maxwell of Kelso.	1874. Do.
1673. Thomas Scott of Whiteslaid.	1880. J. M. Sceales.
1674. James Browne of Kelso.	1883. Charles Steuart.
1818. Charles Nairn.	

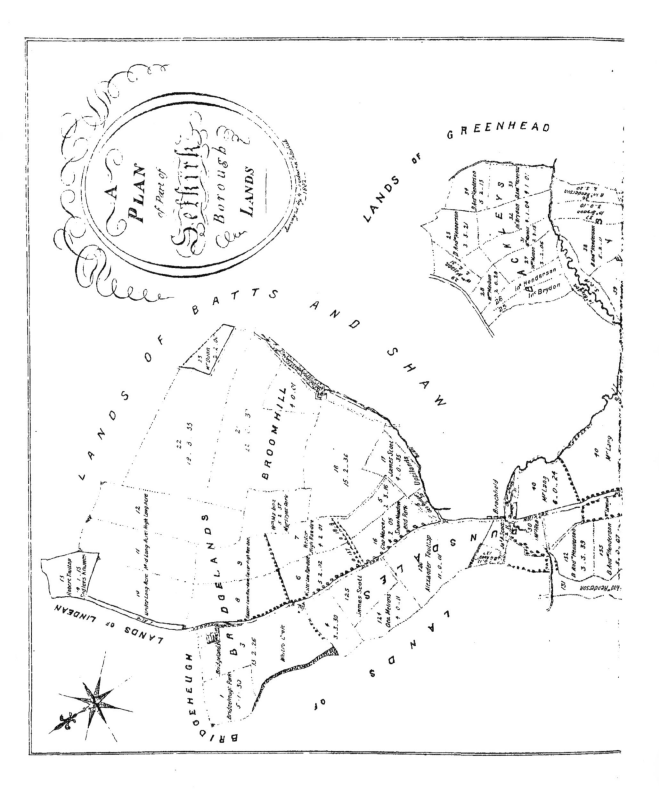

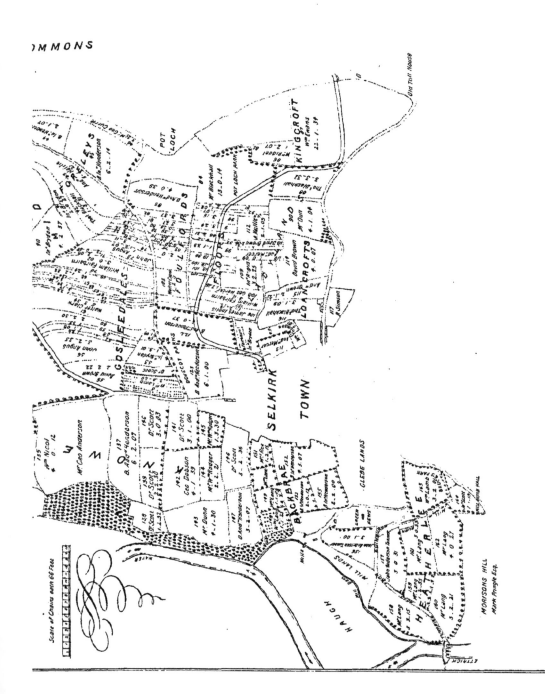

PLAN OF BURGH LANDS 1802.

REDUCED BY PHOTOGRAPHY.

CHAPTER VII.

1661 TO 1699.

UNDER the insensate policy of coercion and retribution pursued by the King's friends in Scotland after the Restoration, Selkirk suffered considerably. Bailie Scot, one of the exceptions to a general pardon granted in 1662, was fined £360 ; and next year Mr. John Shaw, minister of the parish, was summoned before the Privy Council to answer for what they were pleased to call his seditious carriage. Unfortunately another blank in the Council minutes deprives us, at a most interesting period, of information regarding the attitude taken up by the townspeople ; but from ecclesiastical records it may be gathered that there existed a wide divergence of opinion. High and dry Presbyterian or Covenanting Calvinism had its devotees, but there was a strong leaven of the less ascetic, who, if they did not approve the severity of the Secret Council, had little sympathy with the unbending rigour and self-righteous unction of those who defied it.

A. P., vii. 421. Crk., i. 178.

Among the sufferers belonging to the town was George Dun, merchant, who had all he had taken from him, to the value of upwards of 3000 merks. He was arrested while walking peacefully along the road in company with Mr. Archibald Riddel (brother to the Laird of Riddel), and after being hurried through the local prisons, found himself in Edinburgh Tolbooth. Thence he emerged on trial for his life for being at Bothwell Brig. Narrowly escaping, thanks to the uncertainty of a witness who had at first positively identified him, he lived to become tenant of Tinnes, and, according to Wodrow, to possess double what he had lost.

Wod. MSS.

For appearing at Pentland Hill (1666), Patrick, son of Mr. John Shaw, the minister, had to flee to Holland, where he died in a few years, greatly mourned.

Francis Bety or Beattie, merchant in Selkirk, was seized by Will Scott and Billy Murray, Magistrates at that time, who fined him £260. His horse and goods having been taken from him, he was sent into banishment, under which he died.

Wod. MSS.

Another merchant named Robert Haig, incautiously expressing a hope that he might live to see a Protestant fill the throne, was also seized by the bailies, who, after "squeezing from him all that he had," complimented Captain Maxwell, a Papist then in the place, with the sturdy Protestant's horse.

One William Brown was "miserably harassed" by the then Magistrates William Waugh and William Scott, "for baptising his child with a Presbyterian minister." After being stripped of his goods, he was thrown into prison, where he endured great privations. Besides seizing all that he could find in his house, Bailie Waugh compelled Brown to "serve him in all his slavish drudgery most of the time of the persecution." (This Bailie William Waugh's son Andrew was, in 1696, retoured heir to his father, to his mother Joanna Halliday, and John Waugh his grand-uncle. Andrew married Margaret Plummer, and from them are descended the Lairds of Sunderlandhall.)

John Wilson, also a merchant, fled into England, being fined much more than he was worth.

Mrs. Mitchelhill, for giving shelter to Presbyterian ministers, and for other good offices to honest suffering people and gentlemen in the place, was "severely tost by several hands" (in a blanket, or from hand to hand?), and finally was thrown into the prison of Edinburgh, whence they thought to have sent her to the plantations. "But God restrained their rage, and she returned again to her habitation."

Walter Chisholm, Will. Graham, Robt. Thorburn, merchants in Selkirk, were fined by the Magistrates; and James Rae, Alex. Mitchell, Matthew Nicol, Thomas Lauder, and Robert Brown, by the Sheriff—Riddel of Haining. It is to Haining's credit that John Wigham, his own gardener, had to suffer impartial punishment for harbouring George Johnstone.

Extraordinary adventures befell a young lad named John Mein, who with his father, a feuar in Newstead, had been at Bothwell Bridge. Being taken prisoner, he lay a long time in Greyfriars' Churchyard along with the rest, but ultimately found means to escape. Again arrested, and "tossed between the prisons of Selkirk, Jedburgh, and Edinburgh for several months," he once more got free and fled to England, where he continued until the Revolution. After serving in the army under Lord Polwarth, he ended by being one of the bailies of Selkirk.

A. P., viii. 66. One of numerous Acts passed in 1672 authorising new fairs up and down the country was in favour of Selkirk, the bailies of which were empowered to hold an extra fair on the 20th October for buying and selling of horse, nolt, sheep, meal, malt, and all sorts of grain, linen and woollen cloth, and other useful commodities.

In 1681 Parliament approved the report of a committee rejecting Sir Patrick Murray's commission to represent the burgh of Selkirk, " in respect he is not a residing trafficking merchant in the said burgh." It was doubly important that the member for Selkirk in this Parliament should be a man keenly interested in the town's welfare, seeing it was expected to ratify an agreement which had been arrived at for the division of Selkirk Common.

A. P., viii. 237.

This submission and decree-arbitral bears date 20th March 1678, a previous arbitration two years before having fallen through. On one side were the Earl of Roxburgh, James Murray of Philiphaugh, Sir William Ker of Greenhead, Sir John Riddel of Riddel, Alex. Pringle of Whytbank, John Riddell of Haining, Wm. Ker of Sunderlandhall, John Scott of Sinton, John Scott of Clerklands, and Lady Kerr of Fairnilee (for Patrick, her eldest son); for whom Sir Alex. Don of Newtondon and Robert Pringle of Clifton acted as arbiters. On the other side were Bailies William Mitchelhill and William Wauch, representing the burgh of Selkirk, with Sir Patrick Murray of Dryden and John Scott of Woll as "amicable compositors."

According to the preamble, " the great and vast bounds of ground called the Common of Selkirk had for these many ages past not only lain unprofit- able to both parties named, but had also been the seed and ground of much trouble, contention, and debate amongst them." After having perambulated the ground and its marches, seriously considered the interests of the burgh and the respective heritors, taken exact information anent their possessions, and considered the undoubted advantage that may accrue by division, the arbiters and compositors allocated the Common as follows :—

A. P., viii. 419 to 428.

To THE BURGH OF SELKIRK.

That part of the South Common which begins at the east side of Selkirk loaning at the head of the Kingcroft, and then goes eastward by the Kingcroft dyke by the south side of the Potloch, by the lands now pertaining to John Wauch, burgess of Selkirk, and by the lands of Wm. Mitchelhill, present bailie there, until you come to the easter grain of the burn that leads to the Deanhead at the back of the lands belonging to the said John Wauch, and then goes up the said burn until it comes to the easter grain of ane strand that comes from Kettiethristwell; then up the strand to the well, and from thence southward along the highway that leads to Midlem till it come to a march stone upon the west side thereof upon the Rampie Knowe, and then southward to a march stone on the east end of a slack betwixt the Rampie Knowe and the Hog Knowes, then westward by several meiths and marches down the said slack till it come to a march stone upon the east side of Megsmoss; and from thence goes southward by the said meiths and marches upon the west end of the Hog Knowes till it come to a march stone upon the north side of the Trinlie moss-syke, and from thence goes through the syke by several meiths and marches to a march stone upon Newland Braehead; thence down Newland brae to a march stone at the back of Whitmuirhall dykes, and then turns westward as the said dyke goes to Whitmuirhall loch, and then goes up the shore side of the loch by a willow bush within the same to a march stone set up on an old dyke-stead on the north side of Whitmuirlochhead moss, and so on an old dyke-stead upon the south side of the syke coming from the Ker's Well and Kerswell moss; then west the said old dyke-stead upon the south side of the said syke up through the middle of the said Kerswell moss until it comes foreagainst the north end of Whitmuir dykes, and then turns south up the said dykes to a march stone on the north side of Whitmuir loaning.   Thence down south-westward by several meiths and marches through the "flashes" to a march stone on the east side of Crovehall syke, then up the said syke by the meithes set thereupon to another march stone on the east side thereof.   Thence through the said syke up a well strand on the east end of the Mirriecoats to a march stone above the head of the said well.   Then westward by meiths and marches on the south side of Mirriecoats to the Blackhill syke, and so westward down the syke by meiths and marches set thereupon to a march stone on the south side of the same.   Thence northward by meiths and marches through the west end of Mirriecoats by the west end of Logan faulds to a march stone on the west side of the highway that leads through the Mirriecoats.   Thence along the highway to a march stone on the west side of the same, then, crossing the road, north-eastward by meithes and marches to a stone upon the west end of the Longcomb.   Thence eastward along the head of the comb to a stone upon the west side of the Crovehall syke at the head of the moss called the Dryloch, then north-west down the south side of the said Dryloch by meithes and marches to a stone on the south side thereof near to Cusingsheill.   Thence through the west nook of the said moss to a march stone on the west side of the same, on the east side of Gilmiscross.   Then northward by the edge of the said moss to a stone on the west side of the foot of the Nether moss, and from that to the Pickmetburne.   Then down the said burn to the Nether damstead side, and so northward along the head of the said damstead to a syke running through the Clyholls, then down the middle of the said Clyholls to a small green road coming to the said syke on the north side of the King's highway leading to Selkirk.   Then up the said small road to a stone on the head of the knowe on the west side of the said highway; and then turns northward by meithes and marches through the head of a hill to a march stone at the back of the Comb-croft, then eastward to the east side of the said loaning called the King-croft, where the march began.

        That part of the NORTH COMMON beginning at the march stone upon the north side of the water of Ettrick just opposite to the Coble heugh upon the west side of a road that leads from the coble to the holm-foot, and then eastward down the water of Ettrick till it come to the Nettlieburn foot, and then up the said burn till it come to the Linglie moss, and through the middle of the said moss to a march stone upon the north side of the same, and thence northward up the hill by meithes and marches to a march stone upon the head of the Singing Syde, then northward by a march stone on the Blaeberry Knowe, and several meithes and marches through Earnstruther until it come to a march stone on the head of Stonefald brae; thence northward by several meithes to a march stone on Doulie moss Knowe, and then to a march stone on the east end of Douliemoss, and from the said march to a syke that comes from Doulie-moss, and then down the said syke to a march stone on the west side of the same; thence north-westward by a march stone at the Welleyheids to another march stone on the north side of Doulieden syke, and then up the said syke by several meithes to a march stone on the north side thereof, and from thence goes northward along "ane street called the Fannielaw gait" up a green road by several meithes till it come to a march stone upon the south side of the High Street, which leads from Minchmoor at the east end of the Pitlaw and the back of the Hollands.

Thence westward along the said High Street by the south-west side of the Reidscore to a march stone upon the south side thereof. And then northward up the hill by several meithes to the middle cairn of "the three brether" (in Pont's map of 1608, another group of "Three brether's hills" is shown in eastern Eskdale), and from thence turns westward down the hill to a march stone which divides the property of Yair and Fawside, then southward by several meithes and marches by the west end of the Lamblaw and Cairns set thereupon until it come to a cairn on the east side of Philip Burn, then crosses the burn and goes up by the proper meiths of Foulsheills to the west end of Harehead fall; and from thence down the brae eastward by meithes and marches as the syke runs till it come to the Philip Burn running through the middle of the Blackmyres, and then eastward by Dawing syke east the Nar heads to a march stone upon the over Nar of Stainlie. Thence eastward by meithes and marches through How-struther to a march stone upon the west side of the syke—the Holl of Howstrutherhead; then across the said syke and east by several meithes to a "green gait foot" to a march stone upon the west side of a syke at the west end of Archie's moss, *alias* Piper's moss; thence southward down the Linglee Burn till it come to the march stone at the foot thereof, and then turns west-ward along a green gait at the Holme foot to a march stone on the north side thereof, and then southward along another road through the haugh till it come where the said march began. Reserving always to the Duke of Buccleuch's tenants of Fawside and Foulshiels liberty and freedom of pasturage on the west side of the said Common bewest the Peitlaw, according to use and wont.

RESERVATIONS IN FAVOUR OF SELKIRK.

From Clerklands allocation.—Liberty to the said burgh to win and cast peats in the said moss called the Ladywoodedge, with free ish and entry as formerly.

From Haining allocation.—That portion of the commonty lying at the west side of Selkirk loaning and the syke that comes from the Clyholls to remain common betwixt Selkirk and John Riddell of Haining, "ay and while there be ane sufficient and fencible dyke built by him thereupon."

From Philiphaugh allocation.—To the said burgh and inhabitants free ish and entry up and down the Holm-side and up and down Philip Burn, for transporting of turf, heather, and other fuel to the said burgh; excluding them always from any privilege of pasture or other servitude whatsomever, except only to pass and repass for the ends aforesaid. Declaring also that if the water of Ettrick shall alter the present current thereof whereby the mills, caulds, and dams of Selkirk may be prejudiced through want of water, in that case it shall be lawful to the said burghs to make a new cauld and cast a new dam in any place most con-venient for bringing the water to their mills, giving them hereby full power of aqueduct in the case foresaid.

Besides the landowners already mentioned, the laird of Hartwoodburn, William Riddell of Friarshaw, John Curror of Howdon and Whitmuir, Thomas Ker of Ovens Close (Ettrick Bank), and James Elliot of Bridgeheuch, obtained portions of the Common. From the Act of Parlia-ment, which occupies eight large folios of close print, are obtained the following names of subscribing town-councillors—W. Mitchelbill, Wm. Wauch, Philip Scot, Wm. Scot, G. Murray, Simon Halieday, Walter Haliewall, Richard Halliewall, John Haistie, John Sintoun, John Lidderdale, George Johnstoun, Andro Johnston, Wm. Lewes, Henrie Hall, J. B., J. D., James Wilkieson, R. R., John Angus; Andrew Angus, town-clerk.

Regarding the Elliots of Bridgeheuch, to whom a portion of the Common

was allotted, Satchells has something to say.   Maintaining Elliot of Bewlie
to be from the Horsliehill family, he adds :—

> The Elliots of Selkirk they are of the same.
> If James Elliot, late of Bridgeheugh, be a gentleman,
> Then William of Bewlie must needs be one,
> For their grandsirs were two brother-sons :

though in occupation there was a difference—one being a magistrate of
Selkirk, and the other a tender of sheep on the Doun.   For the shepherd
Satchells has much respect—he was a reliever of the poor both with flesh and
fleece.

> But for the magistrate few poor he did relieve,
> He was still ready to take, but never to give.
> "Sir Baillie, if't please your worship,"
> Was the word of every one.

Truly an unpleasant picture of the Selkirk magistracy towards the close
of the seventeenth century.   They were remiss in their duty, too.   Else why
permit the escape from their jail of James Brown, rank Covenanter, apprehended, while he was angling in fancied security, by Claverhouse, who would
have had him shot there and then but for his laird's intercession ?

Crk.,
ii. 359.

Fount.,
48.
1685, April.—A monstrous female child born by a shoemaker's wife in
Selkirk, having two heads, various organs double in place of single, but only
the usual number of arms and legs.

With the object, no doubt, of weeding out Jacobites, all royal burghs
were ordered, in the first year of William and Mary's Parliament, to elect new
magistrates and town-councils "by the poll,"—Selkirk election to be on the
27th April 1689, under supervision of the Laird of Philiphaugh.   Towards
the close of the year William Plummer of Middlestead was made "burgess
and guild-brother of the burgh, in best form, and that because of the entire
love and favour he has and carries towards its wellbeing."   It is to be noted
that Mr. Plummer's burgess-ticket, the earliest that has come under the
writer's notice, has no "birse" attachment, nor any trace of there having
been one.

Poverty, as much as lack of loyalty, may have been the reason why the
Border district did not furnish its proper complement to the new army ; but
no consideration was shown, whatever the excuse.   Lord Newbattle was
A. P.,
ix. App.
25-27.
ordered to march to Roxburgh and Selkirk, and to quarter upon the deficients
until they sent out sufficient horses with sufficient arms.   Next day, on
information of disaffected persons having crossed the Border into Scotland,

seven companies were ordered to Jedburgh and Selkirk, or such other places as might be deemed convenient.

Selkirk had the distinction of contributing one of eight burgh repre- A. P., sentatives in the Parliamentary Committee appointed to treat with English ix. 60. Commissioners for a union of the two kingdoms—the member being Mr. John Murray, advocate, of the Philiphaugh family.

1690.—George Scott, merchant, did acknowledge and testify his sorrow for breaking the P. R. Sabbath day by weighing and delivering of cheeses to Simon Halliday's wife. Ordered to make acknowledgment of his sin, to be rebuked in the meeting of Selkirk, and to pay to the poor £3 Scots.

In 1691 Presbytery urged the Bailies to search for a lost kirk-session book—gone amissing probably during the lax ministry of the shifting, if talented, Dr. Canaries. The quest was unavailing, the oldest session-book now in existence beginning in 1700.

1692.—John Scott of Woll, burgh commissioner to the General Assembly. P. R.

To a register compiled for the Convention of Royal Burghs, we are Blue-indebted for an interesting statement of the condition of Selkirk at this Book, period. In reply to a series of fifteen questions, it is reported that the 1836. common good of Selkirk extends yearly to £2242, 13s. 4d. Scots, and its debt to £25,323, 15s. 4d. There are no mortifications belonging to either town-council, guildry, or trade. No foreign trade, in respect of distance from the sea; and no inland trade, save only shoemakers, who buy rough hides, and work and retail the same in shoes. Have retailed only "two piece" of French wine these five years bygone; and their seck (sherry) and brandy so inconsiderable that it is not worth naming. Ten bolls of malt consumed weekly. No connection, direct or indirect, with shipping. Part of the cess paid by tax and part out of the common good, by reason of the poverty of the inhabitants. Ministers' stipends paid by the heritors; schoolmaster and all other public servants, out of the common good, to the extent of £323, 10s. Scots. All public works maintained out of the common good, the inhabitants being so mean and poor that they are necessitated to contract 500 merks yearly of debt, or thereby. Greatest part of the good houses inhabited by the heritors, to whom they belong; no stranger inhabitants; best houses pay only £42 Scots yearly; rest between that and £2; land not valued; houses and trades stented according to discretion of taxmaster. Five yearly fairs of one day each, and a weekly market. Only one burgh of barony within their precinct, called "Gallowshiels," which they reckon very inconsiderable, having no trade. Taken altogether, an account which Bailies Mitchelhill and Scott, with clerk Halliday, cannot have been proud to sign.

After a long vacancy, during which several calls had been declined, Mr. Hume became minister of Selkirk in 1694—notwithstanding a protest by Mr. Plummer of Middlestead, the Earl of Roxburgh, and Sir William Ker of Greenhead; from which it is clear that Lord Roxburgh's claim to be patron had not then been established.

Francis Hood in Clarilaw, lying under scandal of murder, and his minister asking if he might baptize his child, the Presbytery forbade the minister to suffer him to present the child till he was cleared. Considering what the reverend brethren then believed concerning unbaptized infants, the resolution seems sufficiently inhuman.

The old burgh was evidently a thorn in the side of Presbytery. No sooner had they put down a townsman for calumniously accusing an elder and respectable heritor of stealing the poor's money, than rumours reached them of a "gross abominable scandal and riot committed in the town" on 17th February 1698. Ker of Gateshaw, Ker of Crookedshaw, young Ker of Linton, a lot of other Kers, and a dragoon called Baptie were the principal offenders. Witnesses deponed to Ker of Gateshaw being pulled from his horse by revellers, who danced about in disordered dress upon the street, drinking healths, tossing their wigs and hats, kissing the piper, and pouring brandy down their horses' throats. Arthur Ker and his wife, about whose house the wickedness was committed, confessed and humbled themselves. So did George Little, the piper. Magistrates to be spoken to regarding their neglect of the session's expressions against scandalous persons.

CHAPTER VIII.

1700 TO 1715.

AT the beginning of last century, Selkirk, in common with the greater portion of the Scottish Lowlands, was subjected to ecclesiastical domination as arrogant and intolerable as any ascribed to the Roman hierarchy. New Presbytery was but old priest writ large, so far as regards freedom of thought or opinion. There was nothing into which ministers did not push their meddling fingers; and to a truly reverent spirit nothing could be more offensive than the impious assurance with which they put forward their finite and human deliverances as the will and decision of Almighty God. It was a humiliating result of the noble stand for freedom in years gone by, and can only be accounted for as having sprung by reaction from the unwise prelatic persecution before the Stuarts' flight.

Selkirk kirk-session inaugurated the century by taking steps to render more effective its machinery for terrifying folk into righteousness and conformity.

"Considering that the seat whereon penitents for public repentance are appointed to K. R. sit is incommodiously placed, being the most remote and obscure place in the church, where very few of the congregation can hear or see them when they are rebuked and absolved, the session unanimously appoint that it be removed from the east corner of the church and placed in the middle thereof, that the whole congregation may both see the delinquents that are to sit upon it, and hear what is said to them."

Closely following comes an entry illustrating the means used to establish that rigid and unlovely Scottish Sunday from which people are only now beginning to emancipate themselves. "In order to have the Sabbath more exactly and religiously observed, the elders are appointed to go through the town and fields about it, to take notice of vagrants, and to delate such as they find walking idly, that they may be brought to condign punishment." Six months later, a result of this espionage turns up in the prosecution of four men for going to the house of Walter Minto in Linglee in the time of divine worship, "without any regard to the Lord's Day, the fear of the Lord, or respect to their neighbours." Explained they were there in charge of their masters' horses. They evidently felt the insufficiency of the excuse, for they also expressed sorrow, took the session's rebuke, and paid fines of 14s. each imposed by the Magistrates. It was quite a common custom for the Magistrates to be present at session-meetings, and to cap ecclesiastical censure by civil penalties, according as they were directed. A week or two later, the minister reported that in going through the town last Lord's Day between 9 and 10 at night, he found James Johnston making candles in his house. The Magistrates there and then made James pay £3 Scots to the poor, while the session ordered him to appear next Sunday on the stool of repentance, to be rebuked before the congregation. Not always, however, did the two authorities see eye to eye—

1700, May 12.—The session complains that the Town Council has usurped the right of appointing "a man to ring the hand-bell for warning the people in the town to attend the burying of those who die." Some years before, Bailies James Mitchelhill and Robert Scott had acknowledged that the hand-bell had once been disposed of by the session; but that they had now taken it into their power, and would keep it so long as Mr. Hume was minister. The Bailies had assured the presbytery that so soon as they got a minister with whom they were satisfied they would return the bell, to be disposed of by him and his session as they thought fit; but now they had a minister with whom they were satisfied, the promise was not fulfilled.

Of what a delightful state of feeling within the ancient burgh does this entry afford a glimpse! This cheerful bit of patronage remained for years a bone of contention between laity and clergy, even Mr. M'Ghie's acceptability being powerless to make the Bailies let go their grasp. When the dead-bell was sent round the town the following formula was used by the ringer :—

"Beloved brethren and sisters, I let you to wit that there is ane faithful brother lately departed out of this present warld, at the pleesure of Almichty God (and then he veiled his face with his bonnet); his name is Watty Scott, third son to Jock Scott, a cordiner; he lies at the sixt door within the East Port, close by the forge, and I would you gang to his burying on Thursday before twa o'clock," etc.

It was then a custom of the gentry, possibly of all classes according to their means, to give money to the poor after a death in the family; and there is record in 1700 of £11, 2s. Scots so given by Walter Scott, brother-german to the Laird of Raeburn, at the burying of two of his children, who died one shortly after another. Great care and discrimination was observed in spending poor's money. Two poor boys were sent to "New-work" school, where one William Simpson was schoolmaster. Thirty shillings was paid to Dr. Angus for "purging and blooding a poor man in Philiphaugh who was in great danger of sickness," and to a boy, William Rodger, nine shillings for buying a pound of tobacco to trade with!'

Following is a list of the "utensils of the kirk:"—A large bible. Two table-cloths for the communion-table. Three basins for holding of the bread. Two napkins for covering the basins. Three flagons for holding the wine. Six communion cups. Two boxes for holding poor's money. A pair of leather bags with papers in them. Mention is also made of a sand-glass; but no indication of the time it took to run out, nor how often long-winded preachers were allowed to capsize it.

In a quarrel between Andrew Angus, merchant, and Mr. Ogilvie of Hartwoodmyres, anent a seat in church, Angus declared he got it from Dr. Cannaries when he was minister. Some light is thrown upon the contest by a petition from several inhabitants for a portion of the empty floor within the church whereon to build seats.

No blame can be attached to the session for faltering in discharge of its self-assumed duties in respect to manners and customs. It went so far as to petition Magistrates to forbid "all banquetings, gossippings, or cummerings (feasts at the birth of a child, which the "cummers"—French, *commères*—had all to themselves, no men being allowed to partake along with them) in all time coming;" and on the 25th January (a date afterwards famous as the birthday of the poet who dealt a death-blow to ecclesiastical pretensions) inaugurated a law anticipating Forbes Mackenzie's famous enactment by a century and a half. They appointed a "bell to be rung every night (except the night of the Lord's Day) at ten of the clock, after which time none were to sell any ale or entertain any company drinking in their house." Further, the elders were ordered "to go by turns through the town after ten at night, and whoever they find drinking are hereby, with consent of the Magistrates, fined 12s. a piece, and the landlord or landlady of the house 2s. 6d., *toties quoties*. The Magistrate present gave orders to his officers, in audience of the session, to go along with the elders, and whoever they be that shall prove contumacious, being found guilty, and will not pay their fine and disperse, to take them instantly and carry them to prison." For ringing this 10-hour bell, John Crombie got a fee of 20s. Scots the year following.

1701, September.—Another gift to the poor from the Laird of Raeburn's brother, at the death of a child.

1701.—Compeared John Blackhall, elder, and laboured to excuse himself from breach of the Sabbath-day, alleging that he only walkit through the corn-fields after the sermon. The moderator informed him that this was a stumbling to others, and that he ought to spend the time much better on the Lord's Day at home, by reading and praying and examining his family, which he could not do by vaging abroad. He acknowledged that his walking abroad on the Lord's Day was a great fault, and promised never to do the like again.

No wonder the wretched man, when brought face to face with the terrible consequences of his crime, trembled, and bowed his head for chastisement. Had he refused, he would certainly have collapsed under such a storm of ecclesiastical thunder as was let loose upon an erring and unpitied daughter of the Church—

P. R.   1702, July 2.—The minister of Melrose was appointed to preach at Selkirk, and there, " in the name and authority of our Lord Jesus Christ, denounce the sentence of the higher excommunication in face of the congregation against Isobel Chisholm, and by the same authority cast her out of the Church and Kingdom of Jesus Christ, and deliver her over unto Satan for destruction of the flesh, that the spirit may be saved in the day of the Lord, and that henceforth she may be counted and looked upon by all Christians as a heathen and publican, until God gives her a sense of her sin."

Was there no disciple of the gentle Christ to stand up, and, like Laertes, fling back this impious insolence in the face of the churlish priest? It is not necessary to imagine Isobel amongst the bright and good of this earth to be astonished that clergy capable of such cruelty were not only not hurled from their pulpits, but regarded with reverent dread for full another century. Three weeks later, the doom having been fulminated, brethren within the Presbytery were appointed to warn the people against having any familiar or unnecessary converse with Isobel.

Whether from terror or contempt, trooper Bill Marshall, of Colonel Murray's horse grenadiers, did not respond to the session's summons to come before them.

For the funeral of a Laird of Whytbank the session appeared to have incurred the expense of a new mortcloth. The items of the account may be of interest :—

9 ells double black velvet, ...	£122	8	0
4 lbs. 4 oz. 8 drops black mil'd scrop silk fringes, . .	85	12	6
7½ ells mil'd serge for lining.	6	18	8 .
Making, ...	6	13	4
	£221	12	6

which, with 7s. 6d. to a boy for carrying the mortcloth to and from Melrose at Whytbank's funeral, was a total of £222 Scots, or £18, 10s. sterling.

Considering how little his office shielded Elder Blackhall from the obloquy of Sunday walking, it is not surprising that opposite a list of eligible members for the sacred office there should be frequent entries of "excused."

Against a woman residing in the Batts whom they suspected of child-murder, the session proceeded with characteristic energy and vehemence. The woman and her mother still denying that there ever had been an infant, the minister, two elders, the kirk-officer and a midwife proceeded to the Batts to search into the truth. On their return they reported to Sheriff-depute James Mitchelhill that they had compelled the woman to show her breasts, in which, when they had drawn, they found abundance of milk. It having subsequently been admitted that the child, born dead, had been buried in Lindean Churchyard, woman and mother were committed to prison. The civil authorities found no reason to prosecute; but the minister, not to be balked, resolved to do what he could in the way of clerical penalties. Before going further, advice was asked from the Lord Register (Murray of Philiphaugh, hereditary Sheriff of the county) and his brother the Laird of Bowhill. The latter advised them to limit their accusation.

1703, May 17.—Walter Scott, litster, "acknowledged he had several at his wife's commering; but that there was no excessive drinking, and that they all went out of the house before nine. He confessed Isobel Chisholm was there, but denied that he invited her, acknowledging it was a crime to eat or drink with one lying under the dreadful sentence of excommunication." Congregation again to be advertised of the great danger of conversation with excommunicated persons, and the people to be forbidden from having converse with Isobel Chisholm.

Three men confessing, were sharply rebuked for selling and drinking of ale after ten at night, besides being ordered to pay the penalty. Another, John Rickerton by name, "instead of humbly confessing his fault and showing grief for it, did carry insolently and with such a pertinacious countenance as showed rather design of revenge than of repentance." The screw ecclesiastic having been applied meantime, John humbly "ate the leek" next Sunday. So also did a great number of offenders against the same edict.

Communion Sunday having been fixed earlier so as not to interfere with lamb-speaning and fairs in the towns round about, necessary arrangements are made—so many elders for carrying the bread, so many for carrying the cups, so many for carrying the flagons, so many for "waiting upon the elements in the session-house," and two for collecting the tokens. The following disbursements are recorded :—

		Scots.		
2 basons and laver of pewter,	. . . .	£9	12	0
For wine to the Sacrament and carriage from Leith,	. . . .	2	0	0
„ custom-duty on same,	. . . .	0	7	6
Jas. Trotter for 1200 tickets of lead,	. . . . . .	4	0	0
2 flagons and 2 plates from Newcastle (besides old pewter ones exchanged),		5	11	6
200 nails used in putting up tent,	. . . . . .	0	15	2
3½ yards table-cloth with thread to sew, and silk to mark,	. . .	2	11	4
For washing the cloths, and for " sop and blew,"	. . . . .	1	2	0

For having hastily, and, as he afterwards admitted, without reason, accused William Lidderdale of taking hides out of his neighbour's bark-pits, Robert Scott was subjected to a characteristic censure. "Considering the greatness of his crime in taking away the good name of an elder," he must sit before the pulpit for rebuke. A poor woman, craving protection from the tongue of another who calls her "witch's get," "gleed loun," and other opprobrious names, is not so successful in obtaining satisfaction for her outraged reputation.

More prosecutions for disregard of the ten o'clock bell and of the rules for Sunday observance. From the latter, "dragroons and granadeers" quartered in the town are a great cause of falling away ; while against the early closing movement, the principal inhabitants begin to kick. For drinking late in John Tudhope's house, William Gledstaines of Gledstaines (said to be a collateral ancestor of the Premier), Baillie Mitchelhill, Sheriff-Clerk Halliday and his son, were rebuked in church. A year later the same civic dignitaries and Dr. William Angus were rebuked for drinking with Walter Scott of Tushielaw during time of sermon. A shuffling excuse about Tushielaw not feeling well proved of no avail.

Gled-stones : 1878.

1705, May.—Mr. John Murray, advocate, afterwards Lord Bowhill, ordained elder.

On the first page of a volume of Council minutes beginning 1704 (though bound with much older documents) occurs the following entry :—

SETT OF THE BURGH OF SELKIRK.

The Town Councell consists of ane provost (if the Councell pleass to choyse one), two baillies, ane dean of guild, and ane thesaurer, the old baillies, old dean of guild, and old thesaurer (if they be men of substance within the burgh), fyve deacons and five Colleggs, ten merchant councellers, and fyve treads councellers. They are not chosen yearly ; but as they decreass in their substance are turned out from being councellers, and always thoss off the greatest substance brought in.

At the close of 1704, the debt and revenue of the burgh were taken into serious consideration. The former amounted to 48,500 merks—about £2645 sterling, and a formidable sum enough in those days. Besides, there was owing to the miller 2000 merks, for which they agreed to pay by giving him the mill two years rent free, at the same time compelling burgesses and their tenants to take all their corn to Selkirk mill. He was cautioned, however, to confine his sheep to Bullsheugh Haugh and Green, and keep no more in winter than in summer. The Magistrates were also urged to fine people other than the tacksman who had sheep pasturing on the Common.

1705.—For the confessed crime of resetting hides stolen from two cordiners, thereby subjecting himself to the forfeit of all he had, one Ker, a cordiner, was ordered, under pain of death, never to be seen again within the burgh or shire.

1706.—James Pringle of Buckholm chosen representative elder for the burgh at General Assembly.

Andrew Angus having for forty-four years had the keeping of the town's dead bell, by tolerance from the town allenarly (his father having had it before him in Mr. Patrick Shaw's time, 1596-1634), and being no longer able on account of age to discharge the service due by him in keeping of the bell, it is taken off his hand. Later, the Council, considering that the care of the dead and hand-bells is ordinarily conferred upon poor and indigent fallen-back burgesses, and considering the sad condition of Andrew Riddell, burgess of Selkirk, and of his numerous family, do hereby confer on him the keeping of the bells, and also of the knock (clock), which he is to maintain gratis, and to keep right and exact, furnishing tow, oil, and other materials necessary for the same. He is further to ring the bell at 5 in the morning and 8 at night, and to keep a list of all buried within the churchyard.

The High Street from Thomas Howie's to Bailie Scott's at the East Port being always very "nestie throw its not being casaed," the Council order each to causeway the street before his property—that part in front of the Flesh and Meal Markets to be done half at the town's expense. Concluding they could not have too much of a good thing, they wind up by ordering the causeway to be carried through the whole town. This pavement, or the greater part of it, continued in good repair until the remodelling of the High Street footpaths in 1883.

After riding the Common in August, Magistrates decree that in future it be ridden on the first Tuesday in June. Deacons of crafts to attend with their horses, and see that each man of their trades who has a horse ride likewise, "all in their best equipage and furniture," under penalties; those who have no horses to meet the bailies at Shawburn foot.

In 1706 there was a special meeting of the Council and community to consider the serious scarcity of water, not only for brewing and other purposes requiring large quantities, but for providing families with what is necessary. It was represented that the little water available consisted of two wells that are "mightie unwholesome, being in the summer time all full of small reid wormes, myreclay and dirt," occasioning yearly great sickness in the place, and death of a great many inhabitants—conform to the opinion of several eminent physicians. Moreover, there was great loss to the burgh from the scruples of strangers and country gentlemen against living there, or sending their children to be educated there, on account of the badness of the water. It was decided to close with Mr. Campbell, plumber, in his offer to bring St. Mungo's Well to the cross, a distance of 700 yards, for £95, exclusive of drain-cutting, and of a little lodge and big trough at the cross for gathering the water. In 1882 an old well was uncovered on the south side of High Street opposite the County Hotel, which, from the quantity of small red worms in its water, may have been one of the two here mentioned.

Haining declared not thirled to the town's mill. Mention of a wig-maker in Selkirk. The public ladders let for £5, 4s. Scots; prices for use being 12 pennies a day for the long and half as much for the short ladder, payable by the "theaker," or person whose house is theaked. To insure a monopoly to the lessee, no other ladders allowed to be given out within the burgh.

The authorities of the burgh were now called upon to declare their opinion upon a matter of no less importance than the Parliamentary Union of the two countries. With becoming modesty they first instructed their commissioner to the Convention of Burghs "to do everything needful for the glory of God and good of this kingdom." But Bailie Scott having written for definite instructions, the Council in an evil hour consulted the parish minister (Mr. M'Ghie). That reverend oracle was of opinion that they should strictly require and command their Commissioner not to vote for the alteration or taking away of the Scots Parliament, and that he should not vote for alteration of Church and State as presently established, nor the taking away the fundamental constitution of the nation. Further, that the Commissioner should not vote for settling the succession on the House of Hanover until better terms be proposed and had for the good of the nation than those contained in the Articles. All of which the Council swallowed, and repeated in a long and sententious letter to the Bailie.

A. P., xi. 404-5. Accordingly, when at its momentous sitting of 16th January 1707, the Scots Parliament gave its final deliverance on the Act of Union, Selkirk was found recording its vote against the most beneficent measure ever promoted by British legislators. Its one excuse is that union meant its own extinction as a political entity; for henceforth the royal burgh, which had so long returned a member of its own, was to be absorbed in a group of four, having one member amongst them.

Two serious and very different complaints against people in houses opening on to the churchyard dealt with by the session. One, that they were in the habit of casting their dung and filth into the said yard; and the other, that they allowed people to go to church through their entries, thereby shunning the usual places where elders stand to collect, to the detriment of the poor's money. Resolved to have the doors shut.

Having rebuked two men for pulling nuts on the Sabbath-day, the session summoned other two for "the great offence of going to Galashiels to sell shoes instead of observing the fast-day." Thomas Stoddart was also cited for going to the fields on the fast-day in time of sermon.

In 1707 a duel was fought in the outskirts of Selkirk between two young county gentlemen, one of whom fell pierced through the heart. The combatants were Walter Scott, Laird of Raeburn, and Mark Pringle, younger brother of the Laird of Haining. Scott had been brought up under the care of his uncle, Walter, Tutor of Raeburn, better known by his sobriquet of "Beardie," from his having sworn never to shave until the restoration of the Stuarts. The Pringles, on the other hand, were closely identified with the dominant party, the Laird of Haining having just been returned for the county to the first Parliament of Great Britain. It is said that on the 2d October, a meeting for the transaction of county business had been followed by dinner, at which there was the usual amount of heavy drinking. It was at a time when party feeling ran high in Scotland, there being deep and bitter differences as to the Treaty of Union, just then coming into operation. So that there was material enough for an outburst of antagonism between two hot-bloods of the opposite parties. Whether or not politics was the cause of contention, it seems certain that angry words did pass between young Scott and young Pringle. Next morning Raeburn discovered that he had bitten his glove; and, concluding that he must have done it in token of a deadly insult at some one's hands, demanded from his companion if he had quarrelled with any one the night before. On being informed of his words with Pringle, he determined to have instant satisfaction, maintaining that although he remembered nothing of the dispute, he would never have bit his glove unless for some offence which only blood could wipe out. According to another version it was Pringle who bit his glove, and early next morning roused Raeburn out of bed at Gala, where he had gone to stay overnight with the laird, his brother-in-law. Be that as it may, the two men faced each other early in the autumn morning on a field to the east of Selkirk, still known as Raeburn's Meadow. They fought with swords, and being both skilled handlers of the weapon, had several encounters without hurt on either side. It is said that Pringle repeatedly requested Raeburn, who was a married man and a father, to give up the combat and let the matter be at an end. But the fiery Scott impetuously persisted in fighting till, by a dexterous lunge, his opponent ran him through the body.

The melancholy tragedy caused a great sensation not only in the locality, where the duellists were well known, but throughout the country. Pringle escaped to Spain, where he became a merchant, fell into the hands of the Moors, and was sold into slavery, suffering hardships which seemed to exact Divine amends for his share in Raeburn's untimely death. Eventually he realised a fortune, and returning home purchased the Midlothian estate of Crichton. By the death of many intervening heirs, his grandson Mark (grandfather of the present Mrs. Pringle Pattison) succeeded to the estates of Haining and Clifton.

When he met his tragic end, Scott of Raeburn was in his twenty-fourth year, having married, when only twenty, Anne, third daughter of Hugh Scott of Gala. Besides two daughters, he left an only son William, whose son is pilloried for ever in the diary of his great relative Sir Walter. Considering his family relationship to the man who fell, both by descent and by marriage of collaterals, it is strange Sir Walter, in the precious fragment of autobiography written in 1808, should make two errors in mentioning the duel, giving Raeburn's age as *twenty-one* when he was killed, and describing him as "William, Beardie's elder brother." Other accounts contain blunders which may be allowed to settle into oblivion ; not so, mistakes in a narrative so likely to be held authoritative. It was characteristic of Scott that in his "Lay of the Last Minstrel" he should make use of the incident :—

> Conrad, Lord of Wolfenstein,
> By nature fierce, and warm with wine,
> High words to words succeeding still,
> Smote with his gauntlet stout Hunthill. . . .
> Stern Rutherfurd right little said,
> But bit his glove and shook his head.—

A fortnight thence, in Inglewood,
Stout Conrad, cold, and drench'd in blood,
His bosom gored with many a wound,
Was by a woodman's lyme-dog found ;
And ever from that time, 'twas said
That Dickon wore a Cologne blade.

À propos of the drinking customs of the period, followed as they often were by broils and bloodshed, is a story of another sort, found in the commonplace book of a Laird of Gala, Sir Walter's friend and travelling companion.

Some Border gentlemen were drinking at ——, and the fiddler was regaling them with some tunes. An unfortunate topic drew all their swords forth in an instant, and clash they went to it. The fiddler went under the table, and while the pother was going on overhead, down dropped a hand. He took it up, wrapped it up with great care and put it into his pocket, saying, " Somebody 'll be missin' this the morn."

In common with too many others, the people of Selkirk had been smitten with the speculation fever attending the launch of the African Company, and had even taken advantage of an Act empowering burghs to invest their common good in the enterprise. Accordingly when "the Equivalent"—or compensation money contributed by England in terms of the Act of Union—came to be distributed, the town-clerk was sent to Edinburgh as a "confident" to look after the town's interest, with power to give full receipt for £301, 13s. 9½d. sterling, "noe less or mair." Considerable difficulty attended its redistribution amongst the various investors. A. P., ix. 463. B. R.

Having received a letter from the minister asking payment of the town's share of the kirkyard dykes, and recommending Mr. Jolly for the office of burgh elder, the Council ordered the clerk to write to Mr. Murray of Bowhill, declaring that if he will accept, he will be preferred to Mr. Jolly, "who is an obscure and unknown man to them, and of whom they know nothing." As to the dykes, the Council "will not meddle with them, until the heritors and chamberlain for the Earl of Roxburgh moot."

Thatchers not to ask more than 6s. Scots for one day's work, under penalty of having their burgess ticket torn.

For encouragement to George Curror to prosecute the finding of coal at the Lindean, the Council resolve to maintain a workman with him.

The jealousy with which the townspeople guarded their land from encroachment is one of the most noticeable features in the burgh history—the spirit which led to the first provost losing his life in its defence being always alive, and ready to show itself on provocation. In 1707 the Council being informed that the tenants of Whytbank had reared up marches in a piece of controverted ground between the Red Scaur and the mid cairn of the Three Brethren, appointed "their officer to go and throw down the said marches to-morrow, and that entirely to the ground." So also the tenant in Linglee was directed to take possession of turfs cast in town's ground by William Chyselm, tenant in Bridgeheuch.

For what reason does not appear, proclamation ordered to be made in all Border towns, that barley, oats, peas, beans, wheat, etc., brought to Selkirk Market, and there exposed for sale, should be custom free for three years. Five months later, however, all inhabitants who have corn to sell were ordered to bring the same to the east end of the meal-market, and not sell it privately, whereby the customar was cheated of his custom.

The Dean of Guild ordered to call in all measures within the burgh, to break those not right, and fine as he thinks fit,—an order so complete, unmistakeable, and to the purpose, as to make a modern magistrate sigh for the days when there were no intricate Acts of Parliament for every little duty.

The tenants of Linglee claiming relief from loss by inundations, the Council offer to free them of their tack.

To the poor of the parish, a donation of £90 Scots, on the death of Sir William Scott of Harden.

1708.—The Magistrates and Council having received a letter from Borthwickbrae, as a Justice of the Peace, committing a lass and lad to their prison for pretending they were married, and forging a certificate of marriage, by which letter as Justice of the Peace he appoints the Magistrates to scourge them through the burgh and afterwards separate them, they do (in respect that the burgh is in want of a hangman) appoint the lad and lass to stand upon the Cross for an hour, and thereafter the lad to be put out at the east end of the town, and the lass at the west end thereof, by tuck of drum.

The common good sett for one year from Whitsunday 1708 as follows :—

	Scots.		Scots.
The corn mill,	£666	Bark half-firlots,	£14
Linglee,	473	Flesh-market,	51
Meal-market,	124	Town's common ladle.	12
Tron and petty customs,	77	Town's land,	6
Horse, nolt, and sheep dues,	81	Ground at wells,	15
Malt and barley,	25	Common ladders,	5
The Bog,	41	South Common by the burgesses,	630
Wheat and salt dues,	19	South Common by Midlem,	430

Parliament having increased the monthly cess from 10s. to 33s., "which addition is a heavy burden upon the burgh," Bailie Scot of Scotsbank to go to Edinburgh to do all he can to get it reduced, besides writing about it to the late Provost of Edinburgh at London, and to the Laird of Haining. That so much trouble should be taken to obtain relief from an extra tax of less than £14 a year, payable by the whole burgh, speaks volumes for the unutterable poverty of its inhabitants.

At a meeting to appoint a commissioner to vote for a member of Parliament, the whole Council (twenty-five present)—except the two bailies, dean of guild, and one councillor—refused to take the oath of abjuration. Not being sure, however, of the legality of their proceedings, they consulted the Lord Clerk Register (Murray of Philiphaugh), who advised them to take the oath. Other seven then joined the minority, and the eleven (all the rest having withdrawn rather than take the oath) appointed Andrew Wauch of Shaw, their clerk, to vote for Colonel George Douglas. This obnoxious oath was one abjuring a certain treasonable proclamation issued by the Cameronians.

Two men appointed to act as spadesmen at the Common riding, to get their dinner at the public expense, without further allowance; and, if they refuse, to be imprisoned during the Council's pleasure.

About 50 persons appointed, in their best equipage and order, and with their best horses, to attend the Magistrates at the meal-market, thence to accompany them to Gingilkirk (Channelkirk) to meet the Lord Clerk Register's funeral on its way from Edinburgh, or be liable to a fine of 5 merks.

A sett of standard weights (still in keeping of the town-clerk) received at a cost of £33 Scots.

The Dean of Guild instructed to raise six of the ablest men to go out and assist in making highway to the burgh at Lowrie's Loup and Widdiepath foot.

The tacksman of the mill prays to be relieved of it, the "grist being mightily diminished by reason of several having given up brewing rather than pay the heavy duty exacted by the Excise."

1709.—The Bailies to consider what persons are liable to be "pressed" in terms of the Act of Parliament, and to call for and commit them as they see cause.

Several councillors, absent on account of continued scruples about taking the oath of abjuration, are warned to attend, whereon Bailie Wauch, Geo. Anderson, Thos. Vogan, Robt. Tudhope Wm. Scott, Jas. Wilkieson, James Riddell, Walter Dunce, John Lang, Thomas Curror, and Andrew Halliwell, declared they were not fully clear about it, but would consider further. Most of them took the oath a month later.

The ground on South Common reserved to burgesses is described as follows :—From the Greenhead march to the Kame above the fauld dyke on the north side of Smedheuch, westwards in a straight line of the water-fall of Selkirk hills till you come to a hut on Cauld Kail, and thence westward along the Kame to the market way going to Whitmuir, then westward to a hut on the old dyke stead in Langslack, and then to a cairn on the south side of the Spaining fauld ; and thence along the height of the Kaim to a hut on the west side of the Kaim, then northward by several huts to an old dyke leading to Hayning's march, thence west the dyke stead to the market road leading to Hartwoodburn, then by Haining march to the Loaning head, then down the King's croft dyke and up the dyke on the Forboyds (?) till you come to the road leading to Midlem, thence eastward down the dyke of the Midleys to the burn called the Deanburn, thence to the Greenhead march till where it first began.

Whoever has "calded horses," ordered either to sell or fell the same before Saturday next. Any keeping the same after that date to have their horses taken and be themselves imprisoned. Another instance of prompt, expeditious, and efficient action on part of a self-governing local authority untrammelled by subtle and uncertain instructions from Parliament or Privy Council.

William Elliot, *alias* "the Pyck," having escaped out of prison, his creditor, Eliott of Borthwickbrae, obtained decree against the burgh for the amount of his debt. The Dean of Guild and another having declined to go to Liddesdale in search of "the Pyck," recommend Simon Fletcher as a very fit hand for the job. Fletcher having returned with word from Pyck that Borthwickbrae had been repaid £26 sterling of his debt, the latter denied it, but offered to quit the whole sum (2200 merks) for £100 sterling paid immediately.

Appealed to anent the priority of crafts in public processions, and having consulted the authorities of Edinburgh upon the momentous question, the Magistrates declared order of precedence to be as follows :—

1. The deacon of hammermen and his haill brethren ;
2.   „   cordiners and his trade ;
3.   „   weavers   „
4.   „   tailors   „
5.   „   fleshers   „

all with their banners displayed. For not observing this Act, or for being instrumental in any uproar in going or riding, a deacon to pay £100 Scots, a craftsman £50, any unincorporate person, man or woman, £50. Non-payment to be punishable by banishment from the town, destruction of burgess ticket, and expunging of name from the records. The Act itself to be published by tuck of drum. A banner for the burgh to be provided with all expedition.

1710.—The Magistrates and Council called for John Renwick, " coupper," and bestowed on him the town's drum, who willingly accepted the same and returned his most hearty thanks. For a salary of 20 merks, with other emoluments and exemptions, John bound himself to serve on all occasions as required, without repining or grudging, during all the days of his lifetime, and at all hours and seasons, particularly that he should go through the burgh each lawful day betwixt three and four o'clock of the morning, and at eight o'clock at night, except in such stormy mornings and nights as it was not possible for him to go. Ordered that the drummer and the town's piper each get a coat with the town's livery on it yearly, and a hat with a bunch of " blew " ribbons.

Decided to sell by roup oats sown by the town's herd on the Common without leave; and the tacksman of the customs ordered to restore to Pringle of Haining a sheepskin unwarrantably taken from his servants in payment of burgh dues.

1711.—Bailie Halliday restored the burgh's original charter, taken out of the chest to defend the Incorporation of Tailors before the Justices of Peace, Robert Thorbrand, a member of the craft, having alleged a scandalous libel against deacon John Lang, which the Council deemed the Justices incompetent to try.   Bailie H.'s expenses at the Parliamentary election, £149 Scots.

Cornelius Inglish having been convicted of theft, is afterwards liberated from prison, on signing a bond never to return to the town, "under the penalty of having my face brunt with ane burning-iron, my luggs cut out, and other punishments that may justly be inflicted on me."

1711.—Elders of the kirk to get up lists of all beggar people within the K. R. parish, distinguishing between the old and failed who are not able to work, and such as are able to work and will not.

1712.—Two men, evidently under a crushing sense of sin, "expressed grief for breaking the Sabbath by going to the herd's house in the Common, with the design to get cruds and whey."   They were rebuked, as they richly deserved to be.

1713.—Item of 24s. for setting up the tent for open-air Sacrament, and of 10s. for meat and drink to the workmen.

To defray the cost of digging for springs in Greenyards to lead to the Cross well, the town B. R. humiliated itself so much as to ask for help from the Convention of Burghs, "representing its low condition," and was successful in getting an allowance of 200 merks.

In order to save the threatened cauld, "the hail inhabitants, having horse or no having," ordered to go with sufficient utensils for carrying stones, heather, whins, etc., to stay the new current.

1714.—Parents of children meddling with the water-pipes to be fined 500 merks, or a month in jail, followed by banishment.

The Council having received a letter from the Barons of Exchequer, my Lord Advocate and others, signifying Her Majesty's being taken ill and in danger, and requiring the Magistrates to give such directions as may be most likely to prohibit any disturbance within the kingdom in case of Her Majesty's death, the Council appoint a proclamation to be made by tuck of drum, that all the burgesses keep the peace, and not be seen in tumults or mobs, and that the haill population put themselves in a posture of defence.   Six weeks later, an address to the king was sent for presentation by the Duke of Douglas.

To put a stop to increasing immorality and vice, by drinking at unseasonable hours, and night-walking amongst the younger sort, such as lads and lasses, a warning proclamation to be issued, and the bell rung at 10 o'clock, inquiry being made as to all such as are found drinking after that hour in ale-houses, "except in a modest sober way."

K. R.   Bessie Lang accused of invoking God's curse upon Bailie Tudhope's family, hoping the Bailie's house would come to desolation, and that the hare would kittle in his hearth. Extraordinary as the last part of Bessie's malediction may seem, it had the highest sanction. In a prophecy ascribed to Thomas the Rhymer, an end to the war with Scotland is to be expected when,
Rhym.,   besides other calamities, "hares kendle on the herston," and when "mon
J. A. H.
Murray. makes stables of kyrkes."

1715.—Thanks voted to the Laird of Woll and Sir William Scott of Thirlestane for subscriptions towards a pant or trough at the Cross well, for preserving the waste water. For offering to build the pant, and maintain it during his life, Pringle, a mason, is admitted a freeman of the burgh, "as a tradesman of exquisite art."

The tailors having begun to kick against the custom of working in other people's houses, are ordered by the Council to work in the houses of such burgesses as shall call them, at the wage of 4s. Scots (4d. sterling) per day for each master, and 3s. for journeymen and apprentices that have served a year.

Considering the advantage a race would be to the burgh by the great confluence of gentlemen that would resort thereto, it was resolved to provide a silver plate to the value of £10 sterling, to be run for yearly on the last Tuesday of April, upon the Gala Rig, or where else the Magistrates think fit. Horses to be booked with the town-clerk at least 48 hours before the race.

With the minutes of 1715 is incorporated an interesting and valuable roll of ground-annuals belonging to the burgh, taken from the old Council-books, and of the old and present heritors. Frequent mention of feus for "camps." Distinctive nicknames common, such as John Bryden *alias* Long-sticks, John Bryden *alias* John of the Well, William Dobson *alias* Kip, etc.

1715.—There being a serious conflict of authority betwixt the two Bailies as to administration of the Acts against beggars, Bailie Howie is "advised to do it himself," and ordered, with the Dean of Guild, to shut up a house inhabited by beggars, besides removing them out of the burgh instantly. Among them were "Cripple Andrew, the old piper, a woman out of Peebles (ane Veitch), and a woman in Lady Scotsbank's house."

The ferry-boat let to Gray the miller for £6 yearly, he to keep it tight and right, and ferry people over the water of Ettrick both by night and by day.

An encroachment having been made upon the town's common Green by

the minister enclosing a piece for his own behoof, the "burliemen and landie-
mers" were ordered to cause their "punder," and other persons, throw down
the same entirely. That he had made a mistake was admitted by Mr. M'Ghie,
but he retaliated with a complaint against the Council for interfering with the
kirk-session's right of employing a person to ring the bell. Yielding so far
as to admit the session's right to employ a ringer for church purposes, the
Magistrates stipulated it should be any other man but the man employed
by the burgh. Moreover, he was noways to enter the bell-loft, and was only
to be allowed to ring the bell if he stood in the duchess' loft, with the tow
set down through the bell-loft; or if he stood above the Sheriff's Aisle, with
the tow put out to him at a hole in the head of the bell-loft door.

The men of Selkirk never appear in their ancient records to such
advantage as when there is danger ahead and a scent of fighting in the air.
Just as two centuries ago they answered with alacrity their sovereign's call
to the English border, and as in 1644 they sent half a hundred of their bravest
to fight for freedom of religion, so did they now bestir themselves on hearing
that invasion was threatened by the Pretender.

Bailie Home represented that there was a gentleman in the country who
had been a sufferer in the late times, and who was a person well-affected to
King George, and would take upon him to model the burgesses and others
that desire to be disciplined. Other burghs were arming themselves, and
that it might appear who were friends to the King and Government and who
were not, the Council ordained all fencible men in the burgh to come to the
Green on Monday next, give in a list of their names and what arms they had,
and say whether they will fight for King George or not.

Three weeks later, being satisfied of Torwoodlee's loyalty to King George,
and of his good affections to the present Established Church, the Council
requested him "to accept the character of being their captain," which that
gentleman readily did, expressing readiness to serve the burgh, and advise
upon such measures as might put the burgesses in a posture of defence, in
case they should be attacked.

Though not attacked, Selkirk did not escape without some experience of
war's alarms and discomforts. From their camp at Kelso the rebels sent a
party of horse to Selkirk, demanding a supply of shoes on pain of having the
town delivered up to plunder; whereupon the Bailies, bethinking themselves
that discretion was the better part of valour, gave the Highlanders what they
wanted. So too, when Brigadier M'Intosh demanded £10 sterling, being

what was due of the burgh cess, it was paid at once, and a discharge granted by the rebel collector.

About Martinmas, following an order by the Deputy-Lieutenants that a third of the foot militia in Teviotdale and Selkirkshire should assemble under arms, the Magistrates caused beat the drum for volunteers, who were in all time coming to be exempt from stent. That only twelve men responded to the call indicates a somewhat languid attachment to the Hanoverian dynasty, an attitude in keeping with traditions handed down to the present generation. Even to the beginning of this century there was a strong leaven of Jacobite feeling amongst Selkirk burgesses—probably, however, springing more from sentiment than from opinion.

CHAPTER IX.

1716 TO 1744.

RELIEVED of anxiety by collapse of the Pretender's first adventure, the Magistrates and Council of Selkirk, abetted by a new official in the person of a Deacon-Convener or Deacons' Deacon, soon resumed the even tenor of their way. Sumptuary law followed sumptuary law, and restriction displaced restriction; no word uttered or act done within the bounds being too trivial for their attention. And not satisfied with exercising authority over temporal matters, they did not hesitate, when occasion offered, to do what they could in shaping the spiritual life of the lieges. So universal was their interference in the everyday work of the people, their food, their wages, their marriages, their religion, and even their burial, that it is hard to believe there can have co-existed with a recognition of the Town Council's sphere of action any sincere belief in the working of Providence. They were like the resident magistrate in India, somewhat irreverently introduced as "what stood for the Almighty in these parts." At the same time it has to be admitted that in the absence of anything like modern education and modern means of enlightenment, authoritative repression and encouragement were, to some extent, justifiable.

In 1716 the Council set itself to deal with a practice at public burials of people going to the burial-house, both to the wake the night before and on the burial day, and then "waiting till they get brandie and ale, pyps and tobbacco—to the great oppression of persons concerned, from the inexpressible charges on them, and to disorder in the burial-house at the time of murning." Resolved to prohibit the practice.

Much sensation caused in church by Janet, daughter of the late Andrew Brydon, like a person not in her right wit, crying out in the time of worship, and particularly naming Mr. Wauch for wronging her family in taking away the Lady Well. For this Janet had eventually to make a second public K. R. appearance before the congregation, when she expressed great grief, and promised never to be guilty of the like again. "On begging God's pardon and Mr. Wauch's she was absolved from the scandal."

King George's receiver-general insisting on being paid the stent given to the rebel brigadier, the burgh had to pay it twice,—probably one reason why a sum of 10s. disbursed at the King's Coronation was much grudged, and declared not to be a precedent.

1717.—To obviate fires such as had lately broken out in one of the malt-kilns, fresh clean straw is to be provided for bedding the kiln ; and every time a stap is dried off, the kiln is to be clear of ashes before another is laid on.

This year the town was torn by another great quarrel for precedence among the crafts, who seem to have set as much store by their order of procession as if they had been grandees of Castile. This time it was the new Deacon-Convener who caused embarrassment; and when it was decided that he should walk immediately after the Magistrates and Council, accompanied by the trade with which he was incorporated, the feelings of the hammermen and their deacon were so deeply hurt that they walked out of the room.

A letter from the Laird of Haining, as Bailie of the lordship and regality of Selkirk under his Grace the Duke of Douglas, gave the Council something more serious to think about. It was nothing less than a demand that the burgh servants should attend him with the key of the Tolbooth, that he might hold a court there as Royal Bailie. Though clearly overawed by the boldness of the move, as well as by the influence and standing of its instigator, the Council did not at once surrender. They declared it could not be remembered that ever such a jurisdiction had been in use before; and that as granting the key might prejudice the burgh's rights, it should not be given up. It was intimated to Haining not to take it in ill part the refusing thereof, for it could not be complied with until such time as the Council had ascertained its rights. A week later, it having transpired that what passed in the Council was not so closely kept secret as it ought to be, all the members took a very solemn oath of loyalty and secrecy except Robert Thorbrand and Thomas Halliday, who, for refusing, were expelled. The Council received a bill for five gold guineas from John Brydon, being modified penalty payable by him anent the Lady Well. For more than 200 years this well, with the ground and houses around it, had belonged to the Brydon family, some members of which resented its alienation—Janet, as we have seen, even disturbing public worship in her rage.

Their objections to a "Royal Bailie" did not prevent the Council from celebrating a royal birthday, the King's being ordered to be kept in all time coming after the manner following :—At five o'clock in the afternoon, the Magistrates and Council, with what other burgesses they shall think fit (the town's and trades' officers, with their halberts, accompanying them in their best order), shall go to the Cross and there drink his Majesty King George's health, with other royal and loyal healths. During the time the Council is upon the Cross, the officers, with their halberts, are to stand in order and prevent disturbance. The whole expense not to exceed 13s. 4d.

This year great uproar was caused on Common-riding day by the hammermen. Still sulking under the new order of precedency, they went up and down the town in a body, "tumultuously upbraiding the other crafts, and defying the Council." A threatened fine was evaded only by the hammermen through their deacon acknowledging they had been foolish.

William Wauch, second son of the town-clerk, appointed assistant and successor to his father, "to encourage him to be a good townsman, and to stand up on all occasions for the weal and advantage of the burgh." By his courage in preserving the burgh's rights, liberties, and commonties from being encroached upon by powerful neighbours, Mr. Wauch, senior, had, it seems, excited the great hatred of several in the county. (An energetic remonstrance had just been made against the Duke of Buccleuch's chamberlain for cutting several thousand "divots" on the burgh's North Common.) In face of this enmity towards their clerk, the Council "think it incumbent upon them to testify to the world and to posterity how much the said Andrew Wauch has conscientiously done for the burgh since he entered office in 1701."

1. At his entry the burgh's affairs being in great disorder, the town in great debt, and no account kept to whom the debt was due, nor cause declared for borrowing money, annual rents overdue some for 10 some for 12 years, Mr. Wauch at great pains prepared a list of debt, which was far above what it is now, and put everything into proper order.

2. He also set to rights the charter-chest (a very great and tedious task) and furnished an inventory of all the town's papers, refusing payment for the work.

3. When Patrick Fletcher's heirs demanded a great sum as balance due by the burgh after his two years' treasurership (while Haining was the King's Provost), his accounts not being forthcoming, he did employ himself several months in making up a statement which showed a balance rather due to the burgh, still declining recompense.

4. He bound himself personally with the Council in their bonds, and being fully possessed of their entire confidence, voted and spoke in their proceedings as if he were a Councillor.

5. When the burgh was like to be overrun by powerful neighbours, he did, like an honest and conscientious townsman, stand in the gap, and though threatened with their highest displeasure and resentment, he disregarded all, and would forfeit anything before he acted dishonestly towards his burgh. And we think there has not been a better townsman since the

memory of man, for if God in His providence had not ordered it so that he should be our clerk, our burgh had not been a standing burgh this day. The testimony he gave of his loyalty in Church and State in the late unnatural rebellion won for him the acknowledgment of the Duke of Roxburgh, lieutenant of the shire, who created him a deputy-lieutenant, which was an honour to the burgh and an advantage in preventing more than a just quota of foot and horse being laid upon it. His proving the tacks of the teinds from the Duke of Roxburgh is one among many services not to be forgotten.

It is not satisfactory to reflect that but for these pages the eminent services of this exemplary town-clerk, and of the first Provost of Selkirk, who lost his life in defence of the burgh property, might have remained unknown for ages. Till an enduring monument of brass or granite has been raised to commemorate their public spirit, Selkirk will have before it a duty unfulfilled.

The year 1717 witnessed a wholesale purgation of the Council, somewhat after the Cromwellian fashion. By a plurality of votes no fewer than fourteen members were turned out. No reason is alleged, but it was probably on account of their decay in worldly wealth. Only two new councillors were elected.

An entry curiously illustrating a practice, once more common than it is now, of speaking about certain inanimate objects as if they were of the male or female gender—

Town knock stopt, and rendered useless for going, through the negligence and inability of Patrick Angus to help her. Francis Scott appointed keeper of the knock, maker of graves, and ringer of the bells, on condition that he instantly amend the knock, make her a sufficient going knock, and keep her sae.

1718.—The provost of Sanquhar invited to Selkirk to advise the burgh anent finding out a coal-haugh. At same meeting, Richard Halliwell allowed to be the only snuffmaker and seller in the burgh in time coming, he always making sufficient, and giving good measure.

The Grammar School having been supplied with a master (Mr. Andrew Elliot) by the Council, without consent of the heritors, a dispute arose, which was settled by the Court of Session in favour of the latter; and on a re-hearing, the election in future was fixed to be by each heritor having a vote, and two magistrates each a vote. Long before this the school had enjoyed a high reputation. One of its early masters (about 1680) was John Rutherford, afterwards minister of Yarrow, and great-grandfather of Sir Walter Scott. There is record in 1703 of a " hearty invitation to Mr. Robert Chisholm to be schoolmaster of Selkirk, during his behaving himself faithfully and honestly," at a salary of £200 Scots, payable half by the burgh and half by the heritors. It is startling to find that the books bought for a poor scholar at this date were Ovid's *Trists*, Ovid's *Epistles*, Confession of Faith, and K. R. Erasmus. In 1729 a bell was ordered to be fixed on the school, and four years later the Council, while ordering "safe brods" to be put on the windows B. R. of the English school for shutting at night, declared that in future they shall not be at any expense for windows. An idea of the advanced education to be had a century and a half ago at Selkirk may be gathered from the fact that, in 1731, the Dean of Guild was instructed to erect a stage in the most proper place for acting the play by the boys at the Grammar School. In 1775 the young Haigs of Bemerside were sent to it, but within two months took fever, Haigs of which they communicated to their mother, who had hastened to their side. B., 370. During the eighteen months they remained they had another attack, the fever being probably ague, a disease then extremely common in the south of Scotland. In a narrative by the late General Sir Charles W. Pasley, K.C.B., it is related how, in 1794, he was sent to school at Selkirk, where three of his cousins from Langholm had been domiciled some time before as boarders with Mr. Porter, who had previously been tutor of the young Malcolms at Burnfoot. Hist. Probably a new schoolhouse had just been erected, it having been resolved Poet., three years before to remove the school from the churchyard, where it was xxvii. very improperly situated, both church and burying-ground being much destroyed by the scholars.

1718.—Twelve pints of ale given by the kirk-session to a woman, to infuse herbs for her health, at direction of the doctor.

It is evident from minute particulars concerning the races this year, that at first they were not held on Common-riding day. According to advertisement they took place on the last Wednesday of April, the burgh plate being open to any horse or mare kept in Scotland for six months previous. The distance was three times round the course (being short five miles); eight stone weight allowed, including harness; each horse running to put in six crowns, and to be in the burgh six days before the race. "The drummer to go round the town, and on the second beating of the drum, the running horses to be taken out to the course with all conveniency, so as to be ready to start at the last of three ruffs of the drum at the starting stoup."

1. Mr. Charles Crocket, merchant in Edinburgh, booked a mouse-coloured naig, by name "The Mouse."

2. The Earl of March booked a black mare with a small ratch in the face, two white feet on the far side, by name "Hacked Mary."

3. Sir John Rutherford of that Ilk booked a grey-headed Galloway, by name "The Pearl."

4. Mr. Geo. Lesly, advocate, booked a grey mare, by name "Creeping Kate."

"Creeping Kate" having won, the cup was presented to Mr. Lesly at the Cross by the Magistrates, with a pint of wine in it.

As in later times, there was apt to be difference of opinion between bailies and ministers as to the advantage of race-meetings. On this occasion the kirk-session had to regret a great abuse caused by numbers of people going on Sunday afternoon to the Gala Rig to see some racehorses, to the offence of many good people.

1719, Oct. 24.—John Davis, traveller, having come to this burgh and offered to the Magistrates to supply the office of public executioner during his life, the Council have accepted the offer, and have installed and admitted him to the office accordingly; and have entered him to the perquisites, with power to him to call for and uplift the same, conform to use and wont. And in respect the ladle is sett for one year, the Treasurer is ordained to pay him daily 1s. sterling, until an agreement be made with the tacksman.

Being "exquisite tradesmen" in making and mending ploughs, the Thomsons in Sunderland get a special licence for employment by towns-people, the craft of hammermen being forbidden to stop them.

"The Champion" having disbursed £5, 6s. for "outrigging" (equipping) himself on Common-riding day, the Treasurer is authorised to refund the amount. No light is elsewhere thrown upon the functions of this doughty personage. He may have had a duty similar in kind to that of the hereditary champion of England towards the monarchy, and after the marches were ridden, may have been bound to challenge to personal combat any one who impugned the burgh's rights.

The now venial offence of "chimney-on-fire," was in those days no such trivial matter. Witness the following Act of Council in its most serious vein :—

For soe meikel as there haveing happenned upon Saturday last that a foul lumb did take fire, whereby not only the neighbourhood but the maist part of the toun that lay to the east-ward, was like to have been brunt to ashes by that great threatening conflagration, if the Divine Providence had not miraculously interposed. . . . These are therefore certifying to all that the pains of wilful fire-raising is death without mercy, and confiscation of moveables, one of the four pleas of the Crown that cannot be by the King remitted; therefore it's fit to let them know that he who raises fire by negligence or misgovernance shall be severely fined, his goods confiscat, compelled to pay damage sustained by others, and himself banished three years. If he have no goods, he shall be scourged at the Cross and through the town, and be banished for seven years. (The necessity for this is easily understood when it is remembered that then every house was thatched.)

1720.—George Gray for ever disqualified from holding office within the burgh, for having calumniated and reproached the Magistrates in ale-houses and open streets. That there was room for reproaching the Magistrates, however, is evident from a singularly tyrannical edict against the letting of houses or land to strangers, unless the latter had first obtained their august approbation.

This year, when the town's plate was run for, the Lairds of Gala and Grange stood at the far stoup, the Lairds of Todrig and Middlemill being at the starting-post. For a subscription plate of £25 the Laird of Philiphaugh nominated Sir William Ker and Sir Gilbert Elliot of Minto judges at the starting-point, Sir Robert Baird with the Laird of Fairnington at the distance post, Mr. Pringle of Clifton and Mr. Baird of Newbeith at the far post. Lord Jedburgh's horse won.

Salary of town's herd, 1½ bolls oat-meal (Teviotdale measure), with grazing for ten sheep, a cow, and follower.

The public prints arranged to be sent weekly by the town's Edinburgh agent to the clerk, and by him shown to the Magistrates and other burgesses from time to time.

After a rabid protest against the stage-coach traversing some parts of their district on Sunday, the Synod demanded discontinuance of Saturday s. r. fairs and Monday fairs, on the ground that they led to Sabbath profanation. It is refreshing to note that the Town Council of Selkirk, while willing to oblige the ecclesiastical authorities so far, had one Saturday fair which they would not change—an attitude of independence which so enraged the Synod that they threatened to report the matter to the General Assembly.

In consequence of plague prevailing at Marseilles and other places in French Provence, and seeing that ships from France touched at the Isle of Man, where Jonathan Rodger, tobacco-spinner, and James Riddel, merchant in the burgh, had gone to buy goods, the inhabitants were ordered to use their utmost diligence to stop and hinder the said two persons, their goods and packs, from entering the burgh either in the day or night time. David Murray was appointed an express to go to the coast-side with a letter to them that they must not presume to enter until such time as they report certificate of having performed quarantine. When Murray returned with the intelligence that both were coming home, the Magistrate set men to guard the passes to and from the town, with power to their captain or his men to bring before them such as they might apprehend. The wayfarers on their arrival were able to reassure their panic-stricken townsmen, who "agreed to give them entry."

Lady Philiphaugh having represented that it would be considered a singular favour done to herself were James Laing admitted to be a burgess gratis, the Council, willing to comply, but not willing to make a bad precedent, allowed Laing in as Bailie Waugh's burgess for last year—the Bailies having yearly the naming of a burgess.

Belief in witchcraft died hard in Selkirk. Evidences of superstition linger in ecclesiastical records up to the close of the eighteenth century, in the first decade of which the smoke of witch-fires still ascended to heaven. The circumstances attending the death of one of these unfortunates have been handed down by tradition, though judicial records are awanting, and even the date is unknown. Her name was Meg Lawson. After she was condemned, her guard, composed of burgesses taking duty turn by turn, was surprised one morning to find herring in her cell, though nothing of the kind had been left the night before. The wretched woman seems to have been one of the too many victims whom the fiendish cruelty of witch-finders made glad to confess anything that would hasten their escape from life. She is said to have satisfied her prejudiced questioners, by declaring that she had turned herself into a mouse, escaped by a small hole, ridden on a broom-shank to Edinburgh, and there obtained the fish. But although she had the power to go, she had not the power of staying away to avoid the dread hour which would deliver her to the Evil One, her master. Who can fathom this poor woman's contempt for the intelligence of those wise Magistrates and holy preachers who believed in her familiarity with the Power of Hell? When she was being dragged to the Gallows Knowe to meet her fate, Margaret begged for a drop of water at the Foul-brig-port, as the South Port was sometimes called, from a stagnant ditch in front of it. " Na na," said the man she asked it from, " the drier ye are ye 'll burn the better." So she was hustled up the hill, strangled at a stake, and then burnt to ashes.

It is an added horror to know that she left children of her own behind her, burdened at once with the memory of their mother's unspeakable end, and with the obloquy of their own descent, which followed even her children's children, as appears from an entry in the Session Records of 1721.

July 16.—John Lukup was accused of calling William Scott, late deacon of hammermen, " a warlock and witch, Meg Lawson's kind." Lukup confessed he said William seemed to have overmuch of his luckie-mother Meg Lawson's airt; and that he knew he would have no children, because he had taken instruments on his wedding day, that if he had none his gear would come to William Scott. Lukup further admitted he had said of his own wife and John Middlemist's wife (they being Scott's sisters), that if Meg Lawson was a witch they were of the devil's generation. He was provoked to say so because of the great dispeace he had in his own family, having been married sixteen years and never had twenty-four hours' peace altogether.

1721, August 6.—Reported that on 28th July, John Scott, Laird of K. R. Harden, with William, son of Francis Elliot in Hawick, Thomas Halliday and Thomas Howie, late bailies, and John Tudhope, did in ridicule profanely and P. R. irreligiously administrate the Holy Sacrament of the Lord's Supper in Halliday's house. Halliday and Elliot both denied their share in the profanity. Harden (who was under age) denied profanation of the Sacrament, denied using such an expression as " Here is God, hold Him fast ;" denied looking over the window, and asking passers-by the way to Hell ; denied exclaiming when it thundered, " Can God shoot no louder ?" but admitted singing part of the Psalms to the tune of " Over Bogie wi' my luve." The scandal having been referred to Presbytery, Harden was summoned before a committee ; but, having to be from home on the day appointed, he did not appear. Rather shocking evidence this of reaction which made itself felt about this time against the excessive solemnity and religiosity of the Scotch clergy, not less than against their inquisitorial tyranny in seeking to impose severe views on everybody else. It was heinous even to question their authority, one poor fellow being made to swallow what he had uttered in a moment of independence—" Deil a haid care I for session or Presbytery, let them try their warst "—into which exclamation he had been irritated by an elder reproving him for being too late upon the street !

List of standard weights and measures in custody of Dean of Guild—Brass box holding 2 stone weight from drop upwards ; another holding 16 lbs. avoirdupois from a drop upwards ; brazen metal weights from 1 to 112 lbs. ; a Holland stone ; an iron Stirling pint stoup ; English gallon, half-gallon, quart, pint of mixed metal ; an iron ell and a timber one ; a half-firlot for bark, a corn-full, a peas-full, a half-peck, and a cap.

James, son of George Johnston, merchant, being found in Bailie Wauch's malt-barn during night, advanced the somewhat incredible explanation that the wind had blown him in as he was passing the door. Committed to prison for trial, and afterwards banished, under pain of death.

Decree converting the race-day into a lawful hiring fair, when all sorts of servants may be engaged either in the town or on the muir.

Forty horses to help Philiphaugh to carry lime next week. It is said that up to 1725 there was not one cart in all the town of Selkirk, and that dung was carried to the land on horses' backs. One cart, got after 1725, was soon followed by more ; but many years elapsed before the " muck-creel " was finally dispensed with.

In 1722, the plague being still imminent, instructions were issued to be observed in event of its breaking out; one being that suitable quantities of cheap perfumes be provided, such as pitch, tar, resin, brimstone, vinegar, etc. The burgh to be fenced with a ditch, or proper guards to keep out infectious persons; and an infirmary to be provided, "under inspection of physicians and persons known to be honest and compassionate, and not by such vile prostitute wretches as on former occasions had been employed."

First of a series of.excambions and sales by which Haining eventually obtained possession of a large area of burgh land. Agreed to give the Laird of Haining right of property over a piece of controverted ground at the Dryloch head, provided the burgh has the ground as marked off from the head of Big Moss to Cusinsheill as a servitude, etc.

As little as a King can brook a rival near his throne could the Selkirk Town Council endure any other jurisdiction within the burgh; so James Murray, having appealed to the Justices of Peace against a decision of the burleymen, was at once dismissed from the Council.

B. R.   Much lamentation concerning a great decay of piety and serious godliness, with a corresponding increase in vice and immorality, such as cursing and swearing, drinking to excess, revelling, scolding, thieving, and many other godless and profane practices—more than sufficient to draw down the judgments of Almighty God upon the place. The Town Council, being resolved to improve the power God Almighty had visited them with for the detecting and punishing thereof, invite the elders of the Church and all other persons to discover those godless debauchees, so as justice may be done upon them, and that so the judgments of God may be prevented from falling upon the place. And for encouraging such as are inclined to make discoveries, the Council declared that they should not only be sufficiently rewarded, but have their names concealed.

Truly an ignoble and demoralising board of governors. Did their minds not misgive them, that

> In seeking tales and informations
> Against these men . . .
> They blew the fire that burnt them?

1724.—Necessity to change direction of the river, in order to preserve Lingleehaugh from being altogether carried away. By the coble-pool being left dry, and the boat thereby idle, the market had turned to nothing, and the church no way frequented.

The M.P. for the burghs being dead, the Council unanimously declared they would stand for the Laird of Philiphaugh, and for no other person whatsoever.

Resolved to hire labourers to repair highways in and about, instead of calling out burgesses to the work.

1725.—The Lairds of Philiphaugh and Haining requested to see the Duke of Roxburgh about filling vacancy in parish church, "the Town Council hoping that His Grace will not be refractory, no more than when he gave a call to Mr. M'Ghie." It does not appear whether the Duke was refractory in the judgment of the Town Council; but when he presented Mr. David Brown to the charge, Mr. Henry Davidson, minister of Galashiels, made the following magniloquent protest:—"That patronage, being a remaining branch of the Roman Antichrist, usurped authority over the Church of Christ and consciences of men, was inconsistent with the natural rights of mankind, destructive of Christian liberty in a most valuable and important instance, subversive of the institution of Christ anent the method of planting His Church with a Gospel ministry, contrary to the known principles of this Church ever since the Reformation from Popery, and an invasion of the security granted to the Church by the Articles of Union."

It having become desirable to pass rules for the better regulation of good government in the burgh, it was ordained, *inter alia*—That no prosecutor or defender should presume to drink liquor with any of the Magistrates while a process was pending, and that no Magistrate or Councillor should be drunk when sitting in judgment. This same year, three men in authority—to wit, an ex-bailie, the commissary-clerk, and the messenger-at-law—had to profess publicly before the Synod their sorrow for having "tumultuously gone in upon the Presbytery, refusing to be removed." They were threatened with higher censure if they did not behave themselves more orderly in time coming.

Two houses in Selkirk having been destroyed by fire in 1726, a collection was asked from the Presbytery, for relief of four families who had suffered by it. Of £259 Scots collected, Selkirk gave £104, Yarrow £35, Melrose £34, Galashiels £19, Lilliesleaf and Maxton £12, Roberton, Ashkirk, and Ettrick £10, Bowden £9, Lessudden £5.

As illustrating the functions of ecclesiastical courts at this time, a question of marriage which came before the kirk-session in 1727 is of interest—

Compeared Dr. Gilbert Waugh of Shaw, and William Waugh, Sheriff and town-clerk, his brother, for their own concern and in name of Margaret Plummer, their mother, William Plummer of Middlestead, and Andrew Plummer, doctor of medicine, and complained that their sister Margaret Waugh is intending to marry Mr. Robert Petrie, master of the Grammar School of Selkirk, without advising or asking consent of them, her curators; and they therefore request the minister to desist from proclaiming the said persons in order to marriage. Robert Mercer, commissary-clerk, appeared on the other side, and said Margaret Waugh was gone out of the years of pupillarity. A fortnight later Mr. Petrie produced certificate of his marriage with Margaret Waugh on the 24th July. Mr. Petrie, who was a Master of Arts, became parish minister of Canonbie in 1734, where, after a ministry of thirty years, he died, "beloved, respected, and esteemed by all who were friends to religion, virtue, and polite learning." By his hardly-won wife he had nine children, four of whom by their talents and industry acquired handsome fortunes. Dr. Robert, the eldest, was an eminent physician at Lincoln, and William, the youngest, rose to be second in command at Madras.

Fasti, 631.

The session, which before the institution of Parochial Boards transacted all business connected with the relief of paupers, sold the poor-house in Kirk Wynd to Haining for 100 merks. About the same time they contracted with Minto, one of the elders, that he should have a monopoly of making coffins for the poor at 3s. 4d. each under 12 years of age, and 5s. when above.

So little did William Waugh profit by his father's example, and by his early appointment to the town clerkship, that in 1727 he actually absconded —not because he was a pecuniary defaulter, but in consequence of some political plot connected with the parliamentary election. He absented himself so that Philiphaugh might not be able to get a legal extract of minutes of Council giving him their vote. James Miller was appointed in his place, but after a long litigation, Waugh produced a mandate from the Lords of Session reponing him.

Courant.

At four o'clock in the morning of 1st March 1728, an earthquake shook every house in Selkirk, some persons being tumbled out of bed, though no damage was done. It was also experienced in Edinburgh, and throughout the south of Scotland.

K. R.

The body of a child having been found in a dunghill under the ruins of an old house belonging to John Henderson, flesher, a woman brought from Jedburgh confessed she was its mother, and that it was born dead. Making a long, minute, and touching confession, Margaret begged of the session "that they would have a sympathy with her." She could not read, and entreated the minister to come frequently to visit her in prison, to instruct her and pray for her.

B. R.

Among " certain householders and fallen-back burgesses, whose condition was very pitiful by the cold season and extraordinary dearth of victual," £10 was distributed. An Act was passed abolishing the ladle at markets, and substituting a tax of one penny per sack. There had been complaints from those frequenting the market of the discouragement by the heavy duty of the spoon, although the tacksman had been recommended to be discreet and easy in lifting his custom—not thrusting the spoon against the side of the sack, but in the middle.

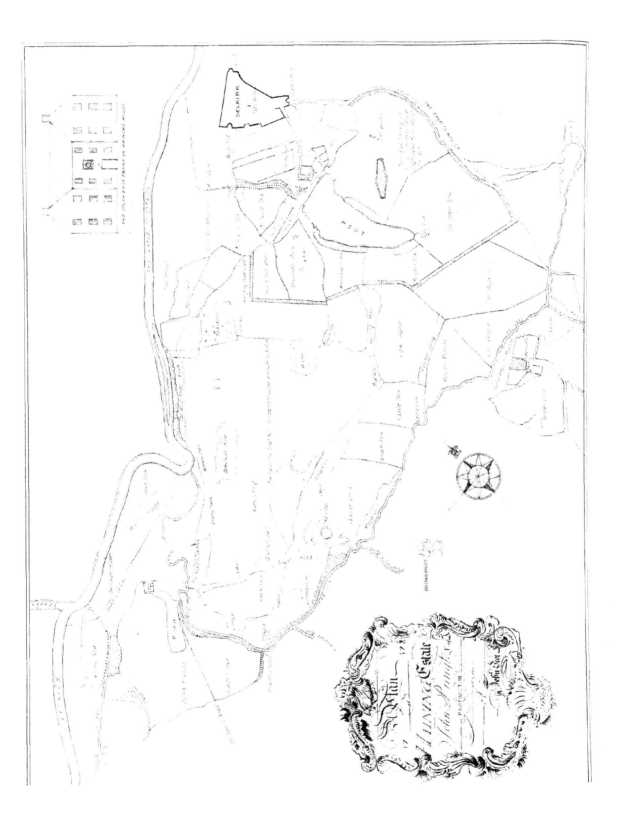

SELKIRK

A blacksmith named John Dods, being a workman "skilled in such business," engaged to put the "knock" right for 25s. Two years afterwards Dods gifted "a globe" to the town, to be put up beside the clock, and declined to take 16s. offered by the Council in acknowledgment. John Renwick, town drummer, craved the Council to receive as a burgess gratis his only son, James, whom he was "instructing in the knowledge of his art as a drummer;" which was granted.

After rejecting a proposal to augment the town's water supply from the Pot Loch (then much deeper than it is now), a right was obtained from Lord Haining to lay pipes from the Haining loch. On completion of the work, John Burns, stone-cutter, got 20s. for making a statue on the top of the Cross-Well, he being obliged to colour the same. In the same enterprising spirit, the Council caused a dial to be put upon the Cross, on the east side of it the town's arms, and on the top a lion. Previous to signing the contract with Haining, it was stipulated that Philiphaugh should, in the event of the loch being drained, take up the empty pipes, and at his own charges bring in a supply from no greater distance than Greenhead meadow.

1730.—Two women ordered to transport themselves out of the burgh, with certificate that if they return they will be pilloried, and then scourged through the town before being put in prison.

My Lord Haining represented to the Council that having purchased land lying between the town head and the loch, on the north side of the road leading to the loch, and there being a piece of ground lying at the corner which obstructs his garden dyke running in a line which can be of no advantage to any one, he desired the Council would allow him to enclose the said piece of ground in exchange for another piece of ground from his park called East Haining, for a more convenient entry to the burgesses in passing to and from the loch, and for watering their horses there. He also offered a spring of water in East Haining Park, on the east of the loch, more wholesome than the loch water, and to which the community of Selkirk had no right. To this excambion the Magistrates agreed.

A twelvemonth later, Lord Haining having purchased more ground at the town's Common Loaning, coveted another small piece of town's land "lying in the bosom of" his new purchase, which was disponed to him for a yearly payment of £1 Scots (1s. 8d. sterling) as fixed by arbiters—Kerr, tenant in Haining-Mote, and Scott, tenant in Oakwood-miln. The Laird of Haining, who had qualified as merchant councillor in 1724, is still entered on the roll as "The Right Honourable John Pringle, one of the Senators of the College of Justice."

1733.—Understanding that there was to be a meeting of Roxburghshire and Selkirkshire gentlemen at Kelso to encourage races, the Town Council offered if the meeting were held at Selkirk to give a plate of £12 out of the public revenue yearly, the innkeepers, butchers, and bakers a plate of £8, and the gentlemen a plate of £25.

1735, May 5.—There was this day given in to the Presbytery a reference from the session of Selkirk that Thomas Inglis, cordiner, and John Riddle, merchant, burgesses in Selkirk, had been guilty of very indecent and unchristian-like things,—to wit, Thomas of selling his wife and John of buying her; that they had been before the session and had acknowledged the same. Both promised never to be guilty of the like again. It is a prevalent idea on the Continent that in Great Britain a man may sell his wife by leading her with a rope round her neck into a public market, and there disposing of her by auction. It has even obtained credence among the very lowest classes in this country. The practice was once common at Smithfield Market, London; and so late as 1834 a man led his wife by halter to Smithfield Market in Birmingham. Three years later a Yorkshireman got one month with hard labour for selling his wife.

1736.—Agreed that as Mr. Andrew Pringle, Lord Haining's son, is entered advocate, it would not be amiss to take him up; and a committee appointed to wait upon him with 5 guineas as an honorary.

1737.—Sergeant Gilray presented an order from the Receiver-General to quarter upon the Magistrates until payment of £14, 7s. 9d. arrears of supply owing by the burgh; and the Council at once took steps to raise the sum.

The big boat being unserviceable for summer traffic, and the little boat ruinous, it was resolved to get a new small one. Convinced, however, of the inconvenience and insufficiency of a ferry, the town authorities in 1738 took estimates for a bridge over Ettrick, a little below the town's mill, to have five arches—two of 40 feet, two of 30, and one of 20 feet. The estimate was as follows :—

5646 feet of freestone, ...	£282	6	0
Rough pend-stone, ...	12	10	0
„ stone, ...	27	0	0
700 loads of lime @ 1s. 4d., including carriage, . . .	50	6	8
Mason-work and service, ...	100	0	0
100 12-ft. deals; timber for scaffolding and founding pillars upon; barrows and mortar troughs; box to found pillars in, . .	50	0	0
Clearing the founds, ...	6	0	0
Iron and lead, £5; Nails, £4, ...	9	0	0
Causewaying and material, ...	11	5	8
Iron clasps, ...	2	10	0
	£550	18	4

A contract was signed for £600, to include the bridge and a road from the south end to the foot of Clock-sorrow (another name for the Clockie-burn or Milburn), besides fixing a sufficient timber frame and lug-stones upon the bank from foot of Philipburn to the bridge.

Glasgow having contributed £10 to the fund, the foundations of the bridge were laid in May 1739, invitations being issued to all the noblemen and gentlemen of the shire. The bailies, who were attended by the merchants and trades in all their pomp and circumstance, entertained the guests in the "gentilest way they could, withal nothing extravagant." Unfortunately the winter was extremely severe, a flood occurred at the founding of every pillar, and the contractors had to be allowed for extra outlay. To assist the miller in breaking ice to let water to the mill twelve men were detailed; and £20 was distributed among families in a melancholy condition from extreme cold, "the like whereof has not been known."

For *naïveté* a minute of Selkirk session, offering suggestions relative to the proper kind of weather, is unapproachable—

The session, considering the present dispensation of Providence with respect to the weather, the Lord having afflicted us with a very bad spring, and yet that He was pleased about a fortnight ago to send some seasonable showers, but it is like to clear up to a great drought again, therefore desiring to show themselves sensible of the Lord's hand in that matter, they appoint Wednesday next to be observed as a day of public fasting and humiliation because of our many sins which provoke the Lord to shake His rod over us, by threatening the fruits of the ground—not forgetting to return Him thanks for the rains we had lately!

In 1740 the coming event of Prince Charlie's rebellion began to cast its shadows before. In the *Caledonian Mercury* of 9th October appeared a report touching the recent election of Magistrates in Selkirk, which contained statements "injurious, false, seditious, and tending to hurt the character and reputation of the community." Therefore the Council, while resolved to do their utmost to discover the author, took an early opportunity of " declaring to the world that they have nothing more at heart than the honour of His Majesty King George, the liberties of their country, and harmony amongst themselves—to the disappointment of those vile and contemptible promoters and publishers of the said paragraph. The clerk was instructed to write to the Lord Provost of Edinburgh, demanding the author's name. Bailie Chisholm, giving evasive answers when asked to declare if he knew anything about the letter, was suspended for four months pending investigation.

1741.—Mr. James Veitch of Glen-isle, depute of the Sheriff-principal, having fined and imprisoned for a riot William Curror, who had already been fined by the Magistrates, the Council considered it an infringement upon their jurisdiction, resolved to apply for a reduction of the sentence, and to prosecute the sheriff-depute for Curror's wrongous imprisonment. Philiphaugh intimated his determination not to depart from the right of jurisdiction he claimed over the inhabitants of Selkirk as Sheriff of the county; but next year an apology was made by his substitute.

Hearing that the Duke of Hamilton was in the town soliciting the burgh's vote for Mr. M'Ghie of Pardowan as member of Parliament, "the Council desired the Magistrates signify to His Grace that they were highly sensible of the honour His Grace had done the burgh by his visit, and on that account would have a high regard for the person His Grace had been pleased to recommend. But, as the election at this critical juncture was of the utmost consequence to the nation in general, and to the estate of burghs in particular, it was hoped His Grace would not take it amiss that the Council take time to consider His Grace's recommendation. At the same time, they begged leave to signify to His Grace that they had in no measure been pleased with the conduct of their present member." What means the Duke had discovered for influencing their judgment is not revealed, but five weeks later the Council decided to vote for his nominee, who was returned.

The Bailies found themselves in a difficulty owing to the Sheriff having committed to them the execution of a sentence passed upon William Blake, a sheep-stealer, then lying in the Tolbooth. He was to be three times scourged through the town by the hand of the hangman, and burnt on his face; but the office of public executioner happened to be vacant. After some looking about, the Bailies alighted on a capable man, whose indenture runs as follows :—

I, John Whyte, residenter in Selkirk, do hereby accept of being executioner or hangman to the burgh during all the days of my lifetime, and to perform all the parts of said offices when I am lawfully called thereto; the Magistrates for the time always paying me the salary hereafter mentioned, to wit—20s. Scots weekly until the 15th May next, at which time I am to enter to the office of "pinder," and to have a right to the usual salary and other perquisites annexed to that office, and besides levy all the spoon-dues from all bags of salt and fish sold in public market; and am to be employed in the town's work as labourer in what may cast up, and receive the usual wages; and to receive 1s. sterling weekly as further wages, and to receive livery clothes, and have £4 Scots paid me for every person I shall be employed to hang, and a merk Scots for each person I shall scourge or burn on the face."

Mr. Finisher Whyte was cruelly done out of a Scots merk on this occasion by the escape of the sheep-stealer from prison, leaving the town to repair a breach in the pend, to build up the chimney of solid work, and to advertise for the runaway in the newspapers.

No doubt in recognition of the Council's acceptance of his nominee, the

Duke of Hamilton sent the burgh £200 in 1742, the interest of one half to be applied in educating children of poor burgesses, the other half to be spent in improving the tolbooth or building a new one, there being no lodging for gentlemen and burgesses thrown into jail for civil debt but that where felons are confined.

With another great Duke the town's relations were not so amicable. His Grace of Douglas having raised an action to declare his right to a jurisdiction of regality within the burgh, it was recalled that a court of regality had first been established in 1717 by John Pringle of Haining, His Grace's commissioner, and a member of the Council, with a view to bring in certain persons to the office of Magistrates and Councillors. Having answered its end, the Court was dropped until 1723, when the said John Pringle used strong endeavours to be chosen a member of Council; but some truly worthy Councillors opposing his views, he was disappointed. The Regality Court was immediately set on foot again, and the apprehensions under which His Grace's vassals dwelt from the regality-Bailie's resentment wrought so far, that John Pringle was chosen into the Council at Michaelmas, though under strong protest. From that year to 1741 there was no more of the regality, but Mr. Pringle's son being then disappointed of his wish to enter the Council, the weight of John Pringle's displeasure was observed to fall on those who had opposed him. In this connection they apprehended this summons was raised, and the Regality Court of new set up, with the plain intention of delivering the liberties and jurisdiction of the town into the hands of the Duke of Douglas and his bailie. John Pringle and James Millar were therefore expelled the Council.

At next meeting these two members rose up and declared they would sit no longer in Council; and John Pringle addressing the Magistrates, thanked them for all their favours, particularly for the treachery and ingratitude he had received from the Council. Then they both withdrew.

The Laird of Haining seems to have set himself at once to revenge his expulsion. Just before Michaelmas of 1743, a species of *coup d'état* was attempted at his instigation. At night, when freemen were going to their several places, some of them were seized by force, carried into houses, and deprived of liberty. The Bailies being called to rescue them, and going to Robert Wilson's house, where Patrick Fletcher was detained, were derided by Mr. Andrew Pringle, younger of Haining, advocate. Upon the Bailies directing their officers to execute their orders, a riot arose. Bailie Laurie was insulted, and the mob being assisted by Lord Haining's servants, and spirited up by Mr. Andrew Pringle, a very great abuse, confusion, and disorder happened, many people fleeing in fear of their lives. Even after the Riot Act was read, the rioters refused to disperse until so instructed by Mr. Pringle.

Considering which, and that for twelve months past Lord Haining and Mr. Andrew Pringle, his son, have been forming parties among the trades, carousing, drinking, and caballing with tradesmen, in order to influence the ensuing election of Magistrates, so as to overturn the present administration of the town; and likewise, considering that my Lord was in town, and in a house near by the place where the mob happened, the Council, being sensible that such practices are highly criminal, tending to destroy freedom of election, and designed to bring the town under bondage and slavery to Lord Haining and his family, who it seems are determined to rule over them in a most absolute manner: RESOLVE to instruct the clerk to proceed forthwith to Edinburgh to take advice anent the prosecution of the rioters.

After the election, certain trades councillors declared they dare not vote, in consequence of a rule passed by the convener and deacons that any trades councillor voting otherwise than directed at a previous meeting should be fined 100 merks. Upon the Council declaring the rule illegal, Councillor Wilkie said that "any vote put to the Council would be carried, if it were even to hang a man;" for which insult he was thereupon dismissed the Council. It was resolved to support the election against an action raised to impugn it, and to defend a summons for misapplying the town's revenues.

In August 1744, on a report that the case anent the elections had gone against the Council, it was resolved to appeal to the House of Lords, "the Magistrates being willing to do what in them lay to preserve the poor oppressed town of Selkirk from being brought under the influence of its powerful neighbours." Next minutes are full of applications for admission as burgesses and free tradesmen, every claim advanced being with the object of swelling the vote-power of the different parties. A Council meeting on the 5th October must have been a scene of great confusion. Forty-three persons were entered in the sederunt as Councillors, and others (including Mr. A. Pringle) were present in spite of the Magistrates' orders to leave the room. Every vote was objected to, and countless protests lodged on both sides. Next year Haining lost a vantage-point by a decision adverse to the Duke of Douglas in the action raised against him by the Town Council relative to his alleged rights of regality. The Duke was ordered to desist from troubling; and in 1748 all heritable jurisdictions were abolished by Act of Parliament. For his regality of Selkirk the Duke of Douglas claimed £2000 compensation, and for his other jurisdictions £34,000; but for the whole he had to be content with a trifle over £5100.

Selkirk Prison.

CHAPTER X.

1745 to 1799.

Notwithstanding their disclaimer, there appears to have been a modicum of truth in the *Mercury's* hints against the loyalty of Selkirk Town Council. In 1742 the souters' deacon-colleague was objected to on the ground that he was loudly talked of in town and country as having drunk the Pretender's health in Peebles, and it was inconsistent with the duty owed to His Majesty to receive into the Council a man disaffected to the King's person and government. Besides, it was argued, John Blackhall being cautioner for his son Thomas, convicted of stealing the Laird of Williamhope's watch, he might, if in the Council, use his influence to get his son's enactment taken off.

Naturally enough, first notice of the rebellion was taken by the kirk, which decreed a fast on Wednesday, 11th September, "because of the civil Sess. Rec.

war with which this island was threatened in consequence of an invasion and rebellion headed by Charles Edward, son to the Popish Pretender." It was duly observed, and Mr. Thomas Boston, minister at Ettrick, did entertain the parish with sermon that day. But news of the Chevalier's victory at Prestonpans ten days after, probably undid the effect of Boston's stern eloquence, and it is difficult not to see between the lines of the following minute, at least an absence of unwillingness to help the rebels—

1745, September 21.—Reported that a letter had been received by the deacon of cordiners from the present deacon of cordiners in Edinburgh, that as the town of Edinburgh was at present under military contribution to supply the Highland army in 6000 pairs of shoes or brogues, therefore, knowing that there were a great many of that kind manufactured in Selkirk, he was authorised by the citizens to entreat they would assist them with 2000 pairs, or what less number their place could afford, and that they be sent to Edinburgh by Sunday night, when their payment would be ordered. The Council *unanimously* resolved that in case the cordiners should not receive payment, or in case the shoes were seized on the way to Edinburgh, they should be paid by an assessment among the inhabitants.

Three days later the same resolution was come to on receipt of a demand for other 300 or 400 pairs of shoes. At a meeting on the 4th October, all present (except John Anderson, deacon of tailors, who refused) took the oath of allegiance to King George; but ten Councillors absented themselves. So that when a division of the Stuart army passed through Selkirk on the 4th November, there would not be wanting sympathisers in the ancient burgh which owed so much to the Prince's ancestors. It is generally believed that on their way towards England, whatever may have been the case on their way back, the Highlanders were sufficiently under discipline to be restrained from violence and plunder. Three of them, however, tried foraging by force in Selkirk fleshmarket. Disregarding the remonstrances of a young man in charge of a stall, one of them was just about to march off with a gigot of mutton, when the flesher, disdaining to use cleaver or knife lying handy beside him, wrenched a stilt from a hand-barrow and knocked the thief down, his comrades making off as hard as they were able. Their assailant was an athletic young man of thirty, John Henderson by name, afterwards known as "The muckle deacon." That night, after dark, he went up on the "riggin" of his house, and what money he had he pinned beneath a "divot," making himself scarce until the army had passed.

Hend.
Lett.

It is remarkable that, as at the time of Flodden and of Philiphaugh, the Council books show at this period a number of blank pages—evidently left for filling in after the subsidence of danger. As the Prince's army disappeared over the English border, the Hanoverian party in Selkirk gathered courage.

1745, November 27.—The Magistrates and Council, considering that several persons liable to suspicion of being concerned in the present unnatural rebellion are passing to and from England, where the rebels at present are, both armed and without arms, they require all persons in the town to give notice of any strangers, that they may be examined by the Magistrates; and if they have not sufficient passes testifying their loyalty to King George, they may be secured and apprehended.

Dateless.—The Magistrates and Town Council being convened, judged it their duty in the present situation of affairs to enter into an association to stand by His Majesty King George, and in defence of our excellent constitution, and to address His Majesty on this occasion.

Then in 1746, after news of the overthrow at Culloden of an enterprise which has won the sympathy of succeeding generations even against their judgment, comes the address congratulating the King on the success of his arms, and " on his great goodness in sending H. R. H. the Duke of Cumberland to command his army."

Probably fears of famine which prevailed early in the year had predisposed the good people of Selkirk to hear with relief that the Prince's chivalrous attempt had been finally crushed. A false rumour having got abroad that almost all the meal in the town had been secretly removed to Ayr and other western ports for transhipment to the Highlands, it was commanded that all such as had meal should at once offer it for sale in the public market.

Proud of their new bridge, the community had in 1743 converted the old boat into a bridge over the Shaw burn, and had passed as efficient the new road along the Scaur. (This path led from the corner of the " Old Bridge Road," along the bank or scaur now enclosed in the private policies of Bridge-park and Wellwood.) The contractor's guarantee of seven years being about to elapse, the bridge was examined by four masons, and passed as sound in the last month of 1746. But the very next November, on the 20th, in a great storm and water-flood, part of one of the pillars and two of the arches fell down, whereby all passage over the river was cut off. Arbiters having declared the contractors free of responsibility, the Council resolved to repair the bridge immediately, and in 1750 it was taken off their hands by the Commissioners of Supply. The old kirk having been taken down just before the bridge was injured, the Council had set about the erection of a steeple above the high pend, at the east end of the Tolbooth, grudging very much the estimated price of £27, 18s. 4d.   What with the bridge, the steeple, and the new kirk, a hole must have been made in the common good.   Allocation of the seats in church leads to insertion in the Council minutes of a long list of names full of interest to Selkirk families of old settlement.

Occasionally the minister and session had to put up with defiance. P. R. Having in vain cited a woman Hogg three times before them, they were curtly told by Janet that, having joined the seceders at Midlem, she did not reckon herself obliged to obey their summons.   After this rebuff it must have K. R. been consoling to receive attention from the Honourable James Carmichael, who in his character of parliamentary candidate, entrusted them with £5 for the poor of the parish.   An appalling picture of the wickedness of the place is limned in their minutes of 1750—

> Three young boys have last Lord's Day been guilty of a very wicked practice—employing themselves in face of the sun, catching of a fish, and taking it out of the water, alarming all the neighbourhood, so that all the idle people gathered to gaze.   By order of a Magistrate the fish had been seized and cut to pieces for distribution amongst the poor.   Confronted with the session, the shaking boys were impressed with the duty of sanctifying the Sabbath, and "instructed how it was to be done according to the questions in our Catechism."   To a general admonition against such practices, leave was taken to add—" Once more your aged pastor would notice how great need there is of such public warnings, as on Tuesday last, when the riotous mob were seen reeling through the street at night, and having got a seasonable rebuke, it was answered with the language of the pit, cursing and blaspheming, as if hell were broke loose."

Upon the death in 1753 of this much discouraged clergyman, great uproar arose regarding the presentation of his successor.   As patron, the Duke B. R. of Roxburgh was petitioned to appoint Mr. Paton, late assistant in the parish ; and the Duke having made a present of the vacancy to Mr. Dundas, younger of Arniston, to him the application was renewed.   Mr. Dundas, irritated by reported collusion between the Town Council and some Edinburgh gentlemen, gave the charge to Mr. Trotter, formerly assistant at Kelso.   In the end the Council resolved to oppose the settlement, and subscribed £5 for that purpose. Accordingly in September, at a presbytery meeting, a petition against it was presented by Bailies William Curror and John Brydon, Dean of Guild Vogan, Convener James Rodger, John Shortreed of Greenhead, the most of the Town Council, six elders, and a great number of heads of families, on the following grounds :—That patronage has always been reckoned a grievance in the church.   That the title of the family of Roxburgh may be called in question, because in the charter of erection of Abbacy of Kelso into a temporal lordship in 1607, the patronage attached thereto, Selkirk among the rest, was particularly reserved to the Crown; and that a like omission occurs in the confirmation by Charles I. in 1634, as well as in the charter of 1647. Whereupon the presbytery decided to ask the Duke to produce his titles. At next meeting the chamberlain of Roxburgh produced a charter of 1663, with others in confirmation, in which the patronage of the parish of Selkirk was expressly mentioned, amongst several others granted to William, Earl of Roxburgh. Notwithstanding a very able statement of objections, the presbytery finally appointed a day for moderating in Mr. Trotter's call, the Rev. gentleman being ordained in July 1754, under protest by part of the congregation.

A strong light is thrown upon the means employed in managing parliamentary elections, by a resolution to prosecute Bailie Scott "for not paying up the money given to him at last general election for behoof of the town by Mr. Laurence Dundas." There cannot be a doubt that for the group of burghs which included Selkirk the seat was a marketable article. Hardly any disguise was thrown over financial negotiations which led to the adoption or non-adoption of a candidate by the town of Selkirk. Bailies were bribed, deacons were bribed, and the councillors at large were bribed. What deacons got had to be redistributed amongst members of their respective crafts, and many a quarrel there was about the sharing. Most commonly the money was spent in drinking and feasting, the town being sometimes the scene of orgies for days together. So notorious was the consequent demoralisation, that the Rev. John Young of Hawick used it as an argument against extension of the franchise :—

"Is it not," he says, "manifest through all Britain that those towns that have no concern in elections have risen to opulence, and are rising apace, while many of our Parliament boroughs are lolling in indolence, strutting in pride, and sinking into insignificance? . . . Hawick and Galashiels are instances of the former: instances of the latter are too common to require specification. Perhaps other causes may concur in producing this effect, but I am persuaded it is not a little furthered by the exemption of those towns from the hurry and bustle, the riot and dissipation, the corruption, perjury, and chicanery that too frequently attend elections. Should we in this town, for instance, ever obtain a vote in elections, it could not better our condition. We might indeed have an opportunity of spending a week or two, once in seven years, in drunkenness and debauchery, without much expense to ourselves. We might have canvassing and cajoling, and swearing and bribing among us, as our neighbours have, on every such occasion. . . . Our people, who now quietly mind their own business, and by honest industry make a decent provision for their families, would acquire habits of idleness and vice. Our trade and manufactures would decline, and we should soon be remarkable for nothing but poverty and pride. Unless we really wish for such a change, we had much better content ourselves as we are."

It is said that at this particular election, when Bailie Scott declined to disgorge what Mr. Dundas had given him, the latter spent £12,000, yet lost the seat. His successful opponent was Mr. Murray of Philiphaugh, who was sorely crippled, financially, by expenses touching £8000. His sporting associate, Lord March, afterwards "Old Q."—"the degenerate Douglas and unworthy lord" of Wordsworth—as good as secured the vote of Peebles in his favour by the following letter to the Provost :—

London, 30th March 1754.

SIR,—Mr. Murray of Philiphaugh proposes to offer himself as candidate for your district of burghs. I hope you and the Council will approve of this intention, and think him a fit person to represent you in Parliament. His birth, fortune, and good character, I doubt not, will sufficiently recommend him. His being my friend will, I flatter myself, likewise incline you to serve him. Be assured you can never do anything more agreeable to me, and I do the more earnestly recommend him to your friendship and assistance, as I am well satisfied you cannot fix upon a more worthy representative, or on one who will be more willing or more able to serve you. Upon this occasion I cannot help repeating to you and the Council the assurance I have often made you of my inclination to be useful to you. I daresay every man in Peebles is convinced of the particular affection I must have to the town where I was born; and every one must see that by your situation whatever services I can do you must, in the end, not only tend to my honour, but to my advantage.—I am, your most obedient and assured friend,   MARCH AND RUGLEN.

Being now reassured as to the stability of the reconstructed bridge, the Council resolved to alter the road from its south end, "bringing it straight up to the top of the brae, then along the foot of the corn rigs the length of John Rae's rig on Luckie's Bunch, and then up the said rig and along to the East Port." From the north end of the bridge to the Linglee, the road fell to be made by the county. To understand this, it is necessary to bear in mind that Ettrick then ran close along the bank or scaur from Forest Mill to near Ettrick Mills, and that the first pier of the bridge stood in the lower half of Yarrow Mill feu. There are men alive who remember the foundations of this and other piers of the bridge, from which there was a long sloping descent towards an alley which still divides the properties of Philiphaugh and Linglee.

1755, May 26.—John Henderson, younger, flesher, having represented that he had a dog gone mad on Saturday last, the Council desired the Magistrates to send the drum round the town immediately, ordering all the inhabitants before to-morrow night to hang or despatch their dogs, under the penalty of 10s. sterling for each dog found alive after to-morrow.

1759.—Captain John Lockhart of the *Chatham* man-of-war, offered himself as a candidate for the burghs, and became member in 1761. He was " brave Admiral Lockhart " of the ballad, the bold actions he performed when in command of the *Tartar* frigate between 1756 and 1759 being proverbial in the navy for nearly half a century. It was at the time of his transfer from the *Chatham* to the *Shrewsbury* that the well-known song was written :—

Logan's Ballads, p. 25.

> Ye sons of old Ocean, who 're strangers to fear,
> On board of the *Shrewsbury* quickly repair;
> Brave Lockhart commands her, rejoice every tar !
> For Lockhart commanded the *Tartar* last war.
> Hearts of oak are our ships, jolly tars are our men,
> We always are ready,
> Steady, boys, steady,
> We 'll fight and we 'll conquer again and again.

Agreed to give £15 sterling towards building Yair Bridge, which is of the utmost consequence to the burgh.

For their extremely lax views of imprisonment, the Town Council had, in 1760, to suffer smartly. An action was raised against them by the Rev. Andrew Dickson of Aberlady for permitting the escape of a prisoner he had put in jail—for debt, presumably. The Council in turn pursued Bailie Curror, through whose remissness the escape had occurred. They assert "it was notoriously known that while George Anderson was prisoner, he went out whenever he pleased, walked into Bailie Curror's house, conversed with the Bailie, acted as a kind of keeper of a child of the Bailie's, carrying it between the prison and the Bailie's house without either challenge or directions for the prisoner's closer confinement; and also the prisoner was allowed to work as a day labourer at the building of the council-house while he was alimented by a creditor." More than a year later the Council compounded with the reverend pursuer for £27, 10s. sterling.

1761.—The charters of the burgh having gone amissing, Mr. Elliot, Edinburgh agent, to be written to, as also Mr. Waugh, late town-clerk, now commissary of Peebles. It was not till 1764 the Bailies were able to return to the chest the Royal Charter of 1540, along with other papers.

1763.—A plantation to be laid down at the Peat Law to east and west of "Green Gate." This was the enclosure of which the ruined walls are still visible on the slope facing Selkirk. Estimates for building them were accepted next year at 3s. 6d. a rood, the dykes to be 58½ inches high, 30 inches broad at bottom, and 18 inches at top.

1764, April 16.—Advertisement to be inserted in the *Courant* offering five guineas for apprehension of man calling himself Alex. Steuart, with short bushy red hair, of a fair complexion, who had broken out of jail, and in quest of whom expresses had been despatched in vain.

In 1765 began the destruction of several buildings which, had they survived to the present time, would have served to give to Selkirk that appearance of antiquity its history would lead one to expect, and of which there is now unfortunately no trace. Untroubled by anxiety for preservation of a relic so reminiscent of dangers that were past, the Council, rather than strengthen the East Port where it was ruinous, decided to sell the stones by public roup, and oblige the purchasers to take down the structure immediately. Only "because it occupied a considerable space of ground in the market-place," the ancient cross was also doomed to destruction. In its case disposal of the materials was reserved, but from no reverence and with no idea of re-erecting it elsewhere; for with its best stones the Pant Well was ordered to be enlarged and repaired, the remainder being disposed of by

The Pant Well.

public roup. There can be little doubt that the sculptured arms of the town still visible on the north side of the Pant Well, though now almost past identification, are those ordered to be put on the Cross in 1730. But where is the statue that once adorned the top of the Well: where the lion that graced the capital of the Cross : where, above all, the venerable shaft itself?

Once more the burgh of Selkirk proved its unfitness for executive authority by being found without a hangman. Bailie Rodger, with an evident sense of humiliation, reported that he was unable to carry out the punishment of a thief, sentenced by the Sheriff to be whipped through the town. Whereupon he and the other bailies were appointed to go over to Jedburgh, and ask a loan of the hangman of that burgh. In case they failed they were empowered to hire any other for the purpose. Jedburgh having proved its willingness to oblige, the Council ordered the several officers of the five trades to assist the town's officer in seeing the sentence carried into execution. They were to prevent all disturbance, being therein assisted by a proclamation, made by tuck of drum, forbidding every person from insulting or molesting either criminal or executioner.

1766, January 2.—In view of the alarming scarcity of corn, it was unanimously decided to apply to Parliament to prevent exportation of wheat or other grain, and to allow Indian corn to be imported from America.

Considering the great inconvenience caused by riding the fairs, taking both Magistrates and trades off their business, decreed that in future fairs will be cried by the drummer, accompanied by two town's officers with their halberts.

This year a chaise, newly arrived in Selkirk, was drawn by two cart Nich. horses along the streets, to the great admiration of a crowd of onlookers; and ^{Recol.} the sixth slated house in the town was erected, for the incongruous purposes of presbytery meetings and county balls. Previously the only slated buildings were the parish church, town-hall, town-prison, and two dwelling-houses.

Having considered the harmony and friendliness that these many years past had subsisted between the town and the family of Philiphaugh, the Bailies and Council intimated that they would be much more ready to serve Mr. Murray than any other candidates that might offer their service, and particularly that he was more agreeable to them than their present member, Captain Lockhart Ross.

In 1767 the Fair Port followed its brother at the east end, its best stones being used to repair the dyke at the Fair Well. By agreement with Haining, certain roads were shut up, and others substituted; but the Council objected to the trustees' proposal to change the road into town from the East Port to the West Port, on the ground that the town's green would thereby be rendered useless, many properties prejudiced, and that the West Port being both steep and narrow, was often dangerous from frost.

1768.—Great summer and winter storms. One Sunday in July, the con- Scots. gregation in the kirk of Selkirk could not see, in consequence of a sudden ^{Lib.,} ^{190.} darkness, and were thrown into the greatest consternation. Lightning played and thunder rolled with such violence that people expected nothing less than the end of the world. By the rain which followed fields were ploughed into furrows, and the rivers were with unexampled rapidity swollen to a high level. In winter two men named Hall and Denham perished in a snow-storm on

their way home from Kelso, having lost their way about two miles from
Selkirk.   On the herd at Bridgeheugh going in the morning to look for his
sheep, he saw two horses at the foot of Shaw Burn, and following certain
traces he came upon the bodies of two men, one dead, the other still with a
little life in him.   In spite of means used to increase vitality, the man expired
at night.   How much more dangerous for winter travelling roads were then
than now, is manifest from an entry in the Burgh Records of Peebles.   It
there appears that the town and the Earl of Traquair co-operated in building
a bridge over the Quair, which "would be of great use in facilitating the
transit of meal from Selkirk to Peebles market, by way of Minchmoor," a considerable part of which road is 1400 feet above sea level.

C. P.,
265.

With all its ancient jealousy of encroachment, the Council in 1770
authorised the Dean of Guild to pursue James Dunlop of Whitmuirhall for
" coming under cloud of night, demolishing two march mounds belonging to
the town, and destroying a considerable quantity of peats, which he broke
and threw into moss holes."

1771.—The march of civilisation further illustrated by destruction of the
West and last remaining port, and by the introduction of street lighting, for
which the inhabitants supplied lamps and the Council oil.   A man who died
within the last three or four years, gave the writer a description of the heavy
oaken beam of the West Port, as it had been given to him in his youth by an
old man who remembered it—stretching across the street just above " the
valley," where the Queen's Head Inn now stands.

1772.—A bit of the town's green between the new road and glebe
annexed to the latter on payment of an annual feu.   Mention of bridge over
" Cloak-sorrow ;" and of another unusual name, "the Cunzie Nook," on a
piece of waste ground at which permission to build was given.   From the
common signification of " cunzie," it has been hastily assumed that where it
occurs there must have been a mint.   It is, however, frequently mentioned in
old Scots burghs, whose names are not to be found on old coins.   Some maintain its identity with the French word *coin*, a corner, used by Shakespeare in
" coigne of vantage," " yond coigne o' the Capitol," etc.   This, however, does
not account for a " Cunzie Neuk" being common to three small towns like
Kelso, Selkirk, and Peebles, where it is mentioned as early as 1473.   Beyond
question it must have been established for a special purpose, possibly for the
distribution of coins after a large coinage.

In 1772, in consequence of the drain upon the common good for public improvements beginning to tell against the town's credit, money could not be found to pay demands upon the burgh. In their extremity the treasurer and clerk applied to Mr. Pringle of Haining, who "in the friendliest manner advanced £150 sterling." Mr. Pringle had his reward. Not only was he soon afterwards allowed to lead a pipe from Mungo's Well to his house (the town's interest being always reserved), but he was permitted to extend his dyke on Peelhill at the loch-mouth a little nearer the loch. Right was taken, however, for the Council to drain the little moss at the back of the Loan when they thought proper; and Haining was held bound to make a sufficient road between the dyke and the loch, to give the inhabitants easy access for watering horses.

1775.—Mason Lodge of Selkirk lent burgh £50 sterling. The parish minister, Mr. Robertson, having been fined for carrying marl from the town's mosses, appealed to the Court of Session. The Council resolved to defend the action, and further, to prosecute the minister for poor-rates, which he had declined to pay. There is a Rhine legend of a cruel Archbishop of Mayence, eaten by mice for his unkindness to the poor. Perhaps it was for declining to pay poor-rates that this Selkirk ecclesiastic was mysteriously invaded by rats. According to a trustworthy chronicler of Newlands parish, N.S.A., the brown Russian or Norwegian rats, which invaded Tweeddale, and totally [136.] exterminated the native black rat, first appeared in the minister's glebe at Selkirk about 1776 or 1777. They were there found burrowing the earth in such numbers as to occasion considerable alarm lest they should undermine houses. After having inflicted chastisement on the poor-neglecting minister of Selkirk, the rats were next heard of in the mill of Traquair, then in the mills of Peebles, and Flemington mill, whence they reached Newlands parish in 1792. Nevertheless, this clergyman was an enlightened person. It was in his reign that the practice was given up of reading every line of the psalm to the congregation—according to the session-book, "only a temporary indulgence granted after the Reformation, to such congregations as contained a number of people who, in that illiterate age, could not read their Bibles."

This year the tenants of the North and South Commons, having spoiled their farms by over-ploughing and over-cropping, and not having paid their rents, application was made for their sequestration.

Once again the business of the town was thrown into confusion, and its communication with a large part of the country interrupted, by the fall of a portion of the bridge. It happened on a Sunday morning in October of 1777.

All Saturday, and during the intervening night, rain had fallen in torrents, accompanied with a furious wind blowing straight down the valley. On Sabbath morning, between ten and eleven o'clock, two of the Haining servants went down to look at Ettrick, which was in great flood, and to note how far the water had risen on the piers. While looking over the parapet, they felt the bridge give way. One drew back in time to escape, but the other was precipitated with the debris into the water. He swam a short way down the river, but the wind, catching his greatcoat, blew it over his head, and impeded his arms so that he sank. Five weeks elapsed before his body was recovered in Tweed. An interesting question for the psychologist presents itself in the very remarkable fact, that in this very part of the river, where he had seen his companion overwhelmed in the flood, and where he had himself experienced so narrow an escape, the survivor drowned himself twenty years afterwards.

In November, a boat was again launched by the Town Council, Robert Clapperton, dyer at Selkirk Mills, being appointed ferryman; and Bailie Broad was authorised to offer £200 sterling, and the materials of the old bridge, towards the construction of a new one, to be built between it and the head of the cauld pool. Higher up than that, a new bridge was at once commenced, and its having withstood the worst rage of a hundred winters' floods to this day is evidence at once of its solidity and of the prudence which fixed its site. The omens were against it, however; for when the first arch had just been finished, the wood beneath gave way, and the whole super-structure fell, injuring many of the workmen. One got his foot so badly smashed the half of it had to be cut away, another had his ribs broken, a third his leg, a fourth was seriously hurt about the head, and there were so many with minor wounds that the carrying of them home was like ambulance work after a battle.

The townspeople's primitive style of living, and the rural character of their occupation, are exemplified in a Council order of 1778—

Swine having become very numerous in and about the town, whereby the barn-yards of the inhabitants have been considerably injured, resolved to intimate by tuck of drum that any swine going at large will, if speedy payment of 2s. 6d. be not made to the informer, become his property.

1781.—Duke of Buccleuch's influence requested in favour of Mr. George Currie, advocate, a town-councillor for whom the whole Council have a sincere regard.

1782.—A great flood in March totally destroyed the cauld. In con-sequence of damage done by the Nettly Burn to the haugh, it was resolved to lay out a plantation along its course. The outlet from the Bog and Foul-bridge Well cleared so as to make a dry and easy passage.

This year the parish crop of corn, generally much more than sufficient for support of its inhabitants, was very deficient, and the poor were reduced to great straits. It being dangerous to increase the poor's-roll, and impossible to relieve all the indigent by gifts of meal or money, a scheme was adopted by the town which proved very effectual. A citizen, acquainted with the country and the victual trade, was empowered to purchase meal of the best quality, to the extent of £50, and to retail it at prime cost. By this means it was reduced from 2s. 10d. to 2s. 2d. per stone, "a more essential service being thus rendered to the parish than if 100 guineas had been distributed." O. S. A., ii. 446.

In 1784, John Moore, Esquire, captain in the 2d Regiment of Foot, was admitted a burgess freeman and guild brother of the burgh, and paid dues of £20 Scots, by way of qualifying himself to become M.P. for the group;— afterwards the distinguished General Sir John Moore, whose burial on the battlefield of Corunna has been recorded in touching and melodious lines that will keep his memory green for ever.

Towards the close of this year the Town Council passed an Act worthy to be recorded in full, animated as it was by a spirit truly generous and honourable.

The Magistrates and Council, taking into their most serious consideration the great losses sustained by John Murray, Esq. of Philiphaugh, who with his ancestors had long represented both county and this district of burghs in Parliament, and more particularly his late sufferings in America for his attachment to king and country, and being animated with the strongest motives of esteem and gratitude for that gentleman, with whose family this burgh for some centuries past has always been on the strictest terms of friendship, and they being anxiously concerned to have his misfortunes as much alleviated as possible, agree to apply to His Grace the Duke of Hamilton, and also to Captain Moore, their representative in Parliament, to use every interest with H. M. Minister of State, to provide for Mr. Murray and his family in such a way as to them seems meet.

Mr. Murray's letter of acknowledgment, dated Edinburgh, 4th January 1785, was as follows :—

GENTLEMEN,—It was with an uncommon degree of pleasure and satisfaction that I received your Act of Council in my favour, and in the warmest manner I thank you for it. I consider it a fresh proof of your friendship and attention to me and my family; and I will at all times think myself bound to you in gratitude. I flatter myself, however, that upon the present occasion there is no necessity for making use of your interest with the Duke of Hamilton and Mr. Moore; yet I am under the same obligation to you as if there had been. It is a pleasing reflection to me that a mutual friendship between the town of Selkirk and my family has sub-sisted without interruption for so many centuries past, and I flatter myself that the same harmony will still continue to the latest posterity. It is my most sincere wish that it may be

so; and as long as it shall please God to spare me in this world, it will be my constant endeavour to show by every means in my power, the real regard which I have for every individual
within the town of Selkirk. As this may perhaps be the last opportunity I may have of
addressing you, as I propose to go abroad soon, I beg leave once more to assure you of my most
sincere and unfeigned good wishes; and with my prayers to God to bless and prosper you all,
I am, gentlemen, etc.,   JOHN MURRAY.

Late in the afternoon of Sunday, 13th May 1787, Dr. Clarkson and Bailie
Anderson were having a quiet tumbler with a friend or two in Veitch's Inn
at the West Port, when the suddenly stopped noise of horses' feet led them
to look out of the window. Two ordinary weatherbeaten travellers having
alighted and sought the shelter of the house, the cronies resumed their seats
and conversation. By and by, the servant-lass coming in with a message from
the strangers, that they would be glad to join the company, Dr. Clarkson,
not favourably impressed by his first glance, thought it prudent to ask what
they were like. " Ane o' them 's gey like a drover, sir; and the tother 's mair
like a gentleman, maybe." " Oh then," said the Doctor, "just give them my
compliments, and say that our company is a private one." And so Robert
Burns and his young friend Ainslie were left to spend the rest of the wretched
rainy day by themselves. To this inconsiderate discourtesy of a Selkirk party,
the world owes one more poem by Burns than it might have had. It is a
mercy he did not pillory the town for ever by scathing verse upon its in-
hospitality, as he did in the inn at Inveraray. Ignoring the repulse of his
friendly advances, Burns passed the night in writing a poetical epistle to his
friend William Creech, who had just left Edinburgh for London, and to whom
he sent it, with the following letter :—

Selkirk, 13th May 1787.

MY HONOURED FRIEND,—The enclosed I have just wrote, nearly extempore, in a solitary
inn in Selkirk, after a miserably wet day's riding. I have been over most of East Lothian,
Berwick, Roxburgh, and Selkirk shires, and next week I begin a tour through the north of
England. Yesterday I dined with Lady Harriet, sister to my noble patron, *quem Deus conservet !*
I would write till I would tire you as much with dull prose as I daresay you are by this time
with wretched verse; but I am jaded to death; so with a grateful farewell, I have the honour
to be, good sir, yours sincerely,   R. B.

The influence of the time and place is apparent in three out of the twelve
verses of the poem :—

> Poor Burns e'en Scotch drink canna quicken,
> He cheeps like some bewilder'd chicken
> Scar'd frae its minnie and the cleckin
>   By hoodie-craw ;
> Grief's gien his heart an unco kickin',
>   Willie 's awa !

Now every sour-mou'd girnin' blellum,
And Calvin's folk, are fit to fell him;
And self-conceited critic skellum
                    His quill may draw;
He wha could brawlie ward their bellum,
                    Willie's awa!

Up wimpling stately Tweed I've sped,
And Eden scenes on crystal Jed,
And Ettrick banks now roaring red,
                    While tempests blaw;
But every joy and pleasure's fled,
                    Willie's awa!

No wonder the poet was "jaded to death." After dining on Saturday night with Sir William and Lady Harriet Don, he had slept at Stodrig. On Sunday morning, in very bad weather, he had set out for Melrose, visited Dryburgh, crossed Leader, ridden up Tweed to Melrose, dined there, visited "its far-famed glorious ruin," and thence, still in very bad weather, ridden by Tweed and Ettrick to Selkirk. He had meant to push on to Yarrow, endeared by song and ballad; but the rain forced him to seek shelter on the way. Next morning he rode past "Elibanks and Elibraes" to Innerleithen. As Doctor Clarkson saw the two companions ride away in the morning, his heart smote him for his want of courtesy to strangers; but when he learned next day that Burns was one of them, his chagrin was immeasurable. In all Scotland there was probably no more enthusiastic admirer of the Ayrshire Bard than Dr. Clarkson, who till his death could never speak with patience of the privilege he had thrown away.

A four-line rhyme known as the Selkirk Grace is now and then spoken of as having been written by Burns on the occasion of his visit to the old burgh. It derives its name, however, from having been said by Burns when dining with the Earl of Selkirk. Contrary to general opinion, it was not Burns' own composing, having been known before his time as the "Covenanter's Grace."

Some hae meat that canna eat,
    And some wad eat that want it;
But we hae meat and we can eat,
    And sae the Lord be thankit.

1790.—Mr. Andrew Henderson appointed town-clerk in succession to his father, who had resigned. Jailer dismissed for liberating from the tolbooth at his own discretion a prisoner lodged there by warrant of the Sheriff.

1791.—Donation of £10 towards building new University in Edinburgh, as the Council "consider that work to be of universal utility." Considering the slave trade most inhuman and against all rules of Christianity, the Council sign a petition for its abolition. Resolved to drain Pot Loch so as to get at marle supposed to be there in great quantity. Mr. Currie offered £50 for the marle, and erected expensive appliances for its recovery—part of the mason work still standing on the present margin of the loch. Finally the Council accepted £20 in full of the £50, in consideration of the great expense Mr. Currie had been put to, and the benefit the inhabitants had received therefrom.

1792.—In order to counteract " certain seditious pamphlets and associa- tions published and entered into by fractious and discontented people," the two Bailies are authorised to "draw up an association for supporting the present constitution, and to lodge the same in the hands of the clerk, to be signed by such people in the town as wish to adhere."

Lawson's
Life,
385.

Two years later the revered and honoured Dr. Lawson of the Secession Church thought it necessary to defend himself against certain reports which had reached Sheriff Plummer's ears as to his sympathy with the French Revolution.

1795.—Having been required to provide two men for the navy, the Council offer a bounty of £21 sterling to each volunteer. This being followed by an order " to raise and levy such able-bodied and idle persons as shall be found within the burgh for service in the navy," the Council declare that there being no persons that fall under that description, they can do nothing therein. Next year, on a call for other three men, volunteers were invited.

1796.—Protest against postal alterations by which letters from Edinburgh would be sent round by Berwick, Kelso, Jedburgh, and Hawick.

1798.—To encourage the establishment of a brewery in Selkirk, John Haldane in Melrose was offered a special pipe from the Well, and exemption from certain town's dues.

Animated by patriotic spirit, the Council voted a subscription to Government of £100 sterling, which they afterwards recalled, devoting it to the clothing and equipment of a volunteer company of infantry, enrolled for defence of the burgh and neighbourhood. In reply to a letter from Sir Ralph Abercromby, Commander-in-chief of the forces in Scotland, the Council stated their ability to quarter one troop of horse without inconvenience. In November a guard of three men was instituted to patrol the town all night for the protection and security of the lives and property of the inhabitants, the watch to have the liberty of the Town Hall as a general rendezvous.

In the last year of last century Selkirk was described as a town of about 1000 souls, many of them subsisting by cultivation of small fields of a few acres each, held in lease or in feu from the burgh. An inkle manufactory employed about 50 hands, and there was also a tannery. " It would seem," adds the author of *Scotland Described,* " that the manufacture of shoes for sale at distant markets must once have prevailed here, for the souters of Selkirk are celebrated in song."

War, famine, pestilence, and rapine had so retarded the growth of the struggling community, that it was little if at all superior either in wealth or numbers to the primitive clachan sheltered by King David's castle seven centuries before.

CHAPTER XI.

1800 TO 1834.

JUST before it went, the dying century bequeathed to Selkirk a legacy destined to add more to its fame than David's Abbey, or its share in Flodden, or King James's favour, or its singled-soled shoon. On the 16th December 1799, Walter Scott, advocate, was appointed Sheriff-Depute of the shire, thereby investing the county-town for ever with interest to the English-speaking world. Little was known of the new Sheriff except that he was a Border Scott of the race of Harden, of no great promise as an advocate, more than a dabbler in literature, a successful translator from the German, and an enthusiastic admirer of the old songs and ballads still floating about town and country. It is interesting to see how Scott identified himself with the somewhat primitive life of the people over whom he was appointed, and to note how the easy geniality of his first reception grew with his growing fame into enthusiastic pride, tempered now and then by fits of restiveness under restraint imposed by the law-enforcing Sheriff.

The nineteenth century dawned on a condition the reverse of prosperous in the town of Selkirk. Foreign war, bad seasons, and lack of employment, had brought about a sad state of matters, so that even in midsummer it became necessary to distribute a considerable sum amongst such of the inhabitants as were known to be in want. Two bills, one for £150 and another for £35, were discounted at Hawick to pay for the loss on oat-meal sold to the poor this winter at a reduced price. To add to its drawbacks the town was torn by opposing factions, Langs and Hendersons being its Montagues and Capulets. To the moralist nothing could be more instructive than the portentous importance attached to these parochial bickerings. Page after page, quire after quire of closely written minutes reveal the keenness with which each little step in public board or council was contested. Strife permeated everywhere; from their worships the bailies, through all grades of officials and councillors, down to the meanest members of the crafts. And, as every partisan looked to his party for such crumbs of employment as were to spare, the result was complete demoralisation of the industrial spirit. No one was a citizen of Selkirk; it was necessary either to swear by Lang and at Henderson, or by Henderson and at Lang. In essence one of the worst evils that can befall a community, the tendency to take sides becomes almost ineradicable. Found to a greater or less degree in nearly every small town, it flourished for many a decade in the burgh of Selkirk, withering its corporate energy, leading to all sorts of unpleasantness, and retarding its natural development. Not that contending parties were always ranged under the same banners; but whichever official represented Montague, there was never wanting a Capulet to focus the efforts of his detractors. In 1832 the system received a blow from the abolition of the political influence of trades-guilds; but the tendency to range in factions was too ingrained to disappear quickly. It needed the gradual establishment of a great industry completely independent of local influence.

1800.—When the Bog was being searched for marle, the workmen came upon the skeleton of a man wrapped in a plaid, with a small wooden dish near by. For a while mystery surrounded the matter, but some of the oldest inhabitants recalled the sudden and unexplained disappearance of a drover many years before. He had been bringing cattle from Crieff fair to England, and had left his lodgings to go out and see his beasts safe before turning in to rest. His companions having come back without him, there had been at the time whispers of foul play. It was considered almost certain this must be the missing man's body, the plaid being like a drover's, and the little wooden dish just such as the Highlandmen used to mix oatmeal in when they came to clear water in their long journeys across the moors.

1802.—The fishing of Ettrick (subject to right of rod-fishing to burgesses) let for a year at £3, 19s. Next year only 21s.

1803.—Andrew Henderson, town-clerk, having resigned, was appointed senior Bailie. George Rodger, senior Bailie, having resigned, was appointed town-clerk. A dexterous shuffling of the cards by the dominant party for the time, not carried out without energetic and unavailing protest from their opponents.

This year witnessed the demolition of ancient municipal buildings which once occupied a great part of the market-place. For a long time they had been crumbling into ruin, and when the Commissioners of Supply agreed to share the expense of erecting a new and suitable Court-house for joint use by county and burgh, they stipulated that after the old tolbooth had been pulled down, no other building would be erected on its site. From the annexed plan it will be seen that there was then no exit from the market-place to the north, the present opening past the Fleece Inn not being made till about thirty years later.

When the old prison wall was being taken down it fell on two men, one of whom had to get a leg taken off, and the other lost an arm. The latter having been hidden beneath the debris, was considered to be killed, but a large stone over the jail-door falling upon him kept the others off, and so preserved his life. The ponderous lock and key of Selkirk Tolbooth are preserved in Sir Walter Scott's collection of antiquities at Abbotsford.

There being now plenty of room in the market-place, the cloth-market was ordered to be removed from the School Yard.

Remote though it was from the centres of political activity, and ill-supplied with news from without, Selkirk was keenly alive to the country's deadly struggle with France. Napoleon's threat of invasion aroused the sleeping valour of the burgesses, who sprang to arms as readily as their forefathers. A remarkable feature of this exciting period was the enthusiastic energy with which old Professor Lawson urged from his pulpit the duties of patriotism, and stimulated the military ardour of his hearers. He not only preached a stirring sermon (subsequently published under the title of " The Influence of Religion on Military Courage "), but after a Monday service at Communion time he mounted the pulpit and specially addressed those in the congregation who had enlisted as volunteers. At the close the venerable man raised his bent figure, and grasping his staff, said, " Though I am not able, friends, to go out and fight with you, I will pray for you if you are called upon to engage the enemies of our country." What made his attitude the more impressive, was that in some places dissenters were looked upon by alarmists as disloyal, if not in active sympathy with Buonaparte. Their teacher's appeal kindled so hot a fire of patriotism in his students' breasts, that, pledged to the peaceful office of the ministry as they were, nothing would serve them but enrolment amongst the active defenders of their country. To Lord Napier, as Lord Lieutenant, they sent a petition for " arms and a drill-sergeant," in which step they had the full approval of their Professor. Stating he had no arms at his disposal, Lord Napier, while thanking the students for their loyalty, had to decline their proffered help. As His Majesty's lieutenant for the county, his Lordship thanked Dr. Lawson

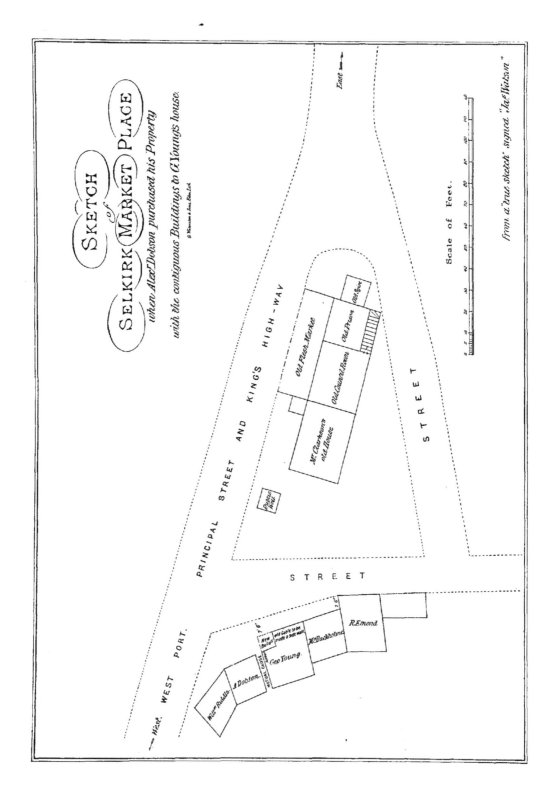

Sketch
of
SELKIRK MARKET PLACE

when Alexr Dobson purchased his Property

with the contiguous Buildings to G. Young's house.

G. Waterston & Sons, Edinr Lith.

East

Scale of Feet.

from a "true sketch" signed "Jas Watson"

PRINCIPAL STREET AND KING'S HIGH-WAY

Public Well

Mr Clarkson's old House

Old Council Room

Old Flesh Market

Old Prison

Old Spot

STREET

STREET

WEST PORT.

West.

Willm Riddle

A. Dobson.

MUTUAL CLOSE

Geo Young.

New Build.

old Gable to be made a Gable wall.

Mc Buckholme

R. Emond

" for the very loyal and zealous exhortation he had delivered on the present momentous situation, and assured him the lieutenancy were unanimous in expressing the high sense they entertained of the propriety of his conduct."

On the second night of February 1804, the glaring bale-fires blazed once more upon the summits of the Border hills—the signal that the French had landed. When at midnight the trumpet and drum played the "assembly" through the dark streets of Selkirk, no one was awakened by the fanfar but knew full well what it meant. In a few minutes nearly every bed in Selkirk was emptied, all rising except the very old and infants. Having assembled at the Cross, where there was many a touching scene between wife and husband, brother and sister, parent and child, lover and lass, the volunteers were escorted as far out of town as the Nettly Burn by a great crowd. One of them, named Will Chisholm, had just been married, and on parting from his new-made bride, said, "Peggy, ma woman, if I be killed ye'll hear tell o't; an' if I live, I'll come back as sune as I can." He was received into the ranks with a tremendous cheer. Their march was continued without incident through the dark night, until on Crosslee Moor they heard a distant rumbling which put them on their guard. Baggage-wagons under the direction of Sergeant Cameron were placed across the road; and each man stood ready with his brown bess should foe appear. On the near approach of the hostile column, however, it turned out to be nothing more formidable than a string of coal-carts. Partly relieved, no doubt, but also chagrined at being hoaxed, the Selkirk company re-formed into order of march, and was just about to start when footsteps were heard coming up behind. It was Sandy Russell, who had been put to bed drunk the night before, and had remained too insensible to march with his comrades. Recovering his senses he had taken in the situation in a moment, got his uniform and gun, and run after the company. When at last he came up, all breathless with his forced march, he was taken to task by the captain, who threatened to have him discharged for his conduct. "Weel, sir," gasped Sandy, "if ye discharge me, I hope it'll be at the cannon mouth," meaning not till he had had his share of danger. He got a cheer all round from the men, who relieved him by turns of the gun and belts his race left him too exhausted to carry. When they reached Dalkeith, about ten in the morning, it was discovered to be a false alarm. The roll was called, and every man answered to his name except one, Gideon Scott, a tailor, who was heartily denounced for his cowardice. Just as the men were getting ready to go to luncheon provided by the Duke of Buccleuch, the "Fly" stage-coach drove up with the truant Gideon upon its top. He had heard a rumour that the alarm was premature, and had hastened to take his place. But his protestations and excuses did not save him from the scorn of his comrades. At the palace the volunteers were handsomely treated by His Grace, who, while he expressed the highest admiration of their bravery and promptitude, could not suppress his regret that the only man to show cowardice bore the name of Scott. On their return home, they were met by a large crowd, and escorted by torch-light, amid great rejoicings, to the spot they had so lately left amid sighs and tears. A strolling actor of the name of Flintoff gave the men, with their wives and sweethearts, free entrance to his theatre, which was in Mr. Lang's barn at the end of Bogie's Close. Next day the volunteers beat to parade and drew up in hollow square at the Cross. Gideon Scott being called into the centre, the buttons and facings were torn off his uniform, and he was drummed home to the tune of the Rogue's March. He lived for many years after, a quiet unobtrusive man, never able to shake off the stigma, which, justly or not, attached to his conduct. It is said that when trying to hide himself in some obscure place after his degradation, he had occasion to require the services of a local barber, who became eloquent in praise of the Border muster. "As for that Selkirk tailor," he continued, as he flourished his razor, "if I had him here, I would slit his throat from lug to lug." The story has it that the miserable man, thinking he had been discovered, and impressed by the barber's evident indignation, rushed from the operating-chair into the street, his face covered with lather.

In 1805 Selkirk had the honour of a visit from the poet Southey, whose unfavourable impressions of the place are thus recorded in his journal :—

Saturday, October 5.—From Hawick eleven miles to Selkirk in the dark, but over a country where sunshine would have been of no use. Selkirk had the true odour Scotic. We had a dirty room, behind which I heard such long echoes that being in a land of bogles, I did not feel much inclined to investigate whence they proceeded till the morning. Then we found it was from a large ball-room; and here was kept a machine to measure militiamen, this being the county town.

Sunday, 6 Oct.—Selkirk is truly a dismal place. The houses all darkly rough-cast and made still more ragged by a custom of painting the window out-frame work exactly to the shape of the wood, which the carpenter always leaves without any attention to squareness. These imperfect squares of dirty white upon dirty rough-cast give a most dolorous appearance. A new town-house with a spire seemed to have no business in such a place. We went to the kirk and just walked through it; it had no other floor than the bare earth. Some vile daubings of Justice, Adam and Eve, etc., on the gallery front, its only ornaments, where there had been till lately a picture of a souter of Selkirk taking measure of a fine lady's foot. . . . The people dismally ugly, soon old, and then bossbent; but I like the plaid, the gray plaid,

Com.
Plce.
Bk. iv.
528.

either wrapping them in wind, or scarft across in sunshine; and I liked the bonnet. The clocks here are stopped by night.

In one of the dozen or more biographies of Sir Walter Scott, it is asserted that on his marriage he went over to the Episcopal Church, mainly to please his young wife. That this cannot have been the case is evident from an entry in Selkirk Council minutes.

1806, April 1.—The Magistrates and Council unanimously elected Walter Scott, Esquire, advocate, Sheriff-Depute of Selkirk, as their member and ruling elder at the next General Assembly of the Church of Scotland.

In compliance with a regulation of Assembly, Scott had two days previously been ordained elder in the parish church of Duddingstone, near Edinburgh, along with his brother Thomas, William Clerk, advocate, and Thomas Miller, W.S., the signatures of all four being attached to the declaration in the parish register.

The Sheriff not only took his seat in the General Assembly, but on being elected burgh representative the year following, again took up his commission. It is not difficult to discern between the lines of *Old Mortality* to which side in the great struggle between Prelacy and Presbyterianism its author's sympathy inclined. But Sir Walter had many likings leading in directions where his judgment refused to follow; and his Episcopal leaning was like his Jacobitism, more a matter of sentiment than of conviction. In any case it was impossible for him to find himself a member of the great ecclesiastical Assembly which had played so powerful a part in moulding the history of his country without being adequately impressed. And though he pricked the cant and assailed the bigotry which made Presbyterianism many a time a laughing-stock, his works will be sought in vain for any expression depreciative of its noble stand for freedom.

1806.—Many delinquencies being allowed to pass in consequence of the expense of prosecuting, it was arranged that Mr. Park (brother to the African traveller), procurator-fiscal for the burgh, should prosecute all petty delinquents, for an annual salary of five guineas.

After much negotiation, it was arranged that the small piece of town's ground at glebe foot should be given in perpetual feu to the heritors, ten plane trees being included. The Council agreed, on conclusion of the matter, to present the minister with a new gown at the town's expense. At the same time they were called on to pay one-third the cost of a new manse.

No doubt at the Shirra's instigation, the Town Council sent an address to Lord Melville, congratulating him on his acquittal from charges of high crimes and misdemeanours. It is well known that Scott's song on this

occasion excited keen resentment amongst the Whigs, and cost its author
the temporary loss of valued friendships. Lockhart describes him as now
plunging into party politics with great vehemence, canvassing electors,
Ch. 15. haranguing meetings, and working indefatigably wherever the Parliamentary
interest of the Buccleuch family was at stake. In this light, interest attaches to
a reply from the Town Council to Sir Charles Ross, candidate for the burghs.
" They will be happy to see Sir Charles whenever he finds it convenient, and
the circumstances of his being connected with the Duke of Buccleuch will
have due weight, it being their anxious wish to cultivate the good understanding that has so long subsisted between his Grace and the burgh." A
few months later the Council approved a proposal that the Duke should sit
for a portrait to be hung in the Town and County Hall.

This year the Common-riding was marked by a delightful incident. It
was reported by the Magistrates that in riding the marches on the 27th June,
they had experienced most marked attention from their neighbouring heritor,
Mr. Pringle of Whytbank. He and almost all his family had met them at
the top of the Three Brethren, the cairn on which he had been at the expense
of raising to a considerable height. From its summit floated the British
Union flag. Mr. Pringle had brought much good cheer, which was liberally
distributed to the Magistrates, burleymen, and attendants. Many toasts
were drunk expressive of the wish of all present that a lasting harmony and
good understanding might continue betwixt the burgh and Mr. Pringle's
family.

Mr. John Anderson requested permission to change his bark mill, erected
in 1799 into a woollen mill, to be supplied with water in the same way; but
a threshing-mill being thought more advantageous for the burgh, the Council
agreed to buy the bark mill and convert it into a threshing-mill !

In 1810, considering subscriptions were being taken for the intended
railroad from Glasgow to Berwick, the Council unanimously authorised Bailie
Anderson to subscribe for ten shares, or £1000, in name of the community ;
and if the plans were altered so as to bring the crossing of Tweed nearer
Selkirk, to offer other £500. Unfortunately the spirited foresight of the
Council was without result; and Selkirk had to wait nearly half a century
before the first locomotive left its smoky track on Ettrick-side.

. The dull unbroken routine of the town was not a little disturbed in 1811
by the arrival of a band of French prisoners, ninety-three in number, all
officers, and many of them surgeons in Napoleon's army. There being no

barracks for their accommodation, they were distributed in lodgings throughout the town. Within a mile radius of the centre milestone at the foot of
Tower Street they were at liberty to move about as they liked; and there is
no record of any of them having attempted to break their *parole.* Up the
Hawick road their limit was "Knox's," now known as the Loanhead; over
the bridge they might stray as far as Philiphaugh entries; and towards
Bridgelands "the prisoners' bush" (still flourishing) marked how far they
might go, and no further. An old man (Douglas "the brave") who well
remembers them coming to his father's tavern in Heatherlie for their morning
glass of rum, says they astonished the Selkirk folk with what they ate.
"They made tea out o' dried whun-blooms, and skinned the vera paddas.
The doctor anes was vera clever, and some of them had plenty o' siller."
Finding exile inexpressibly dull, they tried all sorts of expedients *pour passer
le temps.* In October 1813, they constructed a balloon and set it at liberty,
amid the plaudits of the population. The yeomen were in town that day, but
Captain Ballantyne could not get them together till after the balloon had
ascended, so general was the excitement. Doggerel verses on the event inform
us that Mr. "Selery" blew up the smoke, while Mr. "Bizzizael" led the
balloon along and set it off. Only by a population saturated with names of
the Old Testament could the gallant Frenchman's have been twisted into a
word like "Bizzizael." The balloon was seen to float over Yarrow kirk (eight
miles from Selkirk) at a great altitude, but was never more heard of, notwithstanding a pathetic verse in the ballad—

> O how happy the people
> In Selkirk will be,
> To get back their balloon
> In the air for to flee!

In July 1812 the Council found it necessary to consult the authorities
about a number of infant children of these French prisoners, which were likely
to fall a burden upon the public unless measures were taken to prevent it.
The Transport Office having replied that the prisoners were amenable to the
civil laws of the country in the same manner as British subjects, it was
resolved they should be asked to pay a certain sum of money or go to prison.
Having quarrelled about a daughter of Albion, two of them fought a duel in
a field at Linglee; but it was of the bloodless sort now common amongst
Parisian journalists. After fighting half an hour, one managed to hurt the
other on the lip, and honour was declared satisfied. Such *éclat* as was felt

to pertain to the encounter must have been dimmed by the prosaic view of it taken by the authorities. For having been art and part in a breach of the peace, both wounder and wounded were sent to jail for a month.

In 1814, when the English Government thought they had Napoleon safe in the island of Elba, the French prisoners were allowed to return home in time to rally round their hero in his last desperate effort at Waterloo.

Many years afterwards, in the Southern States of America, two young Selkirk lads were astonished to see themselves looked at with evident earnestness by two foreigners within earshot of their conversation. At last one of them, a distinguished-looking elderly gentleman, came up and said— "*Pardon!* I think from your speech you come from Scotland?" "We do." "Perhaps from the south of Scotland?" "Yes, from Selkirk." "From Selkirk! Ah, I was certain. *Général, c'est vrai*, they are from Selkirk;" on which his companion also came over. The General, looking at one of the lads for a while, exclaimed, "I am sure you are son of ze-ze leetle fat man who kill ze sheeps?" "Faith, ye're richt," said the astonished Scot, "my father was Tudhope the flesher." On which the more effusive of the Frenchmen fairly took him round the neck and gave him a hearty embrace. Making themselves known as two of the old French prisoners, they insisted on the lads remaining in their company, loaded them with kindness, and were never tired of asking questions about their place of exile and all its people, particularly the sweethearts they and their comrades had left behind them.

1812.—On the occasion of the Duke of Buccleuch's death, the Council resolved to attend divine service next Sunday in mourning.

Two letters from Mr. Walter Scott, Sheriff of the shire, engrossed in the minutes of June 1814, refer to the Town Council's liability for the temporary escape of a prisoner from jail. Scott gave it as his opinion that the Council had incurred no responsibility, and was supported by Mr. David Hume, Professor of Law; but when the case was finally decided in 1816, both Sheriff and Professor were found to have been wrong.

1815.—The parish minister having altered the hour of service from 11 o'clock to noon, and resolved to give only one service during winter, in consequence of the uncomfortable state of the church, Bailie Clarkson said he had remonstrated with Mr. Campbell on the subject, which the Council approved of, and requested the Presbytery to order Mr. Campbell to hold two services as formerly.

1816.—A petition of Mr. Dunlop of Whitmuir, and other tenants of South Common, for reduction of rent "on account of changed times," was not entertained.

This year the hopes and fears of Selkirk on a matter closely affecting its

interests were again played upon by speculators, either ignorant or designing.
Mr. Gray, who had contracted to search for coal near Lindean, reported that
he had now cleared out the old pit (dug many years before) to the bottom,
and that appearances were so unpromising as to discourage further search in
that quarter. Certain situations further westward exhibited more flattering
prospects. One of the most likely places was on Lindean Burn, a little above
the small bridge on the Melrose road, nearly opposite to Sunderlandhall,

Selkirk Burgess Cup.

where, according to report, a trial had been made many years ago. Another
situation not unlikely was upon a small runner above the old churchyard,
near a piece of ground called Sadlers Knowes. In these places the rock was
more of freestone nature than anywhere else he had seen in the neighbourhood, whereas at the cleared old pit it was hard whinstone even to the depth
of over 80 feet. The contractor having declined to make further attempts at

his own expense, it was resolved to open a public subscription for the purpose of carrying them out where he suggested.

On the 11th September Bailie Clarkson presented to the Council a silver cup bearing the inscription—

GIVEN BY

THE RIGHT HONOURABLE WALTER, EARL OF DALKEITH

TO

THE ANCIENT BURGH OF SELKIRK

MDCCCXVI.

He further stated that he had been desired by the Earl to entertain the Council that evening to a supper. The invitation was heartily accepted; and it was further unanimously resolved to confer the freedom of the burgh on his Lordship, then only ten years of age.

From Lockhart's Life of Sir Walter, it appears that this handsome gift was tendered by the truly amiable Duke of Buccleuch as a pledge of amity towards the souters, whose susceptibilities had been ruffled at the recent hand-ball match at Carterhaugh. Scott's interest in the matter is sufficiently shown in a letter to the Duke about the design of the proposed gift :—

Edinburgh, Thursday.

My dear Lord,—I have proceeded in my commission about the cup. It will be a very handsome one. But I am still puzzled to dispose of the birse in a becoming manner. It is a most unmanageable decoration. I tried it upright on the top of the cup; it looked like a shaving-brush, and the goblet might be intended to make the lather. Then I thought I had a brilliant idea. The arms of Selkirk are a female seated on a sarcophagus, decorated with the arms of Scotland, which will make a beautiful top to the cup. So I thought of putting the birse into the lady's other hand; but, alas! it looked so precisely like the rod of chastisement uplifted over the poor child, that I laughed at the drawing for half-an-hour. Next I tried to take off the castigatory appearance by inserting the bristles in a kind of handle; but then it looked as if the poor woman had been engaged in the capacities of housemaid and child-keeper at once, and, fatigued with her double duty, had sat down on the wine-cooler, with the broom in one hand and the bairn in the other. At length, after some conference with Charles Sharpe, I have hit on a plan which I think will look very well, if tolerably executed—namely, to have the lady seated in due form on the top of the lid (which will look handsome, and be well taken), and to have a thistle wreathed round the sarcophagus and rising above her head, and from the top of the thistle shall protrude the birse. I will bring a drawing with me, and they shall get the cup ready in the meantime. My cat has ate two or three birds while regaling on the crumbs that were thrown for them. This was a breach of hospitality; but *oportet vivere*—and *micat inter omnes*—with which stolen pun, and my respectful compliments to Lord Montagu and the ladies, I am, very truly, your Grace's most faithful and obliged servant,   Walter Scott.

P.S.—Under another cover, which I have just received, I send the two drawings of the front and reverse of the lid of the proposed cup. Your Grace will be so good as understand that the thistle, the top of which is garnished with the bristle, is entirely detached in working from the figure, and slips into a socket. The following lines are humbly suggested for a motto, being taken from an ancient Scottish canzonetta,—unless the Yarrow Committee can find any better :—

> "The sutor ga'e the sow a kiss,
> Grumph! quo' the sow, it's a' for my birse."

The cup, preserved with great pride by the civic powers, and produced only on special occasions, cannot be said to reflect credit upon either Sir Walter or the silversmith. As a work of art it is strikingly inelegant in proportion, though for massiveness it is a gift worthy the exalted nobleman from whom it came. Clearly Duke and Sheriff alike felt something was due to Selkirk after Carterhaugh; and it is to Sir Walter's credit that he was not deterred from making what amends he could by the discourteous entertainment he had met with at the souters' hands. One Scott, a joiner, nicknamed "The Pea," had the effrontery to tell him to his face he was the better Scott of the two, the Sheriff being nothing but a —— auld ballant-maker. And, but for a fight which distracted the general attention, Scott could not have ventured to leave the County Inn. The crowd even threw stones at him when they detected his departure; but Scott, noways daunted, ordered his carriage to stop at Knowpark entrance, and standing up, disarmed his assailants by exclaiming—"I like my Johnnie's grey breeks for a' the ill they've dune me yet." Unfortunately it was not the last time he was to experience the resentment of a Selkirk mob.

Except in periods of momentary exasperation, the townspeople showed profound respect for "the Shirra" when official business brought him in their midst. It is questionable, to say the least, if even his warmest admirers were aware of the greatness of the man, and the greatness of their own privilege; but after his death it was their delight to recall the homely way in which he used to hobble along High Street to the court-house, many a time having to pace backwards and forwards in the Fleshmarket until the officer came with the keys. One day, in expectation of an interesting trial (no one went to behold the author of *Waverley* sitting on the bench) there was a crowded court. At the beginning, when all was quiet, and the clerk had proclaimed the usual formula, "The Sheriff declares this a fenced Court," old Jamie Inglis (Hyte Tyte) thought it necessary to roar "Silence." Sir Walter, looking first round the Court, and then at the macer, said, "Why, man, ye're the only person making a noise." The merry twinkle in the Sheriff's eye was so contagious as to set every one a-laughing, Sir Walter enjoying the joke as much as any of them,—no idea, apparently, in the mind of the Court to have "laughter instantly suppressed." But it was not always his humorous side Sir Walter showed from the bench. An old soldier named Andrew Kerr, in Selkirk, whose father had been a claimant of the dukedom and estates of Roxburgh, brought home a good share of loot from India, availed himself of his soldier's privilege, and started as a flesher in the town. After being but a short time in business, he failed, paying a very trifling dividend to his creditors. One of these was Andrew Haig, farmer of Batts, a steady hard-working man, who, when his team had no work on the little farm, employed them in carting coals from distant pits. Going, as was then the custom, to have a dram at the settlement of an account with a burgess to whom he had sold coals, Haig found himself in the same room with Kerr, who was boasting loudly of his money. Haig remarked it would be well if Kerr were to pay 20s. in the pound before speaking in that way. Kerr retorted that he did not owe Haig a farthing. Haig declared he did, on which Kerr called him a —— liar. Haig gave his insulter one blow which " streekit him like a sawmon,"—to repeat the expression used in Court. As soon as Kerr could pick himself up he went straight to the fiscal, and lodged a charge of assault. When asked to plead guilty or not guilty, Haig said with his Lordship's permission he would relate the facts as they stood. The story having been told as above, Sir Walter said the law had been violated, and he was set there for defence of the law; but, considering the circumstances, he would be as lenient as the law permitted. Then he turned to Kerr. " Well do I remem-

Hend.
Lett.

ber his look," writes an eye-witness. " His shaggy eyebrows, which we used to call *doo-wings*, covered his eyes altogether; then they lit up like fire, and he dealt to Kerr one of the most scathing rebukes ever I heard fall from lips. At one time, in the middle of it, you would have thought he was going to jump out of the bench. He was never known to exhibit such keen feeling in any other case." Splendidly characteristic was his conduct in an emergency during the later years of his administration. Two rough-looking characters having been sentenced to imprisonment for poaching, one of them was led from Court to jail by the only constables present. The other prisoner, thinking it a good chance to escape, made a movement in direction of the door. This Sir Walter detected in time to descend from the bench and place himself in the desperate man's path. " Never!" said he; " if you do, it will

Selkirk Court House Sheriffship
Time of Sir W. Scott

be over the body of an old man." Whereupon the other officials of the Court came to the Sheriff's assistance, and the prisoner was secured. One of these officials was Mr. Peter Rodger, assistant fiscal, and afterwards town-clerk for more than half a century, to whom we owe not only the incidents of the story, but details of the illustration showing the court-room in Sir Walter's time.

Scott entertained a high notion of the importance and dignity of his office, which he resolutely vindicated when occasion required. In 1816, when the Archduke Nicholas, afterwards Emperor of Russia, was passing through Selkirk, the populace, in their natural anxiety to see the Prince, pressed round so closely that Scott found it impossible to approach. At last, shouting in an authoritative tone, "Room for your Sheriff! Room for your Sheriff!" he cleared a lane through the gazers until he reached the imperial visitor, to whom he apologised for his countryman's rudeness. Allan's Scott, p. 197.

In 1816 there was another violent outbreak of party spirit, which had considerably subsided for a while, after the retirement of Mr. Andrew Henderson from the Council in 1806. Again the old quibbling arguments and protests about trades, freemen, and deacons, took up pages of the council-book, the deadlock of business being so complete that the resignation of twenty-one councillors was necessary to put an end to further political contest within the burgh. At next meeting the Council was made up to its proper number—thirty-four—a consequence of the reconstitution being defeat of the Clarkson-Robertson, and the triumph of the Lang-Lamb-Anderson faction.

1817.—Two addresses to the Prince Regent, one declaring abhorrence of an atrocious attack upon his person, and the other expressive of grief at the death of the Princess Charlotte and her infant.

Messrs. Sanderson & Paterson of Galashiels having estimated the cost of a new cauld at not less than £140, exclusive of wood, it was decided rather to repair the old one.

Strenuous opposition to new road proposed to be made from Melrose Bridge, by Bowden-moor and Lilliesleaf, to Hawick, on the ground that it would probably divert the mail-coach and general traffic between Edinburgh and Carlisle from its present road through the town.

From a printed list of every householder in Selkirk on 16th June 1817, having opposite each name the number of inmates, it appears that the burgh contained a population of 1816 persons—one for every year that had passed of the Christian era.

Several years after the hand-ba' at Bowhill, the late Duke Walter, still a lad, got together several scores of boys from Selkirk and from the Buccleuch estates. These were divided into hostile armies, distinguished by paper caps of different colours, at the head of which the Duke and Lord John fought a mimic battle. Cannons were fired at intervals, and the sham-fight was kept up with so much spirit that there was great danger at one time of its warming into a genuine encounter. How the Duke's liberality and kindness in allowing the people of Selkirk free access to his grounds was requited, may be learned from a letter by Scott, to whom, as Sheriff, complaints had been made anent poaching and mischief :—

Abbotsford, January 11, 1817.

MY DEAR LORD DUKE,—I have been thinking anxiously about the impudent ingratitude of the Selkirk rising generation. . . . I know hardly anything more exasperating than the conduct of the little blackguards, and it will be easy to discover and make an example of the biggest and most insolent. In the meanwhile, my dear Lord, pardon my requesting you will take no general or sweeping resolution as to the Selkirk folks. Your Grace lives near them—your residence, both from your direct beneficence, and the indirect advantage they derive from that residence, is of the utmost consequence ; and they must be made sensible that all these advantages are endangered by the very violent and brutal conduct of their children. But I think your Grace will be inclined to follow this up only for the purpose of correction, not for that of requital. They are so much beneath you, and so much in your power, that this would be unworthy of you—especially as all the inhabitants of the little country town must necessarily be included in the punishment. Were your Grace really angry with them, and acting accordingly, you might ultimately feel the regret of my old schoolmaster, who, when he had knocked me down, apologised by saying he did not know his own strength. After all, those who look for anything better than ingratitude from the uneducated and unreflecting mass of a corrupted population must always be deceived ; and the better the heart is that has been expanded towards them, the deeper is the natural feeling of disappointment. But it is our duty to fight on, doing what good we can, and trusting to God Almighty, whose grace ripens the seeds we commit to the earth, that our benefactions shall bear fruit. . . . The elder boys must be looked out and punished, and the parents severely reprimanded, and the whole respectable part of the town made sensible of the loss they must necessarily sustain by the discontinuance of your patronage. And at the same time I should think it proper were your Grace to distinguish by any little notice such Selkirk people working with you as have their families under good order. . . .   W. SCOTT.

It seems the Council had "its own to do" with mischievous young Selkirk, for in 1818, a reward of 10 guineas was offered for conviction of the persons who had burned heather on the Peat Law, "very much to the prejudice of the poorer classes, who were in the practice of using it for fuel."

1818.—Mr. Watson, schoolmaster, to make a plan of town, showing streets, closes, houses, yards, and everything within its precincts, each property being marked with its owner's name— to lie in the town-clerk's office for the instruction of those having interest in it, without fee. (This map, published in 1823, is here reproduced.)

1819.—Yearly market for sale of lambs to be held on Selkirk Common a short time before Melrose Lammas Fair. Day for rouping the common good to be changed to 8th April in place of day after March fair, "it having frequently happened that people not recovered from the drunkenness common to a fair had attended the roup, interrupting the order and harmony."

Under reservation of rod-fishing to burgesses, the right to salmon-fishing in Ettrick was set for £5, 5s., and a fish worth 5s. to the Magistrates at Michaelmas. Lessee expressly debarred from netting trout.

On the death of Sir John B. Riddell of Riddell, seven candidates came forward for representation of the burghs : Mr. Campbell of Rylie, Mr. Robert Owen of New Lanark, Mr. Chisholme of Chisholme, Mr. Pringle of Haining, Mr. Maxwell of Carriden, the Hon. Captain Elliot of Minto, and Mr. Henry Monteith of Carstairs. Four of these gentlemen, being in town, were invited to state their respective pretensions before the Council, which they did. With respect to a letter from Mr. Owen, the Council was of opinion that it would be proper for the Magistrates to inform him that it would be putting himself to expense altogether needless for him to visit the burgh, as there was not the least chance of his succeeding. This was Mr. Owen, the visionary socialist, who had two years before astonished the world by his *New Views of Society*, and whose practical attempts to establish Arcadia excited keen interest at the time.

In a return ordered by the House of Commons, the sett or constitution of the Council was reported to be the same as in 1709. It was explained that although the burgh may elect a Provost, "in respect it was brought into a great deal of debt by their last Provost, Haining, they had always forborne to choose a provost, and held themselves with two bailies." Their clerk's commission could not be taken from him "without some extraordinar malversation and fault legally tried and made appear." The ancient plan by which the Council weeded itself of poor men and took in men of substance had been superseded by a method of annual election, as follows :—

On the first Thursday after the 14th September, or on that day if a Thursday, the five trades meet in the houses of their respective deacons, and choose long leets for the election of a deacon for the ensuing year. There are six names on the long leets chosen by hammermen, shoemakers, and weavers, and four on those of the tailors and fleshers. Next day the Council shortens these leets to 3 and 2 names respectively; and if there has been any dispute at the trades meetings the night before, the Council settles it. From the short leets the trades that evening elect their deacons for the ensuing year, also colleagues to the deacons, the colleagues being chosen without the Council's interference. On Thursday following, at a meeting of deacons, colleagues, and quartermasters of each craft one of the deacons is made deacon-convener; and on Friday the new men are sworn in members of Council. At the first meeting of Council after, the whole of the old Council as well as those newly elected have votes, so that the constituent members may be forty-three, or any number between that and thirty-three, according as more or fewer changes have taken place. At this meeting the bailies, dean of guild, and treasurer are elected. When a contest is going on the full number of forty-three is generally made up at this meeting, the deacons and colleagues being almost always changed, in consequence of the contending parties being eager to get as many new votes as possible.

By the next or fourth Council meeting may be added "Magistrates from the street" (that is, persons who previous to being chosen Magistrates were not members of Council); and by it also are elected the ten merchant and five trade councillors; such of the old Council as are not re-chosen being removed.

At this period there is an interesting table of revenue and expenditure in 1798, 1808, and 1818, to which the items for 1883 have been added in order to emphasise the comparison—

REVENUE OF BURGH.

	1798	1808	1818	1883
Rent of lands and mills,	£382	£490	£720	£1365
Customs,	37	42	60	31
Burgess dues,	4	2	5	1
Feu-duties,	...	12	15	513
Various,	...	2	179	125
	£423	£548	£979	£2035

EXPENDITURE.

	1798	1808	1818	1883
Interest,	£161	£287	£592	£749
Salaries,	49	70	109	106
Public burdens,	38	121	79	180
Law expenses,	31	38	...	51
Tavern bills,	19	75	50	...
Newspapers for the town,	7	...	5	...
Miscellaneous,	11	41	94	138
Repairs of town mills,	...	414	...	...
Dykes and marches,	...	47	...	73
New paving of streets,	...	180	...	...
Public works,	60	40	92	73
Lighting and cleaning,	...	20	30	143
Officers' clothing,	...	6	2	2
Charity,	...	12	38	...
	£376	£1351	£1091	£1515

From a return of lands, etc., alienated by the Magistrates since 1707, the following have been selected :—

1711.—Liberty to Walter Wilson to bring out his house, and "to build a camp."

1742.—Liberty to build an oven in Kirkwynd if 20s. be given to the poor.

1750.—John Veitch to rebuild ruinous tenement called "Crown's land."

1753.—Andrew Henderson, flesher, to have the gable of his house set out for 1½d. annually.

1768.—For house 25 by 11 feet to carry on the skinner business near the back of the Corn Mill.

1769.—Feued to Andrew Haldane for 4s. 6d., the butt of land lying on the east of Shawburn called "the Hangman's Butt." Commissary Shaw having subsequently claimed the Hangman's Butt, the Council renounced all right thereto.

1772.—Twelve tanpits to be put down at the mills.

1776.—Part of the Porches Pool feued to Bailie Henderson, writer, to bring water to his park. (Porches Pool was part of the half-stagnant ditch leading from the Haining loch by the Bog and Foulport bridge down to Shawburn. A bowling-green and the feu of Thorncroft now occupy the ground formerly covered by Porches Pool.)

1781.—Robert Clapperton, dyer, Selkirk Mills, allowed ground for a house 40 by 16 feet, with liberty to fix stenters on the Green.

1799.—A wet marshy ground called the Green, lying almost in a state of nature, which had been let for £2, 17s., was feued by roup in eleven lots for £9, 12s. 6d.

1806-7.—Several lands at Potloch, and on north side of Greenhead Road, sold; in one instance at rate of £30, 10s. per acre, besides a yearly feu-duty of 10s.

1807.—A piece of land (fully described in minute of 13th May 1809) sold to Walter Hogg in front of his factory at Selkirk Mills at rate of £100 per English acre, and a feu-duty of 5s.

1811.—The Council, having purchased from Bailie Anderson all his property at Selkirk Mills, sold part (including the old back-mill on the north side of the dam, and two thatched houses at Pink's Well, with the ground and trees at back) to Robert Clapperton, dyer, at £70 sterling.

The following is a return of all income (in 1819) from heritable and moveable property.

					Ac.	Ro.	Po.				Rent.
Smedheugh farm,	.	.	.	.	219	3	17	.	.	.	£125
Lochslacks,	.	.	.	.	179	2	12	.	.	.	75
Deepslades,	.	.	.	.	206	3	24	.	.	.	105
South Common,	.	.	.	.	152	2	15	£178 reduced to			126
Linglie,	.	.	.	.	957	1	6	.	.	.	241
Dunsdalehaugh,	.	.	.	.	30	3	39	.	.	.	6
Bog £13, Customs, £49,	.	.	.	.		.	.	.	.	.	62
Town's mill and mill-lands,	.	.	.	.	.	.	.	.	.	.	177
Feu-duties,	.	.	.	.	.	.	.	.	.	.	15
											£932

Note.—Part of South Common retained for time past memory as a cow-gang for cows belonging to the burgesses who pay no rent. It is bare rocky pasture, and has not been measured; but during summer it keeps about 50 cows through the day.

Returning the amount of debt as £12,832, and the interest at £532, the report bears that it is impossible to say at what time or for what purpose the debt was incurred. Probably for more than a century the town had been in debt, and since the commencement of the present century its debt had increased with a rapidity far beyond that of any former period. From 1802 to 1816 it had been nearly tripled, the figures being respectively £4846 and £12,745, representing an average annual increase of £564. To account for this it might be stated that the town had expended considerable sums as follows:—

1. Contributing to erection of new town and county hall and jail.
2. Building new flesh market.
3. Paving anew the streets.
4. Erecting new set of mills, with house, offices, etc., for miller.
5. New onstead for one farm and dykes for others.
6. Rebuilding the public well.
7. Repair of church, and new manse with offices.

The valuable report to the House of Commons from which these particulars have been gleaned bears the attestation of Mr. Andrew Lang, who was re-elected senior Bailie in 1819, with Dr. Thomas Anderson as Dean of Guild.

Within three weeks of his re-election Bailie Lang was called upon to receive as guest of the burgh no less a personage than H.R.H. Prince Leopold, then travelling by advice of his physician. Constant change, it was thought, might wean the Prince from a settled melancholy which threatened to overwhelm him after the death of his wife, the Princess Charlotte, and their infant child.

The royal visit was on 24th September; and word having arrived late the night before, the Magistrates sent to Abbotsford asking the Sheriff to come and help them. " I only," says Scott, writing to Lord Montague, " heard of his approach at eight o'clock in the morning, and he was to be at Selkirk by eleven. . . . Mrs. Scott set out with me in order not to miss a peep of the great man; James Skene and his lady were with us, and we gave our carriages such additional dignity as a pair of leaders could add, and went to meet him in full puff." At the bridge over Ettrick, Prince Leopold was received by the Magistrates and entire population. The horses having been unyoked, a band of willing young souters took their place to drag the heavy carriage up the steep West Port, a regular procession being formed in the following order :—

The town halberdiers in livery.

The town's fifers and drummers.

The five incorporated trades, with their respective banners and halberts ;
the weavers carrying the " Flodden flag."

The U.P. Students attending Professor Lawson's class.

The Merchant Company.

The Town Council.

The Magistrates.

H.R.H. Prince Leopold, accompanied by Sir R. Gardner, and attended by
Walter Scott, Esq., Sheriff of the County.

After arriving in the market-place, they formed a circle near the site of the old cross, and the Prince, passing round, graciously acknowledged the salutations which greeted him on every side. Here he was presented with the freedom of the burgh. According to Sir Walter,

His Royal Highness received the civic honours of the birse very graciously. I had hinted to Bailie Lang that it ought only to be licked symbolically on the present occasion; so he flourished it three times before his mouth, but without touching it with his lips, and the Prince followed his example as directed. Lang made an excellent speech—sensible, and feeling, and well delivered. The Prince seemed much surprised at this great propriety of expression and behaviour in a magistrate whose people seemed such a rabble, and whose whole band of music consisted of a drum and fife. He noticed to Bailie Anderson that Selkirk seemed very populous in proportion to its extent. "On an occasion like this, it seems so," answered the Bailie, neatly enough, I thought. I question if any magistrates in the kingdom, lord-mayors and aldermen not excepted, could have behaved with more decent and quiet good-breeding. Prince Leopold repeatedly alluded to this during the time he was at Abbotsford. . . . If I had had a day's notice to have *warned the waters*, we could have met him with a very respectable number of the gentry; but there was no time for this, and probably he liked it better as it was. There was only young Clifton (Haining) who could have come, and he was shy and cubbish, and would not, though requested by the Selkirk people. He was perhaps ashamed to march through Coventry with them. It hung often and sadly on my mind that *he* (the late Duke of Buccleuch) was wanting who could and would have received him like a prince indeed. . . . I think I have now given your Lordship a very full, true, and particular account of our royal visit, unmatched even by that of King Charles at the Castle of Tillietudlem. . . . The piper is the only one whose brain seems to be endangered; for as the Prince said he preferred him to any he had heard in the Highlands (which by the way shows H.R.H. knows nothing of the matter), the fellow has become incapable of his ordinary occupation as a forester, and cuts stick and stem without remorse to the tune of *phail phranse, i.e.* The Prince's Welcome.

When the long black line of divinity students passed, Prince Leopold asked who they were, and if they had put on mourning in compliment to him. Being informed of their avocation, the Prince expressed a desire that their Professor should be presented to him. Accordingly when the company retired to the Council Chambers, Dr. Lawson was conducted to where the Prince was standing. Accustomed as he was to men of mark and distinction, His Royal Highness was plainly impressed by the striking figure of the venerable divine —tall, spare, stooping, and yet full of dignity. After the ceremony of introduction, the Prince asked him how old he was, and on the Doctor replying that he was over threescore years and ten, remarked he looked rather fresh for his age. "I enjoy tolerably good health," said the old man, "but I am weighed down under infirmities." The Sheriff and others having informed the distinguished visitor more particularly of Dr. Lawson's position, scholarship, and godly life, the Prince said, "Such a man as you need not be afraid of the infirmities of age, nor of any earthly calamity. God is your friend and protector." To which the Professor responded, "Please your Royal Highness, I have long had a wish to see you, not only on your own account and from your connection with the Princess Charlotte, but especially because of your relation to the Electoral House of Saxony, and your descent from ancestors who warmly defended the Reformation. To them Luther, in the hour of need, was much beholden for protection and assistance." The Prince, much pleased, said, "Reverend Doctor, I thank you for so high a compliment—a compliment I have never received before. I am proud to think it is a just one. My ancestors were all zealous Protestants; and, I can assure you, so am I." Having cordially shaken hands with the Professor, the Prince turned to the Sheriff and expressed his especial gratification. Since he came to Scotland he had received many compliments on account of the Princess, but that was the first on his own account and that of his ancestors. Scott remarked to some one standing near that Dr. Lawson had done better than all of them, and gone beyond all in the Prince's favour. On the Sabbath after this interview, the aged pastor preached from the text, "Thine eyes shall see the King in His beauty; they shall behold the land that is very far off;" and alluding to the scene between the Prince and himself, he added, "Yes, we have all been delighted with the sight of an earthly prince; but let us look forward with a good hope of seeing the King in His beauty, and the land that is very far off." A deputation of students, waiting upon the Magistrates to express their gratitude for the opportunity of welcoming the Prince, were all presented with the freedom of the burgh, and received burgess-tickets in the usual form.

Bearing in mind the enthusiasm evoked by Prince Leopold's visit, it is not surprising to find the Council presenting a very loyal address to the Regent, disclaiming all sympathy with the discontent and disaffection prevailing in other parts of the country. And when, four months afterwards, George the Third ended his half-dead life, the Council, "in respect to the memory of our late venerable, most justly beloved and much lamented sovereign, resolved to meet in the Town House on Sunday next in deep mourning, and walk in procession to the Magistrates' seat in the parish church."

1820, February 14.—"By a respectable jury at Selkirk," Sir Walter Scott, Baronet, of Abbotsford, was served heir to his grand-uncle, Robert Haliburton of Newmains. In virtue of this succession, Sir Walter Scott had right of burial in Dryburgh Abbey.

On recommendation of the Honourable Captain Napier, the Council approved a scheme for formation of a railroad from Dalkeith down Gala Water to St. Boswell's Green, thence branching in convenient directions towards Selkirk and Hassendean.

Notwithstanding the discouraging reception of his first advances, Mr. Robert Owen, candidate for the burghs, waited upon the Council and ex-

plained those plans of improvement in political economy for the promotion of
which he desired to obtain a seat in Parliament.

By the very narrow majority of 17 to 16 votes, Mr. Andrew Lang, "a
man fearing God, of the true Protestant religion now publicly professed and
authorised by the laws of the realm, expert in the common affairs of the burgh
and a burgess," was appointed to be commissioner at the election of a member
of Parliament for the burghs. At next trades and council elections, supremacy
was again fiercely contested. Page after page was filled with protests against
admission of this craftsman and that, and against elevation to the deaconship
of men supported by impugned votes. An idea of the interminable nature of
the minutes may be formed from the fact that each of these protests was
followed by a "reply," a "duply," and a "triply," as the successive comments
were ingeniously designated.

In April 1821 it was agreed by a majority of 25 to 3 to offer to Mr. Pringle
of Haining the town's bog, with the ground along the turnpike road from
the end of his new wall to the little park at the Common, and in November
a deed was signed, by which the bog and the loch-mouth road, extending to
5 acres 2 roods 17 poles, were annexed to Haining, at the price of £1500.
Reservation was made of right of access to the loch in case of fire, and for
water-supply. Among the people there was deep grumbling and sore complaint at being deprived of the privilege enjoyed for hundreds of years, by
themselves and their ancestors, of watering their horses and cattle at the loch
mouth.

1822.—Bailies Lang and Anderson appointed to go to Edinburgh and present an address
to the King upon his visit to Scotland. A subscription of ten guineas voted towards an
equestrian statue of His Majesty.

1823.—Bailie Anderson elected senior Magistrate after a long tenure of that office by
Bailie Lang, who was again chosen in 1827.

1826, August 3.—Entry in Sir Walter's diary: "From eleven till half-
past eight in Selkirk taking precognitions about a row, and came home
famished and tired. . . . Can the Sheriff neglect his duty that the author may
mind his? The thing cannot be—the people of Selkirk must have justice as
well as the people of England books. So the two duties may go pull cap
about it. My conscience is clear."

A friendly society which for some years had been at work in Selkirk, in
1819 obtained a grant of £5 from the Council, in acknowledgment of benefits
conferred on the community; and now, after eight further years of prosperity
it proposed to make merry by a public demonstration. Sir Walter Scott

having been applied to for hints about a projected flag on which it was proposed to pay him a compliment, addressed the following reply to Mr. Walter Hogg, manufacturer :—

Sir,—Having been out of town for two days I only this day received your obliging letter. I deem myself much honoured by the flattering expression of kindness and goodwill manifested towards me by the Friendly Society of Selkirk. I have little title to the favour they propose to do me by uniting my armorial bearings with those of the Duke of Buccleuch upon the banner which you are preparing for the approaching joyous occasion. I am no great herald, and unluckily I cannot draw, so I can only give my ideas in writing, leaving some artist to put them into form. On one side of the flag I would place the Duke's arms or crest alone, so as to make the deserved honour designed for his Grace as conspicuous as possible. The other side I would divide into four compartments, which I have marked 1, 2, 3, 4 in the sketch below.

These might be filled up as follows :—

1. My Lord Napier's crest—A bunch of spears upright; the mottoe, *Ready, aye ready.*

2. Since you are disposed to honour me so far—A woman dressed richly, hold a sun in one hand, and a crescent moon in the other; mottoe, *Reparabit cornua Phœbe.*

3 and 4 might bear the crest of any other two gentlemen whom the Friendly Society might delight to honour. Or, at the choice of the Society, 3 might be the crest of the town of Selkirk—the female on her monument; and No. 4 might have that of the county—a stag lying couching under an oack tree; mottoe, *Leal to the Forest.*

I think this would make a very pretty flag; and if I had time, or if you wish it, I could easily get a sketch of it. It would have the advantage of placing the Duke's arms in the principal point of view; and Lord Napier has exerted himself so much on behalf of the country that I am sure the Friendly Society will think him deserving of notice. If I were to intrude my own opinion, the crests of Haining and Whitebank might occupy 3 and 4. But this it is not for me to form an opinion. I am in haste; and with best wishes for the joyful occasion.— Very much your humble servant,   WALTER SCOTT.

Edinburgh, 11th Nov. 1827.

Reference to Lockhart's Life reveals the interesting fact that this letter was written the day after Sir Walter's pathetic visit to Lady Forbes, the sweetheart of his early manhood, probably the one heartfelt passion of his life. Both letter and flag, which are in the writer's possession, are here reproduced.

By the time this nineteenth century had finished its first quarter, the old order of things was fast passing away in the burgh of Selkirk. Before the advances of industrialism, the old feudal system was beginning to fall in pieces; and even burgage, broader-based though it was, showed symptoms of decrepitude. Changes, rapid and complete, came over the habits of people in towns which, at the close of the century, differed little from what they had been for hundreds of years. Still, in crannies here and there, were to be found

Ent.

Sir

Having been out of town for two days I only this day received your obliging letter. I deem myself much honoured by the flattering expression of kindness and good will manifested towards me by the Friendly Society of Selkirk I am little able to the favour they propose to do me by connecting my commercial drawings with those of the Duke of Buccleuch upon the banner which I am preparing, you are preparing for the approaching joyous occasion. I am no great herald and unluckily I cannot draw so I can only give my ideas in writing leaving some artist to put it into form. On one side of the flag I would place the Dukes arms or crest alone so as to make the devices herein designed for Her Grace as conspicuous as possible the other side I would divide into four compartments which I have marked 1. 2. 3. 4 in the sketch below

These might be filled up as follows. 1 say

1. My Lord supports crest – a bunch of Spears ~~upon~~ upright the
motto ready aye ready.

2. Since you are disposed to honour me so far – A woman dress'd
richly hold a ~~full~~ sun in one hand and a crescent moon
in the other Motto <u>Reparabit cornua Phœbe.</u>

3. and 4. Might bear the crest of any other two gentlemen whom
the Friendly Society might delight to honour. Or at the choice of
the Society 3 might be the crest of the Town of Selkirk the female
on her monument and No 4 ~~would~~ might bear that of the
County a Stag lying couching under an oack tree Motto <u>Leal
to the Forest</u>

I think these would make a very pretty flag and if I had
leave or if you wish it I could easily get a Sketch of it. It
would have the advantage of pleasing the Dukes arms in the
principal pannel over and Lord Napier has exerted himself
so much in behalf the country that I am sure the Friendly
Society will think him worthy of notice. If I were to
enumerate my own opinion the crest of Ramsay and White
bank might occupy 3 and 4 But this it is not for me
to form an opinion I am in haste and with best
wishes for the joyful occasion Very much
         your humble Servant
          Walter Scott

Edinburgh 11 November
       1827

Facsimile of Letter from Sir Walter Scott to "Mr. Walter Hogg, Manufacturer, Selkirk."

Flag designed by Sir Walter Scott.

reminders of days bygone, old men and women who had heard stories of war and bloodshed from the actors and sufferers themselves; and with whom lingered much curious lore and superstition the Reformation had not been able to eradicate. The "ingle-neuk" was still a factor in the education of the young, who gathered round it on winter nights to hear tales of Border-raid, fairy adventure, civil war, religious persecution, family feud, or ghostly encounter. Not yet had the morning newspaper banished imagination; for up to 1826 all the weekly journals coming into Selkirk did not exceed half-a-dozen, including two sent from London by the burgh member.

It is told of one of these survivals from the dark period, old William Mabon, who died about fifty years ago at the ripe age of ninety-three, that he never let a new cow into the byre until he had bored a hole through her horn, for the passage of a rowan-tree pin and red thread. And before the beasts were sent to grass in the spring, they had to pass the ordeal of the hempen circle. If Crummie stepped into the ring of rope at the doorstep, she was driven back to her stall, and kept there from day to day until she cleared it. Did a cow fall sick, William boiled a letting of her blood with pins, watching the open door all the while to see the malevolent witch go past. One warm summer evening, a big bee, bumming in at the window, made him yell to his wife, " Pit oot that brute ; it 's some wutch or warlock deil ; ye 'll see what 'll happen, it 's no come here for naething." And so next night when a messenger came running for him to go to the Dean burn, where one of his cows was lying with a broken leg, Willy was at no loss to divine the cause. " Didn' I tell 'ee, Jenny dame, that something wad happen after yon bummer cam' in last nicht ?"

An old woman, who lived in Castle Street in the first years of this century, used to tell of going in the summer gloamin' to the loch-mouth for water, when, just above the gardener's house, she heard a shw-ish-ish over her head, which she knew from familiar stories was the rush of fairies' wings. Peeping over the wall, she saw them alight in the Chicken-Acre, and begin to dance in antic capers, often on one leg, and altogether too fantastic for clumsy human limbs. Withering scorn awaited unbelievers bold enough to hint the slightest doubt about the adventure. To her, at least, it was as sure as the truths of her religion.

Another old matron, less than thirty years ago, procured regularly every Beltane (12th of May) a new rowan-tree pin, which served her as a talisman for the twelvemonth.

And every one knows the story of a souter who, falling asleep in a fairy ring on the slope of Peat Law, awoke in Glasgow. There were people impious enough to doubt his voyage through the air by fairy help, until the discovery of his bonnet on Lanark steeple hushed every whisper. Little more than fifty years ago, the man who questioned this narrative would have been looked upon as he might now be who should doubt Philip's miraculous and instantaneous lift from near Gaza to Azotus.

Where one or two scattered and scraggy trees are still visible at the base of Moat Hill, below Howden, there was in Boston's time a dense forest. Never, or hardly ever, did that powerful wrestler with the Evil One get past "the Woody Path" on his way up Ettrick from a Presbytery meeting without a personal encounter with the foe. Auld Nick would jump up behind, and then begin a struggle, lasting till, at the "whisky yett" opposite Hartwoodmyres, the sablest vanished in a flash of fire. "It's very easy for folk to laugh," said my venerable informant, "but if they had been brought up at the same time as me, they would have believed it a' as sure as their ain existence."

In 1830 the Council was much taken up with proposals for new roads, particularly between Galashiels and Selkirk. Against the plan ultimately adopted, they held out a long time for a bridge at Ettrickbank, towards which they offered £150 and what land was needed.

Naturally they displayed keen interest in a distribution scheme attached to the Reform Bill introduced in 1831. Rather than continue grouped along with distant burghs, Selkirk was fain to be absorbed by the county, but suggested to Parliament as preferable a new district of burghs connected by common interests and by geographical position. It was to comprise Peebles, Selkirk, Galashiels, Melrose, Hawick, Jedburgh, and Kelso.

1831.—Precautions against cholera, which had appeared on the English Border.

Of seven individuals confined in the jail, two escaped. Others in the practice of coming out at night and returning again before the jailer's visit in the morning.

1832.—Andrew Lang, Chief Magistrate, elected representative elder to the General Assembly. In 1833, Alexander Pringle of Whytbank. In 1834, John Anderson, Hawthornbank.

Considering his intimate relations with the burgh, it is surprising that the Council minute-book contains no allusion to the death of Sir Walter Scott, which took place on 21st September 1832. It is known, however, that during the funeral, business was suspended throughout the town, there being many outward signs of mourning. We are afraid it is not to be denied that while he went in and out amongst them, the supreme greatness of the man was not realised by the good people of Selkirk. To the larger part he was probably more illustrious as "the Shirra" than as a man of letters; and only when the grief which his death evoked from every corner of the world became apparent, did they begin to bethink themselves of what they had so long enjoyed, and what they had so recently lost. A feeling arose of intense pride in the neighbour they had so often beheld with unconcern, and whom they had more than once treated with contumely.

If truth must be told, the blame on these occasions cannot be altogether laid upon the souters. Sir Walter (possibly from a feeling connected with an incident mentioned in the nineteenth chapter of his son-in-law's biography) does not seem always to have sat easily with the people of Selkirk; and in several matters about which the burgesses took a keen interest, Scott found himself on the opposite side. His alleged share in turning the fortune of the football match at Carterhaugh was soon forgotten, thanks to his own genial urbanity and kindliness; but his attitude on the question of Reform was not so easily condoned. Not that the Selkirk people heaped such insults on their aged Sheriff as he had to endure from Jedburgh, where they hissed and hooted him, even spat upon him, and called out "Burk Sir Walter." Scott, it seems, anticipated a scene of similar violence at the Selkirk election, over which he had *ex officio* to preside; but though there was unmistakeable manifestation of their Radical sympathies, the people restrained themselves in his presence. Lockhart asserts that the Sheriff with his own hand seized the one man who attempted to hustle an elector. And although Sir Walter was not allowed to leave without pretty plain expression of what the townspeople thought of him in his capacity of Old Tory, Mr. Lockhart expresses his satisfaction that "the ancient capital of the Forest did not stain its name upon this miserable occasion."

On the site of the old Tolbooth stands a monument by which the town and county seek to perpetuate association with their illustrious Sheriff. Though unpretending even to plainness, there is something appropriately simple in its massive elevated pedestal, severe yet well-proportioned, bearing aloft Scott's homely figure, clad in legal robe, that he may look over Ettrick water to the hills he loved so well.

On one panel of the base are engraved the town's arms, on another Sir

Scott's Court-House and Monument.

Walter's own coat-of-arms, while in front are four lines from the immortal *Lay* :—

BY YARROW'S STREAMS STILL LET ME STRAY,
THOUGH NONE SHOULD GUIDE MY FEEBLE WAY;
STILL FEEL THE BREEZE DOWN ETTRICK BREAK,
ALTHOUGH IT CHILL MY WITHER'D CHEEK.

In 1841, two years after its erection, this monument was the scene of an incident touching and picturesque enough for the pencil of a great painter. John Bruce, long piper at Abbotsford, "John o' Skye," as Sir Walter used to call him, came to see the statue of his old master. After gazing earnestly at it for a long time, he sat down on a ledge of the pedestal, apparently in deep thought. Getting up, and, tuning his pipes, he walked round and round the monument, first playing Sir Walter's favourite tunes, and then "The land o' the Leal." It was noticed that the notes of this pathetic pibroch became less and less steady and certain as "John o' Skye" continued his slow march round the statue; and at last, choked with grief, the poor piper had to give up trying. Sitting down again at the feet of his old master, he sobbed for several minutes like a child.

With the year in which Sir Walter passed away, Old Selkirk may be said to have also disappeared; for the Reform Bill by one stroke broke up the constitution by which the ancient burgh had been held together for centuries. Deprived of all political power, and having no longer any useful function as centres of employment, the five incorporated trades one by one collapsed. Fitful efforts to retain and to recover vitality have been made by some of them since that time; but having no reason for existence, they have died a natural death. For two and a quarter centuries they served a more or less useful end; but no one can regret the disappearance of privileged bodies whose very existence was a menace to that spirit of enterprise and of equality which has carried the commerce of Britain to its present marvellous development.

Offering no opposition to the principle of Reform, Selkirk had something to say against certain of the Bill's provisions. It had to be pointed out, for example, that if Parliament limited the suffrage to owners and occupiers of £10 yearly, there would be little or no chance of filling up the Council to its present number, as was required in the Bill. The Council would be nearly one-third of the whole constituency. It was suggested that either the qualification should be £5 in place of £10, or the "sett" should be reduced to 17 or 21, there being scarcely another burgh in Scotland except Edinburgh which had so great a number as thirty-three. These representations were unavailing, and on the 5th November 1833, the following three-and-thirty Councillors were elected by the hundred and odd ten-pounders forming the electorate :—

	Votes.		Votes.
John Blackhall, burgess,	80	Thos. Anderson, surgeon,	75
Wm. Brockie, merchant,	80	Thos. Thomson, merchant,	69
And. Guthrie, smith,	80	Wm. Lamb, nurseryman,	67
John Haldane, brewer,	80	And. Brown, weaver,	62
John Gray, merchant,	79	Thos. Stoddart, smith,	58
Alex. Mercer, inn-keeper,	79	Jas. Cumming, baker,	58
Thos. Mitchell, inn-keeper,	79	Jas. Hume, baker,	56
John Robertson, merchant,	79	Thos. Scott, farmer,	56
And. Hatlie, wright,	78	Eben. Clarkson, surgeon,	54
Wm. Ballantyne, inn-keeper,	78	John Gray, mason,	54
Jas. Chisholm, weaver,	78	Thos. Dryden, Rosebank,	53
Jas. Inglis, Jr., mason,	78	And. Hope, mason,	53
Wm. Muir, hosier,	78	And. Inglis, mason,	53
John Mark, skinner,	78	Wm. Chisholm, weaver,	52
Thos. Hatlie, burgess,	76	Rob. Emond, baker,	52
And. Glen, merchant,	76	Rob. Richardson, merchant,	48
And. Lang, writer,	75		

Mr. Lang having declined the honour, Dr. Clarkson was elected first Magistrate. One of his successors was Bailie Muir, on whose resignation in 1845, Mr. Thomas Mitchell was advanced to the dignity.

The chronicles of the burgh have now reached a period which does not seem to fall within the scope of this survey. After 1833 its public business and social condition became much as they are now; and the events which happened are of easy access either in newspapers of the period or in public records.

From an article contributed by the parish minister to the Statistical Account of Scotland, it appears that in 1833 the population of the town was 1800, and that it might have been greater but for restrictions on trade arising from the jealousy of burghers, which forced many young men to places more open to enterprise.

"The habits of the people are cleanly, their houses comfortable, and kept in good order. Strangers invariably remark the neat and decent appearance of the lower orders on Sunday. Food is good and wholesome, the bread in town being mostly made from wheat, and there being few families without butcher-meat almost every day to dinner. They are for the most part well-informed, disposed to religion, sober and respectful. Though they are much addicted to the smoking of tobacco, drinking of spirituous liquors, at one time common, has in a considerable degree declined, the fifteen inns having of late been little encouraged. The only crime prevalent is that of poaching. Besides the parish church, there is no other place of worship except the Secession meeting-house, built in 1759. At one time there were two, but when the synods were united one was found to be sufficient, and the other was converted into a dwelling-house (now Raebank). Seven schools within the parish provide education at once cheap and adequate, there being few of the population who cannot read and write. In the Savings Bank the average amount deposited during five years was £240, and the amount withdrawn £263, mostly by people emigrating to America. The fund on hand was £1673. To 15 poor in the landward part of the parish an average allowance of 2s. per week is made, while 45 in town require £191 per annum raised by assessment. Of five fairs, one, established in 1820 for the sale of lambs, has not succeeded.

As a description of society and manner of life this would have applied any of the fifty years since it was penned, and applies closely now to a population three times as great. True, the steam locomotive had not then made its loud breathing heard in Ettrick Vale; but it had become a possibility. And although the daily press, the penny post, the electric telegraph, and all the marvellous inventions of the past four decades had not yet revolutionised man's position relative to the earth he lives upon, the past centuries of practical stagnation were surely dead. To the Selkirk burgess of 1834, civil war, English invasion, mosstroopers' raids, religious persecution, armed watch by night, defensive trenches and strong gates, were as foreign and strange as they are to his successor in 1884. It is not to be imagined that further progress is impossible or even unlikely. It is conceivable that before another half century has been paced by the inexorable foot of Time, some continuator of these chronicles may direct attention to the remarkable survival of certain superstitions even in this year of grace. "Highly enlightened as these people were," he may say, "they counted it a sin to whistle on Sunday."

CHAPTER XII.

OLD FAMILIES, NOTABLE PERSONS AND PLACES, OLD CUSTOMS.

CONTRARY to what might be expected in a town with local records more or less complete for four centuries, it is not easy to identify some of its old names. Many that were familiar enough in the mouths of Selkirk indwellers two or three centuries since, are now without a "local habitation." Where were Trinity Hill, the Pillars, the Cunzie-Neuk, Cauldshiels, or the Peel Seuch? Some again are easily traced. Water Row, for instance, is now High Street, for a short time (during an English occupation) called Howard Street, after the southern commander. Castle Street is the old Peel Gait (the gait or road to the Peel or Castle), a far finer name, which it would only be proper in the Town Council to revive. Streets of houses joining the three ports, formed what was called "the Ring o' the Toon," albeit its form was triangular. This was probably the most ancient portion of the burgh—answering to the "old town" mentioned in King David's charter nearly 800 years ago. Outside this ring, outside even the fortified trenches, which enclosed a wider area, there were numerous dwellings probably of a less substantial sort. Many fields now within Haining policy belonged to different burgesses; and it is even asserted that the Selkirk burned by Hertford, about twenty years after Flodden, stood upon the Chicken Acre, a grass park sloping down from Peel Hill. This can only be partly true, and is most likely erroneous. Of two outlets from the Haining Loch, one went by the Bog, South Port, and Porches Pool to Shaw Burn, and the other was the rivulet with the unpoetic name of "Clockie," an ancient word sometimes having the mysterious variant, "Clocksorrow." Another name it bore was Milburn, from its turning a little mill, established no doubt for the service of the King's household when the court was at Selkirk Castle. It is easy still to trace the mill-lade; while a hundred yards or so south of the burgh boundary at Woodburn a heap of stones marks the site of the mill itself. Although as old, it is not to be confounded with the town's mills, granted in tack during Robert Bruce's time. These were where the town's mill yet grinds its daily grist, and were driven by a dam leaving Ettrick lower down than the present cauld. This was Bull-sheugh or Bylliesheugh Dam; and another, called Maldisheugh Dam, left the river about fifty feet above the present bridge. Heugh means "height," and is the opposite of haugh, meaning level ground; though the two are commonly taken to mean the same thing. Further up, the heugh or bank was known as Lauriston Scaur, from a village of that name on the top of it. An old road from Selkirk up Ettrick left the present one about Haining Gate, and after dipping down to cross Mill Burn, went over the face of Morriston Hill to where the Lodge now stands, and thence downwards near the Scaur edge past the village of Lauriston.

It is notable how the bridges have crept up Ettrick since the foundation of the first at Bridgeheugh by Alexander II. in 1234. History is silent as to the date of its disappearance; but there was apparently no means of crossing the water but by the ferry for centuries before the erection, in 1738, of the bridge which, starting from the brae-face at Wellwood, crossed Ettrick by five arches where Yarrow Mill now stands. Part of it fell in 1746, and having been repaired it withstood the furious torrents of thirty winters. So complete was its demolition by the flood of 1777, however, that no attempt was made to restore it; and a site for the present handsome viaduct was chosen about half a mile further up. Bridgeheugh and Old Bridge Road bear witness to this day of its ill-fated predecessors.

No name recurs more frequently in Selkirk records than the Ladywell, Halywell, or Holywell, as it was variously called. Its alternative of Holywell shows the first name to have been derived from "Our Lady" the Holy Virgin, to whom the unfinished Abbey and the churches were all dedicated. In the same way Mungo's Well owed its name to the patron saint of the diocese, that of Glasgow. For a long time Brydones were proprietors of the Lady's Well; and it may have been an earlier guardian of it who assumed the name of Halliwell, once common and prominent in the burgess-roll. One of this family, the Rev. George Holliwell, after taking his degree of M.A. in 1648, became tutor to Sir Patrick Home of Polwarth, afterwards Earl of Marchmont, by whom he was presented in 1664 to Polwarth, in which charge he remained till his death forty years afterwards.

ANDERSON is an old name in the burgh, recurring repeatedly not only in official records but in musty title-deeds. A branch identified considerably more than a century ago with the tanning trade, is now represented by

Mr. George Anderson of Hawthorn Bank and St. Helen's. But it was from incomers the name became most widely known. In 1775 mention is made in the Council Records of Mr. Thomas Anderson, surgeon, who came from Earlstoun, though his family may have been in remoter times of Selkirk extraction. It was under the roof and guidance of this practitioner that Mungo Park learned the elements of his profession, learned also to love his teacher's daughter, afterwards his wife. Park's glowing account of his first adventures led to his being accompanied in the second and fatal journey by his brother-in-law Alexander Anderson, a young man of singular knowledge, enthusiasm, and judgment. Dr. Thomas Anderson, who succeeded to his father's practice, served his apprenticeship under his famous brother-in-law at Peebles, and after a life of arduous work and self-denial, died in 1850. For many years Chief Magistrate, he it was who originated the Border Medical Association. His son, Dr. Henry Scott Anderson, also for several years Provost, was presented in 1881 with his portrait, subscribed for by high and low in town and county—Lord Napier and Ettrick making the presentation in an eloquent and touching speech. The picture, an altogether admirable likeness, bears that it was

PRESENTED TO

HENRY SCOTT ANDERSON, Esquire, M.D.

PROVOST OF THE ROYAL BURGH OF SELKIRK 1868 TO 1880,

BY THE INHABITANTS OF THE BURGH AND COUNTY OF SELKIRK.

Painted by George Reid, R.S.A.

BRYDONE occurs six times in the Flodden roll of burgesses, and was the name of a family or families who not only occupied offices of distinction, but possessed much real and personal property. In order to account for the title "Sir" given to a William Brydone, vicar of Selkirk, in the beginning of the sixteenth century, in his capacity of "Pope's Knight," a story has been invented of his having received the honour in connection with the battle of Flodden. Much regret was caused by the sudden death in 1872 of James Marr Home Brydone, with whose ancient burgess blood was mingled that of an officer of *la grande armée*, and who seemed to combine in himself the best qualities of the two nations once so closely allied. From one of the Selkirk families sprung Mr. Robert Brydone, minister of Renton (1724-61) whose oldest son Patrick, well known as author of *A Tour through Sicily*, had a daughter who became Countess of Minto. In possession of the family of the late William Brydone,

R.N , is an Andrea Ferrara, said to have belonged to the hero of Flodden fame —a very fine blade, whoever wielded it.

CLARKSON, an ephemeral name in Selkirk, is remarkable only for the connection of Dr. Ebenezer Clarkson with Sir Walter Scott, who is said to have had him in mind when he limned the character of Mr. Gideon Gray in *The Surgeon's Daughter*—

"He was of such reputation in the medical world that he had often been advised to exchange the village and its meagre circle of practice for Edinburgh. There is no creature in Scotland that works harder, and is more poorly requited, than the country doctor, unless perhaps it may be his horse. Yet the horse is, and indeed must be, hardy, active, and indefatigable in spite of a rough coat and indifferent condition ; and so you will often find in his master, under a blunt exterior, professional skill and enthusiasm, intelligence, humanity, courage, and science."

A true picture, says Lockhart—a portrait from the life—of Scott's hard-riding, benevolent, and sagacious old friend, "to all the country dear." During the last dark weeks at Abbotsford, Dr. Clarkson watched his illustrious patient slowly wasting to the grave, and was among the last to be recognised by the ruined mind once so keen and quick. In his presence, young Dr. James Clarkson made the *post mortem* examination which revealed the hold taken by disease on Scott's brain. Recording the courtesy with which the dying man to the end saluted Dr. Clarkson, Lockhart observes— "Most truly might it be said that the gentleman survived the genius." Of Dr. James Clarkson's family, one son served in the fruitless naval Baltic campaign, and another sank with H.M.S. *Orpheus* off the New Zealand coast in 1863.

FLETCHER is just such a name as might be looked for in a county where arrows were almost implements of labour. It does not, however, appear in the Flodden roll, albeit tradition ascribes to one of this name the capture of the "Flodden flag." An old tombstone in the kirkyard is commonly pointed out as that of Fletcher who took the flag, although it fixes his birth more than a hundred years after the battle. So facile is ignorance in inventing tradition.

Auld Jock GRAY and young Jock Gray were conspicuous and well-known figures in the township and parish of Selkirk in the beginning of this century. The old man was a packman, of somewhat diminutive stature, silent and sulky, unless concerning religion. When that subject was broached, Gray plunged into it with unvarying fervour, revealing a close knowledge of the Bible, as well as of *The Fourfold State* and other masterpieces of Calvinistic oratory. His wife's father had been minister's man to old Thomas Boston—

a connection with sound divinity of which the packman was proud. He was living up Ettrick when his son John was born—with a want, the gossips said. The last thirty years of his life, his home was in or near the town of Selkirk; but his occupation took him over all the surrounding country. His son Jock (nicknamed "the Ladle" from a song he used to sing) going with him in his rounds, came under the eye of Sir Walter, who made his oddities immortal in the character of David Gellatly in *Waverley*. Daft Jock's power of mimicking the clergy of the district—Russell of Yarrow, Campbell of Selkirk, Lawson of Selkirk, Douglas of Galashiels, and others—procured him ready admittance to many houses of the wealthy as well as those of low degree. One day in Selkirk manse, Mrs. Campbell having asked Jock to imitate her husband's style of preaching, got an answer which made her withdraw in haste. "Dear me," said Jock, "what for div ye ask that? Ye ken I need the paper to dae him." To "use the paper"—to read sermon—was then considered a proof of disgraceful incapacity. A minister entering Ettrick Church one fast-day was astonished to find the pulpit occupied by Jock-the-Ladle, whom he called upon peremptorily to come down. "Na, na," replied Jock, "na, na; just come ye up; they are a stiff-neckit and rebellious people, and it 'll take us baith."

HENDERSONS contributed not a few Magistrates and officials to the Council, as well as deacons to the crafts.

Concerning the JOHNSTONS, numerous and influential burgesses for close on four hundred years, little is to be said in addition to what has been already chronicled. Mr. John Johnston, last surviving freeman of the Tailors' Corporation, was Bailie for many years, and Provost for a term. In his family are most carefully preserved the ancient writs and standard of the craft. According to Professor Aytoun, Burns' friend Johnson, of the "Musical Museum," was born and educated in the neighbourhood of Selkirk; but he was not connected with Johnstons of the burgh.

The LANGS, of all the ancient burgess families of Selkirk, longest maintained a position of influence in the town's affairs. Like the Cardinal, this family,

> Though from an humble stock, undoubtedly
> Was fashioned to much honour.

The name first occurs in the records of the Craft of Taylors, of which John Lang was freeman in 1650, officer in 1656, and deacon in 1680. Members of the family belonged to other Trade Guilds; but entries as freemen taylors are numerous enough to form a genealogy. In 1743 Mr. Andrew Lang was town-clerk, in 1744 procurator-fiscal, and in 1745 clerk of supply—offices which gave their holder a measure of control over the public business alike of town and country. Until within a few years ago his descendants maintained steady possession of one or more such berths in the local public service. To Mr. Andrew Lang, clerk of his Court, Sheriff Sir Walter Scott paid a high and well-deserved compliment in a letter still cherished by his family. Sir Walter was never slow to admit that Lang was as well qualified as himself to be Sheriff. Their relations were those of intimate personal friendship, a friendship which belied Shakespeare's line about

Loan oft losing both himself and friend;

for more than once or twice was the Shirra beholden to the Shirra-Clerk for assistance in emergencies of impecuniosity. Within the last few years the close and intimate connection of this family with the old burgh has been broken by the departure to Australia of the last Sheriff-Clerk Lang, grandson of Sir Walter's friend. It may be permitted to say that the burgesses note with pride the eminence attained by another grandson in the world of letters. Mr Andrew Lang's rare scholarship and facile command of the English language are notable even in circles where literary elegance is common. His "Helen of Troy," full of delicate poetic feeling, proves of what refinement and perfection English verse is capable. Yet it is pleasant among lyrics inspired by far other themes to come upon ballad or song proving the poet's soul still "in touch" with his native land—

Three crests against the saffron sky,
   Beyond the purple plain ;
The dear remembered melody,
   Of Tweed once more again.

Wan water from the border hills,
   Dear voice from the old years,
Thy distant music lulls and stills
   And moves to quiet tears.

A mist of memory broods and floats
   The border waters flow ;
The air is full of ballad notes
   Borne out of long ago.

Old songs that sung themselves to me,
   Sweet through a boy's day-dream,
While trout below the blossom'd tree
   Plashed in the golden stream.

Professor George LAWSON was born in 1749, son of a small and much respected farmer at Boghouse in Peeblesshire. After a distinguished career as student, Lawson was in 1771 ordained pastor of Selkirk Secession Church, recently rendered vacant by the death of its first minister. According to Lawson's biographer, the congregation had its origin in the dissensions and controversy respecting the Burgess Oath, which split the Secession Church at Midlem into halves, those adhering to the Burgher Synod removing the seat of their church to Selkirk. Their first minister was Mr. Andrew Moir, a young man of dignified and commanding appearance, who, by eloquence in the pulpit, attained a high degree of popularity. He died in 1770, in the thirty-ninth year of his age and twelfth of his ministry. When Mr. Lawson preached his first sermon, from the text, "Lord I have loved the habitation of Thy house, and the place where Thine honour dwelleth," he made a powerful impression never belied during a ministry of nearly fifty years. Many stories are told of his extraordinary absent-mindedness. It is even said that paying a visit to his friend Mr. Greig at Lochgelly, so as to be out of the way while a "cried" bridegroom, he suddenly, in the midst of conversation, exclaimed, "Surely this is my marriage-day?" As the ceremony was to be performed at Peebles, he set out in great haste, only reaching that town in the evening to find his fair one so affronted that she would not receive him. At last he found a wife among his own people, a daughter of Mr. Rodger, banker in Selkirk, young, amiable, pious, and accomplished. But within a twelvemonth of their union, Mrs. Lawson died unexpectedly and childless. His second mate was a young widow (daughter of his predecessor), whom he married in 1783, and by whom he had three sons and five daughters. Although a man of rare simplicity of character and naturally gentle, Lawson was capable of inflicting severe rebuke where it was merited, witness many a racy story. When he came to his charge, one old member, Laird Nippy o' the Peel, a penurious consequential Dumbiedykes, thought fit to treat his young minister to a series of dry injunctions, mixed with criticism of such sermons as he had already heard. "We like ye unco weel, sir, we like yer prayers, we like yer rinnin' comments, we like yer sermons, but, sir, we dinna like yer texts." Truth to tell, Lawson had a *penchant* for odd out-of-the-way passages on which to hang his homilies; but not relishing the tone of his critic, he quietly expressed his surprise that Nippy should like all that was the work of a weak and fallible mortal, and find fault with what was taken from God's holy word! The laird's constant refrain to his own remarks—

" Ye see, I aye speak oot my mind "—drew upon him Mr. Lawson's advice to
study Proverbs xxix. 11. "Ay, indeed," quo' Nippy, "and what may the
words o' that vairse be ?" "A fool uttereth all his mind; but a wise man
keepeth it in till afterwards." Lawson's mastery of Scripture in Greek and
Hebrew as well as in English was so thorough, that had every copy been
destroyed he could have restored the greater part from memory; and it was
no doubt this profound scholarship, coupled with a fine gift of exposition,
which led to his appointment as Professor of Divinity in 1787. Dr. Lawson's
eminent services to his church, popularity amongst his pupils, purity and nobility
of life, are set forth in his biography by Macfarlane; and room can be found
here for only the briefest of notices. So absorbed did he become in study,
that he was often not alive to his surroundings long after he had risen from
his book. One day a friend stopped him in the High Street, a short distance
from his house, with a lady's bonnet on his head, his daughter having incautiously hung her hat on the peg usually occupied by her father's. It is said
that riding one day to Hawick he turned his pony when nearing Ashkirk so
as to take snuff with his back to the storm, and, forgetting to turn the
animal's head round again, was within sight of Selkirk before noticing his
mistake. Crossing Minchmoor to Traquair he was suddenly deprived, by the
wind, of hat and wig. As he stood helpless in the blast, unable either to leave
his horse or go on without his head-gear, a shepherd lad appeared on the scene
and recovered both. " I regarded this," he said, " as a striking interposition
of Divine Providence on my behalf, and I think it worthy of record." This
seems rather strained : who blew off his wig ? *A propos* of wigs, a ridiculous
story of his having been powdered by Mrs. Lawson before he went to preach one
Sunday. In the course of a more than usually animated sermon, the Doctor
was surprised to feel a gritty substance mingled with the perspiration on his
face. Suspecting the wig, he took it off, and having detected the powder,
gave it half-a-dozen violent thumps against the side of the pulpit, and quietly
putting it on again, resumed his discourse. He had a habit of interpolating
anything urgent that occurred to him during sermon or lecture in a very
odd way. " I remark, in the second place, that "— Here he would stop and
say, " On Tuesday I intend a pastoral visitation to families residing in, etc.
etc.," and then quietly go on. On the use of strong drink he said, " I think
every minister should be able to take a little. When I came to Selkirk I was
visiting in the country. Among others, I called upon a worthy woman who
lived six or seven miles out of the town. She asked me to taste a little

REV^D HEALEE LAMEN D.D.

spirits, but I declined. I learned afterwards that the good woman's feelings had been hurt; she had sent all the way to Selkirk for some good whisky wherewith to treat her minister. Ministers, therefore, should be able to take a little, just a little spirits." No wonder, remarks his biographer, that such a man of God as this rose high in the vales of Ettrick and Tweed! It is a remarkable feature of his character that although he greatly appreciated the earlier Waverley Novels, he declined to read more after *Old Mortality*, he resented so keenly Scott's representation of the Covenanters. When, in 1820, Dr. Lawson died, the charge was offered to his eldest surviving son George, who declined. His brother Andrew, however, was persuaded to leave Ecclefechan and take his father's place. At his death in 1836, his elder brother left Kilmarnock to come to Selkirk, where he was minister in his father's church until his own death in 1849. The Rev. John Lawson, now pastor of the congregation, is a son of Andrew, who first succeeded the eminent Professor. Carlyle, writing to Dr. Macfarlane in 1870, says :—

"Your *Biography of Dr. Lawson* has interested me not a little, bringing present to me from afar much that is good to be reminded of; strangely awakening many thoughts, many scenes and recollections of forty, of sixty, years ago—all now grown very sad to me, but also very beautiful and solemn. It seems to me I gather from your narrative and from his own letters a perfectly credible account of Dr. Lawson's character, course of life, and labours in the world; and the reflection rises in me, that perhaps there was not in the British Island, a more completely genuine, pious-minded, diligent, and faithful man. Altogether original, too, peculiar to Scotland, and, so far as I can guess, unique even there and then, England will never know him out of any book—or, at least, it would take the genius of a Shakespeare to make him known by that method; but if England did, it might much and wholesomely astonish her. Seen in his intrinsic character, no simpler-minded, more perfect 'lover of wisdom' do I know of in that generation. Professor Lawson, you may believe, was a great man in my boy circle; never spoken of but with reverence and thankfulness by those I loved best. In a dim but singularly conclusive way, I can still remember seeing him, and even hearing him preach (though of the latter, except the fact of it, I retain nothing); but of the figure, face, tone, dress, I have a vivid impression (perhaps about my twelfth year, *i.e.* summer of 1807-8); it seems to me he had even a better face than in your frontispiece—more strength, sagacity, shrewdness, simplicity, a broader jaw, more hair of his own (I don't much remember any wig); altogether a most superlative steel-grey Scottish peasant (and Scottish Socrates) of the period; really, as I now perceive, more like the twin brother of the Athenian Socrates who went about, supreme in Athens, in wooden shoes, than any man I have ever ocularly seen. Many other figures in your narrative were, by name or person, familiar to my eyes or mind, in that far-off period of my life."

The portrait now published, and more in keeping with Carlyle's recollection of Lawson than the expressionless picture of the biography, is from his book on *The Proverbs*.

Dr. Mercer, who lived in Selkirk about the middle of last century, acquired reputation as an enterprising agriculturist. In 1759 his skilful culture had attracted the admiration of Mr. Wight, Government surveyor, who in 1777 reported—

Turnip, barley, and grass seeds were his favourite plan; and well did he conduct every operation. First to begin husbandry improvements about the town, he combined his own interest with that of the people. Many boys and girls, wandering about idle, were employed to weed turnip and clear grass ground from stones. Wages paid regularly spurred them on to industry; and he had the satisfaction of rescuing many young persons from habits of vice and idleness. His enclosures are by ditch and hedges, the ditch lined with the small flattish stones gathered off the land. Owing to great care during the first five years in keeping the thorns clear of weeds, the hedges are excellent. These enclosures are let from 50s. to £3 per acre; and this great improvement has raised a spirit for agriculture, which from the discovery of shell-marl will become more and more vigorous. It gives me pleasure to mention those who have signalised themselves in this art. Mr. Fairbairn excels in turnip, the Reverend Mr. Robertson in cabbage and kail, as well as turnip. Bailie Curror and Bailie Henderson have raised crops of hay this season nothing short of 300 stone per acre.

In 1760 Dr. Mercer and the Laird of Philiphaugh had to be prohibited by the Town Council from taking more marl from the Dry Loch; and his crops having come to nought one year from bad weather, Dr. Mercer gave up practical agriculture in disgust. Related to him was Mr. Andrew Mercer, a Border rhymster connected with the *Edinburgh Magazine*, who first acquainted the Ettrick Shepherd with Scott's projected visit in search of old ballads.

Mitchelhill was long a name of consequence in Selkirk. Its first recorded holder was Sir John Mitchelhill, chaplain and notary-public, in 1512. A hundred years later, James Mitchelhill took his seat in the Scottish Parliament as member for the burgh, being again returned in 1617. John Mitchelhill was M.P. for Selkirk in 1579; William Mitchelhill in 1640; while Bailie William Mitchelhill sat in the Parliaments of 1665 and 1667, being also appointed Justice of the Peace and Commissioner of Supply. At one period this family owned a considerable quantity of land in the neighbourhood of Selkirk. In 1603 William, son of James Mitchelhill and his wife Isabella, only daughter of James Young, burgess, was retoured heir of his grandfather, the said James Young, in a tenement within the burgh, and nine rigs of arable land. Bailie William Mitchelhill, the Member of Parliament, was in 1688 retoured heir of his brother John in the lands of Kingcroft, held of the King for two red roses. Probably the name is derived from the small estate of Mitchelhill in Peeblesshire, mentioned in a popular rhyme :—

Glenkirk and Glencotha,
The Mains o' Kilbucho,
Blendevan and the Raw,
Mitchelhill and Shaw,
There 's a hole abune Thriepland
Would haud them a',—

referring to a pot or hollow in the hill wherein the inhabitants of these places were wont to seek shelter in time of danger. The name itself suggests connection with St. Michael, who was believed to manifest himself on high places, such as St. Michael's Mount in Cornwall and Mont St. Michel in Normandy.

THE RODGERS, though not so old in Selkirk as some other families, have for about a century been prominently and honourably connected with its public business. In the minutes of the Taylors' Craft in 1701, William, son of James Rodger in Oakwood Mill, was registered as "prentice," and five years later Thomas Rodger became "prentice" to John Lang, deacon, William himself became deacon in 1740; and his tombstone records his death in 1763, at the age of 76. As Deacon Lang took a young Rodger as prentice tailor, so Sheriff-Clerk Lang took a young Rodger as prentice lawyer. The office of town-clerk has been held by members of this family since 1795, the present occupant, Mr. Peter Rodger, dating his appointment from 1827. A distinguished member of this family was Captain Rodger, R.N., whose patent anchor was largely adopted by the Royal Navy, after many years' use by merchant vessels.

WILLIAM RIDDEL died at Selkirk in 1788, at the reputed age of 116. During the early period of his life he was deeply engaged in smuggling, and was remarkable for his love of brandy, which he drank in large quantities, as well as strong ale. He was scarcely ever known to take a draught of pure water. Without being what is termed a habitual drunkard, he had occasional paroxysms of drinking, which lasted for several days. After he was ninety he had a fortnight's bout, during which he never was sober, nor took any rest except short sleeps in his chair. His third wife he married when he was ninety-five. To the end he had a good memory and clear mental faculties. For the last two years his subsistence was confined almost exclusively to small portions of bread steeped in ardent spirits or ale.—*Records of Longevity*, p. 319.

SAM RUSSELL had the same undying thirst as the centenarian, but rarely possessed wherewith to buy the assuaging nectar. A new lessee having come to Sunderlandhall Toll, then licensed to sell drink, Sam conceived a brilliant scheme for obtaining there the credit he was denied nearer home. Accompanied by one of the town's officers in livery, Sam walked into the tollhouse, and passing himself off as a gentleman waiting for his coach (sent into Selkirk for repair), drank without stint of the unsuspecting tacksman's rarest and dearest. By and by it became necessary, after uttering objurgations at the coachman's delay, to temper his impatience with further refreshment, which he shared liberally with the servant in attendance. Though rather at a loss to reconcile the stranger's clothes with his position, the toll-keeper was completely taken in by the frequency and elegance of the gentleman's oaths, as well as the lavish ease with which he ordered bottle after bottle of high-priced wine. Suddenly the lackey, who had been on the look-out, came in and whispered in his master's ear that a well-known townsman was approaching. Sending mine host to see if the coach was not yet in sight, the two confederates stole out as silently as they could, running over the fields, and wading Ettrick in their eagerness to escape.

The Rev. WILLIAM SORLEY, first minister of the Free Church in Selkirk, was a man of unusual talent and culture. Noticing his death in 1859, at Birkenhead, the *Scotsman* said—"Within the circle of his intimate friends will long float the memory of flashes of wit rarely equalled and of powers of conversation which for cutting irony, or playful invective, or logical acumen, as occasion required, were never surpassed." It would be hard to find a better pun of its kind than one recorded of Mr. Sorley and his friend Mr. Rashleigh, then residing at the Haining. At their first meeting after the great secession in 1843, the minister, with a twinkle in his eye, said, " Well, we've done it, *Rashleigh.*" " Yes," was the response, "and you'll rue it, *Sorley.*"

JOHN THOMSON, an enthusiastic " souter," died in July 1862, having a few weeks before performed the " casting of the colours " on Common-riding morning for the sixty-ninth time. He was 83 when he died, and was the last person in Selkirk who had enjoyed the privilege of listening to the conversation of Burns. It was in the village inn at Moffat, where he had gone in company with his father. Burns had patted the youngster on the head ; and Thomson used to say it caused a thrill of pleasure to diffuse itself through his whole body when he remembered it.

Among other well-known families and men of Selkirk were the Anguses, one of whom, Bailie John Angus, died in 1662, as is recorded on his tombstone.

One James Ewart, who died in 1683, a year older than the century, had, when he himself was fifty-seven, a son Robert, who became town and sheriff-clerk, but died in 1690, while only in his thirty-fourth year. John Ewart, who was Dean of Guild, died in 1740, aged 81. The Currors and Waughs, who became county families, are mentioned elsewhere; and besides them were the Hallidays, Robertsons, Scotts, Elliots, Chisholms, Douglases, Browns, Lidderdales, and Inglises. The following epitaph is said to be upon a Treasurer Inglis of Selkirk :—

> Here lies a man without a lirk,
> Who was a friend to town and kirk;
> Whilst in his office he took great pleasure
> To manage well the public treasure.

Few places are mentioned oftener in the chronicles of Selkirk than St. Mungo's Well, named so, no doubt, after the famous fount near the Saint's shrine in Glasgow, where Bruce did penance after slaying Comyn. In Roman Catholic times Selkirk was supplied with priests from Glasgow, the headquarters of the diocese. The well was greatly prized by the townspeople, who saw it go into the hands of Haining with a grudge. It is on the slope of what is now the Deer Hill, near the ruins of a deserted washing-house. On Common-riding day the burleymen raced up Peel Gait, down to the Bog and up to the Well, into which the first to arrive popped a stone. Peebles and Penicuik both had wells dedicated to St. Mungo, or Kentigern, as he was often called; and there were few parishes without one or more holy pools famous for their healing virtues. Down to quite recent times kirk-sessions and presbyteries experienced the greatest difficulty in eradicating popular belief in their efficacy.

The Chicken-Acre is that part of the Haining policy sloping down from Peel Hill to the carriage drive, and bounded on the east by the long close. It may have derived its name from being held for the annual payment of a chicken, no uncommon form of rent. Andrew Brown, deacon of weavers, who died about forty years ago, over 80 years of age, used to say he was the last that was born in the Chicken-Acre. The titles of an old house, third on the right going from the Townhead to the South Port, once belonging to Halls, and now to Thomas Nicol, give the proprietor a right of harrow and barrow road through the Chicken-Acre to the Mill Burn.

At the top of the steep road leading from South Port towards Hawick, to the left is Gallows Knowe, the scene of many a last farewell to earth and sky.

Here it was Meg Lawson met her doom as a witch; and here were executed a band of rieving Armstrongs, condemned at what, according to Sir Walter Scott, was the last Circuit Court held in Selkirk. A Teviotdale laird having missed twelve cows, raised his neighbours and traced the thieves as far as Westburnflat, the house of Willie Armstrong, on the banks of Hermitage Water. Being asleep, Armstrong and nine of his friends were secured without difficulty. Although no precise evidence was led proving them guilty of the theft, the cattle never having been recovered, the Armstrongs were convicted on their general character as habit and repute robbers. On hearing sentence of death, Willie o' Westburnflat broke a chair into fragments, which he handed to his companions, offering, if they would stand by him, to fight his way out of Selkirk. His men, however, held his hands, and besought him to let them meet their inevitable fate with resignation. Accordingly they were all executed in form of law, their bodies being buried in Haining deer park just opposite the Gallows Knowe. Close by the wall, small heaps of stones mark the place where side by side the hapless freebooters lie buried.

"Do you see to the left," asks Dr. John Brown in his delightful *Horæ Subseciva* on Minchmoor, "that little plantation on the brow of Foulshiels Hill, with the sunlight lying on its upper corner? If you were there you might find among the brackens and foxglove a little headstone with 'I. T.' rudely carved on it. That is *Tibbie Tamson's grave*, known and feared all the country round.

'This poor outcast was a Selkirk woman, who, under the stress of spiritual despair—that sense of perdition which, as in Cowper's case, often haunts and overmasters the deepest and gentlest natures, making them think themselves

"Damn'd below Judas, more abhorr'd than he was,"—

committed suicide; and being, with the gloomy, cruel superstition of the time, looked on by her neighbours as accursed of God, she was hurried into a rough white deal coffin, and carted out of the town, the people stoning it all the way till it crossed the Ettrick. Here, on this wild hill-side, it found its rest, being buried where three lairds' lands meet. May we trust that the light of God's reconciled countenance has for all these long years been resting on that once forlorn soul, as His blessed sunshine now lies on her moorland grave! For, "the mountains shall depart, and the hills be removed; but my kindness shall not depart from thee, neither shall the covenant of my peace be removed, saith the Lord that hath mercy on thee."'

This outburst of savage superstition took place so recently as 1790. Tibbie, who was a woman of rather weak intellect, had stolen yarn, for which some of her neighbours told her she would be hanged. This so wrought upon her feelings and imagination that she hanged herself. Her house was one of two directly opposite the kirk gate in Kirk Wynd—the one nearest Simpson's

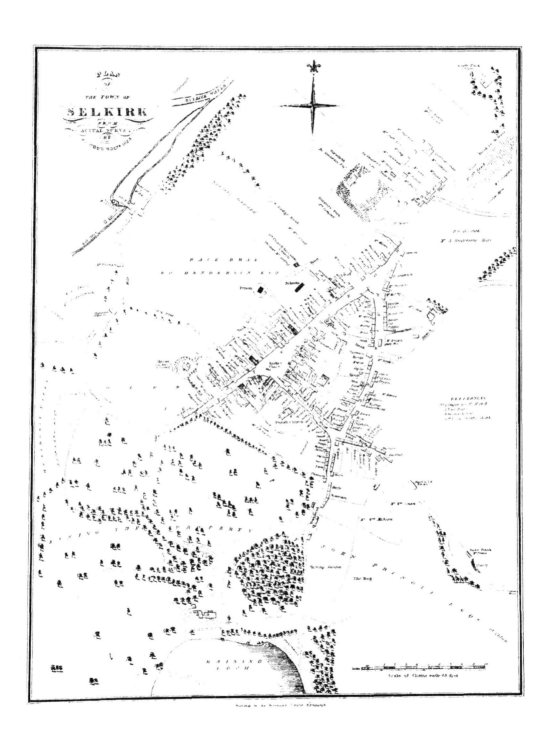

Square ; and old men have told the writer with what awe, as boys, they looked upon the joist to which the wretched woman was suspended. On the site of these houses the present tenement was erected by Mr. Walter Paterson, who bought them. Refused interment in the churchyard, though the door of her humble dwelling-house faced its entrance, Tibbie's corpse was handed over to John Curror, the burgh constable, to be buried at the junction of three lairds' lands, according to the ignorant prejudice of the time. Long before the place was reached the rude coffin had been broken in splinters, and the dead woman was dragged over the ground just as she was cut down. A Christian named Michael Stewart, a dyker in the Duke of Buccleuch's service, placed a rude stone at the head of the grave, which he actually re-opened that he might repair the indecent haste shown at her burial. In the woman's pocket he found one penny and one farthing.

Shrove-Tuesday, or Fastern's E'en, is a movable feast, the incidence of which was indicated in a rhyme well known in the south of Scotland :—

> First comes Candlemas,
> Syne the new mune,
> The next Tuesday after
> Is Fastern's E'en.

It seems to have been a custom observed in every town, and many a rural parish, to indulge in the game of hand-ball on this holiday ; and in Selkirk the practice took a very remarkable form. Up to the close of last century (how long before is unknown) every boy at the parish school provided a game-cock for the annual fight on Fastern's E'en. He who had the best bird was "king" of the school for a twelvemonth ; and as this was the highest ambition a boy could cherish, "Felton greys" and "Carlisle reds" were sought for far and near. The fight came off in school, the chief magistrate sitting at the headmaster's desk as judge. Birds showing the white feather had their necks wrung, and were thrown into a corner—a much-needed perquisite of the dominie. The "king," or owner of the best bird, had to provide a hand-ball, and to carry it a certain distance out of the burgh without being overtaken by those pursuing him. Of course he got an "archcap," or start. While he was at the Haining Gate, the other boys stood at the West Port, both waiting for the signal. This given, they set off, through Mill Burn, up Muriston's Hill, straight through Lauriston, along by the Scaur-heads, until they reached the Woody Path. If the "king" could throw the ball over the burn to Howden Haugh before his pursuers gained on him, he was considered to have added to his laurels; but if not, the royal honours obtained at cock-fighting were considerably dimmed.

Relics of old Selkirk are neither numerous nor very ancient. Of the certainly genuine, the oldest are the burgh records and charters; and next to them come the trades minutes and insignia, elsewhere mentioned. There is, of course, "the Flodden flag," with such claims to genuineness as it possesses; and the Flodden "Ferrara," quite probably used on that disastrous field. Several other old swords have escaped destruction; one found at the side of a service road between Bleachfields and the Batts, another near Howden Moat, and another on the wall-head of an old house in Kirk Wynd. This latter, escaping transformation into a ploughshare, has been shortened and shaped into a screw-driver, an implement quite as emblematic of the arts of peace, though not mentioned in millennial prophecy. Letters on either side are now illegible, except three, D. O. M., for *Deo optimo maximo*—to God, the greatest and best. This fragment of a blade and a pike-head, found at the same time, are in possession of the writer. From the battlefield of Philiphaugh weapons of various kinds have been recovered, and quite a number of coins. Of stone pounds and half-pounds, chipped down to the proper number of ounces, and so lately used that they can hardly be counted old, many survive. If the silver arrow be excepted, the Town Council is without a tangible relic of its long existence and ancient dignity. Two halberts remain, rude in shape and without clue to their age. So poor was the Corporation, that within the present century, a tax of a halfpenny to buy the Bailie's gloves was levied from each stall every fair-day in Selkirk. The abolition of this impost is said to be owing to the contemptuous munificence of a shoemaker from Hawick, who paid for the gloves himself, adding that the magistrates of his town would be d——d rather than have gloves from such a beggarly imposition.

CHAPTER XIII.

THE TEXTILE TRADE OF SELKIRK.

COMMERCIALLY, Selkirk is a daughter of Galashiels, all the large textile factories which have added so much to its wealth and population having been built by incomers from that nursery of the tweed trade. Selkirk, however, must have had weavers centuries before Galashiels appeared on the horizon of history, for they were essential craftsmen in the days when to be self-supplying was the aim of every community. Though not so numerous as the souters, they were the first tradesmen in the burgh to be formed into a corporate craft, their seal of cause being issued in 1608. At that time they wrought both linen and wool, and for two hundred years these two materials were woven in varying proportions, linen for a while having the best of it.

In 1707 Selkirk was early in the field as claimant for a share of English money set aside at the Union to compensate Scotland for past and prospective damage to her industries. The Town Council's petition for a mill did not immediately bear fruit, and equally unsuccessful was a similar request made in 1719, though backed by powerful influence. The year before, one Robert Wilson had got a tack for thrice nineteen years of the waulk-mills (then lying ruinous), on condition that he rebuilt them; from which it may be inferred that a woollen trade once existing had fallen into desuetude and decay. To put a stop to disputes, the Town Council in 1720 issued an authoritative "act anent a standard reel for worsted yarn, to be published by tuck of drum at the Mercat Cross, so that none may pretend ignorance."

The short reel to be a quarter ell long and one ell round about, having six score threads in every cut, three cuts to the hank, and every cut tied by itself. The long reel to be half an ell long, which is two ells about, six score threads to the cut, six cuts to the hank, and eight hanks to the spyndle. Reel for woollen yarn to be half an ell half a quarter long, or ten quarters about, cuts and hanks as in long worsted reel.

In 1731, Robert Scott, stocking-weaver and wool-comber, intimated his desire to settle in Selkirk, " providing the Magistrates and Council would use their interest to have the factory for manufacturing coarse wool in terms of several Acts of Parliament, and the order of the trustees thereanent, fixed at Selkirk, so as he may be entitled to the premium appointed to be made to staplers." Without pledging themselves, the Council provided Scott with a convenient house for lodging his family and carrying on his employment. Scant success followed these various efforts. Six-and-thirty years later, when Bailie Rodger intimated his intention of establishing a woollen manufactory in the town, it was found necessary to erect a waulk-mill, the old one having disappeared. At first it was proposed to build a waulk-mill 20 feet in length "over the malt-mill dam, near the kiln;" but there not being sufficient fall, the site was changed to behind the corn-mill, a cut being taken from the corn-mill dam. Power was given to put up stenters for drying cloth, with privilege to the inhabitants to wash and dry their clothes there when the stenters were not being used. This waulk-mill was kept working in a small way till 1835, when Selkirk began to participate in the budding prosperity of the tweed trade.

In 1771, on a favourable report from Lord Alemoor, the Board resolved to allow James Rodger, manufacturer at Selkirk, £30 in each of three years for a foreman to assist him in carrying on the several branches of his manufactures—"incle making and the spinning of woollen yarn, introduced and carried on by him there." After the three years had expired, the same allowance was continued to William Rodger (probably son of James) from 1774 to 1781. In 1782 it was reduced to £15, and then stopped. This William Rodger had two brothers—James, who built a tannery, and George, townclerk, father of the late George Rodger, Esq. of Bridgelands, and of the present venerable holder of the clerkship.

In 1776, Mr. Loch reported a few looms in Selkirk devoted to jobbing work in wool, but a considerable quantity of yarn was made, as much as £55 a week being paid in the town for spinning. Some of it went to be woven at Musselburgh, but most of it to England. According to Wight, the women were excellent spinners, and fully employed by Yorkshire manufacturers of woollen cloth, who had their wool spun cheaper there than at home.

Application in 1778 for a resident stamper of linen at Selkirk was refused, there being no linen made for sale in or about the town except at two fairs regularly attended by the Melrose stamper.

In 1779, on application by the Rev. William Robertson, minister of the parish, a set of hackles was granted by the Board; but further aid was refused to William Rodger when he applied for it in 1786. Besides his annual allowance, Rodger ten years before had got £30 for putting up a washing-mill at his bleachfield.

1794.—Calender and boiler granted to Robert Chisholm, Robert Orr, Andrew Heatlie, and Patrick Emond, to enable them to carry on the manufacture of linen cloth for sale which they have lately begun. Further, a sum of £30 was given "for the benefit of all the weavers in Selkirk."

1795.—A piece of land at the mills feued to the Incorporation of Weavers for a bleaching-ground.

1803.—A twisting-mill not exceeding £12 in value given to Mary Buckham at Lasswade, to carry on the thread manufacture at Selkirk; and in 1805 a similar grant to Agnes Lawson.

Stimulated by the example of Galashiels, Selkirk began about 1810 to bestir itself for the establishment of a woollen trade in its midst. In 1831 Robert Clapperton, strongly backed by the Duke of Buccleuch, obtained from the Board of Manufactures a grant of £45, to be applied in procuring improved machinery. Less luck attended a petition from William and Simeon Bathgate in 1816, there being some doubt how far the merit originated with them of a certain new construction of mules for which they claimed reward. Next year, on the Duke's recommendation, the weavers of Selkirk got £15 wherewith to buy reeds. As yet there was no factory of any consequence in the town, the weavers for the most part living in poor houses of their own, earning a precarious living from what was called "customer wark." One of these hard-working men of the shuttle who in 1821 lived in an old thatched cottage near the present farm-steading of Philiphaugh, and acted as *cicerone* to visitors, inspired the late Dr. Robert Chambers to a delightful poetic sketch, published in his *Illustrations of the Waverley Novels* :—

> Near Selkrik, where Leslie ance met wi' Montrose,
> And ga'e the King's army its last bluidy nose,
> There lives an old wabster, within an auld shiel,
> As lang, and as ugly, and black as the deil.
> He works e'en and morn for his wife and his weans,
> Till the very flesh seems to be wrought frae his banes;
> Yet canty the wabster, and blythe as a lark,
> Whene'er he gets what he ca's customer-wark!

The black cutty-pipe, that lies by the fireside,
Weel kens it the day when a wab has been paid,
For then wi' tobacca it's filled to the ee,—
And the wabster sits happy as happy can be ;
For hours at a time it's ne'er out o' his cheek
Till maist feck o' his winnings ha'e vanish'd in reek :
He says that o' life he could ne'er keep the spark,
An it werena the pipe and the customer-wark !

.   .   .   .

When the siller grows scarce and the spleuchan gets toom
The wabster gangs back to his treddles and loom,
Where ha jows the day lang on some wab o' his ain,
That'll bring in nae cash for a twalmonth or twain ;

.   .   .   .

Oh, customer-wark ! thou sublime movin' spring !
It's you gars the heart o' the wabster to sing !
An 'twerena for you, how puir were his cheer—
Ae meltith a day, and twa blasts i' the year :
It's you that provides him the bit, brat, and beet,
And maks the twa ends o' the year sweetly meet,
That pits meat in his barrel and meal in his ark !
My blessings gang wi' ye, dear customer wark !

Woollen manufactures were carried on at the old mills in a fitful way for some years, till 1835, when the waulk-mills were enlarged, and the want of further water-power at Galashiels sent some young manufacturers to build mills at Selkirk. Since that the history of the trade has been the history of the different factories. Beginning at the dam-foot and going upwards, these occur in the following order :—

DUNSDALE MILL.—First part built in 1837 for a manufacturer named Inglis. Afterwards it was enlarged, and parts occupied by Thomas Davidson and one Menteith from Galashiels, also by Wilsons and Watsons, who took away all the yarn they made to Hawick. Now possessed by Messrs. Waddel and Turnbull, formerly in Galashiels, who, after being tenants for sixteen years, became proprietors in 1863, and made large additions. Driven by both steam and water power. All operations carried on from wool to cloth. Eight carding setts, and ninety-seven power-looms.

ETTRICK MILLS.—The first part of this large and well-proportioned factory was begun in 1835 by Messrs. James and Henry Brown, only sons of Mr. William Brown, Galashiels ("The Baron"), who won his first premium for cloth in 1798. In recognition of the benefit they had rendered to the town by their enterprise, James and Henry Brown, with their father, were created honorary burgesses of Selkirk. The mill was doubled in 1850. Mr. James Brown, who had bought the small estate of Helmburn in Ettrick, died in 1852; and in 1859 his sons, on a dissolution of partnership, returned to the parent town, where they established a prosperous business at Buckholm Mill. After the death of Mr. Henry Brown in 1860, the firm was carried on by his sons until 1883, when another dissolution left the business in the hands of Mr. James B. Brown and his sons. At the first great exhibition of 1851 this firm obtained a medal, honours having also fallen to them at various succeeding exhibitions, not only in London but on the Continent, in America, and in India. The mills are large, comprising eleven carding setts, sufficient spindles, and 150 power-looms, with the multifarious appliances requisite for conversion of wool into Scotch tweeds. Three magnificent water-wheels are supplemented by powerful steam-engines capable of working up to 400 horse-power.

TWEED MILLS.—First portion, newly erected by Mr. William Brown and his sons on their retirement from Ettrick Mills, is understood to be the nucleus of a larger establishment.

YARROW MILL.—First part begun in 1866 and completed in 1867; main mill being doubled in 1872. Contains eight setts carding, 8780 spindles, and other machinery for manufacture of woollen yarn. Belongs to T. Craig-Brown.

FOREST MILL.—Originally belonged to the town. For several years previous to 1839 was occupied by the Messrs. Hogg, one of whom was recipient of a letter from Sir Walter Scott, elsewhere reproduced. In May 1839 the premises were bought by Mr. George Roberts and others in Galashiels, Mr. Thomas Roberts coming from Galashiels to manage the business. An addition was made in 1842, and in 1844 it was taken into the personal management of the proprietors, Messrs. George Roberts and Andrew Dickson, who made considerable extensions. Eventually it remained in the hands of Mr. George Roberts, who was not only a successful manufacturer but a man honourably and prominently known in public business. From 1848 to 1864 he was Chief Magistrate of the burgh, holding the resumed title of "provost" from 1852. He was chairman of the Selkirk and Galashiels Railway, and second president of the South of Scotland Chamber of Commerce. Four years before his death, in 1877, at the age of 71, he had resigned the business to the care of four sons. Besides this mill, in which every process is carried on, Messrs. George Roberts and Co. own a large spinning factory at Philiphaugh, and a complete tweed mill at Earlston, the latter managed by their partner, Mr. Dunn, also from Selkirk.

BRIDGEHAUGH MILL, built in 1865 by Messrs. Dobie and Richardson, is now in the hands of Messrs. Sellar & Co. Holds four setts carding and fifty looms.

CHEVIOT MILL, first started on a small scale, was slightly extended by Mr. James Bathgate from Galashiels, and now belongs to Messrs. Cochrane and Smith, both from Galashiels, the former a grandson of Adam Cochrane, gainer of a premium in 1788. For weaving only. Fifty-four looms.

ETTRICKVALE MILL is for spinning only, and contains four setts of carding engines. Owned by Messrs. George Anderson and Co. Built by Messrs. Scott and Anderson in 1872.

RIVERSIDE MILL, built in 1875 by Messrs. Gordon and Brydone, and afterwards held by W. H. Brydone and Co. For spinning only. Nine setts of carding engines. Purchased in 1884 by Mr. William Brown, formerly of Ettrick Mills.

On the other side of the river are Ettrickbank Mill, recently erected for weaving by Messrs. J. and R. W. Russell; and Burn Mill, a spinning establishment, belonging to Messrs. Cunningham and Hall.

Selkirk Market Place, 1837.

CHAPTER XIV.

SELKIRK GUILDRY BOOK.

AMONG the parchment-covered books preserved in the Town Hall safe is a " Register belonging to the Gildry of the burgh of Selkirk, bought and begun by Francis Scott, present Dean of Guild, anno 1721." Little of general interest is to be culled from its pages, which are mostly taken up with decisions of "the Dean and his brethren" anent boundaries and gables. From the frequency with which mention is made of houses that have fallen into ruin, it is clear that 200 years ago mason work was anything but substantial. Old houses which have survived till the present time, have at their demolition revealed a prevalent use of clay in place of lime. The guildry had jurisdiction over a variety of affairs. In 1728 they declared the Long Close a church-going road in spite of efforts made by John Curror, "Barron of Howden," to shut it up. Regulation of the food traffic was their peculiar care. On several occasions they seized and destroyed unsound meat, fining the offenders heavily, besides exposing their misdeeds at the Cross. When in 1732 the craft of fleshers tried to shirk part of their service, the Guildry compelled them to kill animals for any of the inhabitants when required (except Thursdays and Saturdays), the fees to be 6s. Scots for every nolt, and 4s. more for " braiking"; 2s. for a calf; 6s. for a sow ; 1s. for a sheep ; and 6d. for a lamb. One of their greatest difficulties was to keep the inhabitants from making a parade of dungheaps before their front-doors. So long ago as 1735 a sanitary prosecution was made of two men " for refusing to remove their dung from off the High Street;" but eleven years afterwards the nuisance again cropped up, " great abuse being committed by dung-middens lying on the street, particularly below the Cross and at the West Port." Upon the whole, no one reading this dusty volume, marking the frequent petty squabbles of neighbour burgesses, the selfish tyranny of the trades, and the unsavoury condition of the town, can fail to congratulate himself on living in better and sweeter times.

The Merchant Company.

Uncertainty hangs over the origin of this ancient Company. Though the designation occurs in the earliest records of the burgh, there is no means of ascertaining at what period the " merchants" were formed into a Corporation. In the reign of William the Lion (1165 to 1214), who appears to have been fond of Selkirk, and held several Parliaments there, it was ordained that " ye merchandis of ye realme sall haif yair merchand gilde;" and, bearing in mind the importance of Selkirk in those days, it may be supposed that its merchants were not slow to avail themselves of the Royal statute. At the same time there is no evidence that the Company was ever instituted a separate guild, as the crafts of cordiners, souters, weavers, and tailors were, early in the seventeenth century. The burgh records of that time are wanting, and the Company's papers neither include a seal of cause nor allude to one. Indeed, when, fully a hundred years later, in 1733, the Magistrates and Council heard that the merchants in the town were about to apply to the Royal Burghs at their next Convention to have themselves erected into a society, they appointed their commissioner to oppose any such design or application, as being oppressive to the inhabitants. The Company's oldest MS. is a "book pertaining to the loft, mortcloth, and rent annuals, with stock they (the merchants) have at this present 1694." Nothing could be less entertaining. Entries about payment of interest alternate with minutes of admission to the Company's seats in the kirk, which indeed seems to have been tantamount to becoming a member. No mention is made of a master or deacon, nor are there any signs of an election by the Company of the ten merchant burgesses who formed a constituent part of the Town Council. It is conclusive that the list with which the old book opens gives the names, not of the members of the Merchant Company, but " of those belonging to the merchants' loft in the kirk of Selkirk." The word " Company" does not occur in the minutes till May 1701. The loft was their sole bond of union, strengthened by the privileges of the mortcloth! In 1709, the merchants convened in their loft, and considering the exceeding troublesomeness of weavers, and especially country weavers, entering their own loft by the door of the Merchant Company's loft, resolve to stop them the very next Sunday. Ten years later it is enacted that " while any proprietors of the Company having right to any seat of the loft is alive (!), it shall not be in his power to allow any person to sit in his place in his absence, under penalty of such a fine as the Company shall think fit," and at the same meeting several inhabitants who " pack and peel with unfrie traders " are recommended to be prosecuted before the Dean of Guild and his brethren—all fines to be handed to the Company. They had the same partiality to flags which pervaded the five crafts, and put great store on the election of standard-bearer. When Archibald Waitt was elected to the responsible office in 1721, he was bound over to " give ane entertainment upon the Common-riding day to the value of 20s. sterling ;" and that it be " handsomely and gently done with," it is certified that " if he fayle in any part either in carrying ye standart or giveing ye entertainment, he shall lose his seat in the loft, his freedome of ye mortecloathe, and be extruded ye Companie." When their thesaurer made his yearly balance, he had delivered to him " the new mortecloath, with ye old litle and big mortecloath, also ye standart, stafe, and halbert." In 1736, it being found that several " upon frivolous excuses absent themselves from attending the standard-bearer upon Common-riding day, and particularly at dinner," it is resolved that in future offenders shall be fined 14s. Scots, the thesaurer to go to their houses and shops and poind for same in case of refusal, if a reasonable excuse is not sustained for absence. Evidently it was a matter in respect of which they could stand no trifling. At the founding of the new bridge designed to be built over Ettrick, on the 24th May 1739, the Company joined a procession of the

Magistrates, with the five deacons and their crafts, as at a Common-riding day, the only difference being that the standard-bearer was to officiate that day " gratis, and not be burdened with treating of the Company, unless what he pleases." The treasurer got *carte blanche* to disburse as much drink-money to the masons as any trade did, and to have music present. They could do handsomely in bestowing charity, too, at a time. In 1749 John Murray, or Candle John, a merchant, in great indigency, is by general consent endowed with the sum of £4 Scots (6s. 8d. sterling) to buy a horse for travelling the country for the maintenance of himself and family. It was an anxious time for the merchants of Selkirk when the building of a new kirk in 1749 rendered necessary negotiations with the Town Council about a new loft, and it was only after many meetings and much hesitation that a seat was finally condescended upon. At a meeting in 1754, it was carried by a vast majority that 40s. sterling be taken out of the funds to aid in " consulting lawyers for making trial at the General Assembly for stoppage of Mr. Trotter being our minister at Selkirk." In 1759, 20s. is given to help build the bridge at Yair. A minute of 13th November 1769 empowers the treasurer " to take six yards of velvet and to line it with a black shaloun, and put a black ribbon round it, and make the old mortcloth in a poke for to had the new one." The Company always possessed a reserve fund, the amount of which fluctuated considerably. Its income was derived from seat-rents, mortcloth fees, and interest, and the expenditure was mostly in careful and judicious benevolence. Of all the ancient guilds it alone survives as a corporate body, numbering as many as seventy members, with a capital fund of about £140. Its functions now are largely social.

THE INCORPORATION OF WEAVERS.

Fortunately, the records of this ancient craft have been so well preserved, that it would be possible to give a succinct account of nearly every meeting and every act since it was first formed in 1608. A little before that date the wabsters within the burgh appear to have become convinced of the desirability of having officers of their own to decide disputes and protect the trade from outsiders. With this view they procured copies of two documents (1603 and 1606), emanating from the webster craft of Edinburgh, setting forth its own constitution, and exhorting the deacon and masters of the same craft in Peebles to fortify the freemen thereof, and put their seal of cause to due and lawful execution against contemners. Armed with these, the websters of

Selkirk applied for like privileges; and on the 13th May 1608 were granted a seal of cause or charter by the Bailies and Town Council. This document is still extant, with the burgh seal attached, in perfect preservation. Its preamble is highly impressive—

To all and sundry whom it effeirs, to whose knowledge these presents shall come, the Provost, Bailies, and Council of the burgh of Selkirk, greeting in God—We make it known that there compeirit before us in our Tolbooth of Selkirk, when sitting in judgement, the best and worthiest persons of the haill craft of websters within the said burgh, whilk presentit to us ane humble supplication, where was containit certain statutes and articles made deviseable baith for the honour of God and for the common weal of this burgh and country, and common benefit and security of the craftsmen, and for other divers causes of good motive, all whilk we have heard, seen, and caused be read, and therewith being reiply advised and considered, and to have our benevolent affirmance and licence thereof, and to have our affirmation and ratification of same in so far as may be necessary to have, Considered the desire and statutes, and finds them consonant to religion, worthy to God, and profit to the common weal of our community and craft, and therefore agree," etc. Article I. authorises the election of a deacon by such freemen of the craft as are also burgesses. II. No weaver to be a master unless examined by the deacon and craft "gif he be worthy and have sufficient graith and wark looms to work upon"—fee thirty shillings Scots and the price of twa pund wax. III. No apprentice for less than five years—fee five shillings Scots, or as he can treat with the craft. IV. No master to take another's apprentice under pain of ten shillings, one pund wax, and restoration of apprentice. A few more rules and penalties are followed by a clause imposing a protective duty of one penny per week on outland websters, to be paid to the burgh craft. The Council then grants to the said craftsmen the liberty that their brethren have obtained in Edinburgh, Dundee, Johnstone, or Peebles, and finds that their statutes are "laudable to God and Holy Congregation, honourable for all the realm, and profitable to the craft." (Signed), GEORGE HALIWELL. GEORGE MITCHELHILL, Provost. JAMES SCOTT, Bailie. GEORGE MITCHELHILL, Bailie.

Though inaugurated under such favourable auspices, the corporation had not enjoyed many years' existence when foreign competition threatened to undo it entirely. On the 29th March 1616, the Council met and threw the ægis of its protection over the infant craft whose birth it had registered with so much magniloquence eight years before. After setting forth the deserts of the craft in respect of its watching and warding when called, its paying stent and all other portable charges whenever imposed either by the kirk-session or the lawful Magistrate, its having to serve all our sovereign lord's lieges in weaving all their yarn, both linen and wool, upon as easy prices as any others within the realm, the Council declares it entitled to protection against the suburban wabsters, who are subject to no such charges. It is declared that the latter wax great, opulent, and rich, while the freemen of the craft within the burgh, by the contrar daily decrease in number and substance, being "almaist not habile to provide for their own private familys." Then follow threats of punishment to all who encourage the landwart unfreemen, and to the latter themselves if caught within half-a-mile of the ports, liberties, and walls of the burgh. This underselling by outsiders continued to be a thorn in the side of the wabsters' craft, for we come upon certificates of proclamation of this Act of Council on the 6th April 1667, 14th February 1671, 8th February 1691, 20th February 1701, and 8th December 1707—after crying of three several " oh yes's," and with tuck of drum.

From 1615 to 1751 the sederunt-book records little save an endless succession of elections and admissions, with now and then an occasional squabble. In 1751 the acquisition of a new minute-book seems to have stirred the craft into new life. Stringent regulations are made by way of thwarting "attempts likely to be made by unfreemen to set up as weavers within the burgh." No apprentices recognised but those who serve six years with a burgess freeman, and every freeman entering to purchase a seat in the weavers' loft in the kirk of Selkirk. The price of a seat in the first pew is £9 Scots ; in the second, £7 ; in the third, £5 ; and in the fourth, £3. In 1761 the Corporation gives a subscription of £1 sterling towards building a new bridge over Tweed at Fairnalee.

A spirit of self-assertion begins to manifest itself in 1789, when a resolution is carried that in important matters such as the election of a member of Parliament, the craft's delegates to the Town Council, the deacon and his colleague (generally spelt " collick " in early MSS.), shall confer with the " haill body " before coming to a decision. The object of this move becomes patent from an entry in the accounts of £2 " saved from the six guineas by the candidate to treat the trade, after allowing the deacon's profits."

The old acts having become so dimmed by age that they cannot well be read, new acts are drawn up and declared to be binding on 7th February 1791. Prosaic enough for the most part, they throw some light upon the mysteries of initiation. Stress is put on the regular payment of 1s. 6d. as the " speaking drink " by the master, and of 3s. as the " binding drink " by the intended apprentice. For a freeman's son the entrance-fee is 10 merks ; if only a burgess's son, 15 merks ; and if neither, 18 merks—in ready money or approved bill ! When a freeman is entered he has dues to pay, also in cash or approved bill, besides four shillings (" one shilling " significantly erased) for " booking drink." Act XII. relates to "reasoning at the meetings," which are to be " carried on with calmness. None shall be allowed to curse or swear any kind of profane oath in his discourse, and one member shall not call another bad names." Considering the determined way in which the drink tributes appear to have been levied, the propriety of Act XII. cannot well be gainsaid. Bad yarn, the subject of Act XV., is treated with proper solemnity, the language becoming almost scriptural—" When a freeman in the trade chances to have a web of very bad yarn, he shall call the deacon and quarter-masters, who shall judge the web, and if it can be woven they shall fix the price for weaving it ; but if the yarn be so very bad that it cannot be woven, then they shall condemn it, and their condemnation shall be holden a sufficient excuse for refusing to weave the web." The new code winds up with a fierce attack on interlopers from without the burgh, who are again threatened with imprisonment in the Tolbooth, "there to be condignly punished."

A little later, at a special meeting held for the purpose, it was decreed that at the dinner on Common-riding day, every man should pay 2s.—eightpence for dinner and dinner-drink, the remaining sixteenpence to be drunk. " Oh, monstrous ! but one halfpenny-worth of bread to this intolerable deal of sack." Even apprentices had to pay in this Falstaffian proportion—sixpence for dinner and dinner-drink, with sixpence more for drink only.

The sale in 1807 of the bleachfield yard and house, lying at Selkirk Mills, seems to indicate the decline of linen-weaving. The trade got forty guineas for the property, and the same year the deacon was presented with a cane to walk with at the Common-riding. In 1809 there were twenty-two members of the Corporation, which appears to have remained almost dormant for about twenty years thereafter. In 1830 they begin to show signs of animation. Partaking the national excitement, they send to Parliament a vigorous petition in favour of reform, municipal, commercial, and Parliamentary, declaring their adherence to the ballot. In curious unmindfulness of their own exclusive laws, they launch out with great bitterness against ruinous monopolies. Preserved with other papers is an acknowledgment of the petition, written by Mr. Joseph Hume's secretary, wrapped in a cover franked by the great economist himself. This was the last articulate utterance of the Weavers' Corporation. At Michaelmas 1832, the deacon and other officers were elected as usual ; but the next entry is in July 1863, when the last four survivors attest the reception as freeman, and election to the diaconate, of James B. Brown, Esq. By "the last of the deacons," the books and documents of the ancient craft have been carefully collected, the tattered leaves of the first sederunt-book being now in a new and handsome quarto, likely to preserve them as lon as paper and ink can hold out against the " inexorable foot of Time." With other effects, there passed into Mr. Brown's hands the tattered remnant of an old flag, said to have been taken by the Selkirk men at Flodden. It is nowhere mentioned in the early records of the craft, the first notice of a flag being in 1796, when it is agreed that each member shall carry "the colour" as he comes into the Corporation, and that no member shall cast the colour round his head to the damage of the colour, under fine of five shillings sterling. The following is a list of deacons since 1617, the loss of nine leaves of the first sederunt-book rendering the names of the deacons from 1608 to 1616 unascertainable. The deacon in 1610 is a witness of the tailors' seal of cause. The date given is the year of election, the time being almost invariably at Michaelmas.

1610. William Dalgleish.	1680. William Fletcher.	1734. Henry Buxton.
1617. Adam Lamb.	1681. Robert Fletcher.	1737. William Dalgleish.
1618. Walter Gowanlocke.	1682. James Dalgleis.	1739. James Simpson.
1619. John Dalgleis.	1684. Walter Dalgleis.	1741. Thomas Dickson.
1622. James Melros.	1685. Robert Fletcher.	1742. James Simpson.
1623. Michael Cathie.	1689. James Kein.	1743. Patrick Fletcher.
1626. John Dalgleis.	1691. James Dalgleish.	1744. John Emond.
1628. James Kein.	1693. James Kein.	1745. William Dalgleish.
1630. Andrew Shortreid.	1695. James Dalgleish.	1747. Thos. Dickson.
1632. Michael Cathie.	1697. Walter Reidfurd.	1749. James Simpson.
1634. James Kein.	1698. James Dalgleish.	1751. William Heatlie.
1635. John Fletcher.	1699. Walter Reidfoord.	1753. Walter Brown.
1636. James Kein.	1701. James Dalgleish.	1755. Robert Lees.
1637. Michael Cathie.	1703. Walter Reidford.	1757. Patrick Fletcher.
1639. Andrew Shortreid.	1705. James Dalgleish.	1759. Robert Orr.
1643. William Fletcher.	1707. Robert Fletcher.	1761. Walter Brown.
1644. James Kein.	1709. John Fletcher.	1763. George Orr.
1648. William Fletcher.	1711. Robert Fletcher.	1765. John Emond.
1649. James Kein.	1713. John Fletcher.	1767. William Heatlie.
1650. Andrew Shortreid.	1715. Robert Fletcher.	1769. Robert Lees.
1653. James Kein.	1716. John Fletcher.	1771. Andrew Murray.
1658. Patrick Fletcher.	1717. William Kein.	1773. Robert Orr.
1665. Walter Gowanlocke.	1719. Geo. Melross.	1775. Patrick Emond.
1666. James Dalgleis.	1721. William Kein.	1777. Andrew Heatlie.
1668. Patrick Fletcher.	1723. John Fletcher.	1779. John Emond.
1671. James Dalgleis.	1724. Thomas Chisholm.	1781. Robert Orr.
1672. Patrick Fletcher.	1726. Adam Simpson.	1783. James Murray.
1674. James Dalgleis.	1728. Geo. Melross.	1785. William Dobson.
1676. Patrick Fletcher.[1]	1730. William Kein.	1787. John Orr.
1678. James Dalgleis.	1732. William Dalgleish.	1789. Andrew Brown.

[1] In Selkirk churchyard the tombstone of this deacon runs as follows :—"Heier lyas Patrick Fletcher, Deicon of the Viveres, vho deseised vpon the 2 of Desember 1675. His age was 59 years."

1791. John Bell (refused office).	1804. William Lauder.	1819. William Lauder.
1792. Andrew Heatlie.	1806. James Chisholme.	1820. James Chisholm.
1794. Robert Chisholm.	1807. William Lauder.	1822. James Inglis.
1796. Patrick Emond.	1808. Andrew Brown.	1824. Ebenezer Brunton.
1798. James Murray.	1810. Walter Dickson.	1826. James Ritchie.
1799. Walter Dixon.	1812. William Lauder.	1828. Elliot Scott.
1800. John Scott.	1814. William Heatlie.	1830. William Chisholm.
1801. Patrick Emond.	1816. James Murray.	1832. Andrew Brown, sen.
1802. John Scott.	1818. Andrew Brown.	1863. James B. Brown.
1803. James Turnbull.		

The Incorporation of Shoemakers.

"Souters ane, souters twa,
Souters in the Back Raw."
Old Rhyme.

Although it was not till 1609 that the souters of Selkirk obtained a seal of cause entitling them to the privileges of a craft of guild, their industry was of very ancient date. When all skins of animals slain in the Royal Forest were sent to Selkirk to be tanned by the King's skinner, some of them, no doubt, were made into shoes and gauntlets. And that the skinner, of whose existence there is documentary evidence, was also a souter, is evident from a statute of guild (thirteenth century) prohibiting "souters" from tanning hides of which the horns and ears are not of equal length. A papal confirmation in the book of Kelso Abbey informs us that in the time of Alexander III. there was a Sutorcroft at Selkirk, and though it is not now recognisable under that name, a retour of 1574 in favour of Walter Scott of Buccleuch enables us to fix its whereabouts with tolerable certainty. It must have been somewhere between Faldonside and Bridgelands, part of the lands transferred with the Abbey from Selkirk to Kelso. Thus as early as the thirteenth century there was a "souter of Selkirk," with a croft of his own, to boot. Probably tanning in early times was superficial, for when the English explored Bruce's deserted camp, after his havoc-working descent upon Northumberland, they came upon some thousand pairs of shoes, made, according to Froissart, of raw hide. In 1426, an agreement was come to between John Brydinson and Thomas Robinson, souters in the town of Selkirk, and the Abbot of Melrose, where- L. M., by the latter let to the former a tenement lying on the north side of the town of Selkirk, with a croft of three acres pertaining to it, with liberty of tanning (*barcandi*), and all other freedoms within the said town, the first year for 10s., the second year for 13s. 4d., in consideration of building the said tenement within two years, and thereafter for 32s. each year, at Whitsunday and Martinmas. "And it is to be understood that the said abbot and monks who shall happen to come to the said town shall have a sufficient lodging chamber and stable in the foresaid tenement, which, after the life of the said Thomas and John, shall freely revert to the said monastery. In witness whereof, the seal of the monastery is set to that part of the indenture remaining with the said John and Thomas; and to the other part remaining with the Abbot, the common seal of the said town, procured by the said John and Thomas." And

E. R.,
v. 312. it is noticeable that in 1448, one Thomas of Selkirk was sent in charge of hides to Flanders. It is not apparent that the large supply of forest leather led to the establishment of an extensive business. Selkirk was no place for the prosecution of a peaceful industry. Lost, recaptured, burnt, sacked, and harried every few years, it never had time to prosper or increase; and when Queen Mary stopped the selling of leather furth of the realm on account of the "butis, schone, and uther apparalingis made thereof" having become too dear, eighteen royal burghs were specified for the proclamation, while no notice whatever was taken of Selkirk. Yet in 1519 it was considered worth recording in the Burgh Books of Council, that Richard Young had agreed to receive John Brown in prenticeship to the craft of cordinership for the space of nine years; and in 1601 Acts and Statutes drawn up by the craft, for its "awin weill, commodity, and profit," were signed by seven-and-twenty masters, many of whom must have had to seek buyers outside the town. In 1609, one year after passing of an Act empowering gentlemen of the shire and burgh magistrates to fix the price of boots and shoes twice a year, the souters obtained a charter, in which by the title of the "Craft of Cordiners," they were duly incorporated under hand of the Bailies and Council. The name cordiners, or cordwainers, is derived, through the French, from cordovan, a kind of leather specially adapted for shoes, and first prepared in the Spanish town of Cordova. The term "souter" appears to have been considered ignominious, if not opprobrious, and does not once occur in the voluminous minutes or numerous papers of the craft. Hogg based a humorous story on this sensitiveness to the name of Souter, and in 1663 an Act of Parliament was actually passed authorising certain of the name of Souter to change it for their true and ancient name of Johnston. It was alleged by the petitioners that their ancestor, fleeing from Annandale to Perthshire in 1460, had sought obscurity under the surname of "Souter," an appellation which two hundred years had not endeared to his descendants.

Shoemaking obtained its title of the "gentle craft" from two brother princes, Crispin and Crispinianus, early converts to Christianity, who went about preaching the glad tidings during day, and maintaining themselves by making boots and shoes at night, until their martyrdom on 25th October 287. Their English historian Deloney, who wrote in 1678, says this story explains the saying, "A shoemaker's son is a prince born," and justifies the couplet—

"The gentle craft is fittest then
For poor distressed gentlemen."

At the hands of the armies which one after another obtained possession of Selkirk, its peaceable and industrious souters suffered great hardship. In 1651 the kirk-session of Stow rebuked certain persons for having resetted shoes stolen by Cromwell's soldiers and the mosstroopers who followed them north. When the Pretender's army lay near Kelso in 1715, a party was despatched to Selkirk, and by force required shoes from the Incorporation, under the alternative of sending forthwith a party of Highlanders to plunder. "To prevent this inconveniency and abuse, the Magistrates, with the deacons of guild, did meet and find it absolutely necessary to comply with the request." Orders were given to the cordiners to provide and make as many shoes as they could in such a short time, and if they got no payment, the burgh should pay them. Accordingly eleven score pairs of single-soled shoes were furnished and carried to Kelso and Jedburgh, where the Highlanders lay. No payment having been received, a stent was ordained on all burgesses and inhabitants for £154 Scots, the value of the shoes. On 10th March 1716, the deacon and office-bearers of the souters gave oath that the shoes taken by compulsion of Lord Kenmuir and Brigadier M'Intosh of Borlum were each pair worth 1s. 2d. sterling. Gratitude for being delivered from Highland plunder appears not to have been a lively emotion in some of the towns-people, for in 1720, the stent officers being threatened with an action by the shoemakers for payment of shoes taken by rebels in 1715, they were empowered to poind the goods of such burgesses as had not paid the stent. When, thirty years afterwards, the second Rebellion occurred, the Selkirk souters found Prince Charlie's little finger thicker than his father's loin. On the 21st September 1745, a letter arrived from the deacon of the shoe-makers in Edinburgh, that their town was under contribution to supply the Highland Army in 6000 pair of shoes, and entreating Selkirk to assist with 2000 pair, or what less number the place could afford. The Council resolved to indemnify the souters for any loss; and when on the 24th, a repeat order came for 300 or 400 pairs, a similar guarantee was given. Strange to say, there is no record whatever of how or by whom the shoes were this time paid for.

As good luck will have it, the archives of this famous society are tolerably complete. Hid in a dirty old sheepskin bag, they were rescued when on the point of being consigned to the rubbish cart; and now both minute-books and documents, carefully arranged and bound, may be seen by the curious in the writer's possession. They are complete from 1609 to 1844. Examining them, one is impressed with nothing so much as the preposterous proportion of revenue spent in drink. For one sixpence of ordinary expenditure they spent three on ale.

> Sometimes they get drunk, and sometimes they do not,
> But the business of drinking is seldom forgot ;
> They drink when they're merry, they drink when they're sad,
> They drink whensoever good drink's to be had.

Witness the following bill at a poinding of skins in 1727 :—

	lbs.	s.	d.
In Baylie Haine's befor and eftir for drink,	00	12	00
in Baylie Ellott's,	00	6	00
To the officers for poynding,	00	14	00
„ burlawmen,	00	13	04
„ nottar,	00	12	00
More, a double gill of brandie,	00	06	00
In Wm. Dobson's for 4 pynts of aill,	00	08	00
In Baylie Ellott's,	00	12	00
	04	03	04

Although the seal of cause itself has disappeared, a copy engrossed in the second minute-book supplies its place, recording the familiar inflated preamble, followed by statutes, plain, practical, and severely protectionist. It was provided—

That every disobedient person to deacon be committed to prison by order of the Magistrate, and there remain until he give full satisfaction. That no man shall be accepted freeman until he shows his burgess ticket, and pays for freedom and liberty such a sum as can be agreed upon, conform to other deacon and quarter-masters within the burgh. That the deacon and quarter-masters sworn for the time shall take an exact trial of all sort of work, as made shoon or barked leather—the same if found insufficient to be escheat, one-half to the King's use, and the other half to the use of the trade. That none be admitted freeman until after an apprenticeship of five years and one year for meat, "sic as usse is." That no unfreeman buy bark either upon the market-day, or off the same, unless he be freeman or burgess of another burgh. That every servant who can make shoon for the market get £8 Scots yearly and two pair of shoes in fee, the second sort £6 and two pair, and the third sort, that have but passed their apprenticeship, six merks. These all bear date 1609, and the following were enacted between that date and 1690 :—That no servant shall leave his master's work in gaming or drinking but he shall pay the sum of 40s. for each break. "That no person shall abusse on another beffor the deacon and quarter-masters under the paine of eight shill., or to speak ireverently to the p'nt deacon and q'mrs, w'out live asked and given." That none of the said members endeavour or presume to wrong or prejudge (prejudice ?) his neighbour, or any of the said trade, at home or abroad, in buying and getting any sort of ware. That if any person will not give to the deacon obedience and satisfaction conform to their transgression committed, but is necessitate to go to the Magistrates, then and in that case whatever expense he shall put on the deacon, he is hereby ordained by the whole trade to pay it.

In 1626, it was "votit, enactit, and statutit be the deacon, q'msters, and haill brethren of the s^d craft, that whensoever any young man newlie admittit a brother and freeman of the same takes up a buith of his awin, to his awin use, it shall in nowyse be lawfull nor leasum to him to indent with ane or more prentises for the space of sievin years next following his uptaking of his awin buith, in na manner of way," under the penalty of 50 merks.

On the 4th May 1628, one John Lidderdale was declared by the deacon and office-bearers to have been "thir tua yeir bygane ane disobedient person, and ane breiker of his aith maid to the craft, and that he still remains obstinat in doing all thyngis contrarie to the weill of the craft in all respects ; . . . and further, that contrair his aith he feyd this present yeir the decone his fey'd servant, callit Wm. Thomsone, sone to umquhyll James Thomsone, quhisler, and cotemptuouslie keipis him cōtrair the haill craftis will, and still trubbilis the haill craft." Also they declare that he has "keipit in his companie, and kept as servants in his house, Wat Hunter, ane approwen theiff and steiller of craft's lether." And the same day, "having considderat that James Thomsone, brother to the said Wm. Thomson, hes purchest and learnit his craft for Godis saik amang the haill craft, as God movit their hartis, and now is becum abill to mak service to any honest man for meill and fie : THEREFORE, they decrie and ordain the said James to fie himself in service with any frieman of the craft where he best pleisses, for sick fie and bounteth as he can maist comodiouslie get."

This is the only instance in which the rigid rules of the craft appear to have been laid aside at the bidding of humanity ; but young men serving as soldiers for the burgh were often admitted freemen without having gone through all the stages. In May 1645, just two months before the battle of Philiphaugh, John Douglas, William Thorbrand, and Robert Walker were so admitted ; and in 1648, Alexander Young, "conditionalie he do not flie, nor run away fra his cullor w^{t}out a pass of his captain." According to Elliot and Scott's MS. account of the shire there were "many souters in Selkirk" in 1649.

Amongst the most interesting entries are those relating to the preparation of skins for shoe leather. The ease with which these could be abstracted from pits rendered necessary the severest penalties against theft. In 1705, one James Ker confessed reset and use of certain hides stolen by Robert Johnston from William Finlaw and James Douglas, thereby putting himself under pain of forfeiting all he possessed, and under pain of death. He was banished for ever from the town and shire. About 1620, English tanners from Chester-le-Street and other towns were brought to Scotland under royal patronage to teach the Scotch their better system. So difficult was it to get the tanners throughout the country to adopt the new mode, and leave off their old practice of letting the leather remain but a short time in the pits, that some of them were proclaimed rebels by way of example.

Various and elaborate contracts were entered into for supply of bark. In 1714, with Robert Elliot of Middlemylne and Robert Paterson of Drygrange, tacksmen of the haill woods on Ettrick belonging to Walter Scott of Harden, for the "haill birk bark" of the said woods. Oak by that time appears to have disappeared from the Forest, for in 1718 the trade bargained for all the oak bark cut in Craigieburn Wood. In 1724, a merchant in Langholm undertook to let them have "five score bolls of oak bark at 14s. sterling per boll, Selkirk measure, hand-waled; that is to say, a little above the wood of the measure, but no heaping."

Owing to the first three leaves of the sederunt-book being lost, and the fourth much dilapidated, the list of deacons from 1609 to 1616 is imperfect; but the following roll is complete from 1616 to 1844, in which year was held the last minuted meeting of the Corporation :—

1617. John Smail.	1638. Robert Curror.	1658. William Dun.
1618. Andro Dobie.	1641. John Mudie.	1661. Thomas Curror.
1619. William Nicoll.	1643. Robert Curror.	1664. Andro Dobie.
1621. John Lidderdale.	1644. John Lidderdale.	1667. John Lidderdale.
1623. William Nicoll.	1646. John Smail.	1669. Robert Smail.
1625. Robert Dun.	1649. Robert Curror.	1671. Andrew Angus.
1627. John Mudie.	1650. William Smail.	1673. John Lidderdale.
1629. William Nicoll.	1653. John Mynto.	1675. Andrew Angus.
1631. Robert Dun.	1654. William Smail.	1677. Robert Smail.
1633. John Lidderdale.	1655. Robert Curror.	1679. John Lidderdale.
1637. Robert Dun.	1657. William Turnbull.	1681. Andrew Angus.

1683. John Smail.
1685. John Curror.
1687. Andrew Angus.
1688. William Smail.
1691. John Curror.
1693. William Smail.
1695. William Lidderdale.
1697. John Curror.
1699. William Smail.
1701. John Curror.
1703. Thomas Curror, elder (*alias* Fairport).
1705. Thomas Curror, yr.
1707. Thomas Curror, elder.
1709. John Curror, elder.
1711. Thomas Curror, elder.
1713. Thomas Curror, yr.
1714. Michael Mitchelhill.
1716. William Smail.
1718. Thomas Curror (Fairport).
1720. James Fairbairn.
1722. William Johnston.
1725. Thomas Curror, yr.
1726. Robert Thorbrand.
1727. John Blackhall.
1729. James Fairbairn.
1731. Robert Thorbrand.
1733. Andrew Laidlaw.

1735. Thomas Curror, yr.
1737. William Douglas.
1739. Andrew Moody.
1741. William Douglas.
1742. Walter Gowanlock.
1744. Thomas Curror, younger, Townhead.
1745. Walter Scott.
1747. James Fairbairn.
1749. Thomas Inglis.
1751. James Gowanlock.
1753. Thomas Inglis.
1755. John Fairbairn.
1757. Andrew Mitchelhill.
1759. John Curror.
1761. James Gray.
1763. Andrew Gowanlock.
1765. William Thomson.
1767. John Blackhall.
1769. John Forsyth.
1771. Andrew Mitchelhill.
1773. Alexander Inglis.
1775. Patrick Tait.
1777. George Mitchelhill.
1778. Andrew Mercer.
1781. William Stevenston.
1783. Patrick *or* Peter Tait.
1785. Alexander Inglis, sen.

1787. Alexander Dobson.
1789. John Curror *or* Currie.
1791. James Inglis.
1793. William Shortreid.
1795. John Tudhope.
1797. Robert Gray.
1799. John Melross.
1800. Alexander Dobson.
1801. John Anderson, jun.
1804. Thomas Inglis.
1805. William Douglas.
1807. William Jameson.
1810. John Anderson, jun.
1812. James Robertson.
1814. James Inglis.
1816. Thomas Inglis.
1818. William Douglas.
1820. Thomas Inglis.
1821. William Scott, jun.
1823. John Melross.
1825. James Hislop.
1827. James Ruthven.
1828. George Turnbull.
1830. Andrew Melrose.
1832. James Scott, sen.
1834-5. James Hislop.
1836-43. A blank.
1844. James Scott.

In 1707 the souters received their share of the equivalent granted to Scotland at the Union by way of reparation for England's part in ruining the Scots Indian and African Company. Smitten with the prevailing rage for speculation, the burgh had in 1695-6 subscribed £500 sterling, the cordiners having indorsed the town books for £34 of that sum. Of this, only one-third really belonged to the trade, the other two-thirds being the property of deacons John Curror and William Lidderdale. The share of the equivalent which fell to each third part was £82, 2s. 8d. Scots (£6, 16s. 10d. sterling). As the equivalent was based on the sum lost, with interest added at rate of five per cent., it would appear that not more than half of the sum subscribed had been paid up.

For thirteen years at the beginning of last century the office of deacon appears to have been monopolised by the Currors, a well-to-do family, whose name emerges frequently not only in the burgh but also in the county records of this period. Immediately after the termination of their reign, a resolution was come to which seems to point to self-seeking on their part. " Considering the great inconvenience that frequently happens and falls out by one, two, or more buying bark for their own proper use, and not communicating the bargain to the Incorporation, so that all may have a share, and that such bargains tend many times to the oppression of the poorer part, and being now resolved to do justice as well to the poor as to the rich, it is hereby ordained that whatever member shall buy bark above three bolls, he shall, within eight days, make offer of the said bargain for the use and behoof of the whole members, a particular answer to be given in three days if or if not the Incorporation is to receive the said bargain."

Another aggravating abuse, dealt with at a meeting held in February 1715, illustrates a weakness inherent in all systems of trade combination. " The Incorporation taking to their serious consideration the great complaints and abuses committed by several members, that when they go to markets they take some by-roads, and serve the country both in selling and couping their shoes, which is very prejudicial both to the members and markets they would frequent, if not served by such an irregular practice ; and, likeways, there are another sort of members that goes to the country and cobbles and mends shoes, and under the colour and pretext thereof, both takes new shoes along with them to sell, either to coupers or any others they can bargain with, and also when they are in houses they fall on and make shoes either of new leather or of old leather, such as boots or the like ; and for remeid thereof that such unjustifiable abuses be not committed in all time coming, it is ordained that no person whatsomever, whether by excuse they may have to go to their acquaintance for free quarters or the like that they may have, when they go to market are hereby discharged that they take no by-roads for the increase of such evil practices,—such as go to Peebles, no other way but by the Quair and up the whole water-side, or through the Ridge ; and alike to all markets, no other way nor the King's highway is to be used or hereby allowed."

A noteworthy bond, dated 11th April 1719 : " I, James Thomson, binds and obliges me myself, being prentice to Thomas Dobson, that I shall never follow the cordiner trade within the kingdom of Scotland, unless within the town of Selkirk, under the pain of £100 Scots."

That such rules were not always put in force without resistance, appears from a petition to the Convention of Royal Burghs in 1720. Five shoemakers had refused obedience to an act anent apprentice dues, and appealed to the four other deacons, who decided against them. An appeal to the Council ending the same way, the five craved redress from the Justices of the Peace; but finding their seals of cause were like to be torn to pieces at the first court, the deacons were obliged to raise declarator to stop the Justices from further procedure, and to ask the Convention to support them in defence of their just rights and privileges. Some notion of the excitement caused by this disruption is obtained from a minute dated 21st April 1719, wherein the disobedient members are styled "dissenting, contumacious, and vexatious brethren, bent on stirring up greater flame among the trades, with no less design than to ruin and rend the Incorporation, to satisfy their malicious and inveterate humours." Such a bad effect had this quarrel, that in January 1720 the Town Council deemed it necessary to rebuke the craft for neglect of its proper business, in not having shoes sufficient to supply the markets, to the manifest oppression of the lieges.

In 1722, it is stated to have been the constant practice and custom of the trade yearly, upon the 26th day of December, being St. Stephen's day, to cause warn the whole servants therein, who are not settled and hired with their masters, to come by eleven o'clock of that day to the Knowhead of Selkirk, in order to their choicing a master. This comes to light in dealing with a member having both an apprentice and whole servant working to him, "which when servants are scarce (as at present) was never allowed." In an indenture bearing same date, William Forsyth, double-soled shoemaker, obliges himself never to teach James Hunter, his apprentice, or any apprentice he shall thereafter have, the single-soled shoemaker trade; and the apprentice binds himself never to make single-soled shoes, under penalty of £20 Scots.

1727.—The deacon in future to consult the brethren before giving an important vote in the Council. In 1742 he is deprived of the choice of his colleague in the Council.

1736.—At a meeting to consider whether the trade should remain idle at Yule as heretofore, it was resolved to sit idle betwixt Yule and eight days before Fastern's Even in all time coming—the act to be observed by all members, under penalty of five merks.

No less than eight boxmasters' accounts not having been cleared in 1762, it was resolved to divide the funds amongst such members as had been admitted seven or more years before.

An action having been raised (1765) against James Melrose, shoemaker at Lauriston (the name of a suburb on the Ettrick Road), to desist from his trade within the privileges of the burgh, in regard he is neither a burgess nor freeman of the craft, James gives in. On condition the process is stopped, he undertakes to pay all expenses, and four shillings yearly for permission to follow his calling.

The trade's standard being much torn and worn out, the officers are empowered to provide a new one out of the funds. At this time (1765) the standard was different from the flag now in use, and formally "cast" on Common-riding day. In the upper half two hovering cupids supported a royal crown, surmounted by a scroll bearing the words, "Up wi' the Souters o' Selkirk," and having below two hands in friendly grasp, with the appropriate motto, "True to the Last." The lower half of the flag was occupied by

The Souters' Halbert.

a group representing a shoemaker measuring a lady's foot. His countenance is said to have shown every evidence of admiration, which found vent in a line of Solomon's Song, "How beautiful are thy feet with shoes, O prince's daughter!" They seem to have used up their flags with considerable rapidity, as in 1791 they paid John Yellowlees, Edinburgh, £5, 10s. for another stand of colours painted on six yards of "rich white lutestring," at 5s. the yard. This, again, has been superseded by a new one from Mackenzie, painter in Selkirk. Besides their flag, the shoemakers, as well as the other crafts, boasted a halbert. It carried an inscription, "God bless the King and the gentile tread." On state occasions the deacon carried a handsome cane mounted with a silver top, on which was engraved the motto, "Up wi' the Souters o' Selkirk." The halbert, deacon's staff, and a late deacon's horn snuff-box, shaped like a boot, are in possession of the writer.

The following advertisement is from the *British Chronicle* (published at Kelso) of 27th April 1792.

"NOTICE TO THE PUBLIC.—The shoemakers of Selkirk beg leave to give this public notice, that on account of the high advanced price of leather of all kinds, they will be obliged consequently to raise the price of shoes. Several kinds of leather have risen a third and other kinds 20 per cent., which is well known to all dealers in that article, so that the shoemakers are unable to serve their customers at their former prices; when the price of leather falls again, they will with great pleasure lower the price of shoes in proportion. Credit is now so short on leather, the shoemakers hope their customers will order payment of their accounts more early than formerly."

Mention has been made of an annual rendezvous of the shoemaker servants at the Knowhead. It would appear the craft had a house there, for in 1785 they put it in thorough repair and let it to William Shortreid for 14s. *per annum*. In the north gable of Abbotsford a sculptured tablet has been built, which, in the absence of positive evidence, may be conjectured to have come from this guild-house of the shoemakers. Above it Sir Walter has placed a new stone bearing the motto of the craft, a sword, and the meaningless date of 1525—probably a misreading of 1535, the date of Hodge's apocryphal story about King James. The mason has also substituted A.B. for A.D.—*anno domini*. In the old tablet, the principal emblem is a crescent-shaped implement used by leather-workers.

Souters' Stone at Abbotsford.

Two years later there is an item of £2, 12s. 6d. paid to William Rule for painting the loft in church. This must have been a reproduction, on a front panel, ot the "Prince's daughter" getting her foot measured, a picture which had ultimately to be painted out because it enticed the minds of worshippers away from the sermon. According to a casual note in the old book, the following motto was upon the forebreast of the shoemakers' old loft in the church :—

> Tradesmen, so long as you do live,
> Honour to your Creator give,
> Who of His goodness thought it fit
> To bless your hands and workmanship.

———

> "Serve the Lord with uprightness."

In 1800 a famine led to the disappearance of nearly all the accumulated funds. Oatmeal being £4 per boll, peasemeal, £3, 4s., and barley-meal, £2, 16s., a sum of £34 was lifted on 20th February, in order to reduce these prices to freemen, journeymen, and widows of the craft. By May 5 all the £34 had gone, and prices had risen to £6 for oatmeal, barley and pease, £4, and flour-meal, £5 sterling per boll. "In order to preserve lives which seem to be in danger," other £30 was authorised to be lifted.

By way of fixing a date in the history of freemasonry within the burgh, it may be noted that in 1816 the souters permitted their flag to be used at laying the foundation-stone of the Lodge on 4th June.

For some time previous to 1818, the members had passed several statutes with the object of transferring to their whole body the privileges enjoyed by the deacon and his colleague as Town Councillors in electing a Member of Parliament. It is no great breach of charity to suppose that desire to have a share in certain bribes given by candidates had something to do with the matter; and one may estimate at handsome figures the unanimity with which the trade instructs Deacon Inglis and colleague Dobson to support William Maxwell, Esq. of Carriden, against Sir John Riddell, Bart., of Riddell. In 1820 Deacon Douglas got into sad grief over a parliamentary election. Instead of voting for Mr. Pringle of Haining, "the late member and candidate of independent principles," as he had promised to do when put into office, the worthy deacon had absented himself from three meetings of the trade, and had "allowed himself to be concealed in the house of Bailie Young in a state of drunkenness for some days previous to the election," when he voted for Mr. Monteith. It was on the 14th March, and that very night the trade "met to consider what mark of disrespect they should put upon him for having betrayed them." They declared Douglas to be totally and for ever unfit to hold office, and accordingly ordered the removal of the box, books, and colour from his custody. To clinch the deacon's downsetting, that minute was ordered to be read at every succeeding Michaelmas before the election. Unwonted activity characterised the souters all the year. At the October fair, the quarter-masters, after searching the market, pounced on a pair of shoes which the assembled trade pronounced not fit to be presented for sale. At a meeting on the 11th December a committee was appointed to draw up an address to Queen Caroline, and "further to contradict a report in some of the public papers that a party of rioters had gone to Sir Walter Scott's at Abbotsford, and assaulted the house, which we are convinced is a false rumour."

Like its brother-crafts, the Corporation of Cordiners sustained a mortal blow from the passing of the Reform Bill. That great measure avenged the Earl of Home, and effectually pronounced the doom, "Down wi' the Souters o' Selkirk."

Well known as they were for their single-soled shoon, the souters of Selkirk owe much of their celebrity to a ballad bearing their name in Scott's *Border Minstrelsy*, and to the gallant obstinacy with which Scott maintained that the doggerel must refer to Flodden. Over his version preference must be given to the following, first published in the *Musical Museum*, restored as its editor Johnson had heard it sung by Border musicians in his younger days :—

> Up wi' the Souters o' Selkirk,
>   And down wi' the fazart Lord Hume !
> But up wi' ilka braw callant
>   That sews the single-soled shoon.
> And up wi' the lads o' the Forest
>   That ne'er to the southron wad yield ;
> But deil scoup o' Hume and his menzie
>   That stud sae abiegh on the field.
>
> Fye on the green and the yellow,
>   The craw-hearted loons o' the Merse ;
> But here 's to the Souters o' Selkirk,
>   The elshin, the lingle, and birse.
> Then up wi' the Souters o' Selkirk,
>   For they are baith trusty and leal ;
> And up wi' the lads o' the Forest,
>   And down wi' the Merse to the deil.

The Minstrelsy copy is four lines shorter, but none the pithier :—

> Up wi' the Souters o' Selkirk,
>   And down wi' the Earl o' Hume,
> And up wi' a' the braw lads
>   That sew the single-soled shoon.

> Fye upon yellow and yellow,
>   And fye upon yellow and green;
> But up wi' the true blue and scarlet
>   And up wi' the single-soled shoon.
>
> Up wi' the Souters o' Selkirk,
>   For they are baith trusty and leal;
> And up wi' the men o' the Forest,
>   And down wi' the Merse to the deil.

In those lengthy and delightful notes which divide with the ballads themselves the ineffable charm of the "Minstrelsy," Sir Walter is at pains to prove that "this little lyric piece relates to the fatal battle of Flodden." He breaks a stout lance with Mr. Joseph Ritson, a celebrated antiquary, who had thus ridiculed the idea in a note to his *Historical Essay on Scottish Songs :*—

"That the souters of Selkirk should, in 1513, amount to fourscore fighting men, is a circumstance utterly incredible. It is scarcely to be supposed that all the shoemakers in Scotland could have produced such an army at a period when shoes must have been still less worn than they are at present. Dr. Johnson, indeed, was told at Aberdeen that the people learned the art of making shoes from Cromwell's soldiers. Away, then, with the fable of the souters of Selkirk! Mr. Robertson, who gives the Statistical Account of the Parish, seems to know more of the matter. 'Some,' says he, 'have very falsely attributed the song to this event (Flodden). There was no Earl of Home at that time, nor was this song composed till long after. It arose from a bet betwixt the Philiphaugh and Home families; the souters or shoemakers of Selkirk against the men of Home, at a match of football, in which the souters of Selkirk completely gained, and afterwards perpetuated their victory in that song.' This is decisive, and so much for Scottish tradition."

Challenging the English antiquary's conclusion, Sir Walter Scott appeals to another passage in the Statistical Account, wherein Mr. Robertson narrates the part taken by a Selkirk contingent in the fight at Flodden. He then continues :—

"Neither is it necessary to suppose, literally, that the men of Selkirk were all *souters*. This appellation was obviously bestowed on them, because it was the trade most generally practised in the town, and therefore passed into a general epithet. Even the existence of such a craft, however, is accounted improbable by the learned essayist, who seems hardly to allow that the Scottish nation was, at that period, acquainted with the art ' of accommodating their feet with shoes.' And here he attacks us with our own weapons, and wields the tradition of Aberdeen against that of Selkirk. But, allowing that all the shoemakers in England, with Praise-the-Lord Barebones at their head, had generously combined to instruct the men of Aberdeen in the arts of psalmody and cobbling, it by no means bears upon the present question. . . . The single-soled shoon made by the souters of Selkirk were a sort of brogues, with a single thin sole; the purchaser himself performing the further operation of sewing on another of thick leather. The rude and imperfect state of this manufacture sufficiently evinces the antiquity of the craft. Thus, the profession of the citizens of Selkirk, instead of invalidating, confirms the traditional account of their valour. . . . Mr. Robertson's authority, though highly respectable, is not absolutely decisive of the question. The late Mr. Plummer, sheriff-depute of the county of Selkirk, a faithful and accurate antiquary, has thus expressed himself upon the subject :—' It is evident the words cannot be so ancient as to come near the time when the battle was fought; as Lord Home was not created an Earl till near a century after that period.' As regards the match at football, ' I was five years at school at Selkirk, have lived all my days within two miles of that town, and never once heard a tradition of this imaginary contest till I saw it in print. Although the words are not very ancient, there is every reason to believe that they allude to the battle of Flodden and to the different behaviour of the souters and Lord Home upon that occasion.' The yellow and green, mentioned in the second verse, are the liveries of the house of Home."

Sir Walter, though ready enough to accept Mr. Plummer's evidence so far as it suits his own hypothesis, declines to admit that the verses allude to the different behaviour of the souters and Lord Home. "So far from exhibiting any marks of cowardice and disaffection, the division headed by that unfortunate nobleman was the only part of the Scottish army which was conducted with prudence on that fatal day. This body formed the vanguard, and entirely routed the division of Sir Edmund Howard to which they were opposed."

How Sir Walter, in face of this, could persist in maintaining that the verses did relate to the battle of Flodden, is hard to understand. Perhaps from an amiable weakness for the seat of his sheriffdom, and reluctance to let go anything that seemed to add to its importance in the romantic past ? He half admits as much. Alluding to the length of his dissertation, he apologises on the ground that he himself is now sheriff-depute, and has the honour to be a souter of Selkirk.

There is really no possibility of the ballad having reference to Flodden. It must be taken for granted that the minister had good grounds for his denial, seeing he had been twenty years in the parish when his account was published. Were further proof of Sir Walter's error needed, it lies at hand in the fact that the souters themselves had no corporate existence in Selkirk till 1601, nearly a hundred years after Flodden. And as a final nail in the coffin of his argument comes the craft's minute, of date 4th December 1815 :—"The shoemaker trade met this morning to consider on the propriety of their appearing as an individual body at the pending football match this day, to be played against the parish of Yarrow; and it was unanimously resolved that the match is to be considered as between the parish of Yarrow and that of Selkirk, and that their appearing in the field is in support of Selkirk parish and not as a body of souters. If, however, the Earl of Home should be disposed with his vassals, as in the days of yore, to meet with the souters, they shall give him an opportunity of regaining a victory lost by his forefathers." This settles the controversy. Beyond doubt, the ballad originated in the football match, and not at Flodden field.

It is curious to note in Pitscottie, Lord Lindsay's appeal before Flodden, that the Scots should not jeopardise their King and his nobility against an auld crookit carle (Surrey), and certain *sutors* and tailors with him in company.

THE INCORPORATION OF TAILORS.

Nothing goes further to prove the importance attached of old to the various trade-guilds within the burgh, than the conscientious care which has been taken of their various records. Of all the charters, confirmations, and other documents in connection with the craft of tailors, not one of value has been lost. Within its box are still to be found not only the original seal of cause (almost illegible on its brown old parchment) and minutes of every meeting since the first, nigh three hundred years ago, but the tattered remnant of the flag, and even the torn old mortcloth, whose sombre folds have covered so many freemen burgesses on their last journey up the steep Kirk Wynd.

It was in 1610, two years after their authorisation of the Weavers' Guild, that the Town Council, with quaint solemnity of phrase and much proclamation of its own dignity, granted a seal of cause to the Corporation of the craft of Tailors.

To all and sundrie to whose knowledge thir present letters shall come, the Provost, Bailies, and Counsell of ye brugh of Selkirk, greeting, in God everlasting—Witte ye : that the day of the date of the making thereof thir present letters, compeard before us Counselors gathered, William Wilkison, Robert Hislop, Thomas Hislop, James Caldwels, John Riddle, and the rest of the masters of the Taylor Craft within this brugh, and presented to us their supplication, containing certan statuts, articles, and rules, . . . to be affirmed by us for the loveing of God Almighty, the honour of the realm, the profit of this good town, and the profit of all our Soveraign Lord's and Ladie's lieges repairing thereto. . . . Considering it is said by common authority that multitudes (but rule) makes confusion, and for to eschew the vice thereof, and to eschew it in time coming, the which desire consonated to reason and therefore is granted . . . thir statuts, etc., following, in the first place, that for all increasment in virtue, pratick, and knowledge stand in good beginning and fundament, and frae thence furth to continue in use, etc." Then follow the usual rules to be observed in the taking on of apprentices, their gradual advancement, first to journeymen, and then to masters. Most jealously guarded of all are the privileges of burgesses, the officers of the craft being invested with such powers as are not now possessed by the Lord Advocate himself, for the summary treatment of unfreemen intruders. It is signed by George Mitchelhill, Provost, Robert Scott, James Mitchelhill, Patrick Kean, John

Scott, John Crook, Dean of Guild, William Lidderdale, Treasurer, James Wauch, Wm. Brown, Wm. Purves, John Smaill, Wm. Dalgliesh, deacon of the webster craft, and remanent councillors, "with our hands touching the notar's pen, because we cannot write ourselves." The witnesses (who presumably could write) are Patrick Shaw, minister of the Gospel, James Bryden, James Sinton, and Wm. Scott, son to umqll James Scott, Bailie.

One wonders, did any of these men hear of Shakespeare? He was their contemporary, and did not die till six years after the signing of the tailors' charter. Quite likely some of them may have had thrown at their heads by overcharged burgesses the verse which Shakespeare incorporated in *Othello* :—

> King Stephen was a worthy peer,
>   His breeches cost him but a crown ;
> He held them sixpence all too dear,
>   With that he called the tailor, lown.

Judging from their sederunt-books, it must be admitted as probable that the honest craftsmen knew little and cared less for anything beyond their own "ports, liberties, and walls." Kings die, a king is beheaded, new kings reign, Cromwell leads his army past their doors, Montrose is defeated before their eyes, a dethroned dynasty strikes twice in vain for restoration, but the tailors of Selkirk go on making deacons and admitting apprentices in unbroken enjoyment of the happiness pertaining to people whose annals are dull. But for an occasional quarrel over the best seats in kirk, and frequent augmentations of liquor dues at new entries, there would be nothing to break the monotony of two hundred and twenty years' dry repetition. Here is a complete list of the deacons who presided over the fortunes of the craft during that long period :—

1610. Wm. Wilkison.	1639. Robert Hislop.	1666. Robert Riddel.
1612. Robert Hislop.	1642. James Wilson.	1667. Wm. Scot.
1613. Wm. Wilkison.	1643. Robert Hislop.	1673. Robert Riddel.
1614. John Riddel.	1645. John Riddel.	1675. Gideon Ogilvie.
1617. Thomas Hislop.	1647. James Wilson.	1677. Robert Riddel.
1618. John Riddel.	1648. David Dun.	1679. Gideon Ogilvie.
1619. Wm. Wilkison.	1649. James Wilson.	1680. John Lang.
1620. —— Riddel.	1650. John Hislop.	1682. Gideon Ogilvie.
1622. David Fletcher.	1651. James Wilson.	1683. Robert Riddel.
1623. John Riddel.	1653. Wm. Scot.	1685. John Wilson.
1624. Robert Hislop.	1654. James Wilson.	1689. Gideon Ogilvie.
1626. John Riddel.	1655. Wm. Scott.	1690. Patrick Wilson.
1627. Robert Wanlaw.	1660. James Wilson.	1691. James Riddel.
1632. John Riddel.	1662. Wm. Scot.	1693. John Wilson.
1633. Robert Wanlaw.	1663. Gideon Ogilvie.	1695. James Riddel.
1635. John Riddel.	1664. Robert Riddel.	1697. Wm. Blaikie.
1638. Robert Wanlaw.	1665. Patrick Wilson.	1699. John Lang.

1701. James Riddel.	1749. John Lang, elder.	1797. Thomas Nicoll.
1703. Wm. Blaikie.	1751. James Rodger.	1799. Wm. Ewans.
1705. John Lang, younger.	1753. John Lang, younger.	1800. Wm. Turnbull.
1707. Wm. Blaikie.	1755. Thomas Kerr.	1802. Wm. Ewans.
1709. John Lang.	1757. Wm. Wilkie.	1803. Wm. Thorburn.
1710. George Easton.	1759. Gideon Thorburn.	1804. John Paterson.
1713. Wm. Blaikie.	1760. John Gowanlock.	1805. James Scott.
1715. Patrick Mader.	1762. John Kerr.	1806. John Paterson.
1717. Robert Thorbrand.	1765. John Johnston.	1807. Wm. Ewans.
1719. Wm. Blaikie.	1767. James Lauder.	1810. Robt. Murray.
1721. Wm. Rodger.	1768. Gideon Thorbrond.	1814. Thos. Nicol.
1723. John Lang.	1770. John Gowanlock.	1816. Wm. Ewans.
1725. George Easton.	1771. John Paterson.	1817. John Paterson.
1727. John Lang.	1772. John Ewans.	1818. Walter Paterson.
1729. George Easton.	1775. James Anderson.	1820. { Walter Paterson.
1731. Wm. Rodger.	1777. John Gowanlock.	{ John Johnston.
1733. John Lang.	1779. Robt. Elliot.	1821. Gideon Scott.
1735. Thomas Ker.	1781. Wm. Thorbrand.	1823. John Johnston.
1737. Wm. Wilkie, elder.	1783. Wm. Turnbull.	1825. Thos. Scott.
1739. Wm. Rodger.	1785. Jas. Anderson.	1827. John Paterson.
1741. Gideon Thorbrand.	1787. Robt. Murray.	1829. Andrew Moyes.
1742. John Lang, elder.	1789. Jas. Scott.	1832. Wm. Welsh.
1744. Andrew Angus.	1791. Geo. Emond.	1834. John Johnston, sen.
1745. John Andison.	1793. Wm. Turnbull.	1836. John Johnstone, yr.
1746. Robert Elliot.	1795. John Gowanlock.	1843. John Johnstone, sen.
1747. John Veitch.		

Importance was attached to the trade's flag or colour, which, along with the mortcloth and halbert, appear to have constituted the paraphernalia of all the Incorporations. In 1722 the "continuing of the banner constant in ane person," is found so inconvenient that the trade statutes in all time coming they shall choose their banner-bearer yearly at their pleasure, and "he who shall happen to be elected shall pay a gallon of ale." This flag was supplanted by a new one in 1770; and it is the latter, which, shorn of "the better half" of its glory, is now among the relics in the trades-box. It must have been quite a work of art. On a piece of fine white silk (60 × 52 inches) was painted a representation of the Fall. Adam and Eve each occupied a half, the flag being divided in the centre by the tree of knowledge, very prolific of apples, and occupied, as regards its upper bole, by the serpent. The tree springs from a pair of gold scissors. The reptile's head is something between those of an ant-eater and a giraffe; it has cat-like whiskers on its upper lip; and, considering its reputation for guile, has an expression wofully weak and vacuous. The figure of the first man remains complete, but of his wife nothing

is left save her hand holding the forbidden fruit. Beneath winds the appropriate scroll, "They sewed fig leaves together and made themselves aprons,"
which are the only garments the artist has allowed his subjects. This might
have been to the end the carrying flag of the Corporation, but for an untoward
accident which befell it on the Common-riding morning of 1804. Enraged at
some affront to his own or to the craft's dignity, Andrew Brown, servant
tailor to George Emond, jumped right through the flag, causing its permanent
damage, and Eve's complete disappearance. An entry relates how it is
resolved to "procekute" the outrageous Brown, and how his brethren "in-
gidge" to pay whatever expense the process comes to. Another flag was
procured in 1820 from Mr. Menzies Bayne, Edinburgh, at a cost of £4.
In acknowledging the money, Mr. Bayne draws attention to an artistic touch
which might otherwise have escaped notice :—"I have properly turned the
head of the serpent t'other way, as the transaction is committed, and he now
begins to shrink from the object of his seductions." This masterpiece is yet
extant, but not in the same keeping as the fragment of its predecessor.

A remonstrance against the settlement of a minister in 1753 is original
enough to warrant transcribing *ipsissimis verbis*.

"Sept. 20, 1753.—The deacon and the members of the Incorption being convend, and
thy taking itt to thir serouss consedration that the Town Concil and the reast of the sevral
Incroption, with the Merchant Companiy, having anomisly agraid that upon on Mr. Wiliam
Troter, minser in Shells, that the Dewke of Roxbrugh having presentd hime to be ther minseter,
and upon Sunday last being order to preach by the presbertr, and the whole trads not being
satisfed with hime, and taking itt to ther considraditon that the Dewke of Roxbrugh having
no right to present a minster to them, the saids majst⁸ and Town Concill having sunk teen
pond sterling, and the hamermen, shoumakrs, weavours, and flesher and Merchant Company
having sunke each of them five pound sterling mony to call the Dewke right of presntion in
question, we, the saids Incorpation of taylor, do sinke the like saids five pound sterling to call
the saids right in question, as itt is a very harde thinge to be introded upon on who is semlingly
not to be satisfing to the pepoll, and is very likly to put a great stope to the success of the
gospell." Signed by sixteen members, including James Rodger, William Rodger, and two
John Langs.

In 1759 a guinea is given for a new bridge at Yair. In 1765 members
are prohibited from turning any coats within their customers' houses, under
penalty of a shilling, the prohibition being affirmed by thirty-one signatures.
A guinea is given in 1803 to assist the public building, if built in Young and
Rodger's property. Probably this refers to the present Town Hall.

An idea of the value attached to the privileges of the trade may be
gathered from the following letter :—"Selkirk, Sept. 17th, 1767.—GENTELMEN,

—As I was formerly a member of your Incorporation, and I having now laid aside the exercise of that imployment, I therefore resine being a member amonge you; always reserving a liberty for me returning to be a member of your Incorporation if I should again exerce my trade; and am, gentelman, your humbel servant, GEO. RODGER." Fifteen years later, in 1782, there is a law account rendered by George Rodger, most likely son of the foregoing. An item, "To extraordinary trouble attending this business," is extended blank, with the following note :—"The above is charged 10s. 6d. below the ordinary rate, owing to this circumstance, that George Rodger wishes to cultivate the friendship of the taylors." The account is for trying to prohibit John Inglis from bringing the Bruntons in Yarrowford to work in the town—a nice pitch of trade protection, truly.

Selkirkshire Conservatives, who have long had to endure obloquy on account of their faggot votes, may derive some satisfaction from learning that they were by no means the first to resort to such questionable expedients. In 1820 the tailors' craft was nearly rent in twain in consequence of some sharp practice in this line by the Whig candidate, Mr. Pringle of Haining, and his friends. At the usual meeting for electing the deacon and his colleague in the Town Council, the votes of a very large number of members were objected to, some of them on the ground that they had been brought from Hounam and Morebattle, a distance of about thirty miles, and illegally admitted at the expense of a party merely to serve a political job. Others were objected to because of their being parties to certain written agreements whereby they bound themselves to support the measures of John Pringle, Esq. of Clifton, and to vote for the leets which he or his friends might propose to the different trades, many of those who signed the said agreements having done so while in a state of intoxication. The retiring deacon himself is appealed to if he was not one of those so beguiled into subscribing the document. A double and disputed election resulted; and political justice was vindicated by the defeat of Haining. That year Henry Monteith of Carstairs was elected Member of Parliament for the joint burghs.

Little remains to be said. Since the last election in 1843, the box and records of the Corporation have been carefully preserved by the family which furnished the last three deacons, and which for a hundred and fifty years has contributed honourable craftsmen to the honourable craft of tailors in Selkirk.

The Incorporation of Fleshers.

In 1679, seventy years after the tailors' craft had been inaugurated, John Cavers, Alex. Tudhope, Walter Scott, Alex. Scott, Andro Hendersone, John Cavers, yr., John Tudhope, James Haldon, Peter Watson, James Chisholme, all fleshers and burgesses of Selkirk, "having with ane consent given in ane supplication to the Baillies and Counsell, desiring their worships to grant them libertie to elect and choyse ane deacon and other officemen of the trade as use in other burghs, the said desire was granted by the said Baillies and Counsell." And the ten petitioners having sent in their long leet of five, from whom the Bailies chose "twae to be in the list of deacons," they met on the 2d October 1680 to elect their first office-bearers, each one of whom being present took the oath of fidelity and obedience.

At no time does the craft thus constituted appear to have attained great dimensions. Unlike the weavers, souters, and to some extent also the tailors, the freemen fleshers seem to have had no business outlet beyond the town, the consequence being that their numbers were limited, rarely exceeding twelve, and often dwindling down to six, five, and even four. Numerous or not, however, they went on electing deacons with admirable punctuality, taking care not to lose any of the privileges which the right conferred upon them. From 1769 to 1790, the Hendersons seem to have usurped control of the trade in much the same way as the Currors did of the cordiners from 1700 to 1714.

List of Deacons.

1680. John Cavers, elder.	1713. Robert Tudhope.	1747. Alex. Scott.
1682. John Cavers, younger.	1715. William Cavers.	1749. Alex. Tudhope.
1684. John Cavers, elder.	1721. James Scott.	1751. John Henderson, yr.
1686. Walter Scott.	1723. Andrew Hadden.	1753. Andrew Henderson.
1687. John Tudhope.	1725. Walter Henderson.	1755. John Henderson, yr.
1689. Walter Scott.	1727. John Henderson.	1757. Alex. Tudhope.
1691. John Tudhope.	1729. James Scott.	1759. Andrew Henderson.
1693. Walter Scott.	1733. John Henderson.	1761. Alex. Scott.
1695. John Tudhope.	1735. John Henderson, yr.	1763. John Henderson.
1697. Walter Scott.	1736. Alex. Tudhope.	1765. Andrew Haldane.
1699. John Tudhope.	1738. John Henderson, elder.	1767. James Douglas.
1705. Robert Tudhope.	1740. James Scott.	1769. Andrew Henderson.
1707. John Tudhope.	1742. John Watson.	1771. John Henderson, yr.
1708. Walter Henderson.	1743. John Henderson.	1773. Andrew Henderson.
1709. Robert Tudhope.	1744. John Watson.	1775. John Henderson, elder.
1711. William Cavers.	1746. John Henderson, elder.	1777. Andrew Henderson.

1779. Basil Henderson.	1800. Walter Henderson.	1810. Walter Henderson.
1781. John Henderson, junior.	1801. John Murray.	1814. John Thomson.
1787. Andrew Henderson.	1803. John Curror.	1816. { George Thomson.
1789. John Henderson.	1804. Robert Tudhope.	{ George Scott.
1791. Robert Tudhope.	1806. John Thomson.	1855. George Scott.

With an occupation not attractive in itself at any time, the brethren of the craft of fleshers have not managed to impart to their records much that is either interesting or significant. In their year of incorporation, they ordained a few rules, of which the very object is now difficult to perceive. No meat, for instance, was to be killed on Monday, "except upon ane Yule even, or ane fair even." Likeways, on Friday they might kill lambs, but not to sell as long as there was any old killed meat in the market. Every year the dues were sold to a tacksman, the price ranging from about £23 to £27 Scots, and to this tacksman the fleshers, either in town or landward, were bound to pay 8d. for every nolt killed, 2d. for each sheep and lamb, and 8d. for every swyne. Not more than two could be partners (joint owners of a slaughtered animal) except in the time of Lent. The necessity for this exception so late as 1681 is worth noting. Either the reformed doctrines had not yet found general acceptance amongst the honest burgesses, or the observances of the old faith had lingered as superstitions after they had ceased to be believed in. No servant was admitted to kill, or take a knife in his hand, until his master paid ten groats to the trade's box-master. And by way of repressing any obliging disposition that might manifest itself in a freeman flesher, a rule was passed forbidding any of them to carry flesh to any house, "but let them either com themselves, or els let them send their servands." Of all their statutes this perhaps died hardest.

As a rule, the election of office-bearers took place at Michaelmas; but a most unusual and apparently important election is chronicled in the following minute, written in a round open hand, and occupying four times the ordinary space :—" At Selkirk, the last day of December 1687 years—There being ane commissione direct from His Sacred Majestie and his most honorable Privie Counsell ffor nominating and appoynting the Proveist, Baillies, Councellors, and Deacons of ye severall Trades and Incorporations within the burgh of Selkirk for the current year till ye feast of Michaelmass 1688 years, as ye samen, daited ye sixth day of December instant, more fullie bears—By which commission John Tudhope being nominatt and appoynted deacon of the fleshers of the said burgh," etc.   There is not a word in the record to throw light on this strange and arbitrary piece of royal interference ; but it probably had something to do with the disaffection produced by the King's outrageous policy.   In less than two years James VII. of Scotland was a fugitive from his throne and kingdom.

On the 22d April 1743, the deacon and quarter-masters were empowered to proceed against John Tudhope (indweller in Edinburgh), eldest son and heir of the deceased John Tudhope, late deacon, for payment of £50 Scots,

The Fleshers' Halbert.

principal and interest, and £5 for failure to pay. In 1774 John Henderson, deacon's colleague, was elected treasurer of the burgh. The same violent political squabble already noticed in the later annals of other crafts, turns up amongst the fleshers. In 1816 another John Henderson's admission was objected to, on the ground that he was not a flesher, but a writer or clerk in Edinburgh, brought out in the heat of a political contest, and James Halden's, because he was a weaver at Hawick. Referring to elaborate reasons laid down in support of the protest, the other side calls them ridiculous—"merely fanciful ideas and suggestions emanating from the protestor's political friend and adviser, Mr. Andrew Lang. Page follows page full of tedious protestations against protests, and objections to objectors, the quarrel ending in the usual disputed election, and the final break-up of the Incorporation.

Not to be behind other and more numerous crafts, the fleshers had their full complement of insignia, their last flag, a broad expanse of fine silk, being still in tolerable preservation. It portrays a deformed little black stot, its horns held fast by a fat old gentleman in blood-red surtout, while an elegant athlete administers the *coup de grâce* with the killing-axe. Over all a ribbon waves in graceful scroll, bearing the words, " Whatsoever is sold in the shambles, that eat, asking no question for conscience' sake.—1st Corinth. 10. 25."   In one corner there seems to have been a representation of the burgh arms, encircled by the motto, " Success to the fleshers of Selkirk," but this has been mostly cut away.   Still to be seen also is the old halbert, its emblems of finely wrought iron half eaten through with rust. It bears no inscription, but in its evidences of decay and neglect one may plainly read that " All flesh is grass."

INCORPORATION OF HAMMERMEN.

The sinewy wielders of the hammer seem to have been excited to imitation if not to envy by the incorporation of their fellow-burgesses, wielders of the felling-axe and slaughtering-knife. For hardly two years had the latter enjoyed the privileges and dignity of guildry, when one-and-thirty smiths, masons, wrights, and coopers begged the Town Council to blend them in one brotherhood, under the style of hammermen. The two-and-twenty Bailies and Councillors accorded a ready consent, lending their dread authority to twenty articles for the government of the young community. So like are these to the statutes of trades already mentioned, that it is not worth while to repeat them. It is the same catalogue of fines for upbraiding the deacon, and of fees, dinners, and drink at entering or passing, while the usual caution is given against crafts-men selling on " the high streets or back-sydes but upon the mercat-day only."

As was to be anticipated, a stringent rule obtained against any " master-man-freed or servant exercising any more crafts but one allenarly." It was not allowed even that the whole body should receive a member unless with the express permission of the candidate's own particular branch. In rather roundabout terms, " the smiths are not to have a vote in taking in a mason, nor a wright, nor a cooper; the masons not to have vote in taking in a smith, nor a wright, nor a cooper; a wright not to have a vote in taking in a smith, nor a mason, nor a cooper; and a cooper not to have a vote in taking in a smith, nor a mason, nor a wright." In 1821, a cry arose of "the craft in danger," in consequence of John Smith, mason in Darnick, having contracted for the different branches of mason and wright work of a house for Mr. Robert Henderson, writer. (The house is now known as " Comely Bank.") Mr. Smith, by payment of a large sum (£15), had previously obtained the privileges of a hammerman, and the craft now declared the said contract a violation of the acts of the seal of cause and of his engagements to the Corporation, he having no right to carry on any branches but a mason's. The Town Council was appealed to, but that body not exhibiting the desired alacrity in calling Mr. Smith to account, the hammermen began to sulk, and refused to send in a list of eligibles for the deaconship that year. Then John Paterson, writer, is authorised to summon the Smiths before the Chief Magistrate; but Mr. John Paterson being both dilatory and exorbitant, the case is transferred to another Mr. Paterson, lawyer in Galashiels. By this time the house must have been about finished; at all events, the matter dropped, and the Smiths appear to have quietly carried out the innovation. Common sense had begun to assert itself even amongst the narrow-minded provincials of old Scottish burghs, and could no longer brook the absurd and tyrannous restrictions put on industry by effete cliques of craftsmen. Though discomfited, the hammermen were not cowed, and knew when to give an unsympathetic Council the rebuke dignified. Being summoned in 1823 to accompany the Royal Archers with their colour, "they find it inconvenient, and therefore decline!" Bluntness may be said to be their characteristic, as witness the following reasons for refusing to entertain a protest:—(1.) Because it is illegally submitted; (2.) Because it is founded upon entire falsehood and unbounded calumnies; (3.) Because it is a mere fabrication of lies.

A strange incident crops up in 1744. At their meeting in September, a fierce altercation takes place over the admission of four men not belonging to either of the orthodox trades. The four attend, and are amongst eighteen who carry Henry Hall for deacon, against seventeen who vote for Hugh Cairncross. By way of adding another to his majority of one, Deacon Hall represented that it was notorious how one of their number, Charles Blackburn, was laid up in prison, and wilfully kept and alimented there in order to disappoint him of his vote; and ended by proposing they should go and get his vote at the prison. The seventeen objected that the vote could not be good, Blackhall being confined in close prison "for ane riot and insult committed on the Magistrates;" but the majority, marching to the Tolbooth, registered the prisoner's vote, and sent in their own leet to the Council. A well-known American poet satirising the canvassing expedients of his countrymen, says—

> Parson Wilbur sez *he* never heerd in his life,
> Thet th' Apostles rigged out in their swaller-tail coats,
> An' marched round in front of a drum an' a fife,
> To git some on 'em office, an' some on 'em votes;
> But John P.
> Robinson he
> Sez they didn't know everythin' down in Judee.

It would appear as if even John P. had something to learn from the ancient hammermen of Selkirk; for it is not yet recorded that the Yankees have taken to scour prisons for supporters.

It is disappointing to find so much enterprise doomed to failure. The Cairncross faction carrying the day, signalised their success by promptly expelling saddler, miller, and dyer at their first meeting. That being in 1745, it is instructive to note how all the points of this village squabble are recorded, while of the nation's throes beneath the Jacobite rebellion there is not a syllable of indication.

In 1753 a grant of £5 is made, to assist in inquiring into the Duke of Roxburgh's title to the church patronage, and to oppose the settlement of a minister " altogether disagreeable to most of the inhabitants." Two years later the price of a seat in the kirk-loft is fixed at 4s. 10d., the deacon to sit uppermost in the fore-seat. On June 8, 1758, Deacon Blackburn (probably hero of the prison-vote) signs an obligation " that he nor his shall not be troublesome to the Incorporation for the future,"—corroborating the charge of rioting and impudence which previously landed him in durance vile. Throughout the entire kingdom great privations were endured at the close of last century in consequence of a scarcity of food, almost amounting to famine; and it was in relieving the sufferings of members that considerable funds amassed by the trades dwindled away. In 1782 the hammermen lifted £15 to cheapen meal for supply of the Corporation, and in 1800 they exhausted their funds in reducing the price of "vittle." For the benefit of those curious in orthography, it may be mentioned that this expenditure is entered in the books as cash lent out for " beihugh" of the trade. In 1793, John Guthrie, slater, is admitted a freeman, there being no other of the trade within the burgh. At a meeting to consider the state of the mortcloth, it is concluded that "by putting a new ribbon round the edges in place of the old chattered fringes, it may appear pretty decent for a considerable time." They were more particular about the flag. So early as 1709, £4 was invested in a new banner, and every twenty years or so a fresh one was provided. The present colour, almost quite new, represents a masonic arch supported by Ionic pillars, and enclosing the implements of the crafts. Its motto, taken from the old flag, is " God's providence is our inheritance." The following list of deacons is complete from 1708 onwards :—

1708. John Fairgrieve.	1724. Simon Fletcher.	1739. Wm. Pringle, wright.
1709. John Tod.	1725. James Shiell, cooper.	1741. Thos. Minto.
1711. John Middlemass, elder.	1728. John Tod.	1742. Jas. Shiell.
1713. John Middlemass, yr.	1730. Andw. Fletcher, cooper.	1743. Rob. Thomson, smith.
1717. William Scott.	1731. James Shiell.	1744. { Henry Hall and
1719. Andrew Fletcher.	1733. John Minto, wright.	{ Hugh Cairncross.
1721. John Mein.	1735. James Shiell.	1745. Hugh Cairncross.
1722. Henry Hall.	1737. John Minto.	1746. John Dods, smith.

1747. Robt. Gotra, smith.
1749. Charles Blackburn.
1751. Aw. Dodds, smith.
1754. Henry Hall.
1757. Wm. Renwick.
1759. Andrew Dodds.
1761. John Dobson.
1763. James Thomson.
1765. James Scott, wright.
1767. John Thorburn.
1769. John Bruce.
1771. Robt. Dalgleish, wright.
1773. Geo. Dun, mason.
1775. Wm. Scott, mason.
1777. James Shiell.
1779. James Scott, junior.
1781. Wm. Pringle.
1783. John Stoddart, smith.

1785. Thomas Gotra.
1787. Robert Glen.
1789. Robert Gotra.
1791. Wm. Dods.
1793. Thos. Hall.
1795. Geo. Dobson.
1797. Thos. Stoddart.
1799. Andrew Inglis.
1800. James Inglis, mason.
1801. John Stoddart.
1802. Andw. Inglis.
1803. Thos. Scott.
1804. Wm. Douglas.
1806. Thos. Scott.
1808. Andrew Cowan.
1809. John Scott.
1812. Andrew Gray.

1814. Andrew Hope.
1816. John Stoddart.
1818. Thos. Cumming, cooper.
1819. David Laidlaw.
1820. Jas. Inglis, junior.
1821. John Thorburn.
1823. Andrew Guthrie.
1825. { Andrew Guthrie.
       { Andrew Hope.
1827. Andrew Inglis.
1828. James Inglis, junior.
1830. Andrew Heatlie.
1832. James Lees.
1833. Robert Inglis.
1835. No election.
1836. Thos. Stoddart.
1858. Robert Hope.

Gate of old Churchyard.

CHAPTER XV.

THE CHURCH AND MINISTERS OF SELKIRK.

1165-
1214.
L. K.,
16.

WILLIAM THE LION, in his charter confirming to Kelso Abbey its lands and privileges, makes mention of "the parish of my town of Selkirk." This, so far as we are aware, is the first time in Scottish history that the word

Reg.
Glasg.,
43, 50,
55.

parish (originally meaning *any district*) was applied to a town, though in the same reign it was used to denote the entire diocese of Glasgow. It is not to be supposed that at this early period there was a parish of Selkirk in the

O. P.,
xx.

modern acceptation of the term—"a district appropriated to one baptismal church;" but it may be taken to signify the extensive country over which the

L. K.,
16.

priest of Selkirk presided in spiritual matters. And although "the places of the King's waste of Selkirk, to which he had transferred his men of Elrehope, as well as of the parish of his town of Selkirk, and all dwelling in these places, with all their possessions," were to belong to the church of Selkirk as their mother church, it was provided that "if in these places a church or chapel should happen to be built, the same should belong, with all its just pertinents, to the church of Kelso," not to that of Selkirk. It does not appear from the Register of Kelso Abbey that this contingency ever occurred.

Concerning the religious men, probably Culdees, who occupied the original Shiel-Kirk, nothing is known, or is ever likely to be; but ancient French and Scottish chronicles name the distinguished monks who presided Mel. over the short-lived monastery established by David I. Chron. Gall. Chris., viii.

1113.—Ralph, first Abbot of Selkirk, was one of the Benedictines brought from Tiron, in France, to which he returned in 1116, on the death of St. Bernard, the founder, whom he was chosen to succeed.

1116.—William, second Abbot of Selkirk, also a French monk, was likewise called to rule the parent foundation on the death of Ralph in 1119.

1119.—Herbert, third Abbot of Selkirk, was a monk of the abbey, and probably a Scots-Craw-man of high rank. He held at the same time the office of chancellor of the kingdom. When ford, the change of situation took place in 1126, he became first abbot of Kelso, and twenty-one Offic., 4. years later, succeeded John, Bishop of Glasgow, in the Episcopal chair. Died 1164. Crown

Of the priests or vicars who filled the charge of Selkirk during the four hundred and fifty years between the abbey removal and the Reformation, only the following can be identified :—

1296.—Richard, vicar of the church of Selkirk, swore fealty to Edward I. of England. Rag.
1296.—Adam de Selkirke, called "parson of the chapel of the camp of Roxburgh." Ro., 156. R. S.
1425.—William Middilmast, vicar of Selkirk, chaplain to the family of Douglas, keepers G. S., of Roxburgh Castle. To St. Michael's altar in St. Andrew's Church at Peebles he gave up ii. 209. several tenements situated in that burgh, in the year 1436.
1489.—The office of parish-clerk was disputed between Alexander Ker, on the one hand, A. L. A., and Robert Scot in the Haining, with his son John, on the other, "ather of thaim claiming the 14. said clerkschip to pertene to thaim."
1494.—Newtown, vicar of Selkirk, mentioned in minutes of Justice-Ayre.
1512.—Schir John Mitchelhill, a "pope's knight," presbyter of Glasgow, combining offices B. R. of chaplain and notary-public, in which capacity he wrote a deed in 1512, conveying the old croft, called Kilcroft, to Elizabeth Ker, daughter of Adam Ker of St. Helen's Shaw, and wife of William Ker. In 1530, Schir John Mitchelhill, chaplain, aged 40 years, deponed on the word of a priest that he set on the locks of the almonry claimed by Janet Lorimer.
1512.—Schir William of Furde, chaplain, a "pope's knight."
1514.—Schir William Bryden, a "pope's knight," styled in 1534 vicar of Selkirk and Auld Roxburgh.
1527.—Schir David Chepman.
1527.—Schir Ninian Brydon.
1531.—Schir John Bryden, chaplain of the Holycross Altar.
1539.—Schir Andrew Ker, elected chaplain of the Rood Altar, two other candidates, townsmen, being Schir Thomas Scoon and Schir Stephen Wilkinson.
1582.—James Beaton, a relation of the Cardinal, styled parson of Auld Roxburgh, but no Hist. mention of Selkirk in conjunction. MSS., iv. 504.

P. C.,
iii. 475,
iv. 522.
1590.—Sir Thomas Ker, "vicar of Auld Roxburgh," charged along with certain indwellers in Selkirk, as "perseuaris and troublaris of ministers in the executioun of thair offices and functioun, and in the possessing of thair mansis and glebis designit to thame."

F. E.,
539.
The first General Assembly of the Reformed Church was held in 1560, since which time the ministers of Selkirk have been as follows :—

P. C.,
ii. 558.
1568.—Mr. John Scott, exhorter at Selkirk, St. Marie Kirk of the Lowes, New Kirk of Ettrick and Rankleburne, with £80 of stipend. In 1576, Johne Scott, minister at Selkirk, complained of Robert, son and apparent heir of Thomas Scott of Haining, trying to dispossess him of the half town and lands of Elliston, of which he and his predecessors had been kindly tenants in the "tymes bigane, past memor of man." Haining had got a grant of the subjects, which the minister maintained was "expres contrair the tennour of the Actis maid in favouris of the auld possessouris of Kirklandis," but the Court decided against tenant-right, and in favour of Haining.

1574 (?) to 1580.—George Cunningham, reader.

—— Shaw of Lauriston.

1580.—Michael Cranstoun, son of a minister of Liberton, to which parish he was translated prior to 1585.

1585.—John Smythe, M.A. of St. Andrews, translated to Mertoun about 1586.

Young,
Life of
Welsh.
1589.—John Welsche, A.M., an extraordinary man, was born 1568-70, son of the Laird of Collieston, in Dumfriesshire. He grew up a wayward, reckless, and passionate boy. To escape from the restraints of school he absconded, and lived with thieves of the English Border, until his clothes were worn out and he had experienced other miseries of the prodigal son. On his way home to the paternal roof, he called on his aunt in Dumfries, partly to obtain food and clothing, and partly to gain her influence in appeasing his father. It so happened that Welsh the elder called at Mrs. Forsyth's house while his son was there ; and on the good woman breaking the subject by asking if there were news of John, his father replied, "The first news I expect to hear of him is that he has been hanged as a thief." He settled down, however, to his parents' satisfaction; and after attending Dumfries Grammar School was sent to Edinburgh University, where he was a "diligent student of great expectation." Taking his degree of M.A. in 1588, he affixed his name to the National Covenant, as required by ordinance of the General Assembly. The year following, Welsh, then about twenty, was appointed to the pastoral charge of Selkirk, there being a law that none be admitted to the ministry under twenty-five, "except those whom the General Assembly judged meet and worthy by reason of singular endowments and rare qualities." Although Welsh was an accomplished scholar, it was probably more to his determined energy of character than to his attainments

he owed his appointment to the destitute region of the Forest, his charge comprehending Yarrow, Ettrick, Rankleburn, and Ashkirk, as well as Selkirk. According to a paper presented by the Assembly to the king in 1587-8, the religious and moral condition of the district was wellnigh desperate, popery having still a strong hold not only upon the minds but upon the affection of people of all grades. There being no manse in Selkirk, Welsh took up his residence with one Mitchellhill—probably James Mitchellhill, a substantial burgess and proprietor of lands within the burgh. He slept with a young boy of Mitchellhill's, who, after he had himself become an old man, delighted in reminiscences of the famous minister. One of Welsh's customs was, he said, to lay a Scotch plaid above his bedclothes at night, and when he awoke, to sit up, cover himself loosely with the plaid, and engage in devotion.

In March 1589-90, the Privy Council appointed Welsh one of the clerical P. C., iv. 466. commissioners for carrying out an Act of Parliament passed in 1587 commanding all Jesuits and seminary priests to leave the country. When preaching to his people, Welsh largely adopted the minatory style—what his biographer calls "making use of the law, as a schoolmaster, to bring sinners to Christ— a style of address well suited to the mental and moral condition of his flock, only then beginning to emerge from ignorance and vandalism." It is perhaps not astonishing that his boldness and plain speaking, while it commanded the admiration of some, did not win the hearts of others of his hearers. "He was hated," says Mr. Young, "by many, especially by some of the influential persons who lived in his neighbourhood. To attempt to awaken men who have been long sunk in the deep sleep of ignorance, superstition, and idolatry, has often excited the deepest hostility, evinced with even more ferocity than that with which wild beasts sleeping in their dens would resent disturbance or the intrusion of light." If he did not spare his people, neither did Welsh spare himself. His custom was, says Kirkton, to preach publicly once every day. "This he did not, indeed, always to the people of Selkirk, few of whom cared to hear him at any time, much less every day of the week, but to such of the inhabitants of the nearest parishes as he could bring together." To overtake the great distances he required to travel, he always kept two good horses, which were not employed in field labour, he having no glebe. Quite possibly he was kept out of it by hostile parishioners; for in 1590, George P. C., iv. 522. Mitchelhill, William Mitchelhill, George Halliwell, George Anisoun, and John Turnbull, indwellers in Selkirk, were summoned at the mercat cross to answer a charge of molesting ministers and dispossessing them of their manses and glebes. His long and frequent journeyings over the wilds of Selkirkshire Welsh performed under great discouragement, few cheering him with their sympathy, and many assailing him with scoffs and taunts. "Yea," says Kirkton, "even the ministers of that country were more ready to pick a quarrel with his person than to follow his doctrine, as may appear to this day (*circa* 1700) in their Synodal records." Those of Ashkirk seem to have been his bitterest persecutors. James Scott, vicar of that parish, was Romanist at heart; and having been deposed by the Assembly for encouraging popish superstitions, many of which were still rampant among the common people, naturally had a deep grudge against so formidable an antagonist as Welsh. From Scott of Headshaw, probably the vicar's relative, came a crowning outrage, which led to the preacher shaking the dust from off his feet and leaving Selkirk. That graceless and inhuman laird cut off the rumps of Welsh's two valuable horses, which bled to death. Probably feeling it vain to apply for legal redress against a man so backed by powerful aid as every landed Scott then was, Welsh went with witnesses to the public cross of Selkirk, and there proclaimed his wrong. It was probably just before he left Selkirk in 1594 that the minister took to wife a lady of illustrious parentage. This was Elizabeth, third daughter of John Knox, by his second wife, Margaret Stewart, daughter of Lord Ochiltree. About two years after the Reformer's death, his young and attractive widow had married Andrew Ker of Faldonside, where Welsh had ample opportunity of visiting and making the acquaintance of his future wife. With not a little of her father's intrepid spirit, Elizabeth Knox was well mated to a man like Welsh, and rendered him signal service in aftertimes of danger and trouble. It is a striking proof of the little love the Selkirk people bore him, or of their dread of his powerful enemies, that when he "flitted" to Kirkcudbright, it was with difficulty a man having the requisite means could be got to convey his moveables. One named Ewart having undertaken the work, and "thus befriended the servant of God in his necessity, thrived ever after in his worldly condition, as was observed by all his neighbours—while the frown of Heaven fell on Scott of Headshaw, whose family forthwith declined and hastened to extinction." Thus, at least, saith the pious Kirkton; but as that reverend author also says he got the details of Welsh's removal from Ewart, which it is impossible to believe, his interpretation of the "ways of God to man" may be equally unreliable. If tradition may be credited, Welsh assumed the mantle of a prophet before he left Selkirk, dealing out both blessings and cursings with a profusion that would have shocked Balaam. He, for instance, invoked sterility on all occupiers of the manse he had found so little rest in ; and when the present incumbent arrived, he was hailed by one old female parishioner as the man in whose time the curse was to be broken. That there had been a long line of childless predecessors was " confirmation strong as Holy Writ " to believers in Welsh's prophetic power—ignorant as they were of his two immediate successors having each had a large family. In 1596-7 a violent sermon delivered by Welsh in Edinburgh, drew down upon him the anger of King James VI., whom he had treated with but little respect in the course of his harangue. Disregarding a summons to appear before the Privy Council, he was outlawed, his forfeited goods and estate being given to his wife's relative Lord Ochiltree, at whose earnest intercession with His Majesty Welsh was pardoned and restored to his own place. Shortly after this he challenged to public debate Gilbert Brown, abbot of Sweetheart, and a prominent defender of Rome ; but Brown declined the contest, and Welsh wrote a treatise attacking the Mass and Antichrist. In 1600 he removed to Ayr, having had indifferent success against the popish influences which, no less than at Selkirk, prevailed around Kirkcudbright. According to his biographer, Welsh also uttered prophecy before leaving this place, telling a gay and reckless young cavalier called Glendinning, that he would live to be his successor, which was fulfilled. At Ayr, also, a man lost his estate in consequence of Welsh hinting at the probability of such a result did he not stop football-playing on Sunday. Surrounding himself with a staff of twenty elders and nine deacons, he established a rigid system of discipline, towards which he employed all the machinery of " stool," sackcloth, money penalties, etc., in vogue at that time. Administered without regard to class or rank, this strict severity would work a certain sort of good amongst his lawless flock ; but while there is enough and to spare of the righteousness which represses, we look in vain for signs of the charity which encourages. Welsh was above all a sincere patriot. Many a time in the fervour of his prayers, often with strong crying and tears, the exclamation burst from his very heart, " O God ! wilt thou not give me Scotland ? " In 1605, Welsh appeared before the Privy Council for having attended a forbidden Assembly of the Kirk, declined to answer the questions put to him, and was consigned to Blackness Castle. For refusing, with his fellow-prisoners, to admit the authority of the Council to judge their cause, as being spiritual, he and they were brought to trial for high treason, which ended in their return to prison, first at Blackness, and afterwards in Edinburgh Castle. In both places he had outbursts of the spirit of divination, and being mocked one evening by a young papist, he entreated the company "not to be afraid to see what God should do among them before they rose from the table, for he would smite some one of them with death." It is unnecessary to add that "shortly after Welsh uttered this warning, the youth fell from his chair a lifeless corpse." In his paroxysms of fanaticism, Welsh actually assumed prophetic powers; and his biographies abound in proofs of their genuineness and unfailing fulfilment. By a letter from the King, Welsh and his five brethren were sentenced to perpetual banishment on pain of death; and they sailed for France on the 6th November 1606, landing safely at Bordeaux. Having quickly acquired the language, he was accepted as pastor of several Protestant congregations, being one of the ministers of St. Jean d'Angely when it capitulated to Louis XIII. Notwithstanding many warnings, he determined to celebrate Protestant worship as usual, and a vast audience assembled, attracted by the novelty of Huguenot services almost within hearing of royalty. Beholding the approach of the Duke of Espernon, sent by the King with some military to apprehend him, Welsh called on the people to make way for the marischal and his attendants, that they might listen to the Word of God. The Duke sat down, heard him to the close, and then conducted him to the King. Louis, much incensed, demanded how he dared to preach heresy so near his person. "Sire," said Welsh, "if you knew what I preached, you would not only come and hear me, but make all France hear me, for I preach not as those whom you are accustomed to hear. First, I preach that you must be saved by the merits of Jesus Christ, and not your own; and I am sure your conscience tells you your good works will never win Heaven. Next, I preach that as you are King of France, there is no man on earth above you; but those whom you hear subject you to the Pope of Rome, which I will never do." To understand the marvellous adroitness of this reply, it has to be borne in mind that Louis at the time was combating pretensions by certain of his Cardinals as to the Pope's supremacy in temporal as well as spiritual matters. "Good," said His Majesty, "you shall be my minister;" and his royal word was kept. When the town was given over to be sacked and dismantled, the King ordered the captain of the guard to place sentinels at Welsh's dwelling-house, to show him all manner of consideration, and to provide wagons for conveying him and his family to Rochelle. After a short visit to Holland, he obtained permission "to come to London to be dealt with;" but as he stubbornly refused to approve the existing government of the Church, he was not allowed to go to Scotland. With great difficulty Mrs. Welsh obtained audience of the King to beseech the necessary permission. "Who was your father?" asked James. "John Knox," was the reply. "Knox and Welsh! the devil ne'er made sic a match as that." "It's richt like, sir," said Mrs. Welsh; "we never speired his advice." The King next asked about her family, and hearing there were but three, all lasses, exclaimed, "God be thanked! for if they had been three lads, I had never bruiked my three kingdoms in peace." Being urged to give the sick man a chance of his native air—"Give him his native air!" said the Monarch; "give him the devil." "Give that," said the undaunted woman, offended at his profanity, "give that to your hungry courtiers." At last the King offered to let Welsh return if he would submit to the bishops; but Knox's daughter holding out her apron towards him, said, "Please your Majesty, I'd rather kep his head there." When he was known to be a dying man, Welsh was permitted to preach in London, and eagerly availed himself of the liberty. But his first sermon was his last. The effort killed him. Two hours after returning to his lodgings he ended his passionate eventful life. No monument marks his grave in St. Botolph, Bishopsgate; but an entry in the registry certifies that "John Welsh, a minister, was buried the 4th of April 1622," eight-and-twenty years after he had left his uncultured and inhospitable charge at Selkirk.

1596.—Patrick Shaw, M.A., grandson of Shaw of Sauchie, declined the vicarage of Greenock, to which he was presented by James VI. in 1594. While minister of Selkirk, he, with fifty-four others, signed the protestation for the liberties of the kirk (1617). Giving up his charge to his son in 1634, Mr. Shaw died previous to 25th July 1646. He gave 40 merks towards building the library of Glasgow College. In 1599 he granted a feu or "onset back Auth. and fore, with the yaird of the same pertaining to him, as ane part of his mans," in favour of MSS. George Anderson, burgess.

(1627.—Thomas Wilkie, reader at the kirk of Selkirk, got the handsome fee of £6, 13s. 4d. Scots, for registering the birth, at Newark Castle, of David, third son of the first Earl of Bucc. Buccleuch. Probably Mr. Thomas Wilkie, minister of Lilliesleaf, or his son the minister of Crailing.)

1634.—John Shaw (M.A., Edinburgh), eldest son of the preceding, was presented to Selkirk by Charles I. in 1634, three years after taking his degree. In 1662 he was ordered to confine himself to the parish; and next year was accused before the Privy Council "of turbulent and seditious carriage." He married Anne, daughter of Sir John Murray of Philiphaugh, who with him had sasine of the eastmains of Selkirk, called Helein-shaw, in 1661. Besides four sons they had a daughter Jean, who married John Pringle, minister of Fogo, only son of Pringle of Balmungo. Their son, John Pringle, succeeded to Yair in 1685. Christian Shaw, granddaughter of the Rev. John Shaw of Selkirk, became wife of the Rev. John Rutherford of Yarrow, and was thus great-grandmother of Sir Walter Scott.

1666.—James Craig (M.A., Edinburgh), was translated from Hoddam after the benefice of Selkirk had been more than a year vacant, and left in ten years to go to Tranent.

1678.—Alex. Cooper (M.A., St. Andrews), came from Sorbie, and continued in 1682, his son Alexander being served heir to him in 1688.

1685.—James Canaries, D.D., son of Mr. Thomas Kinneres, minister of Kinnaird, after a distinguished career at St. Andrews University, seems to have paused a while, finally going to Rome and embracing the popish faith. Returning, he petitioned to be again received into the Reformed Church, which was solemnly done in 1682 by the presbytery of St. Andrews, after a long discourse concerning the temptations he was under to make defection, and of the motives, convictions, and inducements that made him, after some time, "nauseat" that religion. Becoming minister of Selkirk in 1685, he very soon got into grief. On the 16th February 1686, Chancellor Perth moved that a seditious sermon preached by Mr. Kinaries, minister of Selkrig, might be taken notice of, alleging therein that no man of sense could believe the Pope's infallibility, transubstantiation, etc. For this he was suspended, reponed, and suspended again. Archbishop Cairncross of Glasgow had, it afterwards transpired, encouraged Kinaries after his offending sermon to go to London and print it, lending him £20 to pay his expenses. In September of 1689 he was accused before the Privy Council of not reading the proclamation of the Estates, and not praying for their Majesties William and Mary, but for the late king, that God would restore him to his wonted privileges; also of keeping correspondence with papists and not observing the Fast. Although the charges were found not proven and he was acquitted, the parish was declared vacant towards the end of 1691, probably in consequence of a petition from the Magistrates and land parish of Selkirk to that effect, "in respect of Doctor Cannaries his long absence." With a hundred and eighty others, he unsuccessfully petitioned the General Assembly to be received into communion, went to England, and was installed in the rectory of Abington. He married Anne, second daughter of James, Earl of Buchan. He published several sermons and books, some attacking Rome, and one entitled *A Scourge for the Presbyter's back.* It is no great lack of charity to presume that the principles which governed the actions of Dr. Canaries were to a great extent the same as those acknowledged by the excellent Vicar of Bray.

Fount., 163, 207.

P. R.

1694.—George Hume (M.A., Glasgow), ordained 21st September, but remained in Selkirk only three years.

1699.—William Macghie (M.A., Edinburgh), ordained 23d December, remained in Selkirk until his death in 1725, aged about 52. Ecclesiastical records teem with the difficulties encountered by this minister in the discharge of his duties and maintenance of his rights. In 1708 he had a stand-up fight on Sunday with the Laird of Todrig's men for a disputed seat. Two years P. later he complained to the presbytery that " although he had been minister of the parish for ten years, he had all the while had no grass for his kine and horse but what he paid for; albeit by P. R. several laudable laws and Acts of Parliament, ministers obliged to keep a horse are allowed as much grass as feeds two kine and a horse, lying nearest to his manse; and albeit it be of undeniable and incontestable verity that his predecessors did enjoy and possess that part of grass commonly called the Bog for a long tract of time to the best information, from before the '38 until the '86 or '88. But at the Revolution, there being a discontinuance by reason of a long vacancy, the town of Selkirk took it into their own hands, and ever since have sett it as part of their common good." Still concerned for his loaves and fishes, Mr. M'Ghie in 1718 P. R. represented "that there were several houses and yards in Selkirk which did belong to the ministers thereof; and that from the Reformation until the Revolution they were still in use to sett out the same to tenants in tacks, which he had seen." Next year the tenants were reported desirous of entering into submission. On May 9, 1725, the second Sabbath after his death, his brother, James M'Ghie, merchant in Edinburgh, delivered up the bible, tokens, token mould, and K. R. the register of discipline; and special provision was made for the late minister's grave in the kirkyard.

1726.—David Brown, M.A., presented by the Duke of Roxburgh from the parish of Gordon, in compliance with a unanimous call, supported by William Waugh, Town and Sheriff S. R. Clerk, Bailies Chisholm and Scott, Treasurer Curror, Dean of Guild Mein, Pringle of Haining, Plummer of Middlestead, Scot of Todrig, Gilbert Waugh of Shaw, and Stodderd of Williamhope. Mr. Brown was ordained on May 5, and when he died in 1753, he had been twenty-seven years minister of Selkirk. By his wife, Janet Scott, he had a son William, who became minister of Maxton.

1754.—William Trotter. Was minister to a Presbyterian congregation at South Shields when presented to Selkirk in 1753 by the Duke of Roxburgh. After a stout resistance on the part of the town and congregation, he was ordained in July of the following year. After P. eighteen years of pastoral work which is said to have endeared him to his flock, he died in 1771, leaving a widow (Janet Thomson), who survived until 1804.

1772.—Thomas Robertson. Ordained 8th May, died 5th September 1805. His wife was Robina Lang, of Selkirk, who survived him seven years. He contributed a description of the parish to the First Statistical Account (1792), referred to by Sir Walter Scott in his notes on B. M. "The Souters of Selkirk."

1806.—John Campbell, presented by the Duke of Roxburgh in 1805, and ordained 18th April following; died at Bridge of Allan in 1857, in his seventy-ninth year, survived by his widow, Jane, daughter of Mr. Richard Sheriff, farmer at Lugate. Mr. Campbell was minister of Selkirk for one year more than half a century, during which period his broad, charitable, and considerate disposition evoked the affectionate regard of all around him. Essentially " a

moderate," he was of a manly, honest type; not himself ascetic, and not rigid
in his judgment of others—more pleased to do or hear of a good act than
devoted to the exposition of creed and doctrine. Many stories of his *bon-
homie* and humour still float about the parish. One day he had a visit from
a hearer full of anxiety to hear what Mr. Campbell could say in elucidation of
Melchisedec, whose mysterious origin or want of origin had for some time per-
plexed the worthy souter. To this uncongenial task the minister set himself
under a strong sense of duty, and having been at pains to show the doubt-
exciting patriarch in true orthodox light, was gratified to hear his parishioner
express the relief which his clear and lucid explanations had afforded. "By
the bye," said the latter as he was about to leave, "could ye be sae guid, Mr.
Cawmill, as lend me a five-pund note? I'm raal sair pit till't the now, an'
if ye—" "Get out of my sight, you hypocritical scoundrel," cried the
minister, giving the departing frame of the doubter a strong impetus;
"I'll teach you to come here for a five-pound note, riding on the shoulders of
Melchisedec!" Of his father, the Rev. John Campbell, "Roarin' Cawmill of
Lilliesleaf," it is said that he was the most popular minister in the district,
his great aim being to promote the welfare and happiness of all within his
influence. Sometimes his genial sociability led him into situations which
would not now be considered quite in keeping with his profession. Early one
fine Sunday morning, the beadle's wife, on her way to the manse for the kirk
keys, was astonished to find the minister sound asleep on some straw near the
glebe midden. At once connecting the incident with the fact that Mr.
Campbell had been at dinner a short way out of Lilliesleaf the night before,
the woman, as she shook him awake, exclaimed, "Eh, wae's me, Mr. Cawmill,
is this you?" Rubbing his eyes for a moment, he instantly took in the
situation. "Hold your tongue, Margaret," he quickly said, "it was for a
wager;" on which he rose and set out for the manse. Being much importuned
by his wife to take into his own hand the punishment of their boys, who were
getting beyond her powers of chastisement, Mr. Campbell, putting on his
sternest countenance, took a horsewhip from its place in the hall, and sternly
ordered his sons to go up-stairs before him. Upbraiding them in a voice of
thunder, and cracking the whip violently all the while, he drove the offenders
to an attic room, in which he locked himself with them. Still prancing on the
wooden floor, and making the furniture resound with strokes of his whip,
Mr. Campbell told the boys to cry their loudest. "Roar, ye young deevils,
and make yer mother think I'm murderin' ye." Before long, the steps of

the agitated mother hurrying up-stairs were audible through the din, but not until she had shaken the door violently for some minutes, imploring her enraged husband to have mercy on her poor boys, did Mr. Campbell relent. Never again did the good lady ask her husband to assume the office of family corrector. One of the boys became minister of Selkirk, and another, Robert, rendered valuable service to his country during the mutiny at the Nore. At the peril of his life, he went aboard one of the rebel ships in disguise, and discovered the plans of "Rear-Admiral" Parker. He got his post-captaincy for this exploit. Having run a small French fleet into a Mediterranean port, he disputed with his senior officer on the station the claim for prize-money, and succeeded in obtaining £70,000. His brother, the minister of Selkirk, rarely or never ventured beyond the routine of his regular work, the only publication which can be credited to him being an account of the parish (1833), contributed to the second Statistical Account.

Bord.
Mem.
262.

1857.—James Farquharson, M.A.

Ecclesiastically, the church of Selkirk was a prebend of Kelso, in the Deanery of Peebles, Archdeaconry of Teviotdale, and Diocese of Glasgow. It was a church before some of these sub-divisions were effected; but from its foundation it appears to have been subject to the western Bishop. As to where the primitive church of the eleventh century stood there is no evidence whatever, and alike unknown is the site of the Tironensian Abbey founded in the twelfth. Concerning those in existence from the departure of the monks in 1126 till the beginning of the sixteenth century, history and tradition are alike silent; but about this time an entry in the priceless records of the burgh sheds a ray of light. It was before the day of Town Councils, government being then by an Inquisition or Inquest of the "best and worthiest of the burgh," presided over by an alderman and bailies. At a meeting on 17th February 1511-12, the Inquest resolved "Our Lady work, withheld from God, to be completed as is begun." And for the completing of the same, the parishioners shall be "afald" (one-fold, a fine Scots word for sincere. Wallace bewailed Graham as his best brother—his "afald freynd"). "And all burgess-money, and the common goods of this said town, and the bread money shall be given to Thomas Johnston—lending as is permitted to the said work until it may be gotten again. Also, it is ordained that each neighbour who is warned by the kirk-masters shall go to the kirk-work when they are required, or give twelve pence to the kirk-work who so fails." From which we may

understand that the previous church was either out of use or ruinous, and
that the people were putting forth their whole strength for the erection of a
new one.   In April, at a diet to discuss the advisability of going on with the
steeple, Stephen of Lauder thinks the steeple is "maist convenient to be
biggit, as they may win till it;" but George Scott says, "by his grate aith,"
that as it is begun it is most convenient to have it finished.   Others contend
the kirk should be completed.   Not a word is said about plan or dimensions,
but from later entries it seems probable that several side-chapels were attached
to the main building.   From June 1538 the Rood Altar was to stand without
service for a year, while two of the Inquest collected offerings wherewith to
buy ornaments for its repair.   It was further resolved that the service of that
altar be by election of the bailies, aldermen, and community, "as our forbears
gave it aye to ane toun man, burgess or born man therein."   The Inquest
declared three months afterwards that they would cause Sir Thomas Scoon to
say mass at any altar within the kirk, except the Rood Altar, for his wages,
"hecht and promittit within the toun."   Neither in English nor in Scottish
records is there proof that the kirk suffered in the destructive raids made by
Hertford and other English Generals during the first half of the sixteenth
century; but the following extract shows that its sanctity afforded no protection from the sacrilegious assaults of immediate neighbours :—

B. R.,
1512.

P. S.,
xxvi. 67.

February 10, 1553-4.—Remission to George Hoppringle of Torwoodlee; David, William
Robert, and John Hoppringles, brothers of the said George; Robert Blake, Richard Leyis, John
Leyis, James Greif, Alexander Thomson and Robert Leyis, for their absence from the army
assembled on Gladsmuir in 1548, and for art and part of burning the church of Selkirk in the
month of   1534 (?).

This is the last mention of the church prior to the Reformation; but the
same building evidently continued to be used for Presbyterian worship.   In
1617, at a Presbyterial visitation of Selkirk, the parishioners were urged with
all diligence to repair that particular part of their kirk called " Brydone's
Aisle," which wanted all its timber.   This was either the little chapel of which
the Roman Catholic priests of that name had special charge, or that in which
Sir William Brydone, the vicar, left money to provide a shrine.   In 1695, the
presbytery accepted estimates for the repair of both kirk and manse; but the
nature and extent of the repairs may be guessed from the tenor of a petition
to the kirk-session in 1700.   It being therein represented that several
families had no convenience to hear the word, the session agreed to give
them "a portion of the empty room in the floor of the church for building of

P. R.,
1617.

K. R.

seats." In 1704 a porch was built; so late as 1714, the Town Council ordered seats to be made in the area of the church; in 1722 a wire window was put in Ker's Aisle; and two years later a note was sent to Harden, desiring he would order a new door for his loft, the old door being rotten and blown to pieces by the wind.　Mr. Laing, chamberlain to the Duchess of B. R. Buccleuch, having signified that he would not allow the kirk-bell to be tolled 1730. through her Grace's loft, the Dean of Guild was authorised to prevent Mr. Laing building up the rope-hole until the question was settled by the heritors. Things having grown from bad to worse, the heritors found it necessary in K. R. 1735 to take into consideration the ruinous condition of the church.　It was represented that the big door had constantly to be kept open in the time of divine service to give light to those who had their seats contiguous to it, by which the whole congregation was exposed to the inclemency of wind and weather, to their great hindrance in performing their duty.　Next day the Town Council agreed to share the cost of repairing the edifice, on the report that the wester aisle was ruinous, the bell-loft in great disrepair, and the walls of Ker's Aisle shaky.　A letter was read from the Duke of Roxburgh agreeing to pay his share in proportion to his valued rent within the parish; but the Council, being advised that his Grace, as patron of the parish and titular of the tithes, was bound to pay one-third of the entire expense, resolved to go to law on the point, if necessary.　Clearly the sturdy burgesses were not to be daunted by either Duke or Duchess.　Although it soon became evident that no tinkering could save the ancient building, in seven years estimates were received for further repairs.　This time the Merchants' P. R. Aisle was tottering, being eight inches off the plumb at nine feet high. The bell-loft needed renewed attention, as did the north, otherwise called Ker's Aisle, and the west, commonly called the Shoemakers' Aisle.　With these particulars and a mention of the "high steeple with the four turrets," it is possible to form some idea of the kirk's general plan and aspect.　At last came a warning that could not be neglected.　In April 1747, several stones having fallen from the wall into a pew, the session had to ask use of the Grammar School for worship, and by the end of August the venerable pile was levelled with the ground.　No time was lost in erecting its successor, the unroofed and lowered walls of which are now a picturesque ruin in the old churchyard.　A twelvemonth had not passed when the Council approved of the space allocated to the burgh in the new church, and sanctioned the B. R., transference of the bell from the Council-house, it being a parish bell.　Writing 1748.

N. S.
A., 7.
in 1833, the parish minister mentioned the kirk's having been frequently repaired since erection, the last time being in 1829, when it was newly roofed and repainted. We believe it was at this time there disappeared from the panels of the front gallery a series of remarkable paintings emblematic of the various crafts whose members occupied "the lofts" behind. It should be explained that certain portions of the gallery were apportioned amongst the crafts whose deacons, quarter-masters, and office-bearers occupied the front seat. On the panel of the Merchant Company's loft was painted the classic figure of Justice, blindfolded, with scales in her hand, and the motto, " A false balance is an abomination to the Lord." Each trade appears to have reproduced its flag upon its own loft-front. That of the tailors, in which Adam and Eve were represented scantily attired in their first efforts at clothes-making, as also the souters' fresco, in which a brother of the "gentle trade" was engaged in measuring a shapely leg, were objected to by some as foreign to worship and upsetting to feelings of devotion. Not even the fact that each picture was graced by a text from Scripture (that beneath the souter and lady being "How beautiful are thy feet with shoes, O prince's daughter") availed to save them, and they were ruthlessly obliterated. When the church was dismantled and unroofed in 1861, no one appears to have remembered these curious ancient groups beneath the surface paint; and with the other wood work the gallery front went to patch pigsties and outhouses. Of the new parish church the foundation-stone was laid in 1861, and little as is known of the architectural features of its predecessors, it may be safely assumed that none of them surpassed it in hideousness.

Whatever may lie hid

"beneath the clover sod
That takes the sunshine and the rains,"

there are not so many ancient tombstones to be seen in the churchyard as might be expected in a place so long used for burial. Undoubtedly the oldest is a slab built into the wall of the ruined church, on which is portrayed the full-length figure of some one evidently belonging to the higher ranks of life—from the coat of arms and the letters " AIK," probably one of the Scotts of Harden, who lived at "Aikwood," or Oakwood. It is almost identical with one in Melrose Abbey in memory of George Haliburton, and dated 1536.

A strange feature in connection with this stone, found several feet below the surface in the church interior, is that the first name seems to have been chiselled out of the inscription, which is in raised letters. Among the notable headstones standing in the churchyard is one in memory of "Master John Angus, Bailie of Selkirk, who died in 1662, aged 48;" and another to James Ewart, burgess, 1683, aged 84; his son Robert, town and sheriff clerk, 1690, aged 34; as also John, Dean of Guild, 1740, aged 81.

Tombstones in Churchyard.

One commemorates Thomas Curer, deacon-convener of the trades, 1748, aged 88; and another William Rodger, late deacon of the taylors, 1763, aged 76. Fragments of stone of great antiquity have from time to time been removed, among them the shaft of a cross having every appearance of the early Christian period. At different times the school playground and cloth-market, the churchyard has sustained rough treatment; but beneath the surface must lie many a monumental fragment of priceless antiquarian value.

Like most country churchyards, this one has its tale of horror; and it is in keeping with the locality that the incident concerns a souter. Early one winter morning, before daylight, a brother of the craft, whose house opened into the churchyard, had a call from a stranger, who ordered a pair of shoes to be ready at a certain hour next morning. There was something about the appearance and manner of his customer which impressed the souter with the necessity of being up to time, so that the shoes were ready when the stranger called. More than ever struck with his unusual aspect, the trades-man followed him into the dark, walking silently and closely behind him, till at a particular grave he suddenly vanished. Leaving his awl in the mound that he might recognise it again, the shoemaker at daylight brought a great company of the townspeople, who helped him to break open the tomb. In the coffin beside a well-preserved corpse were the newly-made shoes! Oblivious of the fact that they had been paid for by their mysterious owner, Crispin took them away, and had the grave refilled. But next morning, an hour before cock-crow, as he was stitching away at new work, he was confronted by his unearthly customer, glaring at him with a malignity which froze his blood with horror. "You have made me the wonder of the town," said he in ghostly tones, "but I'll make you a greater." At daylight the wretched souter's body was found rent limb from limb upon the violated grave. An aged bedridden father of the craft, when told of what had happened, remembered hearing of a man who had stolen leather from the pits being cursed from the altar, and condemned by the priest to have his eternal slumber broken every hundred years to test the honesty of his descendants.

OAKWOOD TOWER.

pen & ink sketch by T. Scott

CHAPTER XVI.

PLACES IN PARISH OF SELKIRK.

BOWHILL.

If you climb to our castle's top,
I don't see where your eye can stop;
For when you 've passed the corn-field country,
Where farmyards leave off, flocks are packed,
And sheep-range leads to cattle-tract,
And cattle-tract to open-chase,
And open-chase to the very base
O' the mountain,
—And the whole is our Duke's country.

BROWNING.

BOWHILL is now interesting chiefly as the residence of the Duke of
Buccleuch, and as the manor-house of his vast estates in Ettrick Forest. But
to these it is quite a recent addition, having been till after the middle of last
century the property of a family named Veitch, following a branch of the
Murrays of Philiphaugh.

When first mentioned in 1455, the forest stead of Bowhill was in possession of the King and occupied by his own flocks, having been newly taken E. R.,
from Douglas after his forfeiture. Forty years later it takes its place in the vi. 225.
all-embracing record of robbery, but on the suffering side, one of the Turnbulls Pit.,
of Whitehope having relieved Bowhill of eighteen ewes without consent of i. 23.
their owner; and in 1510 David Hoppringle of Tinnes missed sixteen oxen from Pit.,
the place, for which Thomas Dalgleish in Braidhaugh was sentenced to be i. 70.
hanged if he could not find surety. Pending settlement of a dispute between
Janet Borthwick and Isobel, daughter of James Murray, as to ownership, an
agreement was entered into in 1527, between Michael Scott in Oakwood and
Philip Scott in Headshaw, that the said Philip should "put to" a plough to
the stead in lifetime of said Michael. Two years later Michael obtained a
charter of the lands of South Bowhill in favour of himself and his son William, G. S.,
Isabella Murray having surrendered them in their favour for a sum of money iii. 793,
2350.

to be paid at her marriage, and in gratitude for her education and maintenance since her father's death, the grant being confirmed in 1541. In 1546 Robert Ker, burgess of Edinburgh, with Elizabeth Harvey, his spouse, got a nine years' tack of North Bowhill. One of the Scotts taking holy orders, became clerk of St. Mary's Church in Yarrow, but his lawless blood asserted itself on the occasion of the forcible entry of that sanctuary by his fellow-clansmen in 1557. In 1592, "Wattie Scot in Bolhill" so signed himself witness to a deed of caution for one of his turbulent neighbours, John Scott in Foulshiels; and

Sat. 13. among the "chosen men no more but thirty-three" called for by Buccleuch to achieve the rescue of Kinmont, Bowhill's brother William "crossed the strand."

In the first year of the next century happened a double tragedy, involving in grief and hatred two families, almost exactly a hundred years later united by an auspicious marriage—the Scotts of Bowhill (cadets of Thirlestane) and the Napiers of Merchiston. It seems that in the autumn of 1600, young Archibald Napier, a hot-blooded, high-spirited, restless cavalier, had a horse stolen from the House of Mure. Meeting Scott of Bowhill, he described the

Napier of animal, asking if he had seen one like it; whereupon the Borderer, sensitive
Merch.,
309, etc. upon the point of stolen horses, mistook the question for an indirect accusation, and bade the young stranger defend himself or die. Napier, it seems, avoided fighting; but Bowhill "lay all day in wait of him in the way, and at the evning focht him in the stret of the gait (narrow part of the road) betwix low dykes, quhair he culd not flei." Death was the penalty of the "rash intruding fool." There is no indication of the survivor having been prosecuted, the fight having been unsought by him and carried on under conditions which put it beyond legal interference. Above all, it was a fair straightforward encounter—

"foot and point and eye oppos'd,"

—very different from that by which the Scotts of Bowhill revenged their brother's death. Three of them, with others of the name, assisted by Thomas Crichton, cadet of the house of Sanquhar, "under clud of nicht, on foir-thocht felloine, airmed with suird, speir, and pistilettes," waylaid young

Birrel, Archibald Napier as he was "ryding hame to his awen hous," the Wowmet,
52. near Edinburgh, and put him to death with many wounds. This was on 8th November 1600; and was considered so horrible a murder even in those times of daily bloodshed, that King James vowed he would as soon forgive the Gowrie conspirators as the slayers of Archibald Napier. Napier's young

widow (Alesoune Edmeistoune), his father Sir Archibald, with his "brether and remanent kyn and friendis," obtained letters denouncing as rebels Walter Scott, James Scott, and William Scott in Shostanes, all brothers to Robert Scott of Bowhill, and John Scott in Wooplaw, *alias* John of Bonyton. This, however, did not satisfy Alexander and William, the two brothers of the murdered man, who having in vain urged upon Sir Archibald and the famous John Napier of Merchiston the carrying out of some dark scheme of revenge by which they should have blood for blood, declared they felt dishonoured, and must quit the country. In Sheriff Mark Napier's *Life of Napier of Merchiston*, are published touching letters from the parents rebuking their sons for their foolhardiness, and one from young Alexander Napier, in which he deplores the imminent peaceful settlement of the quarrel. He asks his relative young Archibald of Merchiston to "prevent the inequitable petition of the brother of Bowhill, who has stirred up the Lord Buccleuch to suit agreement betwixt us and them." Speaking of the Scotts' offer that " they suld give us a thusand pund and in all tyme cuming to be as brither," he says, " the quhilk offer dois so inanimat me with grit disdaine, that give it war for no moir bot for wilipending so our house and name, and so lichtly accumting of all, that I resolve, God willing, one day to mak thame buy it dearer. . . . For all is dishonorabell quhair thair is not eie for eie, and tuith for tuith ; and as I think nothing sall divert me from the sam, . . . so do I prey you both for your awen and my honor ; bot cheiflie for the remimbrance of him quhois curaguis luve wald niver lyne so long idill in ather your or my errand." Amongst loose papers belonging to the burgh of Selkirk, the writer found a draft deed of compromise, not that which so filled young Alexander Napier with " grit disdaine," but one of much later date. It purports to be an offer by William and James Scot, brothers of the late Walter Scot of Bohill, and Robert, son of said Walter, and on behalf of John Scot, called of Bonnington, to the Right Hon.   Napier, daughter of the late Archibald Napier, and David Balfour of Schannie, her spouse, and to the Right Hon. Lord of Marchinston, treasurer-depute, and to the Right Hon. Alexander, Lord Lowristoun, and William Napier his brother, acknowledging the crime of the slaughter of the said Archibald, and offering to agree to any terms which might be imposed upon them by arbitration, and to pay 2500 merks, etc. Here the infant daughter of the murdered man has become Mrs. Balfour of Schannie, while young Archibald, the fiery Tybalt of his house, from a headstrong cavalier breathing out slaughter against its enemies, has

developed into a grave and learned Lord of Session ycleped Lauriston. As
he was Lord Lauriston only from 1626 to 1629, we learn that up to this
period the Scotts had made no reparation for their cowardly murder of young
Napier. By the church courts they had not been so easily let off.

P. R.   1607, 12th May.—Compt. Walter, James, and William Scotis of Bowhill, and John Scot
of Bonitown, excommunicat for slaughter, having been upon the place of public repentance about
the space of half a year, protesting they were unfenzielie penitent for their sinnis, Mr. Patrick
Schaw, their minister, is ordained to proceed with them."

James Scott, however, was no sooner out of this broil than he got into
another, for which he had to humiliate himself before the reverend court in
1608. So numerous are the "Scotts of Bowhill" mentioned about this time,
that it is impossible to identify them with distinctness. Both the north and
south halves of the estate were held by families of that clan, each ringing the
changes upon the same Christian names. In 1609, for example, Robert Scott
was served heir of his father Walter in the lands of North Bowhill; South
Bowhill coming to Andrew as heir of his father, Robert Scott of Oakwood, in
1616. A Robert Scott, called "of the Pillars," was infeft in North Bowhill in
B. R.,
vol. iii. 1625. In the Taxt Roll of 1628, South Bowhill is entered as the property of
Walter Murray of Oakwood; by 1643 both these places had been acquired by
Val.
Roll. the Master of Harden. North Bowhill still owned for laird a Robert Scott,
who was several times appointed to the war committee of the county.
A. P.,
vi. (1) 51,
etc. Andrew, James, and Adam Scott, follow each other in the Acts of Parliament
up to 1690, when the name disappears for a while to make room for Murray.
James was the theme of one of the most extraordinary of Satchel's extraordinary pastorals in 1686, in which the poet of the clan proved his friend's
descent from Buccleuch in a pedigree much too condensed to be quite satisfactory. The Murray who bought Bowhill (1690-1700) was Colonel William,
brother of the Lord Clerk Register. About 1702 he was succeeded by his
brother John, afterwards Lord Bowhill. Admitted advocate in 1688, John
A. P.,
var. Murray represented the burgh of Selkirk from 1689 to 1702, and the county
from 1703 to 1707. In 1695 he was Sheriff-Depute, and was at various times
nominated in Acts of Parliament to important public offices. Having voted
steadily for union during the preliminary negotiations, he was in 1707 elected
to the first Parliament of Great Britain as member for the county. On 6th
June of the same year, however, he took his seat on the Scotch Bench as
Lord Bowhill, which put an end to his parliamentary career. When, in 1708,
he applied to the Magistrates of Selkirk for a "complement of carriages" for

bringing lime to his new house, they granted him 100 "carriages," every B. R. workman in the burgh that had horses having to assist under pain of fine. Two years afterwards, the Magistrates, " being sensible of many acts of favour received from my Lord Bowhill, and that he stands in need of lime at present," granted a further "complement of 40 horses to bring home 40 bog to his Phil. lordship." This house cost £1500 sterling to build. In 1709, the presbytery MSS. permitted a student of divinity named Moore, to be chaplain to the learned judge while he resided within its bounds. His Lordship, dying about 1714, was lamented in certain remarkable elegiac verses as one

> Who for his virtue might have filled a throne :
> Judicious, great and pious Lord Bowhill.
> His empty seat upon the bench to fill
> Scarce any of our wits he 's left behind
> With such a pious and judicious mind !
> O ! senators, who sable weeds put on,
> Bowhill has scaled the heavens to a throne ;
> And trumpets forth the Mediator's praise,
> Where angels flee about, delight to gaze.
> Who did pronounce pointed decreets 'mongst you
> With open face the Deity doth view,
>
> .   .   .   .   .   .
>
> The sons of Levi cause the pulpits groan
> While for the loss of thee, Bowhill, they moan ;
> (No wonder ; for he amongst great and small
> *Jure divino* Presbytery did call)
> The Acts of Parliament, beyond the Pole,
> Did fill his heart, and his sublimer soul !
> He caus'd Hell's brats find stroke of Justice hand
> When they impanell'd for their crimes did stand ;
> The poor, whom he supported now do mourn,
> While friends prepare his body for the urn."

He was succeeded by his nephew, Lieutenant-Colonel James Murray, son of Colonel William. Concerning the gallant Colonel nothing is known except that he put the presbytery of Selkirk in a flurry, and only escaped their thunder by a timely retreat to Ireland in company with another object of their displeasure. In 1730, Colonel Murray let North and South Bowhill to Andrew Ker in Haining and Philip Scott in Oakwood, at £866 Scots, the parks and gardens at £207 Scots, the timber on the estate being valued at £300 sterling.

A remarkable character next appears for a short while as Laird of Bowhill, in the person of James Veitch—related to the Veitches of North Sinton and of Dawick—a very ancient family. In the beginning of 1745 he attended a supply meeting, which agreed to build a bridge over Yarrow at his request. Being a staunch Jacobite, he joined the rebellion, and is even said to have been one of Prince Charles's bodyguard, but the regular recurrence of his name at justice-of-peace meetings in 1745-6 is not reconcileable with constant attendance in the rebel army. A bit of blue-ribbon, worn by the Pretender, now in the Antiquarian Museum at Edinburgh, is said to have belonged to Veitch. With his pen he printed in clear fine style a copy of the Psalms of David in metre, as used by the Church of England, and at the head of the 31st Psalm he put, in extra large letters, the following words :—" Mary Queen of Scots, when murdered by the she-woolf Queen Elizabeth, upon the scaffold repeated aloud this psalm to the end." The manuscript is marked as " written by Iames Veitch of Bowhill. At Bowhill, September the xxi. 1746."

Very shortly after this, the lands passed into the hands of Buccleuch, the main stem of that family, whose cadets had held them during a century and a half, counting from the hapless reign of James v. It was a fortunate acquisition, inasmuch as it permitted the consolidation of an estate no less beautiful in itself than interesting from its historic associations. The ducal policies of Bowhill, its lakes, and home-farm, now occupy the tongue of land lying between Ettrick and Yarrow at their junction.

> " O, two such silver currents when they join,
> Do glorify the banks that bound them in."

From a rent-roll of the Buccleuch estates it is ascertained that the " holding" of Bowhill in 1766 was 960 sheep, 4 nolt, and 12 bolls sowing, the rent being £60, 10s. Mr. Wight, in the course of his agricultural survey of Scotland in 1777, seems to have been struck by the advanced condition of the land, which was then farmed by General M'Kay for Henry, third Duke of Buccleuch. " In every corner of this county," says Mr. Wight, " a traveller meets with illustrious marks of this young nobleman's zeal for improvements. Here we have no fewer than 120 acres of hill planted by him with fir and other trees." Since the time when King James, coming by Caddon Ford with his 5000 men,

> " saw the dark Forest them before,
> And thought it awsome for to see,"

the woods around Newark have never been denser or more " awsome" than they are at present. (Since this was written they have been sadly thinned by fierce gales, culminating in that of 26th January 1884, when thousands of

Surv.,
iii. 27.

Black Andro's stateliest pines were uprooted and left prone on the hill-side.)
Under the fostering care of successive Dukes, this part of the ancient forest
has been effectually redeemed from its reproach of treelessness, and the hill-
side might furnish as good bows of yew, of ash, or of hazel, as in the day when
it first received its name. By way of seeing what trees would grow naturally
on forest land left to itself, the late Duke Walter, in 1829, caused about 300
acres on the southern slope of Bowhill to be fenced round so as to preserve
it from the intrusion of sheep and cattle. It was hoped that oak-trees would
appear, having been indigenous in the ancient forest, but this rather sanguine
expectation has not been realised. From a paper on the experiment by the
Rev. Mr. Farquharson, minister of Selkirk, and a thoroughly competent B. N. C. 1878.
authority, the following description of the result is taken :—

"With the exception of a few trees which have been planted for ornament, and which
will be more particularly noticed afterwards, all the wood on the ground must be accounted
native, the berries from which it has sprung having been carried by birds, or the seeds transported by the agency of the wind, during the fifty years the ground has been 'hained.' The
Mountain Ash (*Pyrus aucuparia*), the Birch (*Betula alba*), and the Hawthorn (*Cratægus oxy-
acantha*), are the most abundant trees, occurring in nearly equal proportions, although unequally
distributed over the ground. Thus, Birch trees are most numerous, as might be expected, in
the neighbourhood of the old Birchwood at the S.E. corner of the ground. The Hawthorn
appears most abundantly in the middle ground, and under the shelter of the high surrounding
woods ; while the Mountain Ash prevails in the upper regions, and indeed it alone grows in
the highest and most exposed corner, becoming there a stunted tree or shrub, but still holding
its ground, although evidently sore battered by the winter winds. There are a good many
Scotch Firs (*Pinus sylvestris*) along the line of the Bowhill wood, and a few occur at a distance
from the wood. Some specimens of the Ash (*Fraxinus excelsior*) are scattered up and down the
whole area, but not one Oak, Beech, or Elm, nor a single Holly. Next to those already
mentioned, the most conspicuous objects are three species of Sallow,—*Salix aurita, S. caprea*,
and *S. cinerea*,—which are abundant and flourish vigorously, *S. caprea* often rising to the
dignity of a well-stemmed tree. When I have named these eight species, I have exhausted the
list of native trees, and tree-like shrubs growing in Howebottom, for I scarcely think a place
in the list should be given to the solitary Plane (*Acer pseudoplatanus*) on which I lighted.

"As regards smaller shrubs, the Raspberry is pretty abundant ; but I saw only one Rose-
bush (*Rosa canina*), and no trace of the Bramble. A few plants of Juniper (*Juniperus communis*),
which is rare in the district, grow among the heather on the height.

"Turning now to plants of humbler growth, it may be remarked that some species have
occupied large spaces to the exclusion of every other. Taking a view of the whole ground,
perhaps the Bracken (*Pteris aquilina*) is the plant that has most conspicuously asserted itself.
Many acres bear bracken and nothing else, except the scattered trees and shrubs that stand
among the fern. At one spot, where it has found both soil and shelter good, it attains a height
of over six feet, and presents a serious obstacle to the steps of the wandering botanist. Elsewhere, and especially towards the highest part of the ground, the common heather or ling
(*Calluna vulgaris*) occupies large spaces, and is evidently spreading to the eradication of grasses

and other plants around the territory it has already subdued.   I looked for *Erica Tetralix* and *E. cinerea*, but found neither of them.   The grasses I found most vigorous and common were *Aira cæspitosa* (whose local name is, euphoniously, Bull-snouts!), *Holcus lanatus, Agrostis vulgaris,* and *Agrostis canina,* and *Molinia cærulea.*   Among these *Aira cæspitosa* predominates, and may be said to be the grass of the place.   In moister spots, as at the sources of rills, and on flat places by Shielshaugh Burn, *Juncus acutiflorus* prevails.   At the date of my visits, over the whole lower space, and especially where the soil was at all moist, the eye was everywhere caught by strong plants of *Angelica sylvestris, Scabiosa succisa, Senecio Jacobæa,* and *Spiræa Ulmaria.*   At an earlier period of the year perhaps other species might be equally conspicuous.   About twenty-seven years ago, some Deodars, Spruce Firs, and Common Yews were planted in Howebottom. . . .

"The lesson I draw from the Howebottom experiment is that in the old Forest of Ettrick there was not a stately and uniform growth of large timber.   I infer that the ground along the valleys was clothed with a dense brushwood of Hawthorn, Birch, and Sallow, Mountain Ash mingling with these, but flourishing more freely on the hill sides; while above this lower growth rose at intervals "many a semelie tree,"—the Fir, the Ash, the Oak; for although Howebottom offers no evidence that the Oak is indigenous to the district, remains of it preserved in our peat-bogs, attest that it once flourished as a native in the vales of Ettrick and Yarrow."

But no association invests Bowhill with so much interest as its connection with Sir Walter Scott.   Here it was that "his lovely chieftainess, who has more of the angel in face and temper than any one alive," commissioned him to write the ballad which grew into the "Lay of the Last Minstrel."   "If she had asked me to write a ballad on a broomstick, I must have attempted it," says Scott in a letter to Miss Seward.   Drawn partly by a strong sense of feudal attachment, and more—much more—by the inherent courtesy and kindness of his hosts, Sir Walter continued to be a frequent guest at Bowhill to the end of his life.   The last letter he received from Duke Charles was written when his Grace was about to embark at Portsmouth on his unavailing voyage to Lisbon in search of health.   "My prodigious undertaking," writes his Grace, "of a west wing at Bowhill, is begun.   A library of 41 feet by 21 is to be added to the present drawing-room.   A space for one picture is reserved over the fireplace, and in this warm situation I intend to place the Guardian of Literature.   I should be happy to have my friend Maida appear. It is now almost proverbial—'Walter Scott and his dog.'   Raeburn should be warned that I am as well acquainted with my friend's hands and arms as with his nose, and Vandyke was of my opinion.   Many of Raeburn's works are shamefully finished; the face studied, but everything else neglected.   This is a fair opportunity of producing something really worthy of his skill."   In reply, Scott made an effort to have Allan substituted for Raeburn as the painter of his portrait, on the ground that the latter had " twice already made

Lock., cxiii.

Lock., cxliv.

a very chowder-headed person of him ;" but the Duke's proposal was never carried out; and the portrait which now hangs in the reserved position in Bowhill Library was painted by Raeburn in 1808 for Constable the publisher. It has been made familiar by a thousand plates, and is in itself the most attractive object in the now palatial mansion of Bowhill. The spirit of the great minstrel lingers about the whole place. Who can ever forget the lines he wrote in prospect of acquiring Broadmeadows, and seeing

> "Close beneath proud Newark's tower
> Arise the Minstrel's lowly bower."

It was his own old age that he sought to foreshadow in that of the wandering singer—

> "But still,
> When summer smiled on sweet Bowhill,
> And July's eve with balmy breath
> Waved the blue-bells on Newark heath,
> When throstles sung in Hairhead-shaw,
> And corn was green on Carterhaugh,
> And flourished, broad, Black Andro's oak,
> The aged harper's soul awoke !"

Scotts of Buccleuch.

It would be interesting to trace the steps and recount the incidents by which the obscure lairdship of Buccleuch has developed into a conspicuous dukedom, and the barren farm expanded to a magnificent domain. But for this many volumes would be required, and it must suffice to note only such events as associate the family with its cradle county.

Abundant material is furnished in two princely volumes of a History of the Scotts of Buccleuch, written by Mr. William Fraser, to which we are indebted for part of what follows. Adopting his pedigree of the Scotts, as preferable to the mythic tree drawn up by Sir Walter Scott, and to any other that has been attempted, we are, at the same time, not to be held as homologating all his assumptions. Properly, indeed, the Scotts of Buccleuch begin with Robert, fifth in his list, and first distinctly mentioned possessor of Rankilburn—the original name of Buccleuch.

Pedigree by Mr. Fraser.

I. Richard le Scot of Murthockston.	*Circa* 1265-1320.	
II. Sir Michael, his son.	*Circa* 1320.	Died 1346.
III. Robert Scott of Kirkurd, his son (?).	*Circa* 1346-89.	

		Born	Died
IV.	Walter, his son.		Died 1402.
V.	Robert, his son.		Died 1426.
VI.	Sir Walter, his son.		Died 1469.
VII.	David, his son.		Died 1491.
VIII.	David, his son (predeceased his father).		Died before 1484.
IX.	Sir Walter, his son.		Died 1504.
X.	Sir Walter, his son, "Wicked Wat."		Died 1552.
XI.	Sir William, his son (predeceased his father).		Died 1552.
XII.	Sir Walter, his son.		Died 1574.
XIII.	Sir Walter, first Lord Scott, his son.		Died 1611.
XIV.	Walter, first Earl of Buccleuch, his son.		Died 1633.
XV.	Francis, second Earl of Buccleuch, his son.	Born 1626.	Died 1651.
XVI.	{ Mary, Countess of Buccleuch, his daughter.	Born 1647.	Died 1661.
	{ Anne, Duchess of Buccleuch and Monmouth, her sister.	Born 1651.	Died 1732.
XVII.	James, Earl of Dalkeith, her son.	Born 1674.	Died 1705.
XVIII.	Francis, second Duke of Buccleuch, his son.	Born 1695.	Died 1751.
XIX.	Francis, Earl of Dalkeith, his son.	Born 1721.	Died 1750.
XX.	Henry, third Duke of Buccleuch, his son.	Born 1746.	Died 1812.
XXI.	Charles, fourth Duke of Buccleuch, his son.	Born 1772.	Died 1819.
XXII.	Walter Francis, fifth Duke of Buccleuch, his son.	Born 1806.	Died 1884.
XXIII.	William Henry Walter, sixth Duke of Buccleuch, his son.	Born 1831.	
XXIV.	Walter Henry, his son.	Born 1861.	

Rag.
Ro.,
125.

R. S.,
i. 29.

I. "Richard le Scot de Murthoston," was one of the Scottish Barons who swore allegiance to Edward I. of England in August 1296; and his lands were restored to him by a Royal edict issued at Berwick on the 5th September. He is therein styled "Richard le Scot de Murthoston, in county of Selkirk." Murthoston is in the county of Lanark; but this difficulty is ingeniously surmounted by Mr. Fraser. The lands restored, he says, could not be Murthockston, since these were in Lanarkshire. "They were in the county of Selkirk, and we may conclude almost with certainty that Rankilburn and Buccleuch were the lands referred to." A conclusion at first sight somewhat unwarranted; but becoming more probable as the family history unfolds itself. If the assumption is right, the Scotts must quite recently have come into possession of Rankilburn, for in 1236 it belonged to Nigel de Heris, the king's forestar.

L. M.,
ii. 666.

II. "Sir Michael Scot" is in the list of slain at the battle of Durham in 1346, and his name is mentioned amongst those who fought at Halidon Hill. Nothing else is known of him, his relation to Richard of Murthockston being assumed.

Bucc.,
ii. 15.

III. Robert Scott is, in Mr. Fraser's tree, styled Sir Michael's son, but there is no proof whatever of the connection. He is first of the family of whom there is charter evidence, his name occurring in a deed whereby King Robert II. conveyed and confirmed to Walter Scott, son of the deceased Robert, the superiority of Kirkurd (Kirk-Eward) in Peeblesshire. The deed does not say that Robert the father had possessed Kirkurd, but he may have been the representative of a family which had long held lands in the same county. About 1240, an Adam le Scot is mentioned in connection with the lands of Ingliston, near Kirkurd; and in 1296, a Walter le Scot swore fealty to King Edward I. for lands in the shire of Peebles. There were thus two families of Scott, one holding lands in Peeblesshire and another at the

O. P.,
i. 189.
Rag.
Ro.,
144.

same time holding lands in Lanarkshire, both of which lands are later on found in possession of one family of the name. By way of accounting for their amalgamation, Mr. Fraser suggests that Walter le Scot in Peeblesshire and Richard in Murthoston were brothers; and that Walter's line having failed, his property fell to this Robert, third of Murthoston. Should not the supposition be the other way? The non-recurrence of Richard or of Michael's name in the Buccleuch pedigree suggests rather the disappearance of the Murthoston branch; and as strongly does the constant repetition of Walter and Adam confirm the survival of the Peeblesshire family. In absence of documentary proof, it is instructive to find this view supported by tradition. Captain Scott of Satchels, no infallible authority indeed, but none the less a faithful mirror of the common belief, says in his doggerel history of the Clan Scott, written in 1686 :— P. 52.

> The barony of Eward was Buckcleugh's share. . . .
> It was called Scotstoun Hall when Buccleuch in it did dwell. . . .
> When Buckcleugh at Scots-hall kept his house.
> Then Peebles church was his burial-place,
> In the Cross-Kirk there has buried been
> Of the Lairds of Buckcleugh either six or seven ;
> There can none say but it 's two hundred year,
> Since any of them was buried there.

Two hundred years back from 1686 is near enough to 1491, when David Scott, dying at Rankilburn, left instructions in his will that he should be buried in Peebles. If Satchels is as trustworthy about the five or six lairds previously buried there as he evidently is concerning the date of the last interment, the Buccleuch family must be traced to the Peebles Scott, Walter, rather than to Lanarkshire Richard. This would bring the connection with Selkirkshire a generation or two later, but would detract nothing from the antiquity of the family, Walter and Richard having been contemporaries. Before leaving Robert Scott it is proper to remark that but for the casual mention of his name in the charter above mentioned, he would never have been heard of.

IV. WALTER SCOTT got a royal gift of Kirkurd barony, already alluded to. He is also mentioned as owner of a large tract of country between Rankilburn and Tima—really the first O. P., i. reliable notice of the Scotts' connection with their titular lands of Buccleuch. Sir Walter Scott 243, 265. was one of the brave Border barons who fell in the disastrous battle of Homildon in 1402. It Pink., is quite as likely that the Lanarkshire, Selkirkshire, and Peeblesshire lands were united in his i. 72-4. time as in his father's, but in both cases it is matter of conjecture, the identity of Walter of Kirkurd and Walter of Rankilburn being by no means certain.

V. ROBERT SCOTT is really the first baron of whom it can be irrefragably proved that he owned all three estates. Under the designation of Lord of Murthoston, in 1406-7 he confirmed, as superior, the transfer of part of Kirkurd by Thomas Fraser to John of Geddes; and in 1415 he exchanged with the Bucc., monks of Melrose his lands of Glenkery for their lands of Bellenden, both in i. 23. Selkirkshire. By and by the spot thus acquired became the rendezvous of L. M., ii. 547. the clan when it rose to the foray or gathered for war; and to the cry of "Bellenden" the Scotts made their dreaded onset. It was this laird also who, P. in 1420, acquired half of the lands of Branxholm from John Inglis of Menar or

Manor. In 1410 he resigned the lands of Borthwick and Thoft Cotys (now Borthwickbrae) to Regent Albany, who regranted them to Sir William of Borthwick; and in 1426 he resigned the lands of Lempitlaw, in Roxburghshire, to his son and heir, Walter. Archibald, fifth Earl of Douglas, confirmed the gift in a charter dated at the manor of Edibredeschelis, the old name of Newark. Nothing is known of his career or character.

G. S.,
246.

Bucc.,
ii. 24.

VI. SIR WALTER SCOTT, first designated " of Buccleuch," possessed the estates for forty-three years, and added considerably to their extent. He seems to have exerted himself in helping James I. to suppress the lawless borderers after the king's return from his long captivity in England; and one of his earliest exploits was the capture of Gilbert Rutherford, a noted reiver. He obtained the title of knight between March and May 1436—probably at the coronation of James II., to whom he was afterwards of great assistance in counteracting the ambitious and powerful Earls of Douglas. He was a man of bravery and determination, and nothing could be more characteristic than the way in which he became possessed of the second half of Branxholme. When Inglis, its owner, complained of the depredations committed on the lands by English borderers, Buccleuch promptly offered to give him the lands of Murthoston for the remaining half of Branxholme. On the bargain being ratified, Sir Walter remarked that " the Cumberland kye were as good as the Teviotdale,"—a threat of retaliation which neither he nor his successors failed to carry into effect whenever the men of Tynedale were hardy enough to provoke it. In 1436 this laird was designated "Walter Scot of the Bucluche" —first and modest mention of a name now gracing the title of a dukedom. At Langholm, on May-day 1455, Sir Walter Scott and his eldest son David led a strong body of borderers against the last remnant of the army raised to revenge the Earl of Douglas's murder by the king. As a reward for these services, David Scott got a grant from the king of Quhytchestir, in the barony of Hawick; and gradually the family obtained many lands in Selkirkshire long possessed by the Douglases. From this time until the reign of James VI., the designation of Kirkurd, Branxholme, or Buccleuch, was used indifferently, the first gradually giving place to the second, and the second being finally superseded by Buccleuch. Sir Walter Scott died before February 1469, and was succeeded by David, eldest son of his marriage with Margaret Cockburn of Henderland. Another son, James, got Kirkurd and Hassendean, and a third, Alexander, died early, leaving two sons, Walter and Adam.

VII. David Scott was a man of extensive possessions, and though not of noble rank, was considered a desirable connection by no less powerful a baron than the fifth Earl of Angus, who betrothed his sister, Lady Jane, to David, Buccleuch's eldest son. According to the contract, if David Scott were to die his next brother was to marry the lady, and if she were to die her next sister was to marry David, and so down the sons and daughters on either side until the marriage was accomplished. It was consummated by David and Lady Jane, but the bridegroom survived only a few years, and is last mentioned as witness in 1476, with his brother William, to a charter granted by G. s., ii. 1273. Robert Scott of Haining, of certain lands in Peeblesshire. Another brother Robert is expressly mentioned in a royal charter for services on the side of the king at Blackness in 1482, when the royal army encountered the discontented nobles after the execution of court favourites by "Bell-the-Cat" and his associates. David Scott, his father, then too far advanced in years to take the field, supported the royal cause in Parliament, for which the king rewarded him by erecting all his lands into one free barony for ever, to be called the barony of Branxelme. In 1484, David and Robert, his son, were appointed Bucc., ii. 89. by the sub-prior and monks of Melrose Abbey bailies of their lands of Ettrick, Rodonow, etc., with the usual powers. David Scott died in March 1491-2, and in his will left donations to the kirks of Rankilburn and St. Mary of the Forest. He was succeeded by Walter, son of his son David by Lady Jane Douglas. His eldest daughter married Sir James Douglas of Drumlanrig, from whom descended the ducal line of Queensberry, now joined with Buccleuch. A second daughter married Haig of Bemerside. His son William is supposed to have been ancestor of the Scotts of Thirlestane.

IX. Sir Walter Scott, like his father, died early, leaving nothing eventful to be recorded of him. In 1494 he was one of an inquest by which Alexander Erskine was retoured as heir to his father, Thomas Lord Erskine, in the lands of Syntoun and office of Sheriff of Selkirk. Robert Scott of Haining was on the same inquest. The same year he obtained decree against Douglas of Hornyshole as surety for certain Routledges who had sacked and burned the place and manor of Buccleuch. One of his last public acts was when in 1503 he witnessed the act of sasine by Murray of Philiphaugh, as Sheriff of the Forest, in favour of the Princess Margaret of England, queen of James IV. He died before 15th April 1504. His widow, Elizabeth Ker of Cessford, survived him forty-four years—till 9th October 1548—when she was burnt within the

Bucc.,
ii. 187.
tower of Catslack by Lord Grey and a party of Englishmen, accompanied, strange to say, by several Kers, near relatives of the aged dowager.

X. Sir Walter Scott (Wicked Wat), eldest son of his father, whom he succeeded in 1504, was one of the most indomitable of his indomitable race. At the time of his succession he was a minor, probably about fourteen, and his affairs were managed by his kinsman, Walter Scott of Howpaslot, appointed to the office of tutor by his father. While yet a young man, he led his retainers at Flodden; and it may have been his recollection of that bloody field which planted in him an inveterate hatred of "our auld enemies of England," for ever after one of his most striking characteristics. After that date he is styled a knight, so that he was probably one of those leaders who received the honour at the King's hand during the days of dalliance before the battle.

When, after the death of her royal lord at Flodden, Queen Margaret was proclaimed Regent, Sir Walter Scott became involved in a dispute with her in connection with her jointure lands of Ettrick Forest, from the revenues of which he had retained a part worth 4000 merks a year. The Queen having imprisoned both Scott and Ker of Cessford in Edinburgh Castle, in a letter to the Duke of Norfolk gave as a reason that from the feud which existed between them they were the principal cause of the disorder which prevailed on the Border. "These men," she assures the Duke, "do great evil, and specially the Laird of Buccleuch, who did the greatest evils that might be done, and took part plainly with thieves, as is well known." Afterwards we find Buccleuch leaguing himself with the Earl of Angus, whom the fickle Queen had divorced in order to marry Henry Stewart. When at last the Earl was made Warden of the East and Middle Marches, Buccleuch was one of a number of landed men who became bound to keep good rule on the Borders, to attend the Warden when he should call on them, and to "forth-put all Liddesdale men, their wives and bairns, from Teviotdale, Ettrick Forest, and the bounds adjacent." In 1526 occurred the battle of Melrose, caused by Buccleuch's attempted rescue of the young King from the custody of the Earl of Angus; and his defeat did not deter the Border chief from joining Lennox in another attempt having the same object and the same result. It cost Lennox his lands, but Buccleuch, doubtless by interposition of the King, was more graciously dealt with. Angus's animosity, however, was dangerous, and Buccleuch was compelled to remove to France, under a caution of £10,000 Scots not to return without the King's licence. In 1527 His Majesty remitted Sir Walter his "treason" at Melrose and Linlithgow, and on the 10th of February following granted him permission to return to Scotland. In May 1528 the young King escaped from Angus, and in July made public declaration that Sir Walter Scott of Buccleuch in appearing at Melrose had only followed his King's instructions. The autumn of 1527 was marked by the termination of a feud which had existed between Sir Walter Scott and Murray of Philiphaugh. On the 14th October a contract of agreement was made between them, whereby Buccleuch agreed to pay 500 merks Scots to James Murray, for "slauchtering, and spoliatioun of the Hangandschau, quhilkis was committit be the said Walter Scot, knycht, and his freyndis." Murray on his side agreed to give up all apprising of the lands of Kirkurde, and to deliver the charter of sasine to Sir Walter immediately after security was found for payment ; and each swore alliance against the other's foes. Bucc., ii. 148.

The accession of Angus's enemies to the King's Council and favour was not relished in England, where they were deemed no better than rogues. In a letter to Cardinal Wolsey, Lord Dacre (18th July 1528) mentions the Laird of Buccleuch "as a chief maintainer of all misguided men on the Border," and the English ambassador naming the thieves and murderers now become the young King's counsellors, says of Buccleuch that he was the cause of the death of Dan Carre, Warden of the East Marches of Scotland. King James, however, continued to place confidence in him, going so far as to pardon, "for the good, true, and thankful service done to His Majesty by Sir Walter Scott of Branxholm," his friends Robert Scott, tutor of Howpaslot, Robert Scott of Alanhauch, and William Scott of Hassendean, of certain crimes of which they had been convicted, restoring to them, moreover, their escheated lands. St. Pap. Hen. viii., iv. 523-6.

On the principle of setting a thief to catch a thief, the King issued a warrant to Buccleuch to apprehend Cockburn of Henderland, whose incessant robberies and acts of violence had become notorious and unendurable. Sir Walter's great-grandmother had been a Cockburn of Henderland, but no family considerations seem to have weighed with him in an enterprise so much to his heart as the punishment of theft and unruliness, especially when coupled with a royal licence to intromit and dispone as he pleased of the culprit's goods, wherever they could be got hold of. The end is well known. Henderland and Scott of Tushilaw were beheaded in Edinburgh in

May 1530. In the same year the Lord High Treasurer's Accounts show an item, "to the Laird of Buckcleugh for the taking of Penman, 2 elne and half of cloth of silver, price elne ix li.; summa, xxii li. x sh." Notwithstanding his assiduity in the matter, Buccleuch and other powerful Borderers were by the same Parliament which condemned Henderland arrested and warded in the castle of Edinburgh. Having been distributed amongst other prisons, they were detained until a thief-catching expedition by the King into Teviotdale and Liddesdale had been carried out without risk of their interference. Following up a promise to his uncle Henry VIII., King James marched southwards at the head of 8000 men, and executed without mercy all marauders who fell into his hands. In June 1532, the Queen-Dowager essayed to hold a court on her jointure lands of Ettrick Forest; but Sir Walter Scott having some reason to apprehend that the Queen's visit might do him no good, had the audacity to refuse Her Majesty the keys of Newark Castle. Lord Dacre narrating the incident to Henry VIII., says the Laird of Buccleuch " would in no wise deliver the keys unto Her Grace unto such time as he knew the King's pleasure. And so Her Grace did send a complaint upon him to the King, and thereupon the King commanded him to deliver them unto Her Grace. There is in company with Her Grace 60 horsemen and 24 runners on foot." To appreciate the egregious insolence of Buccleuch on this occasion, it is necessary to remember that, just a year before his own accession, his father was a principal witness to the act of sasine in favour of Queen Margaret after her marriage. In the following autumn and winter several pillaging expeditions were made by the Scotch and English into each other's territories. Buccleuch's lands having been ravaged and plundered, and Branxholm Castle burnt by the Earl of Northumberland in October, a retaliatory invasion of Percy's country was conducted by Sir Walter Scott and other Border chieftains. The writer of a letter to the English Earl, after describing the ravages made by two parties detached from the main body of the Scots, says, "The country arose with part of your Grace's garrisons, who scrymaged with the said forays, and pursuing them, did not only perceive two great bushements laid, but also did openly see three standards displayed, as to say, the Laird of Cessfurd, the Laird of Buccleuch, and the Laird of Fernihirst. With these lairds were all the headsmen of the Forest of Ettrick, with all Teviotdale on horseback and foot, 400 tried men from the west part of the Merse, and all the inhabitants of the Forest of Jedworth, and all the best tried men of Morrhowsland and Lawtherdale under the Lord

St. Pap., Hen. VIII., iv. 608.

Buccleuch. And so your Highness' subjects durst not enterprise with them, whereupon they most contemptuously had into Scotland divers prisoners, with great number of horse, nolt, and sheep." Buccleuch, in short, made war like a monarch. In consequence, however, of this bloodshed and anarchy he was again confined in Edinburgh Castle, and no sooner was he released in 1540, than he had to be again put in ward for disturbing the peace of the Borders. Once more he was restored to his liberty and possessions, an act of clemency afterwards confirmed by the Parliament of Queen Mary. A. P., ii. 414-433. Before the Privy Council, Buccleuch gave security for the peace of all his lands, besides promising to assist the King and his wardens against such Borderers as continued unruly. In the negotiations which followed the King's death relative to the betrothal of the infant Queen, Buccleuch, true to his unquenchable hatred of the English, espoused the French connection. His choice may have been disinterested, but it was not without reward, for on 9th November 1543, Sir Walter and his heirs-male were appointed, " by letters of Queen Mary " (then not two years old), with consent of the Regent Arran, " captains and keepers of Her Majesty's Castle of Newark, in the lordship of Ettrick Forest, for nineteen years; and for the exercise of the office Her Majesty granted to them her lands of Cartarhauch, Quhithilwra, Auldwark, and Huntlie." To avenge the Scotch repudiation of the treaty which had been entered into for the marriage of Mary with his son Edward, Henry directed the infliction upon the Scottish Border of an extensive and dreadful raid. Shortly after, the wily Buccleuch is found coquetting with English ambassadors desirous of winning his support, but taking care at the same time not to commit himself. Any hope they may have cherished of his submission must have been dispelled by the active part he took in the battle of Ancrum, when, owing to his stratagem, the English were totally routed and their leaders slain. Like success did not sit upon Buccleuch's helm at Pinkie (1547), where his efforts at the head of a numerous battalion were unavailing to save the Scots from overwhelming disaster. Undaunted by this defeat, the Scotts and Kerrs met shortly afterwards at Cousland, and entered into a bond to remain loyal to the Queen and her authority, to exert themselves against the auld enemies of England, and to uphold the Commonwealth of Scotland to the end of their lives. At two later meetings the oath was renewed by both clans; but the Kerrs proved faithless. Unknown to Buccleuch, the Lairds of Cessford, Fairnyhirst, and Littledean went with their friends to the English camp at Auld Roxburgh, remaining there till the English departed. Following up their treachery by helping Lord Grey to waste the lands of their fellow-countrymen, the Kerrs drove Buccleuch to offer submission to the English monarch, now Edward VI. His offer was accepted, though his sincerity was doubted; and on his engagement being broken, Lord Grey determined that such gross breach of trust should not go unpunished. Finding that nothing could be gained at Branxholme but the winning of the castle, and that was impracticable without cannon, Lord Grey and the Englishmen, assisted by Cessford and many other Kerrs, pushed on to Newark, which they considered might be taken without difficulty. Newark, having succumbed to a short siege, was burned, the victors securing a booty of 3000 sheep and 400 head of cattle. Six months afterwards, in July 1548, Buccleuch attended the Parliament held at Haddington to set aside the treaty with England, and to negotiate a marriage between Queen Mary and the Dauphin of France. John Knox says, "the Lord of Balcleucht, a bloody man, with many Goddes woundes, swore they that should not consent should do worse." Early in October of the same year, Cessford and the chief men of his name were committed to Edinburgh Castle, doubtless at Buccleuch's instigation. This aroused anew the enmity of the Kerrs, at whose solicitation Lord Grey made another inroad on the territory of the Scots. Accompanied by Cessford's brothers and by the whole clans of East Teviotdale, he came to the water of Ale, and there burnt, harried, and destroyed the corn, goods, and houses pertaining to Sir Walter Scott or his friends, carrying like havoc into the valleys of Selkirkshire. The town of Hawick was both pillaged and burnt, a similar fate befalling Selkirk, which had the expensive distinction of having Buccleuch for its provost. It was on this occasion that the tower of Catslack fell a prey to flames lighted by the English and the Kerrs, who were probably unaware that the walls contained their relative the dowager-lady of Buccleuch, herself the sister of a Cessford. At the instance of Sir Walter Scott, the Kerrs were summoned to answer for this raid before the Lords of Council, but the prosecution seems to have fallen through. But Scott was not unappeased. In April 1550 he obtained a Royal Commission appointing him Warden of the Borders between Minto Craig and Craykcross, in which bounds his tenants and retainers dwelt; and in the same month of the following year, he became Governor-general and Justiciar within the bounds of the lands and lordship of Liddesdale, and all other bounds in Teviotdale. Powers of the most ample description were vested in Sir Walter

St. Pap. Ed. VI., i. 75.

Hist. Ch., 175.

Scott by this commission. He was alike the maker, interpreter, enforcer, and avenger of the law throughout this vast territory, largely extended after a few months, when by commission under the Privy Seal, he became Warden and Justiciar of the Middle Marches of Scotland. Although advancing years (he was now more than sixty) and the harassments of Border strife were beginning to tell upon his vigour, the old chieftain set himself strenuously to fulfil the duties of his onerous post. The Privy Council records as well as those of local courts bear witness to his resolute industry in suppression of disorder; but he did not live long enough to effect a complete subjugation of the Border freebooters. Unable to reach him in fair field, and probably exasperated by his newly acquired eminence and power, a party of Kerrs and Humes murdered him in the High Street of Edinburgh on the night of the 4th October 1552. In the indictment, Hume of Cowdenknowes is charged with having stabbed Sir Walter with his own hands, and with having struck his sword through the body of the Knight while he clung to him, and with at the same time calling out to the Laird of Cessford, "Streik, tretour, ane straik for thi faderis saik." Then Hume and Cessford threw their victim into a booth-door, the former saying, "Ly thair, with my malison, for I had lewor gang by thi graif nor thi dure." After the bloody deed, the lairds appear to have sent their servants to "mak siccar." John Peacock, servant to Cowdenknowes, and others, were charged with having returned from the Tron and gone to the booth-door where Sir Walter Scott lay, "and lyfe in him," and with having struck him three or four times through the body. They stripped him of a cloak and "twa bonettis," giving them to a boy to carry. Meeting Bute Herald, who inquired what was the matter, they said, "Thair is ane lad fallin." George Hoppringle of Torwoodlee being "upoun the gait of Edinburgh at the committing of the said murther, sent his twa horce to the Lard of Cesfurd to ryd away upoun." Sixteen years afterwards Torwoodlee was himself miserably murdered in the night-time by a party of Elliots, who, at the same time, burned his house and carried off his property. As fast as they could, the murderers of Buccleuch rode south, eager to gain the shelter of their own mosses and mountains. When they passed Rule Water, one of them said to the people, "Heard ye any tidings of the Laird of Buccleuch? He is put in ward and will never come forth." But the haste of the Kerrs availed them little. They were declared rebels, reduced to absolute want, and to the woods and fells for shelter. Many of them were slaughtered, and none of them dare come forth from their hiding-places to ask protection. Ultimately, the principal men and their accomplices in the murder were banished to France, to serve in the contingent sent by Scotland to aid her ancient ally. Mr. Fraser says that the leniency of their sentence was greatly owing to their alliance with the Homes and to the favour of the Queen-dowager, who probably felt no great regret at the death of the man who had denied her access to her own castle of Newark. Sir Walter Scott was thrice married. By his first wife, Elizabeth Carmichael, he had two sons, who both predeceased him, William, the second, leaving a son, Walter, who succeeded to the estates. His second wife, Janet, daughter of Andrew Ker of Fernihirst, and widow of Turnbull of Bedrule, was within the prohibited degrees of consanguinity with Sir Walter; and the contract provided that a papal dispensation should be obtained. There was no issue; but by his third wife, Janet Betoun, Walter Scott had two sons and three daughters. Janet's father was a cousin of Cardinal and nephew of Archbishop Beaton. Her first husband died, from her second she was divorced, and she survived her third nearly sixteen years. In 1557-58, the Lady of Buccleuch marched at the head of an armed body of two hundred of her clan to the kirk of St. Mary of the Lowes, in Yarrow, and broke open the doors to get at "Sir" Peter Cranston. When she was accused before the Justice for this exploit, a warrant from the Queen Regent put an end to the proceedings. At a later period, she was mixed up with the affairs of Queen Mary and Bothwell, in a way not much to her credit. She appears to have encouraged and fanned their attachment, a part so notorious that she was believed to have brought about their connection by means of witchcraft. Sir Walter Scott has effectively introduced this supernatural accomplishment in his Lay of the Last Minstrel, of which she figures as the heroine, much softened and ennobled, it has to be admitted, by the poet's charitable imagination. "I dare not," says Sir Wm. Drury,

Border
MSS.,
Rolls
House. writing to Cecil, "deliver unto your honour the Lady Buccleuch's speech, yea openly, of her telling the cause she bred Bothwell's greatness with the queen by, nor of her speech of the queen, nor of his insatiateness towards women." To justify the projected divorce of Bothwell from his wife, it was to be asserted that he had had the company of the Lady Buccleuch since he was married; and she was said to be ready, if necessary, to come forward with the evidence. This widow of three husbands, an old woman comparatively, died the year after her paramour's ignominious flight from Scotland.

XI.—Of Sir William Scott, knight, younger of Buccleuch, the only remarkable thing is that he chose for his wife Grissel Beaton, sister of his father's third wife. She bore him one son and three daughters. Of these, the eldest married Kerr of Fernihirst, and had a younger son, Robert, who became Earl of Somerset; the second married a Johnston, and was ancestress of the Earls of Annandale; while the third, after escaping a sacrificial marriage with one of the clan Kerr, became husband of Carmichael of Meadowflat, whose heir was Earl of Hyndford. Sir William Scott predeceased his father by about five months. His widow married Sir Andrew Murray of Black-barony, "from whom," says Mr. Fraser, "the Murrays of Elibank are descended."

XII.—Sir Walter Scott was a child of three when the murder of his grandfather made him heir to the vast possessions of the family. It is he who figures in the Lay of the Last Minstrel, though Sir Walter availed himself of his poetic licence to represent the boy-heir as son of the murdered baron.

> But o'er her warrior's bloody bier
> The Ladye dropped nor flower nor tear !
>
> Until, amid his sorrowing clan,
>   Her son lisp'd from the nurse's knee—
> " And if I live to be a man,
>   My father's death revenged shall be."
> Then fast the mother's tears did seek
> To dew the infant's kindling cheek.

Possibly it was from this incident Lord Tennyson took the motive of his song, " Home they brought her warrior dead." When in the course of the poem, the young lad is tempted into the woods by the goblin-page and left to be captured by English bowmen, one of them thinks—

> " This boy's fair face, and courage free,
> Show he is come of high degree."—
>
> " Yes ! I am come of high degree,
>   For I am the heir of bold Buccleuch ;
> And, if thou dost not set me free,
>   False Southron, thou shalt dearly rue !
>
> Despite thy arrows, and thy bow,
>   I 'll have thee hang'd to feed the crow !"

Whereupon the Englishman prophesies that if ever the young chief should come to his command, he'll give the Wardens work upon the Border. As a matter of fact this laird had but a short lease of life, dying when he was twenty-five; but he lived long enough to prove himself of peaceful disposition rather than warlike. He took an active part in the negotiations and compacts entered into by way of staunching the blood-feud between the Scotts and Kerrs, and which mainly took the form of projected marriages. It is singular that while none of these unions was ever confirmed, the one Ker who was left out of all such arrangements should be the very one to marry a sister of Sir Walter Scott. Before the Scotts were able to patch up their quarrel with the Kerrs they had another with the Elliots, originating in a murder committed by one of the latter in the autumn of 1564. A trial before the Lords of Council resulted in five Elliots and Scotts being condemned, three of them being beheaded the same night on the Castle Hill of Edinburgh by torchlight. Severity had no effect, however, for in spring the Elliots killed a few more Scotts, burned their houses, and carried off their goods. A party numbering 300, harried and spoiled a distance of ten miles round the property of Buccleuch, slaying many men and some women and children. The English took advantage of the feud to side with "the Elwoods," on the ground that the longer the Scottish Borderers continued to quarrel amongst themselves the better it would be for the English. To pacify and subdue the turbulent thieves of Liddesdale several expeditions were made by Regent Murray, who was attended by Sir Walter Scott of Buccleuch. The young knight, however, sided with Queen Mary against those who supported her son, and maintained her cause with all the ardour of youthful chivalry. In 1565-6 he was appointed keeper of Newark, with the lands attached "for discharge of his office." At the same time and for the same period of nineteen years he was constituted "bailie and chamberlain of Her Majesty's lands and lordship of Ettrick Forest," with all powers and privileges belonging to the office. Much disputation has been indulged in as to whether Hamilton's assassination of the good Regent was an act of private revenge, or only part of a concerted plan for the overthrow of the English alliance and the restoration to power of Queen Mary. Be that as it may, on the very day after, Buccleuch and Fernihirst made a hot incursion against England, laying waste the country by fire and sword wherever they went. Queen Elizabeth ordered retaliation, and on the 18th April 1570, a strong body of English under Sussex entered Teviotdale. According to their own account they burned and razed in the country of these two chiefs about fifty castles or strongholds, and 300 villages or hamlets. For his part in an attempt to subvert Parliament at Stirling and for an attack upon Jedburgh for discourteously treating a pursuivant of the Queen's party, Buccleuch was warded in Doune Castle in Menteith, but on giving security he was allowed his liberty in July 1572. During the remaining portion of his life he appears to have busied himself in re-building Branxholm, which work was not finished at his death on 17th April 1574. By his marriage with Lady Margaret Douglas, daughter of the seventh Earl of Angus, he left a son Walter, who succeeded, and two daughters. Margaret, the eldest, was married to Robert Scott of Thirlestane, ancestor of Lord Napier and Ettrick, while Mary married Elliot of Lauriston. Sir Walter's widow afterwards espoused Francis Stewart (a nephew of Queen Mary). He, with base ingratitude, conspired, in 1594, against his cousin James VI. (who had created him Earl of Bothwell and given him the estates of his uncle), was banished, and died a beggar at Naples in the year 1612. His widow survived till 1640—sixty-six years after the death of her first and nobler husband, Sir Walter Scott. Froude identifies this Lady Buccleuch as the evil genius who promoted Queen Mary's passion for Bothwell; but as she survived that villain's flight seventy-three years, her extreme youth at the time of Darnley's murder may be considered to shield her against the charge. It is to the Dowager Lady Buccleuch, widow of her husband's grandfather, the wretched *rôle* is usually attributed.

XIII.—Sir Walter, Lord Scott of Buccleuch, was only nine years old when he succeeded. Before he had reached his teens the old Kerr feud again broke out, but was finally allayed by payment of 1000 merks from Kerr of Fawdonsyde for non-fulfilment of contract by which his son was to marry Janet Scott. Not so easily overcome was the unquenched hatred of the Scotts and Elliots. In April 1581, as two Elliots were passing the gate of Eidschaw at ten in the morning, Wat Scott of Eidschaw, with five or six of his servants, came out and set upon them. They struck the hand from one Elliot, and hurt the other in peril of his life. Much serving of summons, court decreets, and caution-finding followed; but the old scenes of bloodshed and unneighbourly rapine were re-enacted over and over again. Between Buccleuch and his kinsman Scott of Alanehauch, another blood-feud arose and was settled. On one side Adam Scott of Alanehaugh had to answer for his son David's part in the slaughter of one of Buccleuch's servants, while Buccleuch, on the other hand, had to compound for having slain the said David, though he alleged it was an accident. In the winter of 1587, while he was yet but two-and-twenty, Buccleuch made a raid into England, spurred perhaps by indignation at the fate of Queen Mary, with whose fortunes his family had more than once identified itself. He was warded for the act in Edinburgh Castle, but was soon released on the security of two friends. Next year he was appointed for the defence of Selkirkshire against strangers, and in 1590 he was chosen along with Andrew Kerr of Fernihirst and others to put in force the Act for suppressing Jesuits throughout the country. At the coronation of Anne, the Queen Consort, at which he was present, the same year, the young chief received his knighthood. About this time he had the imprudence to become implicated in the lawless acts of his step-father the Earl of Bothwell, in consequence of which he was exiled to France, the King graciously taking under protection his wife and children, and all his lands and possessions. Before setting out, Buccleuch arranged a dispute with Fernihirst relative to a lease of the teind-sheaves of Innerleithen. An altercation had occurred about the matter in the streets of Edinburgh, and swords had been drawn, two of Kerr's servants had been killed, and others severely wounded. A truce was arranged to remain in force till forty days after the return of Buccleuch from France. At first his exile was to be of three years' duration, but he was permitted to come home a year sooner. Eight years later, in 1600, he revisited France, and when there testified that a certain Andrew Scott, Sieur de Savigne, "was descended from our family of Baclough in Scotland," and so being "gentle," was eligible to serve in the King's Scots Body-Guards.

Bothwell's forfeited estates were first granted to the Duke of Lennox, who afterwards resigned them back into the hands of the King, by whom they were gifted to Buccleuch, in token of his great service in the cause of peace within the Borders. The lands included Alemuir in Selkirkshire, with Elvillane and Kirkstead in the same county. This vast addition to his property and influence was made by royal charter dated 1st October 1594; but afterwards it was arranged by King Charles the First that a considerable part of the lands should be restored to the family of the escheated Earl, Liddesdale being the principal property which remained with the Scotts. The real reason of the original transfer from Lennox to Buccleuch was the advance of sundry sums by the latter to the former. Certain rents in Ettrick Forest, payable to the Countess of Bothwell, having been conferred on Kerr of Fernihirst, the latter is found pursuing James Scott of Newark, Chamberlain-depute of the Forest, for the said rents, which Scott had been paying into the Countess's hands since the forfeiture. Sir Walter Scott was himself principal Chamberlain, and in 1603 obtained letters of horning against Sir William Stewart of Traquair for £93, 6s. 8d., part of a tax raised for the baptism of the prince. In 1593 the Scotts contributed 500 men to aid the Johnstons in the bloody conflict at Dryfe Sands, where their enemies, the Maxwells, were smitten hip and thigh, and Lord Maxwell himself slain. As a matter of course, they participated in the collision of the "Reid Swyre," when they were led by Walter Scott of Goldielands, one of the natural sons of " Wicked Wat "—

> "The Laird's Wat, that worthie man,
> Brought in that sirname weil beseen."

In 1594, Sir Walter Scott was re-appointed keeper of Liddesdale, and it was in this capacity that two years afterwards he effected the "rescue of Kinmont Willie." With the circumstances of this gallant exploit every borderer is familiar. Besides being in every collection of deeds of daring, every history of the time, it has inspired a ballad so pithy and stirring that once to hear or read it is to remember its incidents for ever. Buccleuch sits in Branksome Hall when news is brought to him of Kinmont Willie's illegal capture by Scrope's English soldiers, before expiry of the truce entered into by Robert Scott of Haining, as commissioner for his chief :—

> He has ta'en the table wi' his hand,
> He garr'd the red wine spring on hie—
> " Now Christ's curse on my head," he said,
> " But avenged of Lord Scroope I 'll be !
>
> " O is my basnet a widow's curch,
> Or my lance a wand of the willow-tree,
> Or my arm a lady's lilye hand,
> That an English lord should lightly me ?"
>
> And have they ta'en him, Kinmont Willie,
> Against the truce of Border tide,
> And forgotten that the bauld Buccleuch
> Is keeper here on the Scottish side ?

If they had forgotten it, he resolved it should be brought to their recollection. After applying in vain through every channel for the peaceful rendering back of the prisoner, Buccleuch determined to rescue Willie by force from his cell in Carlisle Castle. Accordingly he gathered a company of eighty well-appointed horsemen, mostly men of his own name, who reached the castle two hours before daybreak, on the 13th day of April 1596. Ladders they had brought turning out too short, a breach was

knocked out near the postern gate, by which the storming party forced an
entrance, and guided by information previously obtained, they soon reached
the object of their search.

> Wi' coulters and wi' fore-hammers
> We garr'd the bars bang merrilie,
> Until we came to the inner prison,
> Where Willie o' Kinmont he did lie.

There was no time to loosen his fetters, so they "hente him up" on Red
Rowan's shoulders, "the starkest man in Teviotdale."

> And every stride Red Rowan made
> I wot the Kinmont's airns play'd clang!

> "O mony a time," quo' Kinmont Willie,
> "I have ridden horse baith wild and wude:
> But a rougher beast than Red Rowan
> I ween my legs have ne'er bestrode!

> "And mony a time," quo' Kinmont Willie,
> "I've pricked a horse out owre the furs,
> But since the day I backed a steed
> I never wore sic cumbrous spurs!"

By the time the storming party reached the main body, which Buccleuch had
placed so as to thwart a rescue from the town, the English garrison and city
guard were gathering in numbers that might have overwhelmed his scanty
force. The clangour of trumpets, which Buccleuch had caused sound in order
to impress the sentinels and guards with the hopelessness of resistance, had
succeeded in its object, but it had also aroused the entire population. Armed
men had actually gathered in front to hinder the Scots on their return home,
but impressed by Buccleuch's resolute bearing, they concluded to leave
him a clear passage. Two hours after sunrise, the whole party reached
Scottish ground in safety ; and it was not long before the rescued freebooter
was relieved of his cumbersome anklets. Sir Walter Scott says that the
smith, not very alert at first, showed considerable alacrity when Buccleuch
thrust his spear through the window to arouse him. His daughter lived to
relate how, being then a little child, she saw in the grey of the morning more
gentlemen than she had ever seen before in one place, all on horseback, in
armour, and dripping wet—and much merriment in the company. In Scotland,
the conduct of Buccleuch was everywhere approved, and his splendid vindica-
tion of a lowly countryman's safety during truce hailed with delight. Even
in England, though Lord Scrope was furious and the Queen indignant, there

B. M.
Notes.

were not wanting men who admitted the injustice of Kinmont's capture, and were not slow to express their admiration of his rescue. Strong diplomatic notes were exchanged on the subject between the two Courts, and at one time it seemed as if war must result. Eventually, after eighteen months' argument, Elizabeth carried the day, and Buccleuch delivered himself up to Sir William Selby, Her Majesty's Master of Ordnance at Berwick. Throughout England the border chief was received not as a prisoner but as an honoured guest.

> "For banquets he had store, and that most free,
> Each day by some of their nobility :
> His attendance was by Nobles there,
> As he had been a Prince late come from afar."

When he reached London, and, having been presented to the Queen, was asked by Her Majesty "how he dared to undertake an enterprise so desperate and presumptuous," Buccleuch is recorded to have said, "What is it that a man dare not do?" Unaccustomed though she must have been to such rejoinders from her own courtly nobles, Elizabeth not only did not resent the answer, but turning to a lord-in-waiting, said, "With ten thousand such men, our brother in Scotland might shake the firmest throne of Europe." Sir Walter, in fact, at once stepped into the Royal favour—a distinction of which the family chronicler shows himself passing proud. His halting epic thus reports the Queen :—

> . . . I conceive you're a resolute cavalier,
> At Channel-hall your lodging shall be there,
> Then through our privy-garden to court ye may repair,
> At your own pleasure what time soe'er it be.
> And for your clearer passage ye shall have a private key,
> Except our counsellors and officers in charge
> We do not grant to any, but your merits to deserve.

And when he declined Elizabeth's offer of employment in her own service,

> The Queen answered—"My Lord, since it is so,
> Ye shall be dispatched within a day or two,
> And a letter ye shall carry along with thee
> To our cousin of Scotland his Majestie,
> Wherein your heroic spirit we must commend,
> And intend hereafter to be your steady friend."
> Next day she called her Secretar,
> And charged him a letter to prepare,
> To his Majesty, King of Scotland,
> Wherein she lets him understand
> She had passed from her former wrong,
> By reason Buccleuch was a valiant man.

During his honourable captivity in England, Buccleuch made resignation of all his estates into the hands of James VI. for regrant and new infeftment. The royal charter narrates that it was granted for a recompence and reward to Buccleuch, who with his predecessors, had been kindly tenants of the Crown in certain lands situate in the county of Selkirk; also for sundry large sums of money paid by Buccleuch to the King's treasurer; and for the manifold famous and singular services, acts, achievements, and exploits done by him to the honour, fame, and great commendation of the King and his realm, as well

Bucc.

in his private affairs as in those pertaining to the Commonwealth. Among the lands thus united into the new free barony of Branxholm were Buccleuch, Rankilburne, Kirkurd, Deloraine, Eldinshope, Fastheuch, Huntlie, Carterhauch, Auldwark or Cartermauch, Quhytilbrae or Cathmurlie (now Newark), Mill of Newark, Catslack, Easter and Wester Montbergeris, Schwtingleis, Appletreleis, Meirbank, Sutercroft, Carteleys, etc. etc. After his return from England, and more especially after the King's accession to the throne of Great Britain, Buccleuch set himself with great energy to the discharge of his duties as Keeper of Liddesdale. In one of the most flattering communications ever made by monarch to a subject, Sir Walter was granted complete indemnity for all his acts and deeds while engaged in this work of order. In the execution of His Majesty's commands, runs the letter, "Lord Buccleuch was necessitated to use fire-raising, to cast down, demolish, and destroy castles, houses, and buildings, to use hostile feud in hostile manner against the malefactors, as well in taking of their lives and killing and slaying of them, as in putting them to exile and banishing them from the bounds. In consequence also of the lack of prisons, the most part of these desperate men, immediately on their apprehension, were necessarily hanged, and punished with death by pit and gallows off-hand on the very spot." Concerning all which Buccleuch is formally exonerated from all pains, charges, and peril which may be imputed to him. The doughty chief, in fact, seems to have held the same opinion as Satchells, who, after valiantly defending freebooters and the honesty of their calling, so long as the kingdoms remained separate, adds :—

> But since King James the Sixth to England went,
> There has been no cause of grief,
> And he that hath transgressed since then,
> Is no free-booter, but a thief.

Tired, probably, of inactive peace in the years that followed the union of the Crowns, Buccleuch in 1604 went to take part with the Dutch in their struggle against Spain. In 1609 he returned, but till his death in 1611 he retained his colonelcy in the army of the Netherlands, and had regular reports of his company, which in 1611 is described as "in fine order, and one of the best in the country." In 1606 he was created a Peer of Scotland, with the title of Lord Scott of Buccleuch; but in the popular mouth he was familiarly "Lord Buccleuch." His wife, whom he married in his twenty-first year, was Margaret, daughter of Sir William Kerr of Cessford, and sister of the first Earl of Roxburgh. Elizabeth, another daughter of Sir William, calls Lady Buccleuch her best sister, and adds, "sche was a goud Ker, if ever ther wos any." Besides an only son, there were three daughters of the marriage. A natural daughter, Jeane Scot, called by Satchells "Hollands Jean," married Walter Scot of Whitslaid, who in 1633 granted to Earl Walter, her half-brother, a discharge for 8000 merks of tocher with her.

XIV. Walter Scott, first Earl of Buccleuch, was the first heir for a period of a hundred and forty years of full age at the time of his accession, his predecessors since 1470 having all succeeded during their minority. Soon after he became chief, he narrowly escaped being assassinated by one of the Elliots, one of which name he had evicted from certain lands in Liddesdale. In 1619 he was advanced by King James VI. to be Earl of Buccleuch, and, if one may credit the favourable muse of Satchells, held noble court at Branxholm. Four-and-twenty gentlemen, he says, were kept at the chief's call, all of his name and kin, and each having two servants to wait on him. Besides these, there were four-and-twenty pensioners, each one of whom, for service done and to be done, got a "room" or farm; and Satchells, to prove his veracity, gives the name of each yeoman and the lands he held. It is this catalogue of Buccleuch's household that Sir Walter Scott has paraphrased with such effect in "The Lay:"—

> Nine-and-twenty knights of fame
>   Hung their shields in Branksome Hall;
> Nine-and-twenty squires of name
>   Brought them their steeds to bower from stall;
>   Nine-and-twenty yeomen tall,
>   Waited duteous on them all;
>   They were all knights of mettle true,
>   Kinsmen to the bold Buccleuch.

> Ten of them were sheathed in steel,
> With belted sword, and spur on heel :
> They quitted not their harness bright,
> Neither by day, nor yet by night :
> 　　They lay down to rest,
> 　　With corslet laced,
> Pillow'd on buckler cold and hard ;
> 　　They carved at the meal
> 　　With gloves of steel,
> And they drank the red wine through the helmet barr'd.
>
> Ten squires, ten yeomen, mail-clad men,
> Waited the beck of the warders ten ;
> Thirty steeds, both fleet and wight,
> Stood saddled in stable day and night,
> Barbed with frontlet of steel, I trow,
> And with Jedwood-axe at saddlebow ;
> A hundred more fed free in stall :—
> Such was the custom of Branksome Hall.

In consequence either of profuse expenditure or of extensive purchases of land, the Earl allowed his pecuniary affairs to get beyond his control. A crisis was reached in 1621, when the importunity and eagerness of creditors to secure a preference might have led to the exhaustion of the estate, but for the interposition of Walter Scott of Harden. When Buccleuch went to Holland, he left his possessions in charge of this prudent kinsman, who not only cleared off all incumbrances, but added to the property the lordship of Eskdalemuir. Among other purchases made by the Earl was that of Sinton and its lands, in 1619, from John, Earl of Mar ; and from John and James Pringle of Buckholm, the lands of Tinnies in Ettrick Forest for 20,000 merks. At his death in 1633 his personal estate was £196,000. Like his father, the Earl served for a time in the army of the States-General of the Netherlands, where he went in 1627. Walter Scott, younger of Satchells, whose doggerel lines upon his clan's history have been already quoted, was one of his troop. He says it numbered one hundred men of the name of Scott ; but in rolls of 1632-3, still preserved, not above half-a-dozen of that name occur among a hundred and fifty to a hundred and eighty men. Probably, allowance has to be made for the vain old soldier when the glory of his clan is concerned, and not less, perhaps, when his theme is the greatness of his chief :—

> I saw him in his arms appear,
> Which was in the sixteen hundred and twenty-seven year,
> That worthy Earl his regiment was so rare,
> All Holland's league could not with him compare.

Like Hannibal, that noble earl he stood,
To the great effusion of his precious blood ;
The town was tane with a great loss of men,
To the States of Holland from the King of Spain.
His honour's praise throughout all nations sprung
Borne on the wings of Fame that he was Mars's son,
The very son of Mars, which furrowed Neptune's brow,
And over the dangerous deep undauntedly did plow.
He did esteem his countrie's honour more
Than life and pelf, which peasants does adore.

Other poets than honest Satchells were moved to glorify Earl Walter.
In *Fame's Roll*, by Mrs. Mary Fage, he is the subject of quaint acrostic,
and as " Bucluthius " is thus apostrophised by one Doctor Arthur Johnston—

Arva dedit Scoto Rex Scotus, Belga dat aurum,
Estque triumphatus serta daturus Iber.

which may be rendered—

To Scott the Scottish king gives lands,
With gold the Belgian fills his hands,
While conquer'd Spain embays the brow
Of him who laid her warriors low.

While he was away, the Countess was assisted by a commission of his
kinsmen, among whom were Sir John Scott of Scotstarvit, Walter Scott of
Harden, Sir William Scott of Harden, Hew Scott of Deuchar, ancestor of the
Scotts of Gala, Francis Scott of Sinton (sons of Harden), Laurence Scott of
Harperig, advocate, Mr. William Scott, his son, and Robert Scott of Hartwood-
myres.   In 1631 occurred the death of the Countess (Lady Mary Hay of
Errol), after the birth of her youngest daughter, Lady Mary, on the 11th
April.   The Earl and Countess were staying at Newark at the time.   Next
year there is a curious entry in the Chamberlain Accounts of certain payments
to a little boy of the house of Thirlstane (?) who sang to his Lordship at the
" Dowcat " at Branxholm.   Towards the close of 1633, Earl Walter returned
from a short visit to Holland, and died in London on the 20th November.   His
body having been embalmed, was taken to Scotland in a vessel chartered by
Patrick Scott of Thirlstane, who took charge of the transport.   No fewer than
fifteen weeks were occupied in the voyage to Leith, the vessel having been
driven by a violent storm to the coast of Norway, where the voyagers had to
land and rest before setting sail for Scotland.   In the church of Leith the
corpse lay for twenty days, after which it was carried with considerable

ceremony through Edinburgh, Dalkeith, Lauder, and Melrose to Branxholm. There it lay till the 11th June 1634 (seven months after death), when it was buried with great pomp and circumstance in St. Mary's Church, Hawick. In front of the funeral procession went forty-six "saulies" (hired mourners) in black gowns and hoods, with black staves in their hands. After a mounted trumpeter in livery came "Robert Scot of Houeschaw (?), armed at all pieces, riding on a fair horse, and carrying on the point of a lance a banneret of the defunct's colours—azure and or." Two led horses, and three foot trumpeters "sounding sadlie." The great "Gumpheon of black tafta" carried on the point of a lance. The defunct's spurs carried by Walter Scot of Lauchope. His sword, by Andrew Scot, Broadmeadows. His gauntlets by Francis Scot of Castleside. His coat of honour by Laurence Scot, advocate. Then the arms of eight branches of Buccleuch :—

> Montgomery, carried by John Scot, Provost of Crighton.
> Hamilton of Clydesdale, by Robert Scot of Dryhope.
> Douglas of Drumlanrig, by Robert Scott of Bowhill.
> Douglas of Angus, by John Scott of Headshaw.
> Ker of Fernihirst, by Andrew Scott of Carsehope.
> Beaton of Creighe, by Robert Scot of Hartwoodmyres.
> Ker of Cessford, by Robert Scot of Whitefield.
> Scot of Balcleuche, by Sir Robert Scot of Haining.

Next was borne on a lance point by Walter Scott of Goldielands, the great "pincell (streamer) of black taffata;" the defunct's standard, his streamer and motto of colours, each with its own bearer. Betwixt Sir William Scott of Harden, carrying the defunct's arms in metal and colour, and Sir John Scot of Scotstarvet, bearing the coronet on a velvet cushion, walked three trumpeters and three pursuivants, their blazoned coats in mourning. Last of all, the corpse, on a bier ornamented with various devices in satin and gold, a helmet and coronet on top of the coffin "to show he was a soldiour." "And so in this order, with the conducte of maney honorable friends, marched they from Branxholme to Hawick church, quher, after the funerall sermon endit, the corpes wer interrid amongest hes antcestors." Earl Walter's personal estate was given up at £196,000, including the value of 7000 old sheep, 4000 lambs, and 200 nolt. His library, which contained about 1200 volumes in Latin, Italian, and French, with a few in Spanish and English, was valued at £2666, 13s. 4d. Walter, first son, died in infancy; Francis, second son, succeeded; and there was a third, David, born at Newark Castle on 28th November 1627. The fee paid to the lady-accoucheur on this occasion was £26, 13s. 4d., and at the christening Mr. Thomas Wilkie, reader at the kirk of Selkirk, for registering the same got £6, 13s. 4d. Scots. David, who was provided with a handsome estate in Dumfriesshire, died in 1648, having, it is said, been induced to engage in the civil war by the Earl of Tweeddale, who had designs upon his lands. Of Earl Walter's three daughters, one, married to the Master of Yester, became ancestress of the noble house of Tweeddale; and another, married to Lord Erskine, afterwards Earl of Mar, died without issue. Earl Walter provided liberally for several natural children. One son, William, became Laird of Mangerton on the death of another named Francis. A third, John, by Annas Drummond, cousin of the Earl of Perth, was first of the Scots of Gorrinberrie. He had a brother of the same name, while a third John Scot, provost of Crichton, who received a gift from Earl Francis in 1643 "for advancing his fortoun," died in 1646, his estate passing by escheat for behoof of the Earl. Margaret, a daughter, married John, son of Pringle of Stitchell, the marriage-contract being dated at Newark, 31st August 1632. Another, Janet, brought a tocher of 4000 merks to Andrew Scott of Foulshiels.

XV.—FRANCIS, SECOND EARL OF BUCCLEUCH. Again a minor was in possession of the Buccleuch estates, Earl Francis being scarcely seven years old at the death of his father. By the time he came of age, not only had burdens to the extent of 300,000 merks been cleared off, but a surplus of 500,000 merks had been invested in the estate of Dalkeith. After many years of litigation and delay, Buccleuch found it advisable, on attaining his majority in 1647, to compound with Charles Stuart, grandson of the forfeited Earl of Bothwell, concerning certain claims made for restitution of the Bothwell estates. In consideration of a sum of £50,000 Stuart made resignation to Earl Francis of the lands in question, including the lands of Elmure, Elvillane, and Kirkstead in Selkirkshire. Though, according to Satchells, more inclined to books than arms, the young Earl took a sufficiently decided part in the stirring events of his time. When only fourteen he occupied his place among the nobles in the famous Edinburgh Parliament, which continued from May 1639 till November 1641. Appointed colonel of foot within the sheriffdoms of Roxburgh and Selkirk when scarcely seventeen, at twenty-one he became Sheriff-principal of Selkirkshire by grant of Charles I. That unfortunate A. P., v. monarch had watched the young lord's education with assiduous care. So [303, 330.] early as 1639, Lord Francis being but twelve years of age, the King wrote a very decided letter to his tutors, warning them to beware lest certain efforts to induce Buccleuch to join the Covenanters should prove successful, as such a contingency would much displease His Majesty. Charles's efforts to secure so potent an adherent were, however, unavailing. Buccleuch ranged himself on the side of Parliament, and was a member of the Committee of Estates. He was also one of a committee appointed to control the movements of the Scots army in England, and after having, along with a numerous retinue of gentlemen of his name, been made free of the burgh of Selkirk, he seems to have marched south with the troops. At the storming of Newcastle, Buccleuch's regiment acted with bravery and success, entering a breach at Close Gate side by side with the sturdy burgesses of Selkirk. When, that same year (1643), Montrose attempted a diversion in favour of the King by invading and harassing the south border, the vassals of Buccleuch were called out to resist him by Sir William Scott of Harden and Sir Thomas Ker of Cavers, the chief himself being still three years short of his majority. In the beginning of these troubles a considerable quantity of arms and ammunition had been stored in Newark Castle; and an additional supply was now obtained from the public magazines, for which the Earl of Buccleuch had to pay £3736, 13s. 4d. Scots. An Act was passed approving of what the two knights had done in order to repel the advance of Montrose, declaring that they had carried themselves as loyal subjects of the King, faithful servants of the Estates, and true patriots to the country. Though embarked in the cause of the Covenanters and testifying his attachment by various loans to the Estates, Buccleuch did not submit to the military authorities in their efforts to make him raise more than his proper proportion of men and troopers. When the Duke of Hamilton brought back the remnants of the Scottish contingent routed by Cromwell at Preston, Buccleuch at once took arms against the shattered forces, and joined his troops to Argyll and Leslie's army at Falkirk. From that town he wrote a letter, dated 12th September 1648, to his Countess —" MY DEIREST HEART,—To let you know how desyrous I am and how much I long to bee with you, which I trust in God sall bee shortly, if wee and the othir party agrie, which the Lord of His infinit goodness and mercy grant." Like many another Scottish gentleman who resisted his tyranny, he remained loyal to King Charles I., and was one of the Parliament which instructed its Commissioners to protest against any sentence involving the King's life. When news of his fate reached Edinburgh, Parliament at once proclaimed Charles II.; and on the latter reaching Scotland in 1650, Buccleuch was appointed one of the Commissioners to congratulate His Majesty on his

A. P., vi. (1) 101.

"happy arrival." He assisted in the organisation of a new army after the defeat at Dunbar, he and Lord Lothian being colonels of regiments raised in the counties of Roxburgh, Selkirk, and Peebles. Detained in Scotland as a member of the Estates Committee, he was not present at the decisive battle of Worcester, which was followed by severe measures against the King's party in the North. When General Monk commenced his reduction of Scotland, Buccleuch and the rest of the fugitives found temporary refuge in Dundee, where Anna (afterwards Duchess of Buccleuch and Monmouth) was born. Thence they escaped to Aberdeen, whence he sought refuge in Balveny House, a seat of his brother-in-law, the Earl of Rothes. In the haste of quitting Aberdeen, he had subscribed his name to a blank paper on which the Committee proposed to write a letter calling on their friends to rally. In it Cromwell and his party were styled "a handful of bloody traitors," and this expression was the reason of his successor, Countess Mary, being fined £15,000 sterling, £5000 more than was levied on any other. It was only after explanation of the circumstances, showing that Buccleuch could not be held responsible for any expressions in the letter, that the penalty sum was at last reduced to £6000. On the 22d November 1651, just three months after date of the Aberdeen letter, and in the twenty-fifth year of his age, young Earl Francis died at his castle of Dalkeith, of which he seems in the interval to have regained possession.

In 1650, after the battle of Dunbar, Cromwell's troops had taken possession of both Newark and Dalkeith; but the muniments, plate, and more valuable furnishings had previously been removed to the Bass Rock, and were preserved there in safety till 1652. In 1645, the year in which Montrose was defeated at Philiphaugh, and while Buccleuch's years did not yet number a score, he was appointed justiciar over a very extensive district in the Scottish Border, including the parish of Ettrick, except what belonged to Lord Yester: of St. Mary of the Lowes, except part belonging to Traquair: and of Selkirk, except such as belonged to the Marquis of Douglas and the Earl of Roxburgh. In accordance with the liberal powers with which he was invested, the Earl caused proclamation to be made at the various market-towns within his jurisdiction, and held Courts at Selkirk and other towns for the dispensation of justice. He had further a commission granted to him in 1650 for the burning of witches in the parish of Eckford. Fourteen months after his death his widow married a third husband, the Earl of Wemyss, who had himself been twice previously married, and who proposed to the Dowager Countess of

Buccleuch within two months of the demise of his second wife.   Of the Lady
even Satchells has little good to say :—

> Earl Francis his father, Earl Walter, did succeed
> Into his earldom, but not to his head.
> Yet he wanted neither hand, head nor heart,
> But could not act like to his father's part.
> With the house of Rothes married he
> An equal match by antiquitie.
> He had no heirs-male, but daughters left behind,
> For to enjoy his great earldom and land.
> Their mother was so impudent,
> That she must always have her intent.

After likening her treatment of the Earl to Delilah's dealing with
Samson, he continues :—

> She's like a Gardo countenanc'd like Bendo,
> Cunning as Nilo peeping through a window,
> Which put the wandering Jew in such amazement,
> Seeing such a face look through the casement.

XVI. (1.)—Mary Scott, Countess of Buccleuch, at the time of her accession
was but four years old, and from the first her extensive possessions made her
the object and centre of much discreditable intrigue.   The Earl of Tweeddale,
whose children were next in tailzie after their two cousins, the young ladies
of Buccleuch, framed a project of marrying the eldest to his son.   But he was
thwarted by Gideon Scott of Highchesters (second son to Sir William Scott
of Harden), who won the dowager to his side, and succeeded ultimately (9th
February 1659) in marrying the heiress to his eldest son, Walter, the bride
being not quite twelve and the bridegroom only in his fifteenth year.   Among
other eligible young noblemen competitors for the prize was the heir of the
Earl of Eglinton.   But he, "conveying his father to London, runns away
without any advyce and maries a daughter of my Lord Dumfries, who is a
broken man, when he was sure of my Lady Balclough's marriage, the greatest
match in Britain ; this unexpected prank is worse to all his kin than his
death would have been."   "The best-laid schemes o' mice an' men gang aft
a-gley ;" and the hapless young wife, never strong, died on the 11th March
1661, the touch of majesty availing naught against Death's more powerful
finger.   By her latest will, made under instigation of her managing mother,
her uncle and stepfather got all her personal estate, even to the exclusion of
her husband, who had been created Earl of Tarras.   The marriage, indeed, was

Bail.
Lett.,
iii. 366.

afterwards reduced by the Court of Session, and Tarras thereby deprived of his large benefit under the contract. One of his alternative titles was Lord Alemoor, from an estate of that name in the parish of Roberton and county of Selkirk. Lord Tarras went abroad in 1667, travelling in France, Italy, and the Netherlands, until 1670. On his return he solicited the King for restoration of his annuity under the marriage-contract, or a composition of it; but in vain, His Majesty asking if it were not enough that he had been made an Earl. In 1684, the discontented peer became implicated in the Rye-house Plot, having for its object the displacement of the Duke of York, and the establishment of the Protestant succession. At the entreaty of his wife he turned King's evidence, inculpated many gentlemen, his neighbours of the Scottish Border, and led Robert Baillie of Jerviswoode to the scaffold. At his death in 1693, his life-peerage lapsed, and his eldest son, Gideon Scott of Highchesters, succeeded to his lands. From the Earl of Tarras by his second marriage is descended the present noble family of Polwarth.

XVI. (2.)—Anne, Duchess of Buccleuch and Monmouth, is perhaps the most noteworthy individual of the line. Within two months of her sister's death, her scheming mother had proposed to King Charles II. to marry her to his natural son by Lucy Walters, a Welsh girl of great personal attractions, whom the King met when a wanderer in Holland. To this project His Majesty gave willing assent, and on the 20th April 1663, Anna Scott, Countess of Buccleuch, then in her twelfth year, was married to James, Baron Scott of Tindall, Earl of Doncaster, and Duke of Monmouth. To this union Dryden alludes in the well-known passage from *Absalom and Achitophel* :—

> Of all the numerous progeny was none
> So beautiful, so brave, as Absalon.
>
> . . . . .
>
> In peace the thoughts of war he could remove,
> And seemed as he were only born for love.
> Whate'er he did was done with so much ease,
> In him alone 'twas natural to please;
> His motions all accompanied with grace,
> And paradise was opened in his face.
> With secret joy indulgent David viewed
> His youthful image in his son renewed:
> To all his wishes nothing he denied,
> And made the charming Annabel his bride.

Seldom has a marriage been consummated under so many auguries of

happiness and so bright with the prospect of felicity; and seldom has a
marriage turned out so full of disappointment or so darkened by tragic sorrow.
For a time all went well. The distinguished couple joined freely in the gaieties
of King Charles's merry Court—the Duchess, young though she was, keeping
steadily aloof from the temptations which could not fail to present themselves.
No whisper of scandal ever assailed her. Contemporary writers, with excellent means of forming a correct opinion, speak of her in terms of the highest
respect; and Monmouth himself the day before his death "gave her the
kindest character that could be." Residence in London being a necessary
result of the marriage, the Buccleuch estates were managed principally by
Lord Melville, one of the Duchess's curators under the marriage-contract, and
husband of her half-sister, Lady Catherine Leslie. The curators on both sides
were for the most part relations of the lady, and many of them, such as the
Lairds of Harden, Whitslaid, and Thirlestane, prominent gentlemen of the
Clan Scott. When in 1679 Monmouth was Captain-General of Scotland,
Lord Melville acted as his agent in submitting terms to the Covenanters,
whom the Duke out of his humanity wished to conciliate. During the
estrangement between her husband and his father, the King, the Duchess
appears to have acted with surpassing prudence, endeavouring to counteract
the hot-headed advisers who played with Monmouth's impetuosity, and even
preserving the friendship of the Duke of York—her husband's particular
aversion. Monmouth's mad attempt to seize the Crown after his father's
death, his defeat and execution in 1685, are matters of history. At one of
their last interviews the Duchess asked him "if ever she had the least notice
and correspondence with him about his rebellion, or had ever assented to or
approved of his conduct during these four or five last years; if ever she had
done anything in the whole course of her life to displease and disoblige him, or
ever was uneasy to him in anything but two,—one as to his women, and the
other for his disobedience to the late king, whom she always took the liberty
to advise him to obey. If in anything else she had failed of the duty and
obedience that became her as his wife, she humbly begged the favour to
disclaim it, and she would fall down on her knees and beg his pardon for it.
To which moving discourse he answered that she had always shown herself a
very kind, loving, and dutiful wife towards him, and had nothing imaginable
to charge her with, either against her virtue and duty to him, her steady
loyalty and affection towards the late king, or kindness and affection towards
his children." Monmouth's evil manners live in brass, his virtues were writ

Bucc.

in water; but at least he died with unflinching courage. Of him it is especial truth that nothing he ever did in life became him like his leaving of it, which moved all the bystanders to pity and regret. His title and property having been forfeited by his conviction of high treason, the Duchess obtained a regrant of the honours and estates from the King, who treated her with great consideration. After remaining a widow nearly three years, she espoused, in May 1688, Lord Cornwallis, also a widower. Throughout her long residence in England the Duchess ever retained what she called her "Scotch heart," and in 1701 her longing to return to Scotland was satisfied by a visit made ostensibly to look after her estates. In order to reduce debts incurred by Monmouth's extravagance, the Duchess and Lord Cornwallis had resolved to curtail their expenditure within such limits as would be defrayed by their income in Scotland, the English rents being employed to reduce the sum borrowed. They had not lived long at Dalkeith, where they arrived in October, before the Duchess began to suspect that her agents, whom she had long trusted implicitly in the management of her estates, had abused her confidence to their own aggrandisement. Old Satchells hints as much in his poem, published the year after Monmouth's death, wherein he bewails the impossibility of "inferior friends" getting a groat from the estate whether they "famish, starve, or die;" and recalls "the times of old" when the chief himself requited the attachment of his clan, and "the lawyers got nought." As her years increased the Duchess developed a great hunger for more land. Writing to Lord Royston she says, "I am really grown covettus to incress my land in that part of dear Scotland." Having heard that Scott of Harden was willing to sell an estate in Ettrick Forest, which from its situation would be an eligible purchase, she owned to the same confidential adviser that she "would be glad to buy Scott's land with English money," and that she "greined" to hear more of the proposal. Of her paternal estate she expressed a determination never to part with "one inch that ever did belong to it;" and of the sheep on her lands, she boasts that few could equal them at St. Boswells Fair. Just about this period she received payment from the Queen of "fourteen thousand pounds all at one time;" and to the Buccleuch patrimony were added the Selkirkshire lands of Easter and Wester Kirkhope, Earnhaugh, Deadhope, Howford, Fauldshope, and Gilmanscleugh. From all which it is evident that Evelyn was not far wrong in his estimate of the Duchess as "one of the wisest and craftiest of her sex." A curious trait in her character was her pride of rank, which was no less conspicuous than her love of wealth. Dr. Johnson in his Life of Gay alludes to her as " inflexible in her demand to be treated as a princess," and in several Dalkeith charters she actually adopted the style of " Mighty Princess." In this very sensible and practical woman of the world it is somewhat difficult to recognise the "pitying Duchess" who sat in Newark Castle listening to the Lay of the Last Minstrel—

> Who bade her page the menials tell,
> That they should tend the old man well :
> For she had known adversity,
> Though born in such a high degree ;
> In pride of power, in beauty's bloom,
> Had wept o'er Monmouth's bloody tomb.

In her eighty-first year the Duchess died at London, and was buried, according to her own express desire, beside her paternal ancestors at Dalkeith. She may be said to have been the last of the Scotts of Buccleuch proper. By her marriage with Monmouth, the family in some measure lost its local position and assumed imperial importance, so that her descendants were not so much Scotts of Buccleuch as Buccleuchs of Great Britain. For a long time they were strangers to Ettrick Forest, and it was not until the end of last century, when Bowhill was enlarged, that the Scotts once more attached themselves to those hills and valleys which must be for ever identified with the early history of their race.

XVII.—JAMES, EARL OF DALKEITH, son of the Duke of Monmouth and Buccleuch, died before his mother, in the thirty-first year of his age. In 1692, at Sanquhar, he was proclaimed king by a party of crazy Scotch Covenanters, bent on reasserting Monmouth's absurd claim to the British throne, and thereby securing a Protestant succession after their own hearts.

XVIII.—FRANCIS, SECOND DUKE OF BUCCLEUCH, was thirty-seven years of age at the death of his grandmother, and was the second Scott for two hundred and sixty years who had attained full age before accession. His wife was a daughter of the Duke of Queensberry, a connection by which that title and some of the estates afterwards fell into the hands of Buccleuch. In 1745 Duke Francis called out his tenantry to assist the town of Edinburgh in resisting the Pretender, the half-heartedness of the magistrates and inhabitants on that occasion being a matter of history. He died in 1751.

XIX.—FRANCIS, EARL OF DALKEITH, died the year before his father, in

Bucc.

the thirtieth year of his age. By his wife, Lady Caroline Campbell, daughter of the Duke of Argyll, the family estates were considerably augmented ; and but for a male entail of the western dukedom, the Dukes of Buccleuch would have ruled at Inveraray.

XX.—HENRY, THIRD DUKE OF BUCCLEUCH, was only five years of age when the death of his grandfather left him heir to the distinguished titles and vast possessions of his family. In his youth he had the privilege of travelling on the Continent with Dr. Adam Smith (author of *The Wealth of Nations*) for his companion and preceptor. Leaving London in 1764, they remained abroad until 1766, when the death of the Duke's next brother at Paris led to their return. Meantime Dr. Smith had tenderly and assiduously nursed the Duke himself through a long and dangerous attack of fever— services which were not forgotten, for till the close of his life the philosopher enjoyed an annuity of £300 from his noble patron. His Grace married in 1767 the only daughter of the fourth Earl of Cardigan, afterwards Duke of Montague ; and when, immediately after the event, the young couple paid a visit to their Scottish estates, the occasion inspired " Jupiter " Carlyle of Inveresk to an ode of welcome. The spirit of old Father Tweed inquiring what frantic riot now wakes his dreams, bemoans the many years of peaceful dulness during which he has been bearing his waters to the main :—

> But now my hills with joyful shouts resound,
> And gladness revels o'er my classic ground ;
> My rural Ettrick see in mantle gay,
> With dancing pace comes on his shining way ;
> My tragic Yarrow casts his mournful weeds,
> And like a masker trips it down the meads.
> For shame, my sons ! Tell Ettrick, Yarrow tell !
> What rage, what frenzy, does your bosoms swell !
> Yarrow, the rapture glowing in his eyes,
> With speedy words thus to his sire replies—
> " Roll, Father Tweed ! roll on your silver streams,
> With double splendour shine in sunny beams ;
> A Scott, a noble Scott ! again appears,
> The wish'd-for blessing of thy hoary years."

Duke Henry and his lady lived much in Scotland, displaying to the full that amiability in peace which has become the tradition of the house as much as was their courageous pugnacity in the warlike days of old. Sometimes, like James V. and Haroun Alraschid, his Grace, discarding all outward

appearance of rank, would venture amongst his humble tenantry, often unknown until long after his unpretending visit. Some such incident is the
theme of Henry Scott Riddell's poem *The Cottagers of Glendale*, in which the
storm-caught Duke seeks shelter for the night in the cottage of an old shepherd, whose kindly and garrulous wife becomes nearly demented when her
guest's rank is divulged by a gorgeous groom searching for his lost master:—

> A gentleman folk aye may ken;
> Yet e'en mang sic, though ane were ten,
>   They'd nane be like Duke Henry.

One day when walking to Edinburgh Castle in uniform, his Grace was
accosted by a country lassie, who asked if he could tell her where to find her
brother "Wull," also in the Fencibles. The Duke said he would try, and
asked the girl to go with him to the parade ground. When the sentinels
presented arms as he passed, his companion asked its meaning; and his Grace,
parrying the question, said, "It must have been either to you or me." On
"Wull" asking his sister if she knew who her guide had been, she replied,
"I dinna ken, but he was a very ceevil lad;" and on learning that he was
the Duke of Buccleuch, was lost between thoughts of his Grace's kindness and
her own reckless familiarity. At the death of his mother, Duke Henry inherited Granton and other Argyll estates provided to her, his honours and
possessions being yet further augmented by accession (at the death of "Old
Q." in 1810) to the dukedom of Queensberry, with part of its lands. By his
marriage, large estates in England came to the family. At his death in 1812,
the general grief was thus expressed by Sir Walter Scott—"At the funeral
there was scarce a dry eye among the assistants—a rare tribute to a person
whose high rank and large possessions removed him so far out of the sphere
of private friendship. But the Duke's mind was moulded upon the kindliest
and most single-hearted model, and arrested the affections of all who had any
connection with him." His Duchess survived till 1827—a lady of so much
stateliness that Louis Philippe, afterwards King of the French, said that
though he had conversed with nearly all the crowned heads of Europe, he had
in no instance been so embarrassed as by the formal and dignified bearing of
Elizabeth, Duchess of Buccleuch.

XXI.—CHARLES WILLIAM, fourth Duke, during the short period of his
possession of the estates, devoted himself mainly to their improvement
and administration. He replanted the forests hewn down by "Old Q." and

repaired the old castle of Drumlanrig, left in such disorder that it took £60,000 to make it wind and water-tight. His relations with Sir Walter Scott of Abbotsford were of the most cordial and even affectionate nature; while his kindness to Hogg, the Ettrick shepherd, was as unceasing as it was undemonstrative. He died at Lisbon, where he had gone in search of health, on the 20th April 1819. "Others," wrote Sir Walter, "of his rank might be more missed in the resorts of splendour and of gaiety frequented by persons of distinction. But the peasant while he leans on his spade, age sinking to the grave in hopeless indigence, and youth struggling for the means of existence, will long miss the generous and powerful patron, whose aid was never asked in vain when the merit of the petitioner was unquestioned."

XXII.—WALTER FRANCIS, fifth Duke of Buccleuch and seventh Duke of Queensberry, succeeded, like so many of his race, while yet a minor, being an Eton boy of thirteen at the death of his father. Sir Walter Scott well observed, "The Duke of Buccleuch can never be regarded as a private man;" and the public calls upon Duke Walter led to much of his time being spent in London and various other parts of the empire. It is no secret, however, that of all his princely mansions there was none towards which he turned so gladly as to Bowhill, and that of all his high and eminent titles he bore none more proudly than that of Scott of Buccleuch. He was born at Dalkeith on the 25th November 1806; and for a while after his accession to the title his health was such as to cause no slight anxiety. Sir Walter, who watched his growth with keen and unaffected interest, took comfort in reflecting "how many valetudinarians had outlived all their robust contemporaries and attained the utmost verge of human life"—a hopeful fore- Lock. cast which Duke Walter lived to verify. Indeed, only five years later Sir Walter records in his diary (25th August 1826) that "the Duke has grown up into a graceful and apparently strong young man. I think he will be well qualified to sustain his difficult and important task. The heart is excellent, so are the talents—good sense and knowledge of the world will prevent him from being deceived; and with perfect good nature, he has a natural sense of his own situation. God bless him!—his father and I loved each other well; and his beautiful mother had as much of the angel as is permitted to walk this earth." In 1822, and when only sixteen years of age, the young Duke was called upon to play the part of host to no less exalted a personage than His Majesty George IV., then on his memorable visit to Scotland. One day

when Neil Gow's band was playing to the King at Dalkeith, His Majesty
sent his young host to request a particular air, slapping him on the shoulder,
and saying, "Come, Buccleuch, you are the youngest man in the company, and
must make yourself useful." The King stayed a fortnight at Dalkeith, and
his portrait, painted by Sir David Wilkie, in a full Highland costume which
rendered royalty ridiculous, was presented to the Duke as a memorial of the
visit. Nothing could be finer or in truer taste than the unaffected way in
which the Duke at his majority banquet, taking for granted his "advantages
of birth and fortune," announced his intention " to make use of the station in
which he was placed for promoting the general welfare." And nothing could
be more admirable than the straightforward conscientiousness with which his
Grace tried to redeem the promise. To few men in any position has it
been granted to win so rich a mead of praise as that which followed the fifth
Duke of Buccleuch. From his coming of age, the Duke was the object
of many a hearty welcome and many a sincere encomium. Even political
opponents blunted the arrows of their criticism when they came to deal
with him; and enemies of any other sort he seems never to have created.
Though manifesting a keen interest in political affairs, the Duke did not take
an active share in the work of government. From 1842 to 1846, he was
Lord Privy Seal and Lord President of the Council, joining his chief, Sir
Robert Peel, in that great fiscal change which was the crowning act of his
administration. His Grace died at Bowhill in 1884. He was married in 1829
to Lady Charlotte Anne Thynne, daughter of the Marquis of Bath, who
survives, as do their family of four sons and three daughters—

Wm. Hy. Walter, 6th Duke, b. 1831   m. 1859 Lady Louisa, d. Duke of Abercorn.
Lord Henry John,   b. 1832   m. 1865 Hon. Cecily Susan, d. Lord Wharncliffe.
Lord Walter Charles,   b. 1834   m. 1858 Anna Maria, d. of Sir W. E. Cradock-Hartopp.
Lord Charles Thomas, R. N. b. 1839   m. 1883, Ada, d. of Chas. Ryan, Esq., Victoria, Australia.
Lady Victoria Alexandrina, b. 1844   m. 1865 to ninth Marquis of Lothian.
Lady Margaret Elizabeth, b. 1846   m. 1875 to Donald Cameron of Lochiel.
Lady Mary Charlotte,   b. 1851   m. 1877. to Hon. Walter R. Trefusis.

Lord Henry sat twenty-three years in parliament, first for Selkirkshire,
and latterly for South Hants. Lord Charles, commanding the *Bacchante*,
was intrusted with the charge of H. R. H. the princes Albert Victor and
George of Wales.

XXIII.—WILLIAM HENRY WALTER, sixth Duke of Buccleuch, was born in

Montagu House, 9th September 1831 ; and on the 22d November 1859, was married to Lady Louisa, daughter of James, first Duke of Abercorn. When at a complimentary dinner given by about five hundred gentlemen on the 7th May 1878, his father, Duke Walter, acknowledged the enthusiastic plaudits of the company, he added, " The only satisfaction I have now-a-days, at the end of a life which cannot be much prolonged under the ordinary duration of human nature, is that at all events I shall feel that I have a most valuable legacy to leave behind me, and that the person to whom that legacy will naturally fall is well worthy of receiving it." While Earl of Dalkeith, the Duke represented Midlothian from 1853 to 1868, and from 1874 to 1880, when he was defeated, after a memorable contest, by Mr. Gladstone, whose speeches throughout the county may be said to have hastened the downfall of Lord Beaconsfield's Ministry. The Duke has a family of sons and daughters—

Walter Henry, now Earl of Dalkeith,	b. 1861	Lady Katherine Mary,	b. 1875
Lord John Charles, Lieut. R.N.,	b. 1864	Lady Constance Ann,	b. 1877
Lord George William,	b. 1866	Lord Francis George,	b. 1879
Lord Henry Francis,	b. 1868		
Lord Herbert Andrew,	b. 1872		

LORD JOHN SCOTT, brother of Walter Francis, fifth Duke of Buccleuch, born in 1809, was returned M.P. for Roxburghshire in 1832, after a severe contest, in which he distinguished himself as a ready and effective public speaker. Much hope was entertained of his future services to the Conservative party, but he became early disgusted with Parliament, preferring the pleasures of a rural life, and hunting with great energy across that border country where of yore his ancestors had spurred the horse on far other errands. He was said to be the best hand with a salmon-leister on all Tweed ; indeed there was no form of sport or pastime calling forth dash and energy in which he did not excel. During his later years he entertained deep and earnest religious convictions, and his last public appearance at Melrose in defence of genuine Protestant conservatism is said to have been a remarkable display of vigorous eloquence. It was on this occasion that Lord John enunciated his opinion, since become celebrated, that the " High Church party in Scotland had acted the part of sappers and miners for the Church of Rome." He died in 1860, greatly lamented by the Duke, their mutual attachment being of the warmest and most affectionate nature.

BRIDGELANDS.

L. K.,
309, 179,
460.

In 1234, Alexander II. granted to the monks of Kelso, for the perpetual maintenance of the bridge of "Ecctrick," the land which Richard, son of Edwin, held on either side of the water of Ettrick, the charter being signed before a number of nobles and ecclesiastical dignitaries at Selechirche, the 7th day of June, in the nineteenth year of His Majesty's reign. In a rent-roll attributed to a date before 1300, the monks are said to possess certain lands in Selkirk-Regis called the Bridgelands, containing 16 acres, with pasture in Minchmoor. From time to time the Abbots travelled in state, attended by a powerful retinue, to Ettrick Bridge, for the purpose of holding courts, at one of which, in 1258, Hugh de Reveden resigned his claim to certain lands of "Floris," of which he and his ancestors had long held possession, contrary to justice, and the will of the Abbot. Strict precautions were taken that my Lord Abbot should not ride on the top of his commission. His courts were illegal unless he had the King's Sheriff with him; and there were cases in which he had no jurisdiction. Bridgelands now belongs to the heirs of the late Mr. George Rodger, one of a family long and intimately connected with the burgh of Selkirk, in various offices. The present house was built in 1791.

BROADMEADOWS.

E. R.,
vi. 225.

"Brademedow" is one of the forest-steads entered as paying £6 yearly to the Crown in 1455. In 1502, David Scott in Stirkschawis (Stirches), a notorious cattle-lifter nicknamed "The Lady," produced at Jedburgh a remission for stealing threescore wedders worth 6s. 8d. each, from Ralph Ker, out of "Bradmedowis;" and at the same court, Adam Turnbull, in Hornshole, appeared to answer a charge of stealing fourscore of wedders from Ralph Ker and William Wood "furth of Bradmedowis"—the offence being committed

G. S.,
ii. 3506,
and Phil.
MSS.

during an English raid. In 1510, Patrick, son of the late John Murray of Philiphaugh, obtained a charter from the King of the twenty-two pound lands of "Braidmedowis," in the lordship of Ettrick Forrest, subject to a yearly payment of £30 Scots, and a tenth of all the coal which might be got out of them, with the fishings, except salmon kippers and smolts. Patrick and his heirs were bound to

"build and maintain upon the said lands a sufficient mansion-house of stone, with a hall, keep, balcony, byre, stable, pigeon-house, orchard, garden, bee-hives, with hedges and plantations of oak, etc., and with bridges for passage of the lieges over marshes; forfeiture to follow conviction for murder or theft; and for every £10 land, two mounted men at arms to be furnished, one with a lance and one with a led horse, to do service with His Majesty in war and in the army when called upon."

Patrick Murray left an only daughter, wife of John Cockburn of Glen, whose granddaughter, Margaret Cockburn, was served heir to her great-grandfather in 1607. One John Scot in Broadmeadows, is mentioned as on a jury, who in 1564 convicted five Scots, Elliots, and others of sheep-stealing, for which they were hanged. In 1575, Gilbert Ker of Primsideloch was responsible for the mails of Broadmeadows; and in 1590, the tenant, James Donaldson by name, was caution in £500 that James Scott in Selkirk, called "Mekle Jamie Eister," would not harm the Laird of Philiphaugh. The next proprietors were Scotts, probably connected with the family of Buccleuch, although they have been called cadets of Tushilaw. Andrew, laird in 1628, carried the deceased nobleman's sword at the funeral of Earl Walter in 1633, was appointed to the Committee of War in 1643, and was fined £1800 after the Restoration. Acts of Parliament nominate William Scott of Broad-meadows Commissioner of Supply in the shire; but the family ended in an heiress, married to John Balfour, styled of Broadmeadows, in 1704. Charles Balfour of Broadmeadows (whose wife was Janet, daughter of William Plummer of Sunderlandhall), owned Glenkerry and Midgehope in 1743. Again the family ended in an heiress, their daughter, married to William Scott of Woll, who figures as proprietor in 1785. His son Charles sold it in 1803 to John Boyd, merchant in Leith, who abandoned the old house and built a new one lower down the hill. In 1848 it changed hands again, becoming the property, by purchase, of R. K. Pringle, Esq., H.E.I.C., fourth son of Alexander Pringle, Esq. of Whytbank and Yair. Mr. Pringle, having resigned the Chief Commissionership of Scinde in 1850, laid the foundation-stone of the present mansion-house in 1852, besides greatly improving the amenity and agricultural value of the estate. Purchased in 1863 by the Hon. William Napier, second son of William John, ninth Lord Napier, Broadmeadows once more found a new laird in Hugh M. Lang, Esq., to whom it was sold in 1866, and in whose possession it still remains. By an exploit performed in the recent Egyptian campaign, Mr. Lang's second son, Lieutenant in a Highland Regiment, has shown himself to have the pluck of a true son of the Forest. The troops having been stopped in their advance upon the enemy by a deep canal, Mr. Lang gallantly stripped, swam across, unfastened a boat moored to the opposite bank, and rowed back to his men, who were quickly ferried over. Too eager for the fray to stay and don his uniform, Mr. Lang resumed his place just as

Margin references: Retor. Pit., i. 450. P. C., ii. 492. Taxt Roll. A. P., vi. (2) 52. A. P., vii. 422. 1685-90. A. P., xi. 140. Milne, Melr. C. R.

he came out of the water, and took part in a gallant attack upon the enemy, his name being mentioned in the General's despatch.

Broadmeadows is not without historical interest. In Scott and Elliot's account of the shire, William's Cross, marking the spot where a Douglas was slain by his kinsman in 1353, is said to be in "the heich of an edge beside Broadmeadows." But its crowning interest lies in the fact that it narrowly escaped forestalling Abbotsford as the residence of Sir Walter Scott. "He wrote me once," says the Ettrick Shepherd, "informing me that he was going to purchase the estate of Broadmeadows, on Yarrow ; that he was the highest offerer, and was, he believed, sure of getting it ; and that he had offered a half more on my account, that I might be his shepherd, and manager of all his rural affairs. The plan misgave. Mr. Boyd outbid him, and became the purchaser, on which Sir Walter was so vexed on my account, that he actually engaged me to Lord Porchester." Lockhart, alluding to Sir Walter's expectations, says, "Many a time did he ride round it with Lord and Lady Dalkeith,

' When summer smiled on sweet Bowhill,'

surveying the beautiful domain with wistful eyes. . . . I consider it as, in one point of view, the greatest misfortune of his life that this vision was not realised." Of the same opinion was Laidlaw his amanuensis, for in Broadmeadows, surrounded by independent proprietors, Scott would have been free from the temptations to extend which beset him at Abbotsford, encircled as it was by little lairds, most of them ready to sell their lands as soon as he had money to advance.

Hogg,
Life
Scott,
53.

Lock.,
chap.
xiii.

Cha.
Life
Scott,
189.

CARTERHAUGH.

This fertile farm is not mentioned in the list of 1455, unless it be disguised as one of "2 stedis in Catkermauch,"—a supposition partly borne out by the mention of "Catcarinach (Cartaremauch) et Cartarehauch" in a deed of gift to Alexander Hume of that Ilk in 1489. Considerable confusion existed with regard to these names, Acts of Parliament so late as 1693 giving Cartermauch as an alternative for Auld Wark, which we venture to think must be erroneous. It appears to have been part of the land granted along with the office of King's guardian of the Forest, and as such would be in occupation of Sir Thomas de Charteris and his son from before 1328. Seeing it is spelt " Charterhaugh " in Elliot and Scott's careful MS., its derivation from the name of Bruce's trusted knight is at least possible. As " Carterhalche "

G. S.,
ii. 1921.

A. P.,
ix. 341.

E. R.,
i. 149.

1649,
Adv.
Lib.

it figures in 1502 in Pitcairn's Criminal Records, one Turnbull in Branxholm having stolen from it eight score and eight oxen and cows, two horses, and sundry goods belonging to the Murrays of Philiphaugh, then in possession. Hogg, in his "Pilgrims of the Sun," a ridiculous poem, speaks of "Carelha," and has the assurance to append a note—"now vulgarly called Carterhaugh;" but in the "Queen's Wake" he does not disdain the vulgar rendering :—

> The harp of Ettrick rang again ;
> Her bard, intent on fairy strain
> And fairy freak by moonlight shaw,
> Sang "Young Tam Linn of Carterhaugh."

By common consent, the famous ballad of "Tamlane," familiar in many lands, is identified with Selkirkshire, the well where Janet met her lover being visible to this day close by the house of Carterhaugh.

Tamlane's Well.

It has another claim to notice as the scene of a striking incident in the life of Sir Walter Scott. How the sportive contest which took place here in 1815 came to be called a football match by Lockhart, by Hogg, by Sir Walter himself, and by nearly everybody who has mentioned it in print, it is impossible to understand. That it was really a handball match, many partakers and spectators of the game have united in declaring to the present writer.

It is said to have had its origin in a conversation at Bowhill after a dinner at which the Sheriff was present. Whoever mooted the idea, it seems to have been enthusiastically entered into by Sir Walter, who was at much pains to insure its success. From the tact of the Earl of Home, the Duke's brother-in-law, being appointed to lead the Yarrow and Ettrick men against the souters, it would appear as if the game had been got up as a sequel to the traditional football match of the ballad. At all events there was great excitement throughout the county, and even beyond it, over the approaching event. To the summons of their all-powerful and much beloved landlord the Buccleuch farmers and their men responded in hundreds, and they were joined by all that could be spared for the day from the hill-sides and valleys of the county. These sported sprigs of heather in their bonnets, while the souters had for an emblem twigs of pine, worn also by their allies—a strong contingent of " braw lads " from Gala Water, and about a hundred " callants " full of the *perfervidum ingenium Hawickorum*. When the latter reached Selkirk, they were ranged in single file before Bailie Clarkson's house, treated to a welcome drop of mountain-dew, and then marched with the souters to the field. Monday, the 4th December, was a bright cold day; and those who remember it say the muster of the various bands upon the haugh in the morning was a splendid spectacle. As company after company filed into the ground from the upper waters from many a wild " hope," and over many a winding " swire," the spirits of those whose hearts were with the heather rose with expected triumph; but there were not wanting those who pinned their faith to the suppler sinews and determined energy of the town-bred souters and their friends. Wholly in sympathy with the former was the distinguished party which formed the escort of the noble Duke. It was about 11 o'clock when his Grace came upon the ground, attended by his sons the young Earl of Dalkeith and Lord John Scott, the Countess of Home, the Ladies Ann, Charlotte, and Isabella Scott, Lord and Lady Montague and family, Sir John Riddel of Riddel, Sir Alexander Don of Newton Don, Mr. Elliot Lockhart, member for the county, Mr. Pringle of Whytbank, younger, Mr. Pringle of Torwoodlee, Captain Pringle, R.N., Mr. Boyd of Broadmeadows and family, Mr. Chisholm of Chisholm, Major Pott of Todrig, Mr. Walter Scott, Sheriff of Selkirkshire, and family, and many other ladies and gentlemen. For the first time since the imposing funeral pageant of Earl Walter in 1633, the ancient banner of Buccleuch was unfurled to the breeze, with its blazon of armorial bearings and the old war-cry " Bellen-

Lock. chap. xxxvi.

daine" still as legible as when it left the fair embroiderer's hands centuries before. It was handed by Lady Ann to the Sheriff's oldest son; and the young squire of Abbotsford, suitably mounted and armed, rode over the field displaying it to the sound of the war-pipes amid the acclamations of 2000 onlookers, and doubtless to the heartfelt pride of his great father. " I have no doubt," says Lockhart, " the Sheriff of the Forest was a prouder man than when the Russian Marshall Platoff gave himself a mount for the imperial review in Paris." It was an occasion after his own heart, and he gave vent to his feelings in verse which unites the fire of his *Macgregor's Gathering* with something of the fun of his occasional songs :—

From the brown crest of Newark its summons extending,
   Our signal is waving in smoke and in flame ;
And each forester blithe, from his mountain descending,
   Bounds light o'er the heather to join in the game.

CHORUS.

Then up with the Banner, let forest winds fan her,
   She has blazed over Ettrick eight ages and more ;
In sport we 'll attend her, in battle defend her,
   With heart and with hand, like our fathers before.

When the Southern invader spread waste and disorder,
   At the sight of our crescent he paused and withdrew,
For around her were marshall'd the pride of the Border,
   The Flowers of the Forest, the Bands of Buccleuch.
      Then up with the Banner, etc.

A Stripling's weak hand to our revel has borne her,
   No mail-glove has grasp'd her, no spearmen surround ;
But ere a bold foeman should scathe or should scorn her,
   A thousand true hearts would be cold on the ground.
      Then up with the Banner, etc.

We forget each contention of civil dissension,
   And hail, like our brethren, Home, Douglas, and Car :
And Elliot and Pringle in pastime shall mingle,
   As welcome in peace as their fathers in war.
      Then up with the Banner, etc.

Then strip, lads, and to it, though sharp be the weather,
   And if, by mischance, you should happen to fall,
There are worse things in life than a tumble on heather,
   And life is itself but a game at foot-ball.
      Then up with the Banner, etc.

And after it's over, we'll drink a blithe measure
　To each Laird and each Lady that witness'd our fun,
And to every blithe heart that took part in our pleasure,
　To the lads that have lost and the lads that have won.
　　　　Then up with the Banner, etc.

May the Forest still flourish, baith burgh and landward
　From the hall of the peer to the herd's ingle-neuk!
Then hurrah! my brave boys, for Buccleuch and his standard,
　The king and the country, the clan and the Duke!
　　　　Then up with the Banner, etc.

In quite a different tone, but superior to Scott's in poetic merit, was a poem "On the Lifting of the Banner," by the Ettrick Shepherd, whose soul seems to have caught a quieter enthusiasm :—

　　　　And hast thou here, like hermit grey,
　　　　　Thy mystic characters unroll'd
　　　　O'er peaceful revellers to play,
　　　　　Thou emblem of the days of old ?
　　　　Or comest thou with the veteran's smile,
　　　　　Who deems his day of conquest fled,
　　　　Yet loves to view the bloodless toil
　　　　　Of sons whose sires he often led ?

　　　　Not such thy peaceable intent,
　　　　　When, over Border waste and wood,
　　　　On foray and achievement bent
　　　　　Like eagle on the path of blood.
　　　　Symbol to ancient valour dear,
　　　　　Much has been dared and done for thee ;—
　　　　I almost weep to see thee here,
　　　　　And deem thee raised in mockery.

　　　　But, no—familiar to the brave,
　　　　　'Twas thine thy gleaming moon and star
　　　　Above their manly sports to wave
　　　　　As free as in the field of war :
　　　　To thee the faithful clansman's shout
　　　　　In revel as in rage was dear ;—
　　　　The more beloved in festal rout,
　　　　　The better fenced when foes were near.

　　　　I love thee for the olden day,
　　　　　The iron age of hardihood,—
　　　　The rather that thou led'st the way
　　　　　To peace and joy through paths of blood :

For were it not the deeds of weir,
    When thou wert foremost in the fray,
We had not been assembled here,
    Rejoicing in a Father's sway.

And even the days ourselves have known
    Alike the moral truth impress,—
Valour and constancy alone
    Can purchase peace and happiness.
Then hail, Memorial of the brave,
    The Liegeman's pride, the Border's awe!
May thy grey pennon never wave
    On sterner field than Carterhaugh!

A loud shout from the contending parties greeted the throwing up of the ball by the Duke of Buccleuch. In one impetuous rush the shepherds, led by Lord Home, with Hogg for an aide-de-camp, mingled in furious contest with the souters, led by their bailie, Dr. Ebenezer Clarkson, and his henchman, Mr. Robert Henderson, of Selkirk. In numbers the sides were nearly equal, and though the men from Yarrow braes and Ettrick shaws had the advantage in weight and strength, it was soon seen that they were at a disadvantage with the lithe and agile lads from the towns, skilled by long practice in the game. The shepherds struggled hard for victory, but gradually the centre of the fight appeared to move away from Yarrow, and at last the ball was carried into Ettrick, the souter's goal, by Rob Hall, a Selkirk mason, and perhaps the strongest man upon the ground. Having got hold of the ball a short distance from the river, he succeeded in eluding the clutches of his desperate opponents, and rushing into the stream, held the ball aloft in token of victory.

By the time the breathless competitors had rested, and had refreshed themselves from a booth unsparingly provisioned at the Duke's expense, a change had taken place in the relative strength of the forces. Discarding the pine and adopting the heather-sprig, the blue-fisted weavers of Galashiels now appeared in league with the dalesmen. At whose solicitation this change of front was accomplished was never clearly disclosed; but it was well understood not to have been spontaneous. One of the Duke's daughters is said to have exhibited keen disappointment at the result of the first game, and to have asked if nothing could be done to reverse it in the second tussle. Both the Laird of Torwoodlee and the Sheriff, who had great influence with the people of Galashiels, are said to have had a share in persuading them to change sides; but be that as it may, the effect was visible when the match was renewed.

The Gala lads, familiar with the game from many a Fastern's E'en struggle over the hill at Hollybush, turned the scale effectively in favour of the shepherds; who, in spite of heroic efforts on the part of the two ancient burghs, won the second game, the ball being hailed by George Brodie, from Greatlaws, upon Ale Water. The discontent of the Selkirk players at Gala's defection now broke out into open expression; and so keen were the feelings excited, that attempts to rearrange the auxiliaries from different parishes completely failed. An offer on behalf of Selkirk to play the deciding "heat" with a hundred picked men on either side, could not be carried out for want of time, but was accepted by Lord Home for the first convenient opportunity. This did not calm the indignation of the Selkirk men, however, who are said to have wreaked their vengeance on such stragglers from the Gala contingent as fell into their hands. More crowns were cracked by the banks of Yarrow and Ettrick that night than had been since the day when Cavalier fought Covenanter on the battle-field of Philiphaugh. For a long time it rankled in the hearts of the people in both towns; and to this day it is impossible to have a game of emulation between them without some hostile demonstration by the onlookers. For many years Selkirk folk venturing to show themselves in Galashiels, were assailed with the cry of "Crows, Crows," against which they retaliated by calling the Gala folks "Herons," seriously aggravated by a wretched rhyme :—

"Galashiels herons, lockit in a box,
Daurna show their faces to Selkirk game-cocks."

It is really the case that for some time after the hand-ba', Torwoodlee thought it prudent not to be seen in the county town. Even the Sheriff had his carriage stopped in the market-place that night, as he was returning to Abbotsford, and only his presence of mind saved him from treatment which his assailants would for ever have blushed to remember. Paying no heed to the threatening language of some around him, but conversing in a friendly way with those nearest, he spoke in flattering terms of the skill and ardour they had displayed in the game, and ended by leaving a couple of guineas for their further refreshment. Owing either to the guineas, or the glamour of Scott's compliments, the very men who had been ready to insult him, joined the cheers that rose as he departed. Lord Home leaving the district, the proposed match never came off; and to compensate the Selkirk people for the disappointment, their generous Sheriff sent other £5 to the poor of the parish.

FASTHEUGH.

The earliest recorded Lairds of Fastheugh were Murrays of Philiphaugh; but this powerful family, clothed though it was in majesty of law in virtue of its hereditary sheriffship, could not protect its own lands and tenants against thieves and freebooters. Sandy Turnbull, son of the Laird of Dridane (Dryden, near Ashkirk), robbed Fastheuch of a number of ewes in 1494; and about the same time, Andrew Turnbull, "The Bald," had a share in the "burning of the place of Fastheuch, and stouthreif of certain horses, cattle, and other goods furth thereof." Six or eight years later, the Turnbulls, who seem to have had a special grudge against Fastheuch, again invaded it, bringing with them thieves and traitors of England, who spoiled both it and Hangingshaw of goods, etc., belonging to John Murray. James Murray, "in Skaldynneis," got the lands of Fastheuch from James IV. in 1510; and in 1540 they were granted to James, son of James Pringle of Tinnes, at a rental of £28, rising to £30. In eight years, however, they fell a prey to the earth-hunger of Buccleuch, who got a tack of Fastheugh in favour of himself, his wife, and his son Walter, an Act of Parliament in 1693 ratifying the lands to the Duchess and her heirs for ever. William Scott in Fastheuch was summoned before the presbytery in 1618 for complicity in the horrible slaughter of Adam Dalgleish, tenant of Whitehope, dwelling in Deuchar, for which crime the minister of Selkirk was ordered to enter in process of excommunication against him.

Pit., i. 20, 23, 35.

G. S., ii. 3505, iii. 1540.

P. S., xxii. 25.

A. P., ix. 341.

P. R.

FAULDSHOPE

Was early in possession of the Turnbulls, Thomas of "Fawlishope" being ordered in 1471 to pay to Thomas Folkert, two "sek of gude woll but cot or ter"—good wool without clot or tar. This same Thomas practised the calling of a freebooter on an extensive scale. On the 6th March 1494, he had to answer the following indictment :—

A. L. A.

"Thomas Turnbull in Fawlinshope, knight, under the King's hand, for art and part in the theft of 340 sheep, ewes and wedders, furth of Skaddamness from Patrick Murray; of 80 cattle, 12 horses and mares, besides household goods from nine houses in Carterhauch; of 60 sheep from Patrick Murray furth of Lewynhop; as also for reset of Robert Turnbull of Moodlaw, his sons and others with their booty of 211 sheep, one ox, one cow, 26 oxen and cows, three horses and mares, stolen from David Tait of Prin; also for art and part in the theft of 166 hogs from George Tait of Pirn, and his tenants in Sithope; of 17 she-goats from John Cleghorn; of household goods and 40 ewes from Wm. Cleghorn forth of Leuhanhop; of 7 stirks from John Scott forth of Glensax, and of 24 oxen and cows."

Auth. MSS.

E. R.

To save his estate Sir Thomas appears to have conveyed it to his son and heir John, who in 1484-5 was proprietor not only of East and West Fauldshope but of Huntlie, on the other side of Ettrick. The following letter from King James IV. in his favour was produced at the Justiciary Court in Selkirk :—

JUSTICE.—It is our will, and for certain considerations moving us, we charge you that ye charge not nor compel our lovit knicht Sir Thomas Turnbull to find sourtie in our justice-air, for satisfaction of party, for any accioune that he may be accusit of, committit before our coronation. And this precept be you sene and understanden, deliver the samyn again to the berar. Given under our signet at Linlithgow, the 25 day of Februar, and our regne the sevint yer.

Pit.,
i. 31.

In 1502, John Gray, a tenant in Fauldshope, was accused of participation in another raid on the place of Pirn, and the slaughter of Anthony Tait. Mention is made of Fauldshope as the property of Sir Robert Stewart of Traquair in 1595. Early in the eighteenth century it was sold by Scott of Harden to the Duchess of Buccleuch, and still remains in the hands of her descendant.

Traq
Chrt.

FOULSHIELS.

As the "Middilsted of Fawsyde" this place is mentioned in the list of Forest-steadings taken by the King from Douglas in 1455. In the rental of Kelso Abbey (1567) as in the Taxt Roll (1628) it is called Fawsyde ; but in the County Valuation Roll of 1643, it is entered as Fawsyde and Foulshiels. The first name is still applied to part of the estate ; and in various shapes it is extremely common throughout the lowlands of Scotland.

After the Scotts of Buccleuch succeeded the Douglases and Murrays as keepers of the Forest, they naturally filled its farms or "rowmes" with men of their own name and clan. William, son of Sir Walter Scott, knight, of Buccleuch, obtained charter of the lands in 1532, on their resignation by Scott of Hassendean, and subject to an annual payment of 40 merks, payable to Queen Margaret, and after her decease to the King. In 1593, John Scott of Foulshiels provided caution to the extent of 500 merks for his loyal behaviour, the deed being subscribed before Robert Scott of Oakwood and "Wattie Scott in Bolhill." John, it seems, was suspected of inter-communing with Hercules Stewart, brother of the traitor Earl of Bothwell. Andrew Scott of Foulshiels married, in 1643, a natural daughter of Walter, Earl of Buccleuch : her half-brother, Earl Francis, giving her a jointure of 4000 merks. In 1647 Walter was retoured heir to his brother Andrew in the lands of Faldounsyde, which fifty years later belonged to the Scotts of Gala.

G. S.,
iii. 1159.

P. C., v.
15, 592.

Mungo Park.

As the birthplace of Mungo Park, the celebrated African explorer, Foulshiels may be called one of the sacred spots in Ettrick Forest. On the 10th September 1771, in a clay-built cottage of which the roofless walls are still allowed to stand, he first saw the light; and when, thirty-four years afterwards, his eyes closed in darkness for ever, it was under the whelming waters of the Niger. He was the seventh child and third son of Mungo Park, tenant of the Duke of Buccleuch's farm of Foulshiels, his mother being Elspeth, daughter of Mr. John Hislop, tenant of Tinnes.

His grandfather, Archibald Park, tenant of Foulshiels, died in 1768, at the age of 86, his grandmother, Jean Jeddon or Park, in 1751, aged 73. His father was 79 at his death in 1793, and his mother (twenty-five years her husband's junior) was 74 when she died in 1817. Mungo Park (the traveller's C. R. father) was arrested by the Sheriff's order in 1753, probably for having been concerned in Prince Charlie's intrigues; but cannot have suffered much either in purse or person, for in 1760 he was rich enough to lend 1500 merks to the burgh of Selkirk. After receiving an elementary education at home, young Mungo was sent to the excellent Grammar School of Selkirk, where his industry and proficiency seem to have inspired his parents with a hope of seeing "his pow wag in the poopit." Fortunately the lad himself preferred medicine to divinity, and was apprenticed at the age of fifteen to Mr. Thomas Anderson, surgeon in Selkirk. Three years of apprenticeship and three sessions of attendance at the medical classes of Edinburgh University qualified him for the exercise of his profession; and in 1792, he sailed as assistant surgeon on board an East Indiaman bound for Sumatra. For this appointment he was indebted to Sir Joseph Banks, to whom he had been introduced by his brother-in-law, Mr. Dickson, a seedsman in London. Park's industry as a student of natural history produced good fruit in Sumatra, whence he brought home a valuable collection of plants and fishes. During the two years between Park's return and his departure to Africa he resided in London, with the exception of a short visit to his widowed mother at Foulshiels in 1794. To his sister, " Miss Bell Park, Hartwoodmyres, near Selkirk," he wrote a letter, which displays a simplicity verging on dulness :—

DEAR SISTER,—I have not heard from Scotland since I left it, but I hope you are all in good health, and I attribute your silence to the hurry of harvest. However, let me hear from you soon, and write how Sandy's marriage comes on, and how Jeany is, for I have heard nothing from her neither. I have nothing new to tell you. I am busy preparing my book for the press, and all friends here are in good health. Mr. Dickson is running about, sometimes in the shop and sometimes out of it. Peggy is in very good health, and dressed, as I think, in a cotton gown of a bluish pattern, a round-eared mutch, or what they call here a cap, with a white ribbon; a napkin of lawn or muslin or some such thing; a white striped dimitty petticoat. Euphy and Bill are both in very good health, but they are gone out to play, therefore I must defer a description of them till my next letter.—I remain, your loving brother,   MUNGO PARK.

As advised by his patron Sir Joseph, Park offered his services to the African Association, then desirous to obtain information about the river Niger and the great central mart of North Africa, Timbuctoo. Several persons employed by them had already fallen victims either to the climate or to hostile natives, and news had lately been received of the death of Major Houghton in an attempt to explore the unknown river. Sailing from Portsmouth in May 1795, Park achieved the object of his adventure, and after many narrow escapes from death, reached London again on Christmas morning of 1797. It is said that arriving too early to go to his brother-in-law's house, he wandered for some time about the streets in the vicinity, and eventually went into the gardens of the British Museum, a gate to which had been accidentally left open. As it happened, Mr. Dickson, who had care of the gardens, went there early that morning, and his emotion on beholding at that extraordinary time and place a friend whom he had come to number with the dead, may be more easily imagined than described. An abstract of his travels, published by the Association, made Park a famous man. After a six months' stay in London, during which he refused an offer from Government to employ him in the exploration of Australia, he went in June 1798 to Scotland, spending the summer and autumn with his mother and relations. At Foulshiels he employed himself assiduously in compiling an account of his travels, allowing himself little recreation, except a solitary evening stroll on the banks of Yarrow, and once or twice a long wander among the wild and romantic hills which enclose that classic stream, to every influence of which he was keenly susceptible. Quitting Foulshiels with great regret (which love, not only of his country, had some share in exciting), Park returned to the metropolis, and published his book in the spring of 1799. Its success was instant. Two editions were rapidly sold off, more followed, and to this day the work has not ceased to be popular, and widely appreciated. Park now began to think of settling in life, and, returning to Scotland, was married in August 1799 to Alice, eldest daughter of Dr. Anderson, his first instructor. It is not a little surprising to find "Mungo Park" in the list of young persons admitted to communion for the first time in Selkirk parish church during the same month

Life
and
Trav.

in which he was married. Contrary to what might have been expected of a disposition so adventurous, Park spent fully two years after his marriage at Foulshiels with his mother and brother, who managed the farm. At one time he thought of taking a farm, and at another resumed negotiations relative to the exploration of Australia ; but in October 1801 he went to Peebles to practise his profession. His house was at the head of the Briggate, on the north side, and a small building which projects at the east end of the Chambers Institute is said to have been his surgery. Betaking himself to work in good earnest, he soon acquired a large share of the business in the town and neighbourhood. Much of his spare time was passed with Colonel Murray of Cringletie, and Dr. Adam Ferguson, the well-known Professor of Moral Philosophy ; and he was constantly in receipt of marks of distinction from eminent men throughout the country. The records of the Royal Archers mention him as a distinguished guest on the occasion of their shooting for the silver arrow at Peebles in 1802 ; but he had more enjoyment in his own domestic circle and in the company of select friends than in general society, for which, indeed, he was not particularly suited. There could be but one ending to Mungo Park's settlement in a town pithily described in the epigram, "quiet as the grave, or Peebles." The dull routine of his daily work, contrasted with the romantic occupation of his earlier years, irritated him the more that it presented neither opportunity of distinction nor adequate compensation for the severe labour it entailed. Long rides in all sorts of weather, up the bare valleys and over the bleak hills of Tweedsmuir or Manor Water : wearisome hours spent in dirty houses of poor, ignorant, and often ungrateful patients: and above all, the lack of excitement, effectually disgusted the travelled doctor. A few winters of country practice in such a place would, he declared, tend as effectually to shorten life as another journey into the deserts of Africa. This undoubtedly was the goal of his desires ; and in 1803 he had an interview with the Colonial Secretary relative to a new expedition. After formally consulting a few friends in Scotland, he accepted Lord Hobart's proposal, took leave of his relations, and again went to London in December, hoping to embark in a short time for the coast of Africa. But after being postponed in the first instance till the end of February, the expedition was a second time delayed by a change of Ministry, even after all was ready for embarkation, and part of the troops on board. Being informed that he could not possibly sail before September, Park returned to Peebles in March 1804, accompanied by Sidi Omback Boubi, a Mohammedan teacher of Arabic, whose

Oriental habits remain a traditional subject of wonder in the place. At Whitsunday he took his family to Foulshiels, where he devoted himself with great diligence to astronomy and Arabic. In answer to a summons from London, he left in the end of September, after setting his affairs in order, and taking affectionate leave of his wife and children. He never again saw the green hills of Yarrow.

While living at Foulshiels, Park had been introduced by his brother to "the Shirra," then resident at Ashiesteel. Not finding Park at home one day, and going in search of him, Scott came upon him standing alone on the river bank, casting one stone after another into a deep pool, and intently watching the bubbles as they rose to the surface. Being rallied by his visitor on the apparent idleness of the amusement for one who had seen so much stirring adventure, Park replied—"Not so idle, perhaps, as you suppose. This was how I used to ascertain the depth of a river in Africa before I ventured to cross it, judging whether the attempt would be safe from the time the bubbles of air took to ascend." Though Scott had not then heard of Park's intended second expedition, he instantly concluded that such a purpose was in his mind. Before leaving Scotland for the last time, Park paid his friend a visit, and slept at Ashiesteel. Next morning Scott "convoyed" his guest homewards by a bridle-path over the hills between Tweed and Yarrow. Park was full of his new enterprise, but when they reached Williamhope ridge, Scott saw in the mist floating heavily down the valley "an emblem of the troubled and uncertain prospect which the undertaking afforded." His companion was in no way daunted by the suggestion, and at last they reached the spot where they had agreed to separate. When Park's horse stumbled and nearly fell in going over a small ditch separating the moor from the road, the Sheriff remarked it was a bad omen. "Freits follow those who look to them," answered Mungo, smiling, as he put spurs to his horse and disappeared. Lockhart suggests that the parting proverb was probably borrowed from the old ballad of "Edom o' Gordon":—

Lock., ch. xiii.

> " Wha looks to freits, my master deir,
>   It 's freits will follow them."

Nothing is more likely. "Two verses are restored," says Sir Walter in his notes to the *Outlaw Murray*, "from the recitation of Mr. Mungo Park, whose toils during his patient and intrepid travels in Africa have not eradicated from his recollection the legendary lore of his native country."

Along with Park went two other sons of the Forest—Doctor Alexander Anderson of Selkirk, his brother-in-law, and Mr. George Scott, son of the tenant in Singlee, both of whom had been fired by their friend's stories of his first journey with an unconquerable desire to accompany him on his second. Dr. Anderson, whose experience as a surgeon made him of obvious value in such an expedition, was to be second in command; while Scott, besides taking a share in the direction under Park, had a special post as draughtsman. His skill in drawing having casually come under the notice of the Sheriff, he was recommended by him to the Duchess of Buccleuch, through whose influence he had obtained assurance of a situation in the Ordnance Department of the Tower of London. This prospect he surrendered, that he might go with his old acquaintance. To give Park the advantage of official rank, he was appointed brevet-captain in Africa, a lieutenant's commission being granted to Dr. Anderson. He was further empowered to enlist not more than forty-five soldiers of the garrison at Goree, and such a number of black artificers as he should judge necessary, besides being at liberty to draw upon the Treasury to the extent of £5000.

From Goree, Park wrote to his wife on the 5th April. After mentioning that her brother had sufficiently recovered from rheumatism to dance several country dances at a ball the night before, and that George Scott was also in good health and spirits, he says:—

"I need not tell you how often I think of you; your own feelings will enable you to judge of that. The hopes of spending the remainder of my life with my wife and children will make everything seem easy; and you may be sure I will not rashly risk my life, when I know that your happiness and the welfare of my young ones depend so much upon it. I hope my mother does not torment herself with unnecessary fears about me. I sometimes fancy how you and she will be meeting misfortune half-way, and placing me in many distressing situations. I have as yet experienced nothing but success, and I hope that six months more will end the whole as I wish."

It is unnecessary here to describe the enormous difficulties which were encountered by the expedition, from the time it left Badoo until its final extinction by the death of Park, in a conflict with natives on the banks of the Niger. Poor Scott never reached the river, but died at a place called Koomi-Koomi, where Park had been forced to leave him, ill with fever. A long halt was made at Sansanding, where Park constructed by his own hands the flat-bottomed vessel which was to convey the wreck of his company to the open sea. And wreck it was, for of forty-four Europeans who left the Gambia, only five were alive on the 17th November—three soldiers (one deranged in

his mind), Lieutenant Martyn, and Park himself. Two days later, on the eve
of sailing, he wrote his last letter to his wife, assuring her of his own good
health, and that she might expect him home on the 1st of May, "not unlikely
I shall be in England before you receive this." In a letter to his father-in-
law, Dr. Anderson of Selkirk, Park thus broke the news of Dr. Alexander
Anderson's death :—

> "I know not in what manner to tell you the most sorrowful tidings that ever reached
> your ears, and I sincerely pray that the supporting Spirit from on high may sustain and
> comfort you under this severe dispensation of Divine Providence. You will readily anticipate
> what I am going to say. Your son, my dear friend, has shut his eyes on the scenes of time
> and opened them on the glories of eternity. . . . Death approached gradually, and on the
> morning of the 28th October, as I turned him from one side to the other, he gave a groan. I
> inquired if he felt much pain. He said, 'No, I have had a fine sleep.' Shortly after this, he
> said with clear distinct voice, 'Thou knowest my state, O Lord!' and instantly expired
> without sigh or struggle. . . . My dear father, endeavour to comfort my beloved wife; tell
> her not to be uneasy on my account; I am in excellent health, and, if the thing succeeds,
> expect to be in England in the month of May."

In Selkirkshire the death of these brave sons of the Forest created a
deep impression, and much despondency as to the fate of their undaunted
leader. May, which was to have seen him back in England, passed without
a word even of his safety. As month followed month, faint hope gave way
to dread, and dread became despair. Towards the close of the following year,
unfavourable reports, which had reached the coast settlements, found their
way to Scotland; but it was not till 1811 that authentic information was
received of Park's death, which happened about March 1806, opposite a village
called Boussa. An army of hostile natives attacked his boat from a high
bank which commanded the river; and after vainly defending himself for a
long time, Park, overpowered by numbers and fatigue, jumped with one of
the white men into the river, and was drowned in attempting to escape. Of
the entire crew, only one slave was permitted to live, and from him was
obtained the narrative of the tragedy.

Mungo was not the only remarkable member of his family. It is to his
brother, Archibald Park, farmer in Lewinshope, that Sir Walter refers in
his Introduction to *The Lady of the Lake*, when recalling his doubts of the
poem's success—

> "I remember that about the same time a friend started in to 'heeze up my hope,' like the
> 'sportsman with his cutty-gun,' in the old song. He was bred a farmer, but a man of powerful
> understanding, natural good taste, and warm poetical feeling, perfectly competent to supply the
> wants of an imperfect or irregular education. He was a passionate admirer of field-sports,

which we often pursued together. As this friend happened to dine with me at Ashestiel one day, I took the opportunity of reading to him the first canto of *The Lady of the Lake*, in order to ascertain the effect the poem was likely to produce upon a person who was but too favourable a representative of readers at large. . . . His reception of my recitation, or prelection, was rather singular. He placed his hand across his brow, and listened with great attention through the whole account of the stag-hunt, till the dogs threw themselves into the lake to follow their master, who embarks with Ellen Douglas. He then started up with a sudden exclamation, struck his hand on the table, and declared in a voice of censure calculated for the occasion, that the dogs must have been totally ruined by being permitted to take the water after such a severe chase. I own I was much encouraged by the species of reverie which had possessed so zealous a follower of the sports of the ancient Nimrod, who had been completely surprised out of all doubts of the reality of the tale."

Park, though himself a man of dauntless temperament, was often alarmed at Scott's reckless horsemanship in the mountain rides they had together. "The deil's in ye, Shirra," he would say; "ye'll never halt till ye get a fa' that'll send ye hame wi' your feet foremost." With great gallantry, he assisted the Sheriff in arresting a gipsy accused of murder, from amidst a group of similar desperadoes, on whom they had come unexpectedly in a desolate part of the country. What Sir Walter thought of Archibald Park may be gathered from his letter to their mutual friend, Mrs. Laidlaw of Peel, when the bankruptcy of another brother of Mungo, a writer in Selkirk, involved the whole family in ruin :— ^{Lock., ch. xiii.}

MY DEAR MRS. LAIDLAW,—Any remembrance from you is at all times most welcome to me. I have in fact been thinking a good deal about Mr. Park's (family?), especially about my good merry friend Archie, upon whom such calamity has fallen. I will write to a friend in London, likely to know about such matters, to see, if possible, to procure him the situation of an overseer of extensive farms in improvements, for which he is so well qualified; but success in this is doubtful, and I am aware that their distress must be pressing. Now, ' Waterloo' has paid, or is likely to pay me a great deal more money than I think proper to subscribe for the fund for families suffering; and I chiefly consider the surplus as dedicated to assist distress or affliction. I shall receive my letter in a few days from the booksellers, and I will send to Mr. Laidlaw's care £50, to be applied to the service of Mr. Park's family. It is no great sum, but may serve to alleviate any immediate distress, and you can apply it as coming from yourself, which will relieve Park's delicacy upon the subject. I really think I will be able to hear of something for him; at least it shall not be for want of asking about, for I will bring him in as a postscript to every letter I write. . . .—Very truly yours, WALTER SCOTT.
  Edin., 20th Nov. (1815).

Such a letter tempts one to ask whether the world has not been wrong in thinking Scott most worthy of honour as a writer—he was so great a man. Hardly less to the eternal credit of his kindly heart is his letter addressed to young Mungo Park at Tobermory, Isle of Mull, of date 17th May 1820 :—

SIR,—I was favoured with your very attentive letter, conveying to me the melancholy intelligence that you have lost my old acquaintance and friend, your worthy father. I was using some interest to get him placed on the Superannuated Establishment of the Customs, but God has been pleased to render this unnecessary. A great charge devolves on you, sir, for so young a person, both for the comfort and support of his family. If you let me know your plans of life when settled, it is possible I may be of use to you in some shape or other, which I should desire in the circumstances, though my powers are very limited, unless in the way of recommendation. I beg my sincere condolence may be communicated to your sister, who I understand to be a very affectionate daughter and estimable young person.—I remain very much, your obedient servant,   WALTER SCOTT.

John Park, another brother, four years younger than Mungo, died at Foulshiels in 1851, and was buried at Galashiels, where lie also the father and wife (died 1840) of the great traveller. Park's oldest son, Mungo, assistant surgeon, E.I.C.S., died at Trichinopoly, Madras, in 1823, aged 23; Thomas, second son, a naval officer, died in 1827, aged 24, in Africa, whither he had gone to trace his father's footsteps; and the third, an officer in the Indian army, left a family of sons and daughters, of whom one is married to Mr. Findlater, M.P. for Monaghan. Park's only daughter married a Welsh proprietor of the name of Meredith, whose son and daughter survive.

Mr. Ruskin, the eminent critic and philanthropist, has thought fit to visit with his anger Mungo Park's declaration that he would rather brave Africa and all its horrors than *wear out his life in long and toilsome rides over the hills of Scotland, for which the remuneration was hardly enough to keep soul and body together.*

Fors.
Clav.,
Nov.
1883. "I have," says Mr. Ruskin, "italicised the whole sentence, for it is a terrific one. It signifies, if you look into it, almost total absence of the instinct of personal duty,—total absence of belief in the God who chose for him his cottage birthplace, and set him his life-task beside it; absolute want of interest in his profession, of sense for natural beauty, and of compassion for the noblest poor of his native land. And with these absences, there is the clear presence of the fatallest of the vices, Avarice. . . . He is at that time practising as a physician among his own people. A more sacred calling cannot be;—by faithful missionary service more good could be done among fair Scotch laddies in a day, than among black Hamites in a lifetime;—of discovery, precious to all humanity, more might be made among the woods and rocks of Ettrick, than in the thousand leagues of desert between Atlas and red Edom."

In answer to all which it may safely be said that if Mr. Ruskin had taken the trouble to read what was within his reach concerning Park's tender affection for his family as well as his generous and self-denying treatment of lowlier patients, these scathing words would never have been written. A story told by Mrs. Park's nephew, Dr. H. S. Anderson of Selkirk, illustrates vividly Mungo Park's beneficent gentleness with the poor. Losing his way one stormy winter night among the hills, Park directed his steps to a distant light, which turned out to be the candle of a shepherd's cot. On entering, he found the little household in great anxiety, the shepherd's wife being about to become a mother for the first time, and aid far out of reach. To their joy the stranger revealed his profession, and stayed till all was happily over. Next morning, when Park was being guided by his host to a point whence he could see the road, he asked him why he always walked behind. "Deed, sir," confessed the simple countryman, "the guidwife says ye maun be an angel, and I think sae tae, so I was just keeping a bit back to be sure o' seeing ye flee up."

More than twenty years after all hope had been abandoned in Selkirk-shire of obtaining any relic of the lost travellers, the Ettrick Shepherd was shown by Mr. Nutland, a literary gentleman in London, a copy of the Book of Psalms bound with Watts' Hymns. Richard Lander, who followed Park's footsteps, had found the book in possession of an African king, by whom it was looked upon as a fetish, being wrapped in yellow muslin and hung up for worship. Hogg, to his astonishment, discovered on the title-page the name of his old friend Alexander Anderson in his own writing. On his remarking how much Dr. Anderson of Selkirk would give for this relic of his brother, the owner generously said he would be happy to restore it to the family. And now the little volume, found in the bottom of the boat from which Park leaped into his watery grave, lies, in a case of satin and leather, a cherished relic in the house from which its brave owner set out upon his fateful venture.

A silver-headed bamboo staff which Park is said to have used in his first African journey, now belongs to Mr. Gideon Scott, Selkirk. In 1859 the people of Scotland repaired a long neglect by erecting a monument to the great traveller in the High Street of his county town.

THE HAINING.

In 1535, when James v. was King, certain Acts of James II. and others A. P., ii. 343.
for planting woods were put into "sharp execution," and every owner of £100 yearly, new extent, where there were no trees, was ordered to plant wood, and to make hedges and "hayning" for three acres of land. To cut, peel, burn, or fell new "haynings" was punishable, first time by a fine of £10, second time £20, third time by death. Here "haining" seems to mean plantation. It is identical with the modern German *Hain*, a grove. But that such was the original signification of the name under notice is doubtful. Quite as probably Haining is derived from the old Scotch word *hain*, to save

by setting aside—having its German equivalent in *hegen*, to enclose, to preserve game. It is finely used by Burns in "The Cottar's Saturday Night,"
when the dame brings forth "her weel-hain'd kebbuck." If this be the
proper root, Haining must be held to mean that part of the Forest "hained"
or preserved specially for the King. In the Forest Laws of William the

A. P.,
i. 687.

Lion (1165-1214), who was often at Selkirk, the very first provision concerns "ye hanyt placis of wodis." "The wode is forbodin alswell to thaim
that duellis therin as till other that thai enter nocht in ony hanyt place of the
woddis with thar bestis bot gif thai haf fredom of the forestar." And if the
forester, when he was alone, chanced upon any such "beasts," he was to make
a cross in the earth or on a tree where the beasts were found, and thrice to blow
his horn, and after that to lead them to the king's castle. So that the "hanyt
place," or haining, must have been close to the royal residence. And as the
king's castle of Selkirk stood upon the Peelhill, which is now part of the
Haining estate, there is little room for doubt as to the name's true derivation.

Originally Haining was but a small part of the extensive estate now
covered by the name. It comprised neither Howden, Brownmuir, Greenhill,
Hartwoodburn, North Sinton, nor even the Peelhill, which were all separate
and independent properties. From time to time, by feu and by purchase,
little areas of the town's ground were added to the Haining, whose laird also
got a good slice of the common at the time of its allocation in 1681.

There is nothing to show at what particular date Selkirk castle and its
"hanyt place" passed out of the king's personal occupation; and we are left
to surmise that it may have been after the death of Alexander III. in 1286.

Not until 1463 is Haining mentioned as a separate holding, a family of
Scott being then in possession. In that year Robert Scott of Hanyng acquired

Reg.
Mag.
Sig.,
ii. 771.

by purchase the lands of Grevistoun and Gillishauch in Peeblesshire, David
and Alexander Scot, sons of Sir Walter Scott of Kirkurd (and Buccleuch),
being witnesses to the charter. Fourteen years later the same lands were sold
by Haining, the deed being attested again by two sons of Scott of Buccleuch.

Reg.
Mag.
Sig.,
ii. 1273.

According to Satchells, the Haining family was descended from this
famous race—

> From the family of Buckcleugh,
> There has sprung many a man,
> Four hundred years ago.
> Hassinden he was one.

Sir Alexander Scot of Hassinden was Knight;
With good King James the Fourth he was killed at Flowden fight.
From Hassenden did spring before that time
The families of Wall, Delorain, and Haining.

Satchells' genealogy, when not palpably mythic, is more accurate than his rhyme, or yet his metre; and his derivation of the Scotts of Haining from Buccleuch is confirmed by the fact that in the great funeral procession of the first Earl (1634), the arms trophy of "Scot of Balcleughe" was carried by Sir Robert Scot of Haining.

Against the first "Robert Scot in the Hanyng" and John his son an action was brought by Alexander Ker, claiming to be parish clerk of Selkirk A. L. A., in 1489, for withholding the fees, fruits, and profits of the said parish clerkship [489.] for fifteen years bygone, extending yearly to 20 merks. Only two years later Robert was prosecuted by William Cockburn, younger of Langton, for wrongous occupation of the forest-stede of the Haining, within the forest of A. L. C., Ettrick, for three years, it pertaining to Cockburn by reason of tack of our [208.] sovereign lord (James IV.), and for the wrongous uptaking of the profits of the said stede. Both being present, Scott alleged he had a tack for all the days of his life from "our sovereign lord (James III.), whom God assoilzie." The case was continued for production of Scott's papers. Whether or not he was able to exhibit the tack, Robert was still designated "of Haining" when in 1494 he assisted at an inquest by which Alexander Erskine was retoured heir to his father in the lands of Sinton and office of Sheriff of Selkirk. (The latest mention of Robert is in 1504, when he was included in a long list of persons protected against actions of law during the absence of the Archbishop Pit., i. 43. of Glasgow.) In 1500, there was a sudden break in Scott's possession of the Haining, Murray of Philiphaugh, in conjunction with Pringle of Tinnes, having P. S., i. 124. obtained a nine years' tack of it from the King—"paying mails, grassum, and Phil. duties, and keeping the stede forest-like." This seems to have aroused the MSS. fury of the displaced Scotts, and, indeed, of the entire clan. In 1507, before the nine years' tack to Philiphaugh had expired, the King, with consent of Queen Margaret (who had Ettrick Forest for dowry land), granted in few-form to John Scott and his heirs, the forest-stead and lands of Haining, with lake of the same, extending to £7, 2s. of old extent, and to £21 of new extent, G. S., ii. 3154. in the lordship of Ettrick Forest and ward of the same, with power to build a tower and fortalice, with iron bolts, with stanchions, loopholes, and all kinds of munition necessary for defence against invasion by thieves and malefactors, at a rent of £24 Scots, "and a lance" to serve the King in his wars as often as need is. Acting on this grant, John Scot set portions of his land to certain burgesses for seven years, one of whom, Mungo Brown, died in 1515, possessed of a fourth part of Easter Haining, being 40s. worth of land in the forest-stead. A second intrusion by Murray of Philiphaugh once more put the Scots in a fury. In 1509, James IV. gave Murray the lands of " Pelehill," close by Haining, along with the petty customs of the burgh and sheriffship of the county. Banding themselves together under the leadership of Buccleuch, they attacked Murray's stronghold at Hangingshaw, Murray himself being slain. At a Justiciary Court in Jedburgh (22d November 1510) order was made for distraining the goods of certain accomplices in the bloody deed, and failing these, the goods of John Scot of Haining, one of their sureties. All of which lends colour to the tradition mentioned by Sir Walter Scott, that the fatal arrow sped from Haining's bow. He did not long survive his enemy. The year after Flodden (February 1514) Robert Scott was infeft in the lands as son and heir of his father, an English shaft probably having saved young Philiphaugh the avenging of his father's death. In 1518, Janet Ker, John's widow, let to her " beloved friend Robert Scott of Haining," her wast burn-mill and the mill-croft for sixteen bolls of malt four times in the year. Beyond this there is no mention of the second Robert Scott of Haining. He must have died before 26th February 1531-2, on which day Walter Scott, tutor of Hayning, confirmed a gift by his father and grandfather to the Holy Cross Altar in the parish church. In all probability Walter was a brother of Robert, and tutor during the minority of his nephew Thomas, who was infeft in the lands in 1538, as son and heir of Robert, and is mentioned in 1554 as a pledge for the keeping of good rule by the Rutherfords both anent Scotland and England. Not that Thomas was himself of a pre-eminently law-abiding disposition, for in 1557 he formed one of the sacrilegious band who broke into the chapel of St. Mary of the Lowis in search of Sir Peter Cranstoune "for his slaughter upon ancient feud and forethought felony." Yet in 1561, Thomas figures as a suppresser of Border thieving, having obliged himself to enter before the Warden of the East Marches a man accused of stealing six horses; and is mentioned as one of the very few Border landit men who responded to Queen Mary's command that they should report what progress they had made in apprehending freebooters. At the trial of Elliot of Horsliehill and others for the slaughter of David Scott of Hassendean in 1564, Thomas of Haining appears with other Scotts as prelocutors (the Laird of Balcleuche being pursuer). Two

B. R.

G. S.,
ii. 3388.

Pit.,
i. 69.

B. M.,
i. 372.

Dun.
MSS.

B. R.

B. R.

Haining
MSS.

P. C.,
i. 154.

Pit.,
i. 400.

P. C.,
i. 168.

P. C.,
i. 181.

months later (December 1564), he was one of the assize on a famous case in Pit., i. 456-7.
which Ferguson of Kilkerran, with about 100 associates, were charged with
forcible invasion of a court, and an attack upon Sheriffs sitting in judgment,
"for their slaughter." Mention is made of an action at law in 1576, between P. C., ii. 558.
Robert Scott of Haining, son of the deceased Thomas, and John Scott, minister
at Selkirk. For the minister it was represented that he and his predecessors
had been kindly tenants "in the tymes bygane past memor of man" of the
half-town and lands of Elliston; but that the deceased Thomas Scott of
Haining had obtained a presentation of the property followed by infeftment.
John Scot now pled for non-confirmation of the feu, and produced certain rights
and titles to the property; but the Court decided in favour of Haining.
When, at Holyroodhouse in 1577, Jonet Scot, father-sister to the late Buc- P. C., ii. 671.
cleuch, granted discharge for 1000 merks, payable for the failure of George
Ker to marry her, Robert Scott of Haining was one of the five witnesses; and
in 1589 his was one of the signatures to the "bond" by which members of
the Scott clan were united for mutual defence. Two years later he was
chosen as hostage for the name, for the "brek of the assurance" committed P. C., iii. 381, 396, 404.
by the Scotts in the cruel mutilation of David Elott of Braidlee. Along
with his kinsman Synton, the Laird of Haining was thrown into Edinburgh
Castle, and only released on caution for £1000 by Alexander Scott, burgess of
the city. In 1587 he was in turn caution for Sir Thomas Turnbull of Bedrule, P. C., iv. 189, 191.
and in 5000 merks for his chief, Buccleuch. About this time bad blood seems
to have arisen again between the Scots and Murrays, for in 1590, a band was P. C., iv. 480-3.
forced upon Robert, Laird of Haining, and a number of Selkirk burgesses, that
they would not harm Patrick Murray of Philiphaugh, or his dependants—
Murray and his friends signing another that they would not harm the Scotts.
It was this same Robert who, as deputy warden for Buccleuch, held the truce P. C., v. 290.
on the border which was broken by the capture of "Kinmont Willie;" and his
second son, William Scott, was one of the thirty-three who joined in the famous Sat. 13.
rescue. In 1597-8, Robert Scott of Haining, Provost-depute of Selkirk, was
denounced a rebel for "maist proudly" disobeying an order to apprehend P. C., v. 450.
certain burgesses; and in 1603, was again denounced for inciting the Scotts
of Hundleshope to an outrage on the farm gear and ploughmen of Fethane.
In 1611, Robert's son Robert was entered heir of the lands of Haining, with Reto. Selk., 121.
lake of the same, the lands of Elliston, and the following crofts and acres of
arable land :—A croft called Ladyland, another called Langshot, "Chickinnis"
acre, Hoppringle's acre, Rutherford's acre, the lands of "Hairisbuttis," house

rents in the Water way of Selkirk, in the "Crocegait," in the Well wynd, in Holywell-hill, in Kirkwynd, rents from Minto's acre and from Tait's hill—all in the burgh and liberty of Selkirk. Three years after his accession the young

P. R., 1614.

laird was pounced upon by the ecclesiastical authorities "for not haunting of his parish kirk on the Sabbath Day, and profaning of the fast-day in Kelso." His answer that "he haunted no other kirk, and did not know it was a fast-day," did not avail him, for he was ordered to repair to the session of Selkirk

Bgh. Sas., 1623.

for censure. Having become Sir Robert, he (with consent of Dame Grizel Ker, his spouse) granted his lands to Mr. Lawrence Scott of Harperrig, advocate,

Index Decis.

who is styled "of Haining" in the record of an action by the tenants in 1625, which was decided against him. Although about this time the estate passed into the hands of the family of Riddel, for many years the displaced Scotts continued to be called "of Haining." Sir Robert bore the Buccleuch arms trophy at the first Earl's funeral in 1634; and in 1643 his son being in the second Earl's retinue, was made a burgess of Selkirk. A retour of Agnes Scott, daughter of Lieutenant-Colonel Robert Scott, heiress of Walter Scott,

Gen. Reto., 5205.

portioner of Guilan, brother-german of Robert Scott of Hayning, her grandfather's brother, is the last official mention of the name.

Dun. MSS.

    The disposition by which Haining passed into the hands of the Riddells bears date 3d November 1625. For this family descent from a Norman warrior

Bor. Mem., 181.

who came over with the Conqueror is claimed by Mr. Riddell-Carre, an enthusiastic genealogist, and himself one of them. A better case, it is fair to say, can be made out for the Riddels than for nine-tenths of those who claim that distinction. There certainly was a "Ridel" in the Conqueror's retinue, who obtained lands in England; and in his family the same Christian name prevailed, as is found in certain Scotch "Ridels" of David I.'s time. Adrian IV., the only Englishman ever elected to the Papal chair (1154-9), granted a bull confirming to Auskittel Riddel the lands of Whittun, Lilliesleaf, and others, this same Auskittel being one of the witnesses to Malcolm's charter confirming the removal of Selkirk Abbey to Kelso, and having a daughter married to the

Haigs of Bemersyde, 62.

third Haig of Bemersyde. In course of time they gave their name, it is said, to their lands in Lilliesleaf—a circumstance most unusual if not altogether

Ann. Tevi., 51.

unique. If, as has been asserted, the first Scotch Riddell was descended from an English family settled at Ryedale in Yorkshire, his relationship to the Norman Ridels must be considered doubtful. But beyond all question the race is of extreme antiquity. When in 1576 the Commendator of Jedburgh demanded to be tried by an assize of his Peers, as a lord of Parliament, the

Lord Advocate said, "The Lord of Riddell, being ane barroun of auld blude, suld pas upoun his assyis, and is sufficient thairto." Andrew Riddel of that Ilk, who acquired Haining from Laurence Scott, was twice married (first to a daughter of James Pringle of Galashiels, and second to Violet Douglas of Pumpherston), and it was for Andrew, oldest son of his second marriage, he bought the estate. His oldest son by Miss Pringle became Sir John, the first baronet of Riddel—a title which, after many vicissitudes, ceased to be connected with the old lands in the time of Sir John Buchanan Riddel, who died in 1819. The estate then passed into the hands of Mark Sprot, Esq., in whose family it remains. [Pit., i. (2) 47.]

Andrew, first Riddell of Haining, who took to wife Jean, daughter of Stewart of Traquair, is described as having been a man of much promise, but he did not live to realise it. All that is known of his career is that he sat in the Scottish Parliament as member for Selkirkshire in 1639-40, and that his young son was retoured his heir on 5th January 1643. In 1646 his widow, Jean Stewart, Lady Haining, presented a petition to Parliament anent her losses, and three years afterwards she was married to the Hon. William Douglas, second son of the second Earl of Queensberry, and ancestor of Sir Charles Douglas, who became fifth Marquis of Queensberry in 1812. Among the Haining papers at Dun there is a discharge by John Lidderdaill, chamberlain to the Marquis of Douglas, for £106, 13s. 4d. Scots from Lady Hayning as tutrix-testamentar to her son. [A. P., v. 252, 258. Dun. MSS.] [A. P., vi. (1) 605. Foster, 543.]

John Riddell was destined to play a conspicuous part in the history of his native country—a part that subjected him to much hatred while he lived, and has covered his name with obloquy since his death. He is still spoken of with anger as the persecutor of the Covenanters; at least by those who have not learned to consider that an attitude hostile to these fanatics may have been compatible with a considerate, even a humane disposition. He is first mentioned in public records as a Commissioner of Supply for the shire in the year 1655, the nomination being frequently repeated up to 1690. Becoming associated with Urquhart of Meldrum, who was made Sheriff in 1681, *vice* Murray of Philiphaugh, deprived on suspicion of conniving at conventicles, the Laird of Haining was brought into antagonism with nearly all his neighbours, some of them his near relations by blood and by marriage. While yet a young man he had the misfortune to lose his wife, Sophia, third daughter of James, the fifth Pringle of Torwoodlee, who, according to her brother-in-law, Walter Pringle of Greenknowe, "passed from this world on the 28th September

Pgle.
Mem.,
34, 53.
1663, leaving many of her kindred walking in the way which leadeth to glory." Their marriage had probably taken place in 1656, when a testament of sasine was given to Sophia Pringle of liferent of Bowland, Bowshank, and half of Windydoors, then belonging to the Riddels. A year and a half after his wife's death, Haining used his influence with the Episcopalian or King's party to obtain, in favour of the above named Pringle of Greenknowe, some relaxation of his imprisonment in the Tolbooth of Elgin, whither incurable obstinacy in the cause of the Covenant had led him. In 1661 Riddel was defender in an extraordinary action brought against him by the Mayor of Berwick. It was alleged that by draining the loch into Tweed he caused great destruction
Index
Decis.,
Mor.
12772.
amongst salmon, to the loss of the fisheries at the river mouth. Haining maintained his right to drain the loch, which he had done by its natural outlet, a burn which drove a mill. His argument was sustained, the Court declaring that "it was the proper use of rivers to carry away the corruption and filth of the earth, which should not be hindered by any right of fishing, which is but a casualty given and taken with the common use of the river." According to a tradition, the loch was lowered in consequence of a child of the laird's having fallen into it from a window of the house, which was then washed by its waters. In another legal process (1668) Hayning claimed a right of
Index
Decis.
pasturage in Selkirk Common, which was opposed by the burgesses of Selkirk, but decided in his favour, the dispute being in all probability the first step which led to the Common being divided in 1681. Besides the large area of land which then fell to the share of Haining, Riddell had in 1661 obtained an Act of Parliament ratifying the sale to him and his heirs by the Magistrates and community of Selkirk of the mill called the Burn Mill, with the kiln and "schelinghill" thereof, and its watergate, close, dam and passages. The burn here mentioned is that now known as the "Clockie," and the mill stood on its banks about 100 yards south of the point where it enters the garden at Woodburn. A remarkable contract was made in 1671 between King Charles II. and the Laird of Hayning, in fulfilment of which the latter laid out his estate
Hist.
MSS.,
v. 643.
for the breeding of horses. The promised stud never being sent, the King, to compensate Haining for his expenditure, made him a gift of the Border fines. In 1682 he petitioned to be discharged from the agreement. Besides holding office as Sheriff of the Forest (his duties in connection with which fall more
A. P.,
vii. 527.
properly into the history of the county), Riddell was in 1665 and in 1674 a representative of Selkirkshire in Parliament, the latter election being objected
A. P.,
viii. 214.
to, but finally sustained. Doubtless the landing of the Prince of Orange in

1688 was fatal to his influence; and for the last years of his life, which came to an end in 1696, nothing is known of his position.

He was succeeded by his son Andrew, third and last of the Riddells of Haining. By an agreement dated 4th October 1701, he sold the estate to Andrew Pringle of Clifton, who bought it for his second son, John; and in the same year he disposed of his lands in Gala Water to Robert Rutherford, son of the late John Rutherford of Edgerston. With his cousin, the Earl of Traquair, Mr. Riddell visited Bath in 1706; and amongst the Haining papers are two wills of his, executed at Yair in 1714, evidently in prospect of immediate death. Except a legacy to one of the ladies of Traquair, and another to his sister Jean Riddell, "Lady Butterwhite," he left all he had to his brother-in-law, David Erskine of Dun, one of the Senators of the College of Justice. With his wife, Magdalene Riddel, Lord Dun obtained possession of a most valuable collection of documents relating to the family of Riddell and their possessions, and to the proceedings of the district courts in the troublous times of the persecution. The collection, in admirable order, is now in the keeping of Augustus Kennedy Erskine of Dun, heir of line of the Riddells of Haining. Lord Dun, who died in 1758, in his eighty-fifth year, was described as "a venerable man of very great experience, and greatly distinguished for piety." Dun. MSS. A. P., xi. App. 131. Sen. Just., 491.

Whitsunday 1702 was the term of John Pringle's entry to the Haining, the price he paid for it was 63,000 merks Scots (£3412 sterling), and it comprised Easter and Wester Haining, holding of the King; two husbandlands, holding of the Marquis of Douglas; the Chicken Acre; the seat, pairt, and proportion of the parish church, with the burial-place. The witnesses to the agreement were Robert Rutherford of Bowland and John Murray, advocate.

The first Pringle of Clifton was William, the first Pringle of Torwoodlee, whose father was James Pringle of Galashiels, and whose mother was a Murray of Philiphaugh. In 1509 he got confirmation of a charter by one Henrisoun, a clerk of justiciary in Edinburgh, "for his singular love towards David Hoppringill in Tynnes," of part of the lands and lordship of Clifton. The lands had once belonged to Ailmure of Ailmure, whose paternal acres, strange to say, also fell into the hands of the same Pringles more than 200 years later. William Pringle fell at Flodden; and in 1516, a gift of the land was obtained by Elizabeth Lawson, his widow, Mr. George, his son and heir, Mr. Robert, parson of Morhame, and Alexander Hoppringle, his brother. Remission for G. S., ii. 3370. P. S. v. 91.

P. S.,
xiv. 89;
xv. 71.

P. C.,
ii. 623;
iv. 272.

Ret.
Rox.,
63, 79, 93,
115, 183.

A. P.,
viii. 287.

Cha.
Ann.,
ii. 834.

Scotts
and
Halib.,
58.

the slaughter of David Turnbull was obtained by John Pringle in Clifton in 1535; and mention is made of a George Hoppringle of Clifton in 1541. In 1577, William Ker, younger of Cessford, is ordered to produce Wat Pringle in Clifton and his brother Thomas before the Lords of the Secret Council in connection with a bit of border-thieving, and in 1588, Walter is served with a similar summons. According to the retours, Clifton, or parts of it, were, in 1610, in hands of George of Torwoodlee, as heir of William, his father; in 1616, of John of Tofts, as heir of William, his great-grandfather; in 1618, of John, as heir of John, his grandfather; and finally, in 1622, of Andrew (*alias* Dand), as heir of George, his great-grandfather. After Andrew came Mark, whose son, Robert, succeeded in 1644. In 1661, Robert was a commissioner for the King's bounty, which did not save him from being fined £1200 Scots next year, with other supporters of Parliament' against the King. An Act of Parliament, ratifying his titles to Clifton in 1681, narrates how the various divisions of the estate became united in his possession; and when he died, four years later, his only child, Jonet, was a considerable heiress. His brother Andrew, heir of provision, being desirous to keep the lands in his family, formed a design of marrying his niece to his own son. As, however, Joneta was twenty, and the boy only thirteen, it became necessary to wait till he reached a more marriageable age. Jonet's relations by her mother's side, Murrays of Livingstone, were equally anxious to catch the heiress for Lieutenant George Murray of the King's Guard; and when she suddenly vanished from society, an order was obtained from the Privy Council against her uncle to produce her. Murray urged that as Andrew Pringle had not acted very well towards his deceased brother, he was not well fitted to take charge of his brother's daughter; and Pringle, notwithstanding his oath that he had not been concerned in hiding her, was ordered, on pain of a fine of 10,000 merks, to bring forward his niece by the 5th of November. To make sure of him, he was put in prison. Before long it was ascertained that the missing Jonet was "owre the border and awa" with her boy cousin, to whom she had been married by an English clergyman. For 7000 merks the disappointed lieutenant agreed to withdraw all opposition, and the offence against the laws of the country was wiped out by a fine of 500 merks on the young couple. The juvenile husband seems to have acquired a taste for surreptitious wedlock. When he was upwards of fifty, "being some years a widow, having had several children by his lady, sons and daughters abundantly promising, he married Margaret Rutherfurd, eldest daughter to Fairnington, which was not agreeable to his children and his other near relations, they being married clandestinely to the surprise of his family."

It was the wily match-making uncle and father of this young couple who bought Haining for his second son, John Pringle; and in 1702 John obtained an Act of Ratification, which united Haining and Burn Mill in one barony, holding direct from the crown. Five years later occurred the famous duel in which his younger brother, Mark, killed Scott of Raeburn, great-granduncle of Sir Walter. The laird himself, who had been member for the county during the last four years of the Scottish parliament, had just been returned to the first parliament of Great Britain, in which he retained his seat till 1720, when he became a Judge of Session, as Lord Haining. When he died in 1754, he had reached his eightieth year. Almost from the year of his settlement in the Haining, Mr. Pringle took a keen and active interest in the town affairs of Selkirk. In 1724, he went so far as to qualify himself as a merchant councillor. In 1731 he is designated in the roll as "The Right Honourable John Pringle of Haining, one of the Senators of the College of Justice, merchant member;" but in 1742 he was summarily expelled. ^{A. P., xi., app. 131.}

Andrew Pringle, his son, was an abler man. In 1736, the Town Council of Selkirk agreed that "as Lord Haining's son was entered advocate, it would not be amiss to take him up as ordinary lawyer," and a committee was named to wait on him when he came to the country, and gave him five guineas as an honorary. In 1751, he was appointed Sheriff of Selkirkshire, four years later became Solicitor-General, and in 1759 took his seat on the bench as Lord Alemoor, dying in 1776. "Jupiter" Carlyle says it was a great loss to this country that Lord Alemoor did not live to fill the President's chair, and indeed had not health to go through the labour of it. "He excelled all the laymen of that period for genuine argument and eloquence; and on the bench delivered his opinion with more dignity, clearness, and precision than any judge I ever heard either in Scotland or England." Lord Alemoor, says Dr. Somerville of Jedburgh, "was beyond comparison the most admired speaker at the Scottish bar. His language was pure and nervous, his arguments the most sound and substantial, shortly and distinctly stated, and strictly applicable to the point under discussion. Nothing appeared to be studied for effect; but the native dignity of his manner always commanded attention." It is delightful to find that when in 1757 the General Assembly had under discussion Home's play of "Douglas," Lord Alemoor, in his capacity of lay elder, made his eloquence felt on the side of the reverend dramatist. ^{Auto., 252.} ^{Life, p. 108.}

Lord Alemoor, being unmarried, was succeeded by his brother, Mr. John Pringle, who, at one time a merchant in Madeira, was member for Selkirkshire from 1765 until he accepted the Chiltern Hundreds in 1786. Like his brother, he died unmarried, in 1792, having succeeded to Clifton in 1780.

Mark Pringle, the next laird, a son of John Pringle of Crichton and his wife Anne Rutherford of Fairnilee, was named after his grandfather, who killed Raeburn; was M.P. for county from 1786 to 1802; married a Miss Chalmers in 1795; and died in 1812, aged 58.

John Pringle, his eldest son, officer of the 7th Hussars, served with the army of occupation in France. Retiring from the army in 1819, he was returned M.P. for the local group of burghs, sat for two years, and died unmarried, in 1831. When coming home from a fishing excursion to Headshaw Loch, in a gig, from which his brother and a gamekeeper had already alighted, he was capsized at the stable entrance, his head coming against a sharp stone. He never spoke afterwards. His funeral was the largest ever seen in Selkirk up to that time. Having made use of his abilities to further the public weal, and of his wealth to help the poor, he was greatly lamented.

Mr. Robert Pringle, soon after succeeding his brother in the estates, stepped into the political arena, where he achieved the feat of carrying Selkirkshire in the Liberal interest at the first election after the Reform Bill, though he was never able to repeat the victory. Like his brother, he had served in the 7th Hussars, and like him also he died unmarried, in 1842. He was the last male Pringle of Haining and Clifton, and it is pleasant to quote N. S. A., the following testimony to his own worth and to his family's. "This Rox., gentleman maintains the same high reputation for public spirit, generosity, 152. and interest in the welfare of his tenants, which have distinguished his ancestors. His tenantry are prosperous and happy, and hold him in the highest estimation."

Mrs. Pringle-Douglas, sister of the last two lairds, succeeded to Haining and Fairnilee, Clifton passing to Mr. Elliot of Harwood. She married Archibald Douglas of Adderston, descended from the ancient house of Cavers, who died in 1860. Mrs. Pringle-Douglas survived till 1878, leaving to succeed her an only daughter, Mrs. Pringle-Pattison, whose husband claims descent from a family of Pattison, who once owned the lands of Stonegarthside in the Border country.

Besides the lands from which its name is derived, the estate of Haining includes others which in former times were independent properties. Adderston, near Hawick, Greenhill and North Sinton in the Parish of Ashkirk, lie in the shire of Roxburgh; and in Selkirkshire, there are Peelhill, Howden, Hartwoodburn, Brownmuir, Easter Alemoor, Fairnilee, and Rink.

PEELHILL.—This little holding, which appears to have gone with the Burgh customs and the Sheriffship, was granted to Murray of Philiphaugh in 1503, and remained with that family for two centuries.

GREENHILL.—In 1680, Francis Scott of Greenhill, along with James Scot of Thirlestane and others, was severely fined for absence from the king's host. _Crk., ii. 70._

HOWDEN.—There is mention of a Thomas Minto in Howden, tenant to Wm. Hop Pringle of Howden, having, with one of Ker of Greenhead's men and others, " undir cloude and silence of nicht," stolen 42 sheep from David Roger in Redpath, on the 5th September 1591. In the beginning of the 17th century the place belonged to one of the Turnbulls of Philiphaugh; but shortly afterwards passed into the hands of the Currors, a family intimately connected as bailies and town-clerks with the burgh of Selkirk. From 1648 to the middle of last century there is frequent mention in Acts of Parliament and elsewhere of the Currors of Howden (George, John, and William, in their order) as Commissioners of War and of Supply. Writing in 1722, Hodge mentions the ruins of an old house at Howdine, but no trace of it remains. In 1662, George Curror of Howden was fined £600 by the Royalist Government for having supported Parliament. _P. C., iv. 718._ _Taxt Roll._ _A. P., vi. vii. viii. ix._ _MSS. Adv. Lib._

HARTWOODBURN and BROWNMUIR.—Originally belonging to a family of Scott, Hartwoodburn fell into the hands of the Currors in the middle of the 17th century. In 1713, the estate was divided, Hartwoodburn being given to George, and Brownmuir to Thomas Curror; and in 1748 the latter's grandson, also named Thomas, petitioned for a separate valuation, Hartwoodburn being joined to Williamhope. In 1785 Brownmuir still belonged to Thomas Curror, who is mentioned by Wight in 1777 as having let his own estate at an advanced rent, and set about improving Yair, " a considerable store-farm belonging to the Duke of Buccleuch." Wight devotes several pages to a description of the practice followed by Mr. Curror, whom he calls " a leader in the art of farming." So early as 1690, the name is spelt " Currier;" and among the families who claim kinship with the lairds of Hartwoodburn is that of Mr. Andrew Currie, the well-known sculptor, of _A. P., vi. (2) 30._ _C. R., 1748._ _Wight Hush., iii. 13._

Darnick, and his brother, Mr. J. L. Currie, as renowned a store-farmer in the colony of Victoria as the laird of Brownmuir was a century since in the old country.

In 1794, after by excambion and purchase the Haining estate had become well consolidated, and the land about the loch transferred from the Burgh to the laird, Mr. Mark Pringle set about building the mansion which overlooks the loch. No one, however, who saw it then would recognise it in the bright and stately residence now known as the Haining House. Originally it was built of the dull local whinstone, but when Mr John Pringle came home from the Continent, he had it encased in white free-stone, and added architectural features to give it the appearance of an Italian villa. The daring experiment was successful. In early summer, when the sun is shining and when the loch reflects a sky of blue, the wanderer by its margin might well believe himself on the enchanting shore of Como, or roaming by the lake of the Doria Pamfili Palace at Rome. The pure Italian aspect of the house itself is heightened by marble statues lining the brow of the architectural terrace which lifts it high above the water-level. Numerous touches here and there about the grounds go to deepen the illusion—from the superb bronze Faun sunning himself as he stands with idle grace upon his pedestal to the picturesque front of the cloaca, through which the mill-burn runs to join the river, its two slanting pillars surmounted by white marble busts of water-nymphs or Graces. White marble vases top the pillars of a fine iron screen before the front, looking towards Selkirk; and on either side the stable entrance, where one squire met his death, two busts shine brightly out from niches in the grey walls. During Mr. Pringle's time the people of Selkirk were admitted freely to the Haining grounds, where they revelled in the attractions not only of scenery and art, but of an extensive menagerie of wild animals. It was some time, it is said, before the austerer sort became accustomed to the "graven images," particularly those like Canova's dancer, clad in airy costume. They had not that innate appreciation of art which characterised Thackeray's Irishman at the Crystal Palace—

> The stathues that sthood that noble place in
> Of haythin goddesses most rare !
> Homer, Vanus, and Nebuchadnezzar
> All standing naked in the open air !

Wight,
Husb.
iii 25.   Not inferior to the charms of the loch and of the policy around the house, are those of the green undulating parks and rich woods—laid out for the

greater part in the time of Mr. John Pringle in the latter quarter of the last century. The pleasure-grounds around Haining, writes the Rev. Dr. Douglas of Galashiels, in 1797, "embellished by clumps, detached trees, and shrubs scattered up and down, and diversified with wonderful felicity, attract the notice and admiration of travellers." To Sir T. Dick Lauder in his juvenile days (about 1790), it "was like some dream of the fancy rather than anything real;" but in his declining years it awakened quite other associations. Recalling a visit to Mr. Andrew Pringle, doubtless on some electioneering errand, Sir Thomas describes his host and himself "watching the game-keepers fishing from the boats with their nets, in the enjoyment of the lovely scene and balmy air, and occasionally puffing a cigar, or imbibing a refreshing draught of hock and soda-water. Alas! our amiable and kind host is now no more!" A characteristic bit of bathos. Truer is the note struck by Henry Scott Riddell, in his poem "The Woodland Scene," written at Haining, in 1831.

Though the Haining monkey is extinct, the wolf's cage empty, and the bear-pit become a kennel, the student of natural history would find interesting objects of study in the wonderful variety of wild fowls which flutter the quiet surface of the lake. A herd of fallow-deer, kept at between 50 and 100 head, groups itself picturesquely on the face of a hilly park rising southwards from the loch—diminutive representatives of the great red-deer which once roamed on the same pastures.

Mr. Robertson, minister of Selkirk in 1792, records the existence of "a spring of steel-water at the Haining Lin, from which, though it is but weak, the poor of a scorbutic or scrofulous habit derive advantage;" but, whatever its real nature, the well soon ceased to be resorted to, its very locality being now unknown. Near the Lin, is Howden Mote, a large ancient earthwork, referred to elsewhere. Sixty years ago a remarkable discovery was made by a woodman engaged in splitting timber close by the Haining loch. From the centre of a large wild cherry-tree there escaped a bat of bright scarlet colour, which he was too afraid to capture, thinking it uncanny. Where the bat was enclosed there was a small cavity, but on each side the tree was sound and solid.

HAREHEAD.

In common with its neighbour steadings, Harehead was subjected to the constant ravages of Border thieves. In 1493, Walter Scott of Howpaslot was allowed by the Justiciary Court at Jedburgh to compound for treasonably bringing in William Scott, *the Gyde,* John Scott, and other traitors of Levin to the spoliation of Harehead, and for the treasonable stouthrief of 40 oxen and cows and 200 sheep from the tenants of Harehead at the same time. In 1544, at English instigation, a raid was made on Harehead by certain of John Carre's garrison, who carried away 30 nolt and 3 or 4 horses. Not many years ago, a dirk, with rusty blade and handsome silver-mounted handle, was found near the river at Harewood-Glen, which may have been dropped in one of these thieving scuffles. In 1649, Mr. Elliot and Mr. Scott reported Harehead as one of the few places where parts of the ancient wood of Ettrick Forest were yet to be seen. It is still a part of Philiphaugh estate, as it has been for centuries, Murray being ratified in possession by Act of Parliament in 1701.

MSS. B. M.

A. P. x. 307.

HARTWOODMYRES.

A Scott, as usual, is the first-mentioned laird of this steading, with its name so suggestive of the royal sport of the forest ; and, as usual, the mention is connected with ill-doing. In 1573, letters were sent to "Watt Scott in Hartwodmyris, to enter Thomas Lytill in Megehoip, Sym Littill his broder thair, Alexander Litill alsua his broder thair, Arche Scott callit the Muscatt, and William Portuous in Borthuikbrae," in the Tolbooth of Edinburgh, to underly the law for such crimes as they are charged with. Another letter was sent to Wat in name of "Williame Scott of Tuschelaw, his fader, allegeit presentlie to be visiit with seiknes," charging him to enter certain other accused persons for whom Tushielaw was responsible. This Walter was a true son of the family which afterwards culminated in the King of Thieves, and which prosecuted the levying of black-mail with a methodical assiduity and success not reached by any of their competitors in the same industry. Witness the complaint in 1578 of George Gray and others, " puir tennentis and fermoraris in Galtounsyde ":—

P. C., ii. 306.

P. C., iii. 101.

Walter Scott, younger of Tushielaw, in Hartwoodmyres, has, these diverse and sundry years bygone, since the decease of the late Master Michael Balfour, last abbot of Melrose, taken up at his own hands in forcible manner, without all order of law and justice, the most part of the saids poor tenants' farms, to their great apparent wreck and spoliation ; wherewithal the said Walter, not resting satisfied, but still proceeding in his accustomed manner of oppression, lately by himself, James Scott, his brother, Walter Scott, his son, James Scott, son to the Bailie of Selkirk, William Scott in Selkirk, Dande Scott there, and others his servants and accomplices, came and broke up the complainers' barn-doors, reft, spoiled, and took forth their corn at their pleasure; and because the said George Gray wanted corn, they reft and took from him three oxen and a cow, "and hes thairby laid his pleuch, quhairthrow his mailling is lyke to lye unteillit and lawborit, to his extreme wrak and heirschip;" they being all poor labourers of the ground that have sustained this oppression so long as they could, and now are constrained to lament their wrongous and unreasonable handling unto His Majesty and the Lords of Secret Council, in "esperance of sum remeid." For neither are the said complainers able, nor dare they, enter in process before any other judge, the said Walter being a "clannit" Border man, against whom they will get no execution, although they obtained never so many decreets, and the whole value of the goods taken from them, although it be their all, is not able to sustain the charges of the plea; nor yet have they any assurance to live unoppressed under his Highness's peace and protection in time coming, without His Majesty provide them some present comfort and remedy.

Summoned to answer this complaint, neither Walter Scott nor his friends thought it safe to appear, letters of horning and escheat being ordered against them. In 1589, William Scott of Hartwoodmyres signed the bond betwixt Thrl. Buccleuch and his friends, one with another; and in 1596 he proved his fealty ^{MSS.} by joining in the reckless rescue of Kinmont Willie. When the Earl of Sat. Buccleuch left Scotland for the Dutch Wars in 1627, Robert Scott of Hartwoodmyres was one of the commissioners he left to administer his affairs. In Bucc. 1648 the laird was nominated by parliament to the county committee of war; and nineteen years later William Scott of Hartwoodmyres was com- Acts, vii. missioner for the King's Bounty. From the Scotts the property appears to ^{88-9, 540.} have been acquired by a Mr. William Ogilvy, first mentioned as laird in 1695. George Curror, who is styled "of" Hartwoodmyres in the Session Records of A. P., Selkirk, was probably not laird but tenant. Satchells, in two of the blankest ^{ix. 374 1698.} lines of his blank verse, says—

> George Curror in Hartwoodmyers,
> He is a religious man;

a text which he amplifies further on, in his pastoral to Riddell of Haining :—

> George Curror's then a shepherd swain,
> That gains both corn and store,
> And doth afford both bed and board,
> And much relieves the poor.
> In Hartwoodmyres his barns and byres
> And shepherds do remain. . . .
> But now I'm run ashore;
> Though Jason fetcht his fleece from Greece,
> And was call'd the golden swain,
> George Curror that dwells in Hartwoodmyres,
> For wool more gilt doth gain.

A lintel of the present farm-house, dated 1695, and bearing the initials of William Ogilvy, was brought from an old house which stood by the side of a small burn, where mounds, nettles, and a few stunted trees, bear witness to previous habitation. A feature of the old site is the quantity of broken crystal found near it—an indication, according to our guide, of many a glorious wassail in the old days. It was this house in which Collector Ogilvy was surprised by Prince Charlie's dragoons, and compelled to promise the county cess to his "rightful king," on pain of having the place burnt about his ears. After the death of the last Laird Ogilvie, Hartwoodmyres was offered for sale, and purchased in 1882 for £11,000 by Mr. Scott Plummer of Sunderlandhall.

A large whinstone, called the Bishop-Stone, which used to lie on the ridge of the hill, is now built into the march-dyke between Woll and Hart-woodmyres, a few paces to the west of where it intersects the turnpike to Ashkirk. Beyond the initials of some passing loiterers, no marks are visible on the uncovered portions of the stone; and none, we are informed, were traceable on the rest of it before it was built in. Mayhap, it marked the bounds of abbey lands, or was set to mark the "rest and be thankful" of some fair, round prelate, who loved to sit there, and absorb the glorious view of Ettrick vale. Still more probably, Woll having been originally acquired from the Bishop of Glasgow, the stone was put there to indicate the limits of the bishop's territory. An interesting camp on this estate is elsewhere described.

HEATHERLIE, BATTS, MILBURN, MAULDISHEUGH, Etc.

G. S.,
ii. 2847,
2674.
In 1505, King James IV. granted to William Ker in the Yair, the lands of Batts, Heatherlee, Kincroft, Skinnercroft, eighteen acres on the east side of the stream called Milnburn, upon Morison's Hill, with the lands of Mauldis-heugh, Serjeantlands, Cowperland, and all other crofts and acres within the burgh or county of Selkirk which belonged to Richard Kene, with the offices of coroner and serjeant of the county of Selkirk. For a certain sum of money (£80) owed by Richard Kene, the lands had been apprised to John Murray of Philiphaugh in 1502. The rent was "a red rose on St. John the Baptist's Day, commonly called Midsummer," and the faithful performance of the duties of the said offices. In 1552 these properties formed a distinct lordship, partly possessed by Robert Scott of Wamphray. Mauldisheuch and
Phil.
MSS.

Mauldishauch were in 1601 the property of Philiphaugh, John Murray having Ret. inherited them from his father, Patrick. Heatherlie and Batts about the Taxt Roll. same time belonged to Andrew Ker of Yair ; and in 1643 to Wm. Mitchelhill, J. Lidderdale, and James Elliot.

MIDDLESTEAD.

When James II. disinherited Douglas and took possession of the Forest for the Crown, in 1455, this place was called the Mid-stead of Hartwood ; and part of it appears in the rent-roll of Kelso Abbey, under the name of Black-middings. Its first authentic mention as a separate property is in 1576, when Ker of Primsydeloch was due £31 Scots for the mails of "Braidmedowis and Middilsteid." If it then belonged to Ker, it soon changed hands, a branch of the Scott family coming into possession. According to Satchells, when Buccleuch picked his clansmen for Kinmont's rescue,

> Walter of Deephope, a metal man,
> And John of Middlestead together cam.

The Scotts' term of possession, however, was alike brief. In 1638, Archibald Elliot, third son of "Gibby with the Gowden Garters" by his wife Minto Papers. Margaret ("Maggie Fendy"), who was a daughter of Scott of Harden, and the Flower of Yarrow, obtained the lands by a charter ; and in 1662 Archibald A. P., vii. 421. Elliot of Middlestead was fined £600 for having sided with Parliament against the King. Till 1689 his name occurs in lists of commissioners nominated by Parliament. As was common in those days, he retained his designation "of Middlestead" some years after he had parted with the property, Andrew A. P. viii. 224, ix. 138. Plumber (who married Jean Elliot) being styled of Middlestead in 1678, and so addressed by Satchells in one of his quaintest pastorals. Twelve years C.R., 68. later, Andrew and William Plumber were both made Commissioners of Supply, William alone being mentioned in 1704, and again in 1710, when he became C. R. security for his brother-in-law, Wauch of Shaw, as Collector for the County. William Plummer, by his marriage with Miss Ker, succeeded to the beautiful estate of Sunderlandhall. An eminent laird of Middlestead was Dr. Andrew Plummer, who, born about the beginning of the century, took his degree in 1722, became Professor of Chemistry in Edinburgh University in 1726, and held the chair until his death in 1756, notwithstanding his temporary disablement by paralysis and his possession of private means. His success as a lecturer was marred by extreme diffidence and hesitation ; but his thorough knowledge of medical chemistry caused him to be looked up to

B. R.

as an authority. Moffat Spa is said to owe not a little of its fame to an analytical report Plummer made upon its waters. In 1745, Prince Charlie's year, Dr. Plummer was appointed Commissioner for the Burgh of Selkirk in the General Assembly of the Kirk. His son, also an Andrew Plummer, embraced the legal profession, passing as an advocate in 1771. In 1782, he became Sheriff of Selkirkshire, which office he held until his death, about a year before the close of the century. His successor, Sir Walter Scott, had found in him an early ally in his ballad researches, and frequently refers to him in his notes to the *Minstrelsy* as a scholar and excellent antiquarian. By his wife, Miss Pringle of Torwoodlee, Sheriff Plummer left no issue, being succeeded in his estates by three maiden sisters, "at least as old and musty as any Caxton in his library," writes Scott in a playful letter to his friend Ellis. On the death of the last Miss Plummer, in 1841, Mr. Charles Scott succeeded to the estates, assuming the name of Plummer, with Middlestead as his territorial designation.

Lock., ch. xiii.

As well befitted the mid stead of Hart Wood, this place was in 1774 the scene of the last stag-hunt in Ettrick Forest. The animal was captured by three men, in a fold to which it had been attracted by oat sheaves set out to feed the sheep during an exceptionally severe winter. It was imprisoned in the barn, and in a locality which once harboured

> "The hart, the hynd, the dae, the rae,
> And of all wild beasts great plentie,"

a deer had become so uncommon that many people went a long way to see it. One man having cruelly struck it with a stick, it sprang at him, injuring him in the head with its antlers, so that he died in a few days. Ultimately the gentlemen of the county resolved to revive the glories of the ancient chase— Mr. Scott of Gala to attend with his pack of hounds. With its feet tied, the "poor sequestered stag" was carried in a covered cart to the west end of Midlem, where, on being liberated, it gave itself a shake, looked round upon the great company present, and set off, making straight for Middlestead, where it had fed with the sheep. It was finally caught near Ettrick Bridge, so sorely lamed that it could not be kept for another hunt, as had been intended.

NEWARK TOWER AND OLD WARK.

Although it is the fine imagination of Sir Walter Scott which has surrounded Newark Castle with a charm and with associations which make it the property of the English race, it has a history of its own, which invests it with peculiar interest as the Heart of the old Forest of Selkirk.

From "Newerke," in 1294, King John Baliol wrote a letter to Edward the First of England; but it is by no means certain that this was Newark in the Forest; and its first unmistakable mention was not until 1423, in a charter by Archibald Douglas, Earl of Wigton. The laborious and erudite author of *Caledonia* has concluded that Newark was probably built by William, first Earl Douglas, after he inherited the Forest (1353-84); but this is not likely. The coat-of-arms, built high in the west wall, is not that of any branch of Douglas, but the lion rampant of the King; and the conclusion is unavoidable that the tower now standing must have been built either before Bruce's grant to Lord James (1314-29) or after Ettrick Forest was re-included in the crown lands in 1455. That the latter alternative is correct has been made manifest by the newly published accounts of the Exchequer, from which it appears that Newark was erected about 1466. There is mention of various payments to Sir Thomas Jeffray, master of works at Newark, towards the building of the tower, and to one Gilbert Furde for lime. With the castles of Edinburgh and Stirling, it shares £19, 3s. for furnishings; while no less than £200 is the value put upon twenty oaks cut in the Forest for use in the new building. Before it was quite finished it was intrusted to the custody of John of Moray (ancestor of the present Murrays of Philiphaugh), who got the rent of the half-steading of Whitehill for his fee as keeper. For his disbursements in entertaining the Lords of Council, on their visit to let the Forest lands and hold courts, he was further allowed £18.

As the name "New-wark" implies, it is the successor of a "wark" existing at an earlier period, the site and lands of which came to be known as "Auld Wark." Irresponsible writers have pitched upon the reign of Alexander III. as that in which the first "Wark" was constructed, but there is no authority for the statement. Its origin is enveloped in obscurity, and may have been much earlier. The fact of the present tower being upon a site which was called Newark, at least thirty years before the castle itself

E. R., vii. 452, seq.

was built, points to the probability of the first New-Wark having been itself a stronghold of earthen mounds and entrenchments, which would put its predecessor a very long way back in history indeed. The sites of both are remarkably alike, each being on a high ridge running out from the side of Bow Hill, and terminating in a precipitous slope close to the water of Yarrow. Old Wark enjoys a fine exposure, and a splendid prospect. To the south lies Philiphaugh House with its rounded parks and woods, and all the plain formed by the confluence of the rivers. From the Duchess's Bower, which stands upon the summit, a lovely view is to be had—perhaps the loveliest in Yarrow. Looking downwards through a leafy wood, one can just see the glitter of the stream as it winds along the bottom of the glen, while in the far distance enchanted Newark stands out clearly on its own promontory. Close by the Bower thick strong nettle-beds give evidence of former habitations, ramparts are distinctly traceable, and there are heaps of large stones. Other heaps are said to have been used in building the cottages of a hamlet close by, the clay-built walls of which were levelled in 1878. As the place is known to history only by its name of Old Wark, its uses in the days before it was supplanted can only be imagined. Doubtless it formed the rendezvous for many a merry hunting, in the peaceful and prosperous times before King Alexander's fateful death.

During the period (*circa* 1326 to 1455), when Newark remained in possession of the Douglas, there is no mention of it, except as a place whence the powerful lords of that name issued charters—a distinction it shared with Galashiels and a place called Ettybredshiels, hitherto difficult to identify. Lord Hailes, writing 100 years ago, said, " I wish to know what place is meant by Etlebredschelys ; it is of moment for ascertaining a certain material circumstance in our history ;" and even so recently as 1881, the author of *The Haigs of Bemersyde* has expressed his inability to identify it. It has been hazarded as another name for Lethbertshiels in Stirlingshire, and even an ancient alternative for Galashiels. Without being certain, we are inclined to believe that Ettybredshiels (sometimes Ethelbertshiels) was a manor-house of the Douglas family, situated somewhere near Carterhaugh, probably nearer the cottages now known as Shielshaugh. In 1456, Broadmeadows and the two steads of Catkermauch were in the King's hands and occupied by his own stock. In next year's accounts the two steads are named Bowhill and Ettybredshiels, and in the next again they are described as "in the ward of Ettrick." Now, seeing that in the roll of holdings, the " 2 steads of Catker-

Ann.,
ii. 112.

E. R.,
vi. 226.

mach" occur between Fauldshop and Fastheugh, and seeing further that one of them was Bowhill, we cannot be far wrong in assuming the other (Ettybredshiels) to have been what is now known as Carterhaugh or a part of it. The only other tenable supposition, and one which is strengthened by the mention of "Old Wark or Cartermauch" in 1693, is that Ettybredshiels A. P., may have been the original name of Old Wark; but as Douglas dated one ix. 341. charter at New-Werk in 1423, and a later at Ettybredshiels in 1425, when Auld Wark was presumably deserted, there is a difficulty in accepting this Haigs, solution. There can be no doubt, however, that Ettybredshiels was either 97. Old Wark or a part of Carterhaugh, which is sufficient for all the purposes of history.

After treacherously murdering the Earl of Douglas at Stirling in 1452, James II. lost no time in taking possession of his victim's lands—Ettrick Forest amongst the rest. In the year 1455 he went to Newark with his army, to make arrangements for the management of the Forest and its revenues. Two noblemen were deputed to hold a court at Newark on All Saints' Day (1st November). Divers houses were repaired and plastered, and for the entertainment of the Court there appears to have been a E. R., vi. performance by local actors, dressed in the skins of wild beasts. Again, in 225, etc. 1459, the castle was graced by the King's presence, 21 horses being employed in bringing victuals from Edinburgh for the occasion, and £22 Scots spent in repairing and building a hall, two chambers, and other houses for the royal visit.

> "Then oft, from Newark's riven tower
> Sallied a Scottish monarch's power:
> A thousand vassals mustered round,
> With horse, and hawk, and horn, and hound;
> And through the brake the rangers stalk
> And falc'ners hold the ready hawk;
> And foresters in greenwood trim,
> Lead in the leash the gazehounds grim,
> Attentive as the brachet's bay
> From the dark covert drives the prey
> To slip them as he breaks away.
> The startled quarry bounds amain
> As fast the gallant greyhounds strain
> Whistles the arrow from the bow,
> Answers the arquebuss below;
> While all the rocking hills reply,
> To hoof-clang, hound, and hunter's cry,
> And buglers ringing lightsomely."

G. S.,
ii. 1143,
2721.

Of course Newark Castle went with the Forest when it was given as a dowry to James III.'s Queen, Margaret of Denmark, in 1473, and also in 1502 to the Queen of James IV. Margaret of England. Before that time the

G. S.,
ii. 2199-
2312,
1921.

latter king was frequently at Newark, in March 1493 for example, and the same month in 1496; the custody of the tower having been given to Alexander Hume in 1489, as a reward for his services against the King's father. After her husband's death at Flodden, Queen Margaret found difficulty in collecting the rents of her dowry lands in Selkirkshire. She seems for a time to have intrusted the custody of Newark and the Forest to Murray of Philiphaugh, son of the sheriff who had granted sasine to her English Commissioners in 1503; but when, in 1522, she separated from Angus, she offered him Ettrick Forest to consent to a divorce. Though this

A. P., ii.
323, etc.

proposal was not accepted at the time, when the Queen did obtain a divorce, Angus seems to have acted upon her offer. In 1528 he was accused of treasonable art and part of the munition of our sovereign lord's fortalice of

Pit.,
i. 139.

Newark; the siege of which by the King's party he seems actually to have raised, or attempted to raise. His forfeiture was the result; and though the Douglases were restored to favour in 1542, their connexion with the Forest was never renewed. It was about this time that the Scotts of Buccleuch got possession. In 1532, "Wicked Wat" actually refused to give up the keys of the castle to the Queen Dowager when, attended by sixty horsemen and twenty-four runners on foot, her Majesty came to hold a court upon her jointure lands. But in the end, upon pressure by Henry VIII. on behalf of his sister, Buccleuch was fain to recognise Queen Margaret's rights. Her miserable death, in 1541, restored Ettrick Forest to her son, the King; and after his death, brokenhearted, in the end of the following year, Buccleuch was appointed

P. S.,
xvii. 1.

" captain and keeper of the place and castle of Newark, with power to make deputes and constables"—the gift being repeatedly confirmed by Queen Mary,

P. S.,
xli. 128.

and in 1573 by James VI. Up to this day Newark Castle has remained in the hands of the same powerful family. It was not long in feeling the consequences of having "Wicked Wat" for its master. In the early part of 1548 Lord Grey, with an army composed partly of Englishmen and partly of Kers, took the castle after a short siege, burned the town, and carried away

Sta. Pap.
(Scot.),
i. 75.

3000 sheep, with 400 head of cattle. Returning in October of the same year, they burnt the castle itself; and all its interior fittings, besides slaying four of Buccleuch's servants and a woman within its walls. In 1690, mention

P. C., iv.
538, and
v. 25.

is made of James Scott " of" Newark, who in 1692 is described as chamberlain of part of the Forest, holding office under Sir Walter. James appears to have been succeeded by John, who was rebuked by the presbytery for " ane evil preparatuir" (precedent), in certain high-handed proceedings about the letting of kirk-seats in Selkirk. A heavier charge fell upon him in 1618, when he, his sons, and other relations, were charged with the horrible slaughter of Adam Dalgleish in Whitehope. In 1627, when Walter first Earl of Buccleuch went to the Dutch Wars, his family took up their residence in Newark Castle, where the Countess gave birth to a son named David. On his return Earl Walter joined his family in their Forest home, and here he had the misfortune to lose his wife, who died after the birth of a daughter, Mary. After this, his lordship went to reside at Branxholm. In 1643, William Scott of Mangerton (the Earl's natural son) lived in Newark, the young Earl being only seventeen. The following year, against Montrose's threatened descent upon the Scottish Border, Newark was fortified by a considerable quantity of arms and ammunition obtained from the public magazines; but, if not removed in time, it must have fallen into the hands of Montrose when he pitched his camp on Philiphaugh. According to Sir Walter Scott, the courtyard of Newark was the execution ground of many wretched Irish mercenaries captured at that famous battle. Alarmed by the disturbed state of the country, and apprehensive of further tumult, Buccleuch removed the family muniments, plate, and more valuable furnishings to the Bass Rock, so that when the Protector, after defeating the Scottish army at Dunbar in 1650, took possession of Newark, his troops found it empty. According to Elliot and Scott, the castle was, notwithstanding its rough usage, the principal house within the county in 1649, and one of the few places still adorned with timber; but it was never again occupied by the family. For the fifty years which elapsed between the second Earl's death and the return to Scotland of his daughter, the Duchess of Buccleuch, Newark Castle was left to the tender mercies of agents and factors. *Grande dame* as she was, the Duchess would have despised Newark for a residence; and it is to be feared we owe to Scott's fancy the touching picture of her reception of the Last Minstrel, when—

> " With hesitating step, at last
> The embattled portal arch he pass'd."

Few there are, however, who

> " Pass where Newark's stately tower
> Looks out from Yarrow's birchen bower,"

Margin notes: P. R., 1615. P. R., 1618. Bucc. A. P., vi. (1) 51. MSS. Adv. Lib.

to whom the wandering Harper and the pitying Duchess are not the first
figures in memory's pageant. So magically powerful is the gift of poetry, that
Newark is more famous as the recital-hall of Scott's inspired Lay than as the
actual theatre of kingly courts, of feudal splendour, of fire and rapine, and of
bloody slaughter. To Sir Walter himself it was an undying attraction.
After a stranger arrived at Abbotsford, his first visit was to Melrose Abbey
or to Newark Castle; and the one day Lady Byron could spare, in 1817, was
spent in riding with Miss Anne Scott to Newark. "Her ladyship," says
Laidlaw, "is a beautiful little woman, with fair hair, a fine complexion, and
rather large blue eyes; face not round. I thought her mouth indicated great
firmness, or rather obstinacy." A cattle-show at Bowhill, on 20th October,
was followed next day by a fox-hunt after Dandie Dinmont's fashion among
the rocks of Yarrow, Sir David Wilkie and the Ettrick Shepherd being of the
company. Terence Magrath, a fine singer of Irish songs, was there too, and
saw, says Scott, "his ward Hamlet behave most princelike on Newark Hill"
—Hamlet being a splendid greyhound, re-christened so from *Marmion* on
account of his "inky coat." Deeming nothing trivial that connects Sir
Walter with the hills and dales of his sheriffdom, we offer no excuse for giving
Lockhart's hearty account of a grand coursing-match on Newark Hill, one
clear, bright September morning in 1820 :—

Ch. Life
Scott,
150.

Lock.,
ch. 39.

" Sir Walter, mounted on Sibyl, was marshalling the order of procession with a huge hunting-
whip; and among a dozen frolicsome youths and maidens, who seemed disposed to laugh at all
discipline, appeared, each on horseback, each as eager as the youngest sportsman in the troop,
Sir Humphry Davy, Dr. Wollaston, and the patriarch of Scottish belles-lettres, Henry Mackenzie.
The Man of Feeling, however, was persuaded with some difficulty to resign his steed for the
present to his faithful negro follower, and to join Lady Scott in the sociable, until we should
reach the ground of our *battue*. Laidlaw, on a long-tailed wiry Highlander, yclept *Hoddin Grey*,
which carried him nimbly and stoutly, although his feet almost touched the ground as he sat,
was the adjutant. But the most picturesque figure was the illustrious inventor of the safety-
lamp. He had come for his favourite sport of angling, and had been practising it successfully
with Rose, his travelling companion, for two or three days preceding this, but he had not
prepared for coursing fields, or had left Charlie Purdie's troop for Sir Walter's on a sudden
thought, and his fisherman's costume—a brown hat with flexible brims, surrounded with line
upon line of catgut, and innumerable fly-hooks—jack-boots worthy of a Dutch smuggler, and a
fustian surtout dabbled with the blood of salmon, made a fine contrast with the smart jackets,
white-cord breeches, and well-polished jockey-boots of the less distinguished cavaliers about
him. Dr. Wollaston was in black, and with his noble serene dignity of countenance, might
have passed for a sporting archbishop. Mr. Mackenzie, at this time in the 76th year
of his age, with a white hat turned up with green, green spectacles, green jacket, and long
brown leathern gaiters buttoned upon his nether anatomy, wore a dog-whistle round his
neck, and had all over the air of as resolute a devotee as the gay captain of Huntly Burn.

Tom Purdie and his subalterns had preceded us by a few hours with all the greyhounds that could be collected at Abbotsford, Darnick, and Melrose; but the giant Maida had remained as his master's orderly, and now gambolled about Sibyl Grey, barking for mere joy like a spaniel puppy.

"On reaching Newark Castle, we found Lady Scott, her eldest daughter, and the venerable Mackenzie, all busily engaged in unpacking a basket that had been placed in their carriage, and arranging the luncheon it contained upon the mossy rocks overhanging the bed of the Yarrow. When such of the company as chose had partaken of this refection, the Man of Feeling resumed his pony, and all ascended the mountain, duly marshalled at proper distances, so as to beat in a broad line over the heather, Sir Walter directing the movement from the right wing—towards Blackandro. Davy, next to whom I chanced to be riding, laid his whip about the fern like an experienced hand, but cracked many a joke, too, upon his own jack-boots, and surveying the long eager battalion of bushrangers, exclaimed "Good heavens! is it thus that I visit the scenery of the *Lay of the Last Minstrel?*" He then kept muttering to himself, as his glowing eye—(the finest and brightest that I ever saw)—ran over the landscape, some of those beautiful lines from the Conclusion of the Lay—

> "'But still
> When summer smiled on sweet Bowhill,
> And July's eve, with balmy breath,
> Waved the blue-bells on Newark heath,
> When throstles sung in Hareheadshaw,
> And corn was green on Carterhaugh,
> And flourished, broad, Blackandro's oak,
> The aged harper's soul awoke,' etc.

Mackenzie, spectacled though he was, saw the first sitting hare, gave the word to slip the dogs, and spurred after them like a boy. All the seniors, indeed, did well as long as the course was upwards, but when puss took down the declivity, they halted and breathed themselves upon the knoll—cheering gaily, however, the young people, who dashed at full speed past and below them. Coursing on such a mountain is not like the same sport over a set of fine English pastures. There were gulfs to be avoided, and bogs enough to be threaded—many a stiff nag stuck fast—many a bold rider measured his length among the peat-hags—and another stranger to the ground besides Davy plunged neck-deep into a treacherous well-head, which, till they were floundering in it, had borne all the appearance of a piece of delicate green turf. When Sir Humphry emerged from his involuntary bath, his habiliments garnished with mud, slime, and mangled water-cresses, Sir Walter received him with a triumphant *encore!* But the philosopher had his revenge, for, joining soon afterwards in a brisk gallop, Scott put Sibyl Grey to a leap beyond her prowess, and lay humbled in the ditch, while Davy, who was better mounted, cleared it and him at a bound. Happily there was little damage done—but no one was sorry that the sociable had been detained at the foot of the hill."

During the minority of Henry, third Duke of Buccleuch, Newark Castle was unroofed, the wooden beams and best stones within reach being used to build a farm-house in the vicinity. Thanks, however, to the enthusiastic and liberal spirit of Duke Walter, everything has been done to keep the noble ruin from decay. Its own thick walls, nine feet near the base, are its best security, and, after them, doubtless the interest with which Scott's poetry has

enveloped its every stone. Of this fine example of a Border stronghold, the
following ground-plan is interesting :—

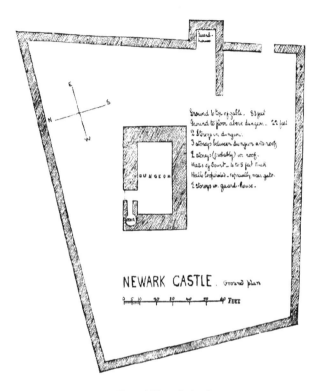

Plan of Newark Castle.

We have seen that the Forest-Warden's keep is not without a moving
history of its own. Even the poorest imagination must be stirred in
contemplating its rugged battlements, which, having so long withstood the
batterings of armed men, still present a brave front to the assaults of " winter
and rough weather." Scenes of long-ago rush through the beholder's mind—
scenes which only the master hand of its inspired Minstrel can adequately
depict in words—

" For some strange tale bewitch'd my mind
Of forayers who with headlong force
Down from that strength had spurr'd their horse,
And home returning fill'd the hall
With revel, wassel-rout and brawl.
Methought that still with tramp and clang
The gateway's broken arches rang ;
Methought grim features, seam'd with scars
Glared through the window's rusty bars."

OAKWOOD.

"Akewood," a Forest-stead paying the King £6 a year in 1455, was in 1478-1482 the possession of one Laurence Rutherford, who was ordered by the Lords Auditors to pay "Bertilmew" Rutherford a chalder and 12 bolls of "vittals." In 1517 it was taken from Alexander Lord Hume and granted by royal charter to Michael Scott, son and heir of the deceased Robert Scott in Oakwood. Michael and his son William got South Bowhill in 1529, and twelve years later a new charter for both estates was granted to William, subject to the liferent of his father and Isabella Kerr his mother. The feus were, for Oakwood £24, and for Bowhill £14, with the conditions of erecting a house and policy, supplying for each £10 two horsemen, one armed with a lance, besides one led horse, to serve in the King's wars. Robert of Oakwood signed the mutual Scott Bond in 1580; next year became involved in the broils which followed Scott of Headshaw's assault upon Hob Elliot of Broadlee and his brother Dand; and in 1590 had to provide Murray of Philiphaugh as his security to the extent of £1000 that he would not harm the Earl of Angus, who had obtained letters of lawburrows against him. A roll of landit men drawn up in 1590-91 mentions *Michael* Scott of Oakwood; but as Robert Scott of Oakwood witnessed a deed in 1592, the recurrence to Michael is probably a mistake. In November 1607 Robert Scott of Oakwood (he who built the tower now standing) appeared before the presbytery for probation of the crime of perjury whereof he accused Mr. Patrick Shaw (minister of Selkirk), and produced a bond made and subscribed by Mr. Patrick to certain persons of his parish to sett their own tack of their vicarage teinds, which he alleged the said Mr. Patrick to have broken. Walter Gledstanes, servitor to the Guidman of Hayning, deponed he heard contentious words between the two, but did not hear Mr. Shaw swear at all; and in the end Oakwood's charge against the minister was found not proven. Likely enough there was some vindictiveness in the minister's subsequent charge against the laird for not repairing to the kirk on Sabbath afternoons, Oakwood's excuse being that, but for having to seek out letters to send to Edinburgh, he would attend, protesting, moreover, that he abode not in contempt of the kirk. To avert the sentence of excommunication against his friends the Scotts of Newark, in 1618, the guidman of Oakwood pled with the presbytery that they were penitent for the slaughter they had committed. This was probably Andrew, who was retoured heir of his father Robert in 1616, and who obtained infeftment in 1626. In Selkirk burgh records mention is made of one Philip Scott *in* Aikwood, who had lent

[Marginal references: A. L. A., 72, 98. — G. S., iii. 160, 793, 2350. — Thrl. MSS. — P. C., iii. 381. — P. C., iv. 538, 784. — P. C., v. 15. — P. R. — B. R.]

the town 1500 merks, which could not be repaid for want of an "active title" in the person of his nearest of kin.   In the taxt roll of Melrose Abbey (1630), there is an entry of £10 payable by Murray of Oakwood—possibly of the Elibank family, and brother-in-law of Sir William Scott of Harden, to whom the place really belonged, his father, "Auld Wat," having died the year before.   Thanks to the complacent credulity of Sir Walter Scott, and the matter-of-fact way in which he is supported by his biographer, a ludicrous tradition about the marriage of this Sir William with "meikle-mouthed Meg" of Elibank has obtained wider acceptance than its probability would have

A. P., vi. (2) 884. warranted.   Sir William's son, "Sir William of Oakwood," was named by Parliament, in 1659, a commissioner to raise money for the navy and army of

A. P., viii. 108. the Commonwealth, and in 1672 obtained an Act of Parliament ratifying him in his wide possessions.   Those in Selkirkshire were :—

> Easter and Wester Oakwood, with mills, mill-lands, etc.
> South Bowhill, with pendicle of Burnfoot and others.
> Eastfield and Wormwood, otherwise called Whitrilburne, (now Hutlerburn) with tower, etc.
> Easter and Wester Kirkhope, with tower, etc.
> Earneshawgh and Singlie, with tower, etc.
> Deidope, with house, etc.
> Dodhead, or Dodbank, with house, etc.
> Whitehawghbraes, with house, etc.
> Howfoorde, with tower, etc.
> Gilmelsclewgh, or Thorniehill, with pendicle called Ettrikside, house, etc.
>   All in the barony of Oakwood.
> Easter and Wester Fauldshope.
> Berrybuss.
> Espinhope and Brockilhope (now Cossarshill or Corsehill and Brockhope).
> Langhope, with house, etc.
> Newhall, or Craigleitch, and Knowes.
>   All in the barony of Harden.

The second Sir William dying in 1680, was succeeded by his son, a third Sir William, who died in 1707, leaving his estates to a brother, who died in 1710, without issue.   The next heir was John Scott, great-great-grandson of Auld Wat of Harden, his predecessors and successors to the present day being as follows :—

1. Walter Scott of Harden, died 1629 ; great-grandson of Robert (second son of Walter Scott of Sinton), who acquired Harden from Lord Home in 1501.
2. Sir William Scott of Harden, his son, died 1655.
3. Sir Gideon Scott of Harden, his son, died 1672.
4. Walter, Earl of Tarras, his son, 1645-1693.
5. { John Scott of Harden, his son, died 1734.
   { Walter Scott, his brother, died 1746.

6. Walter Scott of Harden, his son, died 1793.
7. Hugh, 4th Baron Polwarth, his son, 1758-1841.
8. Henry Francis, 5th Baron Polwarth, his son, 1800-1867.
9. Walter Hugh, 6th and present Baron Polwarth, his son, born 1838.
10. Walter George, Master of Polwarth, his son, born 1864.

It was John, fifth of the above line, who succeeded his distant relation in 1710, and, dying twenty-four years thereafter, left in possession his brother Walter, whose great-great-grandson, the sixth Lord Polwarth, is to-day laird of Oakwood. When Walter Scott who became Earl of Tarras was thirteen years of age, he was united in marriage with Mary, Countess of Buccleuch, then only eleven, but the avaricious designs of the promoters were frustrated by her death two years afterwards. Walter, his son by a second wife, was married four times, his second lady being Agnes, daughter of Wm. Scott of Thirlstane, Yetholm. His third, Ann, only daughter of Scott of Gorrinberrie, was mother of his son Walter, who succeeded him, and became M.P. for Roxburghshire in 1747. This laird's wife, Lady Diana Hume, daughter of the last Earl of Marchmont, attained the age of ninety-four at her death in 1827, and was a great friend of Sir Walter Scott; she had been remarkably Lock., kind to him when a boy, and was the only person "who could give the author ch. 8 and 64. of *Marmion* personal reminiscences of Pope." "She was," says Scott, "the last person whom I recollect so much older than myself that she always kept at the same distance in point of age, so that she scarce seemed older to me two years ago when in her ninety-second year, than fifty years before." It is said that when Lady Diana came to Merton, the minister, as a great compliment, chose for text: "Great is Diana of the Ephesians." Her only son, Hugh, after great difficulty, succeeded in establishing his claim to the peerage of Polwarth, before the House of Lords, in 1835. The present peer, Lord-Lieutenant of Selkirkshire, married, 1863, Lady Mary, daughter of the 5th Earl of Aberdeen. Of the vast estates once held by the family in Selkirkshire, only Oakwood, Oakwoodmill, Fanns, Innerhuntly, and Hutlerburn now remain in its possession, the greater part having been sold by John Scott of Harden to Anne, Duchess of Buccleuch and Monmouth in 1728.

Beyond a slight experience in 1502, when the proverb that "hawks Pit., dinna pike hawks' een" was falsified by one Turnbull stealing 100 sheep from i. 34. another Turnbull, "furth of Aikwode," this place is little identified with mosstrooping, bloodshed, or stouthrief. But if history has failed to invest it with such claims upon our interest, poetry has brilliantly repaired the omission. If merciless documentary evidence has swept away the traditional

foray against Elibank, with its romantic ending, is there not still left the
Last Minstrel's account of Auld Wat's rally to Branksome ?

> " An aged knight, to danger steel'd,
>   With many a moss-trooper came on ;
> And azure in a golden field,
> The stars and crescent graced his shield,
>   Without the bend of Murdieston.
> Wide lay his lands round Oakwood Tower,
> And wide round haunted Castle-Ower. . . .
> Not even the Flower of Yarrow's charms,
> In youth, might tame his rage for arms ;
> And still, in age, he spurn'd at rest,
> And still his brows the helmet press'd—
> Albeit the blanched locks below
> Were white as Dinlay's spotless snow.
>   Five stately warriors drew the sword
>   Before their father's band ;
>   A braver knight than Harden's lord
>   Ne'er belted on a brand."

Of twenty to thirty strongholds of the peel or barmikine type which once
formed the refuge of men of the Forest in time of war, none remains in such
fine preservation as Oakwood. A stone, above a window in the east wall,

Stone in Oakwood Tower.

gives 1602 as the date of its erection ; but, while the first initials are known
to be those of Robert Scott, laird at that time, those of his wife can only be
guessed to point to a daughter of the house of Murray. Walls measuring 38
feet by 23½ feet on the outside, and in themselves 4½ feet thick, do not
permit of spacious chambers within ; but Oakwood is not the smallest tower
in the shire in that respect. Besides the dungeon, there are three " living "
storeys, the gables being bordered with " crow steps " of freestone, distinctive
of ancient Scottish architecture. An old rust-eaten rapier, found near the
Tower, was exhibited in the short-lived Museum of Galashiels. A tradition

about one of the Oakwood rooms, known as the "Jingler's Room," being haunted, has had its origin in another remarkable and wide-spread tradition that Michael Scott (the wizard of the *Lay*) lived in the tower. As this good and learned man flourished from about 1214 to 1300, he cannot safely be identified with a place built 300 years after his departure to another world. There is, moreover, not the slightest proof that he came near Oakwood, the only ground for believing that he ever visited the South of Scotland being the veracious accounts of his

> "Cleaving the Eildon Hills in three,
> And bridling the Tweed with a curb of stone."

When in Scotland, he lived at his own ancestral castle of Balwearie in Fifeshire, first acquired, according to the most reliable genealogy, by his great-grandfather. No doubt the whole fabric of the story is built upon the fact that a Michael Scott did, in 1517, obtain Oakwood by royal charter. In such a case it seems only to require one rash antiquary to identify the new name with the ancient; and whoever was first in this instance has had plenty of responsible writers to follow him, from the Selkirk minister who wrote the latest statistical account to the learned and graceful author of the *History and Poetry of the Scottish Border*. An excellent story, written in pithy Lowland Scotch, affects to give an account of Harden's hiding in Oakwood, and escape from it after "the '45;" and a second deals with an attempt to recover treasure supposed to be buried near Oakwood-Mill. The place seems to tempt invention. "As to the death of the Baron of Oakwood," says the Ettrick Shepherd in a letter, "if Mr. Scott wishes to see it poetically described, he can wait until my tragedy is performed at the Theatre-Royal; and, if that shall never take place, he must sit in darkness and the shadow of death for what light the poets of Bruce's time can shed on the matter." [B. C., Mag., i. 91, 257.]

PHILIPHAUGH.

1265. Fulhope.   Exchequer Rolls, I. 30.
1322. Fulhopehalch.   Great Seal, I. 5.
1567. Phillophauch.   Liber de Kelso, 512.

Under the name of "Fulhope" Philiphaugh contributed 6s. 8d. to the King's Exchequer in 1265; and in 1288 the land of Fulhope, "in which was formerly placed the King's store" (instaurum domini regis) paid £6, 13s. 4d. It is the only place mentioned in the shire accounts of the time, and more than any other it came to be identified with the history of the county. It [E. R., i. 30.] [E. R., i. 35.]

was the scene of Montrose's rout, the one great battle which took place in Selkirkshire, of which for hundreds of years its lairds were hereditary sheriffs. To lovers of romance it is the land

"Where erst the Outlaw drew his arrow;"

and, though the incidents of the ballad have long been discredited, they have no doubt served to enhance the antiquity which is rightly supposed to envelop the relations between the family of Murray and the Forest.

C. S.,
i. 5.

Before the Murrays, however, other families possessed Philiphaugh. About 1315, Robert the Bruce granted to William, called "Turnebul," certain lands and pertinents lying at the west end of "Fulhopehalch," as much as in old times in the Forest was ploughed for a carucate, for the yearly payment of an arrow at the feast of the Virgin's Assumption.

By another charter, there were granted to William Barbitonsor (or Barber) in 1314, the eastern part of "Fulhopehalch" and the "Schelgrene" within the Sheriffdom of Selkyrc; with right to the mills and common pasture of the town of Selkirk, for six shillings of silver annually at Martinmas. To the said William and his heirs was also given the office of Constable of Selkirk, to be held at the royal pleasure, with all that belonged to that office in the time of King Alexander, "our predecessor." These Barbers or Barbours drop

E. R.,
i. 395.
E. R.,
i. 430.

early out of sight. In the Exchequer Accounts of 1331, mention is made of the sale of his ward in Selkirk by William Barber; and next year 40s. is received from his son and heir. In the absence of authentic information as to the parentage of John Barbour, the contemporary and rival of Chaucer, we venture to put in a claim on behalf of this unnamed son and heir of William Barbour of Selkirk. Who so likely to write a poem in honour of "The Bruce," as the son of a man the heroic king had loaded with distinction? As son of the Constable of Selkirk, young Barber was in a position to take advantage of King Edward's leave to study at the English Universities, as we know the poet did : and all the dates in the latter's career are compatible with the supposition that he may have been the son of Philiphaugh. The poet died, a venerable man, in 1396, or 64 years after the mention of our claimant as heir to his father, William Barbour of Selkirk, in 1332, when King David II. may well have taken him, the son of his father's friend, into his favour—a favour which we know the poet never ceased to enjoy. It is therefore no great stretch of probability to say that the first poet of Scotland worthy to be ranked with Chaucer may have been the son of a laird of Philiphaugh. Barbour's name lingered in the Forest long after the family had left it. So late as 1601, John Turnbull was retoured heir of his father George in a fifth part of the lands called Barboursland in the territory of Philiphaugh. Now, however, not a document or tradition remains by which the place may be identified.

The Turnbulls remained in Philiphaugh for quite three hundred years after their first location in 1315. Concerning the first Turnbull of Philiphaugh, it is said that he was one of the family of Rules of that ilk in Roxburghshire, and that he got his second surname from an exploit in the hunting-field, when he saved King Robert from an infuriated bull. Alluding to the clan Turnbull, Leyden describes the incident in verse of somewhat rugged power :—

> " Bold was the chief from whom their line they drew,
> Whose nervous arm the furious bison slew ;
> The bison, fiercest race of Scotia's breed,
> Whose bounding course outstripp'd the red-deer's speed.
>
> On Scotia's lord he rush'd with lightning speed,
> Bent his strong neck to toss the startled steed.
> His arms robust the hardy hunter flung
> Around his bending horns, and upward wrung
> With writhing force his neck retorted round,
> And roll'd the panting monster on the ground ;
> Crush'd with enormous strength his bony skull ;
> And courtiers hail'd the man who *turned the bull.*"

Scenes Inf.

It is a well-known tendency of tradition to invent stories in order to account for names; but this particular tale happens to be sanctioned by authority altogether above cavil. In the Register of the Great Seal the grant of Philiphaugh is made to William, " *called turnebul,*" as if the surname were a *sobriquet*. Further corroboration is derived from the fact that history has no record of the name of Turnbull previous to its mention in the Philiphaugh charter. In grim keeping with his reputation was the champion's death, at the disastrous battle of Halidon Hill, in 1333.

" When both sides were ready to engage, the shock of battle was a while suspended by the appearance of a Scotchman of gigantic stature, who had acquired the name of Turnbull, on account of a brave exploit he had performed in saving King Robert Brus from being gored to death by a wild bull, which had overthrown him while he was hunting. Attended by a great mastiff, Turnbull approached the English army, and challenged any person in it to come forth and fight a single combat with him. After a short pause of astonishment, the challenge was accepted by Sir Robert Benhale, a young Norfolk knight, inferior to the Scot in stature, but of great bodily strength, and yielding to none in military address. The mastiff flying out against Benhale, the brave knight brought a heavy blow upon its loins, and separated its hinder

Storpe. 231.

legs from the rest of its body; and encountering immediately with Turnbull, he eluded, by his address and agility, the blows aimed at him, and first cut off the left arm, and then the head of his adversary."

Thus fell the founder of the warlike Border clan of Turnbull, which still boasts many men amongst its members whose stalwart frames perpetuate the traditional strength and stature of their ancestor.

The mention of a John Turnbull as Sheriff of Selkirkshire in 1360, and again in 1364 as depute sheriff, points to a probability that, from the earliest times, the office was connected with possession of the lands of Philiphaugh. It is, moreover, about the only instance of a Turnbull being mentioned in connection with the administration, or even the observance, of law. As individuals they were notorious and incurable thieves, and as a clan they were perpetually at feud either with their neighbours or with the King's representatives. The record which follows their name in the index of Pitcairn's Criminal Trials, is a register of terrible misdeeds, and of vengeance as terrible. In 1483, we find the Philiphaugh family fighting amongst themselves. James Turnbull claims £100 from Adam for vexation and disturbance in the "breiking" of the lands of Westfield, and for the wrongous spoliation of a cow out of the land of Kirkhope. They seem to have got on better with the Murrays, who acquired part of the lands in 1461; and the gradual merging of the two properties was expedited, towards the close of the sixteenth century, by the marriage of a Murray with a daughter of the other house. In 1506 James IV. granted a deed of remission, in favour of Adam Turnbull of Phillophauch, and William Turnbull, his son and apparent heir, for the slaughter of Thomas Rutherfurd in Jedburgh Abbey.

In 1516 Ralph Turnbull obtained a gift from the Queen Regent of all which belonged to his father, the late Adam Turnbull of Philiphaugh, who with William Turnbull, his brother, "deit under umquhile our Sovereign Lord's banner, wham God assoilze;" doubtless two of the flowers of the Forest, "wede away" on Flodden field. Equally heroic and characteristic of his blood, was the death of another of the name, fighting in the Scots Guard of France against the Spaniards in Calabria, in 1503. "After the battle, they found the standard-bearer, Gilbert Turnbull, stretched in death. As if determined never to part with the colour, he lay above it, the staff in his arms and the flag between his teeth. His companions were here and there around him, and where a Scot lay dead on one side, one or two Spaniards lay on the other." Various retours and entries in the Register of Privy Seal

A. L. A.. 136.

Ruth. that ilk, 78.

P. S., v. 91.

Ecoss. en Frce. ii. 10.

narrate the succession of the Turnbulls of Philiphaugh, John, who died about 1572, being the last who held the family lands in anything like entirety. Divided in five parts among his family, these gradually fell into possession of the Murrays, the last we hear of the Turnbulls being the appearance of William Turnbull, portionar of Philiphaugh, among the jury at Jedburgh ^{Ann.} Circuit Court, in 1623. An early and powerful offshoot from this family were ^{Haw., 289.} the Turnbulls of Minto, the lands of which were confirmed to them by David II. before 1370. John of Minto, called "out wi' the sword," died on field of battle in France, where many of his clan earned knighthood by deeds ^{Ecoss.} of stubborn bravery. ^{en Frce.}

MURRAY OF PHILIPHAUGH.

It was in 1461 that this distinguished family, so long and honourably connected with Selkirkshire, obtained a footing in the Forest; but for a century and a half previous it had enjoyed a prominent and influential position in Midlothian. In direct unbroken male descent no Selkirkshire house traces to a remoter age, the present baronet being twenty-first in uninterrupted line, father and son, from his first-mentioned progenitor, Archibald de Moravia, a signatory of Ragman's Roll in 1296. The name was common among the nobility so far back as the authentic history of Scotland stretches, and Sir ^{Coll.} James Dalrymple mentions quite an array of eminent de Moravias from ^{Pref., 69.} the time of William the Lion till the death of Alexander III. (1286). That this family spread over Scotland from the northern district of Moray is probable enough; and a surmise has been hazarded that Moray, in turn, derived its name from certain prehistoric settlers hailing from Moravia in Austria.

TREE.

1. Archibald de Moravia, mentioned in Fala charter, 1321.
2. Roger de Moravia, son of Archibald, so described in charter to lands of Fala, 1321.
3. John de Moravia, designated son of Roger, in charter by David II., 1356.
4. William de Moravia, designated son of John, in same charter.
5. Patrick de Moravia, styled "Dominus de Falahill," in a precept dated 1413.
6. John de Moravia, of Fallahill, his son or brother, acquired Philiphaugh by royal charter dated 1461.
7. Patrick de Moravia of Fallahill, mentioned in charter by James IV., 1489.
8. John de Moravia, his son, said to be "The Outlaw" of the ballad, killed in 1510.
9. { John de Moravia, his son, died about 1513, probably at Flodden. { James Murray, his brother, died 1529.

10. Patrick, his son, died about 1578.
11. James, his son, died before his father, about 1569.
12. Patrick, his son, succeeded his grandfather, died 1601.
13. Sir John, his son, died 1670.
14. Sir James, his son, predeceased his father in 1637.
15. John Murray, his son, succeeded his grandfather, died 1675.
16. James, Lord Philiphaugh, his son, died 1708.
17. John Murray, his son, died 1753.
18. { Basil, his son, predeceased his father, 1747.
     { John, his brother, died 1800.
19. { Dr. John, his son, died 1830.
     { James, his brother, died 1854.
20. Sir John Murray, Baronet, his son, born 1817, died 1882.
21. Sir John Forbes Pringle Nesbitt Murray, present Baronet, his son, born 1842.
22. Archibald, his son.

Archibald de Moravia, first of the family of whom there is documentary evidence, is supposed to be the same who is entered in Ragman's Roll of 1296, as "Erchibauld de Moreff" in the county of Peebles. Though we find him thus professing allegiance to Edward of England, the only other mention of his name is in a charter wherein James Lord of Douglas endows Roger de Moravia, his son, "for services rendered," with the lands and tenements of Fala, afterwards Falahill. The charter, dated 6th Sept., 1321, is still in admirable preservation amongst the Family MSS. at Philiphaugh. Regarding early members of the house, nothing of interest is known until we reach—

VI. JOHN DE MORAVIA, first of the family connected with Selkirkshire. He acquired the lands of Philiphaugh in 1461, on the resignation of Thomas de Hoppringill. As this was only a year after the death of James II. at Roxburgh Castle, and while the young King was but seven years of age, John de Moravia must have been in favour with the Queen Regent, Mary of Gueldres, and her adviser, Bishop Kennedy of St. Andrews. The ancient accounts of Exchequer represent him as having become Herd-keeper to the Queen in 1462; and thereafter he was appointed Custos of Newark, acquiring with Philiphaugh the Forest steadings of Harehead, Hanging-shaw, and Lewinshope. He appears to have attained to the position of superintendent of the royal forests—keeping the castles and houses in repair, furnishing the necessary wood, and sometimes sending furnishings to Edinburgh Castle; in short, he was royal factor. That he was a man of position in the county is evident from his being named along with John de Turnbull, in 1467, to take inquisitions in Selkirkshire in connection with the tax to defray expenses of the King's marriage. In 1473-4 the Lord High Treasurer's Accounts show an item of 12s. "for a hat to the

King tane be Johne of Murray at Zule." In 1474 he seems to have
crossed over to Normandy with David, a French gunner, to whom £3 was
given on 20th September, at the King's command. Further on, 32s. is
set down for "four elne of blew for the kingis gunnare his govne at the
said passage with John of Murray, who again got £5 to pay for "clathis
coft to Ranald gunnare."

VII. Patrick de Moravia was not so distinguished as his younger brother
Alexander, the ecclesiastic. In 1474, Patrick Murray is mentioned as the
owner of large flocks on "Skaddamness, Carterhauch, and Lewynhop." His ^{Adv.}
^{Lib. MS.}
daughter Isabella was married to Pringle of Galashiels and Smailholm, the
first Pringle of Torwoodlee being one of her sons. Another daughter, Margaret, ^{Phil.}
^{MSS.}
was mother of James Stewart, natural son of James Earl of Buchan, who conferred on his son in 1491 the lands of Traquair, purchased for the purpose ^{Traq.}
^{MSS.}
from Dr. William Rogers, the favourite esquire of James III. From this James
Stewart is descended the noble family of Traquair.

VIII. John of Murray, son of Patrick, seems, like his grandfather, to
have been in high favour at court. A signal mark of partiality from James
IV., in the second year of his reign, is noted by a gift of 20 angels, or £24, "to
Johne of Murray of the Forest, to by him a horss, at the Kingis commande." ^{T. A.,}
^{Sept. 25,}
This was the highest price paid for a horse at that period. The same year he ^{1489.}
got a grant of the lands of Grierston, in Peebles, which had fallen to the King ^{G. S.,}
^{ii. 1927.}
as *ultimus hæres* of David Boswell; and on their resignation by John Murray ^{P. S.,}
of Blackbarony in 1497, he obtained from the king the lands of Cranston- ^{ii. 124.}
Riddel in Midlothian. According to an entry in the Register of the Privy Seal, ^{P. S.,}
^{ii. 146.}
he had a letter of gift from the King of the Forestership of Woodcockar, in
Annandale; and in 1492, a tack of the forest-stedes of Gatehope, Sithope,
Caddonhead, Douglas-craig, and Eldinhope, in conjunction with David Pringle ^{G. S.,}
^{Vol. i.}
of Tinnes. In 1500, his son acquired from James IV. a tack of "oure steid ^{124.}^{P. S.,}
of the hanyng liand within oure foreste of Etrike and warde of the samyne;" ^{ii. 124.}
and in 1509, the steads of Hangingshaw, Lewinshope, and Harehead. A ^{P. S.,}
^{iv. 29.}
curious and inexplicable break in the possession of Philiphaugh occurred in ^{G. S.,}
^{ii. 3206.}
1507, when the Master of Angus got the lands from the King; but in 1508
Murray was confirmed in that part of the land of Philiphaugh called "Quhit- ^{G. S.,}
^{ii. 3267.}
lawisland," besides two husbandlands of Bold in Peeblesshire. On the
accession of James IV. in 1488, all the high offices of State were distributed

amongst those who had been prominent abettors of the young King against
his father; and to Alexander Home, Lord Chamberlain, fell the offices of
"Baillie of Ettrick Forest and Keeper of Newark Castle." In 1501 John
Murray is mentioned as depute of Alexander Erskine; and though the latter
did not formally surrender the office till 1506, Murray was potential Sheriff of
the Forest before that time. In 1503 he granted sasine of her dowry lands
to Queen Margaret, and in the deed is styled "the noble and circumspect
gentleman (*armiger*) John Murray of Fawlahill, Sheriff of Selkirk." On the

G. S.,
ii. 3388.

30th November 1509, the King confirmed Murray in the office, making it
hereditary, and adding to it a tack of the lands of Peelhill, with the small
customs of the Burgh of Selkirk. An idea of the duties attached to the office
of Sheriff, and performed by this laird of Philiphaugh is afforded by a charter
of apprising quoted elsewhere. And yet it is this representative of the family
whom commentators and romancers have with remarkable unanimity pitched
upon as "the Outlaw" of the Ballad. Nothing could be more improbable
than that this orderly "circumspect" and law-enforcing officer of the Crown
should ever take up an attitude of rebellious defiance so diametrically opposed
to all we really know of his character and conduct. Besides his extensive

A. L. C.,
p. 373.

possessions in the Forest and in Lothian, he had a large mansion in Edinburgh,
inherited from his uncle, the Rector of Hawick. He was killed in 1510 by
Andrew Ker of Gateschaw and Thomas Scot, brother of Philip Scott of Aid-
schaw. These, at all events, were the men charged with the crime; but a

B. M.,
i. 372.

tradition lays Murray's murder to the account of Buccleuch and his clan, the
fatal arrow having been sped by Scott of Haining. May the occasion not
have been the "slauchteris and spoliatioun of Hangandschau," compounded
for by Buccleuch to James Murray of Philiphaugh, in the agreement of 1527?
His sons were John, who succeeded him; James, who succeeded John;
William, who married the heiress of Romanno; and Patrick, who became
laird of Broadmeadows.

IX. (1) John de Moravia was not long in possession of the family
estates. Succeeding in 1510, he disappears before 1514, the probability
being that he fell at Flodden with his connections, Murray of Blackbarony
and the young laird of Torwoodlee. By a charter dated 1502 he obtained
Battis, Hadderslie, and King's Croft, in Selkirk; and there is also a precept

G. S.,
ii. 2674.

by George, Master of Angus, in his favour, of eighteen husbandlands in
Selkirk.

IX. (2) James Murray was infeft in Peelhill and the office of Sheriff of Selkirk on 26th March 1514, and in October Queen Margaret granted him a tack of his Forest lands. He possessed a large tract of country—Falahill and Cranstoun-Riddell, in Edinburgh; Philiphaugh, Hangingshaw, Lewinshope, Harehead, Whytupbank, Caldanehead, Peelhill, Newark, Old Wark, and Carterhaugh, in Selkirkshire; Kirkurd and Mounthouses, in Peebles.

In 1525, as one of the " headesmen " of the Borders, he was sworn bound Pit., i. 127. to support Angus as Warden. In 1526, he obtained the lands of Kirkurd by a charter of apprising from Sir Walter Scot of Branxholm, evidently as G. S., iii. 387. security for reparation for the slaughter of his grandfather and other outrages, but the lands were soon reconveyed to Buccleuch, as appears by a contract published amongst the Buccleuch muniments, and dated 14th October 1527.

This document purports to be an agreement "betuix honorable men, Walter Scot of Branxhame, knycht, his kyn, freyndis, seruandis and part takaris on that ane pairt, and James of Murray of Fawlayhill his kyn, freyndis and seruandis on that uther pairt, in maner as efter followis," that the said Walter Scot shall pay the "sowme of five hundretht merkis gude and usuale money" to the said James Murray "for slauchteris and spoliatioun of the Hangandschau, quhilkis was committit be the said Walter Scot, knycht and his freyndis," etc. On his side, Murray undertakes to renounce "and gif oure all apprising of the landis of Kirkurde, and sall deliver the chartar and seising to the said Walter incontinent efter that the sickirnes be fund for payment of said sowme." And they agree to take each other's part in "all honest, gude and lefull querelis aganis all men, exceptand the Kingis grace;" moreover, "without fraude or gile, to cheis foure freyndis be baytht thair avisis" as arbiters in all other actions or quarrels. The witnesses are Robert Scot, tutour of Howpaslot, Walter Scot in Syntoun, Will Ker, and Schir Johne Scot, notary-public.

Less than four years after this, Murray's son and successor, Patrick, signed a bond of mutual aid with Sir Walter Scot's deadly enemy, the laird of Cessfurd; but in 1601 another Murray of Philiphaugh, on his deathbed, left his eldest son to the care and protection of the then Sir Walter Scot of Branxholme. So swift were the changes from enmity to amity in those days. In 1528 James Murray resigned his lands in favour of his son Patrick, who G. S., iii. 740, 813. had a grant of them next year from King James v.

X. PATRICK MURRAY was thrice married, there being issue of each marriage. His name frequently occurs in sasines as Sheriff of Selkirk, and in this capacity he appears to have acted on many occasions—probably in all special sasines of the county. Except Newark and Carterhaugh, he possessed intact the territory belonging to his immediate predecessors; and that he was a man of note and influence is sufficiently evident from his treaty of alliance with another powerful Border chief—Ker of Cessford, founder of the ducal house of Roxburgh. The duplicate signed by Ker, and still in possession of the family, is quaint and suggestive enough to warrant transcription. It is styled a "Bond of Mandril":—

"Be it kend till men be thir present letters me Walter Ker of Saisfurd to be bunden and oblest and be thir present letters faithfully binds and obleses me to ane honorable man Patrik of Murray of Fawlaihill to mentein supple and defend with my kyne frends and servants at my power ye said Patrik in all his rycht honest and just actions causes pleas and quarrels in contrair all others, the King's Grace exceptit or allegeance to ye Crown, And forther never to hear nor vent scaith indurand my lyffetyme to ye said Patrik in body fame or his guids, but to resist reveill and gaynstand at my power. For the observing keeping and fulfilling of thir presents I the said Walter binds and obles me be ye faith and troch in my body in the maist sikerast form and stratest sort of obligation. In witnes of ye quhilk for the mair securitie I the said Walter to thir presents has affixit to my seal at Halleden, and with my subscription manuel the 2d Sept. ye zear of God 1531, before thir witnesses, George Ker of Fawdensyde, Mark Ker of Keppillaw, Ad. Murray, James Murray, Adam Wauchhope, and Schir William Bryding with others diverss."

G. S., iii. 1466.
This laird (1535) resigned in favour of the Countess of Bothwell and her husband, Lord Maxwell, twelve and a half acres of Philiphaugh lands in lieu of £612 due by him and his father James Murray; and the said acres were P. C., i. 283; ii. 307. in turn resigned to Lord Fleming (a kinsman of Philiphaugh) for a sum of money due by the Countess. In 1564 he was ordered to serve the Warden, Kerr of Cessford, with more diligence. Malcolm, his son, was in 1573 charged to enter James and Thomas Inglis in Harehead before the Justice in Edinburgh Tolbooth, to underly the law for crimes of which they were accused. P. C., i. 493. In 1575 John, another son, appeared for John Murray of Blackbarony, to answer a complaint of holding back the mails of his steadings of Glenpot and P. C., ii. 62-5. Priesthope; and in 1578 the said John appears as suretie for John Tait in Skaddoneis, that he should abstain from theft in time coming under a pain of 500 merks. Patrick Murray survived his eldest son, and was succeeded by his grandson, Patrick.

XI. JAMES MURRAY married Margaret, sister of John Stewart of Traquair, and died about 1569. Captain Armstrong, in his *Companion to the Map of Tweeddale*, 1775, says,—"'The Bush aboon Traquair,' the retreat of mutual loves and theme of musical bards, is the place where it is said a son of Murray of Philiphaugh was wont to meet a daughter of Stewart of Traquair." The melody sung to "Hear me, ye nymphs," (written by Robert Crawfurd, a cadet of Dumsoy, who was drowned in returning from France in 1732) still survives, but the old song itself is lost.

XII. PATRICK MURRAY, in May 1578, soon after his grandfather's death, was infeft in Peelhill and the office of Sheriff of the Forest, which designation he often afterwards took in preference to that of his estate. Patrick, though Sheriff, had sometimes to appeal to higher powers for protection against free- P. C., iii. 87. booters. Walter Scott of Tuschelaw was ordered by the Privy Council to find £2000 in surety for his removal from Patrick's steading of Skaddoneis, of which he had taken forcible possession on the 11th July 1578. He obtained in 1588 a precept under the Privy Seal of James VI., feudalizing his Forest properties, and granting them to be held of the Crown at the feu-duty of £27 Scots. This deed, besides narrating the uninterrupted possession by his ancestors "beyond the memorie of man," refers to their gratuitous services to the King and his royal predecessors "without default at any time in their due obedience as became faithful subjects." Patrick Murray's will is a curious Phil. MSS. document. It was made at Hangingshaw in January 1601, the year of his death, when he was "seik in bodie bot heall in mynde and spreit." Almost in the words of Shakspere's will (made fifteen years later) is the first bequest :—

"I recommend my saull throwe the mercyes of God in my Saviour Christ to the partcipa- tioun of yat Glorie and life above quhairof be faith in Christ my Saviour I am sure." Then follows an enumeration of various debts, some of them odd enough, such as "to the sukar baiker's wyfe the sum of £24, 12s. 4d.," and concluding with an equal division of his frie gear amongst his sons and daughters, excepting John, the eldest. The final clauses are quaint and even touching :—"I recommend my eldest sone John to ye protectioun of the Right Honble Sir Walter Scot of Branxholme, Kn^t and it is my will and desyre as he will import my blessing that he follow and obey him under his Majestie. And siclyke in the governing of his effairs that he follows the advice and counsel of my Lord Advocat the Laird of Blackbarronie and his brothers Gedion and Wm Murray the laird of Boujedward, Thomas Hamilton of Priest- field and Robert Scot of Aikwood quhom I be thir presentis do request in maist ernest sort to have a special cair of ye standing of my house and the help of my bairns, and that they give my said sone ane freindlie and fatherlie counsel and concurrance for sic effect. *Item*, I recommend my sone James to ye right nobill and my verray guid lord, my lord Fleming, and because I have the honor to be his lordschippis neir kinisman I will maist ernestly requeist his lordschippe to accept him in servance. *Item*, it is my last and onlie desyre that my eldest son John have speciall cair for the help of my remanent bairnis seing that it hes pleasit God to leve thame na uther father." Etc.

In 1588, Murray was named collector in Selkirkshire for a special tax to P. C., iv. 297; repair Edinburgh Castle; and was caution in 2000 merks that James Lawson iv. 317; iv. 463. of Humbie would not harm Margaret Brown, his mother! Next year he was appointed a commissioner for putting in force an Act for the expulsion of Jesuits. In 1590 he and the bailies of Selkirk had to find security that they would not harm each other; and later on the same year Blackbarony was security in 5000 merks that Philiphaugh would not harm Sir Wm. Sinclair of Hirdmeston.   The Sheriff was as ready to give caution as to take it, for he risked £1000 that his friend Robert Scott of Oakwood would not harm the Earl of Angus or his friends.   Among the witnesses were Malcolm and James

Murray, his father-brothers.   In 1584 Patrick Murray of "Hangitschaw" was one of the assize which sentenced to death three lairds, Douglas, Cunningham, and Edmonston, for art and part in the raid of Ruthven.

XIII. Sir John Murray of Philiphaugh was thrice married; first to Janet, daughter of Scott of Ardross, second to Helen Pringle of Gallosheills, and third to Margaret Scott, who survived him, and was infeft in Hangingshaw as her jointure house in 1677.   This at first was Sir John's principal residence, but he afterwards left it for Philiphaugh, adopting the latter estate as his designation instead of Falahill.   On 19th December 1615, he obtained a crown charter of his whole estates, erecting them into a free barony, to be called the barony of Philiphaugh.   In 1622, Sir John was one of six noblemen and knights appointed under the Great Seal to hold Courts of Justiciary "for the Sheriffdoms of Berwick, Roxburgh, Selkirk, Peebles, Dumfries, and

Stewartries of Kirkcudbright and Annandale"—embracing all the most turbulent part of the Scottish Border.   In 1635, he was foiled in his efforts to prevent the gathering of a company at a marriage in Selkirk, where, as convener of county justices, he had endeavoured to put in force an order designed to prevent the spread of the pest, then afflicting the Border.   When the battle of Philiphaugh was fought Sir John must have been close on sixty, if indeed not older.   He was too advanced in years to take part in the fight; but there can be no doubt with which side he sympathised.   His grief was yet green for a son that had fallen earlier in the same year, fighting against the victorious Montrose at Auldearn.   In 1649, Parliament, in compliance with a supplication from Sir John, authorised payment to him ("for the present subsistance of him, his lady, numerous children and famelie") of the sum of

4000 merks, "before all other debts due by the public," and the sum of 6000 merks to be gifted for the said supplicant's further payment " among the first of these debts most urgent and necessary to be paid," the rest of £12,014, 18s. to be paid "when it may be had."   The following is the supplication :—

"My lordis and vthers of the estates of Parliament now conveined vnto yo[r] Lo/ humlie means and schawis, I yo[r] Lo[ps] servitor Sir John Murray, of Philliphauche, Knight—That quhair in the moneth of September anno 1645 zeirs, befoir and at the battell of Phillophauche againes James Grahame sumtyme Erle of Montrois and his adherentis quhair it pleassed God to grant so happie a succes, that this kingdome was happillie releived, at leist most pairt fred, of thair Tirannicall wicked and rebellious courses vsit and intendit against all honest and religious men, My dwellinghous of Phillophauche and zairds and planting thairof wer all spoyled and rufled and my haill guidis geir and insight plenisching not onlie being thairintill, but all such hors nolt bestiall and scheip with all the cornes that war vpon my maines and lands, thairabout belonging to me and possest be me and my tenentis war spoyled, plundered, and taken away and all reft waist and desolate quhairby I was so vtterlie ruined that nothing was left to me nather within about nor without my house that I had no p^{nt} subsistence; but by the help and charitie of friendis, I being ane aiged man, and haveing reducit myselff (for the weill of my house) to be onlie a lyfferentar of a meane portioun of my estate, being by Godis providence in ane hard conditioun in respect of lyfferentis and greit burdine of debtis— Quhairvpon it pleassed the Cōmittee of moneys and cōmon burdings for the tyme to give commissioun in Apryill 1646 zeirs, to divers gentlemen of the schaire to agnosce and tak tryell of my said skaith and losses, quha haveing led laufull probation thairanent did find the samyn to amount to the sowme of Twelff Thousand fourtene punds, eightine shillingis four pennis as the report maid by the saidis cōmissioners dewlie regrat heirwith producit can testifie. And of the whilk sowme I have as yet resaved no pay't to my heavie loss and prejudice, notwith-standing that my cariage hes bein still, and hopes in Godis mercie sall so continue q'll I leive, to be faithfull and honest as becomes a trew covenantar and good patriot. And that it is notor' how I lossed a hopefull gentleman that was my sone at the battle of Auldairne, who was the staff of my old aige, in the north againes the said Rebell James Grahame, which many of your number can testifie. And that my qualitie and conditioun befoir my sad loss was in ane honest way of leiving with my wyffe, and numerous children and familie qwhich I am forced to declair the veritie to y^r honors, it became now (throu the said loss and want of reparatioun thereof) so meane and poore that we have scarcelie subsistence q'vpon to live, in respect of the meannes of my lyfrent portioun and many cōmon burdens wh. notwithstandg. of the premiss I stil ly vnder and am forced to pay as the rest of the countrey Swa that I am necessitat to have my recourse to yor honors for my supplie. HUMBLIE beseikand thairfoir your Lo^{ps} to tak the premiss to your serious consideratioun, and in respect of my former conditioun and qualitie and present want and miserie to tak such speidie course as y'r honors in wisdome and conscience sall think fitt quhairby I may gett effectuall payment of the said sowme of £12014, 18s. 4d. and annual rentis thairfor sen my loss th'of in maner abouewr'in and that thairby I and my wyffe and childrin may have my own to live vpon in sum honest way according to my rank and degrie which sall obleidge ws ever to pray for and to wisch the blessing of God vpon you and all your labours and interpryses which I pray the lord to grant Humblie expecting y^r favourable answer."

In 1643, Sir John was on the Committee of War. [Acts, vi. (1) 51.]

During the supremacy of the Commonwealth the laird of Philiphaugh was intrusted with a prominent share in the management of Selkirkshire, and [A. P., vi. (2) 884.] in 1659 he was one of the local commissioners appointed to assist General Monk in raising from the county a tax of £150, 14s. 10d. This tax was to provide new troops and equip more ships against " those false brethren, Papists,

A. P., vii. 3.
and other reduced persons, who, for the effecting of their wicked and traitorous designs, had proclaimed Charles Stuart King of England." It is significant of the times that only two years after this Sir John Murray of Philiphaugh was member for Selkirkshire in the "first Parliament of our most high and dread sovereign Charles by the grace of God King of Scotland, England, France and Ireland." In April of the same year (1661), the laird of Philiphaugh figures as one of the principal gentlemen who brought horses to certain races Ch. Anls., ii. 273. held at Cupar in Fife, where a large silver cup of the value of £18 formed the chief prize. He died in 1670, before the endurance of "trew Covenanters" was tried by fresh persecution. He had two daughters married to ministers of the Kirk—Mr. John Schaw of Selkirk and Mr. Robert Knox, minister of A. P., vii. 86. Kelso, grand-nephew of the Reformer. In consideration of her husband's sufferings for his affection and loyalty to his Majesty, Elizabeth Murray or Knox obtained an Act of Parliament (22nd March 1661) conferring on her and her children the stipend vacant since his decease in 1658, which the whole Knox Tree, Menz. heritors were content to pay. Mr. Andrew Knox, grand-nephew of the Reformer and cousin of Sir John's son-in-law, the minister of Kelso, is recorded A. P., vii. 88, 540. to have "died a preacher in Philiphaugh family, without issue." In 1661 and 1667 Sir John's name occurs amongst those appointed Commissioners of Supply.

XIV. SIR JAMES MURRAY, upon his marriage with Anna, daughter of Sir Lewis Craig of Riccartoun, was vested in the Barony of Philiphaugh, under reservation of his father's liferent. Dying in 1637, he thus predeceased his father 33 years, leaving a family of two sons and four daughters. One of the Fount., 253. latter, Janet, married James Scott of Gala 27th July 1646. His second son became Lieut-Colonel James Murray, who obtained a pension on being dismissed from his post in Edinburgh Castle, to make room for Lord Frendrot, a Papist, in 1688.

XV. JOHN MURRAY succeeded his grandfather in 1670, and died five years afterwards. His wife was Elizabeth, daughter of Sir Archibald Douglas of Cavers. Of ten children several died young, their second son John became a Lord of Session by the title of Lord Bowhill; and a daughter, Ann, was A. P., vii. 268. married to Alexander Pringle of Whytbank. In 1661 John Murray was one of a commission appointed by Parliament to try John Oliver and William Fletcher for stealing sheep and oxen. His son, Colonel William Murray, purchased Bowhill.

XVI. Sir James Murray was born in 1655, and in 1678 married Ann, daughter of Mr. Thomas Hepburn, minister of Oldhamstocks. There was no issue of the marriage; but by his second wife, Margaret, daughter of Sir Alex. Don of Newton-Don, there was a family of three sons and five daughters, one of whom, Anne, became wife of John Pringle of Haining. He sat in Parliament for Selkirkshire in 1678 and again in 1681. On the 18th November 1680, he and Urquhart of Meldrum, a commander of one of the King's troops, preferred complaints against each other before the Privy Council. Murray complained that Meldrum had prevented him from sitting in capacity of sheriff of the county, and had at the same time threatened him with imprisonment, without, as he supposed, any such power having been granted by the Privy Council. Meldrum, on the other hand, alleged that the Sheriff and gentry refused to give a list of those in their bounds who had been in the late rebellion. Though he had never been empowered to act alone as a magistrate, and the power granted to him to sit as a justice of the peace had ceased, "yet the Chancellor got him off by an agreement." This insolence (says Fountainhall in his Decisions) may give us a taste of what a military government would be. The case was again brought forward on 21st July 1681, in order to terrify Philiphaugh, who had been elected to Parliament from among the country party. His depute was imprisoned for conversing with rebels and retarding the King's service on his own private piques. On the 6th October, the case having been brought up a third time, " the Council found that Philiphaugh had malversed, and been remiss in punishing conventicles, and therefore they simply deprived him of his right of Sheriffship of Selkirk—it not being heritable, but bought by King Charles from his father—and declared it was devolved in the King's hands to give it to any other." Philiphaugh's share in the Rye-house Plot having been exposed in Carstairs' confession before the Privy Council, he was committed to prison in September 1684. At his examination, being threatened with the torture of " the boots," he made a confession, and threw himself upon the mercy of the Treasurer (Queensberry). He was liberated on bail, under a penalty of £1000 for his re-appearance, but remission was granted that he might be called as King's evidence against his fellow-conspirators. It was on his deposition and that of his associates (Scott of Gala among them) that forfeiture was pronounced against Polwarth and George Pringle of Torwoodlee on the 22d May 1685, and that Baillie of Jerviswood was executed. On the 28th October 1689, he was appointed an ordinary Lord of Session, and took his seat on the 1st November as Lord

Philiphaugh. In 1698 he was disappointed of the office of Lord Justice-Clerk, although supported by the powerful advocacy of Queensberry, who wrote—"He is a man every way qualified for it, both as to his capacity and zeal for the Government, and is a person to whom I owe such obligations as I can in no other way requite, but by endeavouring to make use of what interest I may have with his Majesty and friends about him for his advancement, and by assuring any that assist me in it, that they lay me under a personal obligation." In 1702 he was appointed Lord Clerk Register, which office he held, except a short interval, till his death on 1st July 1708. In token of the respect in which the deceased judge was held by the burgh of Selkirk, about fifty persons were ordered to attend his funeral on pain of being fined five merks. A contemporary described him as "a gentleman of clear natural parts; and, notwithstanding of that unhappy step of becoming evidence to save his life, continued still a great countryman, of a fair complexion, fat, middle stature, turned of fifty years old." He was one of the commissioners

Acts, xi. 404-5. appointed in 1702 to treat for a union of the two kingdoms; and in 1707 he voted in favour of the measure in the Scottish Parliament. In 1701 he obtained Parliamentary ratification of a charter under the Great Seal, dated 15th February 1700, in favour of himself and his eldest son, John Murray.

A. P., x. 307. The Act is a lengthy document, occupying no less than seven large folio pages, as indeed was required from the magnitude of the territory and privileges conveyed. First enumerated are the lands of Hangingshaw, Lewinshope, and Harehead, with their pertinents. Then Philiphaugh, Whitelawsland, lands of Peillhill, the rights and customs of the burgh of Selkirk, the office of Sheriff of the Sheriffdom of Selkirk, the lands of Mauldiscleugh and Mauldishaugh, an acre and a third formerly belonging to the Turnbulls of Philiphaugh—all as incorporated in the free barony of Philiphaugh by James VI. in 1615. In addition, Sir James and his son were confirmed in possession of that part of Selkirk Common allocated to Philiphaugh in 1681, the west half of the Forest-steading of Kershope, the lands of Whiteburn and Daviestoun, in the parish of Livingston and county of Linlithgow. It is astonishing that it should have been this wealthy and prosperous laird who allowed the ancient family estate of Falahill to go out of possession of the Murrays. He sold it in 1682.

XVII. JOHN MURRAY married Eleanor, daughter of Lord Basil Hamilton, and they had eight children. From this connection there was at one time every prospect of the Earldom of Selkirk accruing to the Philiphaugh family.

In 1725 John Murray was elected member of Parliament for the local group of burghs, which seat he continued to occupy till 1734. He was then returned for the county of Selkirk, which he represented till 1753. In 1728, out of his regard, love, and favour for the burgh of Peebles, he gave the sum of £100 sterling to bring in the water of St. Mungo's Well to the town. Commenting on this, Dr. Chambers says: "Why Murray of Philiphaugh should have taken C. P., p. 223. such an extreme interest in Peebles may seem surprising, but is perhaps explained by the fact that he had been lately appointed member for the district of burghs, and looked forward to be re-appointed, which he was in 1754." This is not only ungenerous, but incorrect. It was this John Murray's son that obtained the seat in 1754; and the present to Peebles (also bestowed on the other burghs of the group) was a graceful gift on the occasion of his leaving the burghs for his native shire, and not at all an instance of the gratitude which has been described as a lively sense of favours to come. In 1748, £4000 sterling was paid to this laird in compensation for the heritable Sheriffship of the Forest, so long vested in his family.

XVIII. (1) BASIL MURRAY made up titles to the estate in 1734. He died unmarried in 1747, his next brother having predeceased him.

XVIII. (2) JOHN MURRAY, third son, was laird of Philiphaugh from 1753 till 1802, his reign of forty-nine years proving somewhat disastrous to the fortunes of his house. In 1754 he spent £8000 in contesting the Selkirk group of burghs with Mr. Dundas, who is reported to have disbursed £12,000. Mr. Murray won the seat, but Government failed to implement its promise to repay his expenses in the event of success. So far as Peebles was concerned, Mr. Murray possessed an all-powerful friend in the Earl of March and Ruglen (afterwards Duke of Queensberry, and familiarly known as "Old Q."), who held the town council of that ancient burgh in absolute thraldom. To the heavy expenses of his election were added losses from speculation, from having become security for a defaulting friend, from an inordinate love of horse-racing, and from bad luck on the turf. People used to gather from far and near to see "Old Q." and the laird of Philiphaugh riding their own racehorses. The latter for a while even indulged in the extravagance of a pack of hounds. One of his huntsmen is said to have been drowned in Yarrow, which he rashly attempted to cross when in high flood. From Yarrow, Ettrick carried the body into Tweed, which bore it out into the German Ocean. Finally it was cast ashore on the coast of Holland, a hunting-horn with the name and crest of Philiphaugh leading to the man's identification. In 1764-9, the lavish hospitality he dispensed at Hangingshaw was effectively stopped by the total destruction, by fire, of that noble mansion, described as "the largest, the best, the richest, and the grandest furnished house in the south of Scotland." This was the crowning blow. In 1769 Mr. Murray executed a trust-deed for behoof of his creditors. Hangingshaw was sold to Mr. Johnston of Alva, and other lands to other purchasers. After residing a few years in Philiphaugh House, from which the farmer in occupation removed, the laird went to the West Indies, with his wife and unmarried daughters. When he returned he had gained enough to repurchase the land sold to Mr. Johnston, but was not able to acquire it. One of his daughters, Eleanora (who, when a child, was rescued from her burning home by being extricated through a small window), was married to Sir James Nasmyth of Posso, and is described as "a lady equally attractive from her external charms, and the elegance of her mind and manners." He died in 1802, and was succeeded by his eldest son.

Penne., Tweed. 263.

XIX. (1) Dr. JOHN MURRAY, physician in London, died in 1830, unmarried, and was succeeded by his brother.

XIX. (2) JAMES MURRAY was brought up from his childhood at Inner-leithen, under the superintendence of the Earl of Traquair. At the tender age of eleven, he entered the royal navy, and was present at the relief of Gibraltar, under Admiral Lord Howe, in 1782. After attaining his lieutenancy about 1814, he retired from the King's service, and obtained command of a vessel under the East India Company—then reckoned a sure road to fortune. In 1851 he executed an instrument of disentail of the lands and barony of Philiphaugh, and died in 1854, succeeded by his eldest son.

XX. SIR JOHN MURRAY, Baronet of Philiphaugh and Melgund, born in 1817, died in 1882. By the Sheriff of Chancery, in Edinburgh, he was, in 1863, served heir-male to his kinsman, Sir Joseph Albert Murray, Baronet, Count of the Austrian Empire, since whose death, without issue in 1848, the baronetcy had lain dormant. Count Murray's wife was a daughter of the princely house of Esterhazy. Extensive lands, once possessed by the Murrays of Melgund, passed into the hands of the family of Minto by the marriage of the heiress of Melgund with Sir Gilbert Elliot, third Baronet. Mr. Foster places this baronetcy amongst those "regarding whose claims there does not Peerage, etc., 689. appear to be accessible the *prima facie* evidence which would justify their inclusion among those whose title is unquestioned;" but the title is acknowledged by Lodge, Walford, and all lists of baronets. For that matter, no baronetcy can add to the dignity of the name—Murray of Philiphaugh. By his first marriage in 1840 with Rose-Mary, heiress of W. A. Nesbitt, Esq., of Bombay, Sir John had two sons, the present baronet, and James, married to Mary, daughter of the late Mr. Russel, editor of the *Scotsman;* and a daughter married to William, eldest son of Sir John Trelawny, Baronet, an ancient Cornish family, who died in 1871. By his second marriage in 1877, with Charlotte, daughter of the Rev. Prebendary Burgess of St. Paul's, Sir John had two sons, Hamilton and Charles Richard. At the general election in 1868, Sir John Murray contested the representation of his native county, as a supporter of the Liberal party, failing by only three votes to secure the seat so long and so often held by his ancestors. Immediately after his accession, he began to beautify the barren slopes of the estate with timber, and to improve its expanse of marsh and heath into arable ground. The result has been the conversion of Philiphaugh into one of the most beautiful domains in Scotland.

XXI. SIR JOHN FORBES PRINGLE MURRAY, present Baronet, born in 1842, married Mary Frances Robertson, who died in 1883, leaving one son and three daughters.

Of all the vast estates possessed at one time by the Murrays of Philiphaugh in Selkirkshire, Peeblesshire, and Midlothian, only the original holding, Philiphaugh and Harehead, now remain. The extravagance of the laird who was "Old Q.'s" companion, the disastrous fire at Hangingshaw, and the unfortunate speculations of later proprietors, necessitated the alienation, one by one, of large farms which for years formed part of Hangingshaw estate. What remains of it, however, is enough to make Philiphaugh one of the most delightful seats in the Scottish Border. Thanks to the fine taste of the late Sir John Murray, its barren hill-slopes have been turned into crtile fields, fringed with lines of sheltering timber, thickening here and there into large plantations full of varied foliage. Behind the Manor Hill lies the "Tobacco Knowe." It is said that when a laird of Philiphaugh and a bailie of Selkirk were negotiating an excambion one cold wet day on the hill-top, several hours were spent in an effort of the laird to get this Knowe included with his portion.   At last the bailie, able no longer to endure the comparative comfort of the laird, who lessened the pangs of hunger by successive chews of tobacco, asked a morsel for himself.   The laird ungenerously stipulated for "the Knowe" first; and the bailie, after holding out as long as he could, was fain to capitulate, his craving for a bit of the coveted "weed" being too strong for resistance.   A charming and picturesque nook in the estate is the "Corbie Linn"—a waterfall of considerable height in the course of the Philip Burn.   Formerly it was a series of rapids tumbling through a narrow gorge; but, by slightly deflecting its course, Sir John Murray led the burn to the brink of a perpendicular precipice, over which it falls in lacy beauty between clumps of thorn and mountain-ash, the face of the rock being covered with moss and fern.

Of old, Philiphaugh House was on the haugh proper, just where Lauriston Villa stands at present.   Here it was that Montrose placed his artillery in 1645; and in 1722 it was "an ancient house, with orchards, pigeon house, and planting."   The large and picturesque mansion which now adorns the slope of the hill, overlooking Yarrow just before it pours its waters into Ettrick, was much enriched by additions the first baronet made to it from time to time.   It occupies a fine stance, full "in the eye of Phœbus"— rich wood behind, and in front a roomy lawn from which terraces of easy slope lead down to a level park dotted with trees and fringed with pines. When the family residence of Hangingshaw was destroyed by fire, hardly any relics and heirlooms were saved.   Luckily, the old charter-chest was elsewhere at the time, and from its contents an elegant volume has been compiled, the sere and valued manuscripts serving to illustrate the family history.   Several coins found on the battle-field, a rusty dagger with silver mountings, found by the river-side, near Harewoodglen, one or two bottles hastily hidden by the Cavaliers, and cannon-balls found near Leslie Cottage, are all the relics of local interest in the hall.

Not so capacious, but more picturesque than Philiphaugh House, is Harewoodglen, a charming villa in the Italian style built by Sir John Murray, and now the residence of Mr. Dennistoun of Dennistoun.   It occupies a semi-circle irregularly formed by a line of road and a curve of Yarrow, which here is at its loveliest.   On one side of the water are the woods of Bowhill, through which meander the lines of the Duchess Walk, and, on the other, green sward alternates with rocky scaur, the scaur sometimes covered with rich vegetation, and sometimes bare enough to display strange contortions of

Hodge's MSS.

the silurian rock. One of these is much admired—an almost perfect representation of the Gothic Arch.

On a corner of elevated bank, overlooking the haugh, and fronting the Howden Hills across the river, is Beechwood, the residence of Miss Murray, for whom it was built by her brother, Sir John; while further back, in a slight dip on the hill-side, Thirladean is reflected in a pretty sheet of water, skirted by the road leading to the mansion-house. Its unique appearance and romantic surroundings made it the favourite summer resting-place of Mr. Russel of the *Scotsman*, whose fame quite broke the bounds of anonymity which hedge the journalist. Not to be omitted from notice is the well-planned farm-steading, concerning which the late baronet cherished certain ambitious schemes of agricultural colleges and what not—never to be realised. Like the neighbouring estate of Haining, Philiphaugh boasted a mineral well, which, in 1749, "in regard of its smell, taste, purgative qualities, and other effects, such as colouring money laid into it, differeth little or nothing from the well of Moffat in Annandale, so much frequented." Of this well the present writer has been unable to find any trace whatever.

Cran MSS.

JUNIOR MEMBERS OF THE FAMILY.

ALEXANDER MURRAY, son of John, sixth laird of Falahill and first of Philiphaugh, was a distinguished ecclesiastic during the reign of James III. In 1473, he was Canon of Moray, and, while Rector of Hawick, drew the revenues of the churches of Petty and Brackly, in that diocese. He summoned David Scott of the Bukcleuch in 1478 for "44 merkis the rest of a mair soume of the taxt of the kirk of Hawick." He was Director of Chancery and the King's familiar clerk in 1476, while about 1484 he was Rector of the Forest of Ettrick. Part of his property fell to his elder brother Patrick, and part to ROGER MURRAY, merchant in Edinburgh. This Roger is several times mentioned in the accounts of the Lord High Treasurer. He got £20 for "v. elne of satyne crammacy for a govne to the Quene," 31s. 3d. for the "halue of v. quarteris of veluous for a tippet to the Quene," £45 for "xv. ellis of vellous to be the King a gogare goune," etc.

A. L. A. G. S., ii. 1280. A. L. C., 88.

PATRICK MURRAY, son of John, eighth laird, was proprietor of Broadmeadows, and afterwards of Glen in Peeblesshire. Patrick left an only daughter, wife of John Cockburn of Glen, whose granddaughter, Mary Cockburn, was in 1607 served heir of Patrick Murray in the lands of Broadmeadows.

Retours.

WILLIAM MURRAY, brother of Patrick, married Janet Romanno of Romanno in Peeblesshire, and, settling in that county, became progenitors of the Murrays, Baronets of Stanhope. In 1528 he and Alexander Murray obtained remission for their "treacherous remaining away from the army at Solway;" and in 1532, his son William obtained a charter of the lands subject to the liferent of his parents. They had their own share in the bloody outrages of the time. In 1546, William, son and heir of William Murray of Rommanos, and John his brother, were accused of art and part in the cruel slaughter of Sir Alexander Innes (chaplain) and the muti-

P. S., viii. 23. G. S., iii. 1242.

Pit.,
i. 332. lation of James Geddes; to which was added in the following year a charge of being concerned in the slaughter of Sir Martin Ewmond or Newman, also a chaplain. Murray's cautioners were Sir Walter Scott of Branxholme, Patrick Murray of Philiphaugh, and Alexander Tait of Pirn. P. C., iv.
698, 737;
v. 32. About fifty years later a Murray of Romanno, his son and grandson, implicated in the murder of a neighbouring laird, fled from justice, and four men were sent to occupy the tower, their costs being deducted from the revenue of the estate. A most quaint and importunate protest by their three wives was sent to the Privy Council, and in the end they were left unmolested, after payment of a "grite composicioune." In 1605 the younger of the three lairds figured among "gentleman redders" of a street broil in Peebles, on which occasion he was "hurt and wounded" in the cause of order!

SIR JAMES MURRAY OF DEUCHAR, son or (more probably) grandson of Patrick, tenth laird, was a prominent and prosperous merchant of Edinburgh. He was born in 1570, married 1601, and died 1649. In 1643-4-6-8, he was appointed by Parliament to serve in the Committee of War for Selkirkshire. The Earl of Eglinton in 1647 obtained an Act compelling Sir James to deliver up a bond for the price of 600 muskets, 400 pikes, and some other arms, said bond having been granted to James Murray for the use of the public at the time of the getting of the weapons. His well-known tomb in Greyfriars' Churchyard, Edinburgh, bears the following epitaph:—

"S. D.   I. M.   H. L.   G.

Jacobus Moravius, ex antiqua Morav. a Philiphach familia ortus, civitate Edenburgena donatus, in ea mercaturam fœliciter exercuit, et magistratus honorem sæpius meruit; Gulielmi Mauli civis præclari filiam Bethiam uxorem duxit, ex qua plures liberos suscepit, et ex iis tres filios s̄pstites reliquit, cum filia una, Jacobo Eliseo, civi honorifico, nupta. Opum non tam custos, quam æconomus honestissimus, in literatos munificus, in egenos insigni charitate beneficus. Sic piam vitam placida sequuta est mors, prid. Kal. Maii anno æræ Christ. MDCXLIX; ætatis suæ quarto sexti supra decimum lustri. Optimo ch:q. p. p. p. ff. Jac. eques, Rob. et Pat. Moravii parentarunt."

Stay, passenger, and shed a tear
For good James Murray lieth here.
He was of Philiphaugh descended,
And for his merchandise commended.
He was a man of a good life,
Marry'd Bethia Maule to 's wife;
He may thank God that e'er he gat her,
She bore him three sons and one daughter.
The first he was a man of might,
For which the King made him a knight;
The second was both wise and wylie,
For which the town made him a bailie;
The third a factor of renown,
Both in Camphier and in this town;
His daughter was both grave and wise,
And she was married to James Elies.

His eldest son, Sir James, succeeded to Skirling in Peeblesshire, which had been bought in 1648 for £5200 sterling; but in 1681 the estate passed out of the hands of the family, being bought by a brother of the first Duke of Queensberry. The second son, Sir Robert, was Lord Provost of Edinburgh in 1661, in which year he obtained a ratification of the patronage of the chaplainry in Musselburgh called "the ladie alter," and of the superiority of the lands of

Cameron. He was ancestor of the Baronets of Melgund. A third son, Patrick Murray, succeeded to Deuchar, and frequently represented Selkirkshire in Parliament, a different Patrick Murray being at the same time member for the burgh.

SIR JAMES MURRAY OF KILBABBERTON was second son of Patrick, twelfth Laird of Falahill and Philiphaugh. In early life (1681) he was concerned in the slaughter of David Stewart, brother to James Stewart of Tynnes, a cadet of Traquair, by Andro Pringle, son to the deceased James Pringle of Tynnes. A feud threatened to result, but was averted. James Murray is mentioned in various Acts of Parliament as taking part in public business; and he became Master of H.M. Works, and Keeper of Munitions of Edinburgh Castle. He made his brother Walter Master of Works, with residence at Holyrood-house.

JOHN MURRAY OF ASHIESTEEL, son of Sir John, thirteenth laird, suffered great persecution for his opposition to Episcopacy, and for his strong attachment to the Covenanting cause. According to Wodrow, "he was a gentleman of singular piety, was chased from his house and heritage by Meldrum's oppression, had all his goods driven to the Market Cross of Selkirk, and there sold." ^{mss., v. 37.}

JOHN MURRAY, LORD BOWHILL, second son of the fifteenth chief of the name, is mentioned elsewhere.

Of all the family of Philiphaugh none has left behind him a more creditable record than Colonel Adam Murray of the Romanno branch, who played a prominent part at the famous siege of Derry, in 1689. When, on the 18th of April, Lundy called a Council with design of surrendering the city, Captain Murray was informed by a relation of his own of what was going on. From his station, which was at a considerable distance, though within view of the town, Murray, disregarding an order to lead his men out of sight of the city, marched with his horse straight to one of the gates. A man sent by the Council to remonstrate with him, proposed to have him hauled over the wall by himself; but the captain of the guard opened the gate to him and his troops. Along the streets the multitude followed him with expressions of their respect and affection. He assured them he would stand firm in defence of their lives and the Protestant interest, and assist them to suppress the Council and prevent their surrender of the city—desiring all who concurred with him to put a white cloth on their left arm, which they generally did. Invited to attend the Council, Murray told Governor Lundy, to his face, his late actions had declared him either fool or knave; and, urging him to take the field, assured him of the readiness of the soldiers. He absolutely refused to sign a paper for surrender, and, leaving the Council, returned to the soldiers, whom he knew to be generally as resolute for defending the city as himself. That the pernicious intentions of the Council might be more effectually frustrated, Captain Murray and a party with him went

Mackenzie, Siege Derry.

that night to the main guard, took the keys, and appointed new guards at the gates and on the walls. Murray's opposition was the only thing that prevented the capitulation of the city to King James, and altered the whole turn of affairs. Next day the multitude, having thus broken the authority of the Council, would have made Captain Murray both their general and the sole governor of the town; but he modestly refused it, because he judged himself fitter for action and service in the field than for conduct and government. He was made colonel of the horse. The day after, Lord Strabane, coming to the walls with proposals from King James, Colonel Murray waited on him, rejecting his lordship's solicitation to go over to their party, to become a colonel in their army, and obtain a thousand pounds gratuity. On the 21st, Colonel Murray, at the head of about 150 horse, charged the enemy's cavalry under Lieutenant-General Maumont, with whom he had three personal encounters, killing him in the last. Hardly a day passed in which Murray did not sally out, seldom returning without doing some execution on the besiegers, until the 18th June, when he received some shots in his head-piece, bruising his head, and for a while incapacitating him for service. He and other twelve, going down to flank the enemy's trench before Butcher's Gate, only twelve days before the siege was raised, continued firing till their ammunition was spent, and Murray was so severely shot in both thighs that he did not recover till near November. During the siege, says Dr. Killen, Murray displayed prodigious bodily strength as well as great courage. He is said to have been six feet five inches high. From Kirke, the brutal general who commanded after the relief, "the treatment experienced by Colonel Murray was superlatively base. He had every right to expect the rewards of distinguished fidelity and valour; but it soon transpired that his regiment was to be put under the command of a new colonel, and that he was to be deprived even of the favourite charger which had borne him in many a bloody struggle! His men, no longer permitted to follow a leader whom they admired as the very soul of chivalry, withdrew in disgust from the service; and when one officer ventured to complain, Kirke threatened him with the gallows!" Weakened by wounds, and very likely broken-hearted by this ungrateful treatment, Colonel Murray died the year after the siege, leaving behind him a son and daughter by his wife, Isabella Shaw. The sword with which he slew the French General is now in possession of Mr. J. A. Alexander, of Caw House, Londonderry, a lineal descendant by the female line, who has also a watch presented to the Colonel by King William.

THE SONG OF THE OUTLAW MURRAY.

This well-known and stirring ballad commemorates a transaction supposed to have taken place betwixt a Scottish monarch and a laird of Philiphaugh; but it is impossible to identify any particular laird as hero of the romance. Sir Walter Scott professed himself unable to ascertain the historical foundation of the tale, and considered it improbable that any light could be thrown upon the subject without an accurate examination of the family charter-chest. Professor Aytoun, who enjoyed this advantage, "arrived at the conclusion that the story told in the ballad is, if not altogether fictitious, at least greatly exaggerated;" and after a close perusal, by the courtesy of the late Sir John Murray, of the family MSS., the present writer finds himself confirmed in the same opinion—notwithstanding the elaborate arguments of a learned editor of the family tree to the contrary.

There can, however, be no doubt as to the veritable antiquity of the song, which has been popular for ages in the valleys of Ettrick and Yarrow. Like all other ballads handed down orally from generation to generation, it exists in several versions. That published in the Border Minstrelsy was, for the most part, taken from a copy, apparently of considerable antiquity, found among the papers of Mrs. Cockburn (Miss Rutherford of Fairnalee), authoress of "The Flowers of the Forest." Sheriff Plummer contributed a few verses not in any written copy, and two were obtained from the recitation of Mungo Park, who was born and grew to manhood under the shadow of Newark Castle, the "Outlaw's" stronghold. In Philiphaugh charter-chest there is a copy in manuscript, which, from an allusion to the then Lord Philiphaugh, must have been written between 1689 and 1708. A note which accompanies it is appended, and, while showing what hazy notions of the ballad's origin were entertained by the head of the family two hundred years ago, it at the same time confirms its antiquity :—

(margin note: Published in Aytoun's Collection.)

"IN THE SONG OF OUTLAW MURRAY.

"This Outlaw Murray was ancestor to the now Lord Philiphaugh, the Heretable Sheriff of the Forrest. This King in the   year after the birth of Christ is King James, the Second of the name of Stewart, the 102 King of Scots, by a not interrupted Line from Fergus the First King of Scots; and in the 15 year of this reign he made this raid. He reigned 23 years. Made King in the seventh year of his age, some years he and the Kingdome were troubled with Factions, which being beaten down, and the Kingdome made peaceable, when he had gone into England to help the Northumbrians, as also had besieged the Castle of Roxburgh, by the violence and force of a Faggot burning inwardly, shot out of the Castle in a Timber frame, the rest of his Company receiving no hurt, the King, being with it cast to the Ground, died immediately, in the 29th year of his age, 1460. Cheviot Chase was much about this time. This James Boyd was son to Robert Lord Boyd, High Chancellor of Scotland, and married this King James the Second's sister, and was Earle of Arran when the King sent him on this message to the Outlaw about the sixteen year of his reign, and 23rd of his age. He sent this his Brother of Law Earle of Arran to the King of Denmark to bring his Daughter to be his Queen, and because he did not return so soon as he desired, he denounced him Rebell and Traitor, took away his Estate and Honours, and gave them to this Earle Hamilton, and commanded his sister to marry him, which is their first claim to be Cadits to the Crown at this day. This James Boyd returned with the Queen, and being informed at Leith, where they landed, of the King's unthankfulness to him, returned in that same ship to the King of Denmark, with whom he lived honourably till he died. See the Histories of the Douglases and Drummond of Hawthornden on 5 King James. This James Pringle, Laird of Torsonce, Chief of the Pringles of Scotland, at this time, was Royal Banner-bearer of Scotland, and at this raid by the King was called Hoppringle in French; that is, 'my Princely Cock, keep up a good heart;' now Hoppringle of that Ilk. Albeit by the abbreviation and corruption of the sirname, Pringle by Highland language, yet it is derived from one of their ancestors, a Pilgrim who went to the Holy Land, to the Grave of the Holy Jesus Christ, as is alledged, with the heart of King Robert Bruce in the Company of Sir James Douglas, and returned safe, and was in great favour with Robert the 2nd, the 100 King of Scots, and the first King of the Sirname of Stewart, and by the Highlanders called Pilgrime, which, without altering a Letter, only placing the Letters nearer to the French Pringal, makes it Pringle."

Absurd in its surmises, this note is equally erroneous in its statements of fact, and must have been written by some one ignorant of his country's history. His speculations upon the ancient name of Pringle are only amusing, but his travesty of historical events is almost irritating.

The truth is, that, whatever version be accepted, its anachronisms are not to be got over; and it remains clear that any foundation the story may have had in fact, has been smothered up and hidden by an after-growth of fanciful additions. It appears to us that some clue to the date of the ballad lies in the minstrel's animus against the house of Buccleuch. James Murray, tenth laird, is the last mentioned in the family MSS. as possessed of Newark, which castle passed into the hands of Buccleuch, either in his lifetime or that of his successor, Patrick Murray. After the death of James IV. at Flodden, the widowed Queen-Regent complained loudly of Buccleuch's encroachment upon her dowry lands of Ettrick Forest, the Custos of which domain had Newark for a residence. Buccleuch contrived to keep his hold, and, as he could only do so by displacing Murray, the ill-will of the latter family was a natural consequence. By way of showing the earlier and superior title of the Murrays, the ballad-writer has either invented the story in toto or has amplified the tradition of an actual visit paid to a former Murray by the King. Both Sir Walter Scott and the compiler of the Family Records are of opinion that John Murray, eighth laird, is the presumptive "Outlaw" of the song; and, as he was undoubtedly in great favour with King James IV., nothing is more likely than that the merry monarch may have ended one of his hunting expeditions to the Forest by confirming John in his hereditary sheriffship, interrupted for a few years by the appointment of Lord Home. As a matter of fact, John Murray did, in 1509, obtain a royal charter from his sovereign, of the sheriffship; but, as the office had been vacant since 1506, there is nothing improbable in the supposition that he had already claimed the family rights and taken possession of the castle. Indeed, in 1503, he acted as Sheriff at the Queen's infeftment in her dowry lands of Ettrick Forest. It would have been in thorough keeping with all that it is known of James IV., if his Majesty had taken the opportunity to give his favourite a half-jesting reproof for his presumption; but that Murray was ever seriously outlawed is out of the question. His King heaped honours on him; and, only eighty years after his death, his descendant obtained a feudal precept of his lands for gratuitous services rendered to the Crown by his family, "without default at any time in their due obedience as became faithful subjects." So that, granted a royal progress to Newark, followed by Murray's investiture with the sheriffship, the poet remains chargeable with considerable embellishment. A glorification of the family of Philiphaugh, and a sneer at the rapacity of Buccleuch, are the evident motives of his rhyme; and he must have been one of those of whom it is observed in the old Scots proverb, that, given an ell, they will soon make a web of it. The version subjoined is that given by Sir Walter Scott—not materially different from the charter-chest MSS., but, where it differs, differing mostly for the better.

THE SANG OF THE OUTLAW MURRAY.

ETTRICKE FORESTE is a feir foreste,
  In it grows manie a semelie trie;
There's hart and hynd, and dae and rae,
  And of a' wilde bestis grete plentie.

There's a feir castelle, bigged wi' lyme and
    stane;
  O! gin it stands not pleasauntlie!
In the fore front o' that castelle feir,
  Twa unicorns are bra' to see;
There's the picture of a knight, and a ladye
    bright,
  And the grene hollin abune their brie.

There an Outlaw kepis five hundred men;
  He keepis a royalle cumpanie!
His merryemen are a' in ae liverye clad,
  O' the Lincome grene sae gaye to see;
He and his ladye in purple clad,
  O! gin they lived not royallie!

Word is gane to our nobil King,
  In Edinburgh where that he lay,
That there was an Outlaw in Ettricke
    Foreste,
  Counted him nought, nor a' his courtrie
    gay.

" I make a vowe," then the gude King said,
  " Unto the man that deir bought me,
I 'se either be King of Ettricke Foreste,
  Or King o' Scotlande that Outlaw sall be!"—

Then spake the lord hight Hamilton,
  And to the nobil King said he,
" My sovereign prince, sum counsell take,
  First at your nobilis, syne at me.

" I redd ye, send yon braw Outlaw till,
  And see gif your man cum will he :
Desyre him cum and be your man,
  And hald of you yon Foreste frie.

" Gif he refuses to do that,
  We 'll conquess baith his landis and he !
Or else, we 'll throw his castell down,
  And make a widowe o' his gaye ladye."—

The King then call'd a gentleman,
  James Boyd (the Earle of Arran his brother
    was he) ;
When James he cam before the King,
  He knelit before him on his kné.

" Wellcum, James Boyd !" said our nobil King,
  " A message ye maun gang for me ;
Ye maun hye to Ettricke Foreste,
  To yon Outlaw, where bydeth he :

" Ask him of whom he haldis his landis,
  Or man, wha may his master be,
And desyre him cum, and be my man,
  And hald of me yon Foreste frie.

" To Edinburgh to cum and gang,
  His safe warrant I sall gie ;
And gif he refuses to do that,
  We 'll conquess baith his landis and he.

' Thou mayst vow I 'll cast his castell down,
  And mak a widowe o' his gaye ladye ;
I 'll hang his merryemen, payr by payr,
  In ony frith where I may them see."—

James Boyd tuik his leave o' the nobil King,
  To Ettricke Foreste feir cam he ;
Down Birkendale Brae when that he cam,
  He saw the feir Foreste wi' his ee.

Baith dae and rae, and harte and hinde,
  And of a' wilde bestis great plentie ;
He heard the blows that bauldly ring,
  And arrows whidderan' hym near bi.

Of that feir castell he got a sight ;
  The like he neir saw wi' his ee !
On the fore front o' that castell feir,
  Twa unicorns were gaye to see ;
The picture of a knight, and ladye bright,
  And the grene hollin abune their brie.

Thereat he spyed five hundred men,
  Shuting with bows on Newark Lee ;
They were a' in ae livery clad,
  O' the Lincome grene sae gaye to see.

His men were a' clad in the grene,
  The knight was armed capapie,
With a bended bow, on a milk-white steed ;
  And I wot they rank'd right bonnilie.

Thereby Boyd kend he was master man,
  And served him in his ain degré.
" God mot thee save, brave Outlaw Murray !
  Thy ladye, and all thy chyvalrie !"—
" Marry, thou 's wellcum, gentleman,
  Some King's messenger thou seemis to be."—

" The King of Scotlande sent me here,
  And, gude Outlaw, I am sent to thee ;
I wad wot of whom ye hald your landis,
  Or man, wha may thy master be ?"—

" Thir landis are MINE !" the Outlaw said ;
  " I ken nae King in Christentie ;
Frae Soudron I this Foreste wan,
  When the King nor his knightis were not
    to see."—

" He desyres you 'l cum to Edinburgh,
  And hald of him this Foreste fre ;
And, gif ye refuse to do this,
  He 'll conquess baith thy landis and thee.
He hath vowed to cast thy castell down,
  And mak a widowe o' thy gaye ladye ;

" He 'll hang thy merryemen, payr by payr,
  In ony frith where he may them finde."—
" Ay, by my troth !" the Outlaw said,
  " Than wauld I thinke me far behinde.

" Ere the King my feir countrie get,
 This land that 's nativest to me !
Mony o' his nobilis sall be cauld,
 Their ladyes sall be right wearie."—

Then spak his ladye, feir of face,
 She seyd, "Without consent of me,
That an Outlaw suld come befor a King ;
 I am right rad of treasonrie.
Bid him be gude to his lordis at hame,
 For Edinburgh my lord sall nevir see."—

James Boyd tuik his leave o' the Outlaw kene,
 To Edinburgh boun is he ;
When James he cam before the King,
 He knelit lowlie on his kné.

" Welcum, James Boyd !" seyd our nobil King ;
 " What foreste is Ettricke Foreste frie ?"—
" Ettricke Foreste is the feirest foreste
 That evir man saw wi' his ee.

" There 's the dae, the rae, the hart, the hynde,
 And of a' wild bestis grete plentie ;
There 's a pretty castell of lyme and stane,
 O ! gif it standis not pleasauntlie !

" There 's in the fore front o' that castell,
 Twa unicorns, sae bra' to see ;
There 's the picture of a knight, and a ladye
  bright,
 Wi' the grene hollin abune their brie.

" There the Outlaw keepis five hundred men,
 He keepis a royalle cumpanie !
His merryemen in ae livery clad,
 O' the Lincome grene sae gaye to see :
He and his ladye in purple clad ;
 O ! gin they live not royallie !

" He says, yon Foreste is his owin ;
 He wan it from the Southronie ;
Sae as he wan it, sae will he keep it,
 Contrair all kingis in Christentie."—

" Gar warn me Perthshire, and Angus baith ;
 Fife up and downe, and Louthians three,
And graith my horse !" said our nobil King,
 " For to Ettricke Forest hie will I me."—

Then word is gane the Outlaw till,
 In Ettricke Forest, where dwelleth he,
That the King was cuming to his cuntrie,
 To conquess baith his landis and he.

" I mak a vow," the Outlaw said,
 " I mak a vow, and that trulie,
Were there but three men to tak my pairt,
 Yon King's cuming full deir suld be !"—

Then messengers he called forth,
 And bade them hie them speedilye—
" Ane o' ye gae to Halliday,
 The Laird o' the Corehead is he.

" He certain is my sister's son ;
 Bid him cum quick and succour me !
The King cums on for Ettricke Foreste,
 And landless men we a' will be."—

" What news ? What news ?" said Halliday,
 " Man, frae thy master unto me ?"—
" Not as ye wad ; seeking your aide ;
 The King 's his mortal enemie."—

" Ay, by my troth !" said Halliday,
 " Even for that it repenteth me ;
For gif he lose feir Ettricke Foreste,
 He 'll tak feir Moffatdale frae me.

" I 'll meet him wi' five hundred men,
 And surely mair, if mae may be ;
And before he gets the Foreste feir,
 We a' will die on Newark Lee !"—

The Outlaw call'd a messenger,
 And bid him hie him speedilye,
To Andrew Murray of Cockpool—
 " That man 's a deir cousin to me ;
Desyre him cum, and make me aide,
 With a' the power that he may be."—

" It stands me hard," Andrew Murray said,
 " Judge gif it stand na hard wi' me ;
To enter against a King wi' crown,
 And set my landis in jeopardie !
Yet, if I cum not on the day,
 Surely at night he sall me see."—

To Sir James Murray of Traquair,
  A message came right speedilye—
"What news ? What news ?" James Murray
    said,
  " Man, frae thy master unto me ? "—

" What needs I tell ? for weel ye ken
  The King's his mortal enemie ;
And now he is cuming to Ettricke Foreste,
  And landless men ye a' will be."—

" And, by my trothe," James Murray said,
  " Wi' that Outlaw will I live and die ;
The King has gifted my landis lang syne—
  It cannot be nae worse wi' me."

The King was cuming thro' Caddon Ford,
  And full five thousand men was he ;
They saw the derke Foreste them before,
  They thought it awsome for to see.

Then spak the lord, hight Hamilton,
  And to the nobil King said he,
" My sovereign liege, sum council tak,
  First at your nobilis, syne at me.

" Desyre him mete thee at Permanscore,
  And bring four in his cumpanie ;
Five Erles sall gang yoursell befor,
  Gude cause that you suld honour'd be.

" And, gif he refuses to do that,
  We 'll conquess baith his landis and he ;
There sall nevir a Murray, after him,
  Hald land in Ettricke Foreste free."—

Then spak the kene Laird of Buckscleuth,
  A stalworthe man, and sterne was he—
" For a King to gang an Outlaw till,
  Is beneath his state and his dignitie.

" The man that wons yon Foreste intil,
  He lives by reif and felonie !
Wherefore, brayd on, my sovereign liege
  Wi' fire and sword we 'll follow thee ;
Or, gif your courtrie lords fa' back,
  Our Borderers sall the onset gie."—

Then out and spak the nobil King
  And round him cast a wilie ee—
" Now, had thy tongue, Sir Walter Scott,
  Nor speak of reif nor felonie :
For, had every honest man his awin kye,
  A right poor clan thy name wad be !"—

The King then call'd a gentleman,
  Royal banner-bearer there was he ;
James Hoppringle of Torsonse, by name ;
  He cam and knelit upon his kné.

" Wellcum, James Pringle of Torsonse !
  A message ye maun gang for me :
Ye maun gae to yon Outlaw Murray,
  Surely where bauldly bideth he.

" Bid him mete me at Permanscore,
  And bring four in his companie ;
Five erles sall cum wi' mysell,
  Gude reason I suld honour'd be,

" And gif he refuses to do that,
  Bid him luke for nae gude o' me !
There sall nevir a Murray, after him,
  Have land in Ettricke Foreste free."

James cam before the Outlaw kene,
  And served him in his ain degré—
" Welcum, James Pringle of Torsonse !
  What message frae the King to me ?"—

" He bids ye meet him at Permanscore,
  And bring four in your cumpany ;
Five erles sall gang himsell befor,
  Nae mair in number will he be.

And gif you refuse to do that,
  (I freely here upgive wi' thee),
He 'll cast yon bonny castle down,
  And make a widowe o' that gay ladye.

" He 'll loose your bluidhound Borderers,
  Wi' fire and sword to follow thee ;
There will never a Murray, after thysell,
  Have land in Ettrick Foreste free."—

" It stands me hard," the Outlaw said ;
  " Judge gif it stands na hard wi' me,
Wha reck not losing of mysell,
  But a' my offspring after me.

" My merryemen's lives, my widowe's teirs—
    There lies the pang that pinches me ;
When I am straught in bluidie eard,
    Yon castell will be right dreirie.

" Auld Halliday, young Halliday,
    Ye sall be twa tae gang wi' me ;
Andrew Murray, and Sir James Murray,
    We 'll be nae mae in cumpanie."—

When that they cam before the King,
    They fell before him on their kné—
" Grant mercie, mercie, nobil King !
    E'en for his sake that dyed on tree."—

" Siccan like mercie sall ye have ;
    On gallows ye sall hangit be !"—
" Over God's forbode," quoth the Outlaw
    then,
    " I hope your grace will bettir be !
Else, ere you come to Edinburgh port,
    I trow thin guarded sall ye be :

" Thir landis of Ettricke Foreste fair,
    I wan them from the enemie ;
Like as I wan them, sae will I keep them,
    Contrair a' kingis in Christentie.

All the nobilis the King about,
    Said pitie it were to see him dee—
" Yet grant me mercie, sovereign prince,
    Extend your favour unto me !

" I 'll give thee the keys of my castell,
    Wi' the blessing o' my gaye ladye,
Gin thou 'lt make me sheriffe of this
    Foreste,
    And a' my offspring after me."—

" Wilt thou give me the keys of thy castell,
    Wi' the blessing of thy gaye ladye ?
I 'se make thee sheriffe of Ettricke Foreste,
    Surely while upward grows the tree ;
If you be not traitour to the King,
    Forfaulted sall thou nevir be."—

" But, Prince, what sall cum o' my men ?
    When I gae back, traitour they 'll ca' me.
I had rather lose my life and land,
    Ere my merryemen rebuked me."—

" Will your merryemen amend their lives ?
    And a' their pardons I grant thee—
Now, name thy landis where'er they lie,
    And here I RENDER them to thee."—

" Fair Philiphaugh is mine by right,
    And Lewinshope still mine shall be ;
Newark, Foulshiells, and Tinnies baith,
    My bow and arrow purchased me.

" And I have native steads to me,
    The Newark Lee and Hanginshaw ;
I have mony steads in the Forest schaw,
    But them by name I dinna knaw."

The keys of the castell he gave the King,
    Wi' the blessing o' his feir ladye ;
He was made sheriffe of Ettricke Foreste,
    Surely while upward grows the tree ;
And if he was na traitour to the King,
    Forfaulted he suld never be.

Wha ever heard, in ony times,
    Siccan an outlaw in his degré,
Sic favour get befor a King,
    As did the OUTLAW MURRAY of the Foreste
    free ?

Reading this ballad, one is brought irresistibly in mind of Robin Hood, who with his merry men, clad in Lincoln green, held court in Sherwood Forest as the Outlaw is represented doing in Ettrick Forest. To complete the parallel, Robin, at the invitation of King Edward II. (who had much of the playful familiarity of James IV.), left the forest, and met his sovereign near its out- Brochure, Rev. Jos. Hunter, 1852. skirts, the interview ending in his outlawry being given up for an appoint- ment under the King. Historical investigation has also stripped Robin Hood of much of the romance in which he was clothed by ancient ballads.

It is further impossible to doubt that the "Sang of the Outlaw Murray" was written by some one familiar with Pitscottie's account of the death of Johnnie Armstrong.

THE SHAW.

The lands of The Shaw, lying to the east of the burgh of Selkirk, were granted by James v., in 1528, to William Ker in liferent, and Ade Kerr, his son and heir. The charter conveys "the eastern dominical lands, the east mains of Selkirk, called Saint Helen's Shaw (within boundaries specified), with the tower and mill; with an ancient toft and croft, the Kilcroft; the land called Caponland, and the other land called the Gersland of Selkirk, formerly held by Archibald, Earl of Angus, and now in the King's hand by the said Archibald's forfeiture." These Kerrs were probably of the same stock as the Sunderlandhall family, the wife of Ade Kerr, above mentioned, being Jonet Newtoun, the wealthy heiress of Dalcoif. In 1704, Shaw is found in possession of the Waughs, a family of ancient name, connected for many years with the administration of affairs in both county and burgh. William Waugh had a son, Andrew, and a grandson, William, who both married Plummers of Sunderlandhall, a daughter of the latter marrying Charles Scott, Laird of Woll, whose grandson, Charles, succeeded to the estate of Sunderlandhall, and assumed the name of Plummer. Shaw Tower still stood in 1716, and was probably the house which is recorded as having fallen in 1777, on the 18th December, burying a mother and son. Alarm being given in the town, many hurried out both on horse and on foot, in time to rescue the young man, but too late to save his mother, who was crushed dead beneath the roof.

Margin note: G. S., iii. 645, 2033.

Margin note: P. R.

SUNDERLANDHALL.

The first known possessors of this estate were the powerful Cockburns of Henderland, one of whom, Peter by name, got a charter from Robert II. in 1383, of the lands of Henriland and others in Peeblesshire, and of "Sundreland, with the manor thereof," in the county of Selkirk, resigned by Peter de Cockburne, his father. It appears to have continued in the family till 1463, when it was forfeited by William Cockburn, for assistance given by him to the traitor James of Douglas. James III. then granted the lands to William Douglas of Cluny, creating them (along with the lands of Cranston in Midlothian, Traquair and Leithenhope in Peeblesshire, forfeited by the deceased William Murray), into a free barony, to be held by Douglas and his lawful heirs for ever, upon payment of a red rose at the feast of St. John the Baptist.

Margin note: G. S., i. 163.

Margin note: R. C., 124.

Margin note: G. S., ii. 775.

Douglas was Warden of the Merse from 1466, and was recipient of various F. R.
rents, certain fines in the Court of Ettrick Forest also falling to his share. vii. var.
In 1474, however, the Cockburns again appear in possession, young William
getting a grant of half the lands of Sundirland and Sundirlandhall on their
resignation by his father William.   Young Cockburn married Katherine,
sister to Robert Rutherford of Chatto; and their daughter, becoming the wife
of Sir Walter Scott, was ancestress of the great race of Buccleuch.

In 1498, Robert Ker in Sonderlandhall sold his lands of Esseliebank to A. P.,
Sir William Douglas for 240 merks Scots, to be paid "on one day between Cavers
sunrise and sunset in the Parish Church of Jedworcht, upon the altar of St. Chart.
Mary the Virgin."   Along with Ker of Linton, James Ker in Farnylee, and MSS.,
nine others, "Mr." Thomas Ker of Sounderlandhall was fined in 1528 for not Pit.,
appearing to underly the law for poaching.   Coming to the Park of Ormiston, i. 139.
under silence of night, armed with lances and other invasive weapons,
breaking up the gates thereof, and with bows and dogs chasing and wounding
the "parkit deir," they also attacked and wounded the keepers, mutilating
one of them, named Thomas Anderson.   Ker must have been a man of
learning, as he is again designated "Mr." in 1534, when he was fined for
absenting himself from an assize for the trial of Lord Sympil and his clan for
slaughter.   About this time the lands (still held in separate halves) appear to P. S.,
have passed for a while from the family of Ker; for in 1525 they are mentioned 121.
as the property of Robert Lauder of Lauder, who then gifted them to his son G. S.,
Robert; and in 1566, Robert Lauder of that ilk, in respect of Richard, his son, iii. 344.
who held the lands from his father, granted Sounderland and Sounderlandhall,
along with other lands, to Margaret, sister of Robert Cairncross of Colmslie, in
liferent.   The other half of the estate was granted in 1532 to James Flemyng, G. S.,
one of the King's pages of honour, by reason of the forfeiture of William 2379.
Cockburn of Henderland, executed in 1530 for levying black-mail.   Nine years
later, on James Flemying's death, the lands were confirmed to his brother,
Malcolm Lord Flemying.   Early in the seventeenth century one half of the
lands are mentioned in a taxt roll of the county as belonging to John Lord
Fleming, and the other half to James Lauder of that ilk.   Appearing before
the King and Council in 1591, Thomas Ker of Sunderlandhall and other P. C.,
Border lairds gave their oaths of service to the Wardens, especially in pursuit 810.
of Francis Earl of Bothwell; and some months later Ker, as principal, and
Robert French of Thorniedykes as his surety, gave caution that he would
relieve the Wardens for all attempts by those for whom he was liable.   That

Ker was not at this time *bona fide* proprietor is evident from his being
summoned as "Thomas Ker *in* Sunderlandhall" for contempt of the Word
and the Sacraments.   Neither he nor his wife, who was included in the
summons, thought fit to appear.   In the critical period from 1643 to 1649
Andrew Ker of Sunderlandhall was a Commissioner of War, his place being
mentioned by Elliot and Scott as one of the principal houses in the shire.
From 1661 to 1685 the name of William Ker occurs repeatedly in Acts of
Parliament as on various Commissions.

On the failure of the main line, Sunderlandhall became the property of
William Plummer of Middlestead, who had married Jean, daughter of the
last laird Ker ; and in 1841 the Plummers also ended without male heirs of
the name.   Charles Scott Plummer, son of Charles Balfour Scott, W.S.,
Edinburgh, and grandson of Scott of Woll, inherited the estates through
his grandmother, who was a Miss Waugh, heiress of Shaw, and great-grand-
daughter of the first Andrew Plummer.   He took a deep interest in the
affairs of the county, of which he was convener for some years.   From the
beginning he identified himself closely with the Volunteer movement, becoming first captain of the Selkirk company, and afterwards major of the
battalion.   He died in 1879, in the fifty-eighth year of his age.   By his wife
Sophia, daughter of Joseph Goff, Esq. of Halepark, Hants, he left two
sons and two daughters, one of whom is married to Mr. R. J. Lang, younger
of Broadmeadows.   Mr. C. H. Scott Plummer, the present laird, was born in
1859, and served with the 86th Regiment for some time in Bermuda.   In
him meet the learned line of Plummer, the ancient blood of Scott of Woll
and Sinton, and the fervid race of Kerrs of Yair and Sunderland—a combination fitly representative of the past history of the Forest.

The estate of Sunderland presents several points of historical interest.
By some learned writers it has been identified as the site of a great Arthurian
battle ; and it is near enough the formidable entrenchments of Rink to have
been the scene of some of the hard fighting waged around that stronghold.
Indeed the Catrail, after passing Rink, crosses Tweed at Howden Potts and goes
straight up the outskirts of Sunderlandhall policy to where it crosses the Yair
and Selkirk road.   Mr. Wight gives us a pleasant picture of the young laird
who became Sheriff and a man of letters, realising the Horatian beatitude—

"Ut prisca gens mortalium,
Paterna rura bobus exercet suis,
Solutus omni foenore."

P. R.,
1613.

A. P., vi.
passim.

MSS.
Adv.
Lib.,
1649.

Agr.
Sur.,
1777,
iii. 9.

Sunderlandhall he describes as " mostly of a soil capable of high improvement, and the young gentleman extremely fortunate as to the means, shell-marl being lately discovered there in plenty, which answers the nature of his soil to perfection."   After observing that Mr. Plummer has " luckily both talents and industry to make the most of these advantages," Mr. Wight goes on to attack with some severity his method of cultivation, "regretting particularly that this young improver continues four horses in his plough, excusing himself from the vast quantity of a sort of bramble called the *Lady's Garter*, that overruns the ground with strong roots as soon as laid in grass."   Liberal praise, however, attends his efforts as a store-farmer, by which he has greatly improved the flock on his hill-farm.   Tradition and document are alike silent as to the whereabouts of the first house—no doubt a stronghold of the Border type—the present elegant mansion (a type dear to the eye and heart of Mr. Ruskin), being of warm red stone, framed in green foliage.   The foundation-stone was laid in 1850.   Not many houses stand more pleasantly " fast by the river Tweed."   From its coign of vantage, on the first grassy slope just above the meeting of the waters, Tweed and Ettrick are seen on either side, hastening to mingle at the corner of a broad level delta formed by centuries of denudation.   It is now a beautiful green haugh, broken up by clumps of timber, and plentifully stocked with picturesque " Highlanders " lazily grazing the old pasture.   Mr. Scott Plummer possesses a fine specimen of the old bronze camp-kettle, which was found in the course of excavation in front of the house in 1791.

Now part of the estate of Sunderlandhall is a small farm known at one time as Oven's Close and latterly as Ettrickbank, which the county of Roxburgh steals across Ettrick to enclose.   In all likelihood it is the land on the other side of the river which was set aside by King Alexander at the same time as Bridgelands to defray the costs of keeping Ettrick bridge in repair.   In the Rent Roll of 1567 " Vins Clos " is put down as paying £1 Ret. I. G., yearly to Kelso Abbey; and in 1628 William Brown is retoured heir to his 1411. brother John in Unisclois de Sunderland.

TODRIG.

This estate, a large oblong lying on both sides of Todrig Burn, between the parishes of Kirkhope and Ashkirk—is a wild tract of land, quite detached from the rest of the parish, the farmhouse being six miles as the crow flies

from Selkirk Church, and its extremity two miles further south at a water-
E. R.,
vi. 225.
shed 1238 feet above the sea. In the earliest list of Forest holdings it is one
of the " two westmost steads of Langhope;" but mention of " Archibald of
Todrig" in the Acts of the Lords Auditors only sixteen years later (1471)
would seem to show that even then it had a name of its own. For helping
certain Elliots and Armstrongs to sweep Whitmuir clean of cattle and goods,
Pit.,
i. 19.
and for other acts of interference with the rights of private property, Hector
Lauder, brother to the laird of Todrig, produced a remission at Jedburgh
in 1494. By a charter of James IV., in 1511, the lands of " Todrick "
G. S.,
ii. 3692.
were regranted to John Lord Hay of Yester, and included in the free barony
of Oliver Castle—the rent of Todrig being three arrows at the three principal
courts of Selkirkshire. Before the century had run out, however, the lands,
Thrl.
MSS.
following the fate of most others in the Forest, became the property of the
prevailing clan, and in 1580 Walter Scott of Todrig signed the bond which
united all of his name under the chieftainship of Buccleuch. One result was
P. C.,
iii. 382.
that in the year following he found himself summoned, with innumerable other
Scotts, to hear himself declared liable to the penalties of perjury, defamation,
loss of perpetual honour, with much other high-sounding disparagement which
ought to have made sensitive freebooters wince within their leathern coats.
P. R.,
1614.
" Young Wat Scott in Todrig " seems to have been a thorn in the flesh of the
Presbytery, which had to instruct the minister of Selkirk to enter in process
against him for his contumacious disobedience to the Session. And, as if one
of such a family were not quite enough, the reverend fathers had, in the
course of a twelvemonth, to inhibit the ministers of Selkirk and Ashkirk
against proceeding in the proclamation of " Wat Scot in Ashenside " with
Katrine Ormiston, because Jonet Scott, daughter to Wat Scott of Todrig,
alleged she had a promise of marriage of him. But Jonet was unable to prove
A. P.,
vi. (1)
51, seq.
her claim, and two months later the young farmer of Essenside was made
happy with his chosen love. Thomas, laird of Todrig, appointed in 1643 a
A. P.,
vii. 421,
etc.
Commissioner of War for his shire, was fined £1200 in 1662 for having sided
with the Commonwealth. His son Walter figures as a Commissioner of
Supply in 1690, and is the laird appealed to by Satchells, in his pastoral to
Sat.,
ii. 22.
Whitslade, not to be ashamed of being called a shepherd swain for the
purposes of poetry. The Todrig Scotts were closely related to those of Whitslade, if not in some generations identical, one George of Todrig being an
uncle of William of Harden (Boltfoot), who died in 1563. True to the family
tradition, Thomas of Todrig claimed the attention of Presbytery for a while,

certain disorders which occurred in Selkirk Kirk on two Lord's Days of September 1707 being the immediate reason.

" On the first of these two days, Mr. George Ridpath (a probationer of the Church), and P. R., Mr. William M'Ghie (the minister), went into that seat which is in controversy betwixt the [1708.] laird of Todrig and the said Mr. William M'Ghie, in time of divine worship, where two of Todrig's servants were sitting. One of the latter rose and gave place to them, but the other, to wit Wᵐ M'Millan, would not suffer them to go above him. Thereupon Mr. Ridpath endeavoured to pull down the said William by taking him by the waist, who still resisted, and beat Mr. Ridpath's shin-bones with his heels. Mr. Ridpath took him by the neck and held him for some time, the said M'Millan still threatening to beat him with his fist. The second Sunday Mr. M'Ghie had ordered his own servant and another young man to go to the church and keep possession of the seat. Todrig's servants came between the second and third bells, and Mr. M'Ghie's servants hindered them to come into the seats. M'Millan tried to get over the broadside, but was thrust back upon the ground by James Scott. M'Millan then beat Scott with a staff. The saids persons were then committed to prison and fined by the Sheriff the morrow after."

Thomas Scott, younger of Todrig, was admitted Commissioner of Supply C. R. in 1709, and in 1714 joined in a petition for the disjunction of Whitslade's lands. He sold Todrig in 1748, and in 1785 George Pott was proprietor.

President Lincoln used to say he would give a great deal to know who was the author of a poem which he had cut out of a newspaper and learned by heart—" O why should the Spirit of Mortal be Proud ?" The author was William Knox, son of a tenant in Todrig. Born in 1789 at Firth, near Lilliesleaf, he was well educated, first at the parish school, and then at the Grammar School of Musselburgh. After five years' unsuccessful farming of Wrae, near Langholm, Knox returned in 1817 to the parental roof at Todrig, where he did much to encourage Henry Scott Riddell, another poet of repute, who was then shepherd with his father. Having fallen from easy into straitened circumstances, his parents left Todrig for Edinburgh in 1820, where William devoted himself to literary work, some of it attracting the notice of Sir Walter Scott, Professor Wilson, and other men of letters. But the habits which had hindered his success as a farmer gained a stronger hold, and the too genial poet died of paralysis five years after settling in Edinburgh. His was the poetry of pessimism. *Vanitas vanitatum.* Life's fleetness and death's certainty are the prevailing notes in the poem by which he will achieve immortality—that which so deeply impressed the ill-fated President. So closely was it identified with Lincoln, that nearly the entire press of Canada and the States published as his work the lines which had actually been written by the son of a tenant of Todrig.

WILLIAMHOPE.

A £6 Forest-stead of the King's in 1455, Williamhope is a bleak farm, lying on the watershed between Tweed and Yarrow, mostly on the slope towards Tweed. It is the "summer hill" of Scott's wonderfully-painted picture of winter in the Forest.

> " The sheep before the pinching heaven
> To sheltered dale and down are driven,
> Where yet some faded herbage pines,
> And yet a watery sunbeam shines ;
> In meek despondency they eye
> The wither'd sward and wintry sky,
> And far beneath their summer hill,
> Stray sadly by Glenkinnon's rill."

Alone of all the hopes in Selkirkshire it has a Christian name for its first half; and it is perhaps a pardonable guess that the death near it of William Earl of Douglas, in 1353, may have had something to do with the designation. In 1548 a tack of Williamhope for nineteen years was given to William, eldest son of Sir Walter Scott of Buccleuch ; but he dying in four years, the lands appear to have been granted to Pringle of Newhall. Pitcairn records a violent quarrel, followed by reprisals, between Pringle and Cranston of Cranston, tacksman of the neighbouring stead of Hawthorne. From Queen Mary, Thomas Ker of Mersington obtained a grant "for his sure infeftment in the lands of Williamhope, heritable right having been given to the said Thomas by the father and uncle of her Majesty." The lands were in 1605 bought by John and William Stoddart, descendants of a laird of Baillielees (see Helmburn), and remained in possession of the family until 1770. In Torwoodlee's account of the " Sufferings of the Shire of Forest after the battle of Drumclog " (1679), he says :—

Margin notes: P. S., xxii. 25. / P. S., i. 433. / P. S., xxxii. 132. / Stod. Songs, Pref. x., seq. / Wod. MSS. xxxvi., Art. 37.

> "Mr. Stodheard of Williamhope had long been an eyesore to the oppressors, whom at last they seized, and having tossed him from one person to another to bring him to a compliance with the Episcopal clergy and ensnaring oaths of that time to no purpose, they at length turned him off, at the expense of three years' rent of his estate. One of his brethren, William Stodheard, was so closely pursued after being at Bothwell Brig, as they supposed he could find no shelter but among the hills ; and having endured all the hardships easily supposable in such a way of living, died at length in the fields."

Margin note: B. A., Sept. 1860.

Till recent times there was an artificial subterranean chamber, known as " the Brownie's Cave," near the foot of the steep bank of Glenkinnon Burn, a little below the farm-house. Inside, it was sixteen feet square, surrounded with walls about five feet thick, built of unhewn stones and clay. The slope of the bank came down over the whole, preventing any suspicion that such a retreat existed. This cave was destroyed in the course of agricultural improvements, when an incredible quantity of stones, some of enormous size, were taken out.

John Stoddart, in 1690, was nominated Commissioner of Supply by Act A. P., of Parliament; and in 1749, when Ogilvie of Hartwoodmyres had to resign ^{ix. 138.} the Collectorship on account of his suspicious conduct during the Rebellion, C. R. John Stoddart of Williamhope obtained the post. This laird had previously acquired the lands of Hartwoodburn from the Currors. Besides their own land, the Stoddarts farmed the extensive hill steadings of Tinnis and Lewinshope; but one of them, going into the Baltic trade at Leith, was compelled by reverses in business, and the claims of a large family, to sell his estates in 1770. Williamhope was bought for Mr. Innes of Stow, from whom it descended to the late Alexander Mitchell of Stow, M.P., and after his death to his widow, now Lady Reay. It is recorded of John Stoddart, the Collector, that on account of his great strength and extraordinary length of arm he was called The Beetle of Yarrow; and at Yarrow manse Dr. Russell (elder) used to show a stone which it took four or five men to carry, and which Stoddart had lifted without assistance. He married Martha Muir, widow of Mr. Dalgleish, Fastheuch, the lady after his death marrying a third husband—Mr. John Curror or Currie, Lindean. Her oldest son by Mr. Stoddart, John, married Miss Veitch of The Glen, and lived to the age of seventy-three, being succeeded by his oldest son, Thomas, who sold the paternal acres, and left twelve children. Two of his seven sons held commissions in the army and three were in the royal navy, of whom one had an extraordinary experience of active service. He was the third son, and was born in 1768. When just entered in his teens, he took a voyage to Calcutta, under his uncle's charge, at fourteen was entered midshipman on board the *Exeter*, 64 guns, and two months after was in action with the French off Cuddalore. With permission, he entered the Russian Navy, and was present, in 1788-9, in two engagements with the Turkish fleet, as well as in a desperate fight between the Swedes and Russians, when he was wounded. Re-entering the British service, he was under Lord Howe, in the action of 1st June 1794, shared in Lord Bridport's *rencontre* with the French the year following, witnessed the capture of the Dutch squadron in Saldanha Bay, and from 1796 to 1799 was stationed at the Cape. Attached to the *Kent* in 1801, he was mentioned with praise both by Sir Ralph Abercromby and Sir Sidney Smith, for his services in

Egypt, the Turkish Government presenting him with a gold medal and a sword. Commanding the *Cruizer*, 18 guns, in 1807, he took two privateers of 16 guns each, retook two British merchant brigs, and liberated the crews of three others who had fallen into the hands of the enemy. One son of this hero became Admiral James Stoddart; another was Mr. Thomas Tod Stoddart, author of several passable songs and books upon Angling, and long a familiar form in the best literary circles of Edinburgh and the Scottish provinces. His intense love of Border ballads found expression in "The Incentive :"—

> " Who so fondly, who so truly
>   Loves the country of his birth ?—
> Who will guard it so securely,
>   Knowing best its inner worth ?—
> As the searcher of its story,
>   As the student of its song—
> He who cons its page of glory,
>   When the right o'ercame the wrong?"

But it is as the guardian-poet of Tweed he is perhaps at his strongest :—

> Of our Rivers still the Glory!
>   God defend it! there is need;
> For the Demon of Pollution
>   Campeth on the banks of Tweed.
>
> See the tents of the Invader!
>   How they spread on every hand,
> Pitched by devilish intention
>   O'er the marrow of the land!
>
> Count the forces of the Upstart,
>   Smoke-begrimed and dimly seen
> On and under the horizon,
>   Blackening the blue and green.
>
> Pelf and Self! the double Demon!
>   From its clutch, good God, deliver!
> Save from taint of the defiler,
>   Save, O save, our dearest River!

THE YAIR.

By way of illustrating the frequent change of initial G, to Y, in Celtic names of places, Chalmers instances the river Yare in England; and, following up this cue, a still more accomplished etymologist says there can be no doubt that Yair is from the same root as Yarrow—the British word *garw*—what is rough, rugged, a torrent. Undoubtedly, however, the name has a different derivation and significance—being simply the Scotch word for an enclosure used to catch fish. When King Malcolm IV. confirmed the charter granted to the monks of Melrose by his father, he added to their possessions the fishery of Selkirk (piscaturam de Seleschirche), which he elsewhere called "my fishery." William the Lion indorsed the gift; and, in 1247, Alexander II. issued a special charter of Yair (carta de Yhar) endowing the monks not only "with that fishing upon Tweed which is called the Selkirk fishery," but with seven acres of land, buildings, a meadow, pasture in Wauchope for eight cows and eight oxen, besides timber in the forest for the maintenance and repair of the weir of the said fishery—all in free gift for the honour of God and of the glorious Virgin His Mother, as well as for the salvation of the King himself, his ancestors, and successors. Cruives or Yairs were extensively used for catching fish in early times, and were the subject of frequent and energetic legislation. While those "set in waters quhair the sea fillis and ebbis" were often ordered to be displaced for three years or so at a time, and more than once, "statut to be alŭtly destroyed and put done," yairs in position up rivers continued to be tolerated, as less hurtful to the breed of fish and "the commoun weill." Eventually, however, these also had to succumb, "unless erected under express infeftment of salmon-fishing." The visit of a Royal Commission to Skye, in 1883, brought to light the existence of a "yair," or stone enclosure for catching fish at the head of Loch Snizort. Interdicts against its use proving of no avail, the yair had been broken by order of the Sheriff; but what was destroyed during day was invariably built during night. Even after it had been completely removed, a number of crofters "rose" and rebuilt it. So strong was the determination of the men, that they were prepared to assemble at a preconcerted signal to prevent its destruction, which could only be achieved by strong police or military assistance. "The Yair" must have been some such deadly trap for the finny tribe to be thought worth so many charters and confirmations; and if

> The monks of Melrose had good kail
> On Fridays when they fasted,

Yair must have provided them with good fish as well.

In 1455, two steads of "Yare," in the ward of Yarrow, contributed £12 Scots yearly to the Royal Exchequer; and, more than likely, Thomas of Yare, a thriving merchant of Edinburgh, having great dealings with the Court, owed

[margin notes: Veitch, 53. / L. M., 5, 11, 13. / A. P., Ind., 403. / Glasg. Citiz. / E. R., vi. 225.]

T. A., 19, 112, etc.

it his surname. It does not become identified with any of the great Border families till the end of the fifteenth century, when it is mentioned as the property of a Kerr—related to the powerful family of Fernihirst, now ennobled in the person of the Marquis of Lothian. In 1504, William Kerr of Yair obtained a charter for the lands of Mertoun, in Roxburghshire, and next year a royal concession of the lands of Batts, Heatherlie, Skinnercroft, Kilncroft, 18 acres on Muryson's hill west of the Milnburn, Mauldisheuch, Serjeantsland,

G. S., ii. 2787, 2847.

and Cowperland, and all the other crofts and acres within the burgh and liberty of Selkirk which belonged to Richard Keyne, together with the offices of coroner and serjeant of the county; which, for a certain sum of money owed by the said Richard to the King, had been valued and sold by John Murray of Philiphaugh (Sheriff). In 1510 a letter of licence was issued to William Ker of "the Yair," to sell six husbandlands of Bold, in Peeblesshire, to James Stewart, James Sandilands, William Murray, and others. Five years after Flodden, John Pringle and his brother William obtained a deed of gift of the lands of the late William Ker of Yair, then, through his death, in the King's hands; and a gift of the marriage of Thomas Ker, his "nevoy

G. S., iii. 3133.

and heir." This Thomas married Elizabeth Crichton, got a confirmation of the Selkirk property in 1545, and was one of the Kers who, in 1547, made a

Dalz. Frag., 88.

somewhat unpatriotic alliance with the English under Somerset, and he was also among the "baronis, landit men, and substantious yemen" who got

P. C., i. 283.

letters commanding them to serve Ker of Cessfurd, Warden of the Middle Marches, better than they had been doing. One Henry Zaire was hanged

Bir. Diar., 5.

and quartered at Edinburgh Cross for being at the slaughter of David Rizzio —if not a Ker, probably descended from an earlier occupant of the Forest-stead.

P. C., ii. 118, 493.

It would be with reluctance, if not with a secret reservation, that William Ker of the Yair signed a bond in 1571, to rise against the head of his clan, the laird of Fairnihirst. In 1576, his successor, Andrew by name, was directed by the Privy Council to pay the mails of his steading of the Yair, amounting to £30, in ten days, under pain of rebellion; and fifteen years later

P. C., iv. 709, 791. Bord. Mem., 115.

we find him surety in 1000 merks for George Pringle of Blindlee. When Ker of Linton was killed in 1582, Andrew was party to a bond made at Melrose, referring to the quarrel. Little is known of the family from this time till 1636, when the property was sold to General Patrick Ruthven on his return from the service of Gustavus Adolphus. The last mention of them is in 1645, when Mr. Andrew Ker, quartermaster to the Earl of Lothian's

Regiment, petitioned Parliament concerning a certain part of the purchase A. P., money of Yair, due to his late father and uncle, and now to himself. The $\overset{\text{vi. (1)}}{\underset{350.}{}}$ Kers of Yair lie in Melrose Abbey, their last resting-place being marked by the simple and beautiful inscription—

Heir lyis the race of the hous of Zair.

Patrick Ruthven, the new laird of Yair, a great-grandson of the first Lord Ruthven, sided with King Charles, who created him Lord Ruthven of Ettrick in 1639. After refusing to surrender Edinburgh Castle to the Parliament, he was forced to capitulate, obtaining honourable conditions. Parliament A. P., v. passed a special Act permitting him to return to his house and dwelling of the $\overset{375, 382.}{}$ Yair, and to resort within the parish of Selkirk; and another rescinding his forfeiture, at the earnest suit of General Leslie. Created Earl of Forth in 1642, he was second in command at the battle of Edgehill, the chief command falling upon him after the fatal wounding of Lord Lindsay. He was then nearly 70 years of age, and is described by Lord Clarendon "much decayed in his parts, and, with the long-continued custom of immoderate Hist., drinking, dozed in his understanding, which had never been quick and $\overset{\text{ii. 481.}}{}$ vigorous, he having always been illiterate to the greatest degree. . . . In the field he well knew what was to be done." For defeating the Parliamentary forces at Brentford, that name was added to his title. A second forfeiture, passed upon him in 1644, was recalled in 1647, "in consideration of his deportment abroad in foreign service, his respective carriage to his countrymen elsewhere, his remorse and sorrow for giving any occasion of dislike or offence to his native country, his offer to subscribe the Covenant, and his assurance of good behaviour in time coming." To Yair, however, he seems not to have returned, but died at Dundee in January 1651, about eighty years of age. His affairs being greatly embarrassed, his lands were attached by creditors. Yair passed to James Pringle of Whytbank, who had advanced money to his lordship in his difficulties. Whytbank's brother, Major George Pringle of Balmungo, an old comrade of Ruthven in the Thirty Years' War, had married the latter's daughter Elizabeth; and, as their grandson succeeded to Yair in 1685, the present laird, who is directly descended from them, has the blood in his veins, of the gallant old soldier Patrick Lord Ruthven of Ettrick, Earl of Forth and Brentford. With two interruptions, Yair has belonged to the A. P., xi. Pringles since they first possessed it. The first break was in 1703, when $\overset{\text{App. 143.}}{}$ Mr. John Murray, advocate, after the laird's death, obtained a charter from

A. P. ix.,
App. 143.
Queen Anne of the lands and barony of "Yare," including Craig, and of the lands of Whytbank and others, all of new erected in the barony of Yare. This was ratified by Parliament in 1707, but seems to have concealed a family arrangement; for, both in that year and in 1711, Sir Patrick Scott of Ancrum, B. R. grandfather of the infant heir, acted as tutor of Yair in a dispute with the burgh of Selkirk. Overborne by the expenses of a large family and other burdens, Alexander Pringle was compelled, in 1759, to alienate Yair, which was bought by the guardians of the young Duke of Buccleuch. Twenty-five years afterwards, it was repurchased by his son Alexander, who had acquired a fortune in India, and to whom Duke Henry generously gave the opportunity. By him the present house was built in 1789. The old one was among the Ell. & Sc.
MSS principal houses of the county in 1649, and one of the few embellished by woods. Yair marches with Ashiesteel, where Scott first lived after he became Sheriff of the Forest, and where he wrote *Marmion*. The cordial relations which prevailed between the poet and his near neighbours inspired some of the finest lines in his superb introduction to Canto Second:—

> "From Yair,—which hills so closely bind,
> Scarce can the Tweed his passage find,
> Though much he fret, and chafe, and toil,
> Till all his eddying currents boil,—
> Her long-descended lord is gone,
> And left us by the stream alone.
> And much I miss those sportive boys,
> Companions of my mountain joys,
> Just at the age 'twixt boy and youth,
> When thought is speech, and speech is truth.
> Close to my side, with what delight
> They press'd to hear of Wallace wight,
> When, pointing to his airy mound,
> I call'd his ramparts holy ground!
> Kindled their brows to hear me speak;
> And I have smiled, to feel my cheek,
> Despite the difference of our years,
> Return again the glow of theirs."

Without being in itself beautiful, Yair House is one of the most charming residences on the upper banks of Tweed. Here the river is at its loveliest, well deserving the epithet of "silver stream," bestowed by the poetess, whose residence of Fairnalee confronts Yair from the opposite bank. A somewhat Works,
xii. extraordinary incident took place here in the summer of 1883. Looking out early in the morning, Mrs. Pringle was astounded to see a herd of elephants

disporting themselves in the boat-pool—a sight familiar enough to many of the Indian veterans of Yair, but in quite other latitudes. The elephants, seven or eight in number, belonged to a travelling menagerie, and, overcome with fatigue and the heat of a warm summer morning, had left the dusty road for the inviting river. They sported about in great enjoyment, and

The Yair.

filled their trunks with the cool water only to send it out again in high columns of spray. Wading and even swimming with an evident sense of new-found liberty, it was only with the greatest exertions of their keepers the happy beasts could be induced to leave the stream and resume their weary journey.

It is claimed for Thomas Pringle, author of the *Autumnal Excursion*, that he was the grandson of a grandson of William Pringle "who held the farm of Yair probably, as it would appear, on a feudal tenure as a kinsman of the laird, and lived in an old tower, or peel, at the foot of the Craig-hill." His literary work being unable to support him, Pringle obtained for his friends and himself an allotment of land at the Cape, where he landed in 1820. Here he found a local habitation for familiar names in the old country—

> "And the steep Sarka mountains, stern and bare,
> Close round the upland cleughs of lone Glen-Yair.
> With cattle kraals, associate or single,
> From fair Craig-Rennie up to Clifton Pringle."

In his second edition of the *Excursion*, Pringle changed "paternal Yair and Plora's glens" into "sylvan Yair and Ettrick's glens;" possibly from some doubt of his descent from the ancient family as much as for any improvement it made in the verse. He wrote much rubbish, but we would be proud to claim him for the Forest, were it only for his well-known song :—

> "Home of our hearts! our fathers' home!
>   Land of the brave and free!
> The keel is flashing through the foam
>   That bears us far from thee.
>
> Our native land—our native vale—
>   A long, a last adieu!
> Farewell to bonny Teviotdale
>   And Scotland's mountains blue."

GREENHEAD.

C.D.S.,
ii., 208,
430.
Of the few persons in Selkirkshire who swore fealty to the English King in 1296, Cristine de Greenhead, "del counte de Selkirk," was one ; and although Greenhead is now in Roxburghshire, its retention within Selkirk parish, no less than its ancient connection with the burgh, calls for its mention in these pages. When, in the reign of David II., William Greenhead forfeited the lands of that name, still in the shire of Selkirk, they fell into the hands of R. C.,
31, 36. William Brown, in whose favour the King granted a charter. Early in the sixteenth century, the Kers obtained possession—cadets of that wide-spread family which settled on the lands of Yair, Sunderlandhall, and Faldon- Pit., i.
32, 166. side. Along with Ker of Whitmuir, Alexander Grey in Greenhead was concerned in the cruel slaughter of John Furde, in the town of Selkirk, for which he produced a remission before the court at Jedburgh in 1502.

Andrew Ker of Greenhead was fined in 1534 for being absent from assize; and four years later Gilbert, son and heir of the deceased Andrew, was, with twelve others, charged with the slaughter of Andrew Hall in Bus, and P. S., xiv. 89. William, son of John Hall, upon old malice. The "laird of Greenhead" figures in Hertford's list of those who unpatriotically assisted his expedition Hert. Exp., 88. into Scotland in 1544. Eight years after this, Gilbert was knighted at Jedburgh. His son, Sir Andrew Ker, married a daughter of Wauchope of Haigs, 184. Niddrie, by whom he had seven sons known as "the seven lads of Greenhead." Along with certain Rutherfurds, the laird of Greenhead's sons were forced by King James in 1588 to "enter themselves prisoners into England," as they could not make reparation for the injuries they had done across the Border. In 1591 he gave his oath to assist the King against Bothwell; but his good P. C., iv. 643; v. 81. faith seems to have been doubted, for shortly afterwards another Ker had to become surety for £1000 that he would not reset or intercommune with the dreaded and turbulent Earl. When the Earl of Roxburgh went to London in the train of James VI., on his accession to the throne of England, he P. C., vi. 579. nominated the laird of Greenhead as answerable for the men of his clan. A temporary alienation of the estate was probably the reason why Robert Kerr, who had married the widow of a Haig of Bemersyde, was in 1638 only "*callit* of Greenhead," since fourteen years later he is styled "of Greenhead," Haigs, 244. in an odd horse-shoeing agreement between his stepson, David Haig, and a blacksmith. Sir Andrew, another of the "seven lads," was served special A. P., vii. 421. heir of his father Sir Andrew, created a baronet in 1637, in the Roxburgh-shire Committee of War from 1643 to 1649, sat in Parliament for Roxburgh in 1645 and in 1648-49, supported the Covenant, in 1660 was imprisoned in Edinburgh Castle, and in 1662 was fined £6000. By his first wife, a daughter of Scott of Harden, he left, with other issue, two sons, who both became Members of Parliament. The eldest, Sir Andrew, who succeeded him in 1665, represented Roxburghshire in several Parliaments, and died about 1676, leaving no issue by his wife, a Don of Newton-don. His brother, Sir William, obtained ratification of a royal charter to the lands of Greenhead and others, in 1681; was fined £2000 for adhering to Presbyterianism, A. P., viii. 288. represented Roxburghshire in the last Scottish Parliament, voted for Union, and was returned to the first Parliament of Great Britain. He is said to have been dead in 1721. His eldest son, Andrew, mentioned in 1698, must Fost., 204. either have predeceased or soon followed him; for, in 1726, Sir William Ker A. P., x. 131. of Greenhead was one of a party of gentlemen who demanded a warrant for the apprehension of Sir Gilbert Elliot of Stobbs for killing Colonel Stewart. Quarrelling at a meeting in Jedburgh after an election, Sir Gilbert had used language to the Colonel which made the latter throw a glass of wine in his face, upon which the baronet drew his sword and plunged it in Stewart's body while he was sitting at table.

WHITMUIR AND WHITMUIRHALL.

L. K.,
v. 13,
298, 350,
460, 490,
514, 515.

In the great charter by which King Malcolm IV., in 1159, confirmed the grants of his grandfather David I. in favour of Kelso Abbey, the lands of "Whitemere" are enumerated amongst others, the word in a charter of ratification by William the Lion being spelt Whytemere. In the short original charter by David himself (c. 1150) the town of "Vithemere" is mentioned, "Witemere" being the word in a privilege by Pope Innocent IV., about one hundred years later. From an ancient rent-roll of the monastery, it appears that the grange of "Wittemere," consisting of two plough-gates, was valued at ten merks yearly. In the town of "Wittemere" there were ten husband-lands, each of which paid a rent of six shillings, besides service the same as those in Bowden. That is to say, each tenant of a husbandland had to give four days' work in harvest and one in winter; had to furnish a cart to carry peats from Gordon Moss to the abbey; had to go once a year to Berwick with one horse, to plough every year an acre and a half in the monks' grange at Newton, to harrow one day with a horse, to find one man to assist in washing and another in shearing the sheep, to carry corn one day in autumn and wool from the barony to the abbey, and to find themselves carriages beyond the muir towards Lesmahago. Of seven cottages in the "town" of "Witte-mere," each with an acre and a half of land, three paid 5s., three 4s. 6d., and one 1s. 4d. Another without land paid 6d. Like those of Bowden, these cottagers had to give the Abbey nine days' harvest work, besides assistance in washing and shearing. The original spelling of the last name is maintained till about 1567, when "Quhitmure toune" and "Quhitmure hall" appear as paying to the abbot a rent of £10 and £5, 6s. 8d. Scots respectively, besides certain dues in "quheit, beir, and meill" to the Kirk of Selkirk. There can be little doubt that "muir" or "moor" is a change from the meaning of the original second syllable of the name "mere," signifying moss or lake, as in Winder-mere or Grasmere. Whitmuir was the scene of a sweeping raid by free-booters in 1494. Guided by a brother of the laird of Todrig, two "Elwaldes" or Elliots, and five brethren of the Armstrongs, pounced upon the place,

driving away five score of cows and oxen, besides the "whole household goods Pit.,
of the tenants of Whitmuir." Young Scott of Headshaw became security 31, 32.
that Todrig's brother would satisfy the parties. The tenants do not appear
to have been of a lamb-like disposition themselves, for, in 1502, two of them,
William Ker and James Elwalde, were incriminated in the cruel slaughter of
John Furde, in the town of Selkirk. The same pair were accused of resetting
two sons of an Elwalde, "Hob the King" and "Dand the Man," in their
treasonable deeds, specially the theft of nine score of sheep furth of Tweeddale and Lauderdale. William Dun in " Quhit*mere* " was concerned in the
stouthreif of four horses from Anthony Tait, the cruel slaughter of the said
Anthony, the theft of eight score of sheep from George Tait of Pyrne, forty
sheep from Gaithope, a horse and eighty sheep from William Cleghorn, one
hundred and sixty-six hoggs from George Tait and his tenants in Pirn and
Seathope ; seventeen "gayt" from John Cleghorne, and other goods to the
value of £40. Apparently, when the tenants of Whitmuir lost live-stock
they knew how to replenish it. The Goodman of Whitmuir and the Good- P. C., iv.
man of Whitmuirhall are both in the list of "landit men" ordered to find 783-91.
surety for all attempts done by those for whom they are responsible.

The great "white mere," which gave the place its name, having been
reduced by drainage or by "filling up" to mere morass, came at last to be
drained thoroughly ; and from the ditch works a very fine pair of horns of
the *bos primigenius*, the huge wild ox of the ancient Forest, was obtained.

The first laird of Whitmuirhall was Thomas Ker, who, being tenant at Whit.
the time, obtained a charter in 1566 from the Commendator of Kelso. His MSS.
son John left two daughters, one of whom was married to Andrew Ker,
servitor to the Earl of Roxburgh, brother-german of William Ker of Maisondieu, Andrew obtaining a resignation of the lands from his wife and her
sister in 1619. In 1650, Andrew, styling himself of Maisondieu, conveyed
the lands to Samuel Morrison, merchant burgess of Edinburgh, son of the
deceased Janet Kerr, his sister-in-law. James Morrison succeeded his father
in 1699, and was followed in possession by Margaret, daughter of his brother
Andrew, in 1738. Seven years later, George II. granted the lands of Whitmuirhall and others in gift to John Goudie, Professor of Divinity (afterwards
Principal) in Edinburgh University, as *ultimus hæres* of Margaret, which
was followed by a decree in favour of the said Professor and his son, John
Goudie, minister of the gospel at Earlstoun. The legality of this gift was
stoutly contested in every court, but the House of Lords in 1758 confirmed

the Goudies in possession. In 1761, the preacher at Earlstoun sold the lands to James Dunlop, tenant in Haining-Moat, who made a disposition to himself in liferent and his oldest son Walter and his heirs. In this family the estate has remained ever since, the present laird, Charles Walter Dunlop, Esq., having added very considerably to its extent.

Whitmuir in 1786 came into possession of Walter Dunlop of Whitmuir-hall, who left it to his second son, Archibald, who conveyed it in 1818 to a trustee for behoof of his creditors, Mr. Boyd of Broadmeadows being the purchaser. In 1851, it was bought by Mr. Murray, younger of Philiphaugh (afterwards Sir John, first baronet), from whom it passed for a time to Mr. Hay, Edinburgh. Lastly, it again (in 1880) became the property of the Dunlop family, by its purchase, on behalf of the laird of Whitmuirhall, for £18,000. This estate, like Greenhead, is in the Roxburghshire part of Selkirk parish.

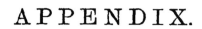

APPENDIX.

I.—CHARTA FUNDATIONIS ABBACIE APUD SCHELECHYRCH (1119-24).

(From the Chartulary of Kelso in the Advocates' Library in Edinburgh.)

DAVID comes, filius Malcolmi Regis Scottorum, omnibus amicis suis Francis et Anglis et Scottis, cunctisque sancte Dei ecclesie filiis salutem continuam. Notum sit, omnibus presentibus atque futuris, me fundasse quoddam Monasterium in Scelechyrca, scilicet, ad abbathiam, in honore sancte Marie, et sancti Johannis evangeliste, pro salute anime mee, et patris, et matris mee, fratrum et sororum meorum, omniumque antecessorum. Hujus vero Ecclesie monachis in elemosynam perpetue donavi terram de Selechyrche, sicut rivulus descendens a montibus currit in Gierua usque ad rivulum illum qui descendens de Crossinemara currit in Twoda et ultra eundem rivulum qui cadit in Gierua quandam particulam terrae inter viam que vadit de Castello ad abbathiam et Gieruam, viz., versus veterem villam. Et haec omnia ita donavi sicut melius habui, in bosco et in plano, et in aquis, et villa de Middleham, et Bothendenam, et Aldonam, sicut melius habui in terris et in aquis et in bosco et in plano. Et totum dominium meum de Malros per medium vicum et per medium fontem usque ad fossam; et sicut fossa dividit, cadens in Twoda, similiter in terris, et in aquis, et in bosco, et in plano; et in Sprostona unam carrucatam terrae et decem acras; et unam maysuram carrucatae pertinentem; et in Berwyc unam carrucatam, et unam maysuram sub ecclesia usque in Twoda : et dimidium unius piscaturae et septimam partem molendini, et quadraginta solidos de censu de burgo per unumquemque annum; et in burgo de Rokesburg unam maysuram et septimam molendini, et quadraginta solidos de censu, septimam partem piscaturae, et decimam caseorum de can scilicet de Galweia, et dimidietatem coriorium coquine mee, et de omnibus occisionibus de quibus alteram partem habeo; et similiter de unctis et de sepis sicut de coriis, et omnes pelles multonum et agnorum, et decimam coriorum cervorum et cervarum quos veltrarii mei capient. Et aquas meas circa Selechirche, communes ad piscandum suis propriis piscatoribus, ut meis; et pasturas meas, communes hominibus suis, ut meis; et boscos meos, domibus faciendis, et ad ardendum ut mihi. Et in Anglia in Hardingestrop quatuor viginti acras de terra in dominio, scilicet, cum pratis ad illud dominium pertinentibus, et unam maysuram dominio pertinentem, et duos bovarios, scilicet, quisque habet decem acras, et in ultro, sex virgatas et dimidiam de terra et sex maysuras versus pontem de Norhamtune, et quandam insulam prati juxta pontem, et molendinum ejusdem villae. Et haec omnia, supradicti monasterii monachis, ita libere et pacifice, jure perpetuo possidenda confirmavi, ut mihi succedentium nullus nihil omnino, nisi solas orationes ad anime salutem, exigere presumat. Hoc factum est Henrico rege regnante in Anglia, et Alexandro rege in Scotia, et Johanne episcopo in Glasguensi ecclesia, et Herberto abbate in eadem abbathia, et hiis testibus; supradicto Johanne episcopo; Matilda comitissa; Henrico filio comitis; Gualthelino capellano; Osberto capellano; Alwyno capellano; Willielmo nepote comitis; Roberto de Bruis; Roberto de Umfravilla; Gualtero de Bolebec; Roberto de Paintona; Gospatrico fratre dalsini; Hugone de Morvilla; Pagano de braiosa; Roberto corbet; Reginaldo de Muscamps; Gualtero de Lyndeseia; Roberto de Burnetvilla; Gospatrico vicecomite; Cospatrico filio Aldeve; Uchtredo filio Scot; Maccho; Colbano; Gillemichel; Odoardo, vicecomite de Babenburch; Lyulf filio Uchtredi; Radulfo Anglico; Aimaro galleio; Rogerio de Lerecestria; Adam Camerario.

[*Translation.*]

CHARTER OF THE FOUNDATION OF THE ABBEY OF SELKIRK (1119-24).

DAVID the Earl, son of Malcolm, King of Scots. To all his friends, French, English, and Scots, and to all the sons of the Holy Church of God, lasting salvation. Be it known to all present and to come, that I have founded a certain monastery in Selkirk, that is to say, at the Abbey in honour of St. Mary and St. John the Evangelist, for the weal of my soul, of the souls of my father and my mother, brothers and sisters, and of all my ancestors. To the monks of which church I have given in alms perpetually, the land of Selkirk from where a rivulet descending from the hills runs into Yarrow, as far as to that rivulet which, coming down from Crossinmara, flows into Tweed; and beyond the said rivulet which falls into Yarrow, a certain particle of land between the road which leads from the Castle to the Abbey and Yarrow, that is, towards the old town. And all these I have so given as I have them, in wood, in cleared ground, and in waters. And the town of Middelham (Midlem), and of Bothendenam (Bowden), and Aldona (Holydean), just as I possess them in lands, waters, wood, and cleared ground, and my whole lordship of Melrose, by the middle street and middle well, as far as the fosse, and as the fosse marches, falling into Tweed, in like manner, in lands, waters, wood, and plain. And in Sprouston, one ploughgate of land and ten acres, and one maisure (house) belonging to the plough-gate. And in Berwick, one ploughgate and one maisure, below the church as far as Tweed: and half of one fishing, and the seventh part of the mill, and forty shillings of the burgh revenue every year. And in the burgh of Roxburgh, one maisure, and seventh part of the mill, and forty shillings of rent, and seventh part of the fishing, and a tenth of the kain[1] cheeses of Galloway. And half of the skins of my kitchen, and half of all the cuttings of which I have the other part; and a like share of the suet and tallow, and of hides, and all skins of sheep and lambs, and a tenth of the hides of stags and hinds which my huntsmen shall capture. And my waters about Selkirk shall be common to be fished by their own fishermen as by mine : and my pastures common to their men and mine : and my wood to be used for building and for fuel as by me. And in England, in Hardingstrop, twenty-four acres of land in lordship, that is to say, with the meadows belonging to that lordship, and one maisure belonging to the same; and two oxgates, to wit, each having ten acres; and besides, six and a half roods of land, and six maisures near the bridge of Norhamtune, and a certain island of meadow next to the bridge; and the mill of the said town. And all these have I confirmed to the monks of the aforesaid monastery, to be possessed freely and peacefully by right for ever; in such sort that none of those succeeding to me shall presume to exact anything whatever but prayers only for the weal of his soul. This is done, Henry reigning King in England; Alexander, King in Scotland; John, Bishop in the Church at Glasgow; and Herbert, Abbot in the said Abbey; these being Witnesses—the foresaid John, the bishop; Matilda, the countess; Henry, son of the earl; Gual-theline, Osbert, and Alwyn, chaplains; William, grandson of the Earl; Robert of Bruis; Robert of Umphraville; Walter of Bolebec; Robert of Painton; Cospatric, brother of Dalsin; Hugh of Moreville; Pagan of Braios; Robert Corbet; Reginald of Muscamp; Walter of Lyndsay; Robert of Burnetville; Cospatric, the sheriff; Cospatrick, son of Aldene; Uchtred, son of Scot; Macchus; Colbanus; Gillesmichel; Odard, sheriff of Babenburch; Lyulf, son of Uchtred; Ralf Inglis; Aimer Welch; Roger of Lerecester; Adam, the chamberlain.

---

[1] Kain is rent paid in produce.

II.—THE CHARTER OF REMOVAL (1147-52).

THIS document was executed by David after he had succeeded to the throne, and bears that having founded a monastery at Abbey-Selkirk while he was Earl (*dum fui comes*) he had, because the place was not suitable for an abbey (*non conveniens abbathiae*), transferred it to Roxburgh at a place called Calkou (Kelso). He added liberally to its possessions. Besides reconveying Midlem and Bowden, he gave thirty acres of land of the territory of "Lyllesclef" between Alna (the Ale) and the stream which divides the land of Midlem and Lilliesleaf; and Withelawe (Whitelaw) with its proper marches. Confusing as are the boundaries of the land of Selkirk in the first charter, the second makes them still more so, the "particle of land beyond the stream which falls into Yarrow," being described as "between the road which leads from the castle and falls into the river above the old abbey, and Yarrow,"—*quandam particulam terrae inter viam quae venit de castello et super veterem abbathiam cadit in eodem rivulo, et Gieruam.* The Lordship of Melrose is omitted, having in the interval been conferred on the monks of the new abbey there. Tacked on to the end of this charter, after the list of witnesses, is a clause conveying also the church of Selkirk, with provision, either that the abbots or priests of that church should be chaplains to the King and his successors for ever, or that the abbots (of Kelso) should be chaplains to the King in the church of Selkirk. Subsequent mention of incumbents "of Selkirk and Old Roxburgh" favour the former interpretation, albeit it is not the most obvious.

III.—CHARTER OF MALCOLM IV., 1159.

IN this charter, confirming all grants made to the monasteries of Selkirk and Kelso by his grandfather King David, Malcolm IV. adds the tithes of Lilliesleaf Mill, and with White-law includes Whitemere (Whitmuir). As if the previously recited boundary presented difficulties, Selkirk is briefly conveyed "with its due bounds;" but there is mention of the "church of the other Selkirk, with half a ploughgate of land." It is dated at Roxburgh, and among the witnesses is Richard the Chaplain, who would be *ex officio* minister of Selkirk.

The chartulary of Kelso has been long preserved in the Advocates' Library, and contains 219 leaves of vellum. The first seven are occupied by an important Rent-roll, written before the year 1300, and prefixed to the book proper, which commences on the 8th leaf. From the handwriting and other circumstances it is probable that the first part of the chartulary was written between 1300 and 1325. To it we are indebted for both of David's charters; King Malcolm's being still extant in its original form. Doubtless it is to errors occurring in transcription that a haziness regarding Selkirk's boundaries in the two earlier documents is to be attributed. Numerous entries in the Chartulary refer to lands in the County of Selkirk.

IV.—RENTAL OF THE ABBACY OF KELSO. [*c.* 1567.]

REDDENE (LINDENE) KIRK.

	QUHEIT.	BEIR.	MEILL.
Cauldscheillis, ...		1 boll	3 bolls
Fadownsyde, ...	1 boll	5 „	8 „
Moselie and Blyndlie, ...		1 „	2 „

	QUHEIT.	BEIR.	MEILL.
The Brige Hauch, ...	2 bolls	2 bolls	4 bolls
Ferinylie and Calfschaw, ...		4½ ,,	9 ,,
Gallawscheillis and Boytsyde, . . .		1 chalder	2 chalders
Langreynk, ...		4 bolls	1 ,,

SELKIRK KIRK.

	QUHEIT.	BEIR.	MEILL.
Quhyt Mure Hall, ...		2 bolls	4 bolls
Quhyt Mure Towne, ...	1 boll	2 ,,	5 ,,
Selkirk Towne, ...		3 chalders	4 chalders
The Schaw, ...		1 boll	1½ bolls
Hartvodburne, ...			2 ,,
Haning, ...		12 ,,	1¼ chalders
Aclintour, ...		2 ,,	6 bolls
Todrige, ...		3 ,,	6 ,,
Phillophauch and Herheid, . . .		1 chalder	1½ chalders
Carterhauch, ...		2 bolls	1¼ ,,
Auld and New Vark, ...		2½ ,,	7 bolls
The Northt Bowhill, ...		1 ,,	2 ,,
South Bowhill, ...		2 ,,	4 ,,
Fawsyde, ...		2 ,,	5 ,,
Bredmedow, ...		2 ,,	3 ,,
Blakmedyngis, ...		1 ,,	2 ,,
Myddilsteid, ...		2 ,,	3 ,,
Harthvodmyris, ...		2 ,,	3 ,,
Fasthucht, ...		1 ,,	2 ,,
Crage and Yare, ...		7 ,,	15 ,,
Sunderland hall and toune, . . .		12 ,,	1 chalder
Faldhoip, ...		3 ,,	5 bolls
Grenheid, ...		2 ,,	4 ,,
Willdunhop, ...			4 ,,
Houdene, ...		2 ,,	4 ,,

THE BARROUNRIE OF BOUDENE.

	£	s	d
Towne of Lyndene, ...	£16	0	0
Mylne of Lyndene, ...	2	13	4
Quhitmure towne, ...	10	0	0
Quhitmure hall, ...	5	6	8
Fadownsyde, ...	10	0	0
Caldscheillis, ...	5	0	0
Vinsclos (now Ettrickbank), ...	1	0	0
Altowne besyde Hatrik (?), ...	5	0	0
Grenheid, ...	5	0	0

LANDIS WITHIN TWEDELL AND UTHERIS.

	£	s	d
Kirklandis of Selkirk, ...	2	0	0

THE VICAREGIS.

	£	s	d
The Vicarage of selcrik, ...	66	13	4

V.—INVENTORY OF GOODS AND GEAR of late JOHN HOPPRINGLE of Smailholm (and Galashiels) (in conformity with his Will dated 13th March 1564), made and given up by his widow MARGARET GORDON and their son DAVID.

1. Horse given by said John to his spous for her awin saddle,		£10 0 0
2. In Gallowschellis, 8 oxen at £6,		48 0 0
3. „ 6 young nolt at £2,		12 0 0
4. In the stack-yard of Gallowschellis 3 stacks of barley, or 48 bolls at 20s.,		48 0 0
5. „ „ 6 stacks of oats,=80 bolls at 11s.,		44 0 0
6. „ „ 4 bolls wheat at 30s.,		6 0 0
7. „ „ 4 bolls peas at 20s.,		4 0 0
8. Upon the steads of Moselie and Gallowschellis, pastured upon "Sisingame," 160 ewes at 10s.,		80 0 0
9. Upon "Magald" 140 ewes at 10s.,		70 0 0
10. „ Sysingame 60 wedders at 13s. 4d.,		40 0 0
11. „ Magald 160 wedders at 13s. 4d.,		106 13 4
12. „ Sysingame 30 "gimmeries and dymmoynds" at 6s. 8d.,		10 0 0
13. „ Magald 20 „ „ „		6 13 4
14. 80 hogs in "Tripirode" and 20 with David Schortred in Mydreseid at 5s.,		25 0 0
15. In Whiteside house 3 stacks barley,=36 bolls at 20s.,		36 0 0
16. „ 6 stacks oats,=60 bolls at 11s.,		33 0 0
17. 1 stack of peas,=8 bolls at 20s.,		8 0 0
18. 8 oxen at £6,		48 0 0
19. In Steichill 8 oxen at £6,		48 0 0
20. In Steichill-yaird, 2 stacks of barley,=16 bolls at 20s.,		16 0 0
21. „ 2 stacks of oats,=40 bolls at 11s.,		22 0 0
22. Utensils, etc.,		50 0 0

(Sum in document is £762, 6s. 8d.) £761 6 8

Owing to John Hoppringle by John Lord Borthwick for the teind sheaves of Stow 1556-57-58-59-60-61-62-63-64, belonging to said John as one of the tacksmen of the Kirk of Stow,	233 0 0
Owing to J. H. by late Wm. Dischington of Ardross and his heirs for the rest of his tocher goods,	66 13 4
Owing to J. H. by Thomas Hoppringle of Torsonce for the rest of his teinds of the Stow Parish,	20 0 0
Owing by Sir Thos. Gothrale of his pension of Stow Kirk,	8 0 0
Owing by And. Hoppringle in Pleuplere ½ of the teind sheaves of the lands of Pleuplere and Torquhan,	8 0 0

(In document £1100, the last £8 being evidently omitted). £1107 0 0

SUMS OWING BY DECEASED.

		£	s.	d.
1. To Andrew, son and heir of Sir James Rutherfurd of Hundalee, Knight, the rest of his tocher goods,	. . . . .	£200	0	0
2. To Andrew Haliburton of Muirhouselaw, the rest of his tocher goods,	.	100	0	0
3. To Thomas Black, ploughman of Galloschellis, 16 bolls of oats at 11s.,	.	8	16	0
4. To John & Geo. Hoppringle, servants of deceased, each for their fees, 10 marks,		13	6	8
5. To other 10 servants of deceased in his place of Gallowschellis, men and women, "ilk ane of thaim our-heid," 20s.,	. . .	10	0	0
6. To Richert Turnor, Myllar in G. Myln, in money,	. . .	10	0	0
„ „ „ 2 bolls meal, at 30s.,	. .	3	0	0
„ „ „ 1 boll malt,	. . .	1	6	8
7. To our Sovereign Lady's comptroller for the "Anderomes" (Andrewmas) mail terms of the lands and steading of Gallowschellis and Moselie, 1564,		45	0	0
8. To Mr. Andrew Hume, parson of Lauder, for twice 19 years' chaff of the teind sheaves of ——, and for the Martinmas mails thereof,	.	110	0	0
9. To John Gordon of ——, for mails of Stichel Mylne and lands within the barony of Stichel,	. . . . .	12	0	0
(In document £508, 9s. 4d.)		£513	9	4
Value of estate and debts owed to deceased,	. . . .	£1107	0	0
Amount of debts owed by deceased,	. . . .	513	9	4
(In document £594, 10s. 8d. ÷ 3 = £198, 3s. 6d.)		£593	10	8

VI.—THE RENTALL OF THE LANDS AND BARRONRIE OF GALLASCHEILES, 1656.

The Rents ar to be payed at two tearmes, viz.: Whitsonday and Mertimes as followes :—

12 SOUME MAILERES.

	Scots.				Scots.		
Williame Wilsone, elder, .	. £26	13	4	Johne Wilsone, elder, .	. £26	13	4
Rot. Haldone (and a bole malt), .	26	13	4	Adame Patersone, . .	. 26	13	4
Alexr. Speiding, . .	. 26	13	4	Robert Mabon, . . .	. 33	6	0
Johne Crouckes, . .	. 26	13	4	Williame Freier, . .	. 32	0	0
Williame Mabon, .	. 26	13	4				
Andro Peca, . . .	. 26	13	4	Summa,	£278	13	4

6 SOUME MAILERES.

George Frier, miller, .	. £15	2	8	Johne Mersell, . .	. £13	6	8
George Dabsone, . .	. 20	0	0	Thomas Gill, . .	. 13	6	8
Williame Clapertoune, .	. 30	0	0	Johne Patersone, .	. 13	6	8
Adame Haldone, . .	. 13	6	8	Jeane Dods, . .	. 13	6	8
Johne Purvis, . .	. 13	6	8	Johne Haldone, elder, .	. 13	6	8

	Scots.				Scots		
Jennet Frater,	£13	6	8	Rot. Speiding,	£13	6	8
Rot. Clekie,	13	6	8	Rot. Broune,	20	0	0
Johne Wilsoune, yr.,	20	0	0	Issobell Young,	20	0	0
Gorge Patersone, burgis,	13	6	8	Williame Wilsone, weifer,	30	0	0
Adame Wilsone,	15	0	0	James Wightman,	6	13	4
Wm. Wilsone, younger,	13	6	8	Andro Scletter,	6	13	4
Gorge Frier, called ballie,	13	6	8				
Gorge Young,	13	6	8	*Summa,*	£370	2	8

COATTERS SOWING A BOLE OF CORNE.

Thomas Patersone,	£10	0	0	Adame Sadler,	£8	0	0
Hew Young,	10	0	0	Johne Persone,	8	0	0
Jennet Blekie,	10	0	0	James Clennane,	8	0	0
James Mophit,	12	0	0	Richart Frater,	8	0	0
Williame Patersone, weifer,	11	0	0	Jo. Patersone, weifer,	8	0	0
Johne Haldone, younger,	10	0	0	(Jo. Clagorne entered at Mert. 1656			
Dand Peca,	13	6	8	and pays £20 in the year.)			
Archbald Wilsone,	10	0	0	Thomas Couke,	8	0	0
Jennet Andersone,	24	0	0	James Taiet,	8	0	0
Jo. Hervie,	8	0	0	Thomas Watsone, garner,	8	0	0
Johne Gill,	13	6	8	Jennet Williamsone,	8	0	0
Robert Frier, talior,	8	0	0				
Robert Morice,	8	0	0	*Summa,*	£219	13	4

COATERS SOWING HALF A BOLE CORNE.

Johne Dobsone,	£6	0	0	Wm. Furgreife,	£6	0	0
Geo. Patersone, wright,	10	0	0	Rot. Ammers,	9	0	0
Thomas Watson, weifer,	4	0	0	Margrat Frater,	4	0	0
Wm. Williamsone,	4	0	0				
Thomas Sadler,	4	0	0	*Summa,*	£47	0	0

UNDER-COATERS THAT HES HOUSE AND YARD.

Archbald Waker,	£6	0	0	James Haldone,	£12	0	0
Wm. Burne,	6	0	0	Thomas Elphinstoune,	4	0	0
Thomas Frater,	6	0	0	Margrat Riddell,	1	10	0
Archbald Frier,	6	0	0	Katrine Dods,	0	15	0
Wm. Couke, drayster,	2	0	0	Jo. Barrie,	6	0	0
Jennet Frier,	6	0	0	Rot. Frier, mille,	4	10	0
Margrat Clekie,	6	0	0	James Donnelsone,	3	0	0
Jennet Aldjoy,	1	0	0	Williame Murray,	2	0	0
Jo. Sadler,	1	0	0	Rot. Wilsone,	1	0	0
Jennet Clennaine,	2	0	0	Robt. Frier, fletcher,	6	0	0
Marrione Couke,	1	0	0	Wm. Speiding,	13	6	8
David Pringill,	2	0	0				
Issobell Maben,	1	10	0	*Summa,*	£101	1	8

	Scots.		
The sowme of the mailes w'in the toune of gallascheiles extends in the year to	£1016	11	0
The 3 walkmilnes payes in the year £60, and 3 stone of napes,	60	0	0

The corne millne of gallascheils pays in the year 1656, 58 bolls of victuall, half meall, half malt, with ane fat sow and two duson of capons.

The nather maines of gallascheils payes this year 20 bolls of victuall, halfe meill, half beir, with ane dousone of fouls, halfe hens, halfe capons, at the candilmest 1658.

The overmaines payes this year 13 bolls of vituall, ye on halfe beir, the other halfe meill, at the candilmist efter in the year 1658.

The teind of Gallaschiels with Boldsyde payes this year 1656,	431	0	0
The customes payes this year, one half at Mertinmes, the other halfe at Whitsonday,	215	0	0
The teind land (?) payes	78	7	0
Mossilies and Chakburne payes, with a dousone of hens and a dousone of capons,	666	13	4
Stolebrige payes, with a dousane of hens and a dousane of capons,	400	0	0
Natherbarns pays, with the half of the Crowne (?)	666	13	4
Boldsyde, with aught hens at Fastrineseven,	156	0	0
Cobels and fichings,	40	0	0
The 12 sowme mailers are to pay for ther longe and short avriages (?) in the year,	4	0	0
The 6 sowme mailers,	2	0	0

Everie 12 sowme mailer payes 2 hens at fastrineseven and 2 capons at pache.

Everie sax soume mailer payes 1 hen at fastrineseven and one capon at pache.

Coaters and under-coaters payes ane hen at fastrineseven.

The new conditiones that was set doune in Hew Scott of Gallascheils his tyme as followes :—

The maillers they ar obliged ay and while the goodman take the land in his owne hand, to work, to teill, harow, to sheir, to leid in alse muche land as will sow sixtine bolles, which he reserves in his oune hand. And also they ar obliged to bring home the elding (turf or peat) or any suche lying about the pleace—all this they ar bound to doe w'out meat or drinke.

At that tyme the coaters was ordined to pay 40 sh. mor for the bole of corne sowing and so was exemted frome worke. And thes that has halfe a bole of corne sowing payed 20 sh. and so was exemted frome worke.

VII.—SUMMARY OF A REPORT OF THE ESTATE OF GALA BY ALEXANDER LOW, Woodend, dated 12th May 1797.

EXCERPTS FROM TACKS.

Corn Mill, with lands of Swine Park; Thomas Cleghorn, tenant. *Rent.*—£50, 1 sow or £2, 6 hens or 6s.

Netherbarns—held by Robt. and James Hunter for 21 years from 1786. Rent £105. Tenants to build a new onstead, and one or two houses and a barn and stable, upon the outfield land, near the vestige of an old camp. Thirled to Galashiels mill. Common conditions as to husbandry.

Boldside, with fishings; Robert Harper, tenant under expiring lease. Rent £40, with 2 salmon and 1 kipper. Liberty to laird and sons to fish.

Hollybush and Boghall.—George Dun, tenant. Rent £70; 24 loads of coal of 10 stones heavy weight, or £2; and 10 hens or 10s. Reserve right of access to Red Moss for marl or peats, or to drain, also liberty for householders of Galashiels to carry off *diviots* from lands of Boghall next the inner moss and 20 yards towards the hill for rigging and skews to their houses.

Parkhouse, upper and nether bogs, south clover parks, etc. Thomas and John Stenhouse, tenants. Rent £44, 3s. 8d.; 26 loads of coal, and 12 hens.

Mossilee.—Robert Harper and Robt. Dickson, tenants. Rent £72, 10s., 12 loads of coal and 15 hens.

Maigelpots and *Blackhopehaugh*, with the fishing on Tweed. George Lees, tenant. Rent £105, 12 loads of coal, and 12 hens.

Blindlie, Mossilee, and *big Meadows.*—John Murray, tenant. Rent £70.

Kilnknow and Blindliehill.—George and John Dun, tenants. Rent £73, and 12 loads of coal.

Hemphaugh and Waterridge.—Thomas Ovens, tenant. Rent £14, 14s., 18 loads and 6 hens. South part of Blankerridge £7, and 6 loads.

Millarland, Harestanelee, Blackwood, Aicken Oak Park, Fadamhaugh, Hatlands, Claydubs, houses and yards. George Bathgate, tenant. Rent £30, 12 loads, 6 hens, and spining 2 lbs. of lint. The Aicken Oak Park not to be ploughed.

Mr. Low now notices the farms and possessions as they occur in the Book of Contents referring to plan of Estate.

1. *Town of Galashiels.*—Small possessions and yards connected with feus or houses. "Must be of considerable value, say 40s. per acre."

"Must be of considerable value, say 40s. per acre."	.	.	28¾ acres	£57 10	0
Haugh and heugh occupied as common, .	.	.	19¾ acres	9 15	0
				£67 5	0

Mill of Galashiels.—Cannot be accurately valued unless by a person fully acquainted with the thirlage and local advantages. If a little more land were added, say £70 *to* £80.

2. *The Eastlands, etc.*—190 acres at from 5s. to 35s., £203, 9s. 6d. Would make a very pretty farm, but onstead would cost £400, and there seems to be a want of water. Recommends it to be laid out in fields of 8 *to* 10 acres and let.

3. *Netherbarns* consists of—

	ACRS.	RDS.	PLS.				
Upper, Nether, and Castle haughs, Blackness, .	63	1	5	22s. 6d.	£71	0	0
Woodmanshaugh, . . .	5	0	8	10s.	2	10	0
Waterside and Salary Heughs, . . .	15	3	14	8s.	6	6	0
Townshott, Kingsknowes, Barnfield, Captain's heugh, and Deadwater field, . .	80	2	15	12s. 6d.	50	6	3
Todhole, New Netherbarns, Belham's bog, Barndyke, and Holmsburn, . •. .	90	3	30	10s. 6d.	47	18	0

	ACRS.	RDS.	PLS.		£	s.	d.
Newfaan Isle, Millars park, Small and Broad Rigs,	63	0	13	8s.	£25	4	0
Old Campbells, Gaasbraes, Bagharvie shott, Tottenbirk hill stell, Netherbarns hill, and Kings Yeats,	201	1	24	6s.	60	6	3
	520	0	29		£263	10	6

Present rent £105, expected rise £158, 10s. 6d. Numerous suggestions as to future management.

	ACRS.	RDS.	PLS.		£	s.	d.
4. Boldside,	83	3	17	10s.	£41	18	6
	62	2	16	7s. 6d.	23	8	9
	44	1	11	3s.	6	12	9
	191	0	4		72	0	0
Fishings,					15	0	0
					£87	0	0

(Let at £90 to a tenant who sublet the fishing at £20.)

Mr. Low directs attention to great advantages to be derived from adding Boldside to Netherbarns. Onstead in a ruinous state, near it a number of trees in balks and rows, many apparently from old stocks, the remains of a wood cut down. Were the half judiciously felled the remaining half would be worth more in 20 years than if all left standing.

	ACRS.	RDS.	PLS.	£	s.	d.
5. Hollybush, Reedmoss Park, etc.,	108	1	39	£22	0	0
Cotters moss, Conter'd Know, etc.,	91	1	12	40	0	0
Boghall, south and north hills, and Gooseholes,	258	2	10	64	0	0
	458	1	21	126	0	0
Present rent,				70	0	0
Expected rise,				£56	0	0
6, 7. *Parkhouse and Bogs*, should be added to Hollybush.	139	1	18	£62	8	0
8. *Mossilie*—						
Cow park and onstead,	42	2	34	20	4	0
Back of the Shank, Blakeburn head, Farmyhill, Stell and Backbrae, Hopehead, face of Maigelt,	498	2	26	124	0	0
Face of the Shank, etc.,	123	2	27	36	0	0
The plain park,	29	3	35	44	16	0
	695	0	2	£225	0	0

9. *Magelpotts.*—823 acres (at about 5s. per acre) £210. All attempts to improve this farm by the plough and converting it into a corn farm ought to be guarded against; but liberty may be given to plough 60 acres.

		ACRS.	RDS.	PLS.				
10. Blindlie, south park, ...		48	1	28				
„ north „		34	2	3				
		82	3	31	10s. 6d.	£43	10	0
11. Kilnknow—								
Blindlee hill, ...		203	3	36		£50	0	0
Meadow potts, Nether and Upper Farnylee, Berrybanks, Wellbraes, . . .		90	2	6		45	0	0
Cookshole, Broadfield, Town shott, Wheatlands, Seguhole, and heugh, . . .		52	0	0		39	0	0
		346	1	2		£134	0	0
12. Hemphaugh consisting of the Town shott, Wilderhaugh, Upper haugh, Leebrae, north and south wa's, etc., . . .		92	0	2		£55	4	3
13. Bay Lands, ...		28	3	23	20s.	28	15	0
14. Windyknowe, ...		7	2	31	15s.	5	17	0
15. Bownty butts, ...		11	2	19		8	8	0
16. Claydubs farm—consisting of Haa lands, Fadamhaugh, Aickenwood, Harestanelee, Blackwood, Millar's land, . . .		33	2	0		35	13	6
17. Weerhaugh, ...		13	0	16		26	15	0
18. Gala parks—including Dryloch yard, Howcroft, little and big horse parks, Broadwood, Longknow, Townhead, Netherlee, Hughfields, etc., ...		183	0	5		137	17	9
19. Drylingshaugh, ...		6	2	35		10	0	0

Several of the parks are too thickly wooded, by which the pasture is spoiled and the wood itself is suffering, especially the oaks, many of which are in a thriving state, but can never grow to be timber unless they have more room.

Mr. Low, considering their advantages, advises planting of strips and clumps of trees, but not of large plantations. "In point of ornament and advantage one plantation is naturally suggested, which is to plant the heughs all the way east from Hemphaugh to the old Tower on Netherbarns, and from thence a strip of 50 feet ought to be continued to the river Tweed, along the east side of the road. A strip of 100 feet broad from north-east corner of Baylands to the old houses in Blindleeparks. Another from the west corner of Gorcum hill along the head of the parks called South Upper bogs, James' Well park, Little and Big parks, Hollybush park, Redmoss park, and thence to turn round to the west march of Bollside to the river Tweed. A third from the old tower on Netherbarns along the marches between that farm and Eastlands to the south corner of Gorcum hill.

The parks and fields proposed to be let to the inhabitants of the town seem to be sufficient for their accommodation, as most of them are (to their credit) so intent on their own business that they have no great desire to be farmers on a small scale.

VIII.—ROLL OF THE CONSTITUENCY OF SELKIRKSHIRE, AS MADE UP AT A MEETING OF FREEHOLDERS HELD AT SELKIRK IN 1790.

Walter Scott of Harden.

John Pringle of Clifton.

John Elliot of Borthwickbrae.

Wm. Johnstone Pulteney, Advocate.

Thomas Scott, second son of Robert Scott, late in Sandyknow (uncle of Sir Walter Scott).

Mr. Steven Oliver, Minr. at Maxton.

Alex. Shaw, late Writer in Edinburgh.

Jas. Cunningham of Hyndhope.

Thomas Ballantyne of Holilee.

Admiral John Elliot.

Robert Ballantyne of Phaaps (Phawhope).

Charles Scott of Wool.

Francis, br. to Walter Scott of Harden.

Walter Scott, Writer to the Signet (father of Sir Walter Scott).

Wm. Oliver of Dinlabyre.

John Rutherfurd of Edgerston.

Andw. Plummer of Middlestead.

Archibald Douglas of Douglas.

John Johnstone of Alva.

George Fairholm of Greenhill.

Henry Murray, late 15th Reg.

Walter Williamson of Cardrona.

Alexander Alison of Glassmount.

John Murray of Philiphaugh.

Sir Alex. Don of Newton, Bt.

Jas. Pringle of Torwoodlee.

Hugh Scott, yr. of Harden.

James Mercer of Scotsbank.

Walter Scott of Raeburn.

Wm. Russel of Ashisteel.

Ad. Ogilvie of Hartwoodmyres.

Wm. Chisholme of Chisholme.

Alex. Robertson of Ettrickhouse.

Alex. Pringle of Whitebank.

Hugh Scott of Gala.

Wm. Caster Anderson, husband to Mrs. Barbara Anderson of Tushielaw.

Mark Pringle of Fairnilie (elected).

Chas. Scott of Howcleugh.

John Scott of Midgehope.

Mark Watt of Bowland.

Total number,—40.

IX.—NOTE OF STOCK UPON SELKIRKSHIRE FARMS OF BUCCLEUCH ESTATE IN 1766.

(From Philiphaugh MSS.)

	SHEEP.	CATTLE.	BOLLS SOWN.	RENT.
Sundhope, .	1260	12	24	(and six horses).
Eldinhopeknow,[1]	440	12 or 15	10	£28, worth £36.
Carterhaugh, .	240	20 (not good)	50	£52.
Bowhill, . .	960	4	12	£60, 10s., worth £70.
Old Wark, .	520	20	24	£65 ; Parks £25 more.
Half Glengaber,	200			£50.
Fastheugh, .	720	8	18	£45, 11s. ; Half Glengaber, £10 more.
E. Kershope, .	520		8	£40.
Ladhope, . .	720	20	30	£43, worth £66, 10s.
W. Eldinhope, .	1000	20	15	£61, worth £100.
Eltrive, . .	1600.			
W. Mountbenger,	1200	30	30	£105, worth £120.
E. Do.,	1000	12	15	£83, worth £100 or more.

[1] Exclusive of Catkerwood, on other side of Yarrow, which pays the tenant about £6.

	SHEEP.	CATTLE.	BOLLS SOWN.	RENT.
Catslack Know,	240	12	26	£31.
Catslack Burn,	720	20	36	£79.
Whitehope & Hanel,	1900	20	for family	£144.
Deuchar, . .	1000	6	30	£100, with Mill.
Tinnies, . .	1000	30	40	£100, worth £122.
Foulshiels, .	720	10	26	£74.
E. Fauldshope,	480	10	24	£54.
W. Do.	480	10	24	£52.
Kirkhope, .	1320	24	40	£115, worth £130.
Newhouse, .	1320	24	30	£108, worth £123.

Note.—Remarkable good sheep 6s. piece.

	SHEEP.	CATTLE.	BOLLS SOWN.	RENT.
Singlie, . .	900	28	30	£75, worth £100.
Gilmanscleugh,	1000	24	40	£115.
Newburgh, .	640	22	16	£55.
Berrybush, .	600	12	none	£40, worth £55, 10s.
Over Delorain,	1800	20	24	£130, worth £180.
Under Do., .	1000	10	24	£85, worth £100.
Howfoord, .	560	24	40	£56, worth £65 or more.
Outerhuntly, .	440	10	30	£40, worth £50 or more.
Corslie, . .	2200	20	for family	£144.
Andleshope, .	...	...	...	Reckoned dear.
Two Buccleughs,	1500	...	...	£183.
Realies (Raelees),	100	3	10	£14.
Cribs, . .	520	6	20	£45.
Yair, . .	720	12	28	£76 (Parks and Garden, about £63).
Craig, . .	480	8	16	£44.
Peel, . .	960	12	26	£83.
Shootinglees, .	1200	...	...	£75, worth £100.
Kirkhouse, .	60	4	20	£30.
Glenlude, .	260	...	...	£18.

X.—EXTENT OF ETTRICK FOREST IN 1628.

In the second volume of the *Retours* (published by the Record Commission, 1811) there is printed among *Inquisitiones Valorum* "A Return of the Extent of the Lordship of Ettrick Forest," dated 9th May 1628. This inquiry was made in the Sheriff Court of Selkirk, held in the Tolbooth (*Pretorium Burgi*), in compliance with an order from the Lords of Council and Session, dated only three days previous. At the request, in October 1625, of Lord Duplin, High Chancellor of Scotland and Principal Collector of the King's Taxes, the King (Charles I.) had commissioned Wm. Douglas of Cavers, Sir Wm. M'Dougall of Makcairstoun, and John Halyburton of Muirhouslaw, Sheriffs in this part of Selkirkshire and Dumfriesshire, respectively, or two of them, to make up the return from evidence furnished by these honest men and faithful to their country :—Walter Veatche of North Syntoun, Francis Scott of Wole, John Scot of

Zorkstoun, Wm. Middlemest of Lillieslie-chapell, Bailie Andrew Ker of Selkirk, Robert Scot, elder, of Satscheillis, Andrew Dowglas of Preistoun, George Ker of Newhall, Wm. Turnebull, Portionar of Phillophauche, James Scot of Johnstoun, Robert Ker of Sunderlandhall, Bailies James Gledstaines and Robert Scot of Hawick, John Veatche of Clerklandis, and Robert Armstrange, called "Rakas" dweller in Langraw. These, being sworn, declared that the lands and dominion of Ettrick Forest, with its camps, towers, fortalices, manors, mills, woods, fisheries, tofts, crofts, outsets, parts, pendicles, and pertinents, being part of the property of His Majesty, lying within the county of Selkirk, extend and are returned at a total of one thousand merks (*mercatas*) Scots of lands; and that the particular lands and pastures undermentioned of the said dominion of Ettrick Forest extend as shown :—

OWNER.	DESCRIPTION OF PROPERTY.	£	s.	d.
Earl of Home.	Reidfurdegrein and Drycleuchscheill,	7	9	5
Earl of Buckcleuch.	Wester Montberger,	16	16	8
	Eister Montberger, and Catslacknow,	16	16	8
	Catslacburne and Schottinglies,	16	15	4
	Blakgrenes,	16	16	8
	Laidhoip,	7	8	1
	Quhithope,	5	19	4
	Wester Delorance and Warldishoip,	6	5	0
	Eister Delorance,	4	15	6
	Newarkmylne,	1	8	8
	Auldwark,	5	13	7
	Cairterhauch,	8	11	10
	Glengaber,	1	18	2
	Fastheuch,	7	3	3
	Tynnies,	11	18	10
	Hertherne,	7	3	3
	Auldishoip,	3	6	10
	Eltrevie,	11	18	10
	Huntlies,	5	5	1
	Fawsydes,	6	6	10
	Quhythilbrea,	7	12	10
	Eldinghoipes,	14	1	10
	Helvellane,	3	3	6
Earl of Traquair.	Gaithope,	10	10	2
	Cithope,	11	18	10
	Gairlacleuch and Blakhous,	11	18	10
	Dowglas Craige,	11	18	10
	Wester Plora,	3	2	1
	Berriebuss,	2	17	6

OWNER.	DESCRIPTION OF PROPERTY.	£	s.	d.
Earl of Traquair.	E. and W. Fauldishoipes,	7	8	0
Sir John Murray of Phillipphauch.	Hangingschaw,	11	18	10
	Levinshoip,	11	18	10
	Hairheid,	12	1	2
Andrew Ker of Oxnam.	Aschiesteill,	6	8	11
Sir Patrick Murray.	Elibank,	7	3	3
	Preisthoip,	1	6	3
	Glenpoit,	5	14	7
	Williamehoip,	6	4	2
Sir James Pringill.	Gallowscheilles and Moysileis,	21	11	0
Walter Scot of Harden.	Kirkhoipes,	9	11	1
	Deidhoip,	2	7	9
	Dodheid, *or* Dodbank,	4	7	9
Wm. Scot of Harden.	Singlie,	6	15	3
	Earneheuch,	6	13	8
	Gamilscleuch,	3	11	7
Dd. Creichtoun of Gilmertoun.	Holylie and Thornieley,	12	9	8
Wm. Ker of Lintoun.	Fairnylie,	12	0	2
And. Riddell of Riddell.	Hayning,	6	0	8
	Windidoris,	6	7	3
	Trinlyknowes,	5	14	8
George Pringill.	Torwodlie,	7	3	3
	Cadounlie,	7	3	3
	Corslie,	5	1	1
Andrew Ker of Zear.	Zear,	14	8	0
Jas. Pringill.	Quhytbank and Reidhead,	6	10	3
	Knowes,	2	17	3
Robert Pringill.	Blindlie,	11	18	10
	Cadounheid,	11	18	10
	Byrop,	1	19	9

Owner.	Description of Property.	£	s.	d.	Owner.	Description of Property.	£	s.	d.
Gilbert Ellot of Stobbis.	Schawes and Helinburne,	10	10	2	Walt. Scot of Girnewood.	Corsecleuch,	2	17	3
	Ballielies,	5	15	7		Bouroppe,	4	6	10
	Midlesteidis and Blakmiddinges,	7	4	7		Sanct Marie Loch of the Lowis,	0	4	9
Wm. Lowes of Plora.	Eister Plora,	3	2	1	Philip Scot.	Dryhoip and Fairmyhoip,	12	9	0
Laird of Cardrona.	Glensax,	5	14	7		Kirksteid,	3	9	2
Geo. Pringill of Newhall.	Newhall, or Craiglatche,	3	14	4	Hugh Scot of Deuchar.	Deuchar,	10	19	9
Robt. Scott.	Hartwoodmyres,	6	13	8	John Murray.	Soundhoip,	5	14	7
Walt. Scott of Huntly.	Langhoip,	4	6	0		Eister Carshoip (part),	1	9	0
	Hyndhoip,	3	14	8	Jas. Murray of Kirkhous.	Do. Do.	1	9	0
Walt. Scott of Quhithaugh.	Hartwoodburne,	6	4	2	And. Scot, formerly of Aikwood.	Do. Do.	3	8	3
Thomas Scott.	Quhithauchbrae,	4	3	6	Walter Murray.	Aikwood,	6	13	8
Robert Scott.	Toschelaw and Cromelaw,	7	12	9		South Bowhill,	3	6	10
	Caltrabank,	4	9	2	Robert Scott.	North Do.	3	4	6
John Scott.	Gilmanscleuch,	4	17	10	Walter Scott of Howfuird.	Howfuird,	6	0	0
	Third of Fawoodscheill,	3	18	2	Andrew Scott of Braidmeddowes.	Braidmeddowes,	7	19	0
And. Scott, Edinburgh.	Two-thirds of Fawoodscheill,	7	16	4	Walter Turnebull.	Hittrelburne,	3	18	9
	Winterbrugh,	5	1	8	Alex. Mitchelstoun,	Blakhaugh,	7	12	9
	Fawodgrainge,	2	18	3			£667	7	10

XI.—OLD COUNTY VALUATION ROLLS.

IN 1643, for the purposes of taxation, Parliament ordered a valuation to be made of lands, teinds, and everything whereby yearly profit arose, prescribing the form of the roll and the mode of ascertaining value. Two original copies of the Selkirkshire Roll then compiled are known to have existed, one lodged in the Exchequer, and the other known to have been, in 1686, in possession of Mr. Alexander Lithgoe of Drygrange, whose father had been collector. In 1785 both these copies had been lost, but the collector obtained four second copies, more or less correct, from Mr. Scott of Woll, Mr. Murray of Philiphaugh, Mr. Plummer of Middlestead, and the representatives of the late William Waugh, collector for many years. Middlestead and Woll's copies were made from the Drygrange original, the former in 1686, by Collector William Plummer. A laborious and careful synopsis of these old Rolls, made in 1785 by the then collector, Mr. John Scott, was printed, but is now difficult to be met with. The following table shows the lairds and valued rental in 1643, the lairds in 1785, and the real rent in 1743, values being given in Scots money:—

ETTRICK PARISH.

Property.	Proprietors, 1643.	Value, Crop 1643.			Proprietors, 1785.	Real Rent, 1743.		
		Scots Money.				Scots Money.		
Riskinhope and Wardlawrig,	John, Lord Hay of Yester, .	£733	6	8	Alex. Hay of Drummelzier. .	£1000	0	0
Muckraw, . .	,, ,,	733	6	8	,, ,,			
Chapelhope and Langbank,	,, ,,	733	6	8	,, ,,	2133	6	8
Summerhope, .	,, ,,	244	8	10	,, ,,			
Cossershall and Brokhope,	Sir Wm. Scott of Harden, . .	733	6	8	Williamson of Cardrona, .	1440	0	0
Braidgarhill and Potburn,.	,, ,,	733	6	8	,, ,,	706 / 933	13 / 6	4 / 8
Thirlestain, .	Patrick Scott of Thirlestain,	833	6	8	Lord Napier, .	1200	0	0
Ramseycleuch, .	,, ,,	666	13	4	,,	866	13	4
Craighill, . .	,, ,,	166	13	4	,,	333	6	8
Stobcleugh, .	,, ,,	353	6	8	,,	400	0	0
Over Kirkhope, .	,, ,,	533	6	8	,.	666	13	4
Fawhope, . .	Scott of Hartwood-myres, . .	533	6	8	R. Ballantyne, .	1200	0	0
Over Dalgliesh, . Nether ,, .	Scott of Whitstaid,	1000	0	0	T. M'Millan, .	1500	0	0
Ettrickhouse, .	,, ,,	433	0	0	Alex. Robertson, .	800	0	0
Shorthope, . .	,, ,,	420	0	0	T. M'Millan, .	516	13	4
Midgehope, . Glenkerry, .	Scott of Tushielaw,	1133	6	8	Scott of Woll, . / Major Rutherford.	800 / 800	0 / 0	0 / 0
Feu-duties, . .	Earl of Haddington,	66	13	4	Duke of Buccleuch.			
,, ,, . .	Earl of Marr, .	10	0	0	T. M'Millan.			

PARISH OF ST. MARY.

Property.	Proprietors, 1643.	Value, Crop 1643.			Proprietors, 1785.	Real Rent, 1743.		
Nether Dellorain,	Erle of Buccleugh,	854	6	0	Duke of Buccleuch,	960	0	0
Wester ,,	,, ,,	1049	17	4	,, ,,	1966	13	4
Easter Buccleugh,	,, ,,	1144	13	4	,, ,,	1813	0	0
Wester ,, .	,, ,,	915	17	4	,, ,,	1000	0	0
Anleshope, .	,, ,,	540	0	0	,, ,,	1066	13	4
Utter Huntly, .	,, ,,	313	13	4	,, ,,	420	0	0
Eldinhope, .	,, ,,	902	0	0	,, ,,	1400	0	0
W. Know, .	,, ,,	366	13	4	,, ,,			
Eltreive, . .	,, ,,	1111	10	0	,, ,,	1300	0	0
W. Mountberger,	,, ,,	1120	0	0	,, ,,	1266	13	4
E. ,, .	,, ,,	947	0	0	,, ,,	933	6	8
Catslack burn, .	,, ,,	878	13	4	,, ,,	900	0	0
Catslack knowe, .	,, ,,	332	13	4	,, ,,	333	12	0
Shootinglees, Alterhouse and Glengaber,	,, ,,	1000	0	0	,, ,,	1100	8	0
Blackgrain, and Whithope,	,, ,,	1341	6	8	,, ,,	1560	0	0

Property.	Proprietors, 1643.	Value, Crop 1643.			Proprietors, 1785.	Real Rent, 1743.		
		Scots Money.				Scots Money.		
Ladhope, . .	Erle of Buccleugh,	£293	6	8	Duke of Buccleuch,	£533	6	8
Tinnes, . .	„ „	1200	0	0	„ „	1200	0	0
Peil and Hathern,	„ „	600	0	0	„ „	866	13	4
Teinds, . .	„ „	588	6	9	„ „			
Kirkstead, . .	Erle of Traquair,	666	13	4	„ „	666	13	4
Blackhouse,					Earl of Traquair,	1866	13	4
Craig of Douglas,	„ „	1933	6	8	„ „	933	6	8
Garcleugh,					„ „			
Over Dryhope, .	„ „	333	6	8	Duke of Buccleuch,			
Eshestiell, . .	„ „	466	13	4	Colonel Russell, .	866	13	4
West Ploraw, .	„ „	116	13	4	Earl of Traquair,	600	0	0
Dryhope and Wardlaw,	„ „	933	6	8	Duke of Buccleuch,	1666	13	4
Gaithopegrain, .	„ „	333	6	8	Ballantyne of			
Sithope, . .	„ „	400	0	0	Hollilee, . .	1000	0	0
Elibank, . .	Lord Elibank,	1000	0	0	Lord Elibank,	1000	0	0
Allanburnhead, .	„ „	600	0	0	Williamson of Cardrona, . .	600	0	0
Priesthope, .	„ „	293	6	8	Ballantyne of Hollilee, . .	266	13	4
Hangingshaw, .	John Murray,	920	0	0	Johnston of Alva,	600	0	0
Lewinshope, and Skadarig,	„ „	1600	0	0	„ „	2129	13	4
W. Kershope, .	John Murray, .	377	0	0	„ „	495	10	0
Deuchar and Mill,	James Murray, .	933	6	8	Duke of Buccleuch,	1000	0	0
Sundhope, .	John Murray, elder	706	13	4	Johnston of Alva,	1333	6	8
Part of Kershope,	and yr., . .	200	0	0	Duke of Buccleuch,	466	13	4
„ „	Robert Murray, .	200	0	0				
Tushielaw, Comlaw and Cacrabank,	Wm. Scott, . .	1666	0	0	Mrs. Anderson, .	2066	13	4
Bowerhope and Corsecleugh,	Patrick Scott, .	1000	0	0	Lord Napier, .	933	6	8
						400	0	0
Redfordgreen and Drycleuchshiels,	Scott of Whitslaid,	200	0	0	Lauder of Carolside,	1200	0	0
¾ Winterburgh,	Buccleugh and Lord Cranstone,	1333	6	8	Duke of Buccleuch,	2200	0	0
¼ „ „	Sir John Scott, .	666	13	4				
Langhope,	J. Scott of Headshaw,	566	13	4	Sir Gilbert Elliot of Minto,	1000	0	0
Langside ?								
Hyndhope, .	Walter Scott, .	333	6	8	Jas. Cunningham,	666	13	4
Gilmanscleuch and Part of Fawoodshiel,	John Scott, . .	866	13	4	Duke of Buccleuch,	1950	0	0
Shaws—two Baillilees and Helmburn,	William Elliot of Stobs, . .	1333	6	8	Johnston of Alva,	2188	0	0
Evellance, . .	Sir James Hay, .	333	6	8	Earl of Traquair, .	400	0	0

Property.	Proprietors, 1643.	Value, Crop 1643.			Proprietors, 1785.	Real Rent, 1743.		
		Scots Money.				Scots Money.		
Plora, . .	Wm. Lowes, .	£266	13	4	Earl of Traquair, .	£466	13	4
W. Fauldshope, .	Sir Wm. Scott of	433	6	8	Duke of Buccleuch,	600	0	0
Kirkhope and Mill,	Harden,	1033	6	8	,, ,,	1333	6	8
Newhouse, . .	„ „	933	6	8	,, ,,	1200	0	0
Singlie, . .	„ „	733	6	8	,, ,,	933	6	8
Berrybush, . .	„ „	240	0	0	,, ,,	400	0	0
Deephope and } Mountcommon, }	„ „	366	13	4	,, ,,	{ 400 400	0 0	0 0
Dodhead, . .	„ „	566	13	4	Mr. Mercer, . .	866	13	4
Whitehopebrae, .	Scott, yr. of Harden,	333	6	8	Scott of Harden, .	666	13	4
Hotrelburne, .	„ „	333	6	8	,, ,,	800	0	0
Innerhuntlie, .	„ „	133	6	8	,, ,,	600	0	0
Howford, . .	„ „	533	6	8	Duke of Buccleuch,	800	0	0

SELKIRK PARISH.

Property.	Proprietors, 1643.	Value, Crop 1643.			Proprietors, 1785.	Real Rent, 1743.		
Fawside and Foul-shiels,	Erle of Buccleugh,	480	0	0	Duke of Buccleuch,	650	0	0
Fastheugh, . .	„ „	500	0	0	,, ,,	566	12	0
Newark or White-hillbrae,	„ „	300	0	0	,, ,,	704	0	0
Oldwark, . .	„ „	143	6	8	,, ,,	192	0	0
Carterhaugh, .	„ „	420	0	0	,, ,,	612	0	0
Bellenden, . .	„ „	306	0	0	,, ,,	666	13	4
Newark Mill, .	„ „	200	0	0	,, ,,			
Teinds, . .	Erle of Roxburgh,	445	6	8	,, ,,			
E. Ailemuir, .} W. „ .}	Scott of Gala,	666	6	8	{ Pringle of Haining, { Elliot of Borth-wickbrae,	666 666	13 13	4 4
Todrig, . .	Thomas Scott, .	666	6	8	George Pott, .	1600	0	0
S. Bowhill, .} Two Oakwoods } and Mill, }	Scott, yr. of Harden,	1333	6	8	{ Duke of Buccleuch, { Lord Polwarth, .	533 800	6 0	8 0
Hartwoodmyers, .	Scott, elder of Har-den,	566	13	4	Adam Ogilvie, .	1000	0	0
E. Fauldshope, .		433	6	8	Duke of Buccleuch,	566	13	4
N. Bowhill, .	Robert Scott, .	466	6	8	,, ,,	533	6	8
Broadmeadows, .	Andrew Scott, .	600	0	0	Scott of Woll, .	733	6	8
Hairhead, . .	Sir John Murray of	133	6	8				
E. „ . .	Philiphaugh, Kt.,	753	6	8	Murray of Philip-			
Philiphaugh and } Mill, }	„ „	600	0	0	haugh, . .	2405	15	0
Yair and Mill, .	Patrick, Erle of Forth, . .	1533	6	8	Duke of Buccleuch,	1800	0	0
Williamhope, .	Lord Elibank, .	466	13	4	Innes of Stow, .	533	6	8
Lands in Selkirk,	"William, Marquis of Douglas," .	906	0	0	Burgh of Selkirk, .	940	0	0

Property.	Proprietors, 1643.	Value, Crop 1643.	Proprietors, 1785.	Real Rent, 1743.
		Scots Money.		Scots Money.
Schaw, . .	John Schaw, .	£240 0 0	Charles Scott, .	£266 13 4
2 husbandlands in Selkirk,	John Bryden and Wm. Mitchelhill,	106 13 4	Burgh of Selkirk,	Not known.
Haning, . .	John Riddell, .	1666 13 4	Pringle of Clifton,	1333 6 8
Hartwoodburn and Brownmuir,	Lieut.-Col. Walter Scott,	466 13 4	" " Thomas Curror,	1000 0 0
Middlestead,	Archibald Elliot, .	666 13 4	Andrew Plummer,	960 0 0
Howden, . .	George Curror, .	266 13 4	Pringle of Haining,	266 13 4
Sunderland and and S. Hall,	Andrew Karr, .	840 0 0	Andrew Plummer,	1400 0 0
Hedderlie and Batts,	W. Mitchelhill, J. Lidderdale, and James Elliot, .	240 0 0	Burgh of Selkirk, Charles Scott,	Not known. 266 13 4
Teinds, . .	Erle of Roxburgh,	1657 13 4	Duke of Roxburgh.	
Feu-duties,. .	Erle of Wigton, .	10 13 4	Heirs of Erle of Wigton.	

GALASHIELS PARISH.

Property.	Proprietors, 1643.	Value, Crop 1643.	Proprietors, 1785.	Real Rent, 1743.
Galashiels, . .	Hew Scott, . .	3723 13 4	Hugh Scott, .	5601 15 8
Blindlee, . .	Robt. Pringle, .	1000 0 0		
Fairnilee and Rink,	Dame Christina Ruthven, Lady Farnlee, and Sir T. Ogilvie, her spouse,	1600 0 0	Pringle of Clifton,	2000 0 0

STOW PARISH.

Property.	Proprietors, 1643.	Value, Crop 1643.	Proprietors, 1785.	Real Rent, 1743.
Caldenhead and Laidlawsteel,	James Pringle of Torwoodlee,	780 0 0	James Pringle, .	1066 13 4 1066 13 4
Torwoodlee, .	" "	836 13 4	" "	933 6 8
Newmilnes, .	" "	90 13 4	" "	
Corslee, . .	" "	233 6 8	" "	306 13 4
Whitebank, . Blackhaugh, . Knows, . . Basha Mill, .	Jas. Pringle of Whitebank,	1319 0 0	Alex. Pringle, . Innes of Stow, . " " Alex. Pringle, .	2333 6 8
Newhall, . .	Jas. Pringle of Newhall . .	222 6 8	Sir John Pringle,	400 0 0
Caldonhead, .	R. Pringle of Blindlee . .	733 6 8	Pringle of Torwoodlee,	included above
Trinlyknowe and Windydoors,	Violet Douglas, Lady Riddel, and Jean Stewart, Lady Hayning, liferenters,	1068 2 8	" "	included with Laidlawsteel. 666 13 4

INNERLEITHEN PARISH.

Property.	Proprietors, 1643.	Value, Crop 1643.	Proprietors, 1785.	Real Rent, 1743.
		Scots Money.		Scots Money.
Holalee and Thornilee, .	Sir David Chrich-toune of Long-towne,	£1000 0 0	Thos. Ballantyne, Innes of Stow, .	£800 0 0
				666 13 4
Feu-duty, . .	Earl of Traquair,	160 0 0	Earl of Traquair.	

HASSENDEAN (NOW ROBERTON) PARISH.

Property	Proprietors 1643	Value Crop 1643	Proprietors 1785	Real Rent 1743
Robertowne, .	Scott of Harden, .		Ad. Scott of Galla-law,	200 0 0
Howcleugh, .	„ „	466 13 4	Walter Scott, .	400 0 0
Hoskott, . .	„ „		John Grieve, .	400 0 0
Craik Midshaw and Whiney-cleugh, . .	Erle of Buccleugh,	700 0 0	Duke of Buccleuch,	2000 0 0
Teinds, . .	„ „	60 0 0	„ „	

HAWICK (NOW ROBERTON) PARISH.

Property	Proprietors 1643	Value Crop 1643	Proprietors 1785	Real Rent 1743
Phillope, . .	Arch. Elliot, .	400 0 0	Duke of Buccleuch,	800 0 0

WILTOUN (NOW ROBERTON) PARISH.

Property	Proprietors 1643	Value Crop 1643	Proprietors 1785	Real Rent 1743
Borthwickbrae, . West Howleugh,	Scott of Hartwood-myres, . .	1000 0 0	John Elliot, .	1333 6 8
Teinds, . .	Lord Borthwick, .	10 0 0	„ „	

ASHKIRK PARISH.

Property	Proprietors 1643	Value Crop 1643	Proprietors 1785	Real Rent 1743
South Sinton, .	Francis Scott,	1600 0 0	John Scott, .	Not given.
Whitslaide, .	Robert Scott, .	266 13 4	Lauder of Carrol-side.	

PEEBLES PARISH.

Property	Proprietors 1643	Value Crop 1643	Proprietors 1785	Real Rent 1743
Easter Glensax, .	Hay of Haystoune,	466 13 4	Hay of Hayston, .	Not given.

After deducting feu-duties and teinds the total valuation of the county (crop 1643) was £79,905 Scots money, equal to £6658, 1s. 8d. sterling.

This seems to have given rise to dissatisfaction; for in 1649 a committee appointed to value the sheriffdom prepared a new Roll by which the net Rental was shown to be £53,316 Scots—a reduction of one-third ! The committee's report states that this valuation was first proposed to be made upon the oath of all the Heritors. "But, finding that by reason of the decay of store, it could not come near the total by that course, they took a more ready way, and summoned so many heritors, tenants, and possessors from each parish to give the true rent

Philip-haugh MSS.

of each parish yearly." *Ettrick Parish*—Adam Laidlaw in Chapelhope, Adam Scott in Ramsay-cleuch, Wm. Laidlaw in Cossarshill, and Wm. Hislop in Dalgleis. *Yarrow Parish*—Wm. Andison in Buccleuch, Walter Dalgleis in Whitehope, John Brydon in Eldinhope, Walter Scott in Catslackburn, Thos. Anderson in Howford, and Thos. Stodert in Hangingshaw. *Selkirk Parish*—Robt. Ker in Sunderland, Robt. Dalgleis in Fastheuch, Jas. Murray in Philiphaugh, John Lidderdale, and Jas. Ewart, yr., burgesses of Selkirk. *Ashkirk* and *Hassendean*—John Home and James Easton. *Stow* and *Galashiels*—John Cruiks and Robt. Freir in Galashiels, Walter Thomson in Windydoors, and James Blakie in Newmylnes. Some of whom attested the roll "with their hands led by the pen of the notar, because they could not write them-selves." The owner of Deuchar is styled Sir James Murray of Skirling; but there are no other changes calling for mention. It is probable that the valuation was not allowed to remain at the low sums fixed by the committee of 1649; for in 1686, the valued rent was £79,865 Scots, within a few pounds of the figures of 1643. A table of the Real Rent in 1743 shows a considerable augmentation; but the valued rent of 1643 continued to be the basis on which the Imperial taxes were levied till 1841.

Philip-
haugh
MSS.

XII.—VALUATION ROLL. COUNTY OF SELKIRK, 1882-83.

PARISH OF ASHKIRK.

FARM OR HOUSE.	PROPRIETOR.	£	s.	d.
Whitslaid, .	Trustees of General David Pott of Todrig, .	400	0	0
Dimpleknowe, .	John Scott of Sin-ton, . .	200	0	0
Sinton Mill, .	,,	140	0	0
Sinton House, .	,,	40	0	0
Sinton Farm and Parks,	,,	284	0	0
Sinton Mains and Whinfield,	,,	307	0	0
Sinton, Parkhead, and Langton,	,,	845	0	0
Plantations, .	,,	57	10	0

PARISH OF ETTRICK.

FARM OR HOUSE.	PROPRIETOR.	£	s.	d.
Cossarhill, .	Miss Williamson of Cardrona, .	£320	0	0
Midgehope, .	William Williamson Ker of Midgehope,	330	0	0
Braidgarhill, .	George Pott of Pot-burn, .	407	0	0
Potburn and Over Phawhope,	,,	640	0	0
Nether Phawhope,	,,	403	0	0

FARM OR HOUSE.	PROPRIETOR.	£	s.	d.
Ettrickhall, .	James Paterson of Whitelee, .	260	0	0
Cacrabank House and Gardens,	B. T. G. Anderson of Tushilaw, .	25	0	0
Tushilaw and Cacrabank,	,,	700	0	0
Scabcleuch, .	Lord Napier and Ettrick, .	210	0	0
Ramseycleuch, .	,,	400	0	0
Ettrickside and Gamescleuch, .	,,	240	0	0
Thirlestanehope,	,,	175	0	0
Wardlaw, .	,,	200	0	0
Thirlestane House and Plantations,	,,	140	0	0
Glenkerry, .	William Aitchison, .	485	0	0
Shorthope, .	W. M. Millar Scott of Wauchope, .	300	0	0
Chapelhope, .	William Turnbull of Fenwick, .	1002	0	0
Over Kirkhope and Brockhoperig,	,,	465	0	0
Riskenhope, .	,,	652	0	0
Rodono with fishing and shooting,	,,	270	0	0

FARM OR HOUSE.	PROPRIETOR.	£	s.	d.
Ropelawshiel, .	Duke of Buccleuch,	295	0	0
Wester Buccleuch,	,,	774	0	0
Annalshope, .	,,	330	0	0
Gair, . .	,,	240	0	0
Crosslee, . .	,,	614	0	0
Easter Buccleuch (exclusive of Henwoodie),	,,	530	0	0
Berrybush, .	,,	40	0	0
Deephope, .	,,	133	0	0
$\frac{54}{58}$ Over and Nether Dalgliesh,	,,	820	0	0
$\frac{2}{56}$,,	D. Milne Home and Andrew Stavert,	30	0	0

PARISH OF ROBERTON.

FARM OR HOUSE.	PROPRIETOR.	£	s.	d.
Bellendean, .	Duke of Buccleuch,	262	0	0
Craik and Midshaw, .	,,	840	0	0
Henwoodie, .	,,	170	0	0
Howcleuch and Borthwickmains,	Charles Scott of Howcleuch, .	258	0	0
Borthwickshiels Farm,	Trustees of General David Pott of Todrig, . .	158	0	0
Borthwickbrae House, Plantings, and Shootings,	William Elliot Lockhart of Borthwickbrae, . . .	110	0	0
Borthwickbrae Farm,	,,	439	0	0
Greenbank, .	,,	15	0	0
Wester Alemoor,	,,	258	0	0
Borthwickbrae Burnfoot,	,,	185	0	0
Easter Alemoor,	Mrs. Pringle Pattison, . .	250	0	0
Philhope and Ringhope, and Shootings, .	Trustees of late W. R. Dickson, . . .	450	0	0
Hoscoteshiel, .	Archibald Stavert of Hoscote, . .	250	0	0
,, House,	,,	65	0	0

PARISH OF SELKIRK.

FARM OR HOUSE.	PROPRIETOR.	£	s.	d.
Batts, . .	Trustees of George Rodger of Bridgelands, . .	94	0	0
Shawburn, .	William McA. Leny and J. S. Pitman,	26	0	0
Smedheugh and Lochslacks,	Burgh of Selkirk, .	278	0	0
Lingle and Shootings,	,,	343	0	0
Deepslaids and Selkirk Common,	,,	280	0	0
Shawpark and Lands,	Mrs. Boylan, . .	100	0	0
Shawmount, .	Trustees of General Dunn, . .	169	0	0
Hartwoodmyres,	C. Plummer of Middlestead, . .	346	0	0
Oakwood and Inner Huntly,	Lord Polwarth, .	490	0	0
Oakwoodmill, .	,,	400	0	0
Williamhope and Shootings,	Baroness Reay, .	244	0	0
Fauldshope, .	Duke of Buccleuch,	200	0	0
Bowhill, . .	,,	250	0	0
Foulshiels, Fastheugh, & Carterhaugh,	,,	1595	0	0
Bowhill Woods,	,,	271	0	0
Philiphaugh Farm,	Sir John F. Murray, Bart., . .	750	0	0
Philipburn, .	,,	70	0	0
Harehead, .	,,	155	0	0
Old Mill Farm, .	,,	386	0	0
Philiphaugh House, Shootings, and Plantings,	,,	155	0	0
Thirladean and Park,	,,	54	0	0
Harewoodglen and Shootings,	Dowager Lady Murray and Sir John F. Murray, Bart.,	145	0	0

Farm or House.	Proprietor.	£	s.	d.
Beechwood, .	Miss Murray, .	50	0	0
Haining Parks, .	Mrs. Pringle Pattison, . .	400	0	0
,, Plantings,	,,	150	0	0
,, House,	,,	100	0	0
Howden, Brownmuir, and Park,	,,	600	0	0
Greenhill and Merrycoat Park,	,,	255	0	0
Todrig and Shootings,	Trustees of General Pott, . .	459	0	0
Sunderlandhall House,	C. H. Scott Plummer of Middlestead, .	100	0	0
Parks, etc.,	,,	172	0	0
Sunderland Farm,	,,	370	0	0
Lindean (part of)	,,	50	0	0
Middlestead, .	,,	450	0	0
St. Helen's, .	George Anderson of St. Helen's, .	70	0	0
Shawfield and Broomhill,	,,	42	0	0
Shaw Farm, .	Robert Haldane, .	136	0	0
Broadmeadows, .	Hugh M. Lang, Esq.	730	0	0
Yair, . .	Alexander Pringle, Esq., . .	933	0	0

PARISH OF KIRKHOPE.

Farm or House.	Proprietor.	£	s.	d.
Fans and Whiteknowe,	Lord Polwarth, .	220	0	0
Part of Oakwood and Inner Huntly,	,,	343	0	0
Hutlerburn, .	,,	400	0	0
Easter Deloraine,	Duke of Buccleuch,	315	0	0
Kirkhope and Newhouse,	,,	900	0	0
Howford, . .	,,	370	0	0
Wester Deloraine,	,,	760	0	0
Outer Huntly, .	,,	140	0	0
Part of Fauldshope,	,,	200	0	0
Newburgh, .	,,	293	0	0
Gilmanscleugh, .	,,	400	0	0
Singlie, . .	,,	366	0	0
Houses and Lands at Ettrickbridge End,	,,	...		

Farm or House.	Proprietor.	£	s.	d.
Houses and Lands at Brockhill,	Duke of Buccleuch,	...		
Hyndhope and Shootings,	J. T. Mercer of Scotsbank, .	750	0	0
Shaws and Shootings, . .	Thomas Anderson,	1230	0	0
Helmburn, .	William Brown, Galahill, . .	220	0	0
Langhope, .	Earl of Minto, .	280	0	0
$\frac{16}{18}$ Easter Redfordgreen, .	Duke of Buccleuch,	71	0	0
$\frac{16}{18}$ Whitehillshiel,	,,	133	0	0
$\frac{3}{4}$ Wester Redfordgreen, .	,,	48	0	0
Shiringcleuch and Shootings, .	,,	90	0	0
Drycleuchlee and Shootings, .	,,	122	0	0

PARISH OF YARROW.

Farm or House.	Proprietor.	£	s.	d.
Easter Mountbenger,	Duke of Buccleuch,	517	15	0
Shootinglees, .	,,	379	0	0
Whitehope, .	,,	750	0	0
Tinnis, . .	,,	821	8	2
Berrybush and Wester Altrive,	,,	760	0	0
Dryhope, . .	,,	788	0	0
Catslackburn, .	,,	522	0	0
Eldinhope and part of Altrive,	,,	616	0	0
Ladhope, and East and West Kershope,	,,	535	0	0
Peel and Hawthorne, .	,,	410	0	0
Deuchar Mill and Land,	,,	49	0	0
Kirkstead and Glebe,	Duke of Buccleuch and Sons, . .	332	0	0
Lewinshope, .	James Johnston of Alva, .	1000	0	0
Sundhope and Eldinhope Knowe and Shootings,	,,	600	0	0

Farm or House.	Proprietor.	£	s.	d.
Hangingshaw and Shootings,	James Johnston of Alva,	95	0	0
Bowerhope,	Lord Napier and Ettrick,	325	0	0
Crosscleuch,	,,	210	0	0
St. Mary's Cottage,	,,	24	0	0
Ashiesteel,	Miss Russell,	529	0	0
Blackhouse and Craig Douglas,	H. C. Maxwell-Stewart of Traquair,	1300	0	0
Part of West Plora,	,,	86	0	0
Part of East Plora,	,,	171	0	0
Birks or Evillane,	,,	140	0	0
Fawnburnhead and part of Cardrona,	Miss Williamson of Cardrona,	200	0	0
Elibank,	Trustees of Lord Elibank,	332	0	0

PARISH OF GALASHIELS.

Farm or House.	Proprietor.	£	s.	d.
Netherbarns,	John Scott of Gala,	368	0	0
Mossilee,	,,	427	0	0
Meigle,	,,	462	0	0
Kilnknowe,	,,	228	0	0
Hollybush,	,,	471	0	0
Eastlands and Parks, etc.,	,,	257	0	0
Galahouse,	,,	100	0	0
Rink,	Mrs. Pringle-Pattison of Haining,	465	0	0
Fairnalee and Calfshaw,	,,	790	0	0

PARISH OF INNERLEITHEN.

Farm or House.	Proprietor.	£	s.	d.
Holylee Farm,	Major J. G. Ballantyne,	631	0	0
Priesthope,	Major J. G. Ballantyne,	128	0	0
Gatehopeburn (Peeblesshire), £111.	,,			
Holylee House,	,,	105	0	0
Thornilee and fishings,	Baroness Reay,	312	0	0

PARISH OF PEEBLES.

Farm or House.	Proprietor.	£	s.	d.
Part of Glensax,	Sir Robert Hay of Haystone,	98	0	0

PARISH OF STOW.

Farm or House.	Proprietor.	£	s.	d.
Newhall,	Sir Norman Pringle, Bart.,	250	0	0
Laidlawsteel Farm,	Baroness Reay,	436	0	0
Blackhaugh,	,,	535	0	0
Laidlawsteel House,	,,	50	0	0
Windydoors,	W. S. Walker of Bowland,	379	0	0
Crosslee,	,,	265	0	0
Galashiels Waterworks,	Galashiels Corporation,	700	0	0
Whytbank Mill and Farm of Caddonmill,	Alexander Pringle of Whytbank,	115	0	0
Whytbank and Redhead,	,,	550	0	0
Caddonlee and part of Millbank,	J. T. Pringle of Torwoodlee,	871	0	0
Torwoodlee Farm,	,,	800	0	0
Torwoodlee House, etc.,	,,	305	0	0
Caddonhead and Shootings,	,,	660	0	0

ABSTRACT.

Ashkirk Parish,	.	.	.	£2,319	10	0
Ettrick ,,	.	.	.	11,651	11	1
Roberton ,,	.	.	.	3,830	14	9
Selkirk ,,	.	.	.	14,517	3	6
Kirkhope ,,	.	.	.	8,247	11	3
Yarrow ,,	.	.	.	12,180	19	2
Galashiels ,,	.	.	.	4,597	1	6
Innerleithen, £1331, 0s. 8d.; Peebles, £106, 15s.				1,437	15	8
Stow,	.	.	.	6,483	5	7
				£65,265	12	6
Galashiels Municipal Extension,		.	.	4,054	15	8
				£69,320	8	2

XIII.—NOTES UPON THE PROGRESS OF AGRICULTURE.

FACTS brought to light in the general history of the shire make it apparent that from the earliest times the Forest consisted of steadings for the production of live-stock, little or nothing being attempted in the way of crops. In accounts of the damage done during inter-tribal forays and English invasions, the burning of corn-stacks is a rare incident compared with the seizure of sheep, nolt, and horses. After the Union of the Crowns had brought about greater security of property on the Border there was no doubt a marked increase of the acreage ploughed and sown; and in Selkirkshire a large part of the lower lands along the margin of the rivers was assiduously cultivated, as the rent-roll of Gala Estate in 1656 conclusively proves.

It is impossible to avoid noticing that in bygone days the proportion of cattle and horses reared and fed upon the hills of Ettrick and Yarrow was much greater than it is now. Hodge in 1722 records it as "remarkable that the Forest is fit for breeding great store of white cattle." Just about this time "The Society of Agricultural Improvers" began an earnest struggle to reform the wretched system of land culture which prevailed all over Scotland; but it was not till after the '45 that potato and turnip husbandry, rotation of crops, drill ploughing, and artificial (lime) manuring came into operation even in the southern counties. *Adv. Lib. MSS.*

Dr. Cranstoun, writing about the middle of last century, says the "commodities afforded by the shire are great store of butter and cheese of the finest sort, for taste and sweetness inferior to none that is to be found anywhere else, and that in such plenty that many parts about are furnished by it. It affordeth also store of neat hides and sheepskins, and great plenty of wool, which is carried to foreign nations, so that the cold Eastern countries bless this happy soil, being warmed with the fleeces of its sheep, which are sold and carried partly to the north parts of Scotland but mostly into England, the custom whereof at the Border is no small increase to his Majesty's revenue. It affords also great plenty of well-spun worset which is sold and carried for the most part into foreign nations." *Adv. Lib. MSS.*

Pennant, who made a tour through Selkirkshire in 1772, corroborates the foregoing, and contributes a few particulars. He says the sheep sell at from £8 to £12 a score, and that the usual weight of a wether is 13 to 18 lbs. (of 22 ozs.) per quarter. The fleece had been so much *Tour, iii. 265.*

improved by the substitution of oil and butter for tar that the wool from 5s. 6d. had risen to 10s. per stone of 24 lbs. He also notices the numbers of cattle reared in the county. In the year 1727-8, 8732 yards of linen cloth, valued at £436, 12s. 6d., were stamped in the county of Selkirk; in the year 1770-1 there were none.

Surv.
III., 2.

An interesting glimpse of the agriculture of Selkirkshire in 1777 is furnished by Mr. Wight's Survey, from which quotations have elsewhere been made. He describes with varying minuteness the methods of cultivation and stock rearing followed by Mr. Scott of Gala, Mr. Plummer of Sunderlandhall, Mr. Curror of Brownmuir, the principal inhabitants of Selkirk, Mr. Pringle of Haining, General M'Kay at Bowhill, Mr. Wm. Scott at Singlie, Mr. Burnet at White-hope, Mr. Wm. Anderson at Henderland, and Mr. Robt. Laidlaw at Chapelhope. "I conclude," he says, "my survey of this county with an observation, that, however barren and comfortless it may appear to a hasty stranger, it contains in its bosom a fund of riches that can never be exhausted while men love mutton and wear broad-cloth."

In 1760 the Board of Manufactures commenced to expend part of the revenue at its command for the encouragement of woollen manufactures, in premiums for wool and rams. The following list, compiled from the official books, kindly placed at the writer's disposal by Mr. Inglis, is of interest not only from an agricultural point of view, but as a list of Forest tenantry :—

PREMIUMS FOR WOOL AND FOR RAMS.

1760. For wool (Winners' names wanting), ...	£20 0 0
1761. ,, ,,	20 0 0
1762. ,, ,,	17 0 0
1763. ,, Alex. Baptie, £10; Robt. Murray, £7; Geo. Pott, £3, .	20 0 0
For rams, Wm. Anderson, £4; Alex. Baptie, £3; Thos. Curror, £2, .	9 0 0
1764. ,, £9, Wool, £20, ...	29 0 0
1765. ,, Sibbald, £4; Ballantyne, £3; Pott, £2, . .	9 0 0
Wool, Baptie, £10; Curror, £7; Aitchison, £3, . .	20 0 0
1767. ,, Brunton, £10; Geo. Pott, £7, ...	17 0 0
Rams, Aitchison, £4; Frs. Scott, £3; W. Scott, £2, . .	9 0 0
1768 to 1778. Premiums for wool and rams, amounting to . .	272 0 0
(After this premiums for wool were discontinued).	
1780-3. Premiums for rams amounting to	36 0 0
1784. Grieve Hoscote, £8; Wm. Scott, Singlie, £4; Jn. Paterson, Philiphaugh, £2,	14 0 0
1785. ,, £8; Jas. Laidlaw, Blackhouse, £4, .	12 0 0
(After 1785 premiums were given for "short sheep," on Mr. Lang's report that in Selkirkshire there was a much greater proportion of them than of "long sheep."	
1786. Walt. Bryden, Phaaps, £8; T. Scott, Dalglieshes, £4; Ja. Cuningham, Thirlstane, £2, ...	14 0 0
1787. H. Scott, Deloraine, £8; W. Bryden, Annelshope and Phaaps £4; Jas. Laidlaw, Mount Benger Knowe, £2, ...	14 0 0
1788. W. Scott, Singlie, £8; Thos. Currer, Yair, £4, . .	12 0 0
1789. Scott, Singlie, £8; Walt. Dunlop, South Common, £4, .	12 0 0
1790. Jas. Burnet, Wheethope, £8; Rob. Gibson, Shaws, £4; John Paterson, Langhope, £2, ...	14 0 0
Carry forward,	£570 0 0

Brought forward,	£570	0	0
1791. Bryden, Phaap, £8 ; R. Welsh, Corhead, £4 ; T. Ballantyne, Craig, £3, .	15	0	0
1792. Gibsons, Shaws, £8 ; Js. Anderson, Whitslaid, £4 ; R. Nicol, Phillop, £2,	14	0	0
1793. R. Horsburgh, Yair, £8 ; Js. Anderson, Whitslaid, £4 ; Gibsons, Shaws, £4,	16	0	0
1794. Gibsons, Shaws, £8 ; Anderson, Whitslaid, £4 ; Paterson, Langhope, £2,	14	0	0
1795. Gid. Scott, Kirkhope, £8 ; Anderson, Whitslaid, £4 ; Nicol, Phillop, £2,	14	0	0
1796. Anderson, Whitslaid, £8 ; T. Knox, Todrig, £4 ; Nicol, Phillop, £2, .	14	0	0
1797. T. Knox, Todrig, £8 ; Anderson, Whitslaid, £4 ; R. Horsburgh, Yair, £2,	14	0	0
1798. T. Knox, Todrig, £8 ; Jas. Inglis, Langhope, £4 ; Ad. Dalgliesh, Fast-heugh, £2, ...	14	0	0
1799. Js. Anderson, Whitslaid, £8 ; Dalgliesh, Fastheugh, £4 ; R. Nicol, Phillop, £2, ...	14	0	0
1800. Dalgliesh, Fastheugh, £8 ; R. Nicol, Phillop, £4 ; J. Scott, Gilmans-cleuch, £2, ...	14	0	0
1802. W. Scott, Mt. Bengerburn, £8 ; Dalgliesh, Fastheugh, £4 ; Js. Stoddart, Newburgh, £2, ...	14	0	0
1803. Jas. Inglis, Langhope, £8 ; Rob. Arres, Rink, £4, . . .	12	0	0
1804. Ad. Dalgliesh, Kirkhopes, £8 ; Wm. Scott, Berrybush, £4 ; Nicol Mill, Newark, £2, ...	14	0	0
1805. Wm. Scott, Berrybush ; Ad. Dalgliesh, Fastheugh ; Nicol Mill, Newark,	14	0	0
1806. Ad. Dalgliesh, Fastheugh ; Thomas Knox, Langhope ; do.,	14	0	0
1807. Ad. Dalgliesh, Fastheugh ; Walter Grieve, Midshaw ; Wm. Nicoll, "Coelficd,"	14	0	0
1808. Scott, Bengerburn, £8 ; T. Milne, Newark, £4 ; A. Park, Lewinshope, £2,	14	0	0
1809. Park, Lewinshope, £8 ; R. Ballantyne, Dryhope, £4 ; Milne, Newark, £2,	14	0	0
1810. Ballantyne, Dryhope, £8 ; Wr. Grieve, Midshaw, £4 ; T. Knox, Langhope and Todrig, £2, ...	14	0	0
1811. Geo. Grieve, Craik, £8 ; W. Scott, Singlie, £4 ; H. Scott, Deloraine, £2,	14	0	0
1812. T. Milne, Newark, £8 ; Ad. Dalgliesh, Fastheugh, £4, . .	12	0	0
1813. T. Milne, Dryhope, £10 ; T. Gibson, Shaws, £5 ; Ad. Dalgliesh, Kershopes, £2, 10s., ...	17	10	0
1814. Brydone, Redford Green, £10 ; Milne, Dryhope, £5 ; G. Brydone, Crosslee, £2, 10s., ...	17	10	0
1815. G. Grieve, Craik, £10 ; W. Grieve, Midshaw, £5 ; T. Gibson, Shaws, £2, 10s., ...	17	10	0
1816. Milne, Dryhope, £10 ; W. Brydon, Bengerburn, £5, . .	15	0	0
1817. G. Brydon, Crosslee, £8 ; Js. Brydon, Moodlaw, £6 ; T. Gibson, Shaws, £4,	18	0	0
1818. T. Gibson, Shaws, £8 ; R. Scott, Dodhead, £6 ; T. Milne, Craig, £4, .	18	0	0
1819. Wm. Anderson, Shootinglees, £8 ; J. Scott, Overdeloraine, £6 ; Mill, Dry-hope, £4, ...	18	0	0
1820. Geo. Brydon, Crosslee, £8 ; R. Scott, Philhope, £6 ; Mill, Dryhope, £4, .	18	0	0
1821. T. Anderson, Sundhope, £8 ; T. Gibson, Shaws, £6 ; Scott, Bengerburn, £4,	18	0	0
1822. R. Scott, Philhope, £8 ; Eb. Beattie, Oakwood, £6 ; T. Gibson, Shaws, £4,	18	0	0
1823. G. Scott, Singlie, £8 ; Brydone, Crosslee, £6 ; T. Gibson, Shaws, £4, .	18	0	0
1824. T. Gibson, Shaws, £8 ; Anderson, Sundhope, £6 ; J. Anderson, Hynd-hope, £4, ...	18	0	0
Carry forward,	£1074	10	0

Brought forward,   . £1074 10 0

1825. G. Brydone, Crosslee, £10 ; T. Gibson, Shaws, £5,   .   .   .   15 0 0
1826. R. Scott, Philhope, £7 ; T. Gibson, W. Kershope, £5 ; Eb. Beattie, Hutler-
     burn, £3, ...   15 0 0
1827. J. Scott, Deloraine, £7 ; R. Scott, Berrybush, £5 ; T. Gibson, Shaws, £3,   15 0 0
1828. Brydone, Crosslee, £7 ; Gibson, Shaws, £5, ...   12 0 0
1829. Gid. Scott, Singlie, £10 ; Jas. Brydon, Phawhope, £6 ; T. Gibson,
     Shaws, £4, ...   20 0 0
1830. Wm. Aitchison, Shootinglees, £10 ; Jas. Brydon, Phawhope, £6 ; T. Gibson,
     Shaws, £4, ...   20 0 0

£1,171 10 0

In Blaeu's Atlas, published at Amsterdam in 1654, the letterpress of which was contributed by Sir John Scott of Scotstarvet, it is stated that in the lower parts of Scotland,
particularly in the neighbourhood of Selkirk, the sheep find the pasturage so good and wholesome (*si bon et si salutaire*), beyond that of all other countries, that they live to be fifteen years
old before they die of themselves by disease. Lord Napier, nevertheless, in his book on
Store-farming (1822), gives a terrible catalogue of years marked by great mortality. From
1672 to 1822 there had been at least twenty-five bad seasons, or one for every sixth year, the
worst beyond all comparison being that of 1674, when tens of thousands of sheep perished in
the snow. Bad weather was the chief but not the only scourge. In 1762 the green hills
around the heads of Ettrick and Yarrow were rendered completely brown by the ravages of a
smooth light-brown caterpillar with dull yellow stripes (*phalaena graminis*, Lin.). Forty years
afterwards, in 1802, a similar visitation took place, when, except in boggy land, the grass was
almost totally consumed. They were so thick on the ground that the palm of a hand would
have covered ten. A few of them, fed in a crystal bottle at Mungo Park's suggestion, developed
into beautiful moths, laid about 100 eggs, and died. While the caterpillars swarmed over
the pasture, countless flocks of crows and sea-fowl were seen for many days hastening to the
banquet. When a burn intercepted their progress, the larvae lay in heaps by the side, so that
when heavy rain swept them into the drains many of the latter were choked. Reappearing in
greatly diminished numbers in 1812, 1824, 1826, they again visited Upper Selkirkshire in
1885.

Peeb.
N.S.A.
29.

Lockhart records Sir Walter Scott's presence at Bowhill in 1817, when a cattle-show at
Bowhill was followed by an entertainment on a large scale to the Buccleuch tenantry and
neighbours ; and, two years later, the Pastoral Society of Selkirkshire was established by the
exertions of Lord Napier. Its annual shows and distribution of premiums have been highly
beneficial. At the first meeting, held at Thirlestane on 17th June 1819, there was a great
gathering of farmers and county gentlemen—every member appearing in a blue coat of Ettrick
Forest cloth, manufactured by Mr. Richard Lees, of Galashiels! To the number of ninety they
dined on the field.

From the Old Statistical Account, written in 1792 by Mr. Russell, we learn that the parish
of Yarrow (which then included Kirkhope) contained 55,000 sheep, 149 horses, and 545 black
cattle. The higher price obtained for Cheviot wool was then leading to the introduction of
that breed in place of the black-faced sheep, at one time universal in the Forest. Much the
completest insight into the agriculture of Selkirkshire is afforded by a laborious "Survey,"
written in 1797 by the Rev. Dr. Douglas of Galashiels, and published in 1798. Estimating

the area at 160,000 acres, which is 2000 less than the ascertained measurement, he valued the county as follows :—

148,000 acres in sheep pasture, at 2s. 9d.,		. . .	£20,350
8,800 acres in tillage,	at 10s.,	. . .	4,400
2,000 acres in wood,	at 25s.,	. . .	2,500
1,200 acres in gardens, pleasure-grounds, etc.,		. . .	1,200
160,000 acres.	Total rent,	.	£28,450

Farm-houses and offices he described as in general paltry and ill-built, most of the former being of one story, low roofed, badly lighted, and covered with thatch. Some stables and byres were so low as scarcely to admit horses and cattle of ordinary size. To repair the waste occasioned by tempestuous weather, it was frequently necessary, in higher parts of the county, to put a new covering of rushes on the houses every year, the accumulated weight of which forced the walls outwards, and exposed both people and cattle to great danger. A beginning had just been made of better things. Farms varied in size from 50 to 6000 acres, from 1500 to 2000 being a moderate size for a farm all pasture, and large where there was a considerable proportion arable. All land was let by the lump, and none by the acre except around Selkirk and Galashiels, the inhabitants of which two places possessed from 1200 to 1500 acres, at rents of from one to two guineas per acre,—more for a few small and select spots. For the few farms below 300 acres £30 to £100 of rent was obtained, the larger farms bringing £100 to £300. "The farmers in general deserve the praise of being frank, communicative, and hospitable. Their tables are much better provided than the appearance of their houses affords any reason to expect ; and there are in their looks and manner a cordial welcome and an urgency to partake of their meat and drink which strongly indicate a kind heart. A few of them live in elegance and plenty, have a plain dinner well dressed and served every day, and a bottle of wine or cheerful glass of punch for a friend. But none of them keeps a chaise, or a man-servant for any household purpose. . . . Attempts to deceive and over-reach purchasers are held in utter contempt by the better sort. . . . Their chief defect is a degree of indifference for that kind of knowledge which can only be acquired from books, or from more frequent and enlarged inter-course with mankind." In his chapter on tillage, Dr. Douglas makes the extraordinary obser-vation that twenty years before he wrote there were scarce 10 acres of turnips in the whole county ; and these, raised in corners of fields in different farms, were generally destroyed by the sheep. A few ridges annually sown around Selkirk and Galashiels were greedily devoured by children and curious people, as soon as the bulb was formed. Potatoes found their way into the county some years before turnips, but were not planted except with the spade till 1772, about which time they began to be dropped in plough-formed ridges, and by 1780 had become quite common.

XIV.—SALMON-FISHING AND FACTORY POLLUTION.

DESCRIBING the food of the people, Dr. Douglas says a number of very good salmon are caught in the Selkirkshire part of the Tweed, and sold at 6d. the Dutch lb., till they begin to fall away, when they are sometimes as low as 1½d., and are purchased by the poorer class to be salted and eaten during winter with potatoes. Yet, twenty years later, Chalmers says the salmon Caled. ch. ii. 897.

with which Tweed formerly abounded, have been nearly destroyed by artifice at the call of interest. "Tweed," he adds, "turns few mills; nor have its waters been contaminated much by noxious manufactures." The first of these remarks was prompted by the great decrease of salmon consequent on legislation, which made the upper proprietors, as Sir Walter Scott put it, mere "clocking hens for the lower heritors," and deprived them of all interest in fish preservation. Half a century after Chalmers had written his certificate of purity, things had so much altered with the noble river as to call forth the burning remonstrances of Mr. Russell, scarcely less renowned as a brother of the angle, than as the cant-hating, clear-headed, and popular editor of the *Scotsman*. "We rejoice to see Hawick, Selkirk, and Galashiels already on their way to be Bradfords and Halifaxes. But contemplate the results of having large towns 50 or 60 miles from the sea sending their whole refuse down the river-channel through five counties! . . . Is that which now spreads health and beauty around to become an eye-sore and a nose-sore extending over half the breadth of the Island? Shall the turrets of Abbotsford be reflected from a monster gutter, all stains and stench? Shall fair Melrose, instead of being viewed aright by the pale moonlight, be nosed in the dark? Forbid it, all the powers of Parliament! If indeed that prohibition could not be uttered without destroying or impeding the brisk and cheerful industry which has sprung up among those sweet hills, there might be nothing for it but to sigh and submit. But can it be doubted that if the people of the towns on the Tweed and other such rivers, shall fail to find the *will*, there will be comparatively little difficulty in the Legislature finding the *way* to prevent their doing what they unhappily like with a river which is *not* their own, but is the property of five counties and the pride of two kingdoms?" This "conversion of Tweed into a pestilential sewer" was in a fair way to be realised at no far distant date, when an action at law by the river proprietors forced the manufacturers to take the provision of a remedy into serious consideration. The result has been the construction of tanks and other means of purification (costing in Galashiels alone upwards of £30,000), which have already brought about an improvement upon which the manufacturers may be properly congratulated, and which ought to be a source of gratification to all concerned.

XV.—POPULATION.

WRITING, in 1792, his account of Yarrow, Mr. Russell says the ancient population of the parish could not then be ascertained; but all aged people agreed that it considerably exceeded that then existing, and their testimony was corroborated from the numerous remains of old houses. One cause of this depopulation might be the monopoly of farms, another the aversion to rebuild cot houses, and a third the attraction of the inhabitants towards manufacturing towns. Dr. Douglas, however, noting an increase of 24 in the county population of 1790 as compared with that of 1755, directly traverses Mr. Russell's conclusions. "It is," he says, "not a little remarkable that in the parishes of Ettrick and Yarrow, where every kind of manufacture is unknown, there are more inhabitants than there were 40 years ago, while there are fewer in Galashiels, where there is a thriving manufacture. The general opinion, that by the union and extension of farms the country is depopulated, is not confirmed by the increasing population of those districts in Selkirkshire and Roxburghshire where the accumulation of farms is most prevalent." Undeniably there is a universal consensus of opinion on the part of early writers that the population of the Forest was at one time much greater than during last century. We are inclined to attribute the falling-off not so much to economical causes as to the complete disruption of that feudal system which tended to gather around each little stronghold and laird-ship a self-supporting community. In the days when every landed man was a soldier, and of importance as " his tail" at a wappinschaw was large or small, it was of the highest consequence for him to have as many dependants as his place could sustain. Each laird had his own mill and miller, his own smith who could wield a sword at need, and as many men of other crafts as could find subsistence in alternate work and warfare. In the course of the 17th century all this was changed, and we read of whole regiments being recruited for foreign service from the hills and valleys of the Scottish Border. Briefly, the constant necessity of defence by force of arms required a stronger population than was necessary during confirmed peace; and the retainers, half shepherds, half moss-troopers, whose families occupied the traditional hamlets of Upper Ettrick and Upper Yarrow, dropped gradually away from a district that could no longer employ them. With the younger sons of lairds many went to foreign wars, and many to found on the other side of the Atlantic a new nation with a destiny of unforeseen greatness.

TABLE OF POPULATION.

Acres.	Parishes.	1755.	1790-S.	1800.	1811.	1821.	1831.	1841.	1851.	1861.	1871.	1881.
21,517	Selkirk, pt.,	1740	1650	2048	2422	2696	2833	3425	4285	4688	5580	7396
5,710	Galashiels, pt.,	850	780	844	986	1358	1364	1935	2832	3181	5869	9529
3,385	Ashkirk, pt.,	200	172	163	162	184	192	171	195	187	143	138
3,579	Innerleithen, pt.,	60	60	67	42	43	64	54	60	73	75	61
42,683	Ettrick,	397	470	445	440	485	530	525	477	454	434	397
10,018	Stow, pt.,	260	282	378	293	328	323	272	358	363	402	441
22,973	Kirkhope,	} 1180	1230	1216	1225	1249	1221	1264	1294	{ 555	565	547
41,859	Yarrow,									643	654	611
3,172	Peebles, pt.,	...	...	...	...	4	...	5	6	...	3	4
11,628	Roberton, pt.,	250	240	237	319	290	306	339	302	305	280	250
166,524	County,	4937	4884	5398	5889	6637	6833	7990	9809	10,449	18,572	25,564

In 1831 the *town* of Galashiels contained 2209 inhabitants, of whom 1079 belonged to the parish of Melrose, and 1130 were in Selkirkshire. The population of the landward part of the parish was 404. The increase of population in Galashiels in 1871 is in great part a conse-quence of the Roxburghshire part of the burgh having been annexed to Selkirkshire by Act of Parliament.

INDEX.

Abbey of Selkirk, 1, 383.
Agricultural Notes, 407.
Ale brewing, 41, 126.
Alemoor, Lord, 309.
Altar of Holy Cross, 36, 41.
America, Emigration to, 413.
Anderson, family of, 35, 81, 87, 134, 146, 155, 162.
Archives of Burgh, 45.
Arrow, Silver, 64.

Bailies of Selkirk, 13, 16, 103, 176.
Banishment, 55, 59, 81, 89, 101.
Bemerside, Haigs of, 97.
Blaikie, Town-Clerk, 51.
Blasphemy, 101.
Boldside, 51.
Borthwickbraes, 86, 88.
Bowhill, 141, 235, 240 ; Murray of, 40, 80, 235 ; Scott of, 53, 59, 235.
Bridges over Ettrick, 11, 107, 113, 121, 162.
Bridgeheuch, 43, 71, 86.
Bridgelands, 11, 280.
Broadmeadows, 59, 280.
Brydone, family of, 23, 25, 35, 37, 49, 94, 163.
Buccleuch, Scotts of, 43, 51, 59, 243 ; Estate, stocks on, 394.
Bullsheugh, 16.
Burgess-roods, 18.
Burgess-rolls, 20, 59.
Burns, Robert, at Selkirk, 124.
Byethorn, 55.

Caldshields, 31, 41.
Carterhaugh, 42, 283.
Cattle, diseased, 37.
Champion of Burgh, 98.
Charters, 38, 39, 42, 383, 385.
Church Offerings, 34.
Clarkson, family of, 164.
Clock, public, 53, 96.
Clockie Burn, 10, 120, 161.
Coal, search for, 85, 96, 137.
Cock-fighting, 175.
Coffin-monopoly, 104.
Common riding, 31, 42, 81.
Common, Division of, 69.
Covenanters, 67.
Creelmen, Act against, 17.

Cromwell's troopers, 63.
"Cummerings," 77, 79.
Cunzie Nook, 120.
Curror, family of, 87, 173, 197, 311, 312, 315.

David I., 3.
Doby, family of, 48.
Drummer, town's, 88, 105.
Duel, fatal, 83.
Dunsdale, 30, 55.

Earthquake, 104.
Ettrickbank, 43.
Excommunication, 78.

Fairnilee, Ker of, 69.
False alarm, 131.
Famine, 104, 113.
Fastheugh, 289.
Fast-day desecration, 83.
Fauldshope, 289.
Ferry across Ettrick, 62, 91, 106, 122.
Flesher's Incorporation, 211.
Fletcher, family of, 25, 109, 164, 190.
Flodden, 21.
Floods, 86, 89, 122.
Football, 54.
Forest peel, 58.
Fortifications of town, 19.
Foulshiels, 42, 60, 290.
Fray, rising to, 31.
French prisoners, 135.
Funeral customs, 59, 76, 78, 81, 87, 93.

Galashiels, Pringles of, 387.
Gala, Scotts of, 84.
Galashiels, roll of crofters, 388.
Gala estate, survey of, 390.
Gallows-Knowe, 173.
Gargunnoch, 30.
Gates of town, 19, 118, 120.
Gilmanscleuch, Scotts of, 60.
Gladstone, family of, 36, 53, 80.
Golf, 54.
Gray, daft Jock, 162.
"Greengate" (Catrail), 117.
Greenhead, Kerrs of, 22, 43, 69, 377.

Guildry Book, 183.

Haining, 10, 102, 104, 105, 109, 299, 312 ; Loch, 10, 121, 149 ; Scotts of, 36, 49, 50, 53, 300 ; Riddells of, 69, 304 ; Pringles of, 47, 69, 83, 307.
Halywellhill, 17.
Hamilton, Roland, 33.
Hammermen's Corporation, 214.
Hangman, 98, 108, 118.
Harden, Scotts of, 59, 86, 101, 328.
Harehead, 313.
Hartwoodmyres, 51, 59, 313.
Hayston, Hay of, 47.
Headshaw, 59.
Heatherlie, 42, 316.
Henderson, family of, 125, 128, 141, 165, 211.
Horse-races, 90, 97, 105.
Howard, Lord, in Selkirk, 63.
Howden, 43, 175, 311.
Huntley, Scott of, 53.
Husbandlands, 34.

Invasion, threatened, 126.
Inventory of a burgess, 37.

Jacobite rebellions, 90, 111.
Jedburgh, Provost of, prisoner, 63.
Johnston, family of, 36, 165, 208.
Justiciary Courts at Selkirk, 14, 62.

Kelso, relations with Selkirk, 8.
Kingcroft, 14.
Kippielaw, Ker of, 48.
Kirk-session, 54, 73.
Kirk-yard, 54, 233.
Kirk utensils, 77.

Ladywell, 162.
Ladywoodedge, 28.
Lang, family of, 49, 87, 89, 90, 128, 146, 149, 155, 165, 207.
Lauriston, 162, 175.
Lawlessness, 15.
Lawson, family of, 126, 130, 146, 167.
Leopold, Prince, at Selkirk, 146.
Lindean, 79.
Lowrie's Loup, 87.

Mad dog, 116.
Mauldsheugh, 18, 31, 41, 42, 316.
Mercer, Dr., 170.
Merchant Company, 184.
Middlestead, 72, 317.
Millburn, 19, 55, 161, 175, 316.
Minstrel, Burgh, 40.
Mitchelhill, family of, 31, 47, 49, 68, 69, 73, 80, 170, 197, 317.
Moore, Sir John, M.P., 47, 123.
Morriston Hill, 162, 175.
Mungo's Well, 82, 121, 173.
Muster-roll of Burgh Soldiers, 60.
Muthag, Provost, murdered, 42.

Napier, Lord, 148.
Newark, 76 ; Tower, 319.
Newburgh, Scotts of, 59.

Oakwood, 327 ; Scotts of, 51, 327.
Old Wark, 319.
Outlaw Murray, 355.

Pant Well, 90, 118.
Park, Mungo, 133, 291.
Parliament, burgh members, 47, 115, 117, 143 ; Shire electors in 1790, 394.
Paving streets, 81.
Peat law, 117.
Peel-hill, 10, 14, 41, 161, 311.
Persecution of Covenanters, 67.
Petty customs, 58, 73.
Philiphaugh, 12, 56, 101, 331 ; Barbour of, 332 ; Turnbulls of, 333 ; Murrays of, 17, 18, 34, 47, 50, 58, 64, 69, 119, 223, 335 ; Battle of, 62.
Piper, town's, 58, 74.
Plague, 35, 58, 99.
Polwarth, Lord, 329.
Population, table of, 414.
Pot Loch, 105.
Pringle of that ilk, 49.
Prison-breaking, 56, 117.
Proclamations, 49.
Provost of Selkirk, 42, 50, 143, 181.

Raeburn, Scott of, 83.
Railway projected, 134, 148.
Rats, the black, 121.
Reformation, 50.
Regality, Burgh of, 37, 94, 109, 110.
Requiems, 36.
Riddel, centenarian, 171.
Riddell of Riddell, 47, 69.
Ring o' the toon, 161.
Riot, 74.
Rodger, family of, 77, 99, 118, 129, 141, 171, 179, 209.
Roxburgh, Duke of, 8, 74, 103, 114.
Russell, Sam, 171.
Russia, Emperor Nicholas at Selkirk, 141.
Ruthven, name of, 52.

Salmon-fishing, 142, 411.
Scots language, 56.
Scott, Sir Walter, 128, 133, 136, 138-142, 146, 149, 150, 156, 158, 242, 288, 297.
Scourging, 55.
Selkirk, Burgh lands, 86, 87, 144 ; burnt, 16, 44, 45 ; Castle, 10, 12 ; Churches, 229; Clergy, 91, 219; Common Good, 86, 144 ; English Kings at, 12 ; Kings-S., 7 ; Royal stud at, 12 ; men in army, 15 ; Mills, 12, 16, 63, 81, 87 ; Monks-S., 7 ; old town, 3 ; Schools, 54, 97, 103, 175 ; Scottish Kings at, 10, 11, 14.
Selkirk, as a surname, 11.
Shaw Burn, 5, 55.
Shaw, Kers of, 34, 120, 362.
Sheep-stealer hanged, 56.
Silver cup, 138.
Sinton, Scott of, 47, 53, 60, 69.
Skeleton in Bog, 129.
Sorley, Rev. Wm., 172.
Souters' Craft, 52, 81, 91, 112, 191, 234.
Stool of Repentance, 75.
Sumptuary edicts, 94.

Sunday observance, 31, 73, 75, 77, 89, 99, 114, 160.
Sunderlandhall, 43, 365 ; Ker of, 51, 59, 69, 362.
Sundhope, Murray of, 60.
Superstitions, 154.

Tailors' Corporation, 207.
Textile trade in Selkirk, 177.
Thirlestane, Scotts of, 53, 56, 59, 90, 236.
Three Brethren Hill, 42, 134.
Tibbie Tamson's grave, 174.
Todrig, Scotts of, 59, 365.
Tolbooth, 62, 109, 129.
Torwoodlee, Pringles of, 91.
Town Council, 16, 80, 96, 107, 109, 143, 159.
Town Cross, 105, 118.
Trade Crafts, 88, 94, 186.
Trevelyan, G. O., 47.
Trinity Hill, 32.
Turnbulls of Philiphaugh, 333.
Tushielaw, Scotts of, 59, 80.

Union with England, 63, 83.
Uplands, 56.

Valuation Rolls, 385, 396, 397, 403.
Veitch of Bowhill, 239.

Watchmen, 17, 31, 36.
Wauch, family of, 95, 103, 104, 173.
Weaponshaw, 21, 31.
Weavers' Incorporation, 186.
Welsh, Rev. John, 220.
Whitmuir, 54, 379.
Whitmuirhall, 51, 120, 379.
Whytbank, Pringle of, 69, 78, 134, 155, 374.
Wife, sale of, 106.
Williamhope, 368.
Witch burned, 100.
Woodburn, 161.
Woll, Scott of, 53, 60, 69, 73, 90.
Woollen factories, 181.

Yair, 41, 51, 371.

PRINTED BY T. AND A. CONSTABLE, PRINTERS TO HER MAJESTY,
AT THE EDINBURGH UNIVERSITY PRESS.

Lightning Source UK Ltd.
Milton Keynes UK
UKHW030606250220
359289UK00007B/639